# A SOCIAL HISTORY OF ENGLAND,
## 1500–1750

The rise of social history has had a transforming influence on the history of early modern England. It has broadened the historical agenda to include many previously little-studied, or wholly neglected, dimensions of the English past. It has also provided a fuller context for understanding more established themes in the political, religious, economic and intellectual histories of the period. This volume serves two main purposes. Firstly it summarises, in an accessible way, the principal findings of forty years of research on English society in this period, providing a comprehensive overview of social and cultural change in an era vital to the development of English social identities. Secondly, the chapters, by leading experts, also stimulate fresh thinking by not only taking stock of current knowledge, but extending it, identifying problems, proposing fresh interpretations and pointing to unexplored possibilities. It will be essential reading for students, teachers and general readers.

KEITH WRIGHTSON is Randolph W. Townsend Jr Professor of History at Yale University. He previously held positions at the Universities of St Andrews and Cambridge, where he was Professor of Social History. His publications include the ground-breaking *English Society, 1580–1680* (1982), *Earthly Necessities: Economic Lives in Early Modern Britain* (2000) and *Ralph Tailor's Summer: A Scrivener, His City and the Plague* (2011), as well as many essays on the social history of early modern England. He is a Fellow of the British Academy, a former President of the North American Conference on British Studies, and an Honorary Vice-President of the Social History Society.

# A SOCIAL HISTORY OF ENGLAND, 1500–1750

EDITED BY

KEITH WRIGHTSON

*Yale University*

# CAMBRIDGE
## UNIVERSITY PRESS

University Printing House, Cambridge CB2 8BS, United Kingdom

One Liberty Plaza, 20th Floor, New York, NY 10006, USA

477 Williamstown Road, Port Melbourne, VIC 3207, Australia

4843/24, 2nd Floor, Ansari Road, Daryaganj, Delhi – 110002, India

79 Anson Road, #06-04/06, Singapore 079906

Cambridge University Press is part of the University of Cambridge.

It furthers the University's mission by disseminating knowledge in the pursuit of
education, learning and research at the highest international levels of excellence.

www.cambridge.org
Information on this title: www.cambridge.org/9781107041790
DOI: 10.1017/9781107300835

© Cambridge University Press 2017

First published 2017

Printed in the United Kingdom by Clays, St Ives plc

*A catalogue record for this publication is available from the British Library.*

ISBN 978-1-107-04179-0 Hardback
ISBN 978-1-107-61459-8 Paperback

# Contents

v

# *Figures*

# Tables

# Contributors

Jeremy Boulton
*University of Newcastle*

Adam Fox
*University of Edinburgh*

Henry French
*University of Exeter*

Alison Games
*Georgetown University*

Malcolm Gaskill
*University of East Anglia*

Adrian Green
*Durham University*

Paul Griffiths
*Iowa State University*

Craig Muldrew
*University of Cambridge*

Linda Pollock
*Tulane University*

Alec Ryrie
*Durham University*

Alexandra Shepard
*University of Glasgow*

Cathy Shrank
*University of Sheffield*

Tim Stretton
*Saint Mary's University*

John Walter
*University of Essex*

Jane Whittle
*University of Exeter*

Phil Withington
*University of Sheffield*

Andy Wood
*Durham University*

Keith Wrightson
*Yale University*

# Acknowledgements

As editor I wish to express my thanks to all the contributors to this volume for their willingness to participate in the project. They were asked to undertake the difficult and demanding task of handling large themes within the constraints of relatively tight word limits, and to do so in a manner that would not only survey the findings and arguments of existing scholarship but also provoke fresh thinking and suggest ways forward in research. Reading and discussing the resulting draft chapters have been the most stimulating and rewarding part of editing this book. I am grateful also for their commitment in speedily writing final drafts, and their efficiency in turning around queries and proofs in the final stages of preparation and production. It has been a privilege to work with them.

The map in Chapter 8 (Figure 8.2) is reproduced from C. Phythian-Adams, *Societies, Cultures and Kinship, 1580-1850: Cultural Provinces and English Local History* (Leicester: Leicester University Press, 1996), xvii (© C. Phythian-Adams 1996). It is used here by kind permission of Bloomsbury Publishing plc.

This book is dedicated to the memory of Christopher W. Brooks, an outstanding historian of this period and a friend to many of us.

# Abbreviations

| | |
|---|---|
| *AHR* | *American Historical Review* |
| BL | British Library |
| *C&C* | *Continuity and Change* |
| DUL | Durham University Library |
| *EcHR* | *Economic History Review* |
| EEBO | Early English Books Online |
| *EHR* | *English Historical Review* |
| *HJ* | *The Historical Journal* |
| *HWJ* | *History Workshop Journal* |
| *IRSH* | *International Review of Social History* |
| *JBS* | *Journal of British Studies* |
| *JFH* | *Journal of Family History* |
| *JMH* | *Journal of Modern History* |
| NRO | Norfolk Record Office |
| *ODNB* | *Oxford Dictionary of National Biography* |
| *P&P* | *Past & Present* |
| RO | Record Office |
| *SH* | *Social History* |
| TNA | The National Archives, Kew |
| *TRHS* | *Transactions of the Royal Historical Society* |

# Framing Early Modern England

## Keith Wrightson

In sixteenth- and seventeenth-century English, the verb 'to frame' meant to construct, join together, shape, form, or devise and invent. 'Framing' was 'the action, method or process of constructing, making or fashioning something'.[1] All historical periods are constructed or devised in this manner. Sometimes they are bracketed by key events deemed to be of particular symbolic importance: happenings 'to which cultural significance has successfully been assigned'.[2] Sometimes they are defined in terms of broader processes that are cumulatively transformative: the 'rise' of capitalism or individualism, for example, or the 'decline' of magic or of the peasantry. But whatever the case, historical periods reflect perceptions of the shape of the past that originate in particular attempts to give it form and meaning, gradually become conventional, and persist while they retain the power to persuade us that they help make sense of it.

The term 'early modern' has become the conventional English-language way of describing the sixteenth, seventeenth and early eighteenth centuries: the period covered in this volume. It is relatively novel in use. The orthodox view is that it emerged from the 1940s, and became more widely adopted from the 1970s in both history and adjacent disciplines (notably literary criticism of an 'historicist' cast). Despite this success, in recent years it has become unusually contested. Those who dislike, or are at least uncomfortable with, its widespread employment tend to emphasise a number of objections. First, it is 'a quite artificial term', unknown in the period to which it refers. It is a retrospective label, 'a description born of hindsight', imposed upon the past. Moreover, it has been uncritically adopted by those unaware of its deficiencies and implications. It is vague and elusive in definition and inconsistently applied. Its chronological boundaries vary not only with country but also with topic. It may be meaningful when addressing some themes, but is inappropriate to others. It is geographically restricted in its applicability, making more

sense when applied to those parts of Europe in which these centuries witnessed significant change than to those that retained more 'traditional'
structures, and is largely irrelevant outside the European context. While
it has been widely adopted in the historiographies of anglophone and
German-speaking countries, it is more rarely used elsewhere. Above all,
the very notion of an 'early modern' period allegedly embodies teleological assumptions about the course of historical change. It is tainted with
'Whiggish' value judgements about 'progress' in human affairs. Worse,
that ethnocentric bias is compounded by its association with the 'modernization' theories prevalent in the social sciences of the 1950s and 1960s.
The very term 'early modern' 'assumes that European culture was travelling towards something called "modernity"'; it contains 'a teleological
modernizing trajectory', a pre-ordained evolution towards 'a uniform,
homogenized world, dominated by western-style economies, societies and
participatory politics'. Softer critics would warn against such linearity and
redefine the period so as to make its chronology even looser: back, where
appropriate, to the fourteenth century; forward, in other cases, to the mid
nineteenth century. Harder critics would abandon it altogether – though
generally remaining coy about what they would put in its place.[3]

Such reservations are to be taken seriously insofar as they promote
reflection on the process of historical 'framing'. Yet they are not so telling as to demand the rejection of the very notion of a distinctive and
meaningful early modern period. To be sure, the concept of such a period
is artificial and retrospective. So is all historical periodisation. It may be
fair to say that it is sometimes employed uncritically. So are many other
historical coinages of disputed meaning and generally forgotten ancestry
that remain in circulation because they are useful shorthands: 'feudalism'; 'Byzantium'; the 'Renaissance'; the 'Scientific', 'Agricultural' and
'Industrial' revolutions; the 'Counter- Reformation'; the 'Enlightenment';
and so on. But it was not adopted simply as a convenient label for a
loosely defined period between (approximately) the late fifteenth and late
eighteenth centuries. Nor did it arrive freighted with twentieth-century
modernisation theory. It emerged earlier, and for good reasons.

The sense that there was something distinctive about these centuries of
European history is hardly a new one. It existed long before the term
'early modern' was coined, and it persists even in those national historiographies that prefer to eschew that term. It originated in the revival
and dissemination of classical culture by the humanist scholars of the
Renaissance, and in an engagement with that recovered legacy that

enhanced their sense of difference from what eventually became known as the 'Middle Ages' and convinced them that they had entered a distinctive 'modern' age (meaning simply the present or recent times). To this extent, our sense of the early modern begins with an acceptance of 'the terms of use laid down by sixteenth-century scholars'.[4] It culminates in the self-perception of another justifiably self-conscious new age: that ushered in by the American and French revolutions, the Latin American wars of independence, and the technological and social transformations of industrialisation. Historians looking back from the vantage point of the nineteenth century came to divide 'modern' history into two phases. The earlier of these could be bracketed by specific events: the opening of oceanic routes to the East, the European discovery of the New World, the Reformation and the shattering of western Christendom at one end, the Age of Revolutions at the other. Alternatively, it could be defined in terms of more diffuse processes: shifts in military technology; the formation of (some) national states; the cumulative impact of print culture; the expansion of commercial and industrial capitalism; the foundation of extra-European colonial empires; philosophical innovation; radical political thought; new ways of exploring the natural world. Whatever the case, this period of European history seemed to have a distinctive texture. It was not discontinuous with the past. All developments have roots. It witnessed continuities as well as changes. All historical periods do. But that did not preclude change and growth of a kind that distinguished the period and laid tracks for what came later. To recognise this does not imply teleology. It is simply genealogy – a tracing of antecedents. Of course these changes were not universal. Nothing ever is. But they proved to be what most mattered.

The specific concept of the 'early modern' is also older than the orthodoxy maintains. It was not, as is often alleged, coined in mid-twentieth-century America in the context of economic history. So far as is currently known, it originated in mid-Victorian England, in the published Cambridge lectures of William Johnson, and in the context of cultural history: specifically, as a means of expressing the way in which the classical revival at the turn of the sixteenth century enabled humanist scholars to engage critically with their own society and to imagine a future. Johnson's notion of the early modern has been described as 'an alternative and indigenous' conception of the Renaissance, one very much influenced by the self-perception of the English humanist scholars of the sixteenth century. As a term it was not immediately successful. But it re-emerged in the early years of the twentieth century in another historical context: in the work of scholars engaged in founding English economic history as a distinctive approach to the past.

The notion that the sixteenth and seventeenth centuries were a period of significant transition in English economy and society was also deeply embedded. It originated in the period itself, in the writings of perceptive contemporaries who believed themselves to be living in changing times, characterised by the erosion of an older economic and social order and the animation of a new one. It was elaborated in the work of Scottish Enlightenment thinkers who traced the emergence of modern commercial society from the sixteenth century; it informed Marx's historical account of the development of industrial capitalism in England; and it was central to the writings of the English Historical Economists, James Thorold Rogers, William Cunningham and W. J. Ashley. The Historical Economists rejected the bleak dogmas of classical political economy and turned to history in support of their contention that the validity of economic theory is relative to the circumstances and values of a particular time and place. They advocated the study of past economic cultures in the round – an economic history that was also social and cultural – and were acutely aware that economic change involved a myriad of factors other than the purely economic. While they might celebrate particular economic achievements, they were also deeply concerned with what has been called 'the distinctive pathology of modern society'.[5] They dismissed teleological triumphalism, stressing instead the complexities and contingencies of economic and social change, – the ironies and human costs of the gradual, complex and uneven process of transition from an older set of institutions, practices and values towards the world of laissez-faire capitalism.

The British and American scholars who followed them with more specialised studies of particular sectors of English economic life between the sixteenth and eighteenth centuries shared that general perception of the period's significance. Indeed, it is hard to see how they could have done otherwise, since it was perfectly evident that the England of the Industrial Revolution was a very different place from that of Henry VII. They were the first rigorous analysts of what Christopher Hill called 'the colossal transformations which ushered England into the modern world'.[6] And it was in the emergent literature of a broadly conceived economic history, among those that pioneered deeper research into those transformations, that the term 'early modern' began to appear more frequently. J. U. Nef, who is sometimes credited with having introduced the term in a paper delivered to the American Historical Association in 1940, was of course one of them. It was adopted because it was more appropriate to their concern with long-term, gradual and diffuse processes than the dynastic and biographical dates or discrete centuries still most commonly applied to frame conventional political history. A broader vision of the past needed a different kind of 'chronological descriptor'.[7]

The notion of the early modern, then, was born of a more expansive approach to the English past. That being the case, it is hardly surprising that its more widespread diffusion occurred in the context of the next major broadening of the range of historical concern: the developments in social and cultural history that constituted the major historiographical innovations of the later twentieth century.[8] That movement was both international and interdisciplinary in nature, and ironically it introduced the concept of the early modern, through the interventions of anglophone historians, to the literatures of countries whose own historians mostly preferred to do without it – notably France and Italy.

In the English case, which is our concern, the rise of social history from the 1960s and 1970s was in direct line of descent from the more inclusive vision characteristic of early-twentieth-century economic history.[9] But it was also creating a new field, sometimes almost from scratch. That involved first of all a massive expansion of the historical agenda to include previously little-studied or wholly neglected dimensions of the English past. It aspired to create a set of histories that were surely there but had been largely excluded from the purlieus of conventional historical study: 'absent presences'.[10] In effect, it amounted to a call to discover a new country: a more fully inhabited country. Secondly, the pursuit of new questions meant identifying and exploring the potential of previously unknown or little-used historical sources (and the institutions that produced them), often at the local level in the county and diocesan archives that were becoming increasingly organised and accessible at the time. Thirdly, it required new methodologies, some of them developed under the influence of adjacent disciplines (notably social anthropology, historical geography and literary criticism) or innovative foreign historiographies (initially the French *Annales* school and later American 'social-science history' and Italian 'microhistory'). These included quantitative analysis where appropriate, or at least a more rigorous and systematic examination of qualitative evidence, both frequently supplemented by forms of record linkage. Finally, interpreting the findings of this research necessitated a higher level of theoretical awareness in the fashioning of historical arguments, both in approaches to particular problems and in thinking about how societies work as interconnected systems. Such interdisciplinarity might begin with an element of imitation: the adoption of concepts and questions appropriate to the problem in hand. But it usually gave way rapidly to critical engagement: the generation of fresh conceptualisation and new interpretative insights as historians in dialogue with the evidence provided by the past sought to characterise unanticipated realities and to construct credible accounts of change.

This movement transformed the sense of the early modern as a distinctive period in several ways. First, it enhanced awareness of its contours. Economic historians concerned with economic growth before industrialisation had already established a more quantitatively precise and chronologically exact account of change in sector after sector of English economic life between the sixteenth and eighteenth centuries: prices, real wages, land ownership, domestic and overseas commerce, the diffusion of agricultural and industrial innovation, and so on. This continued, creating in the process not only a reconnaissance of national trends but also a greater sensitivity to regional and social variations in their impact. But it was now complemented and elaborated by comparable studies (at local, regional and, where possible, national level) of population trends and their constituent elements, urban growth, migration, popular literacy, criminal prosecutions and civil litigation, living standards and domestic consumption, poverty, and much more. People might joke about the existence of an 'early modern curve' in which everything seems to be increasing between the mid sixteenth and mid seventeenth centuries, followed by a century of relative stabilisation and consolidation before renewed growth in the later eighteenth century. In fact, it was much more complex. In some respects, the later seventeenth and early eighteenth centuries saw a reversal of previous trends – for example in the incidence of crisis mortality, criminal prosecutions and litigation. In others they witnessed their acceleration – in agricultural specialisation and industrial production, urbanisation and metropolitan growth, commerce, consumption, intensified communication networks, the expansion and diversification of print culture, and the growth of waged employment. And there were always forms of local and regional variation that were in some respects enhanced over time – some towns stabilised in size; others grew exponentially. The point is that the contours of all this were being charted for the first time and that this mapping seemed to confirm the distinctive identity of an 'early modern' period: one that was not imposed upon the evidence but grew from it.

Within that emergent sense of the broad shape of the early modern period the studies of social institutions, social relations, attitudes, values and patterns of behavior that were undertaken to elucidate particular trends began to create not so much an 'early modern narrative' as a series of related early modern narratives. These were not conventional historical narratives, but analytical narratives, concerned with demonstrating and explaining medium-to-long-term processes of change. They were usually developed to explore specific themes – population trends and their dynamics, for example, or the rise and fall of witchcraft prosecutions, poverty and developments in poor-relief, the growth of popular literacy, or resistance to agrarian change. But each provided context for the others, and cumulatively they contributed to a growing sense of a process of 'social and economic reconfiguration' that took off from the sixteenth century and ultimately produced what E. A. Wrigley terms the 'advanced organic' economy and society that gave birth to industrialisation in the later eighteenth century.[11]

These narratives contained many surprises. Whatever their initial expectations, people found that the evidence presented unanticipated realities, leading them to uncover and address new problems and to make unexpected connections. They opened new perspectives. That meant initially sociological and social anthropological perspectives on continuity and change in social structures, social relationships, attitudes and beliefs. But it soon came to involve both the introduction of gender as a new category of historical analysis, and greater appreciation of the independent role of culture in the construction of historical reality. The narratives of social history began to include, and to be enriched by, those of cultural historians and historicist literary scholars concerned with understanding contemporary concepts in their context; with 'discursive trends' and their relationship to social change – reconstructing 'the discursive spine of English early modernity' – with the creation of a novel 'environment ... congenial to literary creativity'; and with the 'emerging lexicons' that marked change in what could be said, thought, felt and ultimately done. They came to involve attention to material culture and its meanings; to changes in the landscape and in how spaces and places were used, defined, perceived and represented; to changes in the perception of time and in awareness of the historical past. They detected shifts in identity: the interconnected construction of a national identity and regional identities; the recasting of social identities; the shifts in individual identity made possible by what have been called 'the development of technologies and languages for representing the self' and 'an extraordinary burgeoning of the language of reflexivity': new media of self-expression; newly coined self-words.[12]

These early modern narratives were full of new stories: those evocative episodes and accounts of past experience that people scraped up against in the archives and that left indelible marks on their historical skins. They contained new voices: for the most part those of hitherto historically obscure people who nonetheless managed to leave a trace in the records from which we make history. To this extent they constituted a democratisation of the subject, an engagement with hitherto 'under-represented lives' – those of members of subordinate groups in general and of women in particular.[13] As such, they contained a sustained examination and critique of the conventional exercise of power. And they were critical in a further sense also. Specific findings frequently came into conflict with prior assumptions derived from the largely conjectural accounts of 'traditional' society to be found in social theory and with narratives of modernisation based upon them. This was particularly evident in the furore that erupted in the 1970s and 1980s over the history of family relationships.[14] But it was soon to be found elsewhere, for example among historians concerned with class relationships or with nationalism, neither of which was supposed to exist before the birth of modernity. Far from being tainted by teleology, the emergent social and cultural history of early modern England was frequently de-mythologising in its impact on theories of modernisation. It gave rise to a notion of the 'early modern' that involved 'resistance to the master narratives of modernity'; posing questions rather than accepting preconceived answers.[15] And it demanded a heightened sensitivity to the elements of continuity that persisted even within changing contexts, and the perennial problem of the complex relationships between continuity and change as 'people carried on, using both old and new social strategies, as they generally do across moments of change'.[16]

All of this also had an impact upon the ways in which the established themes and central dramas of the history of this period were understood and addressed. The traditional prominence of the sixteenth, seventeenth and eighteenth centuries in English historiography was of course because these were already viewed as formative centuries in political and constitutional, religious and intellectual history. These processes and the convulsive moments of crisis and conflict that they involved could now be understood within a much larger context, and interpreted in ways that drew upon a richer conceptual palette. Historians of the English Reformation concerned themselves not only with doctrinal and ecclesiological change but with the long-term social and cultural adaptations involved in the creation of a plurality of new religious identities. A 'new political history' emerged that placed the familiar landmarks of political crisis and constitutional change within the contexts of processes of state formation, changing governmental priorities, the recasting of local political elites and the emergence of a more participatory political culture.[17]

In sum, the rise of social and cultural history had a transformative influence on the historiography of England between the sixteenth and eighteenth centuries. It massively broadened the scope of our engagement with the English past. It provided a new sense of the shape and dynamics of these centuries as a distinctive period of change, and it justified and advanced the notion of the 'early modern' as we now understand it. That term may well be of limited applicability in the periodisation of other histories. If one considers the whole of Europe, let alone the larger world, it might be said, in Peter Krištúfek's phrase, that 'Every clock in this house shows a different time.'[18] But it works rather well for England, the classic ground on which it was developed. If some of its forms, concerns, debates and dilemmas have aged out of existence, others to which it gave rise continue to resonate. They remain our own. That is why the term is appropriate. It describes a deep past that is not quite past.

This book is not intended as a compendium of what is now known about English society between the sixteenth and eighteenth centuries. It could have had many more chapters devoted to specific issues that have of necessity been subsumed within broader thematic essays. Nevertheless, it will certainly convey a great deal of hard-won knowledge about the structures of English society, its central social institutions, patterns of social relations and cultural values. All save one of the authors of its chapters could be regarded as members of the vital second wave of what used to be called 'the new social history': those who absorbed early the pioneering studies of the 1970s and 1980s, and went on to build upon, greatly extend, modify and where necessary challenge them. This is deliberate. Such scholars are in the best position to survey a particular area of what is now a large field, to know the roads already travelled and to suggest where we could or should be going next. Their chapters can be read as free-standing essays upon particular themes and issues. At the same time, however, they are intended to form a coherent whole, in which each provides context for the others. And taken as a whole, the emphasis of the book is upon the dynamics of early modern English society: sometimes the dynamics of relative equilibrium, more often the dynamics of change. The chapters are ordered in a way that is intended to unfold a panorama of interconnected processes that were cumulatively transformative; how they were experienced; what they meant; how we can understand them.

Part I, 'Discovering the English', is about the English people's discovery of themselves and about our discovery of them. One chapter explores the development of a more elaborate sense of national identity, the institutions central to its discovery (or invention) and how it came to be written. Another details the practice of surveying, listing, and categorising the population for a variety of purposes, a practice that not only enhanced awareness of the nature of English society (and its 'legibility' to the anxious men who tried to govern it) but also collected information that facilitates its historical reconstruction. Two more examine the basic social institutions of the household and the local community. These 'little commonwealths' provided the setting for people's most intimate personal relationships. They were emotionally intense spheres of both inter-dependence and conflict. They were deemed so crucial to the health of a well-ordered commonwealth that they were the foci of a prescriptive literature of 'conduct' books and manuals of governance. And they were also among the first social institutions to be rigorously examined (and argued over) by social historians. Understanding their dynamics is a central part of both recovering the texture of social relations in this period, and grasping the motives and imperatives that so often shaped the course of change.

Part II, 'Currents of Change', is self-explanatory. Its chapters provide pithy interpretative accounts of the processes that collectively reshaped English society. Aspects of demographic and economic change that were an essential part of these processes are constantly alluded to and briefly described. They can be studied in detail elsewhere.[19] Here the focus is on developments that had an impact upon social structures, social relations and social identities: changes in the structures of rural and urban society; in religion, education, literacy and employment of the written word; in access to and uses of the law; in material culture and the consumption of goods; in concepts of authority and the possibilities of protest and resistance. These are well-established themes: some of the staple narratives of the social and cultural history of early modern England. But they are handled here with a difference: sometimes revising the chronology of change; frequently recharacterising its nature; always alert to the need to reconsider its possible meanings.

Part III, 'Social Identities', offers a further shift of focus to chapters exploring the formation of social identities. Three of these examine the worlds of the three 'sorts of people' that by the seventeenth century had largely displaced more elaborate accounts of the social hierarchy in English discourses of social distinction: the ruling elite of landed 'gentlemen', which was itself undergoing redefinition; the 'middle' or 'middling' sort, an increasingly salient group struggling towards the formulation of a distinct and positive social identity; the 'meaner' sort of labouring people and the poor, a greatly increased segment of the population whose place and self-definitions were shaped by their experiences of wage labour, social subordination and the poor law system.[20] Two further chapters examine, first, the significance of gender and sexuality as pervasive criteria of difference, and secondly, how English people defined themselves in relation to a variety of ethnic and racial 'others' encountered either within England or in the larger world in which some of them now moved. Finally, a short coda reflects on how the people of early modern England came to perceive their past, and the extent to which their memories of recent history formed a distinctively early modern sense of the past.

Within this broad structure, the authors of individual chapters have been accorded considerable discretion in their handling of particular themes. They have been obliged to be succinct, but they have worked within flexible chronological boundaries, and their chronological emphasis varies as seems appropriate to them when addressing the trajectories of particular developments. They were encouraged to produce not bland textbook syntheses but interpretative essays that would transcend, where needed, the limitations of pioneering narratives and interpretations, present fresh insights and redirect debate. Beyond this general expectation, however, no attempt has been made to impose any single interpretative perspective or to homogenise approaches to the period as a whole.

There is no party line here. Nevertheless, certain themes and issues tend to recur. First, the chapters tend to underscore the sheer dynamism of the period. Together they offer a multi-faceted account of a complex society in motion, making and unmaking itself, sometimes purposefully, even cataclysmically, more often through gradual adjustments of strategy and aspiration, sometimes by degrees scarcely perceptible to most contemporaries. That dynamism is perhaps what most defines this period: a multiplex quickening – though one that was also uneven in its impact and often paradoxical in its outcomes. English society became more defined, institutionally, ideologically and culturally; better known geographically and socially; more integrated and connected. But it also became more diversified regionally and socially. The processes of change charted here can be said to have affected everyone in one way or another. They entailed generally heightened levels of interaction and the involvement of a myriad of individual actors: a participation that enhanced the social depth of governance, politics, religious initiatives, engagement with the law, access to knowledge and opinion, and the consumption of goods. Yet such opportunity and agency were massively circumscribed by relative social position and by gender. From the mid sixteenth century social inequality was growing. Differentials of wealth, the fundamental criterion of social status, became more pronounced.[21] The social hierarchy was gradually reconfigured, a process that might mean greater fluidity and upward social mobility opportunities for some, but in which life chances for most remained constrained by the dispensations of relative advantage or disadvantage to which they were born. Where change provoked resentment it might be challenged, disputed, arbitrated. But people's capacity to negotiate outcomes was limited by inherited structures of power and authority: in the household, in the community, in the commonwealth. To this extent, if contemporaries were aware that their times witnessed a succession of breaks with the past, the past still stood over them.

It is possible, then, to advance some broad generalisations about the dynamics of English society in this period, and about their outcomes. Its history, like that of all periods, was messy and sometimes muddled in the living. But it was not just 'a mess of separate experiences' or of 'perpetually multiplying exceptions'.[22] At the same time, in interpreting the experiences of change in early modern England, the authors of these chapters share some recurrent theoretical preferences. They are resistant to notions of linearity. They know that change varied in pace and in completeness, that it was selective in its impact and that it was not uni-directional. In interpreting its course and causation, they are sceptical of attributing dominance to any single 'prime mover', be it demographic, economic, political or cultural. Rather, they emphasise the interaction of a range of relevant variables. They reject determinism, drawing attention to the role of contingency in historical change, and the unpredictability of its consequences. And they treat notions of 'modernisation' with suspicion. They are concerned with demonstrating and explaining changes that in many respects remade English society, but these 'early modern' narratives are far removed from the teleological strait-jacket of modernisation theory. Their interpretative perspective is closer to that to be found in the distinctly undogmatic concept of 'complexity'.

Theories of complexity have been developed in order to understand the dynamics of change in complex systems, including social systems, in which large numbers of entities or agents interact with one another. They stress the continuous nature of change in such systems, their adaptability to changing environments and conditions, and their unpredictability. They explain how that adaptability is the consequence of connectivity and interaction: how new strategies emerge in response to initiating events or stimuli, are modified by experience and are diffused through reciprocal influence. Such 'emergent behaviours' can originate in any part of the system, but can gradually exert transformative influence on the whole. Adaptations may be influenced by cultural context – i.e. the agents' perceptions of change and the strategies deemed appropriate to meet it – and other contextual constraints may affect their outcomes. Ultimately, however, their consequences are unpredictable; cumulatively they create new worlds.[23]

Such an approach to social change has much to recommend it to historians. From the historian's perspective it perhaps implies too generous a conception of the agency of interacting 'entities' and says too little explicitly about the costs of social adaptation, the conflicts to which it gives rise and the inequalities of power that often shape outcomes. But these can easily be incorporated. And that done, it offers a model of change that avoids determinism and helps explain diverse outcomes while also permitting generalisation about the nature of the processes involved. It can be particularly helpful in conceptualising the distinctiveness of the early modern period.

In important respects, changes in the 'late medieval' period had already created the pre-conditions for the developments charted here.[24] Nevertheless, from the early sixteenth century English society was galvanised by a succession of powerful stimuli – demographic, economic, religious, political and cultural – that were remarkably concentrated in time. Some were internally generated; some were English expressions of larger shifts and movements. They touched every section of society, albeit to different degrees and with varied chronologies. These experiences triggered adaptations in behaviour, attitudes and strategies that were the more complex because they were in many ways interconnected. They influenced each other, became entangled in the experience of individual lives and intersected to shape the fortunes of particular groups. Over time, these adaptations triggered further responses, not least by increasing the connectedness of society and creating a social environment more conducive to change. In sum, the dynamic of social change was enhanced, sometimes continuously, sometimes in sudden spurts. The sense of rupture that was felt by so many in the later sixteenth and seventeenth centuries, that feeling of standing on the other side of a series of significant watersheds that bred fear of a crumbling order in some, and optimism about the promise of new ways of being in others, was arguably an expression of this accelerated state of becoming.

Such processes gave this period its special texture and flavour as historical experience. Its landmark events and developments no longer have quite the significance that they had to the thinkers of the Scottish Enlightenment, who looked back from the later eighteenth century and saw a pattern in them. They no longer provide the directly 'usable' past celebrated by the historians of Victorian or early-twentieth-century England in support of a particular interpretation of British national identity. They have retreated in time and have become less central to a sense of who we are than the transformations of the twentieth and challenges of the twenty-first century. But to those whose curiosity is aroused by a deeper past, these centuries continue to provide a vital space for knowledge. Much of what they created remains before our eyes, resonates in our deepest assumptions, and is still on our tongues. They present a world that is strangely alien in some respects and immediately familiar in others. The evidence that people generated in such novel abundance allows us to know them better, if never completely. The social history of this period, in its broadest definition, is about recovering that knowledge of what we have been and about broadening our capacity, in Peter Laslett's memorable phrase, for 'understanding ourselves in time'.[25] It contains much to excite the imagination, offers much to engage the intellect, and retains the power to arouse the emotions. It touches on all aspects of the history of this period from a particular point of view. More: it is *central*. Without the perspective it provides, the rest is at best a partial and truncated history; at worst it is scarcely comprehensible.

### Notes

1  *Oxford English Dictionary*, online edn, www/oed.com/view/Entry/74152 and .../ Entry/74162 (accessed 22 January 2016).
2  P. Abrams, *Historical Sociology* (Ithaca, NY: Cornell University Press, 1982), 191.
3  See E. Cameron, 'Editor's introduction', in E. Cameron (ed.), *Early Modern Europe: An Oxford History* (Oxford: Oxford University Press, 1999), xvii; R. Starn, 'The early modern muddle', *Journal of Early Modern History*, 6 (2002), 299; H. Scott, 'Introduction: "Early modern" Europe and the idea of early modernity', in H. Scott (ed.), *The Oxford Handbook of Early Modern European History, 1350–1750*, Vol. I: *People and Places* (Oxford: Oxford University Press, 2015), 7. See also W. Reinhard, 'The idea of early modern history', in M. Bentley (ed.), *Companion to Historiography* (London and New York: Routledge, 1997); and the essays in G. Walker (ed.), *Writing Early Modern History* (London: Hodder Education, 2005).
4  R. Brackman, *The Elizabethan Invention of Anglo-Saxon England: Lawrence Nowell, William Lambarde and the Study of Old English* (Cambridge: D. S. Brewer, 2012), 1.

5 S. Collini, 'For the common good', *Times Literary Supplement* (15 January 2014), 3. Collini was writing of R. H. Tawney, but the same concern was central to the work of the Historical Economists.

6 C. Hill, *The World Turned Upside Down: Radical Ideas during the English Revolution* (Harmondsworth: Penguin, 1975), 384.

7 For the early development of English economic history, see K. Wrightson, *Earthly Necessities: Economic Lives in Early Modern England* (New Haven and London: Yale University Press, 2000), introduction. For William Johnson and the subsequent stages of the emergence of the term 'early modern', see P. Withington, *Society in Early Modern England: The Vernacular Origins of Some Powerful Ideas* (Cambridge: Polity, 2010), Chapters 1 and 2.

8 For accounts of these developments, see A. Wilson (ed.), *Rethinking Social History: English Society 1570–1920 and Its Interpretation* (Manchester: Manchester University Press, 1993), Chapters 1 and 2; S. Hindle, A. Shepard and J. Walter, 'The making and remaking of early modern English social history', in S. Hindle, A. Shepard and J. Walter (eds.), *Remaking English Society: Social Relations and Social Change in Early Modern England* (Woodbridge: Boydell, 2013), 2–10. I use the plural in deference to those who see social and cultural history as separate, and sometimes opposed, developments. I have never personally seen them as other than interrelated and, despite their differences of emphasis and concern, mutually supportive.

9 As noted in Withington, *Society*, 47, 66.

10 The phrase is borrowed from Annie Proulx, 'Big skies, empty places', *The New Yorker* (25 December 2000–1 January 2001), 139.

11 Quoting N. Buxton, *Domestic Culture in Early Modern England* (Woodbridge: Boydell, 2015), 271, 275. For the notion of an 'advanced organic economy', see E. A. Wrigley, *Continuity, Chance and Change: The Character of the Industrial Revolution in England* (Cambridge: Cambridge University Press, 1988), Chapter 2.

12 Quoting Withington, *Society*, 1, 166, 172; and J. Scott-Warren, *Early Modern English Literature* (Cambridge: Polity, 2005), 10, 226.

13 Quoting Lena C. Orlin, *Locating Privacy in Tudor London* (Oxford: Oxford University Press, 2007), 14.

14 See K. Wrightson, 'The family in early modern England: Continuity and change', in S. Taylor, R. Connors and C. Jones (eds.), *Hanoverian Britain and Empire: Essays in Memory of Philip Lawson* (Woodbridge: Boydell, 1998).

15 Quoting Scott-Warren, *Early Modern English Literature*, 15.

16 Quoting C. Wickham, *Framing the Early Middle Ages: Europe and the Mediterranean, 400–800* (Oxford: Oxford University Press, 2005), 831. Wickham's point about the transition from the Roman to the 'early medieval' world remains valid for any period.

17 Quoting P. Collinson, *De republica Anglorum; or, History with the Politics Put Back* (Cambridge: Cambridge University Press, 1990), 14. For state formation and its relationship to elite formation, see M. J. Braddick, *State Formation in Early Modern England, c. 1550–1700* (Cambridge: Cambridge University Press, 2000).

18  P. Krištúfek, *The House of the Deaf Man*, trans. J. Sherwood and P. Sherwood (Cardigan: Parthian Press, 2012), 13.

19  See e.g. C. G. A. Clay, *Economic Expansion and Social Change: England 1500–1700*, 2 vols. (Cambridge: Cambridge University Press, 1984); or more recently Wrightson, *Earthly Necessities*.

20  For shifts in contemporary descriptions of the social order, see K. Wrightson, 'Estates, degrees and sorts: Changing perceptions of society in Tudor and Stuart England', in P. Corfield (ed.), *Language, History and Class* (Oxford: Blackwell, 1991); and '"Sorts of people" in Tudor and Stuart England', in J. Barry and C. Brooks (eds.), *The Middling Sort of People: Culture, Society and Politics in England, 1550–1800* (Basingstoke: Macmillan, 1994).

21  For important new work on the changing distribution of wealth, see A. Shepard, *Accounting for Oneself: Worth, Status and the Social Order in Early Modern England* (Oxford: Oxford University Press, 2015).

22  Quoting Wickham, *Framing*, 13; and Linda Pollock in Chapter 3, 62.

23  For brief introductions to complexity theory, see M. Mitchell, *Complexity: A Guided Tour* (Oxford: Oxford University Press, 2009); E. Mitleton-Kelly and L. K. Daly, 'The concept of "co-evolution" and its application in the social sciences', in E. Mitleton-Kelly (ed.), *Co-Evolution of Intelligent Socio-Technical Systems: Understanding Complex Systems* (Berlin and Heidelberg: Springer, 2013); G. A. Marsan, N. Bellomo and A. Tobin (eds.), *Complex Systems and Society* (New York: Springer, 2013), Chapter 1.

24  See R. Horrox and W. M. Ormerod (eds.), *A Social History of England, 1200–1500* (Cambridge: Cambridge University Press, 2006).

25  The phrase was the title of the concluding chapter of P. Laslett, *The World We Have Lost* (London: Methuen, 1965).

PART I

*Discovering the English*

# Crafting the Nation

## Cathy Shrank

In September 1589, a troupe of professional players – the Queen's Men – arrived in Carlisle at the north-west extremity of Elizabeth I's kingdom.[1] We do not know where they played, but it is probable that, like travelling players in subsequent decades, they performed in the Moot Hall. Nor do we know what they played, but the symbolic restaging of the defeat of the Spanish Armada in *The Three Lords and Three Ladies of London*, penned by one of its members, Robert Wilson, would have made that play a timely choice, coming as it did a mere twelve months after the invading Spanish fleet had been repelled. That being so, the inhabitants of Carlisle would have been greeted in their civic space by an actor, 'very richly attired, representing London', stepping forward to address the audience and to deliver thanks that:

> All England is, and so preserv'd hath bene.
> Not by mans strength, his pollicie and wit,
> But by a power and providence unseen.[2]

Despite the metropolitan focus of the title, these opening lines frame the play as one that concerns a moment of national significance, affecting 'All England', and they testify to a belief in the special favour that God shows the English nation. Those lines also collapse the distance between London and the regions in which this play was almost certainly performed. 'London bids you welcome', the preface ends (sig. A2v), verbally transporting its audience to the capital itself, where they are subsequently enrolled in the action, addressed directly by characters in the play,[3] or at one point participate as judges in a singing competition arranged by the 'everyman' figure, Simplicity, who rejects the adjudication of his 'copes-metes' on stage and instead turns to '*one of the auditory*' (sig. C1v).

This chapter studies the way in which ideas of 'the nation' – as found in *Three Lords and Three Ladies* – were formed and disseminated in early modern England. The nation is more than an administrative unit; as

Benedict Anderson writes, it is a construction: a 'cultural artefact' capable
of arousing 'deep attachments'.[4] Anderson's definition of the nation as 'an
imagined political community' is useful (6). It is imagined because 'the
member of even the smallest nation will never know most of their fellow-
members, meet them, or even hear of them, yet in the minds of each lives
the image of their communion'; it has clearly defined limits ('no nation
imagines itself coterminous with mankind'); and it is perceived as a community because 'regardless of the actual inequality and exploitation that
may prevail in each, the nation is always conceived as a deep, horizontal
comradeship' (6–7).

Anderson's influential work does not itself recognise the existence of
an English nation during much of the timespan covered by this volume.
Nonetheless, his definition – with its emphasis on limits and on powerful emotive connections to an abstract concept – is regularly cited by
scholars of early modern Englishness, for whom the years between 1500
and 1750 encompass a particularly fertile phase in the development of
the 'nation'. During this period, we can trace the coalescence of national
identity around particular institutions; the emergence of processes that
enabled the nationwide dissemination of ideas and standardised practices;
and the deployment of discourses in which the nation is an unquestioned
category of organisation and allegiance predicated on the assumption that
the people of the realm would identify themselves as 'English', with particular customs and duties. As this chapter argues, these discourses had
also cumulative and mutually re-enforcing impact, as the same ideas and
rhetoric about Englishness would have been heard in church, in civic
spaces, in taverns and in the street.

The essay focuses on English, rather than British, identities. In the process, it traces a *longue durée* of ideas: as we will see, many of the elements
that historians such as Linda Colley regard as underlying eighteenth- and
early-nineteenth-century Britishness – namely, Protestantism; a geographically compact unit bound together by an efficient communications network (including a highly developed print trade); urbanisation; a culture
of political participation – are present in the articulation of English identity in the preceding centuries.[5] Moreover, whilst attempts (in 1603–10,
1670 and 1688–9) to formalise the union of the crowns of England and
Scotland into a closer compact of 'Great Britain' were not fulfilled until
the 1707 Act of Union, the labels 'Briton' and 'Britain' were not necessarily new or unfamiliar, at least to those with some schooling.[6] Latin histories, such as Julius Caesar's *Commentaries*, were staple classroom texts
and the island history about which English (and Scottish) boys learned

was therefore that of 'Britain' ('Britannia') and the 'Britons' ('Britanni').[7] The term 'Britain' was appearing on title-pages even before the accession of James VI and I, describing not only an English/British past but also its present, as in Maurice Kyffin's *Blessedness of Brytaine, or a celebration of the Queenes holyday* (1587). Even before the Union, the English were thus well accustomed to wearing different identities simultaneously, be those regional or national, and to appropriating elements of Britishness or, alternatively, of imposing Englishness on the larger landmass, as in the oft-repeated geographical fiction that reimagined England as 'this sceptered isle'.[8] Considering the importance of sustained hostilities with France which Colley identifies as the principal catalyst for cohering 'Britons' after 1707, William Shakespeare's *Henry V* (first performed *c.* 1599) is both oddly prophetic and characteristic of English cultural imperialism, as it co-opts into the war against France not merely representatives of England, Wales and Ireland (regions under English rule), but also of France's ancient ally, Scotland, then an independent nation.[9]

One of the many challenges of writing a social history of early modern nationhood is the difficulty of ascertaining what 'ordinary' people thought in a period in which the composition and dissemination of written records were predominantly conducted by an educated elite whose interests tended to align with the preservation of the status quo. Nonetheless, discourses about Englishness – the practices and beliefs that defined the nation and bound it together – percolated through the social strata. Nationhood was a lived experience in early modern England, encountered consciously or unconsciously through a range of activities and symbols. Even the food you consumed could be inflected with a sense of Englishness, thanks to the wide proliferation of national stereotypes that frequently centred on the preferred diet of each people. An 'English' taste for beef and ale thus set them apart from other nations: the Flemings and Dutch with their reputed love of butter, the Welsh and their enthusiasm for cheese, the Irish and their aqua-vitae, and so on.[10] And, despite Anderson's insistence that nations only emerge after the destruction of the 'legitimacy of divinely ordained, hierarchical dynastic realm' (6), for much of the period 1500–1750, far from being an impediment to national consciousness, the monarchy was a focal point for it. Much of the language and symbolism of nationhood was concentrated on, and sponsored by, the crown, from the coins used in daily purchases, stamped with the monarch's head, to the oaths of loyalty sworn by all office-holders, which – through additions made to the Stuart oaths – internalised allegiance, as its subscribers were required to 'swear from [their] heart'.[11] As Hugh Seton-Watson suggests of sixteenth-century England and France, 'there was a much stronger and wider sense of community [than elsewhere in Europe]. Englishmen and Frenchmen recognised themselves as such; accepted obligations to the sovereign; and admitted the claim of the sovereign on their loyalty at least in part because the sovereign symbolised the country as a whole.'[12]

The years 1500–1750 also saw a series of structural and ideological changes that expanded the range and nature of institutions felt (like the crown) to bind compatriots together. Not least among these developments was the creation of a 'national' Church after England's split from Rome in the 1530s. A foundational part of the legislation that effected this break was the Act in Restraint of Appeals (1533; 24 Henry VIII, c. 12), the import of which the Privy Council planned to have disseminated across the land via the pulpit, proclamations and printed copies affixed to every church door, and endorsed verbally at the dining tables of the nobility and 'the heddes, governers and Rulers of every good town within this realme'.[13] This statute is a productive starting point for unpacking some of the logic and rhetoric underpinning assertions of Englishness in subsequent decades.[14] Its opening statement – 'Where by dyvers sondrye olde autentiyke histories & cronicles hit is manyfestlye declared and expressed/ that this realme of Englande is an Impire, & so hath ben accepted in the worlde governed by one supreme heed and kynge' – affirms the sovereignty of the monarch, who is said to hold 'entire power ... to rendre and yelde Justice and fynall determination ... within this his realme'.[15] As such, it speaks to the power of the past (the 'olde autentiyke histories & cronicles') when forging what is, in essence, a national and legislative fiction. But the Act does more than proclaim the jurisdictional authority of the English monarch. It also asserts the autonomy of the English Church, which 'hathe bene alwayes thought ... sufficient and mete of it selfe, withoute the intermedynge of any exterior personne or persones', and ascribes particular importance to both 'the lawes temporalle', which keep 'the people of this realme in unite and peace without ravin or spoile', and the role of Parliament (comprising king, nobility and commons) in making 'sondry ordynaunces, lawes, statutes, and provisions ... to kepe [this realm] from the annoyaunce as welle as the See of Rome, as from the auctoritie of other foreyne potentatis/ attemptynge the diminution or violation therof' (sigs. B6v–B7r). The Act thus embeds the authority of the crown within a parliamentary system, in which the legislation passed protects not simply 'the prorogatyves, liberties/ and preeminences of the sayde imperyall crowne of this realme', but also 'the jurisdictions spirituall and temporalle of the same' (sig. B7r). In addition, it inscribes a pattern of Englishness in which the 'nation' – characterised by its autonomous crown, Church and laws – came to be defined against the Church of Rome and learned to be suspicious of potential interference from supranational jurisdictions. As Alan Cromartie observes, 'the great advantage of [religious] radicals, even in periods of adversity, was their ability to claim that their antagonists were really "papists", that is, adherents of a foreign power'.[16]

Just as the legislation enacting the breach with Rome served to enshrine the legislative role of Parliament (even as it worked to establish royal supremacy), so too it reified the Englishness of common law. The Act 'concernynge the exoneration of the kynges subjectes from exactions ... payd to the see of Rome' (1534; 25 Henry VIII, c. 21) lays down two criteria for testing the validity of the nation's laws: they must be indigenous ('devised ... within this realme for the welth of the same'), or they must be customary and consensual: taken by 'the people of this your realme ... atte theyr free lybertye by theyr owne consent, and ... bounde ... by long use and custome to the observance of the same'.[17] By the 1560s, the legal system could be used as a key way of distinguishing the governance of England from that of 'Fraunce, Italie, Spaine, Germanie and all other countries, which doe followe the civill lawe of the Romanes', or confidently declared 'to excell aswell the civile lawes of the Empiere, as also all other lawes of the world', as on the title-page of Richard Mulcaster's translation of John Fortescue's *De laudibus legum Angliae* (1468–71).[18] The place of the law as one of the bastions of Englishness is evident in the list of institutions that Martin Parker's broadside *A Scourge for the Pope* (1624?) presents as resisting the foreign, corrupting influence of Jesuit missionaries: 'Our king doth defy them'; 'Our Commons descry them'; 'Our laws will prevent them,/ And shrewdly torment them'; 'Our Parliament Royall,/ Will give them deniall.' But the law did not simply serve as an institution that (like monarchy, Church, and Parliament) commanded allegiance and that came to symbolise the nation and its difference from foreign polities. Successive Tudor governments also continued a process of standardisation (begun in the fifteenth century), establishing a 'national' legal system, through the codification of laws and the appointment and scrutiny of justices of the peace, who were expected to follow 'very specific instructions as to the particular laws "deemed fittest to be put in execution"'.[19]

The institution of a nationwide system of justice was designed and administered by government. A more culturally cohesive nation was also achieved through 'softer' measures. Chief amongst these was the growth of a 'national' system of education, in which, by the end of the sixteenth century, virtually identical school curricula were taught from St Paul's in London to St Bees' in Cumbria, employing textbooks, such as Latin and Greek grammars, 'approved' by royal authority. Many of these institutions were founded (or refounded, from Church schools) under royal and aristocratic patronage, but local communities likewise recognised the value of education and subscribed to found schools, as the village of Willingham, Cambridgeshire did in 1593.[20] Access to this education was admittedly limited to those boys whose families could afford both the sundry expenses that schooling accrued (for items such as books and candles) and the diminution in family income that resulted when one potential wage-earner was removed from employment. Nevertheless, the commonality of the educational experience created a shared cultural resource and set of values that had further impact as they leached into popular culture, through forms such as ballads and plays, which recurrently drew on or alluded to the classical literature and history studied in the early modern schoolroom.[21]

At the core of the school curriculum were the writings of the Roman statesman Marcus Tullius Cicero. The republican ideals of liberty and virtues of deliberative counsel endorsed by Cicero, along with his suspicion of would-be autocrats, might seem at odds with the monarchical structure of pre-modern England. Nonetheless, as John Watt has shown, the years between 1450 and 1530 saw the consolidation and propagation of the powerful and affective term 'commonweal'/'commonwealth', which frames the polity as a mutually participatory body, in which (at least rhetorically) the well-being of all is the proper aim of governance.[22] This did not conflict with traditional ideas of the 'communitarian monarchy', in which monarchs were appointed by God to promote and defend the common good. Rather, in Watt's words, the late fifteenth century witnessed 'a merger of meanings ... between a 1440s coinage for an older notion of "common profit" or common good, and a re-imported and revivified consciousness of *res publica*, based on a fresher and more extensive engagement with Cicero and other late Roman republican writers' (150). Refashioning ideas of 'common profit' along more Ciceronian lines had further ramifications, in the conceptualisation of the holders of public power, including the monarch, as 'officers of the commonwealth', and in the importance of the role of law, to which even the monarch was bound (152, 154). That 'commonweal' became such a dominant concept in early modern England was, in part, due to the extent to which it dovetailed with indigenous ideas and practices, not merely notions of the 'communitarian monarchy' but also the conciliar nature of government; the need for a cadre of 'lesser' governors, below the monarch, to implement policy and dispense justice; and habits of participation and office-holding that extended beyond central government to the administration of towns and parishes, and to the English legal system, with its use of juries.[23] As Thomas Smith wrote in the mid 1560s, 'A commonwealth is called a society or common doing of a multitude of free men collected together and united by common accord and covenauntes among themselves, for the conservation of themselves aswell in peace as in warre.'[24]

In practical terms, the diffusion and implementation of all these processes and ideas were enabled by nationwide systems of communication. As Keith Wrightson observes, 'However much they belonged to their villages and parishes, the country people of the period also moved in a larger world' (41). The early modern English population was a mobile one, even below the social elite, as servants moved between households, and agricultural labourers followed seasonal work. Kinship networks could thus be geographically extensive, and early modern texts regularly depict incomers to London meeting relations already settled, and made citizens, there.[25] Even those who never strayed beyond their parish boundary would consequently have known about, and encountered travellers from, other places. Communications were further enabled by the postal roads, which existed even before the formal implementation of a postal service that, from 1642, promised that 'any man may with safetie and securitie send letters in any part of this kingdome, and receive an answer within five days'.[26] The decades after 1560 saw the expansion of a network of royal standing posts, enabling the rapid relay of the royal packet, as well as the transportation of parcels on behalf of ordinary citizens and the presence of exchequer-funded postmasters who supplied horses for commercial hire.[27] Travel was further aided by mapping and surveying that envisioned the nation on the page, be it in the form of charts, or in cheaper formats, printed as tabular itineraries, listing distances between what become, through repetition across volumes, conventional staging points along a standardised route, or (in the last decades of the seventeenth century) more abstracted diagrams of road networks, such as *Mr Ogilby's and William Morgan's Pocket Book of the Roads* (1691), which depicts 'a nation held together by human mobility'.[28] The development of English cartography served a symbolic as well as a pragmatic function. As J. R. Hale notes, without maps 'a man could not visualize the country to which he belonged'.[29] Christopher Saxton's 1579 *Atlas of England and Wales* broke new ground in the detail and accuracy of its maps; further to that, it placed the local and regional within a national context, each map displaying the royal coat-of-arms, fostering what Richard Helgerson calls 'a cartographically and chorographically shaped consciousness of national power'.[30]

These printed maps and itineraries highlight the crucial role that print played in enabling the nation to conceptualise itself. It was not simply that copies of works could be produced more cheaply in greater numbers, allowing their wider circulation: the editions produced would also be uniform (stop-press corrections aside). The same words could thus be read in Newcastle as in Canterbury, in Plymouth as in Norwich, independent of the personal and professional networks along which manuscript works were transmitted, accumulating multiple variations en route. Print standardised as well as communicated: it meant that the letter of the law or the Latin grammar was identical across the nation, and it allowed people to travel in their minds as much as, if not more than, in person.

It was print, for example, that enabled the Edwardian drive towards uniformity in religion. The preface of the 1549 prayer book announces its intention to combat difference: 'where heretofore, there hath been great diversitie in saying and synging in churches within this realme: some folowyng Salsbury use, some Herford use, some the use of Bangor, some of Yorke, & some of Lincolne: Now from henceforth, all the whole realme shall have but one use'.[31] The Edwardian regime thus began a revolution in worship in which congregations across the nation followed the same form of worship laid down and authorised by the state, and disseminated through texts such as the Book of Common Prayer and (from 1547) ongoing editions of *Certayne Sermons* (the 'Book of Homilies'), which provided a series of sermons 'to be declared and redde, by all persones, Vicares, or Curates, every Sondaye in their churches'.[32] The centrality of religion to national identity is further attested by provisions made for church worship during the Civil War, when the Book of Common Prayer was recalled in 1645 and replaced, on pain of a 40s fine, with *A Directory for Publique Worship of God in the three Kingdoms*. The emphasis that this placed on the communal and uniform sprang from a fear of sectarianism. As the instructions on the 'assembling of the congregation' state, 'when the Congregation is to meete for Publique Worship, the people ... ought all to come, and joyne therein: not absenting themselves from the Publique Ordinances, through negligence, or upon pretence of Private meetings' (sigs. C1r–v). This anxiety bespeaks the importance awarded to conformity of religion in fostering national cohesion (even, or especially, as that cohesion was threatened); and in its concern to promote 'uniformity in Divine Worship' (sig. B4r) the *Directory* shares much of the spirit of the sixteenth-century prayer book that lies at the heart of the Stuart liturgy it (temporarily) overturned.

The standardising effect of church worship was not purely devotional, however: it was also cultural and linguistic. It is striking that the earliest known use of the phrase 'the King's English' dates to Edward VI's reign, a period in which the same centrally prescribed texts were supposed to be repeated on the same day, at the same time, across the land, in exactly the same words: a common cultural experience, but one designed and implemented from above, and delivered in the vocabulary and syntax of south-eastern English.[33] The stipulations regarding Edward VI's injunctions are typical of the Edwardian stress on both intelligibility and uniformity: they are to be read in churches four times a year, 'openly and distinctely', 'in maner and fourme in the same expressed'.[34]

Over the course of the sixteenth and seventeenth centuries, the kinds of demographic, cultural and administrative change outlined above 'drew together provincial communities into a more closely integrated national society'.[35] Yet processes and institutions alone do not explain the emergence of the 'nation' as a meaningful concept capable of commanding affection and allegiance. Much of the work on early modern Englishness has been conducted by literary scholars and focuses on the construction of nationhood in texts – such as Richard Hakluyt's *Principall Navigations* (1589), Raphael Holinshed's *Chronicles* (1577, 1587) or Thomas Wilson's *Arte of Rhetorique* (1553) – which, despite increasing literacy rates, would have reached relatively restricted audiences, on account of the size and consequent cost of these volumes.[36] Significant though these more elite works undoubtedly were in shaping national consciousness, this essay in contrast focuses on three media – plays, ballads and broadsheets, and church worship – which had deep social and geographic penetration, and were thus available to literate and non-literate alike. It uses them to unpack the ways in which the language used in discourses deployed by and about 'national' institutions (such as Church, state and monarch), and the narratives spun about them, helped to cultivate the 'deep attachments' that Anderson regards as a compelling feature of national consciousness (4).

Wilson's *Three Lords and Three Ladies*, with which this chapter began, richly illustrates some of the mechanisms and ideological prisms through which early modern Englishmen and -women were invited to 'imagine' their nation. The play draws on an older tradition of morality drama, in which characters represent moral traits, and infuses it with a politically motivated xenophobia, whereby the antagonists are depicted as morally, linguistically and ethnically 'other'. The Spanish lords are identified as 'Pride', 'Ambition' and 'Tyranny'; their pages 'Shame', 'Treachery' and 'Terror'; and their herald 'Shealty', whose name, 'An Irish word, signifie[s] liberty, rather remisnes, loosnes if ye wil' (sig. G4v). Their otherness is made more evident still in the way that they shift readily among various languages (Spanish, Latin, French). The Vices (personifications of moral failings) also appeal to popular stereotypes of other national and ethnic groups. 'I ... am a Roman', Simony declares, his name (the practice of buying or selling ecclesiastical preferments) and nationality striking a patently anti-papist note: 'Dissimulation a Mongrel, half an Italian, halfe a Dutchman. Fraud so too, halfe French, and halfe Scottish: and thy parentes [Usury] were both Jewes' (sig. F4r).

The play not only demonstrates the use of foreignness as a counterpoint in the construction of national identity; it also reveals one of the peculiarities of England as a nation in the way that the dominance of its metropolis can be deployed as a focus and filter for English identities. It is the 'London' lords who defeat the nation's enemies, collectively defined in stage directions as 'Spaniards'. They then assert their superiority over the provincial 'Lords of Lincoln' to win the Ladies of London in marriage. Despite this apparent show of metropolitan chauvinism, however, London is not a 'closed shop': like many London citizens, the everyman character Simplicity is an incomer, who gave up being 'a meal-man and came to dwell in London' (sig. C3r). 'Time teares out milestones', he tells us: 'Time seasons a pudding well, and Time hath made me a free man.'

That the Queen's Men existed at all and developed the patriotic repertoire that includes *Three Lords and Three Ladies* owes much to the desire of Tudor governments to exert control over and command the loyalty of the disparate parts of the monarch's territories. The Queen's Men were formed in 1583 on the instruction of Elizabeth's spymaster, Francis Walsingham, with the support of the queen's long-time favourite Robert Dudley, earl of Leicester, who supplied many of its original members from his own playing company, Leicester's Men.[37] The primary purpose of this new company was to tour, carrying not only the queen's name to the furthest reaches of her realm but also plays that used English/British history to promote a loyalist and often specifically Protestant ideology, such as *The Troublesome Reign of King John* (printed 1591), *King Leir* (entered in the Stationers' Register, 1594), or *The Famous Victories of Henry V* (Stationers' Register, 1594). The Queen's Men were by no means the only touring company in sixteenth- and early-seventeenth-century England, but they toured more extensively and more continuously than their contemporaries; they also reached more venues by dividing the company in two.[38] In 1589, the year in which they played at Carlisle, for example, there are receipts for members of the company performing at locations as dispersed as Kent, the south-west coast, East Anglia, Ireland and the Welsh Marches.[39]

The county-by-county volumes of the *Records of Early English Drama* are not yet complete, and the sources they collate are often patchy, but there is nonetheless evidence of regular, nationwide visits by touring companies: between 1560 and 1639, for instance, there were 204 payments to licensed players made in Coventry; 133 in Norwich; 94 in York.[40] On these visits, players would perform in a variety of venues (drinking places, churchyards, civic halls, as well as private houses) and some performances would be free to watch, paid for by the mayor or his equivalent. In 1639, a seventy-five-year-old Richard Willis remembered attending a play in Gloucester as a child. The practice he describes is envisaged as both local and national:

> In the city of Gloucester the manner is (as I think it in other corporations) that when Players of Enterludes come to towne, they first attend the Mayor to informe him what noblemans servants they are, and so get licence for their publike playing; and if the Mayor like the Actors or would shew respect to their Lord and Master, he appoints them to play their first play before himselfe and the Aldermen and common Counsell of the City; and that is called the Mayors play, where every one that will come in without money.[41]

Plays, then, were not restricted to metropolitan culture, and they were a powerful way of encouraging the nation to imagine itself, particularly since the Queen's Men established the English history play as a staple part of theatre repertoire that other companies then emulated.[42] As Willis notes of the performance in Gloucester, 'this sight tooke such impression on me, that when I came towards mans estate, it was as fresh in my memory, as if I had seen it newly acted' (113).

The same social and geographic reach, and emotive impact, achieved by early modern players can be ascribed to ballads and broadsides. In Adam Fox's words, 'all manner of information and entertainment was soon produced in broadside and broadsheet format; it was cheap to buy, posted in public places, and distributed throughout the nation in town and country alike'.[43] Cheap print could, moreover, act as 'an instrument of social cohesion, as more people were brought into the reading public, and as stories, images and values permeated multiple tiers of English society'.[44] Not all broadside material was designed to be sung, but much of it was: even sheets mainly composed in prose often contain a summative rhyme, in ballad metre, the short lines of which, with their rhyme scheme and regular rhythm, are easy to remember and thus to disseminate orally. Another advantage of the single-sheet format was the speed with which it could be produced: it probably took one working day to set and print a run.[45] Ballads and broadsheets are thus a useful way of responding to emergencies (rebellions, like the Northern Rising in 1569; threats of invasion, such as the Armada in 1588; the illness and death of monarchs) and of sharing news: about sensational crimes, about war and peace, about prodigious births and monstrous fish.

These ephemeral texts do not simply capture the sense of a nation linked together by networks of news running into and out of the capital, where the English printing trade was primarily based: they also helped shape what it meant to be part of that nation. Particularly striking is the recurrent utilisation of national history, as in the 'disguised ruler' ballads, such as *The Miller of Mansfield*, *The Shepherd and the King* and *The Tanner of Tamworth*, which were reprinted regularly, well into the eighteenth century.[46] These ballads follow a similar formula, in which a king (Henry II, Alfred the Great, Edward IV) encounters a provincial labourer, who fails to recognise him and consequently treats him without sycophancy. By identifying specific rulers, these ballads promote a shared national past, whilst the fantasy of inclusivity and social mobility that they depict speaks to Anderson's conception of the fictions of 'comradeship' on which nationhood relies (7). At the end of each ballad, despite their inadvertent discourtesy – and, in the Miller's case, proof of his criminality (he poaches venison) – the labourers are rewarded with land and honours.

As these ballads also demonstrate, national identity was often focused on the monarch: their named, provincial locations bound into a national story through the king's mobility. This close link between people and sovereign is underscored by the recurrent use of the shared possessive pronoun: 'Henry *our* roiall king would go a hunting,' *The Miller* begins; likewise *The Tanner*: '*Our* king he would a hunting ride' (emphasis added). The choice of the pronoun has emotive effect, closing a temporal gap, knitting auditors/readers into a common past and forging a relationship in which the monarch belongs to them. The niceties of language used thus help mould national identity, as can be seen in the recurrence of coercive adjectives, such as 'true' or 'naturall born', to define the behaviour expected of 'Englishmen' and figuratively to disinherit those who demur. 'True' Englishness might entail living up to a brave and glorious past, epitomised by exemplars such as the explorers 'Gilbert, Hawkins, F[ro]bisher' and the military men 'the Norisses, and noble Veeres, / and

Sidnies[,] famouse many yeares', in order to defend the 'true Religion'.[47] Or it might be demonstrated by working to thwart the 'damnable and hellish Machinations' of 'those bloody men of Rome', as in *A Catalogue of the Names of those Holy Martyrs Who Were Burned in Queen Maries Reign* (1679), which commemorates the Marian martyrs, over 120 years after their deaths: a clearly anti-Catholic intervention at the beginning of the Exclusion Crisis.

Ballads could also coalesce the nation through cultivating a sense of collective responsibility for its fate. As the rhyme at the end of *The forme and shape of a monstrous child, borne at Maydstone in Kent* warns in 1568:

> This monstrous shape to thee England
> Playn shewes thy monstrous vice.
> ...
> Wherefore to ech in England now,
> Let this Monster them teach:
> To mend the monstrous life they show,
> Least endles death them reach.

But it is not merely the active participation of its readers/auditors through prayer or moral reformation to which these single sheets attest. From the early sixteenth century, broadsides comment on and express opposition to government policy, as can be seen in works such as *Questions worthy to be consulted on for the weale publyque* (c. 1548), which lists forty-eight perceived abuses of the commonweal, or Thomas Churchyard's *Davy Dicars Dreme* (c. 1551). As such, these broadsheets evidence the existence of a type of post-Reformation, pre-Revolution public sphere, whereby 'under the rubric of the commonwealth, a range of issues concerned with the workings and maintenance of the social order were discussed'.[48] Nationhood is manifested not merely by the toeing of the loyal line but also by a committed and often passionate desire to contribute to, and profit, the commonweal. The role here played by cheap print was enhanced by the increased range and quantity of material circulating in affordable and accessible formats during the Civil War and Interregnum. Jason Peacey does not make explicit connections between national identity and the 'democratization' of knowledge that he traces from the 1640s and 1650s onwards.[49] Nonetheless, printing information about daily proceedings in Parliament or the conduct of individual MPs would have intensified, and made more widely available, the sense of participating in a national community in which business conducted in Parliament was recognised to be of nationwide significance and a proper concern of all.

Ballads and broadsides thus shape readers and auditors into an imagined community. This was achieved not only through subject matter appealing to patriotic sentiment or fostering xenophobic outrage, but also through style (such as the insistent use of coercive pronouns) and the powerful ideological discourses into which their authors tapped. Not least of these was the idea that their nation was the recipient of divine favour. 'The Lord of Hosts hath blest no land / As he hath blessed ours', asserts *The Joyfull Peace* (1613). For those ballads that were set to music, the emotive resonance of the national community they evoke or the enemies they mock, can only have been enhanced by the communality of singing. Printed ballads usually give a tune by its title only, rather than carrying musical notation; this would seem to indicate that these were known tunes, or ones that could be mastered quickly, and were thus designed to cater to an audience without musical literacy.[50] The 'we' of a ballad text potentially becomes a 'we' experienced through communal performance.

If evocations of national identity encountered in ballads were recurrently focused on the monarch's person, this was still more the case when the English people moved from tavern or street into the church. Aside from two brief hiatuses under Mary Tudor (1553–1558) and during the Interregnum (1649–1660), the years after 1534 saw the establishment and consolidation of a national religion, with the monarch at its head. The use of church worship to cultivate loyal subjects is evident in the prayers for the monarch that formed part of the communion service, and a text such as *The Homelie against disobedience* (first printed, separately, in 1570, in the wake of the Northern Rising) being integrated into regular church worship through its inclusion in the 1571 edition of the *Second Tome of Homilees*. As the *Homelie* indicates, like the 'obedience' ballads (such as *Nortons Falcehood*) that coincided with its initial composition, the Church was used as a mouthpiece for the state at times of crisis. In 1588, *A fourme of Prayer, necessary for the present time and state* not only disseminated appropriate prayers to be read in church, but also instructed 'all Curates and Pastors' how they should 'exhort their Parishioners' to attend church 'not onely on Sundayes and Holidayes, but also on Wednesdayes and Fridayes, and at other times likewise'. The prayers, Psalms and lessons to be 'distinctely and plainly read' included Old Testament readings, such as Exodus 14 or 1 Samuel 17, in which God saved his chosen people in times of tribulation, drawing an implicit parallel between England and the 'nation of Israel'.[51] Preachers were also instructed to 'moove the people to abstinence and moderation in their diet, to the ende they might bee the more able to relieve the poore, to pray unto God to heare his holy worde, and to doe other good and godly workes' (sigs. A3r–v); interestingly, this rubric prioritises not obedience (as we might expect) but charity, fostering a sense of community as a means of buttressing the nation against external threat.

The Church of England was more than an organ for preaching obedience to the monarch, however. As is evident from *Three Lords and Three Ladies* or the 1679 *Catalogue*, protecting the national religion was a powerful rallying cry. 'Englishness' became increasingly identified with Protestantism, and public expressions of loyalty inscribed in oaths of association from 1584 onwards 'redefined allegiance in confessional terms'.[52] 'The conditional nature of allegiance to the monarch' was not 'spelled out' in the Elizabethan and Jacobean associations, but by 'hint[ing] at an implicit relationship between the sovereign's defence of the faith and the subject's duty of obedience', those associations sowed 'intellectual legacies ... which played an important part in English resistance movements of the 1640s and 1680s' (2). Once the interests of Church, monarch and nation were no longer assumed to be one and the same, the nature of what constituted the behaviour and loyalties demanded of 'true' Englishmen inevitably became a site of contestation. The inhabitants of Herefordshire might not have perceived a conflict between their identity as 'faithfull Subjects to his Majesty' and 'as free-borne English-men' when in 1642 they 'joyne[d] in an unanimous Resolution to maintaine: 1. Protestant Religion. 2. The Kings just power. 3. The Lawes of the Subject. 4. The libertie of the Land'.[53] Nonetheless, their belief in the compatibility of all these objectives was not necessarily shared by others. 'True Englishmen' might equally be defined by love for 'the Libertie of this Common-wealth' and an unwillingness ever to be 'reduced again under the Family of the Stewarts'.[54]

The mental uncoupling of the symbiotic relationship among Church, monarch and nation in the mid seventeenth century was not new, however. It happened strikingly early in the life of the English Church, with the restoration of Catholicism under Mary Tudor. During Mary's reign, theories of justified resistance were not only developed and propounded through texts such as John Ponet's *Shorte Treatise of Politicke Power* (1556), John Knox's *First Blast of the Trumpet against the Monstrous Regiment of Women* (1558) and Christopher Goodman's *How Superior Powers Oght to Be Obeyed* (1558). Those works were also accompanied by a campaign of cheap print, produced abroad or at home on illicit presses by printers such as John Day (under the imprint 'Michael Wood') or Hugh Singleton.[55] The radical nature of these publications is evident from *Certayne questions demaunded and asked by the noble realme of Englande, of her true naturall chyldren and subjectes of the same*, printed by Singleton in 1555. From the title onwards (which figures the country, not the queen, as mother and thus the proper focus for the obedience of her 'subjectes'), the pamphlet reframes the nature of the contract between ruler and ruled. 'Item, whether the Realme of England belong to the Quene, or to her subjects?', it demands (sig. A4v). In the process, it delegitimises Mary for violating the laws of the land and positions Parliament as a representative body, constituted not to do the 'pleasure ... of his Prince', but to 'speake ... for the profyte of the poore man, and the wealth of the realme' (sig. A3v). It does all this, moreover, not in a long, complex, expensive text (like Ponet's or Goodman's) but in a cheap and easily disseminated single-sheet octavo, using a series of short rhetorical questions, designed to produce the 'right' response from 'true naturall' Englishmen and women.

The temporary fracturing of the bond among Church, crown and nation under Mary is a reminder that the expression and focus of national identity is often contingent on historical circumstance: Mary's religious policies and her marriage to a foreign prince (Philip II of Spain) shaped a response that would not have been evident should Edward VI have outlived her. The scale of the prosecutions that she authorised also helped harden the correlation between Englishness and Protestantism, as they became etched into national memory, aided by texts such as John Foxe's *Actes and Monuments* (editions from 1563), the ghoulishly illustrated pages of which were supposed to be available in every parish church. Such fusion of religious and national identity would have been compounded by the annual remembrance of other 'deliverances', notably the Gunpowder Treason of 1605. 'Grant that we may still detest / that doctrine and that sinne, / That teacheth us to eate our God, / and eke to kill our King', preaches one ballad, twenty years later, equating the Catholic belief in transubstantiation with the promotion of regicide.[56]

The dynastic circumstances in which England found itself in the last decades of Elizabeth's reign, when political stability was felt to be threatened by the lack of an obvious heir, similarly gave rise to a particular manifestation of national identity. In the words of Patrick Collinson, 'the notion was freely accessible that the crown itself was a public office which existed only to conserve the public safety: even if the public safety was only spoken of, in terms, as the personal safety of the monarch'.[57] Like many of the other texts discussed here, the 1584 Instrument of Association, which bound subscribers to give their 'lyves, lands and goodes' in Elizabeth I's defence, was devised by those in authority: in this case, William Cecil and

Francis Walsingham, who also oversaw its dissemination.[58] Nonetheless, despite the fact that it was engineered from the top, rather than emerging from grassroots, it was still a meaningful expression of national allegiance. The thousands of gentry, clergy, nobility and 'great number of inferior quality' who subscribed to it did so as part of a national community, binding themselves 'joyntly' as 'natural-born subjects of this Realm of England', and swearing to resist 'Publick Enemies to God, Our Queen, and to our Native Country'.[59] At the heart of a document designed by the regime to ensure stable government are thus a rhetoric and process of popular participation. Even if this is a chimera, used opportunistically by those in power to serve their own purposes, it nonetheless creates certain assumptions about the role and place of non-elites in the national polity. As Collinson notes, 'to examine surviving copies of the Bond ... is to be given a vivid insight into both the autonomous political capacity of the Elizabethan republic and its extent and social depth, a carpet, as it were, with a generous pile'.[60] There is thus a tension (sometimes within the same documents) between those discourses designed to encourage obedience and those that cultivate the impression, and therefore expectation, of a more participatory approach. Time and again, from the administration of justice to the royal supremacy (which Thomas Cromwell wanted discussed at dining tables across the land), the policies and propaganda intended to centralise and buttress royal authority paradoxically relied on the devolution of powers and helped to foster a discursive political culture. The efforts to create a loyal, cohesive nation – efforts that saw the Queen's Men arriving in Carlisle – also served to acknowledge that royal power needed to appeal to, and foster, what Thomas Smith described as 'common accord'.[61]

## Notes

1  A. Douglas and P. Greenfield (eds.), *Records of Early English Drama: Cumberland/ Westmoreland/Gloucestershire* (Toronto: University of Toronto Press, 1986), 65.

2  R. Wilson, *The pleasant and Stately Morall, of the three Lordes and three Ladies of London* (London, 1590), sig. A2v. Original spelling and punctuation have been retained in quotations from sixteenth- and seventeenth-century texts, although i/j and u/v have been regularised. For evidence that *Three Lords and Three Ladies* was part of the Queen's Men's repertoire during this period, see S. McMillin and S.-B. MacLean, *The Queen's Men and Their Plays* (Cambridge: Cambridge University Press, 1998), 89. For the Moot Hall as the probable site of performance, see *Records of Early English Drama*, http://link.library.utoronto.ca/reed/venue.cfm?VenueListID=48 (accessed 28 July 2014).

3  See, for example, Nemo's address '*to the audience*', sig. E1v.

4  B. Anderson, *Imagined Communities: Reflections on the Origin and Spread of Nationalism*, new edn (London: Verso, 2006), 4.

5  *Ibid.*, 369–72.

6  For the abortive attempts at union in 1670 and 1688–9, see C. Whatley, *Scots and the Union* (Edinburgh: Edinburgh University Press, 2006), 29–31, 58, 91.

7  The work was available, in English, using these translations of the Latin, from 1530 as *The Commentaryes of Caesar as concernyth thys realm of England sumtyme callyd Brytayne.*

8  W. Shakespeare, 'Richard II', in *The Riverside Shakespeare*, ed. G. Blakemore Evans et. al., 2nd edn (Boston, MA: Houghton Mifflin, 1997), II.i.43.

9  L. Colley, *Britons: Forging the Nation 1707–1837* (New Haven: Yale University Press, 1992), 5–6.

10 See, for example, W. Shakespeare, 'The Merry Wives of Windsor', in *The Riverside Shakespeare*, III.ii.302–4.

11 *An Act for the better discovering and repressing of Popish recusants; 3 & 4 James I c. 4* (1606).

12 H. Seton-Watson, *Nations and States: An Enquiry into the Origins of Nations and the Politics of Nationalism* (London: Methuen, 1977), 8.

13 TNA, SP 6/3, fol. 86r; see J. Gairdner (ed.), *Letters and Papers, Foreign and Domestic, of the Reign of Henry VI* (London: Longman, 1882), Vol. VI, item 1487(2).

14 See G. R. Elton, 'The evolution of a Reformation statute', *EHR*, 64 (1949).

15 *Anno XXIIII Henrici VIII* (London, 1533), sigs. B6v–C3r (B6v).

16 A. Cromartie, *The Constitutionalist Revolution: An Essay on the History of England, 1450–1642* (Cambridge: Cambridge University Press, 2006), 62.

17 *Anno. XXV. Henrici VIII* (London, 1535), sig. F1r.

18 T. Smith, *De republica Anglorum*, ed. M. Dewar (Cambridge: Cambridge University Press, 1982), 144. J. Fortescue, *A learned commendation of the politique laws of Englande*, trans. R. Mulcaster (London, 1567); this was reprinted in 1573, 1599, 1616, 1660 and 1672.

19 K. Wrightson, *English Society, 1580–1680* (London: Hutchinson, 1982), 152. For an overview of fifteenth-century processes, see Cromartie, *Constitutionalist Revolution*, 4–32.

20 Wrightson, *English Society*, 191.

21 The degree to which early modern England was steeped in classical culture is evident from the range of allusions in Shakespeare's plays: for the gate price of 1d, theatre-goers could have seen plays about figures from Roman history (e.g. *Julius Caesar, Coriolanus*), derived from classical literature (e.g. 'Pyramus and Thisbe' in *A Midsummer Night's Dream*), or that bandied allusions to mythical figures, such as Ganymede (in *As You Like It*). For the use of learned allusions in cheap print, see C. Shrank, 'Trollers and dreamers: Defining the citizen-subject in sixteenth-century cheap print', *Yearbook of English Studies*, 38 (2008), 109, 112.

22 J. Watt, '"Common weal" and "Commonwealth": England's monarchical republic in the making, c. 1450–1530', in A. Gamberini, A. Zorzi and J.-P. Genet (eds.), *The Languages of Political Society* (Rome: Viella, 2011).

23 P. Withington, *Society in Early Modern England: The Vernacular Origins of Some Powerful Ideas* (Cambridge: Polity, 2010), 134–68.

24 Smith, *De republica*, 57.

25 See, for example, the goldsmith Yellowhammer in Thomas Middleton, *A Chaste Maid in Cheapside* (*c.* 1613).

26 Anon., *A Full and cleare Answer to a false and scandalous Paper* (London, 1642), 1.

27 M. Brayshay, 'Royal post-horse routes in England and Wales: The evolution of the network in the later-sixteenth and early-seventeenth century', *Journal of Historical Geography*, 17 (1991), 373–4; cf. M. Brayshay, 'Waits, musicians, bearwards and players: The inter-urban road travel and performances of itinerant entertainers in sixteenth and seventeenth century England', *Journal of Historical Geography*, 31 (2005), 431. See also P. Withington in this volume, 183.

28 A. McRae, *Literature and Domestic Travel in Early Modern England* (Cambridge: Cambridge University Press, 2009), 109.

29 Cited in R. Helgerson, *Forms of Nationhood: The Elizabethan Writing of England* (Chicago: University of Chicago Press, 1992), 108.

30 *Ibid.*, 108; for the growth of chorography in this period, see D. Woolf, *The Social Circulation of the Past: English Historical Culture, 1500–1730* (Oxford: Oxford University Press, 2003), esp. 142–63.

31 *The booke of the common prayer and administracion of the sacramentes, and other rites and ceremonies of the Churche: After the use of the Churche of England* (London, 1549), sig. A2v.

32 *Certayne Sermons, or homelies, appointed by the kynges Majestie* (London, 1547), sig. A2v.

33 Thomas Wilson's use of the phrase in *The Arte of English Rhetorique* (London, 1553), sig. P2r, pre-dates the first citation of 1616 in the *Oxford English Dictionary*.

34 *Certayne Sermons*, sig. A3r.

35 Wrightson, *English Society*, 222.

36 See, for example, A. Hadfield, *Literature, Politics, and National Identity: Reformation to Renaissance* (Cambridge: Cambridge University Press, 1994); Helgerson, *Forms of Nationhood*; C. McEachern, *The Poetics of English Nationhood, 1590–1612* (Cambridge: Cambridge University Press, 1996); P. Schwyzer, *Literature, Nationalism and Memory in Early Modern England and Wales* (Cambridge: Cambridge University Press, 2004); C. Shrank, *Writing the Nation in Reformation England, 1530–1580* (Oxford: Oxford University Press, 2004).

37 McMillin and MacLean, *The Queen's Men and Their Plays*, 18–32.

38 *Ibid.*, 36, 52.

39 *Ibid.*, 178–9.

40 S. Keenan, *Travelling Players in Shakespeare's England* (Basingstoke: Palgrave Macmillan, 2002), 166–7.

41 R. Willis, *Mount Tabor* (London, 1639), 110.

42 McMillin and McLean, *The Queen's Men and Their Plays*, 36.

43 A. Fox, *Oral and Literate Culture in England, 1500–1700* (Oxford: Oxford University Press, 2000), 9.

44 T. Watt, *Cheap Print and Popular Piety, 1550–1640* (Cambridge: Cambridge University Press, 1991), 5.

45 H. S. Bennett, *English Books and Readers, 1475–1557* (Cambridge: Cambridge University Press, 1952), 231.

46 The *English Short Title Catalogue* lists editions of *The Miller of Mansfield* (1588–1800), *The Shepherd and the King* (1650–1775) and *The Tanner of Tamworth* (1596–1750). *The Miller* was even adapted into a play by Robert Dodsley in 1737. For the development of a 'sense of a national past' over the sixteenth and seventeenth centuries, see Woolf, *Social Circulation*.

47 Anon., *Gallants to Bohemia* (London, 1620).

48 P. Lake and S. Pincus, 'Rethinking the public sphere in early modern England', *JBS*, 45 (2006), 275.

49 J. Peacey, *Print and Public Politics in the English Revolution* (Cambridge: Cambridge University Press, 2013), 397.

50 Watt, *Cheap Print and Popular Piety*, 33.

51 The significance to English Protestant identity of Exodus 14 (in which, with God's help, the exiled Israelites cross the Red Sea to freedom) is also signalled by the fact that it features as a woodcut on the title-page of the 1560 Geneva Bible.

52 E. Vallance, 'Loyal or rebellious? Protestant associations in England, 1584–1696', *Seventeenth Century*, 17 (2002), 1.

53 *A declaration, or resolution of the countie of Hereford* (1642).

54 W. R., *No Parliament but the Old* (London, 1659).

55 See E. Evenden, *Patents, Pictures and Patronage: John Day and the Tudor Book Trade* (Aldershot: Ashgate, 2008), 29–37; C. Panofré, *Certayne questions demaunded and asked by the Noble Realme of Englande*, EEBO Introductions, http://eebo.chadwyck.com (accessed 26 August 2014).

56 *A Song or Psalme of thanksgiving, in remembrance of our great deliverance from the Gun-powder Treason, the fift of November* (London, 1625).

57 P. Collinson, '*De republica Anglorum*; or, History with the politics put back', in *Elizabethan Essays* (London: Hambledon, 1994), 19.

58 *The Egerton Papers, Camden Society*, 12 (1840).

59 The phrase 'great number of inferior quality' is that of Henry, earl of Huntingdon in a letter to Francis Walsingham on 22 December 1584; TNA, SP 15/28/2, fol. 140.

60 P. Collinson, 'The Monarchical Republic of Elizabeth I', in Collinson, *Elizabethan Essays*, 48.

61 Smith, *De republica*, 57.

# 2

# Surveying the People

## Paul Griffiths

To preserve or augment revenues there must bee meanes: the meanes
are wrought by knowledge; knowledge had by experience; experience
by view and due observacon of the particulars by which revenues doe
or maie arise.[1]

To know the present state of my whole diocess before I would enter
upon my triennial visitation; I thank God I find no cause to say upon
the whole account, *he that encreaseth knowledge, encreaseth sorrow.*[2]

I have been so ravished with the study of numbers, that if any man
will ask me, what is the chiefest Good next to God, that in this life
I take delight in? I must answer, Number; if, what is the second?
Number; if, what the third? Number.[3]

The making of surveys was always important to those who governed
England. Collecting and processing information had long been a tried
and trusted governing strategy, and medieval manorial record-keeping,
with its lengthy surveys of tenants, holdings and obligations, provided
solid grounding for later times.[4] But beyond doubt, the practice of surveying became more vital in all government fields in the course of the
sixteenth and seventeenth centuries, and information cultures and systems
became more sophisticated and widespread with the emergence of what
Peter Burke calls the 'paper state'.[5]

Deep-seated, long-lasting change made the difference. The English state
was transformed by the start of the eighteenth century. The apparatus of
governance had to adapt, alter and grow in response to the seismic shifts
of the two centuries after 1500: a population boom, religious revolution,
economic and commercial transformations in town and country, empire,
and root-and-branch reforms of financing and administering the state (to
name just five). The precise nature of the 'Tudor revolution in government' remains debatable, but this sustained scope and scale of information use by the state had not been seen before. A full list might fill a short

book, but we can start with Henrician muster counts; the mountain of paperwork in fiscal returns to the Great Subsidy (1524–5); Wolsey's corn surveys; enclosure commissions; a nationwide system to register births, marriages and deaths (1538); the *Valor Ecclesiasticus*, which took stock of Church wealth in the wake of Henry VIII's royal supremacy (1535); and a string of state-sponsored surveys in later decades.

At the heart of England's developing practice of surveying was the greater reach of the state into parishes all over the land, crucially through poor laws that could not work without counting and classifying people, articles of enquiry in which Whitehall sought local description and calculation to get to the bottom of all sorts of issues, tax assessments, and Books of Orders to implement whenever dearth or plague struck.[6] And it is in the early seventeenth century that we start to see Whitehall's attempt to collect and collate data on burgeoning trade hitting maturity, with the first Council of Trade set up in 1622 to gauge 'the true balance of the trade of this kingdom' from 'all records and writings as you shall find needful for your better information'. The quest to balance trade generated reams of paper and statistics in the seventeenth century when the state was seeking data on fisheries, shipping, coal, cargos, and the old and new draperies.[7] Data flows if anything picked up pace after 1660 when the Hearth Tax, requiring lists of householders and the number of hearths in their homes; surveys of communicants; the Compton Census of religious affiliation; the Marriage Duty Act; settlement laws that tried to toughen up residence requirements and the right to move somewhere; and the Poll Tax led to countless local 'surveys'.[8]

In seeking information – or 'making knowne'[9] – on myriad matters, the state (and Church) had helping hands in developing local surveying cultures, drawing localities into data grids in which parish and polity worked hand-in-hand to tackle social strains. State and Church officials regularly told local governors to survey their patch, hammering home the elemental essentials of numbers and information. Quite typically, as he was getting ready for a visitation in 1686, Ely's Bishop Francis Turner wrote ahead of time to his parishes asking for their 'light', as he did not want to be 'in the dark'. He asked for presentments and a 'notia', by which he meant:

> an account of every family, expressing the christian and syrname of the house-keeper, the number and names of all persons above sixteen years old in that family by themselves, and of all under sixteen by themselves; setting for a mark the letters A. C. overright the name of every adult, that is the actual communicant in each family, and c. a. for a mark over the name of

every child that has been sufficiently well catechized; and *con* for a mark over every one that has bin already confirm'd.

'By this means', Bishop Turner closed, 'both you and I shall be able to discern at one view what is already done, and what there is yet to do'. A 'good shepherd', he mused in pastoral mode, ought '*to know his sheep and be known by them*' and '*call his own sheep by name*'.[10]

These are census-taking words, but this information-relation between parish and polity was two-way, with local initiatives often in the driving seat. Local surveillance had self-generating priorities and processes that were developed to meet local needs in a frequently distinctive manner. Localities too stuttered from week to week, coping with a hailstorm of troubles. Numbers of poor soared, draining thin resources and deepening concern about need, migration and real or imagined crime-waves that needed quantifying to be understood. Communities up and down England felt that they were 'dayly' under greater pressure.[11]

In towns in particular we hear year after year, with rising heat, that 'the poor' are 'moche increased' of 'late yeares'; 'the number of poore' has 'greatly increased'; or, as Salisbury's bench griped in 1638, 'the number of those [needing] relieefe is growne farr greater then in tymes past'.[12] Reading Southampton's records it feels like a town stunned, as hard-up 'inmates' pour through the gates. The town was 'marvously oppressed' in 1582 and 'so comonlie oppressed as no towne in England the like' a decade later, leaving leaders muttering darkly about 'utter ruin'. The 'abuses' of 'inmates' were 'intollerable' in 1601 and 'highly pesterous' to 'civil government', and their numbers were still 'intollerable' two years later when 'overmuch increasinge' was an even bigger worry as plague swept through the town.[13]

There was little that was not surveyed, and many places like Chester in 1600 had monthly surveys helping governors to keep tabs on most problems under the sun.[14] Surveying the people was a rule of thumb in government from Whitehall all the way down to the smallest parish. England was more linked administratively and magistrates could get guidance on the best way to survey in well-thumbed texts like *An Ease for Overseers of the Poore* (1601) or William Lambarde's guide to *The Duties of Constables, Borsholders, Tythingmen and Such Other Low and Lay Ministers of the Peace* published the year before. Meanwhile, in rural England manorial lords stung by sharp inflation and seeking to squeeze further income from their estates turned to surveyors in an effort to 'know their own'. Conflicts of interest on the land increased the numbers of surveyors stalking the fields and commons, measuring,

calculating and questioning alleged customs as lords tried to redefine
their relationships to tenants through surveys. John Norden advised
'every lord of a mannor [to] cause his lands' to be 'truly surveyed' at least
once a decade, and this became a regular reckoning rhythm in his lifetime. 'What would be more ridiculous', John Lowe asked eight decades
later, 'than for me to go about to praise an art that all mankind know
they cannot live peaceably without[?]'.[15]

Surveying was an art of government that was ever more deeply rooted in
culture and society. Above and below land people peered into dark corners
to survey rivers, buildings, roads, mineral deposits, preachers, teachers,
sewers, forests, money-lenders, wool exports, Quakers and more besides.
Survey was the generic term used for chorographical works describing
England's counties and cities, which multiplied around 1600, and for
accounts of other lands: Venice, Virginia, Turkey, Spain, Sweden, the
East Indies, the West Indies and lavishly with gusto 'the whole world'.[16]
Towns like Colchester in 1598 spent time and money to survey their 'landes, howses, and wast grounds'. As in every year since 1594, Winchester's
mayor ordered a 'view' of land and tenements in the town and its ribbon
developments in 1603. 'Begin at what part of the town you please', David
Jenkins wrote in his surveying guidelines, 'go through setting down every
parcel of land, messuage or tenement distinctly, abutting and bound-
ing it' and the 'tenure and title of the owner or inheritor'. Hospital and
school lands also came under this telling lens and not many acres were left
unmeasured for too long.[17]

This was a world of surveying in a country of counting that looked to
a quantifiable future always better than the unsteady present, when swift
change evident in crammed towns or changes in land-use or tenure soon
made surveys out of date. The underlying reasoning for bringing John
Stow's *Survey of London* up to date was unsurprisingly that London was
'so much alter'd since his time as to be quite another thing'. 'Reviewing'
his Cornish *Survey* in 1602, Richard Carew noted the need for revisions as
his 'countrie hath undergone so manie alterations since I first began these
scribblings'.[18]

It was hard to keep up to date as England's varying fabrics changed
so deeply so quickly. Quite simply there was more to survey. England's
population boom changed things forever. Numbers mattered. What
Southampton's bench wanted in tense times in 1603 was 'knowledge'.
Maidstone's magistrates gave orders to draw up 'a boake of freemen free-
houlders' for 'better knowledge' and also took 'knowledge and notice' of
mischief-makers sitting in pubs, not church.[19] 'Knowledge' came from

'experience', and 'experience' in turn from 'view and due observacon'. Knowledge depended on 'view' or, in another word with equal force survey. To survey was to discover, delineate, calculate and categorise someone or something that needed managing.

Information or 'making known' in narrative and numerical form was the source of knowledge. Long before William Petty called 'political arithmetic' an 'instrument of government' local authorities all over England had been using quantification to survey and govern in a 'more certain and regular' manner (in the words of John Graunt, another key pioneer of the infant science of statistics, who made good use of figures from a single city ·· London – drawn from its most regular form of surveying, the bills of mortality).[20] The dawn of this 'political arithmetic' was in the second half of the seventeenth century, but the steady development of surveying after the middle of the sixteenth century was a long-term process in which the study-based intellectual work of Graunt, Petty, Gregory King and others was not at all separate but a late piece of a jigsaw that began much earlier, when central government and the parishes worked closely together to make governing through surveying a matter of routine.

What are archives for us today were information banks in 1600 to further policy and policing. One Westminster parish noted in 1603 that 'weekely almes' were provided for seventy people, 'whereof xii have been verie good parishioners and have paid all duties'; while 'the number of poore' on the margins and 'likely to come to have reliefe are 123 men and widdowes besides their wives and children'.[21] Like governors back then historians make use of such surveys to draw pictures of families and communities. We use them to map social structures – household size and composition, occupations, distributions of poverty and wealth – as well as keynote social trends like population growth or the widening rifts of a harshly unequal society. Such shrewd detective work is based on individual surveys or combinations of records. But what we lack perhaps is an overall understanding of early modern surveying as a process. We know its intriguing documentary products but it reflects something greater than the sum of its parts.

Our archives, then, were once working papers used to govern from one day to the next, and no historian needs telling that we need to know how they were made in the first place and in what ways they were used to try to put things in order. It was felt that strategies to crack crime and other 'nuisances' had a greater chance of success if first understood through surveying. Localities were governed by numbers. Counting gave something shape, putting governors in better positions to take appropriate action.

'The multitude of the poor must be reduced to number', an anonymous guide advised overseers in 1601.[22] The surge in census-taking after 1550 – 'survey' was often the word used – nearly always arose from troubled times, leading hopefully, like the landmark Norwich Census of the Poor (1570) to more finely tuned regulatory and relief systems.[23]

From the third quarter of the sixteenth century, many cities, some market towns and even rural parishes provided lists of 'the poore surveyed', in the words of a note from Chester.[24] More broadly inhabitants and householders were added up for administrative purposes: like the 'catalogue' or 'kalender' of inhabitants' names also provided for Chester in 1630.[25] 'In this booke are contayned the names of all thinhabitantes yownge and old', taken down by constables, Poole authorities wrote quite proudly in 1574: 1,373 'menn, wymen, and chyldren'.[26] They now had the town quite literally in their hands, in a book, always available when they needed to track something down. Another place surveyed; numbers collected; another little piece of England more 'perfectly' understood.

Numbering and listing were routine practices in 'paper parishes'. Local records are full of lists indicative of this surveying mindset. The sheer range of issues and resulting paper stacks is very revealing of synergies between social change and administrative refinements. A catalogue of papers 'for the towne' was drawn up in Bridport (Dorset) in 1610, and with it we plunge deep into the infrastructure of local-government-by-information. We see: orders 'for seats in the church'; leases; releases; rentals; bonds; vagrant passes; the examination of an anonymous whipped vagrant; 'a note of all such as are rated'; 'divers entries' for 'children'; Bridewell committals; Henry Lack's 'examinacon' and 'writing in greate letters to show cause of his ponnishment'; 'a hue and cry'; an almshouse 'quitans'; 'iiii records for binding of Maniford's children'; a letter requesting 'a booke for the x and xv'; 'a booke for a voluntary benevolence of the best ablest for the sicke'; rates for bells, highways and 'repayringe of the church'; 'examinacons of Robert Burrows that robbed a woman'; more warrants; examinations; certificates; letters to and from Dorchester; and much else besides.[27]

All this was from a small town far from key arteries in one year of dealing with the knock-on effects of a society in transition. A survey was the first course of action if problems piled up. Policy could now follow. In a pattern replicated elsewhere, Salisbury's justices, sitting fretting in the hard 1590s, told constables to draw up a 'certificatt and information' of 'newecomers', 'straungers', 'base borne children', and rowdy houses for the 'better government of this citie'. Their successors two decades later made plans for a 'veywe' of the poor in 1613 to find out 'in what sorte they may be relyved'.[28] Complaints circulated 212 miles to the north in Chester in 1539 about 'the greate nomber and multitude of vcalliant idell persons and vaccabonds' able to work who begged instead, leaving the worthy poor to get by on scraps. 'The nomber and names of all indigent and nedye mendicant people' were 'serched, knowne, and wrytten' down in a 'bill' for 'knowledge' of who should get hand-outs. Three decades later, in an order that word-for-word starts by following the pre-Reformation one – telling us something about how they worked with records – Chester's officers in their 'dowble charged' city went from street to street to take 'viewe and certayne note' of who did and did not deserve help. Six decades later on, following 'consideracon of the multitude of poor vagrant and idle people that of late resorte unto this citty' – 'more than former times' it was said – thereby 'hurting' Chester's own poor, governors asked constables to 'serche' monthly in parishes to get the names of anyone giving room and board to shifty vagrants so that 'some fitting course may be resolved upon'.[29]

This law-and-order arithmetic was a product of its times, embedded in the evolving experiences of England's localities. We see society in surveys coated in the ideological paint of magistrates' prejudices. Records are only a version of what took place: the more so because there was a tug-of-war between the authority of written records and that of oral evidence. It was a drawn-out affair, leaving Thomas Powell wondering in 1622 why 'in many cases records do clear the prescription in question yet in pleading they doe often use no other argument but the memorie of man which may err'.[30] But in the end the power of recorded words was magnified. Archives were representations of authority and necessary to clinch cases. Governors and governed turned to records like custumals in boiling controversies to establish a point in writing as a permanent footprint to follow.[31] The many times something is called accurate because it 'appeareth by the booke' tellingly express the internal power of archives. A Great Yarmouth tussle ended when one side 'appeared [proven] by the particulars thereof' from 'bookes beinge viewed and seene'.[32]

This empirical 'knowledge' on record was elevated when the locality/ parish became the core organisational unit for the 1598/1601 poor laws. A new status was conferred quite suddenly on 'surveying' and record-keeping. Even so there is concern for the safe-keeping and state of records before and after this landmark legislation. Accounts show payments for 'making cleane the books' and 'dustinge recordes'. A Herefordshire Sessions clerk got a few shillings for 'keeping a constant fire in the castle house' in 1688 and 'airing records [that were] soe wett and damp [in] this extraordinary wet winter'. Oxford's 'keykepers' were told to 'bringe upp all suche writings as lye belowe in the treasure howsse and laye them above in chests' in 1583 'for that the nether howsse is somewhat moyste and will hurte the writings'. 'It is thought requisite and soe ordered', Maidstone's magistrates said in 1638, 'that proclamacons that … be brought to this towne shalbee carefuly fyled in the towne hall to the end that the same may there remaine without spoyling, tearinge or looseninge'.[33] Much money was spent on binding, stitching, and 'coveringe' records in 'skynnes' and 'leather'. Norwich's 'old court books and assemblie bookes', needing 'bynding', were 'decently bound' in 1680.[34] And when calamity beckoned in Oxford in 1663 as 'two auntient bookes of records … commonly called the red book and the litle white book' were 'much obliterate and hardly to be read', the recorder hopped on a horse to London 'to have them transcribed in a faire and legible caracter'.[35]

There was much at stake in times when data systems mattered more than ever before. Missing or damaged records impeded authority. Parishes spent significant sums on chests to keep records secure all being well: the 'comon chest', 'parish chest', 'yron cheast', 'strong chest', 'black chest' and 'chest of writings'. Reading had a 'great' and 'little chest' in 1624 and seven years later authorities spent £3 2s for a 'new chest'.[36] The keys to these information-troves were put in the hands of civic officers or trusty elders. Exeter's 'great coffer' had 'nyne keyes and nyne lockes' in 1581, three times more than the usual number, as at Exeter's Heavitree parish, whose 'stronge chest bounded with iron' had 'three lockes and three keyes'.[37] Records were locked in secure vaults for extra safety, like Gloucester's treasury with five locks: the 'cowncell howse', 'armory', vestry or castle gatehouse. Great Yarmouth had a 'hutch' for its 'writings', and nearby Thetford had a 'litle' and 'greate hutche' with three locks.[38]

There is a definite sense of seclusion in these archival arrangements. Records were wrapped in layers of protective clothing with resulting distance, as they nearly always remained out of reach except to an elect few. In fact time and time again people low on social ladders combed through records when, for instance, customary rights were under threat.[39] That said, however, a feeling that records were quarantined under lock and key for reasons of government never goes away. Leaders made calculated choices about who might see records concerning delicate matters of government and authority. Oxford's magistrates decided to hold 'meetinges' in the 'auditt house' in 1640 and also agreed 'that such bookes [as] are fitt to bee kept secrett' would be locked up there with a fire burning 'for the airinge of the writinges' when needed.[40]

Local government was more secretive as social tensions and disparities deepened. More people were surveyed but also excluded.[41] Meetings were run under a veil of secrecy and anyone 'reveal[ing] secrets of the cown-sayle howse' faced a steep fine – 20s in Colchester and Northampton (doubled for a second offence), and £5 in Leicester and Tewkesbury (for a first offence) – or was 'excpellyd' if they 'divulged' the 'private and secrett actings and affaires' of 'assemblies'. Like surveying, 'secresie' was a main-stay of 'good government' and the smooth running of 'publique affaires'.[42] Increased information gathering was linked to tighter limits on who could see records. Maidstone's most sensitive records could only 'be redde, seene', or 'consideyid' when six of the twenty-four common councillors were in the room. It was a similar story in Bridgnorth (Shropshire), where at least three burgesses needed to be around the 'chest or coafer' whenever the coroner, high chamberlain or high bailiff wanted 'to see or use' any 'writeings'. The 'strong chest' in Heavitree parish (Exeter) could only be opened when all four 'sidesmen' were at hand.[43]

'Middling' men like these 'sidesmen' were part and parcel of the basic *Zeitgeist* of these surveying times. Office-holders were recruited for the most part from the burgeoning 'middle sort', whose influence shaped surveying across England.[44] Increasingly able to read, write and add up,[45] these men moved in worlds where life was lived in calculations made leg-ible in accounts. To stay afloat in a commercialising world, shopkeepers, traders and craftsmen referenced records, devised finding guides and drew up inventories, the same skill-sets deployed in office. 'The exact keeping of books', John Hill noted in 1688, 'is one of the hindges upon which trade turns and commerce is held'. Edward Leigh stressed that a consta-ble needs 'these things' to do a good job: 'honesty, science, and ability'.[46] Office-holders were a target audience for 'practical arithmetick' pitched 'chiefly for the benefit and use of tradesmen', and called 'practical', Arthur Leadbetter said, because 'its end is practical' for 'publick commerce'. Joseph Selden's title-page puts it in a nutshell: *The Trades-mans Help, An Introduction to Arithmetick* (1694). 'Practical arithmetic is the soul of mer-chandize', said Edward Cocker in a book directed to 'tradesmen' and 'gen-tlemen' alike.[47]

'Practical arithmetic' can be dated back before 1600 in moves to make mathematics more accessible in 'plaine' form along with advice on how to keep accounts. But the specific spotlight on 'tradesmen' was stronger after 1650 in another revealing overlap with early 'political arithmetic'. These

guides to numbers taught skills essential in life's middle 'station' in or
out of office: making a 'kalender or alphabet' to find something; keeping
things up to date; numbering pages; precise recording; keeping registers
'for the sure keeping and ordering' of papers; summarising entries in the
margins, or painting pointing fingers there, to draw attention to something significant; keeping inventories in 'good order' – 'a merchant can
not display his reckoning too clearly'; and putting tables in neat columns
broken down by date and numbered so 'there can be no mistake'. Always
keep books close at hand, John Hill told tradesmen, 'so that they may be
easily found upon any occasion'.[48]

We see the results of 'practical' experience when turning the pages of
records as they did long ago, and moving from entry to entry following
alphabetical sequencing, indexing and scribbles in margins. 'The order I
observe is altogether alphabeticall', lexicographer Elisha Coles stated, 'for
that best answers the design of informing others'.[49] Alphabetical lists are
common: pensioners, ratepayers, copyholders, prisoners, orphans, 502 sig-
natories of the Oath of Supremacy and Allegiance in Bideford (1660), and a
seventeen-page list of indicted recusants in Oxfordshire.[50] A-to-Z indexes –
'table alphabeticall' – helped to find a particular person or matter. Sessions,
and parish and civic books, often had coloured letters cut down the side –
on as many as twenty-two pages in one Gloucester indictment book.[51]
Exeter's chamberlain, with 'labour and care', finished a twenty-page-long
'index' 'alphabetically digested under proper and particuler heades' for the
third Chamber Act Book (1587–1601), six or seven decades after its last
entry (that distance matters). Kent sessions indictment books had alphabetical indexes with cross-references to indictment rolls in right-hand margins. Pointing fingers in margins made sure that something was not missed.
Any Marlborough inhabitant listed in the clerk's notebook with a 'l[ett]re
B against their names in margents' had 'black billes'. 'A decree to enjoine
secresie' is written in a margin of Tenterden's corporation book next to an
entry slamming leaks from 'comon hall' debates that 'required secresy'.[52]

Surveying at all government levels in all walks of life became more
necessary when the state spread its managerial tentacles across the land,
drawing more information-minded localities into its administrative
embrace. Parishes were loaded down with archival freight. Perhaps to
support a legal claim or to improve their condition, Barnstaple's bench
sent a heap of records to London in two batches in spring 1613: ninety-
seven sets of 'receavors accompts' in eight bundles, three courtbooks, forty
deeds, '19 courte rolles and accompts', '5 olde antient' charters, and five
more granted since the mid 1550s.[53] Middling men who drew up business,

household and personal records to order their lives were more often than not the officers who took care to keep local records secure and did laps of communities, 'surveying' people and problems.

They measured all the time: an action 'marked by the play of power relations' in James Scott's words.[54] Whether measuring in a field or going from door to door in a town, surveyors were creating material and mental images or maps of what they found on the ground. John Lowe's surveyor walked over fields a handful of times to have them 'as it were a map in your head' so 'you may better know where to begin and proceed with your work'.[55] Local officers likewise drew accounts and maps of their territory in their heads and on paper. What they saw and surveyed is the substance of the next section.

What they saw were the impacts of social change, sometimes good but all too often bad. This is what constables found one day in Winchester: 42 alehouse-keepers, 16 recusants, 325 'newcomers' with no right to be in the town, 11 inmates living cheaply, 6 sabbath-day dicers, 6 'fire places danger-ous' and 5 'souldiers married'.[56] Officers crossed communities to 'surveye', 'viewe and see', 'serche', 'enquire', and 'take notice', and to bring back what they found in notes, returns and certificates that were expected to be 'exact'. Precision mattered. It was an aspiration, however improbable, of governors more absorbed in numbers and information. Surveyors were asked to turn in a 'true and perfect accompte', 'perfecte booke', 'perfect bill', 'exact list', 'an exact survey of all the alehouses' in Faversham, a 'true and perfect list' of inmates in Winchester, 'a certayne note' of 'vaccabonds' in Chester in 1571, and 'a perfect list or callender of the names' of all Quakers locked up in prison in the same city a century later.[57]

Ambiguity bred anxiety. Information needed to be certain. Ralph Agas wanted field surveys to be 'sound and inviolate' to 'avoid confusion', and 'exact' in 'callendring and retriving of evidence' for the 'beating out of doubts'; and any magistrate worth his salt would have said the same.[58] Survey once, officers were often told, and then do it again. It was more vital than ever to keep on top of swiftly shifting situations by regular sur-veying. Alehouses were surveyed 'every weeke twysse' in Winchester (1572) and Great Yarmouth (1599) along with 'newe dwellers' and anyone 'dirty-ing' streets.[59] There were monthly counts of 'newcomers' in Colchester (1597); Leicester (1574); St Martin-in-the-Fields, Westminster (1622); and Chester (1590); and anyone under twenty-one living 'at their owne hands' in Norwich (1668).[60] Inmates were added up 'every Munday' in St Margaret's, Westminster (1683) and 'each third Wednesday' in next-door

St Martin-in-the-Fields (1659); quarterly in Northampton (1581); 'every six weekes' in Ashby-de-la-Zouch; and each week 'duly and carefully' in Great Yarmouth (1622) and nearby Norwich (1600).[61]

Concern was expressed in the need for speed. 'With all convenient speed', overseers in St Martin-in-the-Fields were told when instructed to list the 'names of all poore people … that are able to worke' in 1656. 'Give an accompt in writing of ye names of all the poore … forthwith', Norwich parishes were told in 1686. Like Thetford's surveyors in 1578, Great Yarmouth officers were given a week to draw up 'trewe billes of the inhabitants' in 1574. 'Take the names of every householder … in a fayre booke', Rye's constables were told in 1593, 'without delaye'.[62]

Surveying made issues legible, with the potential, at its most eagle-eyed and comprehensive, to dissect communities on paper. A 1656 survey for 'order and government' in Maidstone targeted over thirty types of offend-ers/offences including vagrants, 'unthrifts', sojourners, good-for-nothing tapsters, 'young fellowes and wenches liveinge out of service', crooked officers, and anyone dropping litter. Wardens were asked each Saturday to 'acquaint' the mayor with what they found. Articles from Exeter in 1560 also listed over thirty offences: unruly women, heavy drinkers, appren-tices strutting along streets in glitzy clothes, 'houses of office' considered 'fylthey', bawds, 'decayed' dwellings and – intriguingly five years *before* Thomas Harman's *Caveat for Common Cursetors* first appeared – cant-terms like 'upright men' and 'qyyer byrds'.[63]

The debris of change is in surveys everywhere: 'singlewomen' keeping 'chambers by themselves' who 'goe to thir owne hands', vagrants, idle poor, crumbling buildings, tottering walls, workers without seven-year appren-ticeships under their belts and plague hazards.[64] 'Articles to be inquired of by surveyers' in Cambridge in 1600 are a textbook example of a town dis-covering the dimensions of its difficulties. 'Surveyers' were told 'diligently [to] inquire and faythfully sett downe in writing' the names of anyone who had lived in the town for less than three years; down-on-luck pau-pers who were 'able to gett theire living by labour in whole or in p[ar]t'; 'householders unable to 'maynteyn themselves' without hand-outs; towns-people well off enough to 'give' to the poor; 'all innekeepers [and] ale-housekeepers' and householders giving room and board to beggars; the number of cottages on the fringes of the town; and, lastly, any inmate creeping into the town.[65]

Its people surveyed, Cambridge was better known. Paupers were put in columns in categories in parish after parish and county after county. Recurring headings, designations and strategies were hardly unexpected in a nation increasingly unified by statutes, administrative structures and common problems. There are repetitive chords, as surveys drew from similar concerns but still reflected local needs. The significance of this is that national laws and administrative strategies at all levels created a common vocabulary and process to categorise, list and analyse a viper's nest of growing problems. In Hereford officers surveyed victualling houses, alehouses, inmates and anyone giving them somewhere to stay, apprentices, inhabitants, sixteen traders keeping weights and measures (with ten more names crossed out), whipped vagrants, and 'true' lists of divine service shirkers and 'exact accounts' of paupers able to work. Ipswich surveyed 'all forrenors', vagrants, lodgers, 'poore, nedye, impotent' Gippeswykians, tipplers, victuallers, alehouse-keepers, 'mayds out of service', 'Londiners' as plague hit hard, and people bringing corn to market. And Northampton's leaders surveyed alehouses, 'poore people late come to the towne', tapsters, 'newcomers' – 'continuallie and successivelie' – inmates, apprentices – in a book – communicants – 'a true accompt' – servants – 'speciall notice in writing' – anyone buying or selling corn or cattle, jobbers, poulterers, oatmealmen, 'higlers', maltsters, regrators, engrossers, forestallers, 'newcomers and knitters' in plague time, and 'all maides that worke at their owne handes' – twice every year.[66]

Numbers were organised into local political economies: 46 alehouse-keepers in Newbury (1667), 72 recusants in Loughborough (1686), 1,728 inmates in six Cambridge parishes (1632), 68 Wintonians not paying rates (1599), and 20 Prestonians keeping 'great and unruly doggs' in 1665 (the mayor among them).[67] And governors often counted something again later to check if the tide was turning. Norwich's 'du[t]ch congregacon', noted down in muster lists, was 1,200 strong in 1613, 'but 999' in 1624 and 'but 678' ten years later. (Francis Bacon wrote that 'the population may appear by musters'.) On the eve of the 1570 census in the same city counts showed 752 male 'straungers' living there, 681 women, 1,132 children and 26 servants (2,591); and in the year after the census, officers counted 868 Dutchmen, 203 Walloons, 1,173 women 'of both nations' and 1,681 children – 666 'inglishe borne' (3,925).[68]

This cyclic categorising and counting imposed definition on landscapes. It also imposed authority through inscription. Findings were articulated and ordered in the discriminatory conceptions and felt priorities of the authorities. Surveys, in effect, froze social relations (and realities) in records formulated by articles. Like criminal records, they reproduce (and start with) categories and labels created by elite perceptions. Information flooded in but the most vital step was next when it was put on the magistrates' table and processed, arranged and modified for use as policy to follow including prosecutions and forced evictions.

Surveys done, magistrates were no longer left fumbling to understand something. After going door-to-door they now had the poor in columns, not hidden, with bits and pieces of information that made them more legible in names, ages, addresses and abilities, and slotted into preconceived categories: deserving/undeserving, orderly/disorderly, employed/unemployed.

In Salisbury's 1635 surveys, those on relief rolls in two of the town's three parishes were listed by street, life-course stage, age, ability and weekly payment. Governors saw measly household budgets and profiles of people perched precariously propped up by hand-outs. We see the value of child labour in dragging have-not households from week to week. There are gaps in columns about conditions but there is enough to get us inside the doors of the poor. Eighteen paupers limped through life lame or crippled and five could not get out of bed. Seven were blind, one more was nearly blind, another was blind in one eye and three others had weak eyesight. One could not hear anything at all. Eight were sick, another eight were feeble and three more were impotent. Five wives (one pregnant) had to fend for themselves, having no idea where their husbands were. Twenty-four-year-old Eleanor Macy shared a house with her seventy-year-old feeble mother who was 'sometimes distracted'; Mellor Jones lived along Milford Street with his 'crook-backed' daughter Mary trying to scratch a living on 25d each week; while forty-year-old John Butler languished in prison, leaving his thirty-five-year-old wife with 2s 6d each week to put food on the table for young Crisse, Thomas, Ann, and Nabb.[69]

Similarly gloomy stories of the feckless, luckless and rootless poor run through the Norwich Census (1570), which is a register of need framed by magistrates' questions revealing their deepest concerns: how long have they lived here, where did they live before, are they able to work for their living, how many in the house and who are they? Be specific. Family after family are called 'verie' or 'myserable pore'. Work is hard to come by or nowhere; husbands are missing for years (one wife left reeling with eight children); women with children have no 'helpe'; men are 'not in occupieinge'; needy widows are aged anywhere from 20 to 100; aged people are 'past' work or 'not able to work' but still expected to; and children are breadwinners. Widow Jenkinson would 'spyn when she can get ytt'. Sixty-year-old Robert Barwick, 'longe in pryson for dett', left his wife Anne at home 'that hath no exercise butt traveyle dayelye in hir husbondes behalfe' doing little apparently for her 'ydle' eight children living on 'the labor of others'. Many more were knee-deep in the quicksand of poverty: not long in Norwich like lace-weaver 'Alice-lyve-by-love'; on the wrong side of the law ('unruly', scolds, 'harlots', thieves); or suffering the pitiless scourge of the poor: sickness, disability and everyday pain.[70]

'Publick records, memorials, and evidences' are 'jewels of inestimable value', Gerard Maymes wrote gushingly in 1603.[71] In a vestry room somewhere in an English backwater 'middling' men would have nodded their heads if they read this, and a couple of them might have felt the key in their pocket that unlocked the chest in the cupboard. They might have run through numbers in their heads, maybe turning the pages of a 'book of record' open on the table, tallying and thinking through the most recent threat to the peace and purse. In office or at work, after all, little mattered more to them than numbers.

The true value of surveying was not just what was recorded but the power of paper and the processes that fed it. Writing smugly in 1586, Thomas Hariot bragged that the tribes circling Roanoke had 'no letters nor other suche meanes as we to keepe records'.[72] Settlers were more powerful for their capacity to stitch books of records together. Whether at home or overseas the English surveyed people and felt that they were superior for the winning utility of knowledge in records.

Counting trumped whispering and not knowing. 'In St Martins [-in-the-Fields] I have heard of twenty or thirty thousand' Catholics, Peter Petit noted in 1689, 'but the account was taken there and as exact a one as could be, and I am assured by some that should know' that the real figure 'upon most careful scrutiny was about 600'. 'We hear of the vast numbers' of Catholics in the north, Petit continued, 'but I believe there are much fewer than we hear'. 'People', he said snootily, 'multiply the number of papists … in common talk at least ten-folds'. Nine years earlier, he said to seal his case, 'a sheet of paper' called 'a catalogue' of Catholics in London was published: 'catholics reckoned in St Martin-in-the-Fields are but 22', and – the proof of the pudding – 'the Bishops survey makes it 64'.[73]

Even as he used numbers to put a case, Petit ignored their apparent inconsistency. Not everything went according to plan. Little was 'perfect', 'exact' or 'true', despite great expectations. We lack lists 'of all those yt keepe guns and greyhoundes', Westmorland justices moaned in 1684. 'A very smale appearance', St. Martin-in-the-Fields' vestry complained one day in 1659, only two constables bringing in 'returne of ye inmates'. And a few months later the same vestry slammed 'the greate neglect' of beadles bringing in inmate lists in dribs and drabs.[74]

There were many such defects in surveying. Surveyors sometimes could not even agree on numbers. Four constables were sent to Cambridge's Midsummer Fair in 1626 to keep an eye on 'The Signe of the George' where students boozed all Sunday long. There were twenty there, one of them said, 'drinkinge and conversing' and enjoying tobacco with '4 fidlers playing' in two rooms. No, another one said, 'there were some xii there', and he wasn't sure that it was in time of divine service.[75] Yet we should acknowledge the aspiration to 'exactness' behind one survey after another. 'From hennseforthe', Reading's rulers said in 1591, 'there shalbe a tolboke' kept 'orderly' and 'colours of the cattell and theire proper markes' registered 'with the names' of buyers and sellers.[76] They tried. This is wishful precision on any score. They wanted to get it right to make the place where they lived more ordered and secure. Cattle, Catholics, con-men, citizens, conduits – anything surveyed/counted was a crumb of comfort for magistrates seeking policy.

This was perhaps a predominantly urban phenomenon, but town vaults are exactly where records are more likely to have survived in good order. Surveys cut from the same cloth, under Whitehall's influence, were mostly hatched locally, conducted locally and digested locally. England was not presented in one great national survey – that would have to wait until the census of 1801, the first truly national survey since the Domesday Book. Yet thousands of local surveys revealed England from the bottom up. Long before Sir William Petty decided that surveying was key to government, local officers across the length and breadth of England went up and down streets surveying this and that for the same political practices and principles as those of Political Arithmetic. Each was in a sense a social and economic narrative of a particular place, a response to the experience of change: the raw materials of history.

'Survey the poore', Gloucester's foot soldiers were told in 1640, and off they went back to their parishes to start counting house by house.[77] Another count, another year. Numbers.

England surveyed and revealed in little local particles.

### Notes

1 J. Norden, *The Surveyors Dialogue* (1610), the epistle to the reader, 2.
2 F. Turner, *Letter to the Clergy of the Dioecess of Ely, from the Bishop of Ely before and Prepatory to His Visitation* (Cambridge, 1686), 1 (original emphasis).
3 W. Ingram, *The Secrets of Numbers According to Theologicall, Arithmeticall, Geometricall, and Harmonicall Computation* (1624), 'To the Reader', A4r.

4  O. Coleman, 'What figures? Some thoughts on the use of information by medieval governments', in D. Coleman and A. H. John (eds.), *Trade, Government, and Economy in Pre-Industrial England* (London: Weidenfeld & Nicolson, 1976).

5  P. Burke, *A Social History of Knowledge from Gutenberg to Diderot* (Cambridge: Polity, 2000), 117–19. See also P. Slack, *The Invention of Improvement: Information and Material Progress in Seventeenth-Century England* (Oxford: Oxford University Press, 2014); P. Slack, 'Government and information in seventeenth-century England', *P&P*, 184 (2004); and P. Griffiths, 'Local arithmetic: Information cultures in early modern England', in S. Hindle, A. Shepard and J. Walter (eds.), *Remaking English Society: Social Relations and Social Change in Early Modern England* (Woodbridge: Boydell, 2013). For early America see J. H. Cassedy, *Demography in Early America: Beginnings of the Statistical Mind, 1600–1800* (Cambridge, MA: Harvard University Press, 1969), Chapters 2–4.

6  S. Hindle, *The State and Social Change in Early Modern England, c. 1550–1640* (Basingstoke: Macmillan, 2000); M. J. Braddick, *State Formation in Early Modern England, c. 1550–1700* (Cambridge: Cambridge University Press, 2000); P. Slack, 'Books of Orders: The making of English social policy, 1577–1631', *TRHS*, 5th series, 30 (1980).

7  Slack, *Invention of Improvement*, 51–5, quotation at 52; P. Slack, 'Measuring the national wealth in seventeenth-century England', *EcHR*, new series, 57 (2004).

8  K. Shurer and T. Arkell (eds.), *Surveying the People: The Interpretation and Use of Document Sources for the Study of Population in the Later Seventeenth Century* (Oxford: Leopard's Head, 1992); N. Landau, 'The laws of settlement and the surveillance of immigration in eighteenth-century Kent', *C&C*, 3 (1988).

9  E. Coles, *An English Dictionary* (1673), and E. Phillips, *The New World of Words; or, A General English Dictionary*, 4th edn (1678), s.v. 'information'.

10  Turner, *Letter to the Clergy of the Dioecess of Ely*, 8–9 (original emphasis).

11  C[heshire] RO, Z/AB/1, fol. 265; LE[icestershire] RO, QS/6/1/2, fol. 58v; N[orfolk] RO, T/C1/6, fol. 30v; H[ampshire] RO, W/B1/4, fol. 110; C[ambridge] U[niversity] L[ibrary], CUR 37.3, fol. 126; CRO, QJB/15, fos. 232v–34.

12  NRO, Norwich Assembly Book 5, fol. 273; WILT[shire] RO, G23/1/3, fol. 397.

13  S[outhampton] C[ity] A[rchives], 6/1, fols. 17, 23, 25, 26, 27.

14  CRO, Z/AB/1, fols. 261, 263.

15  Norden, *Surveyors Dialogue*, 30; J. Lowe, *Geodaesia; or, The Art of Surveying and Measuring of Land* (1688), preface, 1; D. Jenkins, *Pacis consultum ... Describing the Court Leet* (1657), 64. See A. W. Richeson, *English Land Measuring to 1800: Instruments and Practices* (Cambridge, MA: Harvard University Press, 1966); A. McRae, *God Speed the Plough: The Representation of Rural England, 1500–1660* (Cambridge: Cambridge University Press, 1996), 169–97.

16 See J. Broadway, 'No historie so meete': Gentry Culture and the Development of
Local History in Elizabethan and Early Stuart England (Manchester: Manchester
University Press, 2006).

17 E[ssex] RO C[olchester], D/B5/Gb1, fol. 160v; HRO, W/B1/3, fol. 136. See,
for instance, San Marino, H[untington] L[ibrary], STTM Box-3, folder 37;
Box-12, folder 33; C[entre for] K[entish] S[tudies], FA/AC3, fol. 153v; Md/
Acm/1a, fol. 71; Md/Acm1/2, fol. 59v.

18 Anon., The Model of a Design to Reprint Stow's Survey (1694), 2; Richard
Carew, The Survey of Cornwall (1602), preface to the reader.

19 SCA, 6/1, fol. 27; CKS, Md/ACm1/2, fol. 2; Md/JLP1/1656.

20 Petty is quoted in T. McCormick, William Petty and the Ambitions of Political
Arithmetic (Oxford: Oxford University Press, 2009), 304; J. Graunt, Natural
and Political Observations ... Made upon the Bills of Mortality (1662), 100. See
also J. C. Robertson, 'Reckoning with London: Interpreting the bills of mortality before John Graunt', Urban History, 23 (1996); Griffiths, 'Local arithmetic'; and J. Innes, 'Power and happiness: Empirical social enquiry in Britain
from "political arithmetic" to "moral statistics"', in her Inferior Politics: Social
Problems and Social Policies in Eighteenth-Century Britain (Oxford: Oxford
University Press, 2009).

21 W[estminster] A[rchive] C[entre], F6039. See also WAC, F3348, F3349,
F3550, F3551.

22 An Ease for Overseers of the Poore (Cambridge, 1601), 17.

23 P. Griffiths, 'Inhabitants', in C. Rawcliffe and R. Wilson (eds.), Norwich since
1500 (London and New York: Hambledon & London, 2004), esp. 63–75. See
also P. Slack, Poverty and Policy in Tudor and Stuart England (London and
New York: Longman, 1988), 48–52, 53–5, 73–80; P. Clark and J. Clark, 'The
social economy of the Canterbury suburbs: The evidence of the census of
1564', in A. Detsicas and N. Yates (eds.), Studies in Modern Kentish History
(Maidstone: Kent Archaeological Society, 1983).

24 CRO, Z/AB/1, fol. 4. And see Peter Laslett's listing of rural censuses in
manuscript and Richard Wall's catalogue of others that have come down
to us in printed form in P. Laslett (ed.), Household and Family in Past Time
(Cambridge: Cambridge University Press, 1972), 74–85 and Chapters 4–5.

25 CRO, Z/AB/2, fol. 24v.

26 D[orset] H[istory] C[entre], DC/PL/B/13/1.

27 DHC, DC/BTB/C88, fols. 30r–v.

28 WILTRO, G23/1/3, fols. 231, 291v, 153v.

29 CRO, Z/AB1, fols. 60, 126v; Z/AB/2, fol. 17v.

30 T. Powell, Directions for Search of Records Remaining in the Chancerie, Tower
[and] Exchequer (1622), 75.

31 A. Wood, The Memory of the People: Custom and Popular Senses of the Past
in Early Modern England (Cambridge: Cambridge University Press, 2013),
Chapter 5; A. Fox, Oral and Literate Cultures in England, 1500–1700 (Oxford:
Oxford University Press, 2000), Chapter 5.

32 NRO, Y/C27/1, fol. 177.

33 CRO, TAB/1, fol. 30; NRO, Great Hospital General Account Rolls, 1618–19; HE[refordshire] RO, Q/SM/4, fol. 225v; O[xfordshire] A[rchives], C/FC/1/A1/01, fol. 261; CKS, Md/Acm1/2, fol. 170v.

34 NRO, N[orwich] M[ayor's] C[ourt] C[ourtbook] 25, fols. 69, 61v; S[hropshire] A[rchives], 3365–523; DHC, DC/BTB/M2/1578; WAC, E5/1574–76; E. M. Ramsay and A. J. Maddock (eds.), *The Churchwardens' Accounts of Walton-on-the-Hill, Lancashire, 1627–1667*, Lancashire and Cheshire Record Society, 151 (2005), 55–6.

35 OA, C/FC/1/A1/03, fol. 311.

36 B[erkshire] RO, WI/AC1 fols. 36v, 53; E[ast] S[ussex] RO, QO/EW/3, fol. 34v; Win/55, fol. 29; NRO, Norwich Chamberlains' Accounts 1603–25, fol. 268v; WAC, SMF1580; WILTRO, G/23/1/3, fol. 375; CKS, Md/Acm1/1a, fol. 66; D[evon] RO, Z19/36/14, fol. 130v; WAC, E2413, fol. 19; BRO, R/AC1/1/2, fol. 80; R/AC1/1/5, fol. 11.

37 DRO, ECA B/1/3, fol. 25; 3004A/PW 2; LERO, BRII/1/3, fol. 31; SA, BB/C/1/1/1, fol. 48v; NORTH[amptonshire] RO, 3/1, fol. 8v; CKS, Md/Acm1/1a, fol. 66; S[uffolk] RO I[pswich], C/4/4/1/34, fol. 9; DHC, DC/LR/D1/3a, fol. 182.

38 G[loucestershire] A[rchives], GBR/B/3/3, fol. 512; NRO, Y/C/19/3, fols. 129, 171; T/C1/1, fols. 11, 65v; GA, GBR/F/4/3, fol. 151; N[orth] D[evon] RO, Bi/3792, fol. 8; WILTRO, G23/1/3, fol. 406; G22/1/205/2, fols. 5, 33v, 74; WAC, F2002, fols. 46, 206; E2413, fol. 93; CKS, TE/S2, fol. 374; NORTHRO, 3/1, fol. 8v; HERO, Q/SM/4, fols. 23v, 89v–90.

39 Andy Wood vividly brings these disputes to life in his *Memory of the People*.

40 OA, C/FC/1A1/03, fol. 103v.

41 Cf. P. Griffiths, 'Secrecy and authority in late sixteenth- and seventeenth-century London', *HJ*, 40:4 (1997).

42 EROC, D/B5/Gb1, fol. 9v; NORTHRO, 3/1, fol. 103; LERO, BRII/1/3, fol. 80; GA, TBR/A/1/2, fol. 36; HRO, W/B2/1, fol. 30v; W/B1/5, fols. 105, 165v; CKS, FA/AC3, fol. 48v; TE/S2, fol. 247.

43 CKS, Md/Acm1/1a, fol. 38v; SA, BB/C1/1/1, fol. 48v; DRO, 3004A/PW/2.

44 H. French, *The Middle Sort of People in Provincial England 1600–1750* (Oxford: Oxford University Press, 2007); J. Kent, 'The rural "middling sort" in early modern England *circa* 1640–1740: Some economic, political, and socio-cultural characteristics', *Rural History*, 10 (1999); S. Hindle, *On the Parish: The Micro-Politics of Poor Relief in Rural England, c. 1550–1750* (Oxford: Oxford University Press, 2004).

45 K. Wrightson, *Earthly Necessities: Economic Lives in Early Modern Britain* (New Haven and London: Yale University Press, 2000), Chapter 1; K. Thomas, 'Numeracy in early modern England', *TRHS*, 5th series, 37 (1987).

46 J. Hill, *The Exact Dealer Being an Useful Companion for All Traders* (1689), 56; E. Leigh, *A Phililogicall Commentary Or an Illustration of the Most Obvious and Useful Words in the Law*, 2nd edn (1658), 48.

47 A. Leadbetter, *Arithmetical Rules, Digested and Contracted for the Help and Benefit of Memory Very Necessary and Useful, as Well for Gentlemen and*

*Tradesmen, as for Youth and Apprentices, in Mercantile Affairs* (1691), A2v, 2;
J. Ayres, *Arithmetick a Treatise Fitted for the Use and Benefit of Such Trades-men
as Are Ignorant in That Art* (1693), A3r; E. Cocker, *Cockers Arithmetick Being a
Plain and Familiar Method Suitable to the Meanest Capacity* ... (1678), A2v.

48  I. C. Gent, *A Most Excellent Instruction for the Exact and Perfect Keeping
Merchants Bookes of Accounts* (1632), 5; Hill, *Exact Dealer*, 52, 59, 58; H.
Oldcastle, *A Briefe Instruction and Maner Hovv to Keepe Bookes of Acompts
After the Order of Debitor and Creditor & As Well for Proper Accompts Partible,
&c* (1588), Chapters 2 and 4. See N. Glaisyer, *The Culture of Commerce in
England, 1660–1720* (Woodbridge: Boydell, 2006), Chapter 3; A. Smyth,
*Autobiography in Early Modern England* (Cambridge: Cambridge University
Press, 2010), Chapter 2; D. E. Harkness, 'Accounting for science: How a
merchant kept his books in Elizabethan London', in M. C. Jacob (ed.), *The
Self-Perception of Early Modern Capitalists* (Basingstoke: Palgrave Macmillan,
2008).

49  Coles, *English Dictionary*, A3r.

50  NDRO, 1064Q/SO1, fols. 12v–13v; HL, EL 2178.

51  DHC, DC/PL/B/1/1/1, fol. 242; SRO, QO/EW7; GA, GBR/B/3/2.

52  DRO, ECA B/1/3, fols. 474–92; CKS, Q/SP1/1–2; WILTRO, G/22/1/107;
CKS, TE/S2, fol. 247.

53  NDRO, B1/46/366.

54  J. C. Scott, *Seeing like a State* (New Haven and London: Yale University Press,
1998), 27.

55  Lowe, *Geodaesia*, 142.

56  HRO, W/K5/8, fol. 35.

57  DRO, ECA B/1/3, fol. 411; NRO, Y/C/19/4, fol. 150; CKS, U120/09, fol. 18;
HRO, W/B2/4, fol. 53; CRO, ML/3/478; Z/AB/1, fol. 126v; ML/3/486.

58  R. Agas, *A Preparative to Platting of Landes and Tenements for Surueigh* (1596),
3, 13 (irregular pagination).

59  HRO, W/B2/1, fols. 3, 24v; NRO, Y/C/19/5, fols. 20v–21.

60  EROC, D/B5/Gb1, fol. 134; LERO, BR11/1/2, fol. 246; WAC, F2001, fol. 162;
CRO, Z/AB/1, fol. 231v; NRO, Norwich City Sessions Minute Book, 1654–
1670, August 1668.

61  WAC, E2416, fol. 134; F2003, fol. 192; HL, HAM Box-2/folder-1, fol. 13v;
NORTHRO, 3/1, fol. 209; NRO, Y/C/19/5, fol. 266; Norwich Assembly
Book 5, fol. 244.

62  WAC, F2003, fol. 97; NRO, NMC 25, fol. 198v; T/C1/1, fol. 8; Y/C/19/3, fol.
91v; ESRO, RYE/5, fol. 282.

63  CKS, Md/Acm1/3, fols. 81–82; DRO, ECA B/1/4, fol. 106.

64  NRO, Norwich Aseembly Book 5, fols. 244–5; Y/C/19/5, fols. 20v–21, 83;
EROC, D/Y/2/2/60; GA, TBR/A/1/1, fols. 8–9; TBR/A/1/2, fol. 9; GBR/B3/
2, fols. 113, 157, 284; HERO, BG11/17/1/5, fol. 45; DRO, ECA B/1/4, fol. 396;
CKS, FA/AC3, fol. 76v; WAC, E2413, fol. 82; E2416, fol. 190.

65  CUL, VC-CT-vi.15, fol. 80.

66 Hereford: HERO, BGII/17/1/4, fol. 14; Q/SM/2, fol. 61; Q/SM/4, fols. 55, 65v; BGII/4/6, fol. 10; BGII/17/1/5, fol. 67; BGII/17/1/4, fol. 34. Ipswich: SROI, C/4/3/1/1/3, fols. 34, 35, 95v, 100v, 127, 210v; SROI, C/4/3/1/1/4, fol. 24. Northampton: NORTHRO, 3/1, fols. 209, 225, 227, 296v, 303v, 422, 423v–424; NORTHRO, 3/2, fols. 8, 54v; NQSi, fol. 96v.

67 BRO, N/JQ/1/1, fol. 11; HL, HAM Box-27, folder-8; CUL, CUR 37.3, fol. 131; HRO, W/B2/3, fols. 22–3; LRO, CNP 3/2/1, fol. 241.

68 NRO, Norwich muster list, case 10/H, no. 11; Norwich Dutch and Walloon Strangers Book, 1564–1643, fols. 22, 69v; Francis Bacon, *Francis Bacon: Major Works*, ed. B. Vickers (Oxford: Oxford University Press, 1996), 302.

69 P. Slack (ed.), *Poverty in Early Stuart Salisbury*, Wiltshire Record Society, 31 (Devizes: Wiltshire Record Society, 1975), 75–80.

70 J. F. Pound (ed.), *The Norwich Census of the Poor, 1570*, Norfolk Record Society, 60 (Norwich: Norfolk Record Society, 1971); M. Pelling, *The Common Lot: Sickness, Medical Occupations and the Urban Poor in Early Modern England* (London and New York: Longman, 1998), Chapters 3–4 and 6.

71 G. Maymes, *England's View, in the Unmasking of Two Paradoxes* (1603), 17.

72 Quoted in Cassedy, *Demography in Early America*, 5.

73 P. Petit, *A Discourse of the Growth of England in Populousness and Trade since the Reformation* (1689), 140–1.

74 Kendal Archive Centre, WQ/O/3, fol. 48; WAC, F2003, fols. 189, 203.

75 CUL, VCT/49, fol. 15.

76 BRO, R/ACI/1/1, fol. 600.

77 GA, GBR/B/3/2, fol. 70.

3

# Little Commonwealths I: The Household and Family Relationships

## Linda Pollock

### Introduction

When early modern people spoke of their 'family' they meant in the first instance the household: those who co-resided under the authority of a household head. The household was central to early modern domestic, social, economic, political and religious life. It was a unit of residence, affective bonds and authority, as well as one of consumption and production, essential to the functioning of the early modern economic and social world. Legal and social thought in many ways regarded the household, rather than the individual, as the main economic entity. Not all household members were connected by birth or marriage, notwithstanding the scholarly focus on the nuclear family. Non-related residents, there by contract, such as apprentices and servants, were also a fundamental element of the early modern household economies and an integral part of family structures. Households typically were bastions of authority, structured by hierarchical differentiation. A member's role was predicated upon basic presumptions regarding the proper place of men, women, children and youths in society, and thus would differ by gender and age.

A household was also the setting for the most intimate personal relationships and the formation of identity. Early modern individuals could not avoid familial labels. Women who came before the authorities were described as 'spinster', 'wife' or 'widow'. Lady Grace Mildmay's epitaph in 1621 depicted her as a 'chaste maid, wife and widow'. Even men, more commonly seen by historians as being categorised according to their occupation, were described in familial terms. William Hoar, 'a dutifull child, a tender fathr, And a most loving husband', was accidentally killed by a musket shot on Lady Day 1679.[1] The ubiquity of these designations testifies to the importance of the household in early modern consciousness, conceptually and materially. Individuals were identified according to familial categories, as well as being secured and connected by domestic ties.

The concept of the family, though, as well as the make-up and culture of any one unit, was constantly changing. A family was not so much allotted – that is given at birth – as continuously created, as members joined or left and intimate bonds were established or broken. Newly married couples quickly added children to the home. The latter in turn would start to leave the natal unit from the mid teens on. Death frequently ruptured personal bonds. Around one-quarter of children would die before the age of ten; many spouses endured the loss of a partner. About 25 per cent of all marriages were remarriages for the bride or groom, sometimes adding step-children, followed by half-siblings to the home. As many as 40 per cent of households had servants, ranging from over 80 per cent in the case of landed to around 25 per cent of those of labourers. Servants were often young – 60–70 per cent were aged between fifteen and twenty-four – and for most service was a transitional occupation. Servants left their employ often, either of their own accord or because they were terminated. Samuel Pepys had 38 servants from 1660 to 1669, 13 of whom stayed less than six months. Only 8 out of the 167 servants employed by Sir Richard Newdigate from 1692 to 1706 worked there longer than five years; 63 lasted just six months.[2] Moreover, personal bonds were not confined to the household: individuals belonged to a family of origin as well as one of marriage, and were embedded in wider social networks that shaped and were influenced by what went on in the home. All of this meant that a household was not a stable entity in the past, if by that we mean unchanging. Rather, demographic realities, life-cycle changes, and the comings and goings of contract members ensured its composition changed often, necessitating constant adjustment on the part of household members.

On so much scholars agree, but the history of domestic relationships has been a notably contentious field. The nature of the early modern family, the strength of English kinship, the prominence of material considerations and the emotional ties of family members, for instance, have been fiercely contested. The impassioned, at times acrimonious, debates may have ended, but furore has not given way to torpor. More recent scholarship has reframed old debates, re-evaluated key concepts, and reshaped the field by incorporating new topics. It highlights the simplistic tenor of the initial questions. No longer do we investigate whether parents loved their children in the past or whether financial concerns or sentiment dominated in the choice of a marriage partner. Rather, concepts like patriarchy, love, obedience, individualism or community are examined anew, focusing more on questions of power, identity and gender, and seeking to relate the household to a wider context. The new research is sensitive to situation and setting, less attached to the mean and more fascinated with deviations around it. It eschews binaries, forced debates and stark interpretative choices; instead it reconceptualises the family as a unit of dynamic, shifting relations and investigates how ideals, values and norms played out in everyday life.

All of this makes the study of early modern households a more intellectually engaging and emotionally satisfying subject, but at the same time renders it difficult to summarise concisely. Scholars have rightly jettisoned the old metanarratives, but to substitute for these a spate of increasingly specialised, local and detailed examples is inadequate. What we are left with is an arch groaning under the weight of perpetually multiplying exceptions. We need to return to some fundamental issues with respect to the importance, role and experience of the household but in a more nuanced and sensitive fashion. One of the ways to do this could be by re-examining the popular conduct books and advice manuals that appeared between the late sixteenth and the early eighteenth century and defined domestic issues and roles as contemporaries saw them. Again and again they dealt with the essential themes of marriage and household formation; the proper nature of marital relations; the dos and don'ts of child-rearing; the duties of kin or 'friends'; the relations of masters and servants; and, running through all this, aspects of the role of the household as an economic unit. This makes them a valuable starting point. But if we follow their lead in examining these central relationships, we need to take into account the diverse ways in which people interpreted, adhered to, dispensed with or reworked prescriptive norms. The implementation of normative values in daily life along with the ever shifting, changing and evolving nature of the household unit are the keys to understanding the dynamism of domestic relationships and the role of change.

## Marriage and Household Formation

Some of the most important decisions people faced in early modern England related to marriage: should they marry, if so when, and to whom? Contemporary moralists had apparently firm views on marriage. It should be to a person with the appropriate social and personal qualities, should take place only if the good will of all interested parties had been secured, and should be undertaken at a sufficiently mature age, when the couple were able to set up and sustain a household of their own. Marital practice, however, was not necessarily in harmony with these opinions. The question of when people married appeared to have been settled in 1981 with the publication of Tony Wrigley and Roger Schofield's family reconstitution of twenty-six parishes. On average, men married around twenty-seven or twenty-eight and women around twenty-five or twenty-six until the nineteenth century, when the mean age at first marriage fell to around twenty-five for men and twenty-three for women.[3] This finding conclusively demolished the long-held myth that people in the past married very young but it was not clear who was marrying younger, nor why. Wrigley and Schofield's concentration on rural parishes, male breadwinners and national averages spurred new research on urban demography, and local and regional differences, along with the marital practices of women and the poor. People in towns married younger. Proto-industrial parishes in West Yorkshire had a low and stable age at marriage. There appears to be both a decline over time in the number of women marrying above thirty and a rise in the number of women marrying around age twenty. Some regions, such as Northern England, sanctioned unofficial but community-recognised unions, thus bringing into question the reliability of data on marriage derived from church registers. As scholars focused on the variation around the mean, they quickly discovered that a declining marriage age was not a national phenomenon: 'variety rather than homogeneity' characterised the marital scene.[4]

Wrigley and Schofield explained the drop in the mean age at first marriage by the fact that improving economic opportunities, especially rising wage rates, enabled more couples than before to fund a household, and to do so earlier. This is probably overly optimistic for those lower down the social scale, overlooking the fact that courtship was sensitive to economic conditions and there could be innumerable hurdles to surmount before the wedding took place. Some unions would not receive the blessing of the community, and thus, regardless of the intentions of the couple, would not take place. Communities preferred stable, economically viable marriages, and poor-law administrators and local authorities tried to stop the poor from marrying. In 1570, the parishioners of Adlington, Kent, unhappy with Alice Cheeseman's choice of a husband, refused to post the bans, demanded that she leave him and threatening her with expulsion from the community if she defied their 'hinderance' of the marriage. Parishioners could also prevent sub-letting, making it difficult for newcomers to get hold of land or a cottage to establish a home.[5]

Wrigley and Schofield's thesis also assumes that early modern individuals viewed their situation in the same light as, or had the same goals as, early modern conduct-book authors and modern-day scholars. Material resources undoubtedly mattered – as Mary Evelyn in 1670 remarked ruefully to her brother-in-law Granville, who was fretting over which one of two widows to marry, 'religion and fortune will come into one's head whether one wills it or no'.[6] But, as Steven King points out, we do not yet fully understand how much influence economic issues had on micro decision-making, nor how early modern individuals assessed risk or balanced economic factors against feelings, duty, hope and the opinions of others.[7]

A couple may not have aimed for immediate financial independence. Certainly, many wed apparently without planning, saving or balancing economic prospects, making marriage a 'triumph of hope over experience'.[8] Job opportunities may have encouraged some to take the plunge without a nest egg. Roger Lowe decided to marry after his business failed when he had no capital, nowhere to live, and knew that his wife Emm would lose her position upon marriage. He did, though, have a job.[9] It may have made sense for some couples to marry early even if they were not in the best of economic circumstances. The most frequently recorded form of hardship affecting the poor was the breakdown or failure of the nuclear family rather than ageing, suggesting that those in straitened circumstances survived better in a family unit. Marriage might have appeared to some as the best option in times of economic downturn: the age of brides, for instance, declined most in those areas where employment opportunities for women contracted. The unpalatable truth for the poorer members of society was that there was not enough money – that life was, and probably would continue to be, financially hard. Even though couples later in life could regret marrying with insufficient resources and long for more ample funds, it was clearly unfeasible for the lower ranks to base all of life's decisions on economic prospects, given that financial security might prove an elusive, often unobtainable, goal. Economic growth, then, provides only a partial explanation for the age at which people married. Cultural norms along with issues of occupation, mobility, perceptions of status and desire all played a role. What we need is a multi-layered interpretation of the practice of courtship, marriage and household formation, one that would explain the entire process of getting married rather than the end stage of the wedding alone.

Economic concerns rarely explained the choice of a particular marriage partner. To gain insight into marriage decisions, we need to move beyond statistics and enter into the realms of personal and family strategies, emotions and perceptions. And we should do so without opposing affection and finances, thereby creating a false dichotomy between romantic love and material concerns. According to English law, marriage had to be based on the mutual consent of the couple, but that 'consent' could take many forms from assenting to the plans of others to finding one's own partner, and the full range is depicted in the historical record. Joan Hayward could have refused to marry John Thynne in 1576 but she agreed, trusting that 'God will put into my father's heart to choose me such a one as God will direct my heart not to dislike'; whereas Elizabeth Rouse in the 1690s married Sampson Bound without her father's approval or knowledge.[10] Initially, historians concentrated on arranged marriage, stressing the active role of parents in organising suitable matches for their offspring. This remained an essential parental obligation for the prosperous ranks and, although there were very few forced matches, their financial resources undoubtedly gave them some leverage. A marriage portion signalled respectability and familial approval ensuring that, even for independently wealthy women, parental refusal to give one could stop the union. Gradually scholars widened their gaze to friends and kin, showing the collective pressures they brought to bear on individual unions. Most marriages, though, were neither arranged nor individually chosen but subject to the 'multilateral consent' of all interested parties. Love and personal choice were only a few of the factors underlying a marriage. The Pinney family papers show that marriage was viewed with a great deal of anxiety and trepidation, particularly with regard to financial matters and religious affiliation. In areas riven by religious dissent, young people sought potential spouses with the same religious views even if that meant searching further afield. The middling sort fretted over 'worth', status and reputation to the extent that some could not find a satisfactory partner. Elizabeth Isham's account of her unsuccessful marriage plans with John Dryden in the 1630s details the emotional aspects of the break-up, revealing the importance that familial love and honour played in the equation. Love for her father rather than lack of love for her suitor ended the negotiations. Material interest, affection, practical considerations, influence of friends and family, parental love, honour, and personal piety, along with a miscellany of other intangibles, shaped marital choice. Any one individual thus weighed countless issues, making marriage, even for those with resources, a leap of faith that things would work out.[11]

## Marital Relations

Scholarship has moved on from the pessimistic stance that early modern marital relationships lacked intimacy and affection and were characterised by submissive wives and domineering husbands. The first wave of revisionism challenged the notion of the relative unimportance of love in marriage and that low expectations were brought to these unions. Later revisionist works portrayed early modern marriages as more mutual and companionate than had been thought, and pointed to the mitigating effect the demands of daily life had on potentially authoritarian relationships. Much of this scholarship, however, assumes rather than investigates the emotional content of marriage. The most recent approaches explore what marriage meant to early modern men and women, emphasising love as a product of the material, social and cultural world, critiquing the privileging of representation over narrated experience, and examining the interaction between values and ordinary behaviour. As Margaret Hunt states, early modern marriages reveal not so much a gap between law and practice, as is commonly claimed, but the creative enactment of cultural ideals in daily life.[12]

Most early modern English men and women believed that marriages should be based on love. Frances Thorold wrote to her husband William in 1683 that 'thy well-being is the joy of my heart ... one hug with thee my dear would set all to rights'.[13] Many couples formed deep bonds and were often heartbroken at a spouse's untimely death. This was the case even for those at the bottom of the social scale for whom grinding poverty and the relentless need for subsistence undoubtedly strained the relationship. But merely affirming the centrality of love to early modern marriages does not get us very far. Even if both parties expected love to be a central theme in their marital relationship, they could have different understandings of what love meant and divergent expectations regarding what constituted loving behaviour, ensuring that love was not so much a recipe for marital bliss as a place where power was continually negotiated. Sarah and William Cowper, for example, argued constantly about domestic authority, especially who regulated the servants. Sarah believed it was her sphere of jurisdiction, regarding William as a tyrant rather than as a loving spouse when he interfered in that arena.[14] Nor did love necessarily increase the status or autonomy of wives because women, even more than men, were meant to sacrifice themselves for those they loved. Ruth Perry goes so far as to claim that marriage and the stress on romantic love detached a woman from her family of origin and from her pre-existing friendships, and turned her into a companion for her new husband, reliant on his benevolence.[15] But to characterise the position of married women as completely dependent on the good will of their husbands misunderstands the early modern concept of obedience, overvalues the power and authority of men, and undervalues the contribution women made to the household.

The loving relationship between spouses in early modern prescriptive literature was based on that between the faithful and God. The scriptural definition of love emphasised performance: love ought to be 'fruitfull in good workes, and not an emptie and idle love, that is, a love in shew onely'.[16] Miles Huggard, in a poem published in 1555 written 'in termes plaine' so that everyone could understand what loving God entailed, declared: 'If thou diddest him loue thou wouldest his wil obay.'[17] Loving God meant abiding by his will, making obedience an integral part of the performance of love. Both God and the faithful had obligations to fulfil in the name of love: God provided support and protection; his flock gave trust, worship and obedience. Conduct-book writers took this model of a loving relationship and applied it to a married couple, gendering the model in the process. Loving, fearing and obeying became a woman's role; loving, providing and protecting a man's.

Obedience thus certainly constituted the core of femininity and marriage in the well-ordered household. Women were urged to make sure they joined themselves to a man whom they could obey. It was as much the husband's duty to command obedience as it was the wife's to give it. Even women like Henrietta Howard, countess of Suffolk, the mistress of the Prince of Wales, unhappy in her marriage, convinced that her husband was not living up to his part of the marriage contract and eager to be liberated from his governance, accepted his right to exercise it. But, despite the portrayal of obedience as necessary and natural, women – along with children and servants – were *trained* to defer to those over them, a tacit acknowledgement that submission did not come naturally, and compliance, on those occasions when it was enjoined, could be hard won.

Women's reflections on what marital obedience entailed reveal that they did not equate wifely obedience with automatically carrying out everything a husband wanted – thereby also showing that agreement with a norm does not mean that a person was unquestioning or unimaginative. Women had ways of getting around unpalatable requests: responding affectionately to commands, for example, but failing to carry them out, or claiming to have misunderstood. A wife could withhold information then challenge her spouse to give a direct order, knowing that he lacked the pertinent knowledge to do so. Love could also be used to justify and excuse actions that might displease a spouse. Obedience was never intended to produce mindless submissiveness – servile obedience was derided in the conduct books – and this allowed women some space in which to voice their opinions. They also adapted the prescriptive literature to suit their needs. A subtle process of selecting what to attend to, of reinterpreting a text's messages or of blending a variety of texts enabled women to use these texts to vindicate rather than guide their conduct. Sarah Cowper, for example, cited from the printed texts to demonstrate her virtue in a trying relationship and thus assert her moral authority vis-à-vis her husband. A wife could also make use of the prescriptive norms to critique a husband's behaviour, as did Henrietta Howard, convinced that she, notwithstanding her adultery, had fulfilled her marital obligations 'in word and deed', whereas her husband was conspicuously derelict in his duty.[18]

Moreover, male control of the family – as revealed by research into the domestic life of men, one of the great growth areas of the history of the family – was neither as complete nor as oppressive as has been thought. The status attached to marrying and heading a household has been a particularly enduring feature of manliness in western society. Men sought to set up and maintain a household, and placed great stock in providing for and behaving towards their family in a proper Christian manner. A man, according to the prescriptive literature of early modern England, should exercise authority over himself and others, demonstrating self-discipline and restraint. This concept of masculinity, however, excluded a substantial proportion of men and was very difficult to live up to for many more. In the case of Sir Thomas Barrington, it was his wife, Lady Judith, and his mother, Lady Joan, who assisted him in his mission to earn governing masculinity, by providing moral support, writing on his behalf and taking on male roles.[19] Masculinities were relational, men usually governed and were subordinate at the same time, and a household was never limited to the patriarch's control alone. Masculine power was also highly situational and frequently nebulous and exploitable. This structure provided plenty of opportunities for the ostensibly governed to exercise authority.[20]

Despite the opinion of the domestic conduct-book writers that a husband should be the one to go abroad, discuss business and procure goods for the family, while a wife should look after these goods, spend money wisely and stay at home, in practice it was essential that all members contribute to a household's economic well-being. Spouses were economically interdependent: a man, for example, faced the loss of income, property, household management and child care on the death of his wife. Marriage was an economic partnership in terms of the merging of the financial assets and skills that each partner brought to the union, and of their management of the household economy. Scholars have assumed that married women did not work because they were busy with home and child care. Certainly, elite women may not have sought employment, although they were more than ornamental: taking over in a husband's absence, offering medical services and running complex households. Married women below the landed ranks usually engaged in paid work in early modern England, either in the labour force or in family trades, shops and businesses. Women were most likely to have jobs – often laborious, at times dangerous – outside the home in their prime childbearing years.[21] Nor was it necessarily the case that women worked because their husbands could not support the family. Elizabeth Harvey, whose husband was an attorney and clerk of Taunton Castle, worked as a cloth dealer. She was the one who travelled on business, leaving her husband at home to tend to domestic affairs and their children.[22]

Notwithstanding the presumption of female passivity in prescriptive literature, that women petitioning the authorities for help presented themselves as helpless and dependent, and the strong link between economic mastery and masculinity, it is clear that women expected to contribute to the family budget and did not view husbands as the primary breadwinner.[23] Women from all ranks of society displayed considerable knowledge of economic and legal systems and were fully capable of operating successfully in the financial world. The ability to provide for a family, however, was an important part of masculinity, and this affected the activity of other household members. Women's contribution to the household did give them a sense of worth and status in the community but it did not necessarily give women more power in the family. Though women were undoubtedly involved in contractual society, their legal agency was curtailed in the interest of maintaining patriarchal authority within the household. Their ability to work was usually dependent on their husband's good will. In many families, a wife's involvement in trade or business created tension, at times spurring conflict. Some wives were far less committed to the concept of male supremacy than their husbands, especially if it cost them their future security, personal possessions, access to their own money or the right to their own trading profits. A husband could assert his right to a wife's possessions to the extent that he threatened the well-being of the family unit. A wife thus had to balance her obligation to ensure provision for herself and her children alongside her duty to her husband.

The importance placed on a reasoned choice of marital partner, the emphasis on both parties fulfilling the expected spousal duties and the expectation that a wife would yield to her husband did not prevent marital breakdown. Discord was a routine part of any relationship in all ranks in early modern England. Its existence does not necessarily indicate fragile bonds of affection and it did offer an opportunity to re-examine roles and relationships. Marital conflict was more complex than merely a result of men demanding rights and wives challenging them. Both spouses deployed gender roles to their advantage in marriage. In cases brought before the courts, men complained of unloving, disobedient wives who had no just cause for behaving that way. Wives were extravagant, mismanaged the household and neglected the children. Husbands also stressed what they considered fraud: the promised marriage portion was not delivered, wives took goods from the home or refused to part with real estate to pay husbands' debts. Women, on the other hand, depicted themselves as victims of cruel men who elevated the prospect of financial gain above justice, equity and family duty. Many women apparently did not agree that they gave obedience in return for maintenance; rather they were entitled to the latter because they were also doing their bit to support the family. Women complained that their husbands refused to provide for them, kept their property from them, denied them their right to manage the household and were negligent fathers. Cases of marital conflict document that many women tried to bypass coverture, felt demeaned if their husband controlled the money and did not bow to a husband's will.

Some conflict did become violent. Men had a legal right to discipline wives until the nineteenth century but there was considerable debate in the early modern period over how far husbands could go: that a man could physically correct his wife but not violently seemed to be the overall consensus. Marital violence affected the whole family, including children, and abuse was broader than beating alone, including material deprivation, isolation and confinement. Though the causes of wife-beating were complex, the main male defence was that violence had been provoked by a wife's insubordination and disobedience. Relatives, neighbours and friends intervened in abusive relationships, offering refuge and material assistance along with efforts to reconcile the couple if possible.[24] Women themselves did not meekly submit to abusive male authority. Anne Dormer, who married Robert in 1668, described how he threatened, confined, isolated and yelled at her. Robert even reprimanded Anne's father when he tried to stand up for her. Despite this dismal situation, Anne managed to carve out a space beyond her husband's control. She wrote letters when he was out of the house and she did not silently accept his abuse; rather she outargued him or gave sharp retorts.[25]

Wives could also take their husbands to court.[26] Despite the disproportionate legal, ideological and practical advantages men enjoyed, they did not always win their case. Common law may have been unkind to married women, but there were other legal systems available. Equity law used in the prerogative courts such as chancery or the court of requests was cheap and user friendly, and enabled married women to maintain some control over their property. Evidence from recognisances shows that even lesser forms of spousal aggression were brought before the authorities. In the sixteenth and seventeenth centuries, society held women's violence to be more threatening, but towards the end of the seventeenth century, men's exploitation of power became increasingly viewed as a cause for concern. By the eighteenth century, court cases stressed the irrationality and barbarous nature of violence. It was becoming unchristian and dishonourable for a man to beat or deprive his wife.

## Children

Many women – almost half by the eighteenth century – were pregnant on their wedding day. Even with a relatively high child mortality rate, and a typical birth interval of two years or more, most married couples would soon begin, as Benjamin Shaw's father put it, 'to feel the effects of a growing family'.[27] The original historiographical debate over whether or not there was a concept of childhood in the past, whether or not children were severely disciplined in the past, and whether or not parents were bonded to their children now seems unproductive and unimaginative. We have a great deal of evidence to show that parenting was taken seriously, that children were wanted and that a great deal of energy was invested in their care. The problem is that scholars overwhelmingly conceptualise parental relations in terms of instruction and restraint. Not only are there many more issues to explore but also, given the fluctuating nature of the household, we need a much more dynamic approach to the topic.

Investigating how children were fitted to early modern society would be one such approach, especially with reference to gender socialisation. The cultural model of manhood in early modern England stressed personal autonomy, independent judgement and self-command, qualities that could be acquired and practised only by knowing the world. Granting sons the freedom to do so was a must, even though this threatened a family's dynastic and financial security.[28] Sons away from home did stretch the rules, running up large debts, becoming entangled in unsuitable romantic liaisons, or failing to make progress in their studies or career. Parents, especially fathers, had to step in to bail them out. Sons needed temptations to test their virtue and this trumped parental concerns about the expense and risk.

For girls, submission to duty and obedience to authority were the most important lessons to learn. At the same time it was recognised how essential wives were to the success of a household, whether this be with reference to a husband's business; to the smooth running of the estate and home; to the economic contribution of a woman's paid work; or to keeping a family clean, fed and housed. This meant that female initiative and capacity for action, problem-solving and exercising authority could not be extinguished. As with the bringing up of sons, parents had to balance competing imperatives delicately. They limited the freedom of girls, especially for the upper ranks, along with their intellectual educational opportunities, and trained them to defer to their husbands, while paradoxically trying to ensure their daughters would be able to rise to life's challenges. Some girls did resent the greater freedom granted their brothers, illustrating that they could think for themselves.

Realising that the views of children were largely absent from histories of childhood, a few scholars have tried to reconstruct the child's perspective. This, unsurprisingly, has proven to be very difficult. Not only are there very few letters or diaries by children left behind, but we also cannot be sure if these actually represent a child's point of view, as opposed to what he or she thought an adult would like to hear. The realm of illness has some potential here because it played a large part in a child's life in the past, and remarks from children trying to describe how they felt when ill have survived. When six-year-old Frances Archer contracted an ague in 1679 she 'could not forbeare shrieking most of the night', saying she 'had the crampe, and alas I know not what to do'. Metaphors of torture, hell, animals or weapons were used to convey the pain. Thomas Darling suffered 'many sore fits' that he said felt like 'the pricking with daggers or stinging of bees', crying out 'A beare, a beare … he teareth me, he teareth me.' Eleven-year-old Christian Shaw told those around her bed 'that cats, ravens, owles and horses were destroying and pressing her down in the bed', shrieking she had been 'pierced with swords'. Testimony such as this provides rare and poignant insight into a child's mind.[29]

There may have been no modern concept of adolescence in early modern England but there was a recognisable period of youth associated with people in their teens and twenties who were in a state of dependence. This was a dynamic, transformative phase for the young, and there was no single path to adulthood. Young people were not passive social constructs of the dominant adult society but had a great deal of creative potential. Youth was not stress-free: young people had plenty of changes and problems to cope with. It was certainly viewed as a time of potential problems relating to sexuality and disobedience. Rebellion, though, has been over emphasised in the historiography. Young adults were fully capable of complicated manoeuvrings to get their own way without engaging in outright defiance. For the most part, young people accepted patterns of behaviour based on respect and deference to superiors, and sought harmony in the household. They regarded adults not just as authority figures but also as providers and as keepers of heritage. In addition, because the household was fundamental to early modern society and economy, the heads had to reconcile multilateral demands to keep it functioning well. This ensured that subordinates had areas of responsibility and privilege, granting youths opportunities to learn decision-making and lessening the need for revolt.[30]

Many of the young adults in a household might be servants rather than offspring, replacing the children who have left for training elsewhere and subject to a quasi-parental authority from master and mistress. The conduct books are quite clear about the obligations of servants: they are to obey and serve. As Robert Cleaver wrote in 1598, servants with respect to their masters are:

> To love them and to be affectioned towards them as a dutiful child is to his father; to be reverent and lowly to them in all their words and gestures, to suffer and forbear them, to obey with ready and willing minds all their lawful and reasonable commandments, to fear them and to be loath to displease them, to be faithful and trusty to them and theirs in deeds and promises, to be diligent and serviceable, to speak cheerfully, to answer discreetly.[31]

Employers, on the other hand, frequently considered servants to be lacking in such devotion; rather, they stole and drank as well as being careless and disobedient. Masters like Sir Richard Newdigate sought to turn servants into model employees – sober, industrious, punctual, deferential and discreet – but often failed. Newdigate had to resort to paying one maid, Mall Porter, to spy and report on the behaviour of the other servants.[32] Servants found plenty of ways to circumvent control: they carved out unofficial leisure time by dawdling on errands, neglected their duties and stayed out all night. Servants were difficult to regulate because they were highly mobile and, even if dismissed, usually had the last word, commenting on their former masters and mistresses to the community at large.

Parents were not the only shapers of childhood development; siblings also formed bridges to adulthood.[33] The initial focus on marriage and parenting meant that sibling interaction was overlooked, but the gradual recognition that sibling ties are the most durable of relationships has led to a flurry of new work on the topic. The emotional and financial interactions of siblings, positioned as they were somewhere between hierarchy and equality, offer a new way to look at the family. Sibling relations were regarded as naturally loving, with siblings owing affection to one another rather than deference or obedience. Sibling bonds could be deep and enduring ones. Siblings helped look after and educate younger brothers and sisters, and could raise them if parents died. Sibling economics – as Amy Harris terms the exchange of emotional and physical labour – were an important component of family financial strategies. Couples had obligations to their sisters and brothers and would also make use of them as an economic resource. Households could have multiple sibling networks tied together by small household expenditures and errands. Siblings were involved in one another's educational, occupational, business and pecuniary successes, supplying child care, advice, nursing, account keeping and loans, among many other activities. Siblings also, however, had to contend with the reality that equality did not mean identical treatment or opportunities. Parental affection for all their children may have been the same, but parental investment was not, setting the stage for sibling wars. It is easy to assume that most sibling conflict would be between brothers, but in fact there are more court cases dealing with brother–sister quarrels over property. This was caused less by resentment of the privileged position of brothers and more by a desire to receive the full provision of a parent's will.

As children grew up, some parent–child relationships turned fraught and a few ruptured, but most parents were committed to assisting their offspring, offering such vital services as financial aid, advice, networks of adult friendships, or help with arranging service or apprenticeship. Leonard Wheatcroft, a tailor who became the parish clerk of Ashover in 1650 and was imprisoned three times for debt in the 1660s, was actively involved in helping his older children find new places. He personally accompanied his daughters to their places of service, and once met with a bone lace weaver 'with whome I burgined to take a doughter of myne apprentis'.[34] Even after children left home, parents provided a range of material and emotional support. They sent money, food or clothes; supervised masters; took back sick children; and helped them find work or somewhere to live. The parental home was a safety net for teens and early adults, offering a respite from problems like debts, illness or unemployment. Benjamin Bangs, for example, opted to become a Quaker after completing his apprenticeship, travelling and preaching around the countryside. When he became ill, he returned to his mother and stayed with her the whole winter.[35] Parents assisted children even after marriage, especially in times of hardship. Jane Adams and her three children returned to her father's house in 1732 when her husband could not look after his family. She stayed there for a year, with her spouse visiting two or three times a week.[36] The parental home was also a refuge for abused wives.

Most parents, to the best of their ability, made a substantial investment in their children, and took care to provide for all of them. Family property was usually passed on to the younger generation over a considerable period of time rather than only at the parental death. There was some privileging of the eldest son at all ranks but primogeniture does not capture the entirety of practice. In towns, equal sharing and exact portions to all children were the norm. In other regions, parents paid apprenticeship premiums or marriage portions, passed on equipment early, or left bequests in their wills that attempted to modify inheritance rules.[37] Parents tried to make sure each child was given some of the family's economic resources to help establish him or her in the world.

Parents certainly felt obliged to support their children but they also hoped that their children would return the favour. The ability of children to reciprocate was restricted by demography and family structure, and parents usually gave more, but even so offspring offered material assistance, particularly helping parents when they were sick or frail. They also provided more intangible benefits, enhancing the prestige and reputation of parents and arousing parental pride and satisfaction. Parents certainly encouraged a sense of reciprocal obligation in their offspring by, for example, placing emotional pressure on grown children to help, and by reminding them of the care their parents had taken of them. This was often a negotiated exchange of mutually agreeable benefits, and though it might not be equal or symmetrical, some meeting of obligations was expected from both parties. Parents who fell short in fulfilling their part might not be able to count on help from their children as they aged. Elizabeth Hewitt, for example, abandoned a father 'who took little care of her when young'.[38]

The lack of adequate financial resources significantly affected family life. Compared to her wealthier counterpart, a poor woman, if she married, married later, had longer birth intervals and probably ended childbearing a few years before menopause. Her children were more likely to die, and if her husband also died she had less chance of marrying again. Bringing up children was a difficult task for poorer families, made even harder by the frequent criticism of their parenting by those in authority.

Not only was a tremendous amount of maternal labour involved in keeping children clean and fed for those lower down the social scale but also, because it cost a minimum of £5 a year to maintain a child and £6 for a youth, it was a real struggle for poor parents to supply adequate food or clothing. Medical care was an additional burden. The lack of resources caused enormous stress. Births were not necessarily welcome, even if a baby was loved when born, because every new addition strained the family budget. If a child died, parents felt simultaneously grief for their loss and relief there was one fewer mouth to feed. Because the poor lived in cramped accommodation, labouring fathers of necessity were involved with family life. These fathers were less concerned with inheritance, had less control over their sons from around the age of fourteen on because they had usually left home to enter service, and had limited involvement in their children's decision to marry. This meant there could be less conflict between fathers and sons than in more affluent families. In general, however, poverty could prevent poor parents from realising even the basics of parental care: a father providing and a mother nurturing. Fragmented families were more common, parents were less able to protect offspring from misfortune, and very poor children may not even have had a home. For the very poor, the family was often not the abiding scheme of life: not a safety net in times of need; not a work unit; and maybe not even a procreative unit, because spinsterhood, prenuptial pregnancy and illegitimacy were all more common among the poor.[39]

## Kin

Individuals did not leave one family behind as they embarked on the next. New couples brought economic and familial obligations along with emotional connections into the household. Population mobility ensured that most early modern English households were unlikely to have dense networks of kin in the immediate locality. Kin ties were therefore believed to be of limited significance beyond the immediate family for the majority of households. Family and kinship as categories, however, are not necessarily linked, developing neither in tandem nor inversely. It is a mistake to underestimate the significance of kin connections dispersed over a larger social area, or those that joined rural areas to major cities. Englishmen and women had a loose but nevertheless systematic way of recognising kin, and bonds could be activated when needed. New work on the language of kinship shows that it could be used to construct a grid of kin links, and endow these ties with social and moral significance. Blood relatives, even distant ones, offered ready-made networks of support to which claims could be made with less of the social and emotional investment required for establishing other contacts. How much energy and time was invested in sustaining kin connections would depend on the goals and temperament of an individual. It would be very difficult to maintain a relationship with all kin, but even so plenty of evidence exists testifying to the vibrancy of kinship ties. They were important for migration, for mercantile networks, for debt and credit relations and reputation, for raising capital, for minimising economic risk, and for supplying charity. Relatives gave material gifts, help in bringing up children and assistance with jobs. They were influential in political and occupational networks and patronage, and involved in marriage negotiations. Kin clearly felt some obligation to help but could not necessarily give all that was needed because they had their own family to consider. Though there was no absolute certainty of receiving aid, near kin, at least, offered much of the strategic support needed through life, and their assistance, typically given at critical junctures, improved the circumstances and prospects of individuals.[40]

At first kin were deemed of more significance to those with property, but as it was increasingly recognised that poor-relief, even for those seen as deserving, did not provide enough support for those in need, so it was uncovered that additional assistance was often provided by kin.[41] Survival for the poorest elderly inhabitants required the combined resources of community, kin and individual, making kinship, along with neighbours, friends and state, a locus of support. The aged poor turned to families and communities only after they had made every effort to be self-supporting and had exhausted all resources at their disposal, but the help that families offered was important. In eighteenth-century Terling (Essex) and Puddletown (Dorset) a half of elderly men and a third of elderly women lived with children. Adult children were a critical supplement to the elderly's attempts at self-sufficiency, and the poorer the parish, the more important it was to have children. Having fewer family members present in the community could lead to greater poverty for an individual, demonstrating the importance of kin support. An adult child may not have wanted to be a residential carer, as in the case of Hester, the youngest child of John Pinney and a successful business woman in London, who resisted staying on the family farm to look after her father although she did visit.[42] But grown children could contribute funds to help the aged in their homes, as well as helping in the house, or with meals and other domestic chores. At the level of the dependent poor, however, adult children, often collecting poor-relief themselves, were not the main pillar of the elderly's economic support.

Kin have been rediscovered more as a social security system, and the questions scholars have asked revolve around the usefulness of kin as an economic resource. Evaluating the significance of kinship in early modern England solely through the prism of material assistance, and deeming it important only insofar as kin supplied aid or not, downplays its role. Even if one never needed support, just knowing kin existed could be a source of comfort, and for more than economic reasons. Historians too readily discount the importance of so-called official kin – those who turned up at major life-cycle events. Apart from the fact that it is doubtful whether early modern English men and women ever divided kin into the categories official or practical, this perspective does not take into account bonds and familial identity. Inviting kin to witness significant rites of passage, for those fortunate enough to be able to do so, gave people a sense of belonging. A person's community may have been based on the household and framed by siblings, friends and neighbours, but the wider kin group formed a supporting cast, anchoring and comforting even when not economically solicited, and immensely useful if called upon. Kin supplied roots, bonds and a place in the world, making them a vital element in the enmeshed connectedness of individual lives.[43]

## Conclusion

All of the relationships within a household that we separate out for the purposes of analysis, in practice impinged upon and influenced one another. This aspect of household life is usually missed by prescriptive texts, with their insistence on examining a series of dyads, hierarchically arranged. Conduct books present a world of clear choices, penalties and rewards. They had their own points of focus: in the sixteenth and seventeenth centuries on order and duty within the 'little commonwealth'; in the eighteenth century on the concept of politeness. They offered mixed and contradictory messages. They had coverage gaps, particularly with regard to women. They had little to say about female civility and apparently did not envisage a world in which sisters sparred as vigorously as brothers. They provided navigational signposts but were of limited practical use in coping with the complex challenges of living in the world.[44]

The most recent scholarship on the early modern family, while remaining indebted to cultural history, attempts to move beyond discourse and representation to investigate the situated use and application of concepts in everyday life – how 'imagined cultural ideals were rendered tangible'.[45]

Individuals, as shown in their diaries, letters and memoirs, had expectations of family members and relationships that were clearly shaped by the prescriptive literature. But, far from viewing these texts as supplying definitive answers, they made use of them in ways the authors probably did not contemplate. They mixed together statements from a variety of texts and merged these with their personal observations and opinions. Furthermore, the act of living inevitably entails prioritisation, negotiation, contest and choice. Obligations and circumstances shift; some norms have more weight at given times or in certain situations than others. Individuals were neither living in an end point nor had a single goal. Decision-making involved an evaluation of the current situation and the vision for the future for multiple – at times competing – objectives.

Family life was a perpetual balancing act of a host of demands, needs, obligations, resources and desires. It involved both contractual relations and affect. It promoted and at times violated important social values. It pursued stability, constantly adapting to its changing make-up, and to changing social and economic conditions. Historians, contending with the twin problems of initial work in the field that emphasised dramatic transformation and improvement, and of revisionist scholarship that stressed fundamental continuities in family life, now postulate a slower-moving, more accommodating, more inclusive change: a process of constant adaptation to shifts in the economic, institutional and cultural contexts within which families pursued their goals, and associated shifts in the manner in which they understood their roles. Putting men back in the Georgian home, for example, brings to light the lack of any straightforward continuity between early modern and Victorian models of masculinity. Early modern individuals were heavily invested in their offspring but they inhabited a different mental world with a less developed concept of emotional or mental development, and little concept of a psychologically damaged child. Contemporaries thought of family ties in the form of reciprocal obligations, rules and sacrifices, but also in terms of affectionate bonds of nurture and sustenance. Each household developed its own particular set of strategies to cope with its own needs and achieve its own priorities. Acts of implementation by a multiplicity of people with diverse experiences and agendas inevitably created different scenarios. Even when an act appears the same, it is neither imbued with identical meanings nor carried out in similar circumstances each time. Thus, because of the unpredictable and unintended effects of contingent human actions, the very concepts and actions of continuity are themselves the seeds for changes, illustrating, as Hannah Arendt stated, the creative potential in human society.[46]

## Notes

1  L. Pollock, *With Faith and Physic: The Life of a Tudor Gentlewoman, Lady Grace Mildmay 1552–1620* (London: Collins & Brown, 1993), 21; P. Sharpe, *Population and Society in an East Devon Parish: Reproducing Colyton, 1540–1840* (Exeter: University of Exeter Press, 2002), 208.

2  P. Laslett, *Family Life and Illicit Love in Earlier Generations* (Cambridge: Cambridge University Press, 1977), 93; S. Hindle, 'Below stairs at Arbury Hall: Sir Richard Newdigate and his household staff, *c.* 1670–1710', *Historical Research*, 85 (2012).

3  E. A. Wrigley and R. S. Schofield, *The Population History of England 1541–1871: A Reconstruction* (Cambridge: Cambridge University Press, 1981), 255.

4  S. King, 'English historical demography and the nuptiality conundrum: New perspectives', *Historical Social Research*, 23 (1998); J. McNabb, 'Ceremony versus consent: Courtship, illegitimacy, and reputation in northwest England, 1560–1610', *Sixteenth Century Journal*, 37 (2006); B. Hill, 'The marriage age of women and the demographers', *HWJ*, 28 (1989).

5  S. Hindle, 'The problem of pauper marriage in seventeenth-century England: The Alexander prize essay', *TRHS*, 6th Series, 8 (1998); D. O'Hara, *Courtship and Constraint: Rethinking the Making of Marriage in Tudor England* (Manchester: Manchester University Press, 2000), Chapter 6.

6  J. Evelyn, *Diary and Correspondence of John Evelyn*, ed. William Bray, 4 vols. (London: Henry Colburn, 1850–2), Vol. IV, 27.

7  King, 'English historical demography', 136.

8  J. R. Gillis, '"A triumph of hope over experience": Chance and choice in the history of marriage', *IRSH*, 44 (1999).

9  S. King, 'Chance encounters? Paths to household formation in early modern England', *IRSH*, 44 (1999), 32.

10 A. Wall (ed.), 'Two Elizabethan women: Correspondence of Joan and Maria Thynne 1575–1611', *Wiltshire Record Society*, 38 (Devizes: *Wiltshire Record Society*, 1983), xix; E. Foyster, 'Parenting was for life, not just for childhood: The role of parents in the married lives of their children in early modern England', *History*, 86 (2001), 319.

11 O'Hara, *Courtship and Constraint*, Chapter 1; Sharpe, *Population and Society*, 274–75, 278; I. Stephens, 'The courtship and singlehood of Elizabeth Isham, 1630–1634', *HJ*, 51 (2008); M. Ingram, *Church Courts, Sex and Marriage in England, 1570–1640* (Cambridge: Cambridge University Press, 1987), 136.

12 M. R. Hunt, 'Wives and marital "rights" in the Court of the Exchequer in the early eighteenth century', in P. Griffiths and M. Jenner (eds.), *Londonopolis: Essays in the Cultural and Social History of Early Modern London* (Manchester: Manchester University Press, 2000), 116, 123.

13 J. Bailey, *Unquiet Lives: Marriage and Marriage Breakdown in England, 1660–1800* (Cambridge: Cambridge University Press, 2003), 28.

14 A. Kugler, 'Constructing wifely identity: Prescription and practice in the life of Lady Sarah Cowper', *JBS*, 40 (2001), 302.

15  R. Perry, *Novel Relations: The Transformation of Kinship in English Literature and Culture, 1748–1818* (Cambridge: Cambridge University Press, 2004), 196–7.

16  J. Preston, *The Breast-Plate of Faith and Love* (London, 1630), 5.

17  M. Huggarde, *A Mirrour of Loue* (London, 1555), image 12.

18  These two paragraphs are based on: I. Tague, 'Love, honor, and obedience: Fashionable women and the discourse of marriage in the early eighteenth century', *JBS*, 40 (2001), 95, 98; L. Gowing, ' "The manner of submission": Gender and demeanour in seventeenth-century London', *Cultural and Social History*, 10 (2013); S. Keenan, ' "Embracing submission"? Motherhood, marriage and mourning in Katherine Thomas's seventeenth-century "Commonplace Book"', *Women's Writing*, 15 (2008), 81; Kugler, 'Constructing wifely identity', 296.

19  J. van Duinen, 'The obligations of governing masculinity in the early Stuart family: The Barringtons of Hatfield Broad Oak', in S. Broomhall and J. Van Gent (eds.), *Governing Masculinities in the Early Modern Period: Regulating Selves and Others*, Women and Gender in the Early Modern World (Farnham: Ashgate, 2011), 125–27.

20  H. Barker, 'Soul, purse and family: Middling and lower-class masculinity in eighteenth-century Manchester', *SH*, 3 (2008); E. A. Foyster, *Manhood in Early Modern England: Honour, Sex and Marriage* (London and New York: Longman, 1999), 139; S. Broomhall and J. Van Gent, 'Introduction', in *Governing Masculinities in the Early Modern Period*, 2, 14.

21  K. Wrightson, *Earthly Necessities: Economic Lives in Early Modern Britain* (New Haven and London: Yale University Press, 2000), 30, 31, 42; M. R. Hunt, *The Middling Sort: Commerce, Gender, and the Family in England, 1680–1780* (Berkeley: University of California Press, 1996), 22, 42, 128; C. Muldrew, ' "A mutual assent of her mind"? Women, debt, litigation and contract in early modern England', *HWJ*, 55 (2003), 52. A. L. Erikson, 'Married women's occupations in eighteenth-century London', *C&C*, 23 (2008), 269; M. K. McIntosh, 'Women, credit and family relationships in England, 1300–1620', *JFH*, 30 (2005).

22  P. Crawford, 'A decade in the life of Elizabeth Harvey of Taunton 1696–1706', *Women's History Review*, 19 (2010), 246, 253.

23  A. Shepard, 'Manhood, credit and patriarchy in early modern England *c.* 1580–1640', *P&P*, 167 (2000); J. Hurl-Eamon, 'The fiction of female dependence and the makeshift economy of soldiers, sailors, and their wives in eighteenth-century London', *Labor History*, 49 (2008).

24  Bailey, *Unquiet Lives*, 113–14, 198; L. Gowing, *Domestic Dangers: Women, Words, and Sex in Early Modern London* (Oxford: Clarendon Press, 1996), 211; E. Foyster, 'At the limits of liberty: Married women and confinement in eighteenth-century England', *C&C*, 17 (2002); E. Foyster, *Marital Violence: An English Family History, 1660–1857* (Cambridge: Cambridge University Press, 2005), Chapter 3.

25  M. O'Connor, 'Interpreting early modern woman abuse', *Quidditas*, 23 (2002).

26 J. Hurl-Eamon, 'Domestic violence prosecuted: Women binding over their husbands for assault at Westminster Quarter Session, 1685–1720', *JFH*, 26 (2001); Hunt, 'Wives and marital "rights" in the Court of the Exchequer', 122; T. Stretton, 'Marriage, separation and the common law in England, 1540–1660', in H. Berry and E. Foyster (eds.), *The Family in Early Modern England* (Cambridge: Cambridge University Press, 2007); J. Bailey, '"I dye [*sic*] by inches": Locating wife beating in the concept of privatization of marriage and violence in eighteenth-century England', *SH*, 31 (2006).

27 P. Crawford, *Parents of Poor Children in England, 1580–1800* (Oxford: Oxford University Press, 2010), 116.

28 H. French and M. Rothery, '"Upon your entry into the world": Masculine values and the threshold of adulthood among landed elites in England 1680–1800', *SH*, 33 (2008).

29 H. Newton, '"Very sore nights and days": The child's experience of illness in early modern England, c. 1580–1720', *Medical History*, 55 (2011), 164, 165.

30 P. Griffiths, *Youth and Authority: Formative Experiences in England 1560–1640* (Oxford: Clarendon Press, 1996), 1–2, 7, 16, 24, 60; I. Krausman Ben-Amos, *Adolescence and Youth in Early Modern England* (New Haven: Yale University Press, 1994), 8, 37.

31 R. C. Richardson, 'Social engineering in early modern England: Masters, servants, and the godly discipline', *Clio*, 33 (2004), 171–72.

32 Hindle, 'Below stairs at Arbury Hall', 73.

33 This paragraph is based on A. Harris, 'That fierce edge: Sibling conflict and politics in Georgian England', *JFH*, 37 (2012); A. Harris, *Siblinghood and Social Relations in Georgian England: Share and Share Alike* (Manchester and New York: Manchester University Press, 2012).

34 Derbyshire Record Office, Ashover MS, 'A history of the life and pilgrimage of Leonard Wheatcroft of Ashover', 2079M/F1, fols. 19, 20, 21.

35 I. Krausman Ben-Amos, 'Reciprocal bonding: Parents and their offspring in early modern England', *JFH*, 25 (2000), 294.

36 Foyster, 'Parenting was for life', 315.

37 Wrightson, *Earthly Necessities*, 61, 62–3; I. Krausman Ben-Amos, *The Culture of Giving: Informal Support and Gift-Exchange in Early Modern England* (Cambridge: Cambridge University Press, 2008), 19.

38 Ben-Amos, 'Reciprocal Bonding', 304.

39 Sharpe, *Population and Society*, 204; Crawford, *Parents of Poor Children*, 113, 22, 27, 29, 208, 41, 43–5.

40 This paragraph is based on: K. A. Lynch, 'Kinship in Britain and beyond from the early modern to the present: Postscript', *C&C*, 25 (2010); N. Tadmor, 'Early modern English kinship in the long run: Reflections on continuity and change', *C&C*, 25 (2010); R. Wall, 'Beyond the household: Marriage, household formation and the role of kin and neighbours', *IRSH*, 44 (1999); K. Wrightson and D. Levine, *Poverty and Piety in an English Village: Terling, 1525–1700* (Oxford: Clarendon Press, 1995), 99–102; D. Cressy, 'Kinship and kin interaction in early modern England', *P&P*, 113 (1986); I. Krausman

Ben-Amos, 'Gifts and favors: Informal support and gift-exchange in early modern England', *JMH*, 72 (2000).

41 S. Hindle, '"Without the cry of any neighbours": A Cumbrian family and the poor law authorities, *c.* 1690–1730', in Berry and Foyster, *The Family in Early Modern England*; J. Healey, 'Poverty in an industrializing town: Deserving hardship in Bolton, 1674–99', *SH*, 35 (2010); L. A. Botelho, *Old Age and the English Poor Law, 1500–1700* (Woodbridge: Boydell, 2004), 79, 83, 98–102, 134–5.

42 Sharpe, *Population and Society*, 300.

43 P. P. Viazzo, 'Family, kinship and welfare provision in Europe, past and present: Commonalities and divergences', *C&C*, 25 (2010); Tadmor, 'Early modern English kinship in the long run', 25–6.

44 Gowing, 'The manner of submission', 26; Barker, 'Soul, purse and family', 12; Harris, *Siblinghood and Social Relations*, 89.

45 French and Rothery, 'Upon your entry into the world', 403.

46 H. Arendt, *The Human Condition*, 2nd edn (Chicago: University of Chicago Press, 1998), 95–6, 175–7, 237.

4

# Little Commonwealths II: Communities

## Malcolm Gaskill

### Introduction

Everyone in early modern England belonged to a community. Membership entailed not just shared space but a social arrangement that organised lives, managed relationships, and shaped identities within lifespans and across generations. Communities were built on values, informing the collective evaluation of conduct to determine reputation and status. Yet ideals were honoured as much in the breach as the observance, especially at times of rapid change, which suggests why contemporaries worried about them so much. This chapter will explore both enduring and evolving characteristics of English communities, in terms of physical appearance and, less tangibly, how community was experienced – a more transcendent sense of attachment sustained by feeling and emotion.

Community was so fundamental to existence that contemporaries made little effort to define it. Unlike the household, the term conveyed only a vague sense of identity and engagement. In 1604 the schoolmaster Robert Cawdrey, drawing on the Roman concept of *communitas*, gave it simply as 'fellowship', offering 'communion' as a synonym. Throughout the seventeenth century, lexicographers elaborated on this without much deviation. One described 'Fellowship in partaking together', another 'injoying in common or mutual participation'. The best definition that some dictionaries managed was 'to commune', derived from *communicare*, hinting that communities were arenas for making human connections. Communities, then, grew from dynamic social relations. The radical Robert Coster sought in 1649 'to advance the work of publick Community' by challenging landed tyranny. Only by levelling its gentry and clergy, he argued, could England enjoy 'Brave Community'. Thus 'community' had overtones of both 'charity' and 'commonwealth', fusing ideals of spiritual and economic unity. Hobbes conceived community in terms of 'concord' and 'covenants', which like 'peace' and 'love' struck him

as vital pre-conditions for stable government.[1] By this time, the secondary definition of 'a Corporation or Company incorporate' was emerging,
shifting the meaning from 'spiritual congregation' to 'political and commercial collective'.[2] This is not to imply, however, that the habit of lay
association was not already established in the Middle Ages, nor that the
community's spiritual dimension had disappeared by the modern period.[3]

Early modern social historians have made 'the community' a category
of analysis, essential to understanding the intersecting currents of continuity and change that characterise their period. Their early work generated debate, much of it rooted in older sociology where 'community'
was coterminous with the local and implied wholesome consensus prior
to the atomising effects of industrialisation. The distinction between
*Gemeinschaft* ('community') and *Gesellschaft* ('society') formulated in the
nineteenth century by Ferdinand Tönnies left an important legacy.[4] The
idea was taken up by Tönnies's contemporary Max Weber, who made
a profound impression on the 'new social historians' of early modern
England between the 1960s and 1980s.[5] Some wondered whether communities were best characterised by individualism and conflict or by collectivity and harmony. According to John Bossy, the Church regarded
parishes as hostile arenas where unity was 'an exceptional, temporary
and exceptional feeling'.[6] Lawrence Stone went further, branding the village 'a place filled with malice and hatred', a view James Sharpe found
'extremely pessimistic'.[7] The debate never really went anywhere, perhaps
because it addressed the wrong questions. It was, in any case, overtaken
by a more sophisticated appreciation of community and society, one that
neither assumed wholesale change from the Middle Ages nor simplisti-
cally equated change with decline.[8] The best accounts treated community
'not as a feature of the social prehistory of Europe but [as] part and parcel
of the developing historical process itself'.[9]

The problem remains, however, our inclination to simplify and stiffen
an infinitely complex, varied and flexible entity. Not only did the early
modern world sustain different types of community, but people belonged
to several at once. Some communities were subsets, others entire alternative ways of belonging, and yet few were mutually incompatible. The
dichotomy implied by Tönnies was a false one, contrasting life in pre-
modernity (rural and introspective, organically bonded) with modernity
(urban and expansive and fissiparous), as if these were discrete geographical and temporal zones. In fact, village communities co-existed comfort-
ably and productively with regional, national and even trans-national
groupings. And identities extending from community membership were

multi-faceted, intersecting and layered, without any necessary tension or contradiction.[10] People might simultaneously belong to an ecclesiastical parish, the manor from which they held land, the neighbourhood, or a religious guild or fellowship. Urban guilds were exclusive associations, but their members also belonged to a *wider* community of citizens and a *parallel* community of neighbours, adding scope and depth to self-awareness. Even the 'strangers' ghettoised in cities identified with communities of kinship and trade and religion, near and far.

Every community had complex relationships with other communities, and was complex in itself. Neither inherently conflictual nor inherently consensual, communities were marbled with contradiction and contingency, ambiguity and ambivalence. The essential processes of inclusion and exclusion were shifting and uncertain; the demarcation lines were fuzzy; the rules were prescriptive and proscriptive yet subjective and changeable. Furthermore, narratives supporting the concept of community were unstable: different social groups envisioned things differently. Cherished norms were challenged and circumvented, as well as quietly compromised by 'the daily workings of communities made up of flesh-and-blood individuals'.[11] Habits and protocols that allowed conflict and harmony, co-operation and individualism, to co-exist in low tension were fundamentally important, leading us to a view of community as a set of contingently enacted thoughts rather than a predictably mechanical structure. Community itself is not a thing, as Keith Wrightson reminds us, 'it is a quality in social relations which is, in some respects, occasional and temporary, and which needs periodic stimulation and reaffirmation'.[12]

Moreover, as interests clashed in this era of profound social, economic and political transformation, even dominant visions of the ideal community diverged. Before the Reformation, the perfect parish had been a holy congregation, focused on rituals of common prayer and communion. And it made sense within the 'great chain of being' that this spiritual assembly should mesh with temporal orderings of patriarchy, hierarchy and polity. In the sixteenth and seventeenth centuries, however, demographic growth, social polarisation, internal migration and urban expansion – not to mention cultural upheavals in faith and worship – led to rival ambitions that multiplied versions of community. Essential ideals survived, even in towns and cities and divided rural communities, yet these became strained and contested. As Peter Burke has observed, 'if real communities are messy affairs, ideal ones ... have clear boundaries'.[13] And most of the tension that transformed early modern communities, and indeed all society, lay in the emotional gap between the dogmatic insistence of clear-cut ideals and an endlessly various day-to-day reality.

## Continuity

In 1500 the majority of English people lived in the countryside, as they did in 1750 at the end of the period. Most inhabited hamlets and villages, the rest market towns or cities, among which Norwich, York and London were pre-eminent. Administratively, England was divided into counties, and counties into 'hundreds' (or similar). Counties formed regions with varying densities of settlement, a pattern determined as much by topography as by human design. Some people, especially in the uplands of the north and west, lived remotely, relatively free from interference by Church or magistracy or manorial lords; others, in the downland south and east, were cheek-by-jowl and felt the constant glare of authority. Throughout England, the course of life followed the seasons; weather; and availability of food, fuel and raw materials; but also social and political imperatives. Ties extended vertically and horizontally: between people of different social rank through patronage and deference; and between neighbours of equal rank who shared interests, for example upholding the right to use common land for grazing and gathering firewood. Such concerns even aligned landed manorial tenants with landless labourers, while excluding the nobility and gentry. Rural communities, especially the more compact ones, were mini-commonwealths of work and worship, reproduction and recreation. Pre-Reformation calendar customs persisted in adapted forms, tracing the rhythms of life, satisfying basic spiritual needs and giving meaning to existence. Common cultures also consisted in shared dialect, proverbial wisdom and biblical phraseology to form 'communities of speech'.[14]

The parish church lay at the heart of communal life – a focal point for civic and administrative activity as well as for devotion. In the vestry, the minister, churchwardens and other 'principal and ancient inhabitants' met as an informal parish council. Vestries were also storerooms for everything from fire buckets to hobbyhorses (used in festivals) to the oak chest where parish registers, manorial deeds and custumals were kept – the written memory of the community. Tradition was also upheld by funerary statues – the community's memory in marble – bearing silent witness to the ancient legitimacy of authority. Like the religious wall paintings obliterated in the 1540s, these monuments to the aristocracy and gentry reminded ordinary folk of their worldly place as they filed into church and took their pews in order of rank.

Often the manor house, another monolithic symbol of power, stood nearby. Many lords would open their doors at Christmas time, treating locals to cakes and ale, and there were other similar rituals intended to reinforce the patronage–deference relationship. In Hampshire, it was customary for the Tichborne family to give the poor doles of flour or bread on Lady Day. A painting from 1671 depicts the entire parish arranged before the manor house, a portrait of an unequal relationship seen through the dispensation of charity. The common people, drab and supplicatory, contrast with the silk-clad Tichbornes, whom the artist made glow with privilege.[15] Besides great houses, larger villages and towns had guildhalls and corn exchanges, where trade and tradesmen were regulated. Market crosses, broken by Protestant iconoclasts but not completely destroyed, served as rendezvous points for more substantial communities. And in this post-Reformation era, former church buildings were put to secular uses, and new town halls built to meet the civic needs of administration and local government. Architecture drew people together, concentrating attention in a way that preserved social difference and promoted respect.[16]

At the same time, quite how such institutions were used lay beyond the control of the ruling elite. Sites where the status quo was reaffirmed were also where it was challenged. Most social protest was conservative, not proto-revolutionary, however, and demanded that those who governed abide by their obligations. Anonymous petitions and rhymes were pinned to church doors and manor gates and market crosses, and it was in such places that demonstrators gathered in times of dearth. Precincts of officialdom were put to other informal uses. Church porches saw 'clandestine marriages' and sheltered watchers for spirits on All Hallows' Eve, both practices condemned by the Church. As well as a burial ground, the churchyard was a site for spells, oaths, transactions, courtship and games. Completing the picture were alehouses, the venues for sociable events such as 'ales' to boost parish coffers, and quotidian routines of relaxing with beer and tobacco, storytelling, singing, dancing and gambling. Puritans reviled such disorder and ungodliness, although some in authority valued the 'good fellowship' that alehouses promoted.

Churches and mansions and alehouses were connected by neighbourhoods, mini-communities in themselves, where people saw and heard and smelled each other – their cooking, refuse, livestock, children, disputes. Even in London, neighbourhoods constituted a primary setting for social experience.[17] This was where food and fuel were bartered and borrowed, begged and pilfered, and favours exchanged – likewise news and gossip. Most people lived face-to-face lives. Busybodies peered through cracks in the shutters; they eavesdropped, made mock and started rumours. Pleasantries and insults were traded, promises kept or broken, invitations accepted and declined. If the Church and other institutions were the community's vital organs, this activity, for good or ill, was its lifeblood. Social relationships were thus constantly renegotiated, in practice often to further selfish or sectional ambitions, but always theoretically to promote neighbourliness. After the Reformation, 'good works' to aid the disadvantaged were declared worthless as a means to salvation but continued to benefit the community socially and politically.[18]

The households that neighbourhoods comprised were more than just homes or families: they were thrumming machines of work and reproduction, instruction and devotion, nurture and sustenance. They were also political communities – indeed symbolic microcosms of the hierarchical state. Fathers and masters were seen as kings ruling their own realms, and accordingly their murder was punished as petty treason. A blow even at plebeian patriarchy struck at the overarching ideology, which stood for the integrity of the parish and the nation. Every aspect of life was connected. An individual's honour did not exist in a vacuum, but was subsumed by the collective reputation of his or her household. Lives were, for the most part, lived in plain sight of all, and for most people privacy was not just unobtainable but undesirable. What for us might be a personal aspiration or right was, to the early modern community, furtive and suspicious.

To escape supervision and censure, subordinate groups did form alternative miniature communities both within the whole and distinct from it: 'companies' of sociability.[19] Female activities such as spinning bees, visits to the bakehouse, milking in the pasture, washing clothes, attending births and serving on 'juries of matrons' all mattered for the well-being of ordinary women. On these occasions, words could tumble out, unpoliced by men. Adolescents of both sexes sought relief from the pressure to conform. Servants and apprentices made friends, and in some towns ran riot on May Day and Shrovetide. This was not revolutionary conduct: it was bounded, limited, and akin to the sanctioned appointment of boy bishops – a ritual of temporary inversion to validate the orthodox order of things, however much alarm boisterous behaviour caused law officers.[20] These displays were communal lessons in conformity: demonstrating right through wrong. Witches and murderers, their crimes luridly described in pamphlets, were exemplars not just of ungodliness but of bad neighbourliness and unsociability.[21]

Communities, then, did not cohere through unanimity or full obedience but through structures of authority that permitted a degree of dissent and clamped down on the rest. Arthur Dent's *The Plaine Mans Path-way to Heaven*, first published in 1601, denounced the sins that poisoned the community's soul. Drunkenness was particularly injurious, causing misery, beggary, shame, strife, quarrelling and fighting. Idleness, too, corrupted commonwealths. 'There be many lazie losels & luskish youthes, both in Townes and Villages', wrote Dent, 'which do nothing al the day long but walke the streetes, sit upon the stalles and frequent Tavernes and Ale-houses'.[22] Malefactors might be legally whipped or pilloried, but even formal sanctions required local assent. Many offences tried by Church courts received punishments inflicted by the community for the sake of the community, for instance forced repentance before the congregation wearing a white sheet. Other sinners were ordered to 'purge' – that is made to find witnesses to their good character. Ecclesiastical justice, meted out *pro salute animae* ('for the good of the soul'), was meant to restore errant sheep to the flock and correct communal imbalances. Like manorial courts, Church courts settled disputes cheaply and quickly, and were therefore popular.[23]

Communities also regulated themselves by extra-legal means deemed legitimate through long usage. These included spreading satirical ballads, humiliating adulterers and cuckolds with 'rough music', and silencing outspoken women with scolds' bridles and ducking stools. Like Church court punishments, these sanctions reinscribed the moral boundary of the community. Counter-measures against witches also reveal communal values and their defence. Mostly these were tests, such as the dubious 'ordeal by water', which required popular participation. The intention was a theatrical demonstration of guilt, of which at least some community members were convinced but could not prove. The custom of requiring murder suspects to touch corpses, which might 'bleed afresh' to identify their killers, operated on similar lines. The local application of such controls promoted a sense of mutual reassurance, good will and harmony.

Communities, then, were places to observe hierarchy and discipline, but also stages for displays of mutuality and obligation. Horizontal ties were both constraining and sustaining, and put individual liberty second to collective security. Neighbourhood snooping was a means of self-regulation linked to the 'moral economy', an unwritten code by which fairness and propriety in everything from sexual mores to grain prices was fiercely upheld. Protests defended custom, censuring miscreants and compelling superiors to abide by paternalist rhetoric. The idea of the 'politics of the parish' is also relevant here. If communities were building blocks of the state, then they shared in its political character, from villagers' adherence to faiths and factions in the national 'public sphere', to the local calculus of reputations and negotiation of relationships. Customary rules were constantly reappraised and protected, made and remade.[24] Even fun was literal 'recreation': feasts and celebrations repaired the frayed social fabric. Community consisted in bounded territory and its people, but also in activities that promoted 'intercourse between man and society, man and the material world, and man and the supernatural universe'.[25]

## Change

Village communities, for all their introspection, were not islands. Like towns and cities, they were connected through local institutions; lines of kinship; and networks of work and trade and religion to other villages, and to towns and cities and regions. Irrespective of size or particular identity, a community belonged to a dynamic social and economic world beyond. And through restless dynamism came constant change. In the later sixteenth and seventeenth centuries, population expansion, urban growth, the enclosure of open fields, industrialisation, expanding markets, and increased road and river traffic had a significant impact on how communities looked, felt and functioned. Migrants came and went, as did pedlars and traders, beggars and vagrants. To geographical mobility was added social mobility, further complicating the picture of the community as the fortunes of individual families, and sometimes whole groups, waxed and waned. The scale and pace of change varied according to local society and topography. By 1700 the parish of Myddle in Shropshire had remained remarkably unaffected, yet Highley, just forty miles away, was transformed by enclosure. In Cambridgeshire even proximate parishes had contrasting histories. The social structure of Chippenham became more polarised, but that of Willingham more egalitarian. The experience of Terling, as reconstructed by Keith Wrightson and David Levine, does not stand for all Essex.[26]

Economic change was matched in scale and pace by state formation, the extension of royal policy through law into communities. From the mid sixteenth century, parishes were increasingly hard-wired into a national framework through the enforcement of common law and proliferating statutes by justices of the peace, who also participated in local government and the 'county community'.[27] These magistrates belonged to a structure of local office-holding where constables were responsible to them, and they to assize judges at Westminster. The imposition of Protestant uniformity reinforced this hierarchy, with churchwardens answerable to archdeacons and bishops and their delegates. The Reformation made faith a test of allegiance policed by officials, from unpaid amateurs (whose authority derived from local standing) to crown appointees. Traditional religious practices were proscribed, as were informal counter-measures against sin, which were deemed disorderly and disrespectful to the law. After 1600 English life met with higher expectations from within and without, although the growth of state roles performed locally diminished distinctions between internal and external pressures. Nor were ideals of civil and godly order easily separable, with religion and the law forming two halves of an ideology that fitted parish and state alike. Local campaigns against everything from healers' prayers to maypole dances contributed to a puritan 'reformation of manners'. New standards were imposed by a burgeoning 'middling sort' whose increasingly self-conscious identity as a community within a community was cemented by what offended them – drunkenness, idleness, fornication and superstition – as much as by social aspiration. There were many barriers to realising their imagined ideal community, but focusing on 'the other' offered practical reassurance. Witches handily epitomised, indeed personified, the chaos to be confronted.[28]

In the course of the seventeenth century, select vestries, dominated by middling sorts (including parish officers), cast the same influence over their communities as magistrates had over counties – probably greater, given their propinquity with neighbours. This local autonomy may even justify a view of the state as a 'monarchical republic' comprising some 10,000 parishes, each of which, with its self-appointed, self-determining oligarchy, bore republican characteristics.[29] To compensate for the absence of resident gentry, in 1596 vestrymen in the Wiltshire parish of Swallowfield drew up their own moral and legal code, 'to the end we may the better and more quyetly lyve together in good love and amytie'. Swallowfield reminds us what the English state owed to the industry and initiative of the chief inhabitants of its constituent communities. 'Swallowfield was in some sense the Privy Council writ small', notes Ethan Shagan, 'and the Privy Council was in some sense Swallowfield writ large'.[30]

Once again, however, the picture is not only diverse – political conditions varied widely from place to place – but we find ambiguous meanings and ambivalent attitudes even within specific communities. Whereas justices of the peace largely represented the policies of central government, parish elites hovered between 'two concepts of order' – on one side adhering to the law, and on the other making decisions that satisfied the community (or, at least, people most like themselves). Discretion was not just possible: it was essential for keeping communities on an even keel. Magistrates and constables and grand jurors were not perhaps obvious guardians of the customs of the poor, but nor were they immune to such pressures.[31] Under the Tudors and Stuarts the spectre of popular rebellion and civil war hung heavily over English life. One local consequence was that defending authority and maintaining order required sensitivity to the needs of working people, who often felt that superiors were not rewarding their deference with patronage.

Another key office-holder in the vestry was the overseer. After 1600, ad hoc responses to poverty had evolved into the poor law, administered at parish level. A fault-line in communities was thus given legal definition, separating those who paid the poor rate from the recipients. Ratepayers qualified through property and income, but who received their money was subject to the officers' discretion. Paupers might be refused on moral grounds – for example because of absence from church – and even men of modest means, assuming they were ratepayers, might endorse these decisions. Desire to keep the rate low, in times of escalating poverty, informed judgements about who was deserving or undeserving, creating a community of self-interest in the haves and the alienation of the have-nots. Distinctions between 'ancient inhabitants' and newcomers or 'strangers' were also made, to the extent that different grades of wine might be provided at Christmas. If they were lucky, vagrants were returned to the parishes of their birth: whipped *and* sent home if unlucky. Once again, we see how exclusion and inclusion worked together, creating a moral majority in the community by castigating a minority. Hospitality, meanwhile, became similarly discretionary – a 'private virtue' and more rarely incorporated into 'a holistic view of community'.[32]

The waning of affect in communities was widely observed. Ballad literature, in particular, reveals a widespread feeling that English charity – meaning love between neighbours, rather than just generosity to the poor – had dwindled, and with it hospitality and willingness to offer credit. One tale of poverty and woe was addressed to 'hard-hearted' landlords, another mused on days gone by: 'Good hospitality was cherisht then of many / Now poore men starve and dye, and are not helpt by any.'[33] Much of this was pure nostalgia for a golden age that may never existed. And yet before the Reformation, religious houses did care for the poor and 'good works' had contributed to the soul's salvation as well as harmonising parish life. The poor, back then in stable and manageable numbers, furnished sinners with an opportunity to imitate Christ, and were therefore not just accepted but valued. By the reign of James I, if not earlier, the poor had become a burden to be treated with suspicion and, if in doubt, active hostility. Christmas cheer for the needy had vanished from the great halls; the gates were closed.

The same people in communities who feared losing wealth to the poor rate also feared that the 'many-headed monster' would burgle their houses and rob them on the highway. Laments for the passing of a merrier England did not disclose the full extent of growing social polarisation and the bitter emotions that came with it. It was one thing to neglect the poor, another actively to fear them – and indeed for the poor to resent this fear and neglect by the very people, principally their own neighbours, who once might have gladly helped them. Many witchcraft accusations, their rise coinciding with the rise in poverty-related tension, began with doorstep confrontations over alms – the so-called 'charity-refused' model.[34] In 1646 Elizabeth Crossley, a poor woman 'in evill report for witching' in her community, left Henry Cockcroft's house at Heptonstall, Yorkshire, discontented with some milk she had been given. The death of Cockcroft's son three months later was attributed to her rage, encouraging other people to make their own accusations. Emotions ran high because the refusal of alms signified deterioration in community relations rather than their disappearance, resulting in a stressful ambiguity of status and obligation. Feelings were raw, not dead, and where there was hope there would be disappointment – and guilt (in the rich) and fury (in the poor). 'The very intensity of the charitable impulse', writes Robin Briggs, 'helped to create serious tensions for all participants'.[35]

English communities were also frequently divided over religion. Grassroots puritanism grew after 1600, clashing with the Church of England, whose orthodoxy became militantly anti-Calvinist during the reign of Charles I. Dissent led to persecution, and persecution to emigration to New England. The policies of Bishop Matthew Wren drove as many as 1,350 people from Norfolk, mostly travelling as families, including fifty households from Norwich alone. Some belonged to select subcongregations that had crystallised around puritan ministers, who now led them into the wilderness. The Revd Robert Peck, excommunicated for ignoring Anglican liturgy, led the first wave from Hingham, Norfolk, to Massachusetts in what became an exodus from the parish. His 'violent schismatical spirit', inimical to peace at home, was thus channelled into creating a new community.[36] In America, puritans reinforced the amity and unity they already felt with regional godly networks, for example in East Anglia and the West Country, and built communities in the more traditional sense of like-minded people working and worshipping in the same place.

The thinking behind emigration was not entirely religious: there was a feeling that the public good on which communities thrived was being weakened by selfishness. Some pointed to 'want of duty in the people'. Others feared the explosion of litigation ('for matters of commodity') and an epidemic of private gain. The Digger Gerrard Winstanley perceived how 'the heart of covetousness swells most against community, calling community a thief'.[37] Landowners and merchants, it was said, prospered at the expense of others. Competition made it hard for people to live together. 'There is such pressing and oppressing in towns and country about farms, trade, traffic, etc.', wrote Robert Cushman, one of the founders of new Plymouth in 1620, 'so as a man can hardly live anywhere but he shall pull down two of his neighbours'.[38] 'Swarms' of idle paupers posed the greatest threat, breaching the peace and draining resources. Both helping and punishing the poor were wasted opportunities. On plantations, these people would support themselves and create markets for textile exports, demand for which had slumped. Instead of collecting the poor rate, communities should raise money to send paupers to America.[39]

Pragmatic considerations were framed by emotion. A minister in Jacobean Virginia had pitied the beggars in England's streets who 'day and night call upon the passers by, and yet remaine unprovided for', and yearned for the restoration of faith and hope, charity and love. Without these virtues the English were spiritually dead, their communities redundant.[40] 'Selfe-Love is setled farre into everie mans heart', deplored Michael Sparke, whereas in America a lost world of Christian love might be recreated, inspiring the Old World to reform itself. Witness the title of the puritan leader John Winthrop's call to New England, 'a model of Christian charity', which proposed colonisation as an antidote to selfishness in communities by promoting compassion and trust. It was a crying shame, Winthrop felt, for children to be seen as a burden and poor neighbours called 'vile and base'. His friend John White never gave up hope 'that the love that waxeth cold and dyeth in the most part yet may revive and kindle in some mens hearts'.[41]

Around 350,000 English hopeful people went to America in the seventeenth century. Many, however, were sorry to find the new communities as bad as the old ones, or worse. Within two years of the foundation of Jamestown, Virginia, in 1607, 'Ambition, Sloth and idlenes had devoured the fruits of former labours.' After tackling America's vast emptiness, colonists were, as the earl of Stirling noted, 'quickly entangled with the other extremities, grudging to be bounded within their prospect, and jarring with their neighbours for small parcels of ground'.[42] Puritan expectations were higher than those of Virginia's settlers, which made the disappointment that much greater. A year after the arrival of the *Mayflower* in 1620, Robert Cushman was bemoaning New Plymouth's disregard for charity, hospitality, brotherly love and the common good. In 1637 the joy felt by the Revd John Davenport and his congregation at finding a godly community in Boston was marred by puritan controversy. Peter Bulkeley, a minister who swapped Bedfordshire for Boston, was shocked by the worst breaches of amity he had ever experienced.[43] By this time Boston was full, and its satellite communities began arguing over boundaries. Satan, it was supposed, had 'cast a bone of division' among colonists at Hingham, named for the Norfolk village they had left a decade earlier. This helps to explain why a third of the godly ministers who emigrated in the 1630s returned home.[44]

As in England, colonial exclusion went hand-in-hand with inclusion, rancour with harmony. Puritans in England deplored the heartless divisiveness of New England's congregationalism, which produced communities of saints distinct from a disenfranchised reprobate majority. By the time of John Winthrop's death in 1649, his shining 'city upon a hill' seemed more like any unregenerate English town: venal, fractious and ungodly. The first fifty years of Watertown, Massachusetts, were marked not by a consensus that eluded England's communities but by a dissension all its own.[45] And the witch-trials that flared up in Salem, Massachusetts, in the 1690s reflected a catastrophic failure of community. Colonial townships were blighted by the same sins listed by Arthur Dent, and the counter-measures were the same: a Boston drunk made to wear a white sheet and placard, a Maryland murderer identified by a bleeding corpse, and a suspected witch in Connecticut subjected to the water ordeal.[46] By 1700 colonisation had demonstrated that the quality of an English community consisted not in its land or laws or institutions or religion, nor in the prevention of discord, which was impossible. Instead, it lay in people's willingness to moderate selfish impulses with consideration for each other and the common good, and also in an ability to settle perennial disputes and to absorb inevitable conflict.

## Conclusion

How to sum up change in early modern communities? Most obviously, the religious ideal of parish unity through *caritas* ('charity') faded. By 1750 hospitality was no longer a realistic goal but instead became 'a rhetorical weapon, to challenge the dominance of the market-place ... by a return to a mythical past of open generosity'.[47] As economic horizons widened, so too did the focus of economic morality, from the village to the nation. Disputes emerging from commercial sophistication were resolved with the dispassionate language of the law, displacing more emotional appeals and 'elevating universal calculated social good above ... interpersonal community values'. 'Community' was redefined negatively as the need to find new ways for individualistic and competitive households to trust each other. The meaning of 'commonwealth', an idea once so binding and altruistic, shifted towards 'government' rather than 'common good', implying exclusivity rather than inclusivity.[48] Commonwealth by the old definition was not repugnant, just difficult to attain; as such, its politicisation from the mid seventeenth century was yet another sign of 'the slow decline, and intermittent efflorescence, of medieval commonalty'.[49] Increasingly, then, 'territorial' and 'interest' communities, united by proximity and shared aims, were overlaid with 'attachment' communities – emotional projections of collectivity across space and time, or what Benedict Anderson once called 'imagined communities'.[50]

Economic change in larger, denser local populations was mainly experienced as social class: heightened consciousness, differentiated relationships and mutual antagonism. Such feelings, which later acquired regional and national scope as imagined class communities, at first crystallised locally and interpersonally. Parish elites retreated from the lower orders, encouraged by enclosure and capitalist investment in land. Absentee landlords exploited people they never met, and squirearchy wielded an authority that cared nothing for popular assent. The 'division of cultures' was so profound, even the *rhetoric* of community was redundant. Shared pastimes and beliefs became a thing of the past. The witchcraft accusations that offered a quick unifying fix for communities only signified a widening gulf. Educated people decried the brutality and superstition of the masses. The drowning of a suspect by her neighbours at Chatham in 1675 was condemned by the naval surveyor Sir John Tippetts as 'a piece of such cruelty as I have rarely heard of'.[51] Such words came from sincere horror, yet also served to sharpen a sense of civility. In urban areas especially, middling sorts gradually formed a national community called 'the middle class', aided by the discrimination central to the administration of poor-relief. By the mid eighteenth century, the burden of poverty had overwhelmed some regions, hardening reluctance to assist 'strangers' and concentrating attention on 'the familiar neighbourhood needy'.[52]

(The Tichborne dole was suspended in 1796 by local magistrates owing to abuse by vagrants, despite a curse on the family if the custom ever ended.) To belong to a class community was to be locked into 'a hierarchy of economic advantage or disadvantage', depending on who you were.[53]

Even medieval communities had been to some extent 'imagined': they reinforced subordination by concealing it behind politicised rhetoric, nurturing unity and obedience to serve the interests of lordly government. Tangible aspects aside, pre-modern communities were conjured into life with beguiling language. As Bob Scribner once said, 'concepts of community embodied universal, virtually hegemonic values, that led everyone to seek to appropriate them'. An individualistic reality was exactly what made the imagery of community so desirable – for preserving the common peace as well as for advancing sectional interests.[54] Rituals of patronage, like the Tichborne dole, were collective social therapies; but they were also cynically coercive, demanding plebeian complicity in the invention of common goals. What had happened by 1750 was largely that the mask had slipped to expose the true face of hierarchy and self-interested wealth and power.

Does this risk slipping back to the narrative suggested by the *Gemeinschaft* and *Gesellschaft* model – the demise of community as state and civil society took over? In fact, the shift towards collective identities beyond the local context is better characterised by the evolution of the parish within a regional and national framework. The reigns of Elizabeth I and James I saw the strengthening of the idea of the Protestant nation state, glorifying its monarchs and anathematising popish enemies. Saints' days were replaced with propagandist commemoration, such as providential delivery from the Gunpowder Plot in 1605. Villagers continued to celebrate ancient festivals, but with a psychic connection to a larger, enclosing national community. The quasi-religious flavour of all this makes preference for 'communion' rather than 'community', expressed by Jacobean lexicographers and modern sociologists alike, particularly apposite. Other, often competing, religious identities emerged. Sects like the Quakers and Baptists created an imagined community of extraordinary range and intensity, while puritans across the Atlantic world preached Protestantism in danger. Then there was the development of 'the public', the most potent rhetorical iteration of national wholeness, uniting political people and political space as a 'community of the imagination'.[55]

Perhaps, then, we should think in terms of restructuring rather than one paradigm replacing another, and return to the idea that communities were a constant feature of a historical process, not its primitive stage.

State formation, one of early modern England's most distinctive characteristics, did not act *upon* community and so did not displace it. Instead, the state grew *through* communities, meaning that parishes, politically self-conscious and active in law and administration, did not just belong to the wider nation: they constituted it. By the later seventeenth century, communities drew as much strength from external forces as from internal ones, specifically dynamic regional and metropolitan connections. This change was visible in a transition from religious to civic institutions, and with it a shift towards 'civic community', an identity that looked outwards as well as inwards. The moral regulation formerly undertaken by parish vestries became work for public bodies such as the Societies for Reformation of Manners, who operated locally but with a national uniformity of rhetoric in pursuit of national ambitions.[56]

An ability to maintain order and resolve disputes indicated the versatility of English communities existing in inextricable partnership with an expanding nationhood, public and civic society. After all, the secularisation of local institutions resulted in no Hobbesian civil war of man against man, nor even the spread of atomised mini-republics. The restructuring of communities can also be seen in class antagonism, which was unifying in the very act of its divisiveness. Working people in eighteenth-century Derbyshire clashed with clergymen demanding tithes, but drew huge strength from 'their continuing membership of the community of pugnacious independent free miners'.[57] Disrespect for custom nurtured plebeian solidarity in its defence. From friction came fraternity. In the towns, corporations and craft fellowships were reinvigorated, and communities constantly remade using languages of fellowship and brotherhood – more 'imagined communities', secured by emotion and imagination and a common language.

These adaptations suggest that all communities – the traditional rural parish governed by religious values and the imagined communities of faith, class, state or nation – were shaped by emotion: its needs and eruptions, rules and restraints, manipulations and appeals. 'Emotional communities' are, according to Barbara Rosenwein, 'precisely the same as social communities' except for an emphasis on 'systems of feeling'. Emotional codes governed attraction and repulsion in local society, and defined good and bad behaviour.[58] Emotions are also a guide to early modern continuity and change in that they bridged theory and reality in community life, for instance guilt over neglecting charity and the growth of other selfish impulses. This did not amount to some transition between positive and negative emotions in public life, but rather a long-term reconfiguration of universal emotions, which changed the meaning of community. What remained constant was both the persistent self-interest central to human nature, and a natural urge to combine and to improve.

### Notes

1  R. Cawdrey, *A Table Alphabeticall* (London, 1609), Crv; H[enry] C[ockeram], *The English Dictionarie* (London, 1623); E. Phillips, *The New World of English Words* (London, 1658); S. Skinner, *A New English Dictionary* (London, 1691); R. Coster, *A Mite Cast into the Common Treasury* (n.p., 1649), title-page, 6; T. Hobbes, *Leviathan* (London, 1651), 55, 62–3, 68–70, 86–7.

2  T. Blount, *Glossographia* (London, 1656), K3; P. Withington, 'Agency, custom and the English corporate system', in H. French and J. Barry (eds.), *Identity and Agency in England, 1500–1800* (Basingstoke: Palgrave, 2004).

3  S. Reynolds, *Kingdoms and Communities in Western Europe, 900–1300*, 2nd edn (Oxford: Oxford University Press, 1997),      Chapters 4–5; Z. Razi, 'Family, land and the village community in later medieval England', in T. H. Aston (ed.), *Landlords, Peasants and Politics in Medieval England* (Cambridge: Cambridge University Press, 1987).

4  J. Harris (ed.), *Tönnies: Community and Civil Society* (Cambridge: Cambridge University Press, 2001).

5  M. Weber, *Economy and Society: An Outline of Interpretative Sociology*, ed. Guenther Roth and Claus Wittich, 2 vols. (Berkeley: University of California Press, 2013), i, 40–3.

6  J. Bossy, 'Blood and baptism: Kinship, community and Christianity in western Europe from the fourteenth to the seventeenth centuries', in D. Baker (ed.), *Sanctity and Secularity: The Church and the World* (Oxford: Oxford University Press, 1973), 143.

7  L. Stone, *The Family, Sex and Marriage in England, 1500–1800* (London: Weidenfeld & Nicolson, 1977), 98–9; J. A. Sharpe, *Early Modern England: A Social History, 1550–1760*, 2nd edn (London: Arnold, 1997), 93.

8  R. M. Smith, '"Modernization" and the corporate medieval village community in England: Some sceptical reflections', in A. R. H. Baker and D. Gregory (eds.), *Explorations in Historical Geography: Interpretative Essays* (Cambridge: Cambridge University Press, 1984); K. Wrightson, 'The "decline of neighbourliness" revisited', in N. L. Jones and D. Woolf (eds.), *Local Identities in Late Medieval and Early Modern England* (Basingstoke: Palgrave, 2007); K. Wrightson, 'Mutualities and obligations: Changing social relationships in early modern England', *Proceedings of the British Academy*, 139 (2006).

9  P. Collinson, *De republica Anglorum; or, History with the Politics Put Back* (Cambridge: Cambridge University Press, 1990), 17–18, quotation at 18.

10  M. J. Halvorson and K. E. Spierling (eds.), *Defining Community in Early Modern Europe* (Aldershot: Ashgate, 2008), 1; C. J. Calhoun, 'Community: Toward a variable conceptualization for comparative research', *SH*, 5 (1980). Cf. the model of 'subjective' village life versus 'objective' city

life devised by Tönnies's follower Georg Simmel: 'The metropolis and mental life', in K. H. Wolff (ed.), *The Sociology of Georg Simmel* (New York: Free Press, 1950), Chapter 4.

11 Halvorson and Spierling, *Defining Community*, 21.

12 K. Wrightson, *English Society, 1580–1680*, 2nd edn (London: Routledge, 2003), 61–5, quotation at 62.

13 P. Burke, *Languages and Communities in Early Modern Europe* (Cambridge: Polity, 2004), 6.

14 D. Rollison, *The Local Origins of Modern Society: Gloucestershire, 1500–1800* (London: Routledge, 1992), Chapter 3, quotation at 69.

15 G. van Tilborch, *The Tichborne Dole* (1671), Tichborne House, Hampshire.

16 R. Tittler, *Architecture and Power: The Town Hall and the English Urban Community, c. 1500–1640* (Oxford: Oxford University Press, 1991).

17 J. Boulton, *Neighbourhood and Society: A London Suburb in the Seventeenth Century* (Cambridge: Cambridge University Press, 1987), Chapters 8–11; I. W. Archer, *The Pursuit of Stability: Social Relations in Elizabethan London* (Cambridge: Cambridge University Press, 1991), 74–82.

18 For the spatial dimension see Amanda Flather, *Gender and Space in Early Modern England* (Woodbridge: Boydell, 2007), Chapters 2–4.

19 M. T. Crane, 'Illicit privacy and outdoor spaces in early modern England', *Journal for Early Modern Cultural Studies*, 9 (2009); P. Withington, 'Company and sociability in early modern England', *SH*, 32 (2007).

20 B. Capp, *When Gossips Meet: Women, Family and Neighbourhood in Early Modern England* (Oxford: Oxford University Press, 2003), Chapters 5–8; P. Griffiths, *Youth and Authority: Formative Experiences in England, 1560–1640* (Oxford: Oxford University Press, 1996), Chapter 3.

21 M. Gaskill, *Crime and Mentalities in Early Modern England* (Cambridge: Cambridge University Press, 2000), Chapters 2, 6.

22 Arthur Dent, *The Plaine Mans Path-way to Heaven* (London: Robert Dexter, 1601), 175–90, quotations at 178, 185.

23 M. Ingram, *Church Courts, Sex and Marriage in England, 1570–1640* (Cambridge: Cambridge University Press, 1987).

24 K. Wrightson, 'The politics of the parish in early modern England', in P. Griffiths, A. Fox and S. Hindle (eds.), *The Experience of Authority in Early Modern England* (Basingstoke: Macmillan, 1996).

25 F. Braudel, quoted in N. Schindler, *Rebellion, Community and Custom in Early Modern Germany* (Cambridge: Cambridge University Press, 2002), 134n.

26 D. G. Hey, *An English Rural Community: Myddle under the Tudors and Stuarts* (Leicester: Leicester University Press, 1974), Chapter 6; G. Nair, *Highley: The Development of a Community, 1550–1880* (Oxford: Blackwell, 1988), Chapters 1–6, 10; M. Spufford, *Contrasting Communities: English Villagers in the Sixteenth and Seventeenth Centuries* (Cambridge: Cambridge University Press, 1974), Chapters 3–5; K. Wrightson and D. Levine, *Poverty and Piety in an English Village: Terling, 1525–1700*, 2nd edn (Oxford: Oxford University Press, 1995).

27  S. Hindle, *The State and Social Change in Early Modern England, c. 1550–1640* (Basingstoke: Palgrave, 2000), Chapters 4–6; M. J. Braddick, *State Formation in Early Modern England c. 1550–1700* (Cambridge: Cambridge University Press, 2000); J. R. Kent, 'The centre and the localities: State formation and parish government in England, c. 1640–1740', *HJ*, 38 (1995).

28  M. Ingram, 'Reformation of manners in early modern England', in Griffiths, Fox and Hindle, *Experience of Authority*; A. Reiber DeWindt, 'Witchcraft and conflicting visions of the ideal village community', *JBS*, 34 (1995).

29  P. Collinson, *Elizabethan Essays* (London: Hambledon, 1994), Chapter 2; M. Goldie, 'The unacknowledged republic: Officeholding in early modern England', in T. Harris (ed.), *The Politics of the Excluded, c. 1500–1800* (Basingstoke: Palgrave, 2001).

30  S. Hindle, 'Hierarchy and community in the Elizabethan parish: The Swallowfield articles of 1596', *HJ*, 42 (1999); Collinson, *De republica Anglorum*, 30–4, quotation at 30; E. H. Shagan, 'The two republics: Conflicting views of participatory local government in early Tudor England', in J. F. McDiarmid (ed.), *The Monarchical Republic of Early Modern England* (Aldershot: Ashgate, 2007).

31  K. Wrightson, 'Two concepts of order: Justices, constables and jurymen in seventeenth-century England', in J. Brewer and J. Styles (eds.), *An Ungovernable People: The English and Their Law in the Seventeenth and Eighteenth Centuries* (London: Hutchinson, 1980).

32  S. Hindle, 'Civility, honesty and the identification of the deserving poor in seventeenth-century England', in French and Barry, *Identity and Agency*; S. Hindle, 'Power, poor relief, and social relations in Holland Fen, c. 1600–1800', *HJ*, 41 (1998), 94; S. Hindle, 'A sense of place? Becoming and belonging in a rural parish, 1550–1650', in A. Shepard and P. Withington (eds.), *Communities in Early Modern England: Networks, Place, Rhetoric* (Manchester: Manchester University Press, 2000); F. Heal, *Hospitality in Early Modern England* (Oxford: Oxford University Press, 1990), 387–93, quotations at 388.

33  *A Lanthorne for Landlords* (London, n.d. [c. 1620]); [M. Parker], *Times Alteration: Or the Old Mans Rehearsall* (London, n.d. [c. 1620]).

34  K. Thomas, *Religion and the Decline of Magic* (London: Weidenfeld & Nicolson, 1972); A. Macfarlane, *Witchcraft in Tudor and Stuart England* (London: Routledge, 1971). Macfarlane later backdated individualism by several centuries: *The Origins of English Individualism: The Family, Property and Social Transition* (Oxford: Blackwell, 1978).

35  TNA, ASSI 45/1/5/38–9; M. Gaskill, 'Witchcraft and neighbourliness in early modern England', in S. Hindle, A. Shepard and J. Walter (eds.), *Remaking English Society: Social Relations and Social Change in Early Modern England* (Woodbridge: Boydell, 2013); R. Briggs, *Witches and Neighbours: The Social and Cultural Context of European Witchcraft* (London: Penguin, 1996), Chapter 4, quotation at 139.

36 Oxford, Bodleian Library, Tanner MS 68, fol. 332; J. Britton and E. Wedlake Brayley, *A Topographical and Historical Description of Norfolk* (London, 1810), 262 (quotation).

37 E. F., *Englands Deplorable Condition Shewing the Common-wealths Malady* (London, 1659), title-page; T. Stretton, 'Written obligations, litigation and neighbourliness, 1580–1680', in Hindle, Shepard and Walter, *Remaking English Society*, 189; T. Scott, *The Belgicke Pismire* (London, 1623), 29–30; G. Winstanley, quoted in Hindle, 'Sense of place?', 111.

38 R. Cushman, quoted in John Demos (ed.), *Remarkable Providences: Readings on Early American History*, 3rd edn (Boston, MA: Northeastern University Press, 1991), 8; W. Symonds, *Virginia: A Sermon Preached at White-Chappel* (London, 1609), 19–22; F. Higginson, *New-Englands Plantation* (London, 1630), C3v.

39 R. Gray, *A Good Speed to Virginia* (London, 1609), B2–B3v; J. Hagthorpe, *Englands-Exchequer* (London, 1625), 24–5; J. Smith, *A Description of New England* (London, 1616), 40; R. Eburne, *A Plaine Path-Way to Plantations* (London, 1624), 9–16, 47–9; T. Morton, *New English Canaan* (London, 1637), 55–7; C. Levett, *A Voyage into New England* (London, 1624), 35–6.

40 A. Whitaker, *Good Newes from Virginia* (London, 1613), 4–6, 18–21, quotation at 6; W. Bradford, *A Relation ... of the English Plantation Setled at Plimoth* (London, 1622), 67.

41 M. Sparke, *Greevous Grones for the Poore* (London, 1621), 3; A. Heimert and A. Delbanco (eds.), *The Puritans in America: A Narrative Anthology* (Cambridge, MA: Harvard University Press, 1985), 71, 81–92; J. White, *The Planters Plea* (London, 1630), 79.

42 R. Johnson, *The New Life of Virginea* (London, 1612), C1v; W. Alexander, *An Encouragement to Colonies* (London, 1624), 5.

43 R. Cushman, *A Sermon Preached at Plimmoth in New-England* (London, 1622), 3–5, 10–11, 15–16; I. MacBeath Calder (ed.), *Letters of John Davenport, Puritan Divine* (New Haven, CT: Yale University Press, 1937), 5–6; Boston Public Library, MS Am. 1506/2/7.

44 E. Winslow, *New-Englands Salamander Discovered* (London, 1647), 4; S. Hardman Moore, *Pilgrims: New World Settlers and the Call of Home* (New Haven, CT: Yale University Press, 2007), 55.

45 R. Thompson, *Divided We Stand: Watertown, Massachusetts, 1630–1680* (Amherst, MA: University of Massachusetts Press, 2001).

46 Boston Public Library, MS fAm. 2176, p. 72; W. Hand Browne (ed.), *Judicial and Testamentary Business of the Provincial Court, 1649/50–1657* (Baltimore: Maryland Historical Society, 1891), 536–7, 539–40; Connecticut State Library, Wyllys Papers, fol. 22.

47 Heal, *Hospitality*, 403.

48 C. Muldrew, 'The culture of reconciliation: Community and the settlement of disputes in early modern England', *HJ*, 39 (1996), 942; C. Muldrew, *The Economy of Obligation: The Culture of Credit and Social Relations in Early Modern England* (Basingstoke: Macmillan, 1998), 4; C. Muldrew, 'From

commonwealth to public opulence: The redefinition of wealth and government in early modern Britain', in Hindle, Shepard and Walter, *Remaking English Society*.

49 P. Withington, *Society in Early Modern England: The Vernacular Origins of Some Powerful Ideas* (Cambridge: Polity, 2010), Chapter 5, quotation at 166.

50 P. Willmott, *Community Initiatives: Patterns and Prospects* (London: Policy Studies Institute, 1989), 2–5; D. Lee and H. Newby, *The Problem of Sociology: An Introduction to the Discipline* (London: Routledge, 1983), 57–8; B. Anderson, *Imagined Communities: Reflections on the Origin and Spread of Nationalism*, 2nd edn (London: Verso, 1991).

51 TNA, ADM 106/313.

52 P. Rushton, 'The poor law, the parish and the community in north-east England, 1600–1800', *Northern History*, 25 (1989) 152.

53 H. French, 'Living in poverty in eighteenth-century Terling', in Hindle, Shepard and Walter, *Remaking English Society*, 314.

54 R. Scribner, 'Communities and the nature of power', in R. Scribner (ed.), *Germany: A New Social and Economic History*, Vol. I: *1450–1630* (London: Hodder, 1996), 317.

55 G. Baldwin, 'The "public" as a rhetorical community in early modern England', in Shepard and Withington, *Communities*, 212.

56 C. Muldrew, 'From a "light cloak" to an "iron cage": Historical change in the relation between community and individualism', in Shepard and Withington, *Communities*, 163; P. Withington, 'Citizens, community and political culture in Restoration England', in Shepard and Withington, *Communities*.

57 A. Wood, *The Politics of Social Conflict: The Peak Country, 1550–1720* (Cambridge: Cambridge University Press, 1999), 194.

58 B. H. Rosenwein, 'Worrying about emotions in history', *AHR*, 107 (2002); J. Plamper, *The History of Emotions: An Introduction* (Oxford: Oxford University Press, 2015), 67–74.

# PART II

## *Currents of Change*

# 5

## *Reformations*

### *Alec Ryrie*

The Reformations of the 1530s and thereafter were the most significant extrinsic shock experienced by English society between the Black Death and the Civil Wars of the 1640s. The magnitude of the shock has never been in doubt. What is now clear, however, is the extent to which it was genuinely extrinsic. England's religious life until the late 1520s was remarkably stable. Naturally there were points of stress, and when the earthquake came, they were where the cracks first appeared. Yet they did not cause it. This crisis came on England unawares, and it came in two distinct forms: a political and an intellectual assault, often but not always in alliance. Between them, they remade English society. This chapter will survey how they did so, and how the English responded to, adapted to and resisted the new world in which they found themselves.

Pre-Reformation English religion has been a playground for modern prejudices. It is easily caricatured either as a swamp of superstitious corruption or as a bucolic paradise of communal faith. We do not need to accept either view to recognise that, in its own terms, it was working fairly well. By European standards, the English Church was unusually well disciplined and well led. Its sacramental, pastoral and practical service to its people was generally adequate. There were frictions over predictable matters of land, money and law, but they did not coalesce into the sort of more widespread anticlerical prejudice that was common in contemporary Germany, Scotland or elsewhere. Instead, the Church drew on – and replenished – a deep well of legitimacy and affection. The signs of this cycle of loyalty can be seen in the consistent support that the living and the dying of all classes provided for all manner of local ecclesiastical services, whether in money, in kind or in effort.

It is hard to gauge the balance among love for this establishment, contented conformity to it, disgruntled compliance with it and alienated withdrawal from it. Clearly, however, open dissent was rare. Since the expulsion of the English Jews in 1291, England had been religiously uniform in law, and nearly so in fact. A few foreign Jews apparently found a discreet home in London at times.[1] There were isolated sceptics, scoffers and freethinkers. A rather more substantial irritant for the Church was the loose movement of dissidents who called each other 'brethren' or 'known men', but who were known to their orthodox neighbours and are still known to historians as Lollards. This scabrously anti-ceremonial and anti-hierarchical movement was vaguely attached to the memory of the fourteenth-century Oxford theologian John Wyclif, but retained little of his particular doctrines beyond a passionate commitment to the English Bible. Lollards' religion consisted chiefly in clandestine meetings to read the Bible and other English texts aloud. Otherwise, they generally conformed outwardly to the public Church, albeit with misgivings and with occasional outbursts of scorn at its practices. Periodically a bishop took it upon himself to root out these heretics, whereupon most of those arrested readily recanted their errors and returned home to carry on. Only a handful of repeat offenders were sentenced to death by burning. Lollardy was numerically tiny, a low-level, endemic presence in London, Bristol, Coventry and some rural areas of southern England – in particular the Chiltern hills, the closest thing it had to a heartland. Its chief significance was indirect. It primed the English Church and people to be aware of heresy, one simple sign of which is that 'heretic' and 'Lowler' were widely used as all-purpose insults almost devoid of specific meaning.

This was not the most promising terrain for the Protestant Reformation. As everywhere in Europe, certain small but important social groups showed an early interest in the religious novelties coming out of Germany after 1517: merchants whose travels exposed them to foreign ways, scholars struck by the appeal of Luther's ideas. The persistent Lollard minority showed some interest too. But that hardly made the new heresies dangerous. As the formidable machinery of the English Church and state began to mobilise behind orthodoxy in the late 1520s, it made sense to expect that this movement would at worst become another annoying heretical minority, and at best would be squelched altogether.

In the event, however, the state threw its weight on the other side of the balance. King Henry VIII's marital and dynastic crisis, and his bloodily quixotic solution to it, merged improbably with the new religious movement to take England into unexplored territory. A ratchet of legislation between 1529 and 1536 successively restricted the privileges of the English clergy; broke the legal ties connecting the English Church to Rome; and asserted that the king was supreme head, immediately under Christ, of the Church of England: a sententious title, made more ominous by the regime's refusal clearly to define what it meant.

The assertion of that title in 1534 is usually taken to be a decisive turning point, and sometimes counted as the foundation-date of the independent Church of England, but at first relatively few English subjects took much notice. The first changes actually to affect the parishes were some amendments to the liturgy. Hitherto the pope had been prayed for daily at mass, both in Latin and in English: now he was not to be mentioned, and scratched out of the service books. In the canon of the mass, the prayer for pope, bishop and king often became a prayer for king and bishop. These were on one level minor tweaks, but, given the familiarity of liturgy, impossible not to notice.[2]

Following close behind was a more momentous imposition. Royal commissioners required all adult males in England to swear an oath acknowledging the king's new marriage and disavowing his first, on pain of treason. (A second oath, acknowledging the king's newly discovered supremacy over the Church, was administered much more sparingly.) Virtually no-one resisted. It was not a matter to die for. But the sheer oddity of the policy – subjects were not normally required to consent to a royal marriage – was a sign that England was in uncharted waters. The entire population was being conscripted to, and implicated in, forging a new religio-political identity. Henry VIII and Thomas Cromwell did not see themselves as enfranchising the population, but they were creating, or acknowledging, an unprecedented variety of popular politics.[3]

Other clues began to materialise in the parishes. Old taxes ('Peter's Pence') ceased; new, more arduous dues took their place. Preachers (a rare breed) obediently extolled the king's supremacy. Some, more daringly, questioned the value or even the legitimacy of the old ceremonies and sacraments. Royal commissioners nosed into every church, tallying incomes and recording goods. Rumours of all kinds began to canter.

In 1536 some of them came true, in what was, for most English people, the defining episode of the Reformation: the dissolution of the monasteries. No other event of the sixteenth century was carved so deeply into popular memory.[4] For generations to come, the division between 'abbey time' and the emptier years since would remain a reference point, and for good reason. The seizure of all monastic property by the crown in 1536–40 was, and remains, the largest single transfer of landed wealth in English history. It also remains weirdly under-researched. The roots of the policy have been much discussed: in short, greed sauced with humanist and evangelical distaste for monks, and political fears for their loyalty.

Its effects, however, remain much less clear. This was partly because 'the dissolution of the monasteries' was a composite event made up of hundreds of local dissolutions, in which institutions whose local significance had varied hugely were destroyed in different ways and were succeeded by different arrangements. A few of the greatest abbeys became secular cathedrals; some became parish churches. More were sold by a king who burned through this unprecedented windfall so fast that he was facing bankruptcy again before the monasteries were five years gone.

Two effects stand out. First, the destruction of the monasteries probably damaged England's structures for social welfare more than any other single event has ever done. Most of the hospitals, education, employment and charity that the monasteries had provided simply disappeared. Royal promises to use parasitic monks' wealth to aid the poor turned out to be worthless. In upland regions, where parishes were large and the monasteries' role had been that much more vital, the effect was catastrophic. Archaeological research on childhood mortality suggests that it leapt in the years around 1540 and remained high thereafter.[5] And if the dissolution only served to accentuate adverse economic trends that were already under way, it also became a by-word for them and the perceived injustices they represented. It is no coincidence that the largest and most dangerous mass rebellions of the age, the northern risings in the autumn of 1536 known collectively (and misleadingly) as the Pilgrimage of Grace, were sparked by the dissolution. As the regime had taught them, the Pilgrims bound themselves to their cause by means of an oath.[6] Only now was England waking up to the fact it was in a new world.

Secondly, once the out-manoeuvred Pilgrims had been suppressed and the futility of further resistance was plain, the monasteries' lay neighbours began to be drawn in. The greatest winners were the gentry, who ended up holding not only most of the former monastic lands, but also a series of legal rights that went with them. The majority of English advowsons – the legal rights to present priests to rectories, vicarages and other benefices – had belonged to monasteries. Now, almost by accident, these rights were transferred to the new owners of the land. Even more bizarrely, this arrangement endured, and endures even to the present. To many it was a mere scandal, but it also fitted the new owners' sense of their emerging social position. They were often longstanding patrons and benefactors of the religious houses they now owned, and sometimes saw some continuity between these two different forms of stewardship. And many of them professed to see their new duties to parish churches as a solemn charge, to be executed faithfully. It at least justified their sudden enrichment.[7]

However, as it became clear that the monasteries were doomed, others too rushed to snatch what they could from the communal ruin. Unless royal commissioners managed to intervene, fabrics and furnishings were spirited away and roofs stripped of lead. Even the building-stones of the abbeys themselves disappeared in the night. In some cases, this was intended as pious salvage. Relics, images, vestments or other precious items were stored away in hope that the world would turn and normality would return. But more often it was a matter of scavenging from the old Church's corpse. Were such scavengers imbruing their hands, too, in the blood, and so making themselves stakeholders in Henry's Reformation? Or were they merely making pragmatic use of objects that the royal commissioners' depredations had already desacralised? We do not know, but whether willingly or not, they were helping to ensure that the old world could not easily be restored.[8]

The monasteries were not all that vanished from England's inherited religious landscape in the late 1530s. Pilgrimages were suppressed: all relics were now classed as idols, and England's premier shrine, that of Thomas Becket at Canterbury, was pulverised for memorialising a man now vilified as a traitor. Pardons and indulgences, the small change of the Catholic economy of salvation, were prohibited. The Lenten fast was relaxed by royal proclamation. The English Bible, long banned because of its association with the Lollards, was not only legalised but, in 1538, ordered to be placed in every parish church so that all comers might read it. Rumours spoke of more to come. Would priests be allowed to marry? Would parish churches be seized like the monasteries had been? Surely the new royal order to make a record of all baptisms, marriages and burials could only portend onerous taxes?

Instead, in 1539–40, Henry VIII made it clear that his Reformation was not going to go much further. An illusory stability appeared. In many parish churches, not much had changed. The mass continued in all its Latinate glory, albeit that a new English-language litany was introduced in 1544. Heretics continued to suffer reassuringly traditional deaths. It only took a little effort for many English people to convince themselves that England's religion was basically unscathed. When Henry VIII made an emotional appeal for religious unity before Parliament at Christmas 1545, lamenting that his subjects were quarrelling about religion and labelling one another heretics and papists by turn, it was possible to hope that the unity of which he spoke might materialise. For whatever else had been shaken, one feature of England's unofficial religion had been powerfully reinforced: the king's own authority. Henry VIII had given his subjects ample reason to doubt his good faith and piety, but not enough to outweigh the deeply entrenched national faith in good lordship, a faith that the regime bolstered with a canny mix of idealistic propaganda, nationalist drum-beating and well-calibrated bursts of exemplary violence.

In fact, the quarrelsome nation that Henry described was going to become England's new reality. The most fundamental change wrought by the Reformations that he started was one neither he nor anyone else wanted: a nation that had been unified in religion became divided by it. The remainder of the story of the Reformations is one of how those divisions were negotiated and how the lives of the men and women who took the different paths now open to them were changed in the process.

The imaginary peace of Henry VIII's last years gave way to a decade-and-a-half of bewildering, switchback religious lurches, a string of crises that made clear how much had in fact already changed.

The chaos of Edward VI's short reign (1547–53) owed less to his regimes' radical religious policies than to the strains of a catastrophic war in Scotland and deeper, ongoing shifts of social and economic power. The social significance of religious change in this context was twofold. First, this was the period when religious change became impossible for even the wilfully uninformed to ignore. The mass was progressively replaced with a series of English liturgies that changed the daily and weekly rituals of Church life almost beyond recognition. The Tudor state's insatiable hunger for ecclesiastical property reached the parishes in earnest, stripping churches of their imagery, plate and furnishings, and closing the chantries that had maintained thousands of priests in parishes across the country. The resulting religious vacuum was filled, amongst other things, by officially approved homilies that all parish clergy were required to read aloud to their people, a way of ensuring that all English subjects were exposed to the new doctrines – if they listened, and if their priest read them in a manner that made it possible for them to do so.

We might expect that such an unheralded revolution would provoke fury, and in one of England's most traditionally rebellious regions it did. In the summer of 1549, much of Devon and Cornwall rose in rebellion against religious change in general and the new Book of Common Prayer in particular. Remarkably, however, the south-westerners were alone. Elsewhere, very few of those who loathed what was being done to their Church did anything about it. Although print censorship nearly collapsed in 1547–9, very few religious conservatives published anything. There was a degree of foot-dragging and passive resistance, but precious few had the

stomach for confrontation. Some had already been bought off, or compromised. Most of those who had reconciled themselves to Henry VIII's
changes had already gone too far to turn back. Some evidence hints at a
lethal fatalism settling onto English conservatism. Nothing could now be
done, except wait for the young king to come of age, hoping and trusting
that he would put things right. The truth – that the Tudor kings were the
root of the problem, not part of the solution – was so unwelcome that
most of their subjects shied away from it.[9]

Many of them, instead, interpreted the combination of social and religious change in a second, surprising way. A major theme of evangelical
preaching was the state of the 'Commonwealth': lamenting the growing
economic woes of the age, and diagnosing them as moral failings. This
rhetoric had started outside the state establishment, with the many evangelicals who felt the waves of seizures of Church property to be somewhere between a missed opportunity and mere robbery. With the new
reign, some of those same evangelicals had come into the regime but had
not softened their views. Whether sincerely or cynically, they managed to
stake out a decent claim to the moral high ground. As a result, when, in
the desperate summer of 1549, there was unrest driven by enclosure and
other socio-economic grievances across most of southern England and the
Midlands, many of the 'campers' who assembled to press their demands
aligned themselves with, not against, reforming religion. They borrowed
its language to appeal to the regime, and they heard its preachers at their
encampments. Again, how sincere any of this was is beyond our knowing,
but it is the first tangible sign of what would come. The English, or many
of them, would find a way of building a new identity around this religion and of making it work for them.[10] This is not to say that the English
now welcomed the Reformation, but they were sufficiently inured to and
divided by it that the chance to present a united front against it was gone.
The comparison with the wall of opposition that the Tudor Reformations
were already meeting in contemporary Ireland is instructive.[11]

First, however, a new set of crises brought a tantalising alternative. For
all the emerging enthusiasm for the new religion and the helpless confusion of the old, there is little doubt that the restoration of Catholicism
under Mary I (1553–8) was both popular and on course to succeed. A huge
effort to rebuild the material fabric of parish Catholicism achieved an
extraordinary amount in a short time, especially given that these were
years of dearth, war and epidemics. But the clock could not simply be
turned back. There had been too much looting and destruction, and the
new owners of the monastic lands would only consent to the Catholic

restoration once their right to keep their ill-gotten gains had been protected. For that and other reasons, English Catholicism was not so much restored as recreated in this reign, with the new spiritualities and disciplines of what would become the Counter-Reformation beginning to make themselves felt.[12]

The sudden end of the restoration and the return to Protestantism, with the death of Mary and the accession of Elizabeth I in 1558, cut this process short. Yet the Marian interlude had lasting consequences. Although it did not restore a Catholic England, it ensured there would be no united Protestant England either. The religious conservatives who had been left voiceless and bewildered by Edward VI's Reformation had now rediscovered their steel. Those who had once been lured into abandoning the papacy by intertia and loyalty to the Tudor crown would not make the same mistake again. A small but self-confident minority of determined Roman Catholics now remained in England, and for all that subsequent centuries of persecution, discrimination and prejudice could throw at them, they would persist. Around them and to some extent sustaining them was a larger periphery of sympathisers whose outward conformity to the established Protestant Church was half-hearted or, indeed, wholly cynical.

A similar splintering was emerging at the other end of the spectrum. The Marian regime had tried to deal with England's stubborn minority of Protestant converts by intimidating its leaders into recantation or driving them into exile. The policy half worked. Some prominent Protestants did recant, but many more stuck to their guns: for them, too, the battle-lines now seemed far clearer than before. The regime was eventually compelled to follow through on its threats, and between 1555 and 1556 a swathe of imprisoned bishops, clerics and theologians were executed. Those who had escaped to exile, meanwhile, organised an impressive campaign of printed propaganda that the regime struggled to stifle. In the pressure-cooker of exile, exposed to the heat of Protestant Reformations more full-blooded than England's, they were also fired with new zeal. All this ensured that the purge did not end with the leaders. From 1556 to 1558, the regime was rounding up and burning underground congregations of clandestine Protestants from London, Kent, Essex and elsewhere. Some 300 died in all.

Given a few more years, these policies might well have bled English Protestantism to death, but in the event they only angered it. The memory of the persecutors' cruelty and of the martyrs' heroism was cherished and burnished until it became the centrepiece of an emergent national myth of Catholic cruelty. As an ever-loyal nation swung behind the lead of its new queen, it learned that murdering good English men and women was what Catholics did: a lesson that it was slow to forget. It has been said that although England became a Protestant nation under Elizabeth I, it did not then, or indeed ever, truly become a nation of Protestants.[13] It did, however, become and long remain a nation that hated and feared Catholics.

Not that even the anti-Catholic majority was united. If the Marian regime did not succeed in exterminating the Protestants whom it exiled and persecuted, it did succeed in splitting them. The exiles divided bitterly between those who were determined to remain in lockstep with each other and with the orderly Reformation of Edward VI, and those who wished to dash to a more complete renewal of their religious lives without waiting for the laggards to catch up. In 1558–9 they brought this unresolved quarrel home with them, where it became overlaid on another: what was to be done about those who had conformed to Mary's restoration, but who now claimed to be good Protestants? Surely those who had faced death or exile for their faithful witness could not simply keep company with such faint-hearted turncoats as if nothing had happened? Did they not need to repent of their complicity, and demonstrate their good earnest by pressing the Reformation forward?[14] Hence the split between the new would-be centrist establishment Protestants – 'moderate' in the sense that they were as keen to bridle enthusiasm as to spur on laggards – and those who quickly came to be labelled 'puritans', whose determination to purge the English Church of its popish remnants was fuelled by their distrust of an establishment whose religion, they feared, was not sincere or reformed at all. The battle-lines thus formed would divide English religion for generations to come.

The quarter-century of turmoil from 1534 to 1559 was followed by eighty years of formal religious stability, which only broke down with the political crisis of 1640 and the subsequent Civil Wars. The social history of the Reformations during this long period of supposed peace is, therefore, a matter of how the religious divisions that opened up in the preceding era worked their way through English society at large, and what effect they had on the way.

It has been traditional to see the great drama of this period as the struggle between 'Puritans' and an establishment Protestantism that has sometimes been labelled Anglicanism. This is a myth created by partisans who claim their descent from both parties, and like most myths it has some truth to it. From the 1560s onwards, a broad party of self-consciously 'advanced' Protestants pressed with increasing urgency for Elizabeth's

Reformation to be purged of its remaining popish structures and rituals, only to be stymied at every turn. The regime – above all the queen herself – refused to yield an inch to opponents who, if they could, would plainly have taken a mile. Petitions and policy proposals were stonewalled. Attempts at further reformation from the ground up in regions like East Anglia, by bringing groups of like-minded ministers together to support one another and to build (informally) the kind of structures of collective self-governance typical of Calvinism, were blocked and at times fiercely suppressed. In 1588, Puritan impatience boiled over with a published set of viciously satirical, populist attacks on the alleged hypocrisy and corruption of episcopacy, under the pen-name 'Martin Marprelate'. This provoked a determined counter-attack in which Puritanism was effectively stamped out as a public presence within the Elizabethan Church. It remained, however, as a stubborn and vocal, though contained, minority of malcontents through the 1590s and the reign of James I (1603–25). His son Charles I pushed for a more thoroughly Anglican discipline, enforcing this policy with more zeal than discretion. This, and secular discontent with Charles's (mis)rule, stirred up a hornet's nest of opposition in both England and Scotland that eventually brought England's unprecedentedly long civil peace to an end.

The difficulty with this narrative is that no such clearly defined parties existed. Many who clearly had puritan tendencies liked to think of themselves as a small, persecuted minority at odds with the mass of the godless around them, but this was a theological rather than a sociological opinion. These people were doctrinally primed to see themselves as a faithful remnant, a little flock of God's elect amongst a reprobate mass.[15] In fact, the evidence increasingly suggests that some puritan characteristics spread themselves very widely in English society, at least by the end of the sixteenth century. 'Anglican', by contrast, is an anachronistic category that virtually all historians of the pre-Restoration period now take care to avoid. How we should think about the obedient, conformist Protestantism that became England's default is not so clear.

The traditional category of 'puritan' can only be used to define the earnest, Calvinistic Protestantism that became firmly rooted in England by the late sixteenth century if we broaden its membership considerably.[16] For at the same time as puritan agitators were banging their heads against the brick wall of royal intransigence, others were quietly cultivating their own godly gardens. Richard Greenham, vicar of Dry Drayton, Cambridgeshire from 1570 to 1591, was a puritan of another kind. The further Reformation he had in mind was not institutional but pastoral and spiritual: changing ordinary Christians' lives through painstaking parish ministry. A generation of earnest, idealistic but clear-sighted ministers, many of them Cambridge graduates who had served informal apprenticeships with Greenham, set out to complete England's Reformation retail, soul by soul, rather than wholesale through changes to its laws. If Greenham was the morning-star of this quiet second Reformation, its brightest ornament was William Perkins, a Cambridge theologian who, at his premature death in 1602, left both a small library of succinct, humane guides to Christian living that were translated across Protestant Europe, and also a cohort of enthusiastic students and successors who turned his message into Jacobean England's public orthodoxy.

The most recent studies of both Greenham and Perkins have both denied that their subjects were Puritans at all, on the grounds that they largely conformed to and were undoubtedly loyal to the established Church of England.[17] Whatever labels we choose to apply to them, it is clear that their kind of religion seeped deep into English life. And if idealistic ministers always saw the glass of popular religion as half-empty, booksellers knew there were fortunes to be made selling anthologies of prayers, printed sermons and handbooks to pious living that inculcated a Calvinistic 'practical divinity' of Greenham and Perkins's kind. Bishop Lewis Bayly's *The Practise of pietie*, for example, consists of over 800 pages of earnest practical advice on Christian living, printed in cramped type on tiny pages so as to keep the price as low as possible. Between 1612 and the Civil War it ran through over fifty editions.[18] Other popular imprints that failed to match Bayly's volume of sales made up the difference in variety and accessibility: moralising ballads imbued with Protestant principles, stirring tales of the Protestant martyrs, collections of prayers that used Protestant doctrines as their framework, advice on household management that presumed a self-consciously Protestant piety. Insofar as we can reconstruct lists of best- and steady-selling religious imprints, unabashedly Protestant texts dominate them.[19]

Other evidence points in the same direction. The sermon, advanced Protestantism's chosen medium of religious change, became widespread, carefully constructed and rhetorically effective in the post-Reformation era, and valued by parishes that saw learned preaching as a point of local prestige.[20] Protestant scepticism drove traditional polyphonic church music to a few traditionalist redoubts (mostly cathedrals and collegiate churches), to be replaced by the singing of metrical Psalms, 'Geneva style' (that is, men and women in unison). This practice turned out to be not only hugely popular but also a Trojan horse for sometimes aggressively

Protestant presumptions.[21] Although we have long believed that English
Protestantism's rejection of religious imagery in worship extended to a
general suspicion of all visual images, we are increasingly aware that biblical and other explicitly Protestant visual imagery pervaded domestic decoration and public spaces such as inns.[22] In religious practice itself, what we
know about the patterns of public, family and solitary prayer belies any
sharp division between Puritan and conformist Protestants. 'Conformists'
fasted, wept for their sins, and pursued fervour and zeal in their religious
exercises. 'Puritans' embraced such traditional-seeming practices as making pious vows; used set forms of prayer, including the Book of Common
Prayer, in their private devotions; and found spiritual comfort in the ministry of the established Church.[23] Undoubtedly many English Protestants
were, sometimes, either puritans or anti-puritans. But rather than
attempting to divide the nation into these parties, we would do better to
acknowledge that 'zealous Protestantism could ... be a popular religion'.[24]

Not all zealous Protestantism, however, tended towards puritanism. A
small avant-garde of ceremonialist clerics and traditionalist laypeople persisted throughout the period and discovered new verve, and royal encouragement, from the late 1610s onwards. Some such people were, as their
opponents alleged, undoubtedly flirting with Catholicism, whose rich
spirituality continued to have an appeal and which both won and lost
converts throughout this period.[25] But generally, this was a libel. The new
English Church had built up a genuine mass allegiance from people who
were not drawn by the Calvinist doctrines that had become their preachers' orthodoxies: an allegiance built above all on loyalty to the new English
liturgy, the Book of Common Prayer, which puritan campaigners wanted
so badly to reform. If England cannot be divided into puritans and conformists, it can perhaps be divided into Bible Protestants and Prayer Book
Protestants. Certainly, when the Church of England was dismantled by
the wartime Parliament in the 1640s, its defenders found that the Prayer
Book was their most popular cause, and its use (though formally illegal
throughout the later 1640s and 1650s) continued to be widespread.[26]

What this religion meant to its adherents remains the great mystery.
Conformity, by its nature, does not leave much mark on the record, and a
religion that is almost defined by praying in set words tends not to speak
for itself. We may see a glimpse of it from outside in a jaundiced but
sharply observed portrait painted by Arthur Dent, in his 1601 bestseller
*The plaine mans path-way to heauen*.[27] The book consists of a lengthy dialogue between idealised types: a Protestant minister in the Greenham–
Perkins mould (backed up by a zealous layman), an 'ignorant man' of

good will but of corrupt religion, and a 'caviller' or malicious fault-finder. After nearly 400 pages of conversation, the ignorant man is converted and the caviller departs, contemptuous and evidently hell-bound.

The ignorant man, however, initially jibs at the religion his more self-consciously pious neighbours recommend:

> If a man say his Lords praier, his Ten Commandements, and his Beliefe, and keepe them ... no doubt he shall be saued, without all this running to Sermons, and pratling of the Scripture ... As long as I serue God, and say my praiers duly, and truely, morning and euening, and haue a good faith in God, and put my whole trust in him, and doe my true intent, and haue a good minde to God-ward, and a good meaning; although I am not learned, yet I hope it will serue the turne for my soules health.

Working men who lack the leisure or inclination to bury themselves in the Bible 'cannot liue by the scriptures: they are not for plaine folke, they are too high for vs'. In any case, he adds almost in passing, he cannot read.[28] Two decades earlier another zealous pastor, George Gifford, had produced a similar sketch of what he called 'the Countrie diuinitie'. Gifford's plain man liked a modicum of preaching, but also believed that the Prayer Book service and the official Homilies were 'as good edifying' as any sermon.[29]

'This age', Dent's minister commented, 'is full of such carnall Protestants', and although we might prefer the designation Prayer Book Protestants, we might well agree.[30] Indeed, what else could the religion of the illiterate have been? Again, however, we should beware of the Calvinist instinct to divided the world sharply between the godly and the ignorant: this is preachers' rhetoric, not sociological analysis. And whereas in 1581 Gifford's country-divine rejected his godly neighbour's entreaties, in 1601 Dent's ignorant man eventually embraced the teaching he was offered. Along with the affection that many undoubtedly zealous Bible-Protestants continued to feel for the Prayer Book, this is a sign that, if we must draw lines here, we should not do so too sharply. Zealous Protestantism, of the kind that was often labelled puritan, was a diverse and expansive – not to say quarrelsome – category. By the turn of the century, it had become the most readily available model of what Christian piety meant for most English people. Ministers wanted their people to define their entire lives by it, and so naturally were disappointed. But its reach into national religious life was pervasive.

This establishment Protestant–puritan continuum dominated English religion as nothing since has done, but even so, significant minorities lay outside it. The most obvious were the Catholics – whether 'church papists', who compromised and concealed their faith to various degrees,[31] or recusants, who refused to conform to the established Church and faced a series of consequences ranging from fines, discrimination and civil disabilities to, in extremis, exile or execution. England was openly at war with Spain from 1585 to 1604, and unofficially so for a decade or more before, and during this period Catholics were readily seen as foreign agents. Most of the executions of missionary priests or their lay protectors fell during those years. The Gunpowder Plot of 1605, however, ensured that peace did not bring an outbreak of tolerance. The struggle for England's Catholic community was not merely to negotiate these dangers, but to forge a sense of what its own identity might be. Its exiled leaders, training and sending back missionary priests into terrible danger, were naturally inclined to confrontation, pressing for Catholics to rebel. In 1569, some of them had done so, supporting the northern earls who proposed to replace the queen with her Catholic cousin Mary, queen of Scots. But the revolt was a fiasco, which crumbled at the first show of strength from the regime, and was followed by a bloody programme of exemplary reprisals. After that, rebellion was a dream.

For most Catholics who actually remained in England, therefore, the exiles' purism seemed self-defeating. A slice of England's nobility and gentry remained stubbornly but discreetly Catholic. They and their affinities pioneered what would eventually become the mainstream view of English Catholics, that their political loyalty to the English throne and state was compatible with their spiritual allegiance to Rome. In the wake of the Gunpowder Plot, James I attempted to exploit this by imposing a new oath of allegiance on Catholics, which disavowed any belief that popes may depose or excommunicate kings. Since it was theologically almost impossible for Catholics to accept this, the oath was in one sense a success: it made the Catholic clergy look extreme, while expressing a view that many lay Catholics already tacitly held. However, as the sense of immediate danger receded, the project of splitting, isolating and exposing English Catholicism no longer seemed so urgent. A new reality was becoming clear: English Catholicism was going neither to surge back to retake the country, nor to die out. In some regions, such as the north-west, it was deeply entrenched. And as is often the case with stable religious minorities, once a generation or two of both fears and hopes have turned out to be groundless, both sides of the divide relax and adapt themselves to a new normal.

There was no such relaxation towards a smaller minority: Protestant radicals and separatists. Since the reign of Henry VIII, England had been subject to periodic panics about 'Anabaptists', who would supposedly tear up all godly society and sound doctrine to replace them with profanity, polygamy, common ownership of goods, rebellion and slaughter. The bloody disaster of the apocalyptic Anabaptist kingdom established in Münster in 1534–5 remained a staple of alarmist English thought right through the seventeenth century, and a handful of supposed Anabaptists, most of them foreigners, were burned as heretics by successive regimes: the last two in 1612. There was a panic in the early 1580s about a secretive, mystical sect of Dutch origins, the Family of Love, which had certainly built up networks of sympathisers in Cambridgeshire and elsewhere, but which paranoia began to spot everywhere.[32] The significance of these episodes is not the presence of tiny numbers of sectarians, but the fear that they generated in the rest of society. With hindsight we can see that this fear was excessive, but the far boundary of the Calvinist settlement was less clearly defined than it can look in retrospect. As would become clear in the mid seventeenth century, the possibility of the Reformation dissolving into a welter of chaotic radicalism was very real.

For the present, however, the threat came not from exotic sects but from just beyond the establishment's boundaries. The repeated puritan disappointments of the 1570s and 1580s drove a handful of unblinking radicals to abandon hopes for a comprehensive national Reformation and instead to press ahead on their own. These separatists, often named Brownists for one of their most prominent early leaders, remained few in number, and tended to slip into exile in the Netherlands and elsewhere. It was such a group of Dutch exiles who took the lead in establishing a colony in Massachusetts in 1620. Tellingly, they chose the hardships and risks of an ocean crossing to a potentially hostile environment over the danger that they might 'lose our language and our name, of English'.[33]

These formal separatists, however, were the tip of a much larger iceberg. The phenomenon of what Patrick Collinson has called 'semi-separatism' was pervasive in puritan circles by the end of Elizabeth's reign. Like church papists, such people's formal loyalty to the established religion was belied by a subculture of voluntary structures, meetings and disciplines alongside it, which was often the real heart of their religious practice.[34] They tended to maintain not only that this was compatible with conformity to the Church of England, but also that they were truer to its avowed principles than most others. Their neighbours, and the hierarchy, found their excess of enthusiasm subversive. Who was right is a matter of opinion, and partly depends on how the denouement is interpreted. As the definition of conformity was narrowed and its enforcement was stepped up in the late 1620s and 1630s, the dilemmas of the semi-separatists became sharp. Possibly as many as 20,000 emigrated to New England in that period, as the only way of remaining faithful to both their consciences and their king.[35] Many of those who remained at home heard the siren call of open opposition. Small conventicles of Baptists, antinomians and other radical groups emerged in London and elsewhere in the 1630s.[36] And when the established Church's discipline collapsed after the 1640s, an array of Independent and then other, more radical groups took shape. Did this prove that the establishment was right to use a degree of repression to keep order, or that, in the end, the repression had been counter-productive?

One question that remains unsolved is how, and whether, the alarms about separatism and radicalism connect with another, bloodier phenomenon. England's involvement with the great witch-hunt of the early modern period was marginal. As was the case in many large, law-governed states, bureaucratic procedures tended to prevent local rumours and temporary panics translating into large-scale purges. Our records of witch-prosecutions are poor, and give us systematic coverage only of the Home Counties. Some fifty convicted witches were hanged in Essex, with cases peaking in the 1580s, and with four times as many acquittals as convictions. The numbers are much smaller but the pattern similar in other counties. So perhaps a few hundred died across the country as a whole, overwhelmingly women. For the most part, this seems primarily to reflect long-established patterns of popular belief in, and fear of, malign magic. The novelty, both in England and elsewhere, was that suspected witches were now being put on trial, with new laws passed to criminalise various magical acts in 1542, 1563 and 1604. For some theologians – Catholic and Protestant alike – this piecemeal approach, focusing on witches who had used magic to inflict tangible harm, was profoundly mistaken. Witches' fundamental crime was devil-worship, and they should be punished as heretics and blasphemers, not as common felons.[37] Recent scholarship on the far bloodier witch-hunts in central Europe has suggested that this view arose from the experience of hunting down and rooting out Anabaptists and other radicals, who, like witches, were seen as having been in league with the devil.[38] Whether the same connection was made in England is a question that has, as yet, scarcely been asked. One intriguing straw in the wind is that the most robustly sceptical contribution to the Continent-wide debate over witchcraft in this era came, strangely enough, from an Englishman. Reginald Scot's *Discouerie of Witchcraft* (1584) argued bluntly that witchcraft was a fiction, a product of credulous fears and, implicitly, popish superstition. The book was roundly condemned on all sides.

Intriguingly, Scot has been linked – suggestively, not decisively – to the Family of Love.[39]

If, as Scot argued, the contemporary preoccupation with witches was no better founded than the parallel fear of English Anabaptists, the same is not necessarily true of a final category of religious dissidents, who were the focus of equally vivid fears: atheists. The English word 'atheist' was coined in 1553, and entered common parlance so quickly that it was clearly filling a need. Anti-atheist polemic became a distinct genre by the early seventeenth century. Whether the phenomenon it was attacking existed is less clear. A few outspoken freethinkers, or blasphemers, can be identified, but there is no real hint of consistent or serious atheism, or even deism, in England before the mid seventeenth century. There were certainly committed believers who found themselves tempted to doubt such core Christian doctrines as the inspiration of scripture, the immortality of the soul and the incarnation of Christ, though we tend to hear of such private struggles with doubt only once the doubters had resolved them in favour of orthodoxy.[40] The most widespread form of 'atheism', however, was what William Perkins called 'the common Atheisme that is in the world', meaning those who lived 'as if there were no God'.[41] Such people might profess orthodox Christianity; even sincerely regard themselves as believers. Yet their actions, clerics warned, told another story.

Much of this is simple moralising, but it should be taken seriously at least to this extent. If some of England's carnal Protestants were like Arthur Dent's 'ignorant man' – that is, willing at times to be pious according to their own lights – others clearly were like his 'caviller', whose main interest in religion was that it leave them alone. Perhaps it is always so. But in post-Reformation England the social environment was unprecedentedly friendly towards 'cavillers'. The formal requirements that the English Church laid on its people were not onerous, compared either to the medieval past or to confessional states elsewhere in Europe. The English no longer had to fast rigorously in Lent, nor was there social pressure to support the Church with substantial gifts of money, goods and time as once there had been. The Church's disciplinary structure was not intrusive. All that was needed was occasional physical presence at church, which need not involve ever attending a sermon. An unprecedented space for mere withdrawal from religious life had opened up. The ferocious religious quarrels of the age did not necessarily convince all observers that one party was right and the others wrong. If there was no open and avowed 'atheism', the authors of diatribes were perhaps right that a creeping secularisation and irreligion were beginning to pervade England's spiritual life.

Perhaps that is how such change always comes: as a social reality before, a generation or two later, the theorists arrive to catch up with and to justify what has already begun to unfold.

The long 'Jacobethan' religious peace ended during the reign of Charles I, a new king thoroughly entranced by a ceremonial revival led by a coterie of brilliant, divisive churchmen. What began as a daring insurgency quickly became a new orthodoxy under its most pugnacious proponent, William Laud, bishop of London and then, from 1633, archbishop of Canterbury. Laud and his allies progressively sought to squeeze puritan practices out of the established Church: imposing ceremonial changes that puritans found intolerable, questioning the previously uncontentious doctrine of predestination and raising misplaced but widespread fears of a slide towards 'popery'. Those who opposed the new agenda found themselves deprived or silenced. A minority chose exile, but a far weightier body were now reluctantly persuaded by their experience of 'tyrannical' bishops that England's Reformation needed at last to be finished. And so, when Charles's regime collapsed in 1640 under the weight of multiple crises – above all, the Scottish rebellion against his religious policies – it quickly became plain that returning to the Jacobethan *status quo ante* would not restore religious peace. Fears of popish tyranny mixed with long-cherished hopes of reformation to make the Civil War that followed, at least in part, 'the last of the wars of religion'.[42]

Perhaps a swift parliamentary victory, or a negotiated peace, would have produced the outcome sought by the largest and most vocal parts of the Protestant-puritan establishment: a national Church shorn of bishops and ceremonies. Or perhaps that was already impossible, and the Dutch model – an established Reformed Church but with widespread non-conformity – was a more realistic hope. In the event, however, the trauma of a long war, and of the drawn-out politicking that followed it, created a space for impatient separatism to burgeon into florid radicalism and angry dissent. The Protestant establishment that had kept radicals at the margins was now overwhelmed, not least because London, centre of the parliamentarian cause, and the victorious New Model Army, proved themselves the most fertile incubators of sectarianism. The era's taxonomists of heresy were kept busy inventing labels for the jungle of antinomian, apocalyptic, spiritualist, messianic, pantheistic and utopian movements that sprang up across the country. A few of them achieved durable form, notably the Baptists and the Quakers. Others merged, transformed, withered or gave way to new green shoots appearing in their place.[43] The total numbers of people involved remained small, but the army-dominated republican regimes of 1649–60 were persistently unwilling to suppress them. Some of their leaders, notably Oliver Cromwell himself, were openly sympathetic. They also had no wish to hand the spiritual government of the nation to an intolerant Presbyterian clique.

That clique's hopes slowly crumbled. It was not simply the encroachment of radical sects and the rejection of national Presbyterian structures by self-governing 'Independent' congregations. They also found themselves unable to bring the Prayer Book Protestants with them. The old Prayer Book was supposedly banned, the old bishops expelled from office. But the republican regimes generally only took action against these people – whom we can now, cautiously, begin to call 'Anglicans' – if their religious practice strayed into open royalism. Only around a quarter of the old parish clergy were ever expelled from office. Remarkably, the majority of men ordained during the Republic were ordained illegally, by deprived bishops, rather than by the new presbyteries.[44] Anglicans experienced these years as persecution, but they also brought opportunities. Freed of the need to be a comprehensive national Church and of the constraints of legal uniformity, these believers began to experiment with their traditional religion in untraditional ways. Some adhered to the old Prayer Book rigidly. Some adapted it, whether from political prudence or religious adventurism. Either way, this emergent Anglicanism was something new: not a domineering national Church, but the largest of the new sects. And, ironically, the least frightening of them – a fact which became crucial when the republican regime itself tottered in 1658–60 and a Stuart restoration beckoned. The rump Presbyterian establishment was now more alienated from the army and alarmed by the radical sects than it was scared of resurgent Anglicanism. Blithely promising religious inclusion, Charles II was welcomed back to his throne.

It turned out that Anglicanism had some bite left to it, after all. For all his promises, the new king restored the old Church of England's structures almost unchanged, and once again a quarter of England's parish ministers, over 2,000 men, were ejected from their churches in 1662 for failing to conform to it. But while the Presbyterians, Independents and sectarians of the war years could be expelled and discriminated against, they could not be wished away. The 'Great Ejection' confirmed that the Church by law established was, despite its name, no longer truly the Church of England; and the 'Great Persecution' that followed (in truth, a matter of discrimination and imprisonment rather than of mass execution) proved futile. One of the ironies of the revolution of 1688–9 is that both James II and

William III's regimes were, for very different reasons, committed to instituting a fair measure of tolerance for Protestant dissenters.

The Toleration Act of 1689 has, in retrospect, acquired some of the glory traditionally attributed to the 1688–9 revolution. At the time, in an age when 'toleration' was an admission of failure, it did not seem so. It was a truce, born of pragmatism and exhaustion. This was not how anyone had expected the Reformation would end. But it turns out that the Reformation had not, after all, been a matter of replacing Catholic England with Protestant England, much less of forging one of the various godly commonwealths of which successive reformers had dreamed. Its enduring achievement was, instead, to ensure that the English would never again be a nation united under the same God.

## Notes

1 D. S. Katz, *The Jews in the History of England, 1485–1850* (Oxford: Clarendon Press, 1994).
2 A. de Mezerac-Zanetti, 'Liturgical developments in England under Henri VIII (1534–1547)', unpublished Ph.D. thesis, Durham University (2011).
3 J. Gray, *Oaths and the English Reformation* (Cambridge: Cambridge University Press, 2013); E. Shagan, *Popular Politics and the English Reformation* (Cambridge: Cambridge University Press, 2002).
4 A. Wood, *The Memory of the People: Custom and Popular Senses of the Past in Early Modern England* (Cambridge: Cambridge University Press, 2013).
5 B. J. Penny-Mason and R. L. Gowland, 'The children of the Reformation: Childhood palaeoepidemiology in Britain, AD 1000–1700', *Medieval Archaeology*, 58 (2014).
6 Gray, *Oaths and the English Reformation*, 145–53.
7 L. Kaufman, 'Ecclesiastical improvements, lay impropriations, and the building of a post-Reformation Church in England, 1560–1600', *HJ*, 58 (2015); B. Lowe, *Commonwealth and the English Reformation: Protestantism and the Politics of Religious Change in the Gloucester Vale, 1483–1560* (Aldershot: Ashgate, 2010).
8 Shagan, *Popular Politics*, 162–96; D. MacCulloch, M. Laven and E. Duffy, 'Recent trends in the study of Christianity in sixteenth-century Europe', *Renaissance Quarterly*, 59 (2006), 725–6.
9 A. Ryrie, *The Age of Reformation: The Tudor and Stewart Realms, 1485–1603* (Harlow: Pearson, 2009), 162–7.
10 E. Shagan, 'Protector Somerset and the 1549 rebellions: New sources and new perspectives', *EHR*, 114 (1999); A. Wood, *The 1549 Rebellions and the Making of Early Modern England* (Cambridge: Cambridge University Press, 2007).
11 H. Jefferies, 'Elizabeth's Reformation in the Irish Pale', *Journal of Ecclesiastical History*, 66 (2015).

12 E. Duffy, *Fires of Faith: Catholic England under Mary Tudor* (New Haven and London: Yale University Press, 2009).

13 C. Haigh, *English Reformations: Religion, Politics and Society under the Tudors* (Oxford: Oxford University Press, 1993), 280.

14 R. Harkins, 'Elizabethan puritanism and the politics of memory in post-Marian England', *HJ*, 57 (2014).

15 P. Collinson, *The Religion of Protestants* (Oxford: Oxford University Press, 1982), 189–205.

16 A process ongoing ever since the publication of P. Lake, *Moderate Puritans and the Elizabethan Church* (Cambridge: Cambridge University Press, 1982).

17 K. L. Parker and E. J. Carlson, *'Practical Divinity': The Works and Life of Revd Richard Greenham* (Aldershot: Ashgate, 1998); W. B. Patterson, *William Perkins and the Making of a Protestant England* (Oxford: Oxford University Press, 2014).

18 I. Green, *Print and Protestantism in Early Modern England* (Oxford: Oxford University Press, 2000), 348–51.

19 T. Watt, *Cheap Print and Popular Piety* (Cambridge: Cambridge University Press, 1991); A. Walsham, *Providence in Early Modern England* (Oxford: Oxford University Press, 1999).

20 A. Hunt, *The Art of Hearing: English Preachers and Their Audiences, 1590–1640* (Cambridge: Cambridge University Press, 2010).

21 A. Ryrie, 'The Psalms and confrontation in English and Scottish Protestantism', *Archiv für Reformationsgeschichte*, 101 (2010).

22 T. Hamling, *Decorating the 'Godly' Household: Religious Art in Post-Reformation Britain* (New Haven and London: Yale University Press, 2010). Cf. P. Collinson, 'From iconoclasm to iconophobia: The cultural impact of the second English Reformation', in P. Marshall (ed.), *The Impact of the English Reformation* (London: Routledge, 1997).

23 A. Ryrie, *Being Protestant in Reformation Britain* (Oxford: Oxford University Press, 2013).

24 Walsham, *Providence in Early Modern England*, 325.

25 M. Questier, *Conversion, Politics and Religion in England, 1580–1625* (Cambridge: Cambridge University Press, 1996).

26 J. Maltby, *Prayer Book and People in Elizabethan and Early Stuart England* (Cambridge: Cambridge University Press, 1998).

27 An argument made in C. Haigh, *The Plain Man's Pathways to Heaven: Kinds of Christianity in Post-Reformation England, 1570–1640* (Oxford: Oxford University Press, 2007).

28 A. Dent, *The plaine mans path-way to heauen* (London, 1607), 25–8.

29 G. Gifford, *A briefe discourse of certaine pointes of the religion, which is among the common sorte of Christians* (London, 1581), fols. 2r, 3r, 18v–19r, 24v, 50r–v, 65v.

30 Dent, *The plaine mans path-way*, 125.

31 A. Walsham, *Church Papists: Catholicism, Conformity and Confessional Polemic in Early Modern England* (Woodbridge: Boydell, 1993).

32 C. Marsh, *The Family of Love in English Society, 1550–1630* (Cambridge: Cambridge University Press, 1994); C. Carter, 'The Family of Love and its enemies', *Sixteenth Century Journal*, 37 (2006).

33 K. L. Sprunger, *Dutch Puritanism: A History of the English and Scottish Churches of the Netherlands in the Sixteenth and Seventeenth Centuries* (Leiden: Brill, 1982), 139.

34 Collinson, *Religion of Protestants*, 242–83; P. Collinson, 'Night schools, conventicles and churches: Continuities and discontinuities in early Protestant ecclesiology', in P. Marshall and A. Ryrie (eds.), *The Beginnings of English Protestantism* (Cambridge: Cambridge University Press, 2002).

35 S. Hardman Moore, *Pilgrims: New World Settlers and the Call of Home* (New Haven and London: Yale University Press, 2007).

36 D. Como, *Blown by the Spirit: Puritanism and the Emergence of an Antinomian Underground in Pre-Civil-War England* (Stanford: Stanford University Press, 2004).

37 J. Sharpe, *Instruments of Darkness: Witchcraft in England, 1550–1750* (London: Penguin, 1996).

38 G. K. Waite, *Eradicating the Devil's Minions: Anabaptists and Witches in Reformation Europe, 1525–1600* (Toronto: University of Toronto Press, 2007).

39 D. Wootton, 'Reginald Scot/Abraham Fleming/the Family of Love', in S. Clark (ed.), *Languages of Witchcraft: Narrative, Ideology and Meaning in Early Modern Culture* (Basingstoke: Macmillan, 2001).

40 L. Dixon, 'William Perkins, "atheisme", and the crises of England's long Reformation', *JBS*, 50 (2011).

41 W. Perkins, *A godly and learned exposition of Christs Sermon in the Mount* (Cambridge, 1608), 233; J. Dod and R. Cleaver, *Ten sermons tending chiefly to the fitting of men for the worthy receiuing of the Lords Supper* (London, 1611), 3.

42 J. Morrill, 'The religious context of the English Civil War', *TRHS*, 5th series, 34 (1984).

43 J. F. McGregory and B. Reay (eds.), *Radical Religion in the English Revolution* (Oxford: Oxford University Press, 1984); B. Reay, *The Quakers and the English Revolution* (New York: St Martin's Press, 1985); A. Hughes, *Gangraena and the Struggle for the English Revolution* (Oxford: Oxford University Press, 2004); A. Hessayon and D. Finnegan (eds.), *Varieties of Seventeenth- and Early Eighteenth-Century English Radicalism in Context* (Farnham: Ashgate, 2011).

44 K. Fincham and S. Taylor, 'Episcopalian conformity and nonconformity 1646–60', in J. McElligott and D. L. Smith (eds.), *Royalists and Royalism during the Interregnum* (Manchester: Manchester University Press, 2010); K. Fincham and S. Taylor, 'Vital statistics: Episcopal ordination and ordinands in England, 1646–60', *EHR*, 126 (2011).

6

# Words, Words, Words:
# Education, Literacy and Print

*Adam Fox*

Polonius: What do you read, my lord?
Hamlet: Words, words, words.

(W. Shakespeare, Hamlet (1601), II.ii.195)

Among the greatest changes to come over English society between 1500 and 1750 were the expansion of educational provision, the growth in literacy levels, and the increased use of the written word in both manuscript and print. The consequences of these developments were profound and wide-ranging, and taken together they transformed the experience of almost everyone in England. By the mid eighteenth century, the ability to read the printed word had become a normal part of adult life; the capacity to wield a pen was an increasingly familiar accomplishment; and in books, pamphlets, single-sheets and all manner of printed ephemera people found the words that expressed their mental worlds and the ideas that structured their lives.

These changes were neither linear in their progress nor even in their effects. They were experienced in different ways by different people, in different times and places, and their selective impact provides graphic illustration of some of the fundamental distinctions that defined English society. In many ways there is no more powerful demonstration of the basic divisions – of wealth, rank and gender – that characterised the early modern period than the extent to which people had access to education and its fruits. In other ways it may be said that the proliferation of the written word and the diffusion of print culture contributed to the gradual reconfiguration of these hierarchies. New avenues of social mobility opened up; novel forms of information and opinion became available to more people; and all English men and women were, at some level, incorporated into a national culture founded upon text.

For the social elite education began at home under the guidance of a private tutor. The great families of the land could afford to employ the best: the philosopher Thomas Hobbes acted as tutor to the Cavendish family, earls of Devonshire; Lady Anne Clifford, daughter of the third earl of Cumberland, was mentored by the poet and historian Samuel Daniel. For the gentry, domestic instruction was no less the initial stage of a child's career. In the 1560s the future Lord Chancellor, Francis Bacon, was educated on the family estate in Norfolk before being sent to Cambridge at the age of twelve. Edward Hyde, the future earl of Clarendon, 'was bred up in his father's house' in Wiltshire, under the guidance of the local clergyman.[1]

For some well-to-do boys education started at the 'petty' school kept by a local schoolmaster or a parish clerk. George Villiers, son of a Leicestershire squire and the future duke of Buckingham, began and ended his formal instruction at the village school in Billesdon; John Evelyn's first educational experience was at the age of four when he attended class in the church porch on his father's estate at Wotton in Surrey. The main function of these petty schools was to teach pupils to read English, and they could be quite inclusive, accepting girls as well as boys and the children of labourers alongside those to the manor born. Thereafter, however, experience diverged. At the age of eight Evelyn moved on 'to learn my Latin rudiments and to write', before going to the grammar school at Southover, at which point other boys were sent to work and girls were taught to spin, weave and sew.[2]

The sixteenth and seventeenth centuries experienced considerable expansion in the number of grammar schools like that at Southover. This was a result in part of the stimulus to classical learning given by the Renaissance, the drive to found new educational establishments in the wake of the Reformation, and the growth of charitable giving to secular bodies. Between the accession of James I and the outbreak of the Civil War, private philanthropy contributed almost £400,000 to institutions of learning in England. As a result the numbers of grammar schools doubled between the reigns of Elizabeth I and Charles II, and when Christopher Wase surveyed them in 1673 he found a total of 704, or roughly one for every market town. They varied in size and prestige, from long-established endowments such as Eton or Westminster, and large urban foundations like Shrewsbury or Merchant Taylors', which had several hundred scholars, to small country establishments of no more than a few dozen pupils. Some of the latter might teach English and even admit girls in the lower forms, but in essence their purpose was to instruct boys of upper and middle rank in Latin, and some of the older ones in Greek. The social composition of a typical provincial grammar school is illustrated by the surviving registers of that at Colchester in Essex, under the mastership of William Dugard, between 1637 and 1642. During these five years, 165 boys enrolled, of whom only 18 received 'free' places, the reminder paying 10s per quarter in tuition and other charges. Thirty-one per cent were the sons of knights or gentlemen, 20 per cent from clerical or professional backgrounds, 37 per cent the offspring of merchants or tradesmen, and 12 per cent the sons of yeomen farmers.[3]

The grammar school curriculum was relatively consistent. Lily's Latin Grammar was a standard text between its introduction in 1547 and its replacement by the Eton Grammar in 1758. Once boys had mastered Latin vocabulary, accidence and syntax, and could translate both into and from English, they moved on to the study of a corpus of ancient texts that included the histories of Caesar, Livy and Sallust and the poetry of Virgil, Horace and Ovid; the orations of Cicero and the plays of Terrance; the fables of Aesop and the precepts of Cato. This regimen helped to develop a common cultural repertoire and consolidate a set of shared mental reference points among its beneficiaries. It drove a wedge of classical language and learning between the social elite and the lower orders. Into the eighteenth century, many gentlemen continued to regard those who could not read Latin as 'illiterate'. It also contributed to the sense of intellectual and cultural distance between elite men and women.[4]

Like the grammar schools, the two universities of Oxford and Cambridge experienced considerable expansion up until the mid seventeenth century. Eight colleges were founded, or refounded, at Oxford between 1509 and 1624, and seven at Cambridge between 1505 and 1596. By the 1630s some 2 per cent of all seventeen-year-old males were in attendance. Some were 'gentlemen commoners' seeking the varnish of learning and the social connections that would fit them to take their place as governors of the realm or leaders of county society. But the majority were mere commoners, or 'plebs', who frequently waited upon their betters as servitors or 'sizars'. They more often undertook the four-year course of study that led to the degree of Bachelor of Arts and might prepare them for careers in the Church, teaching or government service. The extant admissions records of four Cambridge colleges from the seventeenth century reveal that 33 per cent of matriculands were of gentle status, of whom less than one-third were likely to graduate; 22 per cent came from clerical or professional families, of whom more than two-thirds became graduands; however, of the 16 per cent that hailed from the ranks of merchants and tradesmen and 15 per cent from the yeomanry, around 80 per cent took a degree.[5]

For some able and fortunate boys of humbler birth a 'free' place at the grammar school and the scholarship to a university college could open up the possibility of a career in Church or state, pedagogy or the professions, and thus represent a route to economic and social advancement. At the end of this period Archbishop Moore was the son of a butcher just as Cardinal Wolsey had been at its beginning. In the seventeenth century, Bishop Richard Corbett of Norwich was the son of a Surrey gardener, and Archbishop Samuel Harsnett of York the son of a Colchester baker. The father of the lawyer and scholar John Selden had been a village fiddler from West Sussex, and the step-father of the famous poet and playwright Ben Jonson a London bricklayer. But these beneficiaries of the edifice of classical learning in endowed institutions were exceptions. For the most part this was a system that reflected the social order as it was, and it may have done more to ossify the rigidities of rank than to provide a vehicle for their dissolution.[6]

Meanwhile, traditional education at home remained the lot of most well-to-do women. Learning to read English, and perhaps French, together with the skills of household management and other 'feminine' accomplishments, were its chief intention. Writing was considered to be less important, and knowledge of Latin generally regarded as irrelevant or inappropriate. Typically Margaret Cavendish, daughter of an Essex gentleman, was tutored at home in the 1630s by an 'ancient decayed gentlewoman', learning 'singing, dancing, playing on music, reading, writing, [needle]working, and the like'. By this time, however, boarding schools for young ladies and daughters of the comfortable middle ranks were appearing, particularly around London at Deptford, Stepney and Hackney. In the early 1640s the future poet Katherine Philips, daughter of a prosperous cloth merchant, was educated at Mrs Salmon's in Hackney. Such private academies for girls soon sprang up in cities such as Oxford and Exeter, and towns like Shrewsbury, Manchester and Leeds. After the Restoration, the daughter of Lancashire minister, Adam Martindale, was 'bred at home, to her booke and pen, and in Warrington and Manchester, to her needle and musick'. The Essex clergyman Ralph Josselin spent roughly £6 per year on the education of each daughter, as compared with £10 annually in supporting each son, but this included sending Mary and Elizabeth to a Hackney boarding school in 1675.[7]

The growth of these girls' establishments benefited from a general elaboration and diversification of educational provision in the century after the Restoration. Following the disruptions of the Civil War a long period of stagnation began to overtake both the grammar schools and the universities. The regimented grounding in the classics on which they were founded began to lose some of its appeal among the elite, while the mercantile and professional ranks increasingly questioned its relevance and purpose. Entrants to Oxford, who had numbered 460 per annum in the 1660s, had fallen to below 200 a year by the 1750s. When various 'neare relations' tried to persuade Henry Martindale to take his son Adam away from St Helens grammar school in the early 1630s, and set him 'to somewhat that might be me a subsistence; alledging too many instances of such as made no advantage of their learning, though they had been brought up so long to it as to be fit for nothing else', they expressed a scepticism about the value of such education that was common among middling families and becoming more widespread. Whereas some 55 per cent of entrants to Oxford in the years 1577–9 had been non-gentle, or 'plebeian', this figure had fallen to 37 per cent in the late 1630s, and just 17 per cent by 1760.[8]

One manifestation of changing attitudes was the increase in domestic tutors: a rough estimate suggests that by the eighteenth century perhaps a quarter of the peerage, a third of the gentry, a quarter of the clergy and a fifth of the professions were being educated at home. Another consequence was the growth of private academies offering an alternative to the classical curriculum of grammar school and university. Some were founded by dissenting ministers ejected from their livings after 1662, such as that at Newington Green, north of London, established by Charles Morton, or the Rathmell Academy opened at Settle, North Yorkshire, by Richard Frankland in 1670. Others were established subsequently by non-conformist denominations and congregations, like Northampton Academy launched by the Revd Robert Jennings in 1715. They were joined by numerous small private schools, sometimes short-lived, offering a more technical or vocational training and aimed at the sons of the urban commercial classes. Such academies placed more emphasis on mathematics and some even offered elementary science, or 'natural philosophy': practical subjects such as surveying, navigation and accounting held an important place alongside emerging disciplines like geography, history and modern languages. When Bathsua Makin opened an academy for girls at Tottenham High Cross in 1673, offering Latin, arithmetic and astronomy alongside more traditional 'female' subjects, it prefigured gradually changing attitudes, as did the few properly co-educational grammar schools that first appeared in the 1680s. From the second quarter of the eighteenth century, provincial newspapers became full of advertisements for private tutors, new schools for boys and girls, and dozens of lecture courses on all manner of subjects aimed at an adult audience. Between 1726 and 1760 about 200 teachers from seventy-eight towns across the West Country placed notices in the pages of the *Salisbury Journal*.[9]

Thus, the century after the Restoration transformed the opportunities for learning open to boys, and to a lesser extent girls, of the 'middling sorts'. New educational provision was both cause and effect of the development of religious pluralism, the changing face of the English economy and the more fluid nature of the social order that are such features of this period. Even for those lower down in society this rapidly evolving scene was not without impact. For poorer children education was no less likely to begin at home. For centuries it had been incumbent upon Christian mothers, when they could, to instruct their children in letters, and one legacy of the Reformation was the conviction among ardent Protestants that an ability to read the Word of God was necessary for salvation. This is what inspired the godly Alice Heywood, wife of a fustian weaver from Bury in Lancashire. Her son Oliver later recalled that in the 1630s 'she was continually putting us upon the scriptures and good bookes and instructing us how to pray'. Moreover, 'it was her usual practice to help many poore children to learning by buying them bookes, setting them to schoole, and paying their master for teaching, whereby many a poore parent blessed god for help by their childrens reading'.[10]

Many women clearly helped the children of others by becoming school dames themselves. From 1555 all teachers required a licence from the Church, but the records are full of those minded to ignore this: like Grace Coates of Baseford in Nottinghamshire, prosecuted in 1625, who 'sayeth that all such as cannot read are damned'. But there were many others like the woman at Reculver, Kent, who in 1619 'with the minister's consent teacheth two or three children their hornbooks', or the 'two poor, honest, sober, and well meaning persons' from the Yorkshire village of Bilton who in the early eighteenth century were said to 'teach children to read, and instruct them in ye Church catechism'. An ecclesiastical survey of Eccleshall in Staffordshire between 1693 and 1698 found that, together with one man, there were five women acting as teachers in the parish, four of whom were the wives of day-labourers and local craftsmen.[11]

The extent of such offerings varied greatly across the country and over time, but they often formed part of quite extensive networks of licensed establishments. Even in the Elizabethan period, 258 out of the 398 parishes in the county of Essex had a school at some point, as did fully forty-four of the fifty-three parishes in Hertfordshire. In adjacent Cambridgeshire, meanwhile, roughly 20 per cent of villages had a continuously licensed schoolteacher in the fifty years between 1570 and 1620. In Kent, half the towns and villages had a school running for some period during the first four decades of the seventeenth century: thirty-four of these lasted for at least two decades and twenty-four continued for three decades or more. It may be that at this time the more prosperous and densely populated counties close to London were better served than the regions with poorer ecclesiastical livings, larger parishes and scattered settlements further to the north and west. If this was so, however, the balance was to some extent being redressed by the later seventeenth century. Thus in Cheshire, while there were licences granted to just 53 schoolmasters in the period 1555–1600, this figure rose to 79 between 1601 and 1650, and increased again to 105 in the half-century before 1700.[12]

It was also the case after the Restoration that the number of endowed schools under the supervision of the parish vestry began to increase, often presided over by the curate and meeting in the church. Bishop William Nicolson would discover many of them when he held his primary visitation of the diocese of Carlisle in 1703. In addition, the 1680s saw a pioneering initiative in London to establish 'charity schools', on the basis of subscriptions. By 1705, there were 54 operating in the city, and in 1723 as many as 123 were catering for 5,223 pupils. This model was taken up by the Society for the Promotion of Christian Knowledge, founded in 1699 to provide free education for the poor nationwide. The impact of these developments was beginning to be seen in the returns to Archbishop Herring's visitation of the large diocese of York in 1743: it revealed that of 645 responding parishes, 379 had a school of some kind, variously described as either 'English', 'petty', 'free', 'endowed', 'private', 'public' or 'charity'.[13]

Attendance at all schools was usually from the age of about five or six, and the ability to read print could be instilled within a year or even a few months. 'When I was about six years of age', recalled the timber merchant's son Oliver Sansom, brought up at Beedon, Berkshire, in the early 1640s, 'I was put to school to a woman, to learn to read, who finding me not unapt to learn, forwarded me so well, that in about four months' time, I could read a chapter in the Bible pretty readily'. Writing, which required a quill pen and knife and the ingredients to mix ink, together with costly paper and blotting equipment, could take up to two more years to learn. Girls were far less likely to be taught this skill than boys, and poor lads less liable than wealthier ones. The age of about seven, when instruction in writing might begin, was also that at which a youngster could start work. Typically, Thomas Tryon, the son of a Gloucestershire tiler and plasterer, was put to school at the age of five in 1639 but had 'scarcely learnt to distinguish my letters, before I was taken away to work for my living'. He was unusual only in that at the age of thirteen, when working as a shepherd, he began 'thinking of the vast usefulness of reading' and bought himself a primer, 'and now got now one, then another, to teach me to spell, and so learn'd to read imperfectly, my teachers themselves not being ready readers'. Even more exceptionally he was then 'desirous to learn to write'. Although 'at a great loss for a master, none of my fellow-shepherds being able to teach me', he finally found 'a lame young man who taught some poor people's children to read and write' and 'agreed with him to give him one of my sheep to teach me to make the letters, and joyn them together'.[14]

In consequence it was quite common for poorer children, especially girls, to leave school with some reading capacity but without being able to write, or even to decipher script. For this reason, the concept of 'literacy' in early modern England is difficult to define. Being able to sound out a simple printed text in English represented the lowest threshold of attainment, although even here the gothic, or black letter, typeface of simple didactic and devotional texts remained easier for most people to manage than the roman, or white letter, font of other works. Furthermore, the majority of those contemporaries who understood 'print hand' still struggled to fathom 'written hand'. And handwriting itself came in a variety of forms, some of which were less intelligible than others: from the widespread but very difficult secretary hand, through a variety of arcane legal styles, to the somewhat more recognisable italic script. Thus when it was said of a Lancashire timber merchant in the 1590s, or a Suffolk yeoman's wife in the 1620s, that they could 'not write or read a written hand' these limitations were familiar, but did not preclude the ability to comprehend some print. A poor Kentish seaman made this explicit in 1633 when claiming that he could not 'writte or read anie other hande then printed hande'. One late-seventeenth-century Yorkshire woman was clearly noteworthy in that 'she reads also written-hand as well as print', but Thomas Highway, the parish clerk of Myddle in Shropshire around 1700, was far more typical: 'hee can read but litle' of the printed word, and 'can scarce write his owne name, or read any written hand'.[15]

Calculating the extent to which people could write their own name, as opposed simply to making a mark, on formal documents such as legal depositions, marriage registers or subscriptions to oaths, provides some measure of the expansion of educational provision over these centuries. The relative infrequency with which girls were taught to use a pen is confirmed by the estimation that in 1500, perhaps 10 per cent of adult males but only 1 per cent of adult females could form a signature. On the accession of Elizabeth I in 1558, these figures had risen to 20 per cent of men and 5 per cent of women; at the outbreak of the Civil War in 1642 they stood at 30 per cent and 10 per cent, respectively; and by the time George I came to the throne in 1714 an average of 45 per cent of men and 25 per cent of women could sign, or more than one-third of the total adult population. The evidence yielded by Hardwick's Marriage Act of 1753, which required brides and grooms to sign a specially printed register, reveals that between 1754 and 1760, fully 64 per cent of men and 39 per cent of women were able to write their names, or just over half of all people.[16]

Predictably enough, the evidence of signatures also betrays the ways in which educational opportunity was the product of social status. Thus in the counties of East Anglia over the period 1580–1700, all those of clerical and professional status could sign their names, as could 98 per cent of aristocracy and gentry. At the same time, however, this skill extended to 65 per cent of yeomen, 56 per cent of tradesmen and craftsmen, 21 per cent of husbandmen, and 15 per cent of labourers. A sample of depositions made across northern England during the period 1700–70 indicates that whereas three-quarters of both craftsmen and tradesmen, and yeomen farmers, were able to sign their names, only one-third of labourers could do so.[17]

To some extent, there was also a hierarchy of signing ability in terms of environment. As might be expected, cities evince higher levels of penmanship than market towns and, in turn, small urban centres betray greater capacity than rural areas. The evidence from four London parishes in the 1640s suggests that even at this date as many as two-thirds of adults could sign their names; by the 1720s, some three-quarters of the metropolitan population were so equipped. Between 1754 and 1762, male signing ability had also reached 74 per cent in the university city of Oxford, 66 per cent in the major port of Bristol and 60 per cent in the textile town of Halifax. Out in the countryside, meanwhile, there could be marked differences in levels of signing between neighbouring parishes at any given time, explained perhaps by the capricious availability of local schooling or any number of contingent factors. In mid-seventeenth-century Surrey, for example, the spectrum ranged from one parish where 71 per cent of people could sign, down to another in which only 9 per cent were so able; in Nottinghamshire the parameters were similarly between 73 per cent and 7 per cent.[18]

Although making a signature might be only the most basic form of writing ability, what these statistics suggest is just how widespread the ability to wield a pen was becoming. Whereas in 1500 writing had been a particular skill, largely confined to a narrow cadre of the social, clerical and professional elite, by 1750 it was a relatively common accomplishment, diffused at every level and found in every part of English society. Moreover, if most of those who managed the quill had already learned to read, and very many people, especially women, learned to read without ever picking up a pen, the implication of these figures is that the great majority of the population could understand words on the page by the close of the early modern period.[19]

A number of changes flowed from these developments. As writing was 'democratised', simple italic script became the common mode and the old gothic cursive and stylised legal hands were gradually outmoded. By the late seventeenth century, black letter type was being replaced even in popular texts with white letter. A greater uniformity between script and print thus ensued and the distinction between 'print hand' and 'written hand' reading ability was undermined. English completed its triumph over Latin as a learned medium: after 1733 all legal proceedings moved into the vernacular, and over the eighteenth century a decreasing proportion of books were published in classical languages. Use of the very word 'publication' gave insight into another triumph: that of print culture over manuscript. In the seventeenth century, 'publication' was still used in the sense of simply 'to make public', for which scribal circulation was often sufficient and sometimes preferable: in the eighteenth century, its conflation with 'printing' was completed.

The rise of print was a phenomenon that was both cause and effect of the expansion of education and literacy in early modern England. Both processes were also inseparable from the progress of the English Reformation. A large part of the market for print was for basic devotional and didactic texts such as the officially sponsored *ABC with the Catechisme* and *The Primer and Catechisme*. From the 1560s to the 1630s, *The ABC* was selling anything between 20,000 and 100,000 copies every decade, while the records of the Stationers' Company of London suggest that something like 2 million copies of the *ABC* and the *Primer* were produced between 1677 and 1700 alone. Their consumers were people like Hannah Gifford, teacher at the borough school in Dorchester, who was supplied in May 1666 with a parcel of twelve hornbooks at 1d each and thirteen primers at 3d a piece, together with eleven psalters, used for teaching Latin, and eight New Testaments.[20]

These centuries produced the standard texts of Christian doctrine, worship and edification that entered popular consciousness and became embedded in the national culture. Chief among them, of course, was the English Bible. Between William Tyndale's rendition of the New Testament in 1526 and the Authorised Version of 1611, there were eight major translations of all or part of the scriptures into English. By 1729 at least 664, and possibly as many as 732, different editions of the complete vernacular text had been published. Its greater issue in smaller formats over time is indicative of an expanding market down through society. In the 1630s, an unbound octavo cost 6s or 7s in London, and a duodecimo between 3s 4d and 4s; in the reign of George II, octavos were being sold for 3s and duodecimos for 1s 9d. By this time the family Bible had become a familiar object even in the households of husbandmen and labourers.[21]

Another text that became increasingly familiar to the English people was the Book of Common Prayer. Whereas in 1549 a folio edition unbound cost 2s 2d, by 1600 it was just 10d; a century later it could be bought for between 5d and 9d in quarto or duodecimo, and for only 3d in abbreviated form for binding up with small Bibles. Equally canonical were the metrical psalms. Thomas Sternhold and John Hopkins began translating them in the late 1540s and a complete edition of all 150 appeared in the vernacular in 1562. Over the next century-and-a-half, 'Sternhold and Hopkins' went through some 790 editions. Perhaps 400,000 copies were published in the last quarter of the seventeenth century, by which time prices were as low as 3d for the smallest sizes.[22]

These foundational texts permeated the imaginations of all men, women and children in England: they articulated the rites of passage that punctuated their lives, they supplied the parables and lessons that informed their moral compass, and they coined the words and phrases that entered their linguistic currency. Thanks to print and collective repetition these works came to provide the foundation of a national culture. To them were added a supporting cast of popular devotional works that became the 'best sellers' of their day, the kinds of works of which most people had at least heard. Arthur Dent's *A Plain Man's Pathway to Heaven* (1601) was, in abbreviated form, said to be in its fifty-third edition by 1675; Lewis Bayly's *The Practice of Piety* (1612) had entered its fifty-seventh English edition by the 1720s; and Richard Baxter's *A Call to the Unconverted* (1658) was already in its twenty-eighth incarnation by 1696. In due course even these old favourites were overtaken by John Bunyan's *The Pilgrim's Progress* (1678–84), of which 160 editions would be printed by 1792, in additon to numerous bowdlerised versions. It was, thought Dr Johnson, one of the three works written by 'mere man' that we wish was longer.[23]

Religious and didactic works were just one part of the market for print. These centuries witnessed an increasing profusion of works published on almost every conceivable subject. Philosophical treatises took their place alongside political tracts; plays and poems mingled promiscuously with prose narratives and picture books; practical guides and self-help manuals poured out on everything from midwifery to manners, and gardening to gastronomy. As a result the printed word entered the fabric of daily life in English society and the period saw the emergence of something like a national literary canon.

Yet for most of this period printing was closely controlled. Licensing of the press began under Henry VIII, and from 1557 the Stationers' Company of London exercised the power to inspect all works before issue. Their authority lapsed during the tumultuous years of the Civil War and Interregnum but a new Printing Act came into force in 1662, operating with interruptions until 1695, after which pre-publication censorship came to an end. Within this oscillating regulatory framework, the production of texts burgeoned. Fifty-nine surviving works are known to have been printed in England in 1500, rising to 401 by 1600; 4,198 remain from the spectacular year of 1642, falling back to 2,756 from 1700, and increasing again to 3,383 by 1750. In total, almost 210,000 separate domestically produced titles are now extant from the period 1500 to 1750, and many more were imported from abroad. It has been suggested that only around two-thirds of seventeenth-century publications have come down to us. Assuming actual output of 300,000 works, and print runs of 1,000 copies each, both of which are conservative estimates, there was a total of 300 million individual items printed in the country between the beginning of the sixteenth and the middle of the eighteenth century.[24]

One reflection of this growth in production is the increasing size of the libraries built up by individuals over time. The selection of about 2,000 learned volumes assembled by Thomas Bodley in November 1602 to refound the university library in Oxford might be compared with the 50,000 eclectic works that the physician Sir Hans Sloane bequeathed as one of the founding collections of the British Museum in 1753. The greatest aristocratic library of the Elizabethan and Jacobean period, that left by John Lord Lumley in 1609, amounted to 3,600 books and manuscripts; by contrast, when the library of Richard Maitland, fourth earl of Lauderdale, came to auction in 1689 it totalled some 20,000 items.[25]

Perhaps even more telling in terms of the role of books in society at large are the expanding, if more modest, stocks accrued by the provincial gentry across the period. Typically, when Sir William More of Loseley

House near Guildford, Surrey did an appraisal in 1556, he found that he had about 140 manuscripts and 100 printed works. When the bibliophilic Derbyshire gentleman Sir William Boothby died in 1707, however, his collection was said to number 'near six thousand books' and occupy at least 122 shelves of the 'inner library' at Ashbourne Hall. Meanwhile, the emergence of women as distinct consumers in the market is suggested by the closet of Frances Wolfreston, wife of a country squire from Statfold near Tamworth in Staffordshire. By the end of her life in 1677, she had over 100 of her own books, 92 per cent of which were in the vernacular with about half comprising imaginative literature.[26]

No less striking is a propensity both to buy and to retain books that extended down to the middle ranks of urban society. A sample of the probate inventories of almost 3,000 Kentish townsfolk reveals that by the early seventeenth century as many as 40 per cent of men and 25 per cent of women possessed books of some kind. Another analysis of inventories indicates that whereas 18 per cent of London households owned books in 1675, as many as 56 per cent did so by 1725. Even in the small towns of east Kent and Hampshire 42 per cent of sampled inventories listed books by the later date. The mason from Coventry who was said in the 1570s to own more than sixty volumes, including romances and histories, jests and riddles, almanacs and poems, together with 'a bunch of ballets & songs all auncient', was probably exceptional. A century later the library of the non-conformist preacher and sometime town clerk of Rye, Samuel Jeake, which then amounted to some 2,100 items, was no less extraordinary. But such examples demonstrate the limits of possibility for the prosperous urban 'middling sorts'.[27]

At the same time, many cases of more modest bookishness across society illustrate just how deeply the reading habit was penetrating rural life. In the middle years of the seventeenth century, the Yorkshire yeoman Adam Eyre was avidly buying books on his visits to Wakefield and Sheffield. Among his prizes were copies of Foxe's edifying *Acts and Monuments*, Raleigh's inspiring *History of the World* and Dalton's practical *Country Justice*. But he also had sermons and treatises by puritan divines that were borrowed by his neighbours around Hazlehead in the West Riding, from whom he received similar material in return. In the decades following, Leonard Wheatcroft, a craftsman from Ashover in north-east Derbyshire, established a remarkable lending stock of religious, educational and miscellaneous works. By the time his son Titus finished the catalogue that he began in 1722 it contained 392 titles. Meanwhile, a villager from Charlton, near Pewsey in Wiltshire, who had been in service in London and begun to buy books there, was building up a collection of two or three dozen works for sharing. Classics such as Ovid, Seneca and Epictetus were set alongside staples of the emerging English canon – Shakespeare's plays; Dryden's Virgil; Butler's *Hudibras*; the poetry of Milton, Waller and Prior – and were leavened by the topical commentary on metropolitan manners of Tom Brown, Ned Ward and Joseph Addison.[28]

Or consider the experience of John Cannon, born in 1684 in the Somerset village of West Lydford. Although his farming parents said that 'buying books was beyond their circumstances', their teenage son managed to have 'always, some book or other in my pocket'. He 'delighted' in works tracing 'the lives and actions of great men and worthy heroes', and in 'books of divinity … (a thing not common in many)'. He bought *Aristotle's Masterpiece* for a shilling, 'which I got to pry into the secrets of nature especially of the female sex'; a copy of Culpepper's *Directory for Midwives* served the same purpose, until his mother caught him in the act. Cannon scrimped and saved to acquire such titles from a bookseller on market days in the little textile town of Bruton. It was here, in 1701, that he met Philip Whitacre, a local gardener 'who had in his house the large history of that learned and warlike Jew, Josephus Ben-Gorion', which he allowed Cannon to read. A couple of years later he befriended John Read, a self-taught shepherd who 'gave himself to know English learning, figuring, poetry, and a smack of astronomy'. Read 'had a good store of valuable books, which he would bear about him in his daily employments, & when we met, he would not only read, but lend me some of them'. By the turn of the seventeenth century, therefore, it was possible to find, in the small towns and villages on the edge of the Somerset levels, farm boys reading erotica, gardeners owning esoteric histories, and shepherds sharing their vernacular libraries.[29]

Clearly both the geographical range and the social depth of the book trade were growing all the time. London remained the centre of the industry. In 1586 it was already home to 25 printers operating some 53 presses. By the mid eighteenth century it supported 120 printers, who were still producing some 86 per cent of the national output, and about 70 bookshops mostly clustered around St Paul's Churchyard and Paternoster Row, along Fleet Street and the Strand, on London Bridge and in Little Britain. With the lapse of the Printing Act in 1695, however, presses began to spring up beyond London and the small university enterprises in Oxford and Cambridge. This gave a boost to the book trade across the country: one contemporary source suggests that by the mid 1740s there were 381 individuals involved in some aspect of the business in 174 towns nationwide.[30]

From an early date certain centres of education and cathedral cities had been well served by retailers of the printed word. During a period of less than ten months in 1520, the Oxford stationer John Dorne sold fully 1,850 works. In 1585 the stock of the Shrewsbury bookseller Roger Ward amounted to 546 separate titles in more than 2,000 individual copies. Michael Harte held in excess of 4,500 volumes ready for sale from his Exeter premises in 1615; and Eden Williams's 'great shopp' in Lincoln contained over 2,000 books and pamphlets in 1671. During the seventeenth century, however, such premises were also springing up in the rank and file of county centres. In 1644 John Awdley's shop in Hull was carrying a stock of 832 copies; the inventory of a Warrington bookseller listed over 1,200 volumes in 1648. And by the end of this period weekly stalls in small country towns, like the one patronised by John Cannon at Bruton, were a familiar sight. Up until his death in 1736 the prominent Lichfield bookseller Michael Johnson also maintained market stands in Birmingham, Uttoxeter and Ashby-de-la-Zouch.[31]

In addition, itinerant sellers had, from the first, taken portable texts out into the countryside, connecting even the most isolated communities to a national print network. Before the Reformation, John Dorne had 170 broadside ballads for sale at ½d each, but the fact that he was also offering batches of seven at 3d, or twelve for 5d, suggests that they were already destined for the carrier's pack. In 1578 we find a man 'sellinge of lytle bookes' in the churchyard of the remote Cambridgeshire village of Balsham. In the early 1620s, a 'poor pedlar came to the door' of the Baxter family in the Shropshire community of Eaton Constantine offering 'ballads and some good books': he sold a copy of Richard Sibbes's *Bruised Reed*. In 1696 a basket containing about 200 ballads, probably belonging to a hawker, was stolen from the marketplace in Kirby Lonsdale, Westmorland. One broadside ballad produced by William Dicey of Northampton in about 1730 listed no fewer than thirteen printers and booksellers in neighbouring counties from whom 'chapmen and travellers may be furnish'd with the best sort of old and new ballads, broadsheets, &c.'.[32]

Indeed, there is no more graphic evidence of the growing depth of the market for print over these centuries than the proliferation of the kind of cheap, unbound and often ephemeral works that were the stock-in-trade of such vendors. Some 3,000 distinct ballads are estimated from the second half of the sixteenth century alone which, assuming print runs of 1,250 copies each, would mean total production of 4 million sheets. Small wonder that in the 1590s one Suffolk preacher witnessed them 'bought up a pace' in markets, discovered them in 'the shops of artificers, and cottages of poore husbandmen', and found that people had them 'set up in their houses, that so they might learne them, as they shall have occasion'. At this time about one-third of the themes of these popular songs were religious or didactic, but during the seventeenth century, when they came to sell for 1d each, they peddled an eclectic mix of news and politics, romance and bawdry, stories and jests. Sung in the streets and plastered on ale-house walls, they were one of the most ubiquitous and familiar sources of the printed word in English society: despite their extreme fragility some 15,000 specimens printed before 1700 still survive.[33]

In the second and third decades of the seventeenth century ballad publishers also began reissuing popular titles in octavos or duodecimos of twenty-four pages or less at a cost of 2d, as well as in twenty-four-page quartos (later known as 'double-books') costing 3d or 4d. Some of these were 'small godlies' containing morality tales or simple works of edification; others were 'penny merriments' featuring collections of jokes or comic tales; and still others were 'pleasant histories' including the legends of medieval heroes or abridged adaptations of more recent fiction. What came to be known by the second half of the eighteenth century as 'chap-books' were a foundation of English popular reading from the reign of James I to that of Queen Victoria. Generations of well-to-do boys were introduced to them in their nurseries and swapped them at their grammar schools. Working youngsters, no less, found in them their first introduction to literature and a powerful formative influence. The poor brazier's son from Bedfordshire, John Bunyan, grew up in the 1630s bewitched by such works as *George on Horsebach* or *Bevis of Southampton*. Sixty years later the young John Cannon spent all his spare money on 'pamphlets & small historys of low price', such as '*The Seven Champions, Fortunatus, Parismus, Dr. Faustus, The Wars of England, Extraordinary Events,* & the like'. Around 1750 the first reading of the Berkshire shoemaker's son Thomas Holcroft was chapters from the Old Testament together with two of the same 'delightful histories' that 'men called chapman's books', namely *Parismus and Parismenes* and *The Seven Champions of Christendom*.[34]

Nor was such literature only for children. It could form a staple of edification and entertainment for readers of all ages and stations. The Staffordshire lady Frances Wolfreston owned fifty of these small 'godlies', together with about sixteen little 'merry' books mostly published between the 1640s and 1660s. The admiralty official Samuel Pepys acquired 193 such works during the last two decades of the seventeenth century. Lower down in society, his contemporary John Bunyan noted how his Bedfordshire 'brethren' remained as devoted to such cheap print as he had been in his youth. A century later, the Northamptonshire thresher Parker Clare, 'the lame man of Helpstone', was no different: he 'could read a little in the Bible, or Testament, and was very fond of the superstitious tales that are hawked about the streets for a penny, such as *Old Nixon's Prophecies, Mother Bunches Fairy Tales,* and *Mother Shipton's Legacy,* etc., etc.'.[35]

Just as popular were almanacs. Part astrological predictions, or 'prognostications'; part calendar and diary; and part digest of useful information; they were being been produced from at least the early sixteenth century. By the 1660s they sold at the rate of 400,000 per year, and a century later Moore's almanac alone was vending 82,000 copies annually. The last decades of the sixteenth century saw the emergence of the 'pamphlet', made from a single sheet in folio or quarto format. Selling for anything between 1d and 4d, pamphlets became a common vehicle for topical comment and polemical opinion in both prose or verse. Quick to run off, cheap to buy and easy to distribute, they were one of the most potent weapons and influential vehicles of the printed word. During the two remarkable decades between the beginning of the Long Parliament and the return of Charles II, when the nation was plunged into political chaos and censorship broke down, the London stationer George Thomason managed to collect some 14,942 separate examples. In the reign of Queen Anne, Jonathan Swift found them so numerous that 'it will very well employ a man every day from morning till night to read them'.[36]

Alongside the pamphlet came the serial publication of news. The year 1620 saw the appearance in London of the first folio 'newsbook', and from October 1621 'corantos' in quarto format were produced intermittently over the following twenty years. They were highly regulated and dealt only with foreign affairs, but with the collapse of licensing at the Civil War the first newspapers carrying domestic content burst onto the scene. By 1644 a dozen of them were appearing in London every week, some with a circulation of over 500 copies. In total, no fewer than 350 separate news titles came and went in the revolutionary years between 1641 and 1659: Thomason gathered up 7,216 specimens. After the reimposition of licensing the long-lived *London Gazette* became the official government mouthpiece in 1666, and before the end of the century it had been joined by rivals such as the *Post Boy, Post-Man* and *Flying-Post.* By 1712 there were ten single-sheet newspapers appearing in the capital every week, selling 25,000 copies between them. 'All Englishmen are great newsmongers', observed a foreign visitor to London in 1725. 'Workmen habitually begin the day by going to coffee-rooms in order to read the latest news. I have

often seen shoeblacks and other persons of that class club together to purchase a farthing paper.'[37]

The eighteenth century saw the arrival of the provincial newspaper.
The first was the *Norwich Post*, around 1701, and early followers were the
*Bristol Post-Boy*, the *Exeter Post-Man* and the *Worcester Post-Man*. By 1760
such publications were being produced in thirty-five centres across the
country with total sales of 200,000 copies a week.[38] A parallel innovation
was the periodical magazine, carrying topical commentary, correspondence from readers and essays on all manner of subjects. John Dunton's
*Athenian Mercury* was an early example in the 1690s, but the reign of
Queen Anne saw the periodical come of age with Daniel Defoe's *Review*
(1704–13), Richard Steele's *Tatler* (1709–11) and Steele's collaboration
with Addison on the *Spectator* (1711–14). The last came out daily, sold
for just 1d and went through a remarkable 635 numbers. Edward Cave's
*Gentleman's Magazine*, launched in 1731, was perhaps the most successful periodical of the eighteenth century, and in 1744–6 Eliza Heywood
edited what was the first women's magazine in England, the *Female
Spectator*. By the 1760s more than thirty periodicals were being published
in London alone.[39]

This remarkable literary efflorescence in early Georgian England
brought with it the novel in its fully fledged form. Scarcely have so many
enduring classics been produced in such a short period: Defoe's *Robinson
Crusoe* (1719) and *Moll Flanders* (1722); Swift's *Gulliver's Travels* (1726);
Richardson's *Pamela* (1740) and *Clarissa* (1747); Fielding's *Joseph Andrews*
(1742) and *Tom Jones* (1749); Smollett's *Roderick Random* (1748) and
*Peregrine Pickle* (1751); and Sterne's *Tristram Shandy* (1759), to name only
some of the best known. Their sales were prodigious – Fielding's *Amelia*
(1751) shifted 5,000 copies within a week – and like other popular works
they benefited from some of the marketing innovations of the period: the
advent of serial publication, where large works were issued in weekly
instalments to stagger the costs; the issuing of cheap editions of popular
works; the 'remaindering' of overstocks; and the advent of the circulating
library from which books could be borrowed for a small fee. All of these
initiatives helped to transform people's access to the printed word.[40]

In the process, the whole business of literature – production, distribution
and reception – was placed on a different footing. A new breed of hack-
writer emerged – Johnson's 'drudges of the pen': journalists and essayists,
critics and reviewers, who lived by their words and fed off those of others.
The stereotypical image of the 'Grub Street' scribbler in his garret reflected

the changing social profile of the author. A new gender profile was also emerging. The published female of modest origins was a legacy of the seventeenth century – in Restoration England the poet and playwright Aphra Behn had been the daughter of a Kentish barber; the prolific cookery writer Hannah Wolley was a widow in straitened circumstances; and the author of one of the best-known manuals on childbirth, Jane Sharp, was a practising London midwife. But the early Georgian age saw ordinary women forcing their way into the male-dominated world of letters to an unprecedented degree. The contributions of Eliza Haywood, Penelope Aubin and Delarivier Manley to the development of the novel, for example, were significant. Among other things, they created both the demand for and the supply of literature among an ever-growing feminine readership.[41]

In so many senses the England of 1750 would have been unrecognisable to the English of 1500. This was no more so than in relation to the availability, form and content of words in script and print. By the reign of George II, tens of thousands of sheets were scribbled, and pages published, every year, in ways and for purposes that would have been difficult to conceive of in the days of Henry VIII. They were both produced and consumed by a diversity of people, in a range of circumstances, and for a variety of reasons that were equally unimaginable to previous generations. To some extent, this process of transformation not only expressed, but also elaborated, the essential cleavages and fissures of the social order: it added a new level of cultural differentiation to economic divisions and gender inequalities. Only gentleman and 'scholars' were fluent in learned languages; fewer women could write than men; the 'middle sorts of people' had a greater ability to read than the labouring classes; and urban dwellers were more likely to own books than their rural neighbours. Yet, for all this, something more positive had happened. Information and communication on paper had the potential to liberate the mind and empower the subordinate in altogether new ways. Apprentice shopkeepers kept diaries, and farm boys composed autobiographies; workers left threatening squibs for their employers, and the poor sent petitions to their betters; daughters addressed letters to their fathers, and servant girls wrote notes to their lovers. Country people perused newspapers alongside shoeblacks; cookmaids read novels after their mistresses; and seamstresses bought magazines no less than ladies. All this enabled them to broaden their mental horizons, to imagine new possibilities, and to claim some share of a cultural repertoire that could belong to everyone.

**Notes**

1 *Oxford Dictionary of National Biography*, 60 vols. (Oxford: Oxford University Press, 2004); J. Lawson and H. Silver, *A Social History of Education in England* (London: Methuen, 1973), 136.

2 *ODNB*; J. Evelyn, *The Diary of John Evelyn*, ed. E. S. de Beer, 6 vols. (Oxford: Oxford University Press, 1955), Vol. II, 6.

3 J. Simon, *Education and Society in Tudor England* (Cambridge: Cambridge University Press, 1966); W. K. Jordan, *Philanthropy in England 1480–1660* (London: Allen & Unwin, 1959), 283; W. A. L. Vincent, *The Grammar Schools* (London: Murray, 1969); R. O'Day, *Education and Society, 1500–1800* (London: Longman, 1982), Chapter 4; D. Cressy, 'Educational opportunity in Tudor and Stuart England', *History of Education Quarterly*, 16 (1976).

4 F. Watson, *The Grammar Schools to 1660* (Cambridge: Cambridge University Press, 1908).

5 Cressy, 'Educational opportunity in Tudor and Stuart England', 311–13; O'Day, *Education and Society*, Chapter 5.

6 J. Aubrey, *Brief Lives*, ed. A. Clark, 2 vols. (Oxford: Oxford University Press, 1898), Vol. I, 184; Vol. II, 11, 219, 308; *ODNB*.

7 *ODNB*; A. Martindale, *The Life of Adam Martindale, Written by Himself*, ed. R. Parkinson Chetham Society, 4 (Manchester: Chetham Society, 1845), 207; O'Day, *Education and Society*, 186–8.

8 Martindale, *Life*, 24; O'Day, *Education and Society*, 196–208.

9 N. Hans, *New Trends in Education in the Eighteenth Century* (London: Routledge, 1951), 26–7; O'Day, *Education and Society*, 208–16; R. Porter, *Enlightenment* (London: Allen Lane, 2000), 78.

10 M. Spufford, 'First steps in literacy', *SH*, 4 (1979), 435.

11 A. Fox, *Oral and Literate Culture in England 1500–1700* (Oxford: Oxford University Press, 2000), 46; Lawson and Silver, *Social History of Education*, 113; T. Laqueur, 'The cultural origins of popular literacy in England 1500–1850', *Oxford Review of Education*, 2 (1976), 257–8; Spufford, 'First steps in literacy', 435.

12 B. Simon, 'Leicestershire schools 1625–40', *British Journal of Educational Studies*, 3 (1954); M. Spufford, *Contrasting Communities* (Cambridge: Cambridge University Press, 1974), 183–91; P. Clark, *English Provincial Society from the Reformation to the Revolution* (Hassocks: Harvester, 1977), 199–203; K. Wrightson, *English Society 1580–1680* (London: Hutchinson, 1982), 186; K. Charlton and M. Spufford, 'Literacy, education and society', in D. Lowenstein and J. Mueller (eds.), *The Cambridge History of Early Modern Literature* (Cambridge: Cambridge University Press, 2002), 26.

13 Lawson and Silver, *Social History of Education*, 181–92.

14 Spufford, 'First steps in literacy', 410, 415–16.

15 K. Thomas, 'The meaning of literacy in early modern England', in G. Baumann (ed.), *The Written Word* (Oxford: Oxford University Press, 1986), 100; Fox, *Oral and Literate Culture in England*, 47–8, 91–2.

16  D. Cressy, *Literacy and the Social Order* (Cambridge: Cambridge University Press, 1979), 176–7; Lawson and Silver, *Social History of Education*, 192–3; R. S. Schofield, 'Dimensions of illiteracy, 1750–1850', *Explorations in Economic History*, 10 (1973).

17  D. Cressy, 'Levels of illiteracy in England, 1530–1730', *HJ*, 20 (1977); Cressy, *Literacy and the Social Order*, 136; R. A. Houston, 'The development of literacy: Northern England, 1640–1750', *EcHR*, 2nd series, 35 (1982); R. A. Houston, *Scottish Literacy and the Scottish Identity* (Cambridge: Cambridge University Press, 1985), Chapter 2.

18  Cressy, *Literacy and the Social Order*, 73, 191–201; Lawson and Silver, *Social History of Education*, 194.

19  S. E. Whyman, *The Pen and the People: English Letter Writers 1660–1800* (Oxford: Oxford University Press, 2009).

20  I. Green, *Print and Protestantism in Early Modern England* (Oxford: Oxford University Press, 2000), 183–4; D. Underdown, *Fire from Heaven* (New Haven and London: Yale University Press, 1992), 247; M. Spufford, *Figures in the Landscape* (Aldershot: Ashgate, 2000), 258–9.

21  Green, *Print and Protestantism*, Chapter 2.

22  *Ibid.*, Chapters 5 and 9.

23  *Ibid.*, Appendix I; Laqueur, 'The cultural origins of popular literacy', 262–3; *Johnsoniana; or, Supplement to Boswell* (London, 1836), 91. (The other two were *Don Quixote* and *Robinson Crusoe*.)

24  F. S. Siebert, *Freedom of the Press in England, 1475–1776* (Urbana: University of Illinois Press, 1952); *The English Short Title Catalogue*, available at http://estc.bl.uk (accessed 13 October 2016).

25  W. D. MacRay, *Annals of the Bodleian Library Oxford*, 2nd edn (Oxford: Oxford University Press, 1890), 29; M. Hunter, A. Walker and A. MacGregor (eds.), *From Books to Bezoars: Sir Hans Sloane and His Collections* (London: British Library, 2012), 11; L. Stone, *The Crisis of the Aristocracy, 1558–1641* (Oxford: Oxford University Press, 1965), 705–7; J. Lawler, *Book Auctions in England in the Seventeenth Century* (London: Stock, 1906), 170–5.

26  H. S. Bennett, *English Books and Readers 1475–1557*, 2nd edn (Cambridge: Cambridge University Press, 1969), xiii–xiv; P. Beal, '"My Books are the great joy of my life": Sir William Boothby, seventeenth-century bibliophile', *Book Collector*, 46 (1997); P. Morgan, 'Frances Wolfreston and "hor bouks": A seventeenth-century woman book-collector', *Library*, 6th series, 11 (1989).

27  P. Clark, 'The ownership of books in England, 1560–1640: The example of some Kentish townsfolk', in L. Stone (ed.), *Schooling and Society* (Baltimore: Johns Hopkins University Press, 1976); L. Weatherill, *Consumer Behaviour and Material Culture in Britain 1660–1760* (London: Routledge, 1988), 88; R. Laneham, *A Letter* (London, 1575), 34–6; M. Hunter, G. Mandelbrote, R. Ovenden and N. Smith (eds.), *A Radical's Books: The Library Catalogue of Samuel Jeake of Rye, 1623–90* (Woodbridge: Boydell, 1999).

28 Wrightson, *English Society*, 199; M. Bell, 'Reading in seventeenth-century Derbyshire: The Wheatcrofts and their books', in P. Isaac and B. McKay (eds.), *The Moving Market* (New Castle, DE: Oak Knoll, 2001); J. Spence, *A Full and Authentick Account of Stephen Duck, the Wiltshire Poet* (London, 1731), 7–8.

29 J. Money (ed.), *The Chronicles of John Cannon*, 2 vols. (Oxford: Oxford University Press, 2010), Vol. I, 28, 30, 35–6, 37, 42–3.

30 J. Raven, *The Business of Books* (New Haven and London: Yale University Press, 2007), 47; J. Brewer, *The Pleasures of the Imagination* (London: HarperCollins, 1997), 137; J. Feather, *The Provincial Book Trade in Eighteenth-Century England* (Cambridge: Cambridge University Press, 1985), 29.

31 Fox, *Oral and Literate Culture*, 15–16; J. Barnard and M. Bell, 'The English provinces', in J. Barnard and D. F. McKenzie (eds.), *The Cambridge History of the Book in Britain*, Vol. IV: *1557–1695* (Cambridge: Cambridge University Press, 2002), 674; Wrightson, *English Society*, 198; M. Spufford, *Small Books and Pleasant Histories* (London: Methuen, 1981), 75.

32 T. Watt, *Cheap Print and Popular Piety, 1550–1640* (Cambridge: Cambridge University Press, 1991), 11; Spufford, *Contrasting Communities*, 208; R. Baxter, *The Autobiography of Richard Baxter*, ed. N. H. Keeble (London: Dent, 1974), 7; Spufford, *Small Books*, 121; Feather, *Provincial Book Trade*, 108.

33 Watt, *Cheap Print and Popular Piety*, 11–12; P. Fumerton and A. Guerrini (eds.), *Ballads and Broadsides in Britain, 1500–1800* (Farnham: Ashgate, 2010).

34 Spufford, *Small Books*, 7, 72–5; J. Fergus, *Provincial Readers in Eighteenth-Century England* (Oxford: Oxford University Press, 2006), 161–79; Money, *Chronicles of John Cannon*, Vol. I, 30, 35; E. Colby (ed.), *The Life of Thomas Holcroft*, 2 vols. (London: Constable, 1925), Vol. I, 10–11.

35 Watt, *Cheap Print and Popular Piety*, 315–17; Spufford, *Small Books*, 3, 7, 131.

36 B. Capp, *Astrology and the Popular Press* (London: Faber & Faber, 1979), 23; Raven, *Business of Books*, 134; J. Raymond, *Pamphlets and Pamphleteering in Early Modern Britain* (Cambridge: Cambridge University Press, 2003); *Catalogue of the Pamphlets … Collected by George Thomason, 1640–1661*, 2 vols. (London: British Museum, 1908); Porter, *Enlightenment*, 93.

37 G. A. Cranfield, *The Press and Society from Caxton to Northcliffe* (London: Longman, 1978), Chapter 1; *Catalogue of the Pamphlets … Collected by George Thomason, 1640–1661*; M. Harris, *London Newspapers in the Age of Walpole* (London: Associated University Presses, 1987); M. Van Muyden (trans. and ed.), *A Foreign View of England in the Reigns of George I & George II* (London: Murray, 1902), 162.

38 G. A. Cranfield, *The Development of the Provincial Newspaper 1700–1760* (Oxford: Clarendon Press, 1962); R. M. Wiles, *Freshest Advices: Early Provincial Newspapers in England* (Columbus: Ohio State University Press, 1965).

39 Brewer, *Pleasures of the Imagination*, 141–4; Porter, *Enlightenment*, 79–82; K. Shevelow, *Women and Print Culture* (London: Routledge, 1989).

40 R. D. Altick, *The English Common Reader* (Chicago: University of Chicago Press, 1957), 49; R. M. Wiles, *Serial Publication in England before 1750*

(Cambridge: Cambridge University Press, 1957); P. Kaufman, *Libraries and Their Users* (London: Library Association, 1969); J. Raven, 'Libraries for sociability', in G. Mandelbrote and K. A. Manley (eds.), *The Cambridge History of Libraries in Britain and Ireland*, Vol. II: *1640–1850* (Cambridge: Cambridge University Press, 2006).

41 P. Rogers, *Grub Street* (London: Methuen, 1972); P. Crawford, 'Women's published writings 1600–1700', in M. Prior (ed.), *Women in English Society 1500–1800* (London: Methuen, 1985); C. Turner, *Living by the Pen* (London: Routledge, 1992).

# 7

# Land and People

## Jane Whittle

Robert Loder was a prosperous Berkshire farmer who made over £100 a year selling malted barley, which was shipped down the Thames to London. His account books for 1610–20 record his concerns for the business and profits of farming: issues such as the balance between wheat and barley in his fields and the expense of feeding his live-in farm servants. The Loder household consisted of Robert, his wife, their children and five farm servants – three men and two women. All the adults were actively engaged in farming. While the men worked in the fields and transported grain to market, the female servants malted the barley, milked cows, and picked and marketed fruit from the orchards. Mrs Loder and the female servants baked bread, brewed beer, made cheese and cured bacon, providing all the basic foodstuffs for the household from the products of the farm. Everyone helped in the fields at harvest time.[1] In the same decade of the seventeenth century, Alice Le Strange, the wife a gentleman with an income of over £2,000 a year, began running the home farm on his estate in Hunstanton, Norfolk. Among her employees were the Wix family. Richard Wix, his wife Anne and their son were all occasional agricultural labourers for the Le Stranges, but they also had other means of making a living. Richard's main occupation was as a thatcher, while Anne earned an income from knitting stockings. She also spun wool and made butter and cheese. They had a smallholding; grew a small amount of grain; and kept cows, pigs and poultry. When Richard died in 1628 their moveable goods and livestock were worth £11 12s.[2] A century later, another account keeper, Richard Latham of Scarisbrick, Lancashire, spent his whole adult life living on a 19-acre life-leasehold farm inherited from his father. He rented out some land but also grew wheat, oats and occasionally barley, and kept cows. His wife and daughters spun linen and cotton, both for income and to make household textiles. This farm economy provided them with enough to get by but they were far from self-sufficient. Richard worked for wages and employed others on his farm; the family purchased grain, other foodstuffs such as sugar, and textiles. The Lathams were deeply enmeshed in a local economy of informal loans and exchanges of money, goods and labour.[3]

Up until the 1980s the history of rural England was dominated by two grand narratives of revolutionary change told from different ideological viewpoints. On the one hand, economic historians described 'agricultural revolutions' led by the likes of Robert Loder and the Le Stranges. They argued that profit-orientated farmers and landlords led increases in farm productivity, made possible by the modernising institutional changes of engrossing, enclosure and the spread of leasehold tenure. On the other hand, social historians focused on the proletarianisation of rural population, describing how small farmers like Richard Wix and Richard Latham were torn from the land and forced to become impoverished wage labourers. There is no doubt that between 1350 and 1850 the English countryside was transformed from a society of small family farmers to one based predominantly on large farms employing wage labourers. But the issues of when and where these changes took place, let alone why and how they occurred, are far from resolved. Recent research has undermined many of the grand narratives' assumptions. Change was not as clear-cut as was once thought. Medieval agriculture could be highly productive: crop yields on Norfolk's manorial demesnes in the early fourteenth century were not exceeded there until after 1700.[4] The idea of a peasantry being transformed into wage-earners between 1500 and 1750 has been qualified by the realisation that the rural population was already strongly proletarianised at the start of the period: it is estimated that 'both in 1381 and in 1522–5 those who depended on wages for most of their income accounted for a little below half of the population in most of the country, but more than half in the eastern counties, from Kent to Lincolnshire'.[5]

This chapter examines the disputed claims about the changing nature of rural society between 1500 and 1750. It aims to identify what changed most during the period and what the possible causes of those changes were. The next section focuses on enduring features: structures that formed the backdrop to the change. This is followed by a section examining those aspects of rural society that experienced most change between 1500 and 1750. Finally, the possible mechanisms of change, such as demography, class conflict and commercialisation are explored.

**Enduring Features**

Throughout the early modern period England remained a rural society: 95 per cent of the population lived outside large urban centres in 1520 and 79 per cent in 1750.[6] More than that, land remained deeply embedded within the social structure and culture of English society. It was of course the most important means of production. Agriculture usually fed the population without significant imports of grain,[7] and the land also provided the raw materials for the other basic consumer necessities: clothing, fuel and shelter. In the era before formal banking, land was the most secure means of investing and storing wealth. It generated wealth through farming, selling such resources as timber or pasture, or being rented to tenants, and provided security for loans via mortgaging. Land was the key indicator of status. Ownership of manorial land allowed entry into the gentry. Village society was stratified partly according to the size of landholdings and types of tenure. Rural inhabitants who lacked rights to land – wage-workers, most women, the young – also lacked status. Finally, land was the world within which people lived, in a landscape created by generations of human actors: cleared, drained, ploughed, planted, hedged, walled, built upon, argued over, looked at and remembered. The land and landscape both were shaped by people and shaped the way people could lead their lives.

In early modern England, landownership was a system of overlapping rights. All land was owned and used, but almost always by more than one person. The roots of this system were medieval and feudal. Lords held units of land, manors, from the monarch. In turn, lords granted land to manorial tenants, while those tenants sometimes leased their land to sub-tenants. Serfdom, whereby many tenants had unfree status, had largely disappeared by the sixteenth century, but the manorial system remained. The classic manor divided land into the manorial demesne, tenanted freehold and customary land, and common pasture shared by lords and tenants. The demesne belonged to the lord and was either managed directly as a home farm or leased out. Freehold was a privileged tenure, originally held by free tenants. Its terms were usually clear-cut, with rents low and fixed. Customary land had been unfree during the medieval period. It was held 'according to the customs of the manor', which varied widely in terms of the rents, fines and rights assigned to tenants. By the sixteenth century the most common types of customary tenure were copyhold of inheritance and copyhold for lives. Copyhold of inheritance gave the tenant the right to pass land on to an heir, or to sell it, without the lord's interference as long as the transfer was reported and rents and fines paid. Copyhold for lives was held for the lives of three named people (normally the tenant, his wife and one of their children), and the tenant had no right to the land beyond this. As well as rents, customary tenants paid entry fines when a new tenant took possession of a holding, and sometimes a heriot or death duty when a tenant died. There had been an active market in all these types of land since at least the late fourteenth century. Manors, freeholds, customary land and leaseholds were not only rented out, but were bought and sold between tenants. Thus land could be acquired by grant of a landlord, by inheritance or by purchase, or sometimes by a mixture of methods. The inheritance custom of primogeniture, inheritance by the eldest son, dominated for all types of land, but often the heir had to pay cash bequests to his siblings as soon as he acquired the land.

Lords had the right to hold manorial courts, which recorded the transfer of land between tenants and regulated the agricultural system of the village. Across much of England systems of 'open field' agriculture operated, requiring forms of co-operation among tenants. Arable was held as strips of land in large fields. When land rested fallow, or between harvest and new sowing, the village livestock grazed these fields. Meadow land was also often held jointly by tenants who took an agreed share of the hay and grazed animals in the meadow after haymaking. Most manors had 'commons': areas of rough pasture used by lord, tenants and other inhabitants. It was this complex system of grazing rights, or use rights, as well as the complexity of different types and layers of tenure, that was so characteristic of early modern landholding in England. It meant that in many cases, neither lords nor tenants had an absolute right to decide what to do with their land, leading to many bitter disagreements about who owned what and what they could do with it.

Viewed from a global perspective, early modern England had one basic system of agriculture: mixed farming, which combined grain crops (primarily wheat, barley and oats) with raising sheep and/or cattle and relied on plough cultivation. Less significant in terms of land use, but vital to diet, were the fruit, vegetables, pigs and poultry raised on small plots close to the farm house. The ideal farm was an integrated, self-contained and sustainable system. It included arable and pasture and raised crops and livestock. The plough was pulled by horses or oxen, which were fed with fodder crops from the farm. Livestock provided manure, which recycled nutrients into the soil. Rotations of crops and fallow kept the land in good heart. Peas and vetches were grown for fodder, but also had the characteristic of fixing nitrogen in the soil, providing extra nutrients for the next crop. Farm buildings were constructed of timber from hedges and copses, and either stone or mud and straw. Fuel was cut and collected from hedges, copses and rough pasture land. The waste products of dairying, brewing and kitchen scraps were fed to the pigs and poultry.

The variety of rural society came not only from differing property rights and social structures but also from regional and local differences in landscape, farming types and settlement patterns. Farming types reflected differences in climate, topography and soil. The lower rainfall of eastern and midland England made these areas more favourable for arable farming, while the high rainfall in the west provided rich pasture for livestock. Upland areas had a shorter growing season and poorer soils suitable only for less intensive forms of livestock farming. Clay soils were fertile but difficult to cultivate, requiring more animals to draw the plough. Lighter sandy or chalky soils were easier to cultivate, but lost fertility easily: here arable farming was often combined with keeping large flocks of sheep, grazed on rough pasture by day but folded on the arable at night to provide dung for the fields. Joan Thirsk's mapping of the farming systems in early modern England shows both the extent of local variations in farming systems, and the degree to which they changed over time.[8]

Perhaps of even greater significance are the persistent regional differences in settlement patterns and landscape between the 'champion' and 'wood pasture' regions of England. The champion landscape dominated in a broad central band of England stretching from east Yorkshire in the north to Dorset and Hampshire in the south.[9] It was characterised by large nucleated villages; carefully regulated open-field systems; and a lack of hedges, woodland or extensive pasture. This region saw the largest number of deserted villages in the fifteenth century and the most extensive parliamentary enclosures after 1750. To the east and west of this area lay wood pasture regions with more scattered settlements of small villages, hamlets and isolated farms; irregular field-systems that incorporated small enclosed fields; and a greater abundance of trees and pasture. Rural industry was more common in wood pasture regions, and the communal regulation of agriculture and village life weaker. These regional differences had their origins before the Norman Conquest, were recognised by sixteenth-century observers such as John Leland and William Harrison, and are still apparent in the English landscape today.

## Patterns of Change

Both economic and social historians begin their accounts of the transformation of rural society with institutional changes in the structure of landholding. For economic historians these were the prerequisites for increased agricultural productivity, which in turn allowed the non-agricultural population in towns and industries to grow, laying the foundations for the Industrial Revolution. For social historians they were the means by which the peasantry was dispossessed. Therefore, this section begins by exploring institutional changes before moving on to consider productivity and farming methods, and then wage-earning and non-agricultural occupations in the countryside. In each case it is necessary to consider the quantitative data available in some detail. Such data has the potential to reveal the general trends across the whole country over long periods of time, but its reliability needs to be carefully established.

Together the institutional changes of engrossing, enclosure and the spread of leasehold had by the mid nineteenth century transformed a medieval system of landholding into a capitalist one: replacing small farms with large farms of over 100 acres; multiple-use rights with clearly defined proprietors; and manorial land tenures with contractual lease-holds based on market-determined rents. Engrossing, the enlargement of farms, is often seen as a prerequisite for enclosure, and leasehold as a consequence of enclosure, but the three processes were not necessarily closely connected. Of all three, engrossing had the most direct relationship with landlessness and depopulation: increasing farm size tends to reduce the number of farmers. Large farms of 100–300 acres, in the form of manorial demesnes, had long existed, but as the system of labour services by unfree tenants broke down by *c.* 1450, manorial lords leased out these farms. The presence of these large leasehold farms in sixteenth-century England was one the reasons why R. H. Tawney, in his classic account of agrarian change in the sixteenth century, mistakenly concluded that lords were evicting customary tenants and engrossing their holdings into large leasehold farms. In fact, there is no evidence of widespread evictions to support this theory.

Nonetheless, quite apart from demesne farms, a myriad of local studies do suggest that tenant numbers decreased and the land area of individual tenancies increased throughout the period from 1500 to 1750, as well as before and after those dates. But the tracing of changes in farm size over time has been obstructed by one important issue: the amount of land sub-let also increased rapidly over the same time period. Plentiful documentation survives recording the amount of land manorial tenants held from their lords. If those tenants had all farmed the land themselves, this would reveal the size of farms. However, this often was not what happened. Some tenants sublet their land, and thus the size of farms could be quite different from the size of manorial tenancies. Records of subtenures are rare. C. J. Harrison, in a ground-breaking study of Cannock, Staffordshire, found that in 1554 two-thirds of the 1,400 acres of manorial land was sublet. Some tenants sublet all their land and did not farm; others sublet parts of holdings or rented land from others. The real structure of farms was quite different, and more polarised, than the structure of manorial tenancies: there were more farms over 200 acres in size and more smallholdings of less than ten acres.[10] Recent research by Joseph Barker using evidence from poor rates and tithe accounts from fifty communities in four different regions of England demonstrates that subtenure was widespread and significant from at least the late sixteenth century: Cannock was the norm rather than a peculiarity.[11]

The difficulty of documenting subtenures in order to measure farm size has been ingeniously side-stepped by Leigh Shaw-Taylor. He suggests the most important issue in the modernisation of farming, the development of agrarian capitalism, is not the acreage of farms, but whether farmers had to rely on employing wage labour. Rather than reconstructing the exact size of farms, he suggests we should examine the ratio of male farmers to male wage labourers (adequate records for women are lacking). By the time of the 1851 census all the counties of south and east England recorded seven or more hired workers per farmer, showing that the great majority of farms were large capitalist enterprises by that date. Occupational data from early-eighteenth-century parish registers reveals that the ratio was 2.8 hired workers per farmer. This is considerably less than in 1851, but still indicates a capitalist system of farming in which hired agricultural workers outnumbered farmers.[12] Similar types of data can be gathered for earlier dates. In Gloucestershire in 1608 the ratio was 0.6 hired workers per farmer,[13] while in sixteenth-century Norfolk it was 0.8.[14] These figures suggest that in the period before 1650 farms worked with family labour alone were considerably more common, and that the number of wage workers employed in agriculture increased over time.

Enclosure was the physical process of placing a hedge, wall or ditch around a piece of land; but it was also a legal process by which common rights, such as seasonal grazing by other people's animals, over a piece of land were extinguished. In the sixteenth century the Tudor government was alarmed by both engrossing and enclosure, fearing they would undermine England's ability to feed its population. Tawney took his cue from sixteenth-century commentators, assuming engrossing and enclosure were closely connected to each other and reached a peak in the mid sixteenth

Table 7.1 *The chronology of enclosure: percentage of land enclosed during each period.*

| Time period | Wordie (Leicestershire) | Allen (south Midlands incl. Leicestershire) | Wordie (national estimates) |
|---|---|---|---|
| Pre-1550 (W)/pre-1524 (A) | 9.1% | 10.0% | *c.* 45.0% |
| 1500–99 (W)/1525–74(A) | 8.4% | 2.1% | *c.* 2.0% |
| 1600–99 (W)/1575–1674 (A) | 33.7% | 16.7% | *c.* 24.0% |
| 1675–1749 (A) | — | 5.0% | — |
| 1700–99 (W)/1750–1849 (A) | 42.2% | 54.8% | *c.* 13.0% |
| 1800–1914 (W)/1850+ (A) | 6.7% | 3.0% | *c.* 11.4% |

*Sources*: (A) R. C. Allen, *Enclosure and the Yeoman* (Oxford: Oxford University Press, 1992), 31; (W) J. R. Wordie, 'The chronology of English enclosure, 1500–1914', *EcHR*, 36 (1982), 498 and 502.

century. In fact, engrossing and enclosure could be quite independent: small pieces of land were often enclosed and many large farms were open, and attempts to track the chronology of enclosure by Wordie and Allen both suggest that the sixteenth century was a low point in enclosure, as shown in Table 7.1.

Enclosure varied strongly by region. Some English counties, such as Cornwall, Devon, Essex, Kent and Cheshire, had always been very largely enclosed and saw little extra enclosure in the early modern period. Other predominantly wood pasture regions, such as Norfolk and Suffolk, had open but flexible field systems in the medieval period. Regions such as this experienced substantial piecemeal enclosures by individual initiative or local agreements from the fifteenth century onwards. Taking these broad trends into account, J. R. Wordie estimated that for the country as a whole, perhaps 45 per cent of land was already enclosed by the mid sixteenth century. The situation in the champion region of central England was different. Here, stricter open field systems meant it was difficult for lords or tenants to enclosure small pieces of land. Robert Allen's 'south Midlands' and Wordie's Leicestershire, shown in Table 7.1, fall within this region. Here enclosure occurred later, with less than 50 per cent of land enclosed by *c.* 1700, compared to more than 70 per cent nationally.

Table 7.2 *Land values, wheat prices and men's wages compared.*

| | Land values | | Wheat prices | | Male labourers' wages | |
|---|---|---|---|---|---|---|
| | d per acre | index | s per qtr | index | d per day | index |
| 1500–24 | 5.9 | 100 | 6.4 | 100 | 4.0 | 100 |
| 1550–74 | 10.1 | 171 | 14.6 | 228 | 7.3 | 183 |
| 1600–24 | 86.5 | 1466 | 36.6 | 572 | 8.6 | 215 |
| 1650–74 | 106.8 | 1810 | 41.4 | 646 | 11.3 | 283 |
| 1700–24 | 133.0 | 2254 | 33.1 | 517 | 10.7 | 268 |

*Sources*: Land values are market rents per acre for the south Midlands from R. Allen, 'The price of freehold land and the interest rate in the seventeenth and eighteenth centuries', *EcHR*, 41 (1988), 43. Grain prices from J. E. Thorold Rogers, *A History of Agriculture and Prices in England*, Vol. IV (Oxford: Oxford University Press, 1882), 292 (for 1500–74); J. E. Thorold Rogers, *A History of Agriculture and Prices in England*, Vol. V (Oxford: Oxford University Press, 1887), 276 (for 1600–1674); and W. G. Hoskins, 'Harvest fluctuations and English economic history', *Agricultural History Review*, 16 (1968), 30 (for 1700–24). Day wages from G. Clark, 'The long march of history: Farm wages, population and economic growth, England 1209–1869', *EcHR*, 60 (2007), 100 (raw wages).

Unfortunately Wordie's national estimates of the amount of land enclosed in different periods are little more than informed guesses: the variety and intricacy of local patterns of landscape change have discouraged regional studies of enclosure outside the Midland region.

Engrossing and enclosure were associated with a third type of institutional change, the spread of leasehold tenures. Tenure mattered because it determined what proportion of the profits of farming were kept by the farmer, and what proportion were paid to the landlord as rent. Customary tenures such as copyhold and freehold normally had fixed rents that could not be increased. Table 7.2 shows the extent to which land values increased over time (that is sale values and market rents, not manorial rents). Copyhold rents were fixed by custom at around 8d per acre: this was slightly above the market value of land in the early sixteenth century, but by the early seventeenth century it was approximately a tenth of the market value. This transformation over time made customary rents extremely favourable to the tenants and problematic for landlords. Robert Brenner followed Tawney in his influential account of English agrarian change by arguing that landlords attempted to recoup their losses by converting customary tenures to leaseholds or by raising entry fines on customary tenures. Some customary tenures were converted to leasehold in the sixteenth and seventeenth centuries, but the change was often resisted by tenants making it legally complicated and expensive. In addition, the new leasehold tenures were often a form of customary leases known as 'beneficial' leases, which were actually very similar to copyholds for lives and not equivalent to modern contractual leaseholds. Entry fines on customary tenures could not always be raised, as some were fixed by custom; variable entry fines were increased over time, but not enough to compensate fully for the steeply rising land values. Table 7.2 shows that land values rose very rapidly in the late sixteenth and early seventeenth century, a period when the degree of tension between lords and tenants was particularly high, judging by disputes brought to the central courts. While some tenants lost the legal battle to protect their tenures, throughout the sixteenth and seventeenth centuries royal courts upheld customary tenants' rights if they were clearly documented.

Customary land tenures that during the medieval period had served to subjugate the population to manorial lords, had, by the early seventeenth century, become a privileged form of tenure that offered low returns to landlords in comparison to demesne land, which could be leased at market-determined rents. Not all customary tenants were poor farmers; some were gentlemen or lawyers themselves, and collectively tenants often had the wealth and resources to mount legal resistance to manorial lords. Additionally, customary tenants increasingly became landlords themselves. The lack of correspondence between manorial rents and actual land values meant they could choose either to make a living from farming or to follow another occupation and rent out their land for extra income. In many communities it was subtenures let at market rates, rather than the conversion of customary tenures, that led to the spread of contractual tenancies and market-determined rents.

Established accounts of the transformation of early modern rural England from widely differing ideological viewpoints were based on the assumption that institutional changes such as increased farm size, enclosure and leasehold tenures were a necessary prerequisite for increased agricultural productivity. Yet a direct relationship between institutional change and increased productivity has never been established, and a number of recent studies challenge the existence of a close connection. Robert Allen argues that significant productivity increases in the early modern period were achieved on medium-sized yeoman farms in the open fields.[15] Pushing improvements back in time, Bruce Campbell's work on the productivity of manorial demesnes in medieval Norfolk demonstrates that

Table 7.3 *Estimates of crop yields: gross yields per acre.*

| Year | Wheat | | Barley | | Oats | |
|---|---|---|---|---|---|---|
| | Norfolk | England | Norfolk | England | Norfolk | England |
| 1300–48 | 15.6 | 7.8 | 17.2 | 11.7 | 15.0 | 9.9 |
| *c.* 1550 | — | 9.99 | — | 9.0 | — | 10.6 |
| *c.* 1600 | 11.7 | 11.1 | 11.7 | 12.4 | 15.4 | 13.2 |
| *c.* 1650 | — | 13.5 | — | 17.9 | — | 12.1 |
| *c.* 1700 | 14.7 | 14.1 | 15.3 | 19.7 | 20.0 | 10.8 |
| 1750–70 | 25.5 | 15.5 | 30.9 | 26.5 | 38.3 | 23.3 |
| 1800 | 20–24 | 18.7 | 36 | 29.7 | 40.0 | 25.2 |

*Sources*: B. M. S. Campbell and M. Overton, 'A new perspective of medieval and early modern agriculture: Six centuries of Norfolk farming *c.* 1250–*c.* 1850', *P&P*, 141 (1993), 70; S. Broadberry, B. Campbell, A. Klein, M. Overton and B. van Leeuwen, *British Economic Growth, 1270–1870* (Cambridge: Cambridge University Press, 2015), 97.

agricultural innovation and high crop yields were possible without enclosure or leasehold.[16]

The most detailed information about early modern crop yields comes from probate inventories, which survive in their thousands for the period from *c.* 1560 to 1750, but have never been studied comprehensively. Campbell and Overton's most recent estimates for the whole of England are based on inventories from eight English counties, weighted to represent the country as a whole.[17] Their findings show that for England as a whole, yields of all the main crops except rye exceeded medieval levels by the 1600s, improved gradually across the seventeenth century and increased more rapidly after 1700 (see Table 7.3). Norfolk was exceptional in its medieval productivity.

Inventories can only be used to calculate gross yields: that is, how much grain was harvested from a particular area. This is a crude measure. Gross yields can be increased in many ways that do not indicate new and improved agricultural methods. Sowing crops only in the best soils would increase yields, as would sowing a crop more densely, but neither of these strategies would necessarily increase a farmer's profits. Yields can also be raised by using more labour to intensify cultivation, but this reduces the labour productivity of agriculture. It is labour productivity (the amount of crop yield that can be produced with a given number of days' labour) that is most important for the development of the economy as a whole: increased labour productivity releases a higher proportion of the population from agriculture to work in industry or live in towns. Moreover, it should also be emphasised that grain yields reveal nothing about the other farm products – most importantly, livestock.

Early modern agriculture was more pastoral than earlier or later periods: more land was put down to pasture rather than ploughed. Pastoral agriculture requires less labour than arable, but produces fewer food calories per acre. The technical improvements in agriculture that were introduced or became more widespread in England between 1600 and 1750 were all concerned with improving fodder for livestock. These included the floating of water meadows to improve hay production, the increased sowing of 'improved' grasses such as vetches and clover, and the introduction of turnips and clover into crop rotations. While livestock numbers held fairly steady over the early modern period, the meat and milk produced per animal increased.[18]

Estimates of the growing proportion of the population not working in agriculture and the absence of any severe subsistence crises in early modern England do suggest that the labour productivity of agriculture increased between 1500 and 1750. It is possible that the increased reliance on wage labour, rather than unpaid family labour, encouraged farmers to be more efficient in their use of labour as a resource. However, labour is not just another 'input' into the farm economy, it is a way of life. Transforming the nature of agricultural labour meant transforming the nature of rural society.

To what extent did this transformation take place in early modern England? Shaw-Taylor's ratio of 1 farmer to every 2.8 labourers in the early eighteenth century translates into a farming population where 26 per cent were farmers and 74 per cent wage labourers. The ratio for sixteenth-century Norfolk, one of the most highly commercialised agricultural regions at that time, of 0.8 hired workers per farmer translates into a farming population of 56 per cent farmers and 44 per cent hired workers. Dyer uses tax returns to estimate that in 1522–5 around 50 per cent of the population were dependent on wages for a living.[19] For the early eighteenth century, Muldrew estimates that 70 per cent of the rural population were dependent on wages.[20] All these figures suggest the increase over time is not as dramatic as some earlier commentators assumed, but nonetheless indicate a tipping of the balance away from small family farms towards large farms that relied on wage labour during the seventeenth century.[21]

As well as the numbers of wage workers, the nature of wage labour, and its relationship to landholding, were also important to the nature of rural society. In early modern England, wage earners were a mixture of servants and day labourers. Servants were mostly young, unmarried people who lived with their employers, receiving around three-quarters of their wages in the form of board and lodging. In contrast, day labourers tended to be married householders who were paid by the day or task. They too often received food and drink with their wages, but it rarely made up more than one-third of the payment. Servants outnumbered day labourers in rural England throughout the early modern period. Muldrew found that there were 1.9 male servants per male labourer in Gloucestershire in 1608, and 1.7 servants per labourer (of both sexes) in various village censuses dating from 1688 to 1750.[22]

The growing gap between land values and wages altered the structural role of wage earning. Wage earning was transformed from a predominantly life-cycle phase to a lifetime condition. In the early sixteenth century it was possible for young men and women who had not inherited land to pool their earnings from years in service to purchase a landholding. After the late-sixteenth- and early-seventeenth-century rise in land values this was no longer possible. Instead, they could only hope to rent a house and continue to make a living from wage-earning or industrial work. That is not to say that labourers were always landless. Probate inventories, despite being likely to record only the better off, reveal that even in the early eighteenth century, 44 per cent of labourers owned cows.[23] The examples of Richard Wix and Richard Latham at the start of this chapter illustrate how households combined a number of ways of making a living, including earning wages. Muldrew's detailed reconstruction of labourers' household budgets, which factors in home production and the work of wives and children, suggests that there were significant fluctuations in standards of living over time. The household surplus, once food, clothing, fuel and rent are allowed for, stood at £8 10s in 1568, but deteriorated markedly to a deficit of −£11 6s in 1597 and was still in deficit at −£1 8s in 1625, largely as a result of high grain prices. This indicates that such households were failing to make ends meet in the early seventeenth century, and may well have had to sell capital assets such as land, livestock or tools to purchase food. But incomes recovered in the late seventeenth and eighteenth century, to a positive balance of £4 1s in 1690 and £19 2s in 1760. An important contribution to this upturn in fortunes was women's increased earnings from spinning, a consequence of the expanding textile industry.[24]

This last point is a reminder that the agricultural and industrial economies were not separate in early modern England, but intertwined within rural households. Wrigley makes a rough estimate that the 'rural non-agricultural population' grew almost as fast as England's urban population between 1520 and 1750, from 18.5 per cent to 33 per cent of the national population.[25] Wrigley's assumptions about increased non-agricultural employment in the countryside are supported by other studies. Men's occupational descriptions in East Anglian wills demonstrate significant increases in the number of rural parishes supporting common trades such as tailors, carpenters, shoemakers and butchers between 1500 and 1700. The number of parishes with retailers also increased from 1.6 per cent to 8.6 per cent, while the biggest increase was found in occupations associated with the linen industry, found in only 1.1 per cent of parishes in the sixteenth century, but 23.0 per cent by 1650–99.[26] With regard to women's employment, it is possible that the proportion of women and girls across England employed in spinning increased from 11.5 per cent in 1590 to 22.6 per cent in 1750.[27]

Research over the last forty years indicates that social and economic change in early modern rural England was less dramatic than had previously been assumed: farm size grew, more land was enclosed, leasehold became more common, agricultural productivity increased, the proportion of wage labourers increased and non-agricultural employment became more important, but in many cases significant change had already occurred by 1500, and more rapid changed occurred after 1750. However, it is nonetheless clear that an important tipping point in rural society, from one dominated by small farmers to one in which wage labouring was the main occupation for men, did occur between the late sixteenth and early eighteenth century. It is also clear that the period between *c.* 1580 and *c.* 1640 was one of particularly rapid change and social distress, during which land prices rose beyond the means of wage earners and small farmers, and wages failed to provide an adequate living.

## Mechanisms of Change

There are a number of competing models of economic development in pre-industrial societies: demographic models stress the consequences of population growth and decline; Marxist models emphasise the importance of property rights and conflict between classes; neoclassical models prioritise market forces and commercialisation in determining change over time. While demography, class conflict and commercialisation are often seen as separate models, the most effective explanations of change over time combine elements of all three approaches.

The contours of population change in early modern England are shown in Table 7.4. From a high point of perhaps 4.8 million in 1348 on the eve

Table 7.4 *Population totals, age at marriage and proportion never married, 1524–1751.*

| Year | Population totals (millions) | Average age at first marriage for women | Percentage of population aged 40–4 but never married |
|------|------|------|------|
| 1524 | 2.4 | — | — |
| 1551 | 3.1 | — | — |
| 1576 | 3.4 | — | — |
| 1601 | 4.2 | — | 6.7 |
| 1626 | 4.8 | 25.2 | 17.4 |
| 1651 | 5.3 | 25.6 | 23.6 |
| 1676 | 5.2 | 26.2 | 20.8 |
| 1701 | 5.2 | 26.0 | 24.9 |
| 1726 | 5.6 | 25.9 | 14.7 |
| 1751 | 5.9 | 25.0 | 10.7 |

*Sources*: E. A. Wrigley, R. S. Davies, J. E. Oeppen and R. S. Schofield, *English Population History from Family Reconstitution* (Cambridge: Cambridge University Press, 1997), 134 and 614; E. A. Wrigley and R. S. Schofield, *The Population History of England 1541–1871: A Reconstruction* (Cambridge: Cambridge University Press, 1989), 260 and 568.

of the Black Death, England's population levels fell significantly before beginning to grow again sometime between 1450 and the early sixteenth century.[28] From 2.4 million in the 1520s, the total had doubled by the 1620s, and continued to grow to a peak of 5.4 million in the 1650s. The late seventeenth century brought a slight decline to 5.0 million in the 1680s, followed by renewed growth to 5.4 million in the 1710s and 6.0 million by the 1750s. Thereafter, population grew rapidly to 8.7 million by 1801.[29] Thus the high point in England's medieval population before the Black Death was not significantly exceeded until the mid eighteenth century.

In relatively self-contained, organic economies, like that of early modern England, population change is intimately connected to agricultural production. As Thomas Malthus observed in his *Essay on the Principle of Population* (1798) population levels could not exceed the supply of food necessary to support that population. If the population began to outstretch the food that could be produced by the agrarian economy, a 'positive' check of increased mortality via malnutrition, increased susceptibility to disease or starvation resulted. This situation could be avoided by 'preventative' checks, which reduced fertility levels. In early modern England, a powerful preventative check operated via marriage conventions. A 'north-west European household formation system' existed in which couples married relatively late and set up a new household at marriage, once they had acquired the wealth and skills necessary to live independently from their parents.[30] Late marriage and the accumulation of wealth were facilitated by the fact young people circulated between households, working as live-in servants and earning wages before marriage. Ann Kussmaul estimates that 60 per cent of the 15-to-24 age group were employed as servants in early modern England.[31] As the population grew, real wages fell and property prices increased, making it more difficult for young people to acquire the necessary resources to marry and set up a household. This caused the average age at first marriage to increase, and encouraged a larger proportion of the population not to marry. As social conventions strongly discouraged births outside marriage, the birth rate fell. This mechanism can be seen in operation in the seventeenth and early eighteenth centuries when the average age at first marriage for women was as high as twenty-eight in many parishes, and by 1701 a quarter of the population reached their early forties without marrying.[32]

Robert Brenner's Marxist account of England's economic development observes that population growth (or decline) can have opposite effects depending on the nature of property rights and the balance of class forces. He pointed out that in the medieval period population growth led to the fragmentation of farms, as landholdings were split to accommodate more people, whereas in the sixteenth century, population growth led to engrossing, with farms increasing in size. Karl Marx argued that in feudal, pre-capitalist societies the two main classes – lords and tenants – were locked in conflict over the level of rent. It was this conflict or 'class struggle' that determined who accumulated the profits of farming, the main form of wealth produced by the economy, and it was this, Brenner argues, that determined the course of economic development. Class conflict between lords and tenants over the level of rents and other payments, and land-use issues such as enclosure, certainly existed in early modern England. And the consequences of the (mostly) legal battles fought by lords and tenants over those issues were of great significance for particular communities. However, Brenner argued that tenants were the overall losers of these conflicts in the sixteenth century, and this allowed landlords to create large leasehold farms worked with wage labour. This account, borrowed from Tawney, has been shown to be largely erroneous: on the whole customary tenants were quite successful in defending their use-rights and terms of tenure, as argued above.

Significant though it was, over-emphasis on the conflict between manorial lords and tenants risks overlooking other types of conflict that were

inherent in early modern rural society. Subtenants (the tenants of manorial tenants) suffered higher rents and less security of tenure than manorial tenants, and their numbers swelled from the mid sixteenth century
onwards. Large farmers sought to keep labour costs down while agricultural workers sought a living wage. When actual disputes over enclosure
or rents are studied, there is very rarely a clear division between 'modernising' landlords on one hand, and impoverished tenants on the other.
Sometimes lords sided with the majority of tenants against individual
tenants who sought to enclose. In other cases, the tenants who opposed
higher rents or new tenures included wealthy gentlemen who had purchased customary land. The shared resources and conflicting economic
interests of rural society created multiple tensions and alliances.

Looking more closely at how the prices for different elements of the
agrarian economy changed over time in relation to each other can be surprisingly informative (see Table 7.2). A combination of population growth
and monetary inflation is one explanation of why the price of grain and
land rose during the sixteenth century: with the population doubling,
less was available per person. But population growth does not explain
why land values had increased so much more steeply than wheat prices
by the mid seventeenth century. Instead, it is necessary to consider who
was participating in the land market, and what resources they had. In the
medieval period, the unfree status attached to peasant landholdings discouraged gentlemen and townsmen from purchasing them. This placed a
ceiling on the price of land, and ensured land circulated only within the
peasantry. In the sixteenth and seventeenth centuries, customary land no
longer held this taint, and was increasingly purchased and accumulated by
wealthy landowners. As land values outpaced the customary rents paid to
manorial lords, customary land became an increasingly attractive investment, pushing land values still higher.

It is also important to note that variations in grain prices affected different sections of the rural population very differently. It is clear enough that
when grain prices rose faster than wages, the standard of living of wage
labourers, who relied on purchasing bread, was adversely affected. What
is less commonly realised is that fluctuations in grain prices caused by
harvest quality had varying effects on different-sized farms. Good harvests
caused the price of grain to fall, and bad harvests caused it to rise steeply.
A small farmer with 10 acres might make a profit of £2 10s in a normal
year, after grain had been put aside for next year's seed and household
consumption. If the harvest was 50 per cent better than normal, profits
increased slightly to £3, because although prices fell the farmer had more

to sell. If the harvest was 50 per cent worse than normal, however, the small farmer fell into debt, making a loss of £13 17s. Not only did he have no surplus to sell, wiping out his profits, but he also lacked enough grain to feed his family, and therefore had to purchase grain at very high prices. A large farmer with 100 acres might make a profit of £70 in a normal year by selling grain. In a year with a very good harvest and low grain prices, this profit fell to £48. However, in a year with a bad harvest, when small farmers fell into debt, the large farmer could still feed his household and make bumper profits of £110 12s by selling his reduced surplus at very high prices.[33] Bad years provided the incentive and means for small farmers to abandon farming, and large farmers to accumulate more land. Historians have struggled to find widespread examples of manorial lords evicting small customary tenants. The effects of bad harvests and rising land values combined offer an alternative mechanism by which small tenants abandoned farming, farm size grew over time, and the proportion of wage earners and those with non-agricultural occupations increased.

In a subsistence economy the incentive is for farmers to raise as wide a range of crops and livestock as possible in order to spread the risk of crop failure and animal disease and provide varied consumption. Elements of this strategy are evident in medieval England, with crops grown in every locality. The switch towards a more pastoral economy in early modern England was a movement towards greater specialisation. Farmers in upland and western England, and other areas with poorly drained soils, increasingly abandoned arable farming.[34] To do so they must have been sufficiently confident that they could buy the grain they needed, and thus that England had an effective internal grain trade. In some cases this confidence may have been misplaced: parts of north-west England suffered from severe dearth and some deaths from food shortage in the late sixteenth and early seventeenth century.[35] On the other hand, the great famine of 1315–18, in which an estimated 15 per cent of the population of southern and eastern England died, was never repeated.

Another way of viewing the extent of commercialisation is to consider geographical scales of self-sufficiency. Peasant households are often presented as self-sufficient; however, this mode of existence had already died out by the date of the first detailed documentation of English rural society in the thirteenth century. Instead medieval England was characterised by a high degree of self-sufficiency within localities, defined as village communities grouped around particular market towns, although some foodstuffs and fuel were traded beyond this scope, for instance to supply London. Wool was the main export. By the period 1500–1650 the English economy was more regionally integrated, with a long-distance internal trade in grain and livestock well established. Trade with continental Europe increased: England exported growing quantities of woollen cloth, while the majority of imports were also agricultural products, most significantly linen and silk cloth, wine, dried fruit, and sugar.[36] After 1650 there was another qualitative change in the nature of trade. England became integrated into global networks importing calicoes from India and sugar from the Americas, as well as expanding exports of woollen cloth.

These changes permeated rural England. Shops were rare outside urban centres before 1600. Yet it is estimated that by 1750 there was one shop for every 41.4 people in England, with almost as many shops per person across rural southern and eastern England as there were in London.[37] Small rural shops sold local foodstuffs such as butter and cheese, and English textiles, but also foreign goods that had rapidly become everyday necessities: sugar, tea and tobacco. Many rural inhabitants depended for their living on producing goods from the international economy, particularly spinning and weaving textiles. Agricultural profits benefited from the growing number of non-farmers needing food. The self-contained English economy dependent on the products of the land, as presented by Malthus and others, was further undermined by the increased use of coal. English coal production increased from 177,000 tons in the 1560s, to 24 times that amount in the 1750s (over 4 million tons). Coal replaced fuel such as wood and charcoal which took up land, freeing land for other uses. Wrigley estimates that in 1700, when English coal output stood at 2.2 million tons, 'to have provided the same heat energy from wood on a sustained yield basis would have required devoting 2–3 million acres to woodland'.[38]

The changing nature of rural society underpinned the increased commercialisation of early modern England. In the late sixteenth and early seventeenth century the class of prosperous farmers, wealthy yeomen and gentry, like Robert Loder and the Le Stranges, grew in size. They rebuilt their houses, furnished them with an increasing range of goods, and ate and dressed well. The number of wage earners also grew as many small farmers lost access to land (or failed to acquire land in the first place) and relied more heavily on wages. Out of necessity, rural households with little land, such as that of Richard Wix, were heavily dependent on the market. While many rural workers in the early seventeenth century suffered the dire consequences of low real wages and barely scraped a living, in the late seventeenth and early eighteenth century industrial production and foreign trade combined to improve employment prospects and reduce the cost of purchased goods.

While it is almost impossible to measure changes in farm size over time, the attitude towards small farms certainly changed. For late-eighteenth-century commentators like Arthur Young, farms of 4 acres or less were not farms at all, they were an irrelevance to the business of agriculture. For Elizabethan legislators, 4 acres was the amount of land a cottager needed to retain a degree of independence and avoid reliance on charity or crime. In thirteenth- and fourteenth-century Norfolk 4 acres was a peasant landholding: on many manors the average size of land-holding was between 2 and 6 acres – having such a smallholding was the majority experience. The old stories of social and economic change in rural England between 1500 and 1750 stressed either the forcible dis-possession of the peasantry to create a new class of wage labourers or triumphalist economic improvements in which enclosure removed feudal inefficiencies and agricultural yields rose paving the way for England's industrialisation. New accounts are less clear-cut, and the fragility of the evidence means that much is still open for further investigation. Rather than landlords evicting tenants, the role of the land market and subtenure loom large. Enclosure was not closely linked with agricultural improve-ment, and the scale and motivations of enclosure before 1750 need careful reconsideration. While there is evidence of increased agricultural produc-tivity, it is less spectacular and more uneven than was once supposed. The same can be said about the increasing number of wage earners in rural England. Changing patterns of waged work in agriculture and the growth in non-agricultural forms of rural employment demand further research attention. The spread of village shops in the eighteenth century demonstrates the emergence of a new form of consumerism, dependent in part on imported goods, but the exact progress of commercialisation, measured as the increased dependence of rural households on purchased goods over time, is still unclear. After 1750, as Wrigley has convincingly argued, came the biggest rupture of all: reliance on coal as an energy source meant that England ceased to be an organic economy. From the 1790s England became a net importer of food, and by 1841 the majority of England's population was urban: it was no longer an agrarian society and agriculture was just one type of industry among many.

### Notes

1 G. E. Fussell (ed.), *Robert Loder's Farm Accounts 1610–1620*, Camden Society, 3rd series, 53 (London, 1936).
2 J. Whittle, 'The house as a place of work in early modern rural England', *Home Cultures*, 8 (2011).

3  C. Foster, *Seven Households: Life in Cheshire and Lancashire 1582–1774* (Northwich: Arley Hall, 2002), 142–71.

4  B. M. S. Campbell and M. Overton, 'A new perspective of medieval and early modern agriculture: Six centuries of Norfolk farming *c*. 1250–*c*. 1850', *P&P*, 141 (1993), 70 and 74.

5  C. Dyer, *An Age of Transition? Economy and Society in England in the Later Middle Ages* (Oxford: Oxford University Press, 2005), 220.

6  E. A. Wrigley, *People, Cities and Wealth* (Oxford: Oxford University Press, 1987), 170.

7  M. Overton, *Agricultural Revolution in England: The Transformation of the Agrarian Economy 1500–1850* (Cambridge: Cambridge University Press, 1996), 75.

8  J. Thirsk, *England's Agricultural Regions and Agrarian History, 1500–1750* (Basingstoke: Macmillan, 1987).

9  T. Williamson, *Shaping Medieval Landscapes: Settlement, Society, Environment* (Macclesfield: Windgather Press, 2003).

10  C. J. Harrison, 'Elizabethan village surveys: A comment', *Agricultural History Review*, 27 (1979).

11  J. Barker, 'The emergence of agrarian capitalism in early modern England: A reconsideration of farm sizes', unpublished Ph.D. thesis, Cambridge University (2013).

12  L. Shaw-Taylor, 'The rise of agrarian capitalism and the decline of family farming in England', *EcHR*, 65 (2012).

13  A. J. Tawney and R. H. Tawney, 'An occupational census of the seventeenth century', *EcHR*, 5 (1934), 47.

14  J. Whittle, *The Development of Agrarian Capitalism: Land and Labour in Norfolk 1440–1580* (Oxford: Oxford University Press, 2000), 236.

15  R. C. Allen, *Enclosure and the Yeoman* (Oxford: Oxford University Press, 1992), 208; R. C. Allen, *The British Industrial Revolution in Global Perspective* (Cambridge: Cambridge University Press, 2009), 59.

16  Campbell and Overton, 'A new perspective'.

17  S. Broadberry, B. Campbell, A. Klein, M. Overton and B. van Leeuwen, *British Economic Growth, 1270–1870* (Cambridge: Cambridge University Press, 2015), 84 and 97. The counties are Cornwall, Durham, Hertfordshire, Kent, Lincolnshire, Norfolk, Suffolk, Worcestershire.

18  *Ibid.*, 100–10.

19  Dyer, *An Age of Transition?*, 220.

20  C. Muldrew, *Food, Energy and the Creation of Industriousness: Work and Material Culture in Agrarian England, 1550–1780* (Cambridge: Cambridge University Press, 2011), 283.

21  For national estimates of the number of wage labourers see Chapter 14 in the present volume, 317–318.

22  Muldrew, *Food*, 222.

23  *Ibid.*, 250.

24  *Ibid.*, 215, 217, 257.

25 Wrigley, *People, Cities, Wealth*, 168–71.

26 J. Patten, 'Changing occupational structures in the East Anglian countryside, 1500–1700', in H. S. A. Fox and R. A. Butlin (eds.), *Change in the Countryside: Essays on Rural England, 1500–1900* (London: Institute of British Geographers, 1979).

27 Calculated from C. Muldrew, '"Th'ancient distaff" and "whirling spindle": Measuring the contribution of spinning to household earnings and the national economy in England', *EcHR*, 65 (2012), 518.

28 Broadberry *et al.*, *British Economic Growth*, 20. Other estimates put the medieval high point at 5–6 million; see J. Hatcher, *Plague, Population and the English Economy 1348–1530* (London: Macmillan, 1977), 71.

29 E. A. Wrigley, R. S. Davies, J. E. Oeppen and R. S. Schofield, *English Population History from Family Reconstitution* (Cambridge: Cambridge University Press, 1997), 614.

30 J. Hajnal, 'Two kinds of pre-industrial household formation system', in R. Wall (ed.), *Family Forms in Historic Europe* (Cambridge: Cambridge University Press, 1983).

31 A. Kussmaul, *Servants in Husbandry in Early Modern England* (Cambridge: Cambridge University Press, 1981), 3.

32 Wrigley *et al.*, *English Population History*, 134 and 184–5; E. A. Wrigley and R. S. Schofield, *The Population History of England 1541–1871: A Reconstruction* (Cambridge: Cambridge University Press, 1989), 255 and 260.

33 Overton, *Agricultural Revolution*, 21.

34 Thirsk, *England's Agricultural Regions*.

35 A. B. Appleby, *Famine in Tudor and Stuart England* (Liverpool: Liverpool University Press, 1978).

36 C. G. A. Clay, *Economic Expansion and Social Change: England 1500–1700*, Vol. II: *Industry, Trade and Government* (Cambridge: Cambridge University Press, 1984), 125.

37 H. Mui and L. H. Mui, *Shops and Shopkeeping in Eighteenth Century England* (London: Routledge, 1989), 40.

38 E. A. Wrigley, *Energy and the Industrial Revolution* (Cambridge: Cambridge University Press, 2010), 37–9. The total area devoted to arable agriculture in 1700 is estimated at 9.56 million acres; Broadberry *et al.*, *British Economic Growth*, 74.

# 8

## Urbanisation

### Phil Withington

In 1621 Robert Burton moaned that 'The Low countries have three cities at least for one of ours, and those far more populous and rich', singular in their 'industry and excellency in all manner of trades'. England, in contrast, had 'swarms of rogues and beggars, thieves, drunkards and discontented persons, many poor people in all our Towns, *Civitates ignobiles* as Polydore calls them, base cities, inglorious, poor, small, and rare in sight, and thin of inhabitants'. In sum, '*England ... (London only excepted) hath never a populous city, and [is] yet a fruitful country.*'[1]

Until recently this depiction of English towns and cities has resonated with English urban historians of the early modern period in at least three respects. First, just as Burton invoked a depleted urban culture haunted by the spectre of poverty, so the prevailing interpretative paradigm has been 'crisis'.[2] The thriving communities of the medieval era are understood to have experienced cultural decline, economic trauma, and pronounced social stratification and conflict during the sixteenth and early seventeenth centuries.[3] It was only after 1660 that an English 'urban renaissance' is thought to have seen the rejuvenation of many older settlements and the emergence of new industrial centres that broke the mould of the traditional urban system.[4] Secondly, just as Burton singled out London as the exception to this rule, so historians have viewed the metropolis as an English urban anomaly – a place that experienced its own problems but also had a distinct and, indeed, positive impact on English society and economy more generally.[5] The division of labour between metropolitan and provincial historiography has only served to compound this sense of London's uniqueness.[6] Thirdly, and perhaps most importantly, just as Burton described a relative urban deficit in England so 'the urban' is a less than conspicuous feature of English social historiography. Peter Laslett did not regard towns and cities as a prominent part of 'the world we have lost', describing early modern England as 'a rural hinterland attached to a vast metropolis through a network of insignificant local centres'. Even metropolitan London was less 'a civic site', than a landscape of 'village communities'.[7]

This chapter argues, in contrast, that early modern England was a more urban society than has generally been acknowledged and that it became more so over time. As Burton intimates, towns and cities undoubtedly faced challenges over the period. However, more recent studies suggest that there were fair amounts of economic opportunity and affluence as well as cultural fecundity and innovation.[8] More to the point, while English towns and cities themselves underwent considerable expansion over the period, they were also implicated in, and often integral to, a wide range of practices, processes and identities that are not generally recognised as especially 'urban'. As a result, the full importance and burgeoning extent of urbanism in early modern England is less appreciated than in the Low Countries or Italy, where, as both Burton and Laslett note, cities were much more prominent as places and urban culture more celebrated.

The argument takes its cue from Jan de Vries's observation that urbanisation can be understood in three ways: as 'demographic', or increased numbers of people living in cities and towns; as 'structural', or the kind of institutions and activities situated in urban centres; and as 'behavioural', or the kinds of attitudes and practices associated with urbanism whether situated in towns and cities or not.[9] In demographic terms alone, urbanisation was a defining feature of the era: by 1700 the number and size of English urban settlements was growing faster than in any country in Europe, and London, at the centre of a national and international urban system, had become the continent's largest city. But the structural and behavioural aspects of urbanisation mean that its significance in England extended far beyond the city walls. This is because many of the historical processes now associated with early modernity depended on institutions that were primarily – if not uniquely – urban. This is as true of commerce and the emergence of the early modern market economy as it is of schooling, literacy, print technology and the communication of knowledge and ideas; of law and litigiousness; of governance and the growth of the state; of transatlantic colonialism and empire. All of these processes were rooted in and articulated through the English urban system, even as they had national and international ramifications; but rarely is the urban dynamic of these more general social developments recognised.

What follows suggests that these wider ramifications can be understood in three, interrelated ways. First, the urban system played a *connective* role in English society that was altogether more than the sum of its individual or collective parts. Secondly, the proliferation of urban institutions – both 'medieval' and 'modern' – was *constitutive* of more general social and economic processes to a degree that belies their historiographical neglect. Thirdly, urban culture was *congruent* with some of the key cultural trends and characteristics of the era, so much so that the urban provenance or antecedents of these trends are often lost. These connective, constitutive and congruent aspects of English urbanism were mutually reinforcing and therefore difficult to disaggregate: people visited or lived in cities because of the institutions and resources they provided; they learned and disseminated urban-based habits and goods as a result. The connective, constitutive and congruent consequences of English urbanisation nevertheless reveal the wider social, economic, political and cultural importance of towns and cities long before the 'urban renaissance'. They also point to a particular kind of urbanism that is different from the Dutch and Italian models: one that is not distinct from other kinds of social organisation, in the manner of the autonomous city state, so much as integral to regional, national and imperial life – so integral, indeed, that it can often be invisible to either the contemporary or the historical eye.

In 1500 just over 3 per cent of English and Welsh people lived in cities of over 10,000 people or more – a larger proportion than in Scotland, Ireland and Scandinavia; a similar proportion to the much more populous France; a much smaller proportion than northern Italy, Belgium and the Netherlands (Table 8.1 and Figure 8.1). By 1600 that figure had risen to almost 6 per cent; by 1700 it was over 13 per cent; by 1800 it was over 20 per cent – this when the national population rose from just under 3 million people to above 6 million people over the same period. This rate of urbanisation remained similar to France until 1700, when the French urban population reached a plateau of 9.2 per cent, declining slightly thereafter; it was much higher than Scotland until the second half of the eighteenth century, and it completely eclipsed rates of urbanisation in Scandinavia and Ireland. Comparison with urbanised regions offers a different perspective again. Northern Italy and Belgium retained relatively large and stable urban populations throughout the period; but England was proportionally more urbanised than northern Italy by 1750 and Belgium by 1800. Indeed, of the countries grouped here, only the Netherlands surpassed English and Welsh rates of urbanisation over the period, and even these regressed in the eighteenth century.

These figures show that the British Isles were unusual in their constant urbanisation across the entire period. Moreover, in England and Wales this trajectory coincided both with rapid national increases in population

Table 8.1 *Urban percentage of total population, 1500–1800 (cities over 10,000).*

|  | 1500 | 1550 | 1600 | 1650 | 1700 | 1750 | 1800 |
|---|---|---|---|---|---|---|---|
| England/Wales | 3.1 | 3.5 | 5.8 | 8.8 | 13.3 | 16.7 | 20.3 |
| Ireland | 0 | 0 | 0 | 0.9 | 3.4 | 5.0 | 7.0 |
| Scotland | 1.6 | 1.4 | 3.0 | 3.5 | 5.3 | 9.2 | 17.3 |
| Scandinavia | 0.9 | 0.8 | 1.4 | 2.4 | 4.0 | 4.6 | 4.6 |
| Netherlands | 15.8 | 15.3 | 24.3 | 31.7 | 33.6 | 30.5 | 28.8 |
| Belgium | 21.1 | 22.7 | 18.8 | 20.8 | 23.9 | 19.6 | 18.9 |
| Northern Italy | — | 15.1 | 16.6 | 14.3 | 13.6 | 14.2 | 14.3 |
| France | 4.2 | 4.3 | 5.9 | 7.2 | 9.2 | 9.1 | 8.8 |

*Source*: J. de Vries, *European Urbanization 1500–1800* (London: Methuen, 1984), 38–40.

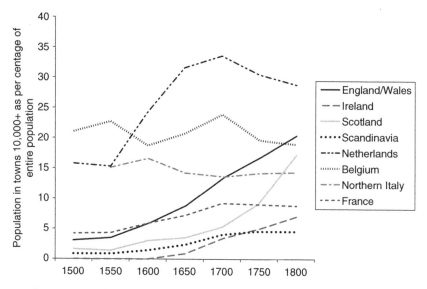

Figure 8.1 Population in towns over 10,000 as a percentage of entire population.

(between the 1520s and 1640 and again after 1750) and periods of national stagnation and decline (most notably in the fifty years after 1650). Of course, the threshold of 10,000 or more is a crude index of urbanism. Even if urbanisation is understood purely in demographic terms then many urban settlements, especially in this period, were much smaller than

Table 8.2 *Cities in England and Wales by size of settlement, 1520–1750*
*(population figures in 000s).*

| | 1520 | | | 1600 | | | 1700 | | | 1750 | | |
|---|---|---|---|---|---|---|---|---|---|---|---|---|
| | (no.) | pop. | % | (no.) | pop. | % | (no.) | pop. | % | (no.) | pop. | % |
| London | (1) | 55 | 1.9 | (1) | 200 | 4.5 | (1) | 575 | 10.6 | (1) | 675 | 11 |
| 10,000+ | (4) | 40 | 1.4 | (5) | 55 | 1.3 | (10) | 143 | 2.6 | (20) | 346 | 5.7 |
| 5–9,999 | (5) | 30 | 1.1 | (14) | 85 | 1.9 | (22) | 145 | 2.7 | (30) | 210 | 3.0 |
| 2.5–4,999 | | | | (15) | 45 | 1.0 | (37) | 120 | 2.2 | (79) | 245 | 4.0 |
| **Total population** | | 2,850 | | | 4,400 | | | 5,400 | | | 6,100 | | |

(no.) = number of settlements; pop. = population estimates; % = proportion of national population.
*Source*: J. de Vries, *European Urbanization 1500–1800* (London: Methuen, 1984), 64.

this. Neither does it give any sense of the hierarchy of settlement within England and Wales, nor the proportion of population living across the urban system. Table 8.2 attempts to provide some nuance by dividing urban settlements by population size and showing the number of types, their aggregate population, and their proportion of the national population between 1520 and 1750. Immediately striking are the importance of London to English and Welsh urbanisation, particularly during the sixteenth century, and the increasing prominence of smaller settlements, especially settlements of over 10,000 inhabitants, after 1600. Even as late as 1800 the metropolis accounted for almost half the urban population of England and Wales.

E. A. Wrigley demonstrated long ago that the importance of the metropolis extended far beyond its urban and suburban boundaries. Wrigley argued not only that England was unique in sustaining demographic urbanisation throughout the early modern period, but that this growth precipitated a host of economic, demographic and sociological changes that together point to the deep urban roots of the Industrial Revolution. Economically these included the formation of a national market, a doubling of agricultural production, greater demand for and provision of raw materials (like coal and lead), the better provision of credit and commercial facilities, improved transport networks, and higher real wages. Demographically, the realities of urban morbidity insured a balanced regime in which population did not expand too rapidly beyond available resources. Sociologically, it institutionalised what he styles 'rational' rather than 'traditional' attitudes and behaviour, allowed new kinds of social mobility and social groupings, and encouraged more fluid and emulative patterns of consumption. For Wrigley, all of these urban-induced or urban-related changes help to explain England's industrial 'take off' in the second half of the eighteenth century.[10]

Wrigley's 'simple model' is the obvious starting point for any consideration of the wider significance of English urbanisation. The aim here is not to engage with its central hypothesis – the deep urban origins of English industrialisation – so much as to backdate and historically situate his story. Wrigley focuses on demographic urbanisation *after* 1650 because it is the concentration of large populations in both London and the northern industrial cities that precipitates economic modernity. What this focus misses, however, is that in the hundred or so years before 1650 the metropolis was already becoming the burgeoning hub to an increasing number of cities and towns within this system: that early modern urbanisation involved the revivification, invigoration and expansion of medieval urbanism as well as the emergence of what Ann Kussmaul styled new urban 'agglomerations'.[11]

The geography of the medieval urban system is nicely captured by Charles Phythian Adams's depictions of 'pre-modern' England and Wales as fourteen 'cultural provinces'. These 'cultural provinces' were amalgamations of counties and 'local societies' that shared a common cultural inheritance based on their ecology and environment; customs and dialects; spatial propinquity; and, most importantly, water-borne transport networks by which goods and people moved. According to Phythian Adams, rivers, estuaries and coastlines 'orientated' these provinces in particular directions and gave them their primary characteristics, and he named them accordingly (see Figure 8.2).[12] Far from being static and immemorial organic entities, however, these provinces and local societies were defined by geographical mobility both internally, in terms of quotidian movement and settlement over short distances, and externally, in terms of regularised long-distance commerce, exchange and migration according to their geographical orientation. Moreover, each cultural province possessed an urban hierarchy that included provincial capitals, such as Norwich and Chester; county towns and specialised urban centres, such as Yarmouth and Ipswich, or Preston and Liverpool; and market towns and townships, such as Thetford and Wigan.

Each of these types of settlement performed important roles within their locale and together formed provincial urban systems that structured the mobility and commerce that defined local and provincial life. On the one

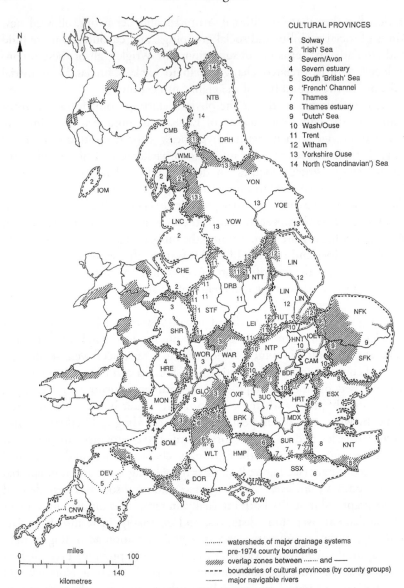

Figure 8.2 The 'cultural provinces' of pre-modern England and Wales. From C. Phythian-Adams, *Societies, Cultures and Kinship, 1580–1850: Cultural Provinces and English Local History* (Leicester: Leicester University Press, 1996), xvii. © C. Phythian-Adams 1996. Reproduced by permission of Bloomsbury Publishing plc.

hand, therefore, cultural provinces formed distinct 'countries' in which towns and cities were integral to a local sense of identity and belonging. On the other hand, local and provincial urban networks also connected with the national urban system, through London, and also international trading systems, via both the metropolis and the provincial ports.

The connective role and power of cities and towns that this suggests is most clearly evidenced by the economic structures and developments that underpinned the early modern growth of London. As Keith Wrightson argues, *circa* 1500 'the market' already existed as 'four overlapping spheres of commercial activity'. At the most basic level was 'the intensive small-scale dealing which took place among the inhabitants of an immediate locality', whether a lordship, village or town. A second sphere of activity 'comprising rural–urban and inter-urban trade at the level of the district, 'country' or sub-region' centred on larger and smaller market towns. These 'market areas' fed into a 'third level of interconnection': 'trading networks' based first and foremost on provincial capitals that 'tied particular countries into regional and interregional systems of interdependence, and on occasion connected them further with international networks of exchange'. It was through these networks that domestic foodstuffs, raw materials, manufactured goods and luxury products circulated around the country, and foreign luxury goods like wine, spices and fine finished fabrics were imported and distributed inland. Finally, at the apex of these networks was London: like other capital cities it was by far the largest market for domestic goods and services and the principal hub for international trade.[13]

In the early sixteenth century, cities and towns experienced challenges precipitated by the 'ruralisation' of certain industries – in particular cloth – whereby manufacturing began to be concentrated in deregulated rural settlements rather than urban craft economies. This trend itself represented a new kind of urban connectivity, as urban-based merchant capitalists took advantage of cheap labour and the lack of regulation in rural pastoral areas to establish new cloth-manufacturing districts. Certain towns and cities suffered as a result. In Yorkshire it was West Riding townships like Leeds rather than established cities like York that became centres of the textile industry. Elsewhere conglomerations of small towns and villages that were incorporated into 'putting out' or 'domestic' systems of production engendered new kinds of urban/rural interpenetration and relationships: in eastern Somerset and western Wiltshire, in south-east Lancashire and the Kentish weald, on the uplands of north-central Wales, and in the Stour Valley between Suffolk and Essex. By the middle of the eighteenth century agglomerations of industrial townships – for example around Leeds, Halifax, Sheffield, Birmingham, Sunderland and Manchester – had become as important as old and new imperial ports like Bristol, Liverpool and Glasgow in reshaping the scale, weight and culture of the English and Scottish urban systems.[14]

While this preference for deregulated rural manufacture over traditional craft production set an important precedent for subsequent industrial development, it did not mark the demise of the traditional urban system. On the contrary, from the middle of the sixteenth century it began the sustained period of demographic growth outlined above, despite the pronounced problems of both 'background' and 'crisis' mortality – always present and sometimes catastrophic – that inevitably characterised urban living.[15] Urban migration could be seasonal or permanent, desperate or opportunistic, reactive or part of household strategies. It also involved the thousands of immigrants who settled in London and the cities of the south-east after the onset of Europe's religious wars, bringing with them new skills and production techniques. In the meantime the intensification of agricultural production and the specialisation of urban manufacture saw the need for larger and more integrated markets. Market towns were busier with goods and people, their hinterlands wider, their consumers more sociologically diverse, their reach into the country deeper. In the meantime the greater volume of long-distance transactions saw the popularisation of fiscal practices, such as inland bills of exchange, and a proliferation of litigation in Westminster and urban courts when transactions went wrong.[16]

The traffic and commerce of provincial capitals and the metropolis likewise intensified. They facilitated the growing integration of regional economies and the more gradual but cumulatively transformative expansion of overseas trade: first with the ports and entrepôts of the Baltic, Iberia and the Levant from the 1570s; then with Asian cities and markets from the early 1600s; and finally with the establishment of the American colonies from the 1610s.[17] Urban centres connected and constituted each sphere of commercial expansion and colonisation; and it was through the metropolis, provincial capitals and market towns back home that the increasing volume of new commodities reached consumers.[18] Moreover, the emergence of the joint stock company as the preferred institution of global commerce connected city and country in new financial webs of inter-dependency. Rather than citizen-merchants forming regulated companies and undertaking to trade themselves, as was customary in Europe and the Levant, stockholders from disparate backgrounds increasingly invested in a company organisation, like the East India Company, which then oversaw the business of salaried employees.[19] In the meantime, 'interlopers' or non-company members sought to trade independently of these corporate monopolies. Either way, traditional urban communities were unable to dominate the profits of empire in the same way that they were unable to control and exploit modern manufacturing.

Two modes of urban-based communication epitomised the connective importance of the urban system. From the 1560s postal routes and towns created 'corridors of inter-urban communication and contact' between the provinces and metropolis: whereas in 1566 two postal roads connected London to Dover in the south and Berwick in the north, by 1605 Portsmouth, Penryn and Padstow (Cornwall), Barnstaple, Holyhead (via Birmingham), Carlisle, Penrith, Dale (via Bristol and Swansea), Ludlow, Margate, and Sandwich were final destinations. In the seventeenth century the system was formalised and timetabled, and was 'crucial in shaping the social, political, and economic geography of England and Wales'.[20] Equally indicative of the connective nature of early modern urbanisation are the coastal trade and ports. Their increasing business is retained in port books: customs records for domestic and overseas trade that were introduced for 122 maritime centres in 1565.[21] Diachronically these records show the steady increase in both the volume and the variety of domestic and overseas trade before 1650 and the rapid proliferation of both thereafter.[22] They also suggest that while London remained the primary urban hub – as both the main destination and point of redistribution for domestic and overseas goods – provincial urban systems like the Bristol Channel could also be transformed by the burgeoning weight of traffic.[23]

Witness statements from a probate dispute in the city of York in 1681 illustrate the extent and social depth of urban connectivity by the second half of the seventeenth century. The will was that of Elizabeth Smith and the dispute centred on whether her son, William, was alive to inherit her modest fortune. William's existence was in doubt because nearly twenty years earlier, in the 1660s, he had been transported at the instigation of his parents to 'Barbados or Virginia' on account of his 'Extravagant and riotous ways of living'. That the colonies should already be somewhere for the Smiths to send their profligate son is one indication of England's extended urban connections: William was accordingly shipped from York to Hull to London and so on to Bridgetown. The ship, however, never arrived;

and a second intimation of England's urban reach is the account of the York mariner Peter Buttery spending the next ten years enquiring after William in the many ports he visited – from Bordeaux to La Rochelle to Stockholm.

But it was the provenance of the rumour that William had in fact survived his journey that really brings home the quotidian mobility of early modern lives. Catherine Beckwith recalled that in 1678, 'being then at London on board a vessel on the River Thames at Billingsgate designed for York ... she heard one by the name of William Ellis of Kingston-Upon-Hull call of one William Smith saying "What cheer?"'. Intrigued, Beckwith 'made enquiry (hearing Smith answer) what Smith he was and where he was born'. Smith answered 'I am William Smith son of York and was born in St Andrew Gate', and 'he inquired how his father and mother did and desired this examinant to present his duty to them and told her if time permit he would send a token to his father and mother by her but being at some distance could not ... being then bound for Virginia'. Beckwith did, however, take note of the mark that confirmed, for her, his identity as her friend's son: a scar on his cheek accidently given him as a child by his mother.

This casual description of an ordinary woman waiting to sail back to York from London points to the everyday impact of maritime traffic. Even more striking is what William allegedly did next. Dorcas Semore deposed that Elizabeth had visited her house three years earlier and asked her to read a letter that 'she had lately received from her son William'. It transpired that he was 'married and very well and desired his said mother to make much of herself and withal had sent her a five shilling piece'. Whether the letter was sent from Jamestown or London is unclear. What it does show is that the prospect of ordinary householders exchanging letters and tokens nationally or internationally was well within the bounds of possibility, even when the recipient had to ask a neighbour to read it for her.[24]

The connective impact of urbanisation stemmed from the intensification of inherited practices and technologies – to do with markets, for example, or shipping – as well as the development of newer configurations and infrastructures such as industrial agglomerations and postal routes. This mutable continuity also characterised English structural urbanisation and the manner in which urban institutions came to shape and constitute ostensibly national processes and developments. This is particularly true of the early modern state, which appropriated medieval urban institutions in order to regulate manufacture and commerce nationally, and also to cope with the social consequences of capitalisation and commercialisation intimated by Burton.[25]

Early modern people inherited a very clear sense of the urban based on medieval notions of corporatism, citizenship, freedom and common-weal. Conceptually this legacy involved independent householders par-ticipating in the formal urban community: becoming a burgess, freeman or citizen, and undertaking public roles and responsibilities in return for economic liberties, such as the right to practice a trade and access to common lands. Institutionally, medieval urbanism centred on the coun-cils, assemblies, courts and offices in which public decision-making was organised and implemented and communal resources protected.[26] Before the Reformation, associational bodies like guilds, chantries and fraterni-ties supplemented the formal community: these were often powerful and wealthy institutions that could exert decisive power in a town. Moreover, townsmen often shared urban space or were subordinate to powerful insti-tutions outwith their formal and informal communities: for example, bishoprics, abbeys and monasteries; colleges and universities; royal and noble lordships.

An important assumption of the 'crisis' interpretation of early modern urbanism is that over the course of the sixteenth and early seventeenth century this medieval inheritance was denuded and destroyed. Not only did the Reformation hit towns badly, leaving them institutionally thread-bare and culturally bereft, but the political powers, autonomy and com-munity of townsmen were compromised both by external encroachments and by new oligarchic hierarchies of power.[27] More recently, however, an alternative narrative of structural urbanisation, as opposed to degradation, has emerged. This centres in the first instance on the surprising fate of the formal urban community: the institutions upon which urban freedom and citizenship traditionally depended. First, from the early decades of the sixteenth century burgesses and citizens increasingly petitioned for char-ters of incorporation from the Attorney General in London. These expen-sive and valuable documents enhanced the power and status of citizens by formally recognising in law urban communities and the corporate institu-tions, resources and powers they claimed. In so doing, they also acknowl-edged the inter-dependency of urban and central authority and the lines of communication upon which this relationship rested. This facilitated, secondly, the systematisation of the institutions, procedures and offices of urban citizenship. Over time the nomenclature of mayor, aldermen and common councilmen became standard; the appointment of legal officers like recorders, clerks and high stewards became normal; elective and bureaucratic procedures were regularised; and the extension of governmental responsibilities was accepted. The result, thirdly, was an amplification of public powers within the urban community. On the one hand, citizenship became a palimpsest for state power: it became standard for aldermen and mayors to serve as magistrates, and the number of cities and towns able to elect parliamentary representatives increased significantly over the period. On the other hand, the associational diversity and material wealth that characterised the late medieval town were not so much destroyed by the Reformation as repositioned within the body of what contemporaries styled 'city commonwealths'. Indeed, as Robert Tittler has shown, one of the main reasons behind incorporation was the need for citizens and freemen to ratify and guarantee this transfer of resources.[28]

This resulted, fourthly, in a certain homogenisation of urban space and association. Just as the urban corporation increasingly formed an umbrella institution under which guilds, companies and other citizen bodies legitimately functioned, so the dissolution of religious institutions and liberties gave citizens the opportunity to exert greater authority over the urban environment (indeed, by the seventeenth century only the bishoprics survived as serious governmental rivals).[29] But this process also led, fifthly, to social reconfigurations and conflict within urban communities. Affluent elites – especially merchants, wholesalers and wealthier artisans – exhibited 'aristocratic', 'patrician' or 'oligarchic' pretensions that justified their monopoly of civic governance and enhanced their claims to social status and superiority. Others resisted and in some instances espoused a 'plebeian', 'popular' or 'democratic' position in order to defend what they presented as 'customary' rights, liberties and access to resources.[30] Finally, and perhaps most importantly, there was a huge proliferation in the number of towns and cities that became formally incorporated or experienced at least some of the infrastructural developments associated with 'city commonwealths' – a process that Tittler nicely associates with the rise of the town hall.[31] Far from witnessing the death of medieval corporatism, that is, the early modern period saw its revitalisation and expansion into a national corporate system of city commonwealths with London as its hub. The scale and extent of this process is suggested by Figure 8.3, which shows not only how intensive English incorporation was compared to Scotland after 1500, but also how it became a tool of colonisation in the Ulster plantations in the 1610s. Thereafter the reproduction of chartered and incorporated settlements across the Atlantic became a crucial dynamic of English colonial settlement.[32]

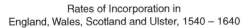

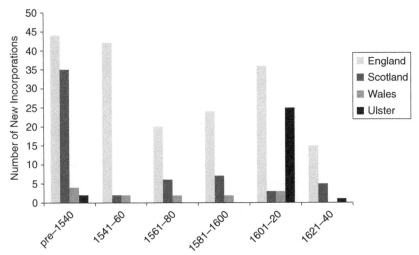

Figure 8.3 Rates of incorporation in England, Wales, Scotland and Ulster, 1540–1640. From P. Withington, 'Plantation and civil society', in É. Ó Ciardha and M. Ó Siochrú (eds.), *The Plantation of Ulster: Ideology and Practice* (Manchester: Manchester University Press, 2012), 70.

The revitalised structures of medieval urbanism were a constitutive feature of the early modern state and political economy. Some of the key parliamentary statutes of the era originated in governmental practices and experiments in larger cities like London and Norwich.[33] The procedures of apprenticeship as outlined in the definitive 1563 Statute of Artificers marked one such translation from the urban to the national; the series of acts establishing parochial poor-relief between the 1570s and the 1600s another.[34] That these traits of urban citizenship were successfully inscribed in statute reflected, in turn, the burgeoning presence of MPs representing urban constituencies in the House of Commons. The proportion of urban MPs was four-fifths by 1641. Likewise, the implementation of legislation provincially depended in large part on the corporate system. Although historians of early-modern state-formation have almost entirely neglected its urban dimensions, contemporaries did not. The Council of Ireland in Dublin rehearsed a familiar argument in 1552 when it explained to the Privy Council in London that it was 'Cities and towns from whence all Civil and good orders sprang: and thereby doth chiefly continue through

the universal world where any Commonwealth remains'.[35] More prosaically, Michael Dalton observed in *The Country Justice* that there were
three types of justice of the peace (JP): a small number of senior clerics
appointed by 'act of Parliament'; the large number of county justices who
were commissioned by the Lord Chancellor (and who have monopolised
historiographical attention); and the significant number of JPs appointed
'by Grant made by the king by his Letters Patent': 'as Mayors and chief
officers in diverse corporate towns'. Dalton explained that the crucial difference between county and corporate JPs was that while the former could
be relieved of their office by simply having their commission removed,
the king was unable either to select or to discharge the latter 'at his pleasure'. Indeed, once an urban community was granted the right to select
its magistrates no rival authority could be commissioned to serve within
its jurisdiction until the charter was legally revoked.[36] That the Tudor and
early Stuart regimes proceeded to empower urban communities despite
this remarkable discrepancy reflects the symbiotic relationship between
city and state in the century after 1540 – a degree of trust and reciprocity reflected in the proliferation of urban parliamentary constituencies.
Equally revealing is the chronic instability and partisanship that overtook
the state after 1640, when urban communities were politicised and con-
secutive regimes challenged the magisterial autonomy and parliamentary
influence of citizens by attacking their charters.[37] No ruler distrusted or
attacked the privileges of citizens and freemen more than James II; his
eventual abdication suggests, among other things, just how integral their
place in the commonwealth and state had become.[38]

Urban apprenticeship was likewise fundamental to the political economy of the period, not least because the 1563 Act applied the rules prac-
ticed in London nationwide. Apprentices were contracted to a master for
seven years, during which time they worked in exchange for instruction
and could not marry. In urban communities, successful completion after
the age of twenty-four gave apprentices access to freedom and the right to
establish their own working households. Stephan Epstein and others have
accordingly argued that by effectively providing skills, knowledge, and
human capital the institution contributed to the technological innovation
and economic growth that precipitated industrialisation.[39] In contrast,
Sheilagh Ogilvie claims that apprenticeship and the guilds more were
generally protectionist, exclusionary and an economic hindrance: it was
the relative weakness of English corporatism compared to the Continent
that explains its economic success. The answer probably lies somewhere
between. On the one hand, it is incontrovertible that guild organisations

in general and apprenticeship in particular remained foundational economic institutions in England until the second half of the eighteenth century. As late as 1700, 'over 9 per cent of English males became apprentices' in London alone and provincial centres continued to serve their hinterlands.[40] Whatever its consequences, apprenticeship structured economic training either in the regular contracts recorded in urban archives or as a template for the innumerable unrecorded arrangements made outwith the corporate system.[41] On the other hand, recent work suggests that, in terms of its practice, apprenticeship was a much more open, fluid and flexible institution than its formal rules suggest. Urban apprenticeships were characterised by trial periods and early terminations; absenteeism was common, as was movement between masters, trades and cities in the course of an indenture. Completion rates were surprisingly low, with four years an alternative preferred period of training to seven; and in London and Bristol at least, only 40 per cent of apprentices progressed to citizenship.[42] All this suggests that, like early modern magistracy, apprenticeship was characterised by discretion and the need to make the institution work for all parties involved: apprentice, family, master, craft. Perhaps more importantly, it also points to the cumulative creation of a mobile and skilled labour market of journeymen and servants capable of working for others or setting up house beyond the boundaries of the corporate system – not least in the newer manufacturing agglomerations that characterised the period.[43]

In important respects the story of the English state was also one of urbanisation: it developed through, rather than despite, the structures of medieval urbanism. This was concurrent with a second set of changes involving not so much traditional urban citizenship as the efflorescence of cultural and professional services – in education, in law, in communications, in sociability – that were located primarily, if not uniquely, in cities and towns. The urban system inculcated the massive expansion of England's urban educational infrastructure: in the petty schools; in 'free', 'public' and 'private' schools; and in the university colleges, academies and legal Inns that proliferated from the late fifteenth century.[44] It facilitated the well-documented increase in legal provision and legal business that made England in the later sixteenth and early seventeenth century a more litigious society than the contemporary USA: in the borough courts, in the central courts in London and their provincial outlets meeting in county towns (quarter sessions, assizes and extraordinary commissions), and in the ecclesiastical courts centred in cathedral precincts and the universities.[45] It was integral to transformations in communication and representation: most obviously in the establishment of the metropolitan-based print trade but also in the emergence of professional theatre companies and a vernacular literary and playing tradition.[46] Finally it was in the urban system that the less-heralded expansion of licensed and commercial sites of consumption and association occurred. This latter development – sometimes known as the 'town' in contradistinction to the traditional 'city'– involved at once the growing nexus of traditional venues such as alehouses, taverns and inns, and the opening, from the middle of the seventeenth century, of newer establishments like coffeehouses, assembly rooms and gin-houses.[47] From the 1590s in London, and subsequent decades in provincial capitals and market centres, these institutions structured new modes of urbane (and not so urbane) behaviour.[48] It is for these reasons that Peter Borsay describes an 'urban renaissance' by the last quarter of the seventeenth century, whereby provincial urbanity had become intrinsic to the formation of polite and civil society for the gentry and middling sorts more generally.[49]

Viewed in these terms it is not difficult to see how urban culture was congruent with cultural patterns and trends more generally. Institutional intensification and innovation across the urban system were the most obvious marker of these developments: more schools and colleges; busier law courts and taverns; new theatres, booksellers and coffeehouses: districts outwith the traditional city known for their cultural and legal services. There were sociological ramifications, too. On the one hand, the producers and professionals who manned and ran these institutions, and who were versed in the skills and expertise associated with them, formed a growing and influential section of the urban populace. Schoolteachers, clerics and academic fellows; the host of legal occupations, from clerks and solicitors to barristers and judges; publishers, translators, authors, hawkers; impresarios, victuallers, vintners, cooks – together they formed an emergent social grouping that did not fit at all easily in the established social order, and that demarcated the interface between town and country in new ways. On the other hand, the groups attracted to use or visit the institutions – whether as students and apprentices, litigants and readers, groundlings or gallants, visitors and shoppers – not only made for more heterogeneous urban environments. The wider appropriation of urban services and resources could not help but impact on the generations of rural inhabitants attending schools, bringing suits, reading almanacs, listening to sermons or visiting a tavern. In this respect it was not just the urbane gentry and intelligentsia who embodied, as it were, the emergence of the town, but also the host of urban and non-urban inhabitants who appropriated the services and expertise located in the urban system.

Literacy rates are perhaps the most obvious marker of urban congruency, with literariness and legalism not far behind.[50] Whether they corroborate Wrigley's model of a move from 'traditional' to 'rational' society is much less obvious. Certainly the career of a man who in many respects personifies the extent of English urbanisation by the middle of the seventeenth century was no harbinger of Weberian modernity. John Lilburne hailed from a lesser gentry family in Durham with interests in Sunderland industry; attended the free grammar schools in the market town of Bishop Auckland and provincial capital of Newcastle; was apprenticed to a London wholesale clothier with extensive trading and religious connections; imported illegal books from Amsterdam into London and became a polemicist himself (encountering the wrath of the law in the process); was set up as a London brewer by his Sunderland uncle while keeping company with London separatists and marrying Elizabeth Dewall, daughter of a London merchant; was involved in the 'apprentice' riots against Strafford in 1641 and a year later enlisted to fight for Parliament. Even before he became a propagandist of that quintessential London movement – the Levellers – Lilburne was formed and empowered by the urban system.[51]

The resonance among urbanism and the two cultural tendencies with which this chapter concludes likewise suggests a more complicated story than Wrigley tells. The first of these was the associational basis of urban life and the proliferation – rather than diminution – of associational possibilities within urban environments over the course of the period. Such possibilities included the formal corporate organisations of city commonwealths: the common councils, assemblies, guilds and companies that provided the institutional basis of urban citizenship. They included the proliferation of informal sociability and more formal clubs, societies and voluntary associations that gathered in the drinking places and other social spaces of the town. They encompassed parochial communities and, over the course of the seventeenth-century, the proliferation of dissenting churches, congregations and 'parties'. By the eighteenth century they also included working men's combinations and middle-class subscription groups. In a very real sense, that is, early modern urbanism was defined by the capacity for collective action and agency, or what contemporaries came to describe as 'society'; and urbanisation marked the proliferation of this capacity both within urban environments and as a template for purposeful association elsewhere.[52] But these associational habits were also rooted in the more perennial webs of relationships and emotional ties – the friendships, enmities, kinship, neighbourliness and reciprocities – that were simply inherent to the propinquity of urban living. Such bonds were never better revealed than when they were most challenged. As Wrightson has found, 'the response to the plague of 1636 in Newcastle confirms the power and resilience of the associational life of the city'. Rather than a disintegration into the kind of apocalyptic dystopia envisaged by plague treatises, the catastrophe prompted the 'refusal of people who shared a space, knowledge of one another (good and ill), and obligations to one another (reluctant or willing) to renege upon those commitments'.[53] The same sense of society was revealed by the host of witnesses drawn into the dispute over Elizabeth Smith's estate. In the course of their respective testimonies they described a range of behaviours – relating to commerce, retail, literacy, travel and litigation – characteristic of, though not unique to, urban living. Elizabeth's female friends in particular also demonstrated a palpable sense of neighbourliness rooted in everyday propinquity, familiarity and reciprocity.

The second congruence is that between urbanism and the assortment of social values and skills known as 'civility' or 'honesty'.[54] The appropriation of classical norms of behaviour and conduct is one of the defining characteristics of the early modern period and has been well charted by Anna Bryson, who uses behavioural handbooks to trace the gradual shift from a culture of medieval courtesy to early modern civility and politeness.[55] Yet what is missing from Bryson's account is the role of English urbanism in popularising these norms and translating them into practice. While this absence is unsurprising given English urbanism's more general historiographical neglect, it is historically incongruous given the urban provenance of civility. As Bryson points out, in classical texts 'civil' was primarily a term of political description associated with the 'city' and 'citizen', carrying connotations that have subsequently been applied to 'civic'. These semantics made sense to the Italian Renaissance writers who first introduced the concept into European vernaculars, as it 'fitted easily enough with the predominantly urban context of their own culture'. But Bryson suggests that it was nonsense in a place like England, which, 'like France, was a country dominated by a rural aristocracy'. Indeed so convinced is Bryson that there was no aspect of English society that could 'in any concrete sense, be defined as "civic", still less "bourgeois"', she is forced to contradict the claims of the first English proponents of civility that she cites.[56] However, subsequent work on everyday notions of 'honour', 'credit' and 'civility' has shown that permutations of these values were widely promulgated, enforced and appropriated in the century or so after 1550. The codes of conduct and discourse that characterised the institutions of urban citizenship have been found to be expressly civil in nature: the expansion of the corporate system standardised and disseminated these norms.[57] The civil sociability of the town and the urban renaissance were likewise predicated on emulating classical conventions.[58] But perhaps most strikingly, the increasing recourse of ordinary male and female householders to urban-based courts of civil and ecclesiastical law in order to protect and contest their honour, credit and reputation was one of the defining features of the age.[59] Not only were these courts situated in cities, and so drew thousands of plaintiffs, defendants and witnesses into the urban system, but urban inhabitants were also much more likely to become embroiled in legal business than their rural counterparts.[60] The widespread and complicated appropriation of these legally enforced norms has been found to be fundamental to social relations and economic exchange and 'is likely to have *informed* processes of identity-making rather than simply recorded them'.[61] It also encapsulates the centrality – and invisibility – of urbanisation to early modern English society.

When Robert Burton described the pauperism and paucity of England's urban culture in 1621 he was looking to answer a specific question: 'Our land is fertile we may not deny, full of all good things, and why doth it not then abound with Cities, as well as Italy, France, Germany, the Low Countries?' For Burton the answer was simple: 'idleness is the *malus Genius* of our nation'. Drawing on classical authorities, Burton argued that 'fertility of a country is not enough, except art and industry be joined unto it'. And for Burton urbanism – or the lack of it – was the proof of the pudding.[62]

In certain respects Burton was not far off the mark. In crude demographic terms, England was much less urbanised that either the Low Countries or Italy in 1621. Nor is there any doubt that just as English towns and cities had faced significant economic and social challenges over the last hundred years, so Italian, Dutch and Flemish cities were the cradles of the most advanced political economies in Europe. What Burton could not appreciate is that the absence of many large, populous and autonomous cities did not reflect the lack of 'art and industry' so much as their national distribution by other means. On the one hand, manufacturing and extractive industries were increasingly concentrated in agglomerations of households that were outwith the traditional urban system. On the other hand, this system had itself been revitalised as a hub for local, national and international commerce and services, as a constitutive feature of the early modern state, and as a cultural crucible. Burton himself was educated at the grammar school in the market town of Nuneaton (founded 1552) and lived his adult life in Oxford; but like John Lilburne, his persona is taken to be English rather than urban. Economically connective, politically constitutive, culturally congruent: it was not the decrepitude of English urbanism so much as the integrative power of English urbanisation that characterised early modern English society. In this respect it is perhaps best to leave the last word to William Smith. The York merchant William Bell deposed in 1676 that he was drinking at York River in Virginia 'in one Mrs Leake's house there' when 'one William Smith by name came into his company'. Bell recalled that when he asked this forced migrant 'what Smith he was [Smith] told him he was a Yorkshire man born and was born at York'.[63] Like the childhood scar observed by Catherine Beckwith, the city lived with him still.

## Notes

1 R. Burton, *The Anatomy of Melancholy* (1621), 52–3.

2 P. Clark and P. Slack (eds.), *Crisis and Order in English Towns, 1500–1700: Coventry and the Urban Crisis of the Late Middle Ages* (Cambridge: Cambridge University Press, 1979).

3 P. Clark, '"The Ramoth-Gilead of the Good": Urban change and political radicalism at Gloucester', reprinted in J. Barry (ed.), *The Tudor and Stuart Town* (Harlow: Longman, 1988).

4 P. Clark and P. Slack (eds.), *English Towns in Transition, 1500–1700* (Oxford: Oxford University Press, 1976); P. Borsay, *The English Urban Renaissance: Culture and Society in the Provincial Towns, 1660–1770* (Oxford: Oxford University Press, 1989).

5 E. A. Wrigley, 'A simple model of London's importance in changing English society and economy, 1650–1750', *P&P*, 37 (1967); I. Archer, *The Pursuit of Stability: Social Relations in Elizabethan London* (Cambridge: Cambridge University Press, 1991); P. Griffiths, *Lost Londons: Change, Crime and Control in the Capital City 1550–1660* (Cambridge: Cambridge University Press, 2008).

6 P. Griffith and M. Jenner (eds.), *Londonopolis: Essays in the Cultural and Social History of Early Modern London* (Manchester: Manchester University Press, 2001).

7 P. Laslett, *The World We Have Lost – Further Explored* (London: Taylor and Francis, 2000), 56–7.

8 J. Barry, 'Bourgeois collectivism? Urban association and the middling sort', in J. Barry and C. Brooks (eds.), *The Middling Sort of People: Culture, Society and Politics in England 1550–1800* (Basingstoke: Macmillan, 1994);

P. Collinson, *The Birthpangs of Protestant England: Religious Change in the Sixteenth and Seventeenth Centuries* (Basingstoke: Macmillan, 1988), 28–60; R. Tittler, *Architecture and Power: The Town Hall and the English Urban Community, 1500–1640* (Oxford: Oxford University Press, 1991); R. Tittler, *The Reformation and the Towns in England: Politics and Political Culture, c. 1540–1640* (Oxford: Oxford University Press, 1998); P. Withington, *The Politics of Commonwealth: Citizens and Freemen in Early Modern England* (Cambridge: Cambridge University Press, 2005).

9 Jan de Vries, *European Urbanization 1500–1800* (London: Methuen, 1984), 10–17.

10 Wrigley, 'A simple model', 65–8; E. A. Wrigley, 'Urban growth and agricultural change: England and the Continent in the early modern period', reprinted in P. Borsay (ed.), *The Eighteenth Century Town* (Harlow: Longman, 1990), 79–80.

11 A. Kussmaul, *A General View of the Rural Economy of England, 1538–1840* (Cambridge: Cambridge University Press, 1990), 138–40.

12 C. P. Adams, *Societies, Cultures and Kinship, 1580–1850: Cultural Provinces and English Local History* (Leicester: Leicester University Press, 1996), 9–23.

13 K. Wrightson, *Earthly Necessities: Economic Lives in Early Modern Britain* (New Haven and London: Yale University Press, 2000), 93–7.

14 Wrigley, 'Urban Growth', 78–9; Wrightson, *Earthly Necessities*, 107–8.

15 P. Slack, *The Impact of Plague in Tudor and Stuart England* (Oxford: Oxford University Press, 1990); K. Wrightson, *Ralph Tailor's Summer: A Scrivener, His City and the Plague* (New Haven and London: Yale University Press, 2011), 28–42; Wrightson, *Earthly Necessities*, 164.

16 C. W. Brooks, 'Interpersonal conflict and social tension: Civil litigation in England, 1640–1830', in A. L. Beier, D. Cannadine and J. M. Rosenheim (eds.), *The First Modern Society* (Cambridge: Cambridge University Press, 1989), 357–99; C. Muldrew, *The Economy of Obligation* (Basingstoke: Macmillan, 1998), Chapter 8, 338–44.

17 Wrightson, *Earthly Necessities*, 176–7.

18 N. Zahedieh, *The Capital and the Colonies: London and the Atlantic Economy 1660–1700* (Cambridge: Cambridge University Press, 2010); D. Hussey, *Coastal and River Trade in Pre-Industrial England: Bristol and Its Region 1680–1730* (Exeter: Exeter University Press, 2000).

19 Thanks to William Pettigrew for discussions on this point.

20 M. Brayshay, 'Royal post-horse routes in England and Wales: The evolution of the network in the later-sixteenth and early-seventeenth centuries', *Journal of Historical Geography*, 17:4 (1991), 377, 387.

21 Hussey, *Coastal and River Trade*, 7.

22 T. S. Willan, *The Inland Trade* (Manchester: Manchester University Press, 1976), 26–41; T. S. Willan, *Studies in Elizabethan Foreign Trade* (Manchester: Manchester University Press, 1959), esp. Chapter 3.

23 Hussey, *Coastal and River Trade*, 78–99.

24 Borthwick Institute, CPH 3497, 1681, Mabson C. Richardson and Saltmarsh. Depositions of Grace Harrison; Richard Moore; Peter Buttery; Catherine Beckwith; Dorcas Semore.

25 The main accounts almost entirely ignore the urban. See M. Braddick, *State Formation in Early Modern England, c. 1550–1700* (Cambridge: Cambridge University Press, 2000); S. Hindle, *The State and Social Change in Early Modern England* (Basingstoke: Macmillan, 2000).

26 Withington, *Politics of Commonwealth*, 85–99.

27 Collinson, *Birthpangs*, 56–9.

28 Tittler, *Reformation*, 57–103.

29 Barry, 'Bourgeois collectivism?', 108–9.

30 For a nice example see 'Government and politics in Ludlow, 1590–1642', *Transactions of the Shropshire Archaeological Society*, 56 (1957/8), 282–94; Withington, *Politics of Commonwealth*, 66–75.

31 Tittler, *Architecture and Power*, 14–16; Withington, *Politics of Commonwealth*, 18–24.

32 M. Peterson, 'Boston pays tribute: Autonomy and empire in the Atlantic world, 1630–1714', in A. I. Macinnes and A. H. Williamson (eds.), *Shaping the Stuart World, 1603–1714: The Atlantic Connections* (Leiden: Brill, 2005).

33 J. Bishop, 'Utopia and civic politics in mid-sixteenth century London', *HJ*, 54 (2011).

34 Wrightson, *Earthly Necessities*, 156; C. Minns and P. Wallis, 'Rules and reality: Quantifying the practice of apprenticeship in early modern England', *EcHR*, 65:2 (2012), 556.

35 TNA, SP 61/4/5, Council of Ireland to the Privy Council, 27 January 1552 (Dublin). I'd like to thank Jennifer Bishop for this reference.

36 M. Dalton, *The Country Justice* (1619), 10.

37 P. Halliday, *Dismembering the Body Politic: Partisan Politics in England's Towns 1650–1730* (Cambridge: Cambridge University Press, 1998).

38 P. Withington, 'Public discourse, corporate citizenship and state-formation in early modern England', *AHR*, 112:4 (2007).

39 S. R. Epstein, 'Craft guilds, apprenticeship, and technological change in preindustrial Europe', *Journal of Economic History*, 58 (1998); J. Humphries, 'English apprenticeship: A neglected factor in the first industrial revolution', in P. A. David and M. Thomas (eds.), *The Economic Future in Historical Perspective* (Oxford: Oxford University Press, 2003); J. van Zanden, 'The skill premium and the "Great Divergence"', *European Review of Economic History*, 13 (2009), 139–40.

40 C. Minns and P. Wallis, 'Rules and reality: Quantifying the practice of apprenticeship in early modern England', *EcHR*, 65:2 (2012), 559; Wrightson, *Earthly Necessities*, 165; C. Galley, *The Demography of Early Modern Towns: York in the Sixteenth and Seventeenth Centuries* (Liverpool: Liverpool University Press, 1998), 134–6.

41 T. Leunig, C. Minns and P. Wallis, 'Networks in the pre-modern economy: The market for London apprenticeships, 1600–1749', *Journal of Economic History*, 71:2 (June 2011), 421.

42 Minns and Wallis, 'Rules and reality', 562, 567, 570, 574–6.

43 Thanks to Patrick Wallis for talking about these issues.

44 L. Stone, 'The educational revolution in England, 1560–1640', *P&P*, 28:1 (1964).

45 C. W. Brooks, *Pettyfoggers and Vipers of the Commonwealth: The Lower Branch of the Legal Profession in Early Modern England* (Cambridge: Cambridge University Press, 1986), 79.

46 E. S. Eisenstein, *The Printing Press as an Agent of Change* (Cambridge: Cambridge University Press, 1980); T. Rutter, 'Issues in review: Dramatists, playing companies, and repertories', *Early Theatre* 13:3 (2011).

47 I. W. Archer, 'Social networks in Restoration London: The evidence of Samuel Pepys's diary', in A. Shepard and P. Withington (eds.), *Communities in Early Modern England* (Manchester: Manchester University Press, 2000); P. Withington, 'Intoxication and the early modern city', in S. Hindle, A. Shepard and J. Walter (eds.), *Remaking English Society* (Woodbridge: Boydell and Brewer, 2013); B. Cowan, *The Social Life of Coffee: The Emergence of the British Coffeehouse* (New Haven and London: Yale University Press, 2005).

48 M. O'Callaghan, *The English Wits: Literature and Sociability in Early Modern England* (Cambridge: Cambridge University Press, 2007); P. Withington, 'Intoxicants and society in early modern England', *HJ*, 54 (2011).

49 Borsay, *English Urban Renaissance*, 311–20.

50 Wrightson, *Ralph Tailor's Summer*, 66–7, 176; D. Cressy, *Literacy and the Social Order: Reading and Writing in Tudor and Stuart England* (Cambridge: Cambridge University Press, 1980), 119–22; C. Brooks, 'Apprenticeship, social mobility and the middling sort, 1550–1800', in Barry and Brooks, *Middling Sort*; C. Brooks, 'Professions, ideology and the middling sort in the late-sixteenth and early-seventeenth centuries', in Barry and Brooks, *Middling Sort*.

51 Withington, *Politics of commonwealth*, 13, 80, 122; A. Sharp, 'Lilburne, John (1615?–1657)', *ODNB*, online edn, October 2006, www.oxforddnb.com/view/article/16654 (accessed 8 December 2014); P. Withington, 'Urban citizens and England's civil wars', in M. Braddick (ed.), *The Oxford Handbook of the English Revolution* (Oxford: Oxford University Press, 2015), 323–4.

52 Barry, 'Bourgeois Collectivism?', 85–8; P. Clark, *British Clubs and Societies 1580–1800: The Origins of an Associational World* (Oxford: Oxford University Press, 2000); P. Withington, *Society in Early Modern England: The Vernacular Origins of Some Powerful Ideas* (Cambridge: Polity, 2010), 102–34.

53 Wrightson, *Ralph Tailor's Summer*, 160–1.

54 Brooks, 'Apprenticeship', 77–8; P. Withington, 'Honestas', in H. Turner (ed.), *Early Modern Theatricality* (Oxford: Oxford University Press, 2013).

55 N. Elias, *The Civilizing Process*, trans. E. Jephcott (Oxford: Blackwell, 2000); A. Bryson, *From Courtesy to Civility: Changing Codes of Conduct in Early Modern England* (Oxford: Oxford University Press, 1998).

56 Bryson, *From Courtesy to Civility*, 60–1.

57 Barry, 'Bourgeois collectivism?', 106–7; J. Barry, 'Civility and civic culture in early modern England', in P. Burke, P. Harrison and P. Slack (eds.), *Civil Histories* (Oxford: Oxford University Press, 2000); Withington, 'Public discourse', 1028–34.

58 O'Callaghan, *English Wits*, 6, 29; Borsay, *English Urban Renaissance*, 257–63.

59 Muldrew, *Economy of Obligation*; L. Gowing, *Domestic Dangers: Women, Words and Sex in Early Modern London* (Oxford: Oxford University Press, 1998); A. Shepard, *Meanings of Manhood in Early Modern England* (Oxford: Oxford University Press, 2003).

60 A. Shepard, *Accounting for Self: Worth, Status and the Social Order in Early Modern England* (Oxford: Oxford University Press, 2014), 16–17.

61 *Ibid.*, 23–4.

62 Burton, *Anatomy*, 52–3.

63 Borthwick Institute, CPH 3497, 1681, Mabson C. Richardson and Saltmarsh, deposition of William Bell.

# 9

# The People and the Law

## Tim Stretton

## Introduction

During the sixteenth century, surprising numbers of English men and women fell under the spell of the law. By the early eighteenth century the love affair was fading, but the attachment and habits of mind remained strong, and it is difficult to overemphasise the law's influence on the nation in the decades and centuries following 1500.

Law courts, legal agents, legislation and proclamations constituted the main sinews of the emerging centralised state, and the willingness of ordinary English women and men to engage with the law, seen in record levels of criminal prosecutions and an explosion of civil litigation, proved central to the success of the whole state-forming process. Inter-personal litigation and a growing reliance on legal instruments contributed to a rise in contractual thinking that altered conceptualisations of personal and professional interactions and relationships. In literature, legal subjects saturated English Renaissance drama and developing courtroom concepts of proof and probability helped shape new narrative forms. Most obviously of all, laws and lawyers were at the centre of the great constitutional upheavals of the age, from the legally engineered reformation of religion and Henry VIII's and Edward VI's attempts to appoint their successors, to the lawyer-dominated parliaments that challenged and then executed King Charles, and later framed the Bill of Rights that supposedly made the Glorious Revolution glorious. Participants in these and other political dramas drew heavily from a deep well of legal language and concepts that resonated in the public imagination, including Magna Carta, habeas corpus, the ancient constitution and the true liberties of the freeborn citizen. Scholars used to examine each of these parts of the law in isolation. Now – thanks to decades of pioneering work in a range of related fields – social, as well as cultural, political, economic and gender historians are beginning to realise the astonishing extent to which law in all its varied forms permeated early modern society and acted as a key determinant of change.

## Legal Structures

Almost all of the defining elements of the English justice system were already in place in 1500. The monarch presided at the apex of the legal system, as the font of justice, supposedly protecting the life, liberty and property of English subjects and dispensing mercy to temper the harshness of the criminal law. The Privy Council regulated the nobility and sought to shape behaviour through proclamations and prosecutions. Parliament passed statutes to supplement the existing common law and the largest central courts in London's Westminster Hall, King's Bench and Common Pleas; administered those laws; and heard appeals from the vast array of lesser courts that operated on manors and in cities, towns and boroughs all over the country. Judges went on circuit twice a year to hear common law actions at the assizes held in major urban centres and market towns, alternating venues year by year to deliver justice to as many communities and districts as possible. Supporting this fusion of regional and central justice, ecclesiastical authorities operated their own elaborate jurisdiction dealing with marriage, property inheritance and matters of sin, and local magistrates held quarter sessions four times a year. For matters that ecclesiastical and common law courts could not adequately address, the other court in Westminster Hall, Chancery, engineered equitable solutions tailored to individual circumstances. This framework altered little over the period, but the structures it supported and the roles it played underwent significant transformations between 1500 and 1750.

## Litigation Growth and Its Effects

The sixteenth century witnessed a number of innovations, including the development of new prerogative courts: such as Star Chamber, which provided subjects with relief against misuses of power and the crown with a means of controlling its political enemies, and the court of Requests, which sought to extend equitable relief to the less powerful. However, the major catalyst for change during this century was a quickening of flows of legal business in existing jurisdictions. Beginning in earnest around 1550, the English experienced the fastest and largest growth in levels of litigation in recorded history. The number of cases initiated in the two largest common law courts grew from just over 2,000 cases a year in 1500 to over 23,000 cases a year by 1600, and continued expanding in the decades prior to the disruptions of the 1640s. The drop during the civil wars was temporary and litigation levels remained high until the last decade of the seventeenth century, when they fell away sharply. Surveying central court litigation from the year 1200 to the present day, 1640 appears to have been the high point, in terms of per capita litigation, and 1750 the low point.[1]

An even greater number of legal actions proceeded through England's local jurisdictions: the customary courts of rural manors, and the borough and mayors' courts in towns and cities (in addition to the criminal prosecutions that will be discussed later). In Kent, for example, in the year 1602 at least 183 residents participated in legal actions in Queen's Bench and 117 in Chancery, but 1,208 or more involved themselves in legal actions in local hundreds and manors or urban boroughs and liberties. The cathedral city of Canterbury alone had six different courts, hearing over 580 cases in that year. Yet in per capita terms, this caseload was actually below average for the period. Courts in Shrewsbury in Shropshire at this time heard around 1,100 cases a year when the population was approximately 5,500, the equivalent of one case for every five residents. The borough court of Romney Marsh in Kent heard 52 suits in 1602 when the town's population was only about 400 – the equivalent of one case for every four residents – and the average for the whole of Kent in 1602 was at least one case for every five inhabitants.[2] One speculative estimate puts the total number of lawsuits in England and Wales towards the end of the sixteenth century at over 1 million cases a year when the population had not yet reached 4 million. Given that each case required at least two parties, and often involved multiple plaintiffs or defendants, it soon becomes apparent that almost everyone in the country had direct experience of the law, whether as litigant, witness, juror or curious observer.[3]

The reasons for this dramatic expansion were social and economic more than legal. From about 1520, slow but steady population growth after a century of stability produced a rise in demand for goods and foodstuffs that produced inflation and helped fire an expansion of credit. Sales of interests in land also increased, especially after the dissolution of the monasteries, placing an even greater premium on capital and credit. More and more people formalised financial, property and sales agreements through legal means, both written and unwritten, and went to court if these arrangements or interactions went wrong.

In purely economic terms, an escalation in sales and extensions of credit produced a proportionate growth in defaults and lawsuits, but the relationship was not simply arithmetical. The majority of suits in the seventeenth-century Chancery, for example, represented not new causes or quarrels, but complaints about existing suits proceeding at common law. In other words, rising litigation levels helped to produce a culture of law, as knowledge of the law spread, aided by the rapid expansion of the legal profession, and as one outraged defendant after another became an adamant plaintiff in another lawsuit. Commentators throughout the period frowned on legal actions for breaking Christian codes of neighbourly charity, but as going to law increasingly became an acceptable response to dissension, litigation and the rule of law cemented themselves at the heart of the English psyche.

Church court defamation and common law slander actions also reached record levels between 1580 and 1620 (the majority of the former brought by women), revealing concerns about honour and reputation and the fragility of personal credit during a time of large-scale migration from rural areas to urban centres. Neighbours who sued each other for verbal slights almost invariably knew each other, but many of those who felt driven to defend their credit had an eye to their economic standing and honest character in a world where markets and marketing were becoming increasingly anonymous.

The cultural effects of recourse to law on such an unprecedented scale spread far and wide. In terms of governance, a significant proportion of local court activity was administrative in nature, dealing with the election of officers, the regulation of trades, the maintenance of infrastructure and responses to poverty. On a more central level, the assize justices on their twice-yearly circuits schooled local populations through their charges or instructions to grand and trial juries, highlighting current crown concerns and driving home the principles and ideological importance of obedience to law. They then reported local problems and disaffections back to their superiors and royal officials in Whitehall and Westminster. This process proved as essential to the maintenance of good governance, centralised power and the growth of civil society as the reading of proclamations in town and village markets and squares, or of sermons from the pulpit.

The linkages between law and politics became even stronger with the dramatic expansion of the legal profession and a growing recognition in intellectual circles of the 'scientific' qualities of legal reasoning. Critics were quick to lambast lawyers as 'pettyfoggers and vipers of the commonwealth' but men with legal training soon became influential figures in local and central circles of governance, serving as stewards on manors, as sheriffs and Justices of the Peace (JPs), and making up the largest single grouping in the House of Commons. It is telling that at the beginning of the seventeenth century, of the sixty Kentish men acting as JPs, mayors and jurats, forty-two had served as MPs.[4]

Sheriffs, messengers and litigants helped consolidate the law's power and reach as they criss-crossed their counties and braved the roads to and from London, carrying and serving the parchment writs that signalled court proceedings. Courts issued writs to get parties into court; to proceed to the issue, amend the proceedings or have a cause transferred from one court to another; to call jurors, ensure their attendance or find replacements; to ensure the losing party accepted a court's decision; to attach the defendant's pledges; and to collect the damages the court awarded. The officials, litigants and allies carrying these writs discussed their legal burdens in alehouses and turnpike taverns, adding yet more links to the spreading chains of legal communication.

The diffusion of legal parchment and paper had other effects, as more and more individuals employed legal instruments to organise their lives and transactions. Increasing numbers of apprentices put their signatures or marks to indentures that set out the terms of their apprenticeships, especially after the 1563 Statute of Artificers mandated apprenticeships or service for unmarried adolescents 'living at their own hand'. In response to changes in land conveyancing, growing numbers of married couples arranged jointures rather than rely on customary widow's rights to dower, and many chose to set down these arrangements in marriage settlements drawn up by scribes or lawyers. The elites had long been accustomed to creating 'uses', the forerunners of trusts, to control the descent of their lands, but after the passing of the Statute of Wills in 1540 individual choices set out in wills and testaments further displaced traditional customs of inheritance. The single most pervasive instrument, however, was the conditional bond, made famous by Shakespeare in *The Merchant of Venice*: a sealed document in which parties set down their agreement with a money penalty for default that could be sued for as a debt. Hundreds of thousands of English women and men turned to bonds to secure all manner of transactions and activities, and the penalties could be severe – typically double the amount of a loan, even if the term was only a few weeks or months. Liability was strict, meaning that penalties could be claimed even if payment was only a day late, or if the bondholder had repaid the loan in full but had neglected to have the bond cancelled. Equity courts could intervene to provide relief in severe cases, but for a growing number of bondholders, failure to pay the penalty resulted in imprisonment for debt – a severe enough result to evoke, if not to mirror, the pound-of-flesh penalty in Shakespeare's play.

## The Rise of Contract

Reliance on all of these legal instruments familiarised whole generations of English men and women with the effects of legal terms and conditions, and of the dangers that could lurk in lawyers' fine print. These were early days in the evolution of the modern law of contract, but it is possible to argue in the broadest terms that the English were becoming accustomed to thinking contractually, a point brought home by the emergence in the seventeenth century of the concept of the social 'contract' that borrowed heavily from ideas and vocabulary associated with marriage contracts. In inheritance, the customary practice of primogeniture increasingly gave way to personal choice (in the form of bequests in wills, and terms and conditions in family settlements), and provision for widows relied less on dower (a life interest in a third of a husband's property) and more on jointures (specified interests in land or annual payments during widowhood). Dower was a customary right that applied universally, whereas jointures were contractual interests that had to be arranged, a shift with varied effects depending on a woman's resources, knowledge and access to legal representation.

The nature of litigation also tended to shift focus away from customary practices and community habits of mind towards individuals. Although many unprincipled litigants used legal process to dominate opponents with fewer resources, lawsuits could also undermine hierarchies of status and wealth, and challenge unfair uses of power and authority. In terms of social status, the majority of plaintiffs sued their equals or social superiors. Some apprentices sued their masters and mistresses; middling-sort property owners sued members of the gentry; and tenants on manors brought suits against lords, ladies and stewards, challenging exploitative practices and so weakening local powerbases.

Litigation could also confront patriarchal divisions. Around a third of legal actions in most English jurisdictions involved at least one woman, and women made up between 10 and 15 per cent of litigants in most courts, a proportion that rose as the sixteenth century gave way to the seventeenth. Female litigants challenged male adversaries in court in ways that had previously been unthinkable. In a direct blow to 'coverture', the common law principle that a husband's legal identity and property rights 'covered' or subsumed his wife's, some married women even managed to sue their husbands in equity courts, seeking assurances of their personal safety during periods of estrangement and asserting control over property that coverture customarily gave to their husbands.

Observers rightly identified litigation as a symptom of the failure of neigh-bourly relations, but the opportunities it gave people from all but the poor-est backgrounds to protect their interests contributed to an emerging notion of individual rights. Resources remained key – the litigant with the most financial, social and legal assets enjoyed a huge advantage – but a rhetoric that placed the virtue of the legal cause above the status of the contestants provided a significant alternative to existing hierarchical registers of power.

Alongside this capacity to act as a solvent against tradition, interpersonal litigation also brought huge pressure to bear on conceptions of personal trust, during an age when financial credit and moral or personal credit were inextricably intertwined. What might be characterised as a legal loss of innocence proved to be painful for many parties, but as Craig Muldrew has shown, despite the unprecedented number of personal clashes at law, and the resulting erosion of friendships and professional relationships, the commitment to the values of Christian neighbourly charity and the ideal of personal trust they supported held firm. And while criticism of lawyers and of legal officials was common, the target of the near constant cho-rus of angry voices was the corruption or failings of particular lawyers or judges rather than the shortcomings of the system itself. Virtually no-one shared the desire of Dick the Butcher in Shakespeare's *Henry VI, Part II* to 'kill all the lawyers' and pull down and replace the whole legal structure.[5]

As the seventeenth century gave way to the eighteenth, disillusionment with the heartache and cost of litigation led to a precipitous drop in the number of lawsuits that still has not been adequately explained. It appears that growing numbers of people sought alternative ways of conducting business and dealing with indebtedness and disagreements that did not require frequent confrontations in court. Credit instruments emerged that offered greater flexibility than conditional bonds and a means of transferring debt without recourse to court. Falling demand led lawyers to increase their fees, and the contracts, documents and pleadings they framed became increasingly technical and more expensive. A typical Chancery bill from 1500 includes a single paragraph, whereas those from 1800 fill multiple tabletop-sized pages. The combination of these effects created barriers that made the law less and less accessible to ordinary peo-ple, in terms of its alien nature as well as its costs.

## Crime and Criminal Justice

Alongside the rise in interpersonal litigation, the century from 1540 to 1640 witnessed a dramatic focus on regulation, with law-making bodies intensifying efforts to influence or control the behaviour of the general population. Parliamentary statutes, royal proclamations and an avalanche of regulations sought not only to combat crime through statutory extensions to the common law, but also to license all manner of trades and occupations and clamp down on disruptive or immoral behaviours including drunkenness, vagrancy, profanity, blasphemy, gambling and idleness. These further expressions of the state- (and Church-) building impulse met with varied success, but rarely fulfilled their makers' ambitions. Attempts to impose restrictions on dress and diet based on social status, for example, soon revealed the limits on law as a mechanism of social engineering. In this and other instances, the co-operation of the community proved vital, in particular the sheriffs, magistrates, mayors, aldermen, churchwardens and constables charged with putting orders and regulations into practice. These officials proved adept at using legal means to maintain order in their communities, and while some favoured harsh enforcement, others moderated their zealousness according to local conditions and the mood of the community. From the regulation of alehouses and drunkenness to the policing of profane oaths, the will and desires of central authorities were 'tempered by the realities of local social relations'.[6]

These realities proved particularly complex and fraught in London during its long history of sustained population growth beginning in the mid sixteenth century. Aldermen, JPs and parish officials shared a strong impulse to maintain order, or at least to contain disorder, but the sheer scale of the problems attending high migration and mobile populations in the jumbled streets of this port capital produced dramatic variation from ward to ward and magistrate to magistrate. Local efforts to reform and increasingly to regulate the city's vagrant poor filled the hospitals of Bridewell and Bethlem, transforming them into houses of correction where punishments included whipping and hard labour, while the vast bulk of legal charges – for petty theft and other misdemeanours – were dealt with without recourse to criminal trials.[7] The interplay between residents and under-resourced local and central authorities could resemble a loud and at times chaotic dance, as individuals and groups shifted their civic allegiances and made choices based on the acceptance, appropriation, modification or rejection of elite orders, aspirations and values. The same neighbours who fought Church court battles over defamation informed on or covered for each other as they used, evaded or fell victim to the law.

London represents a unique case, but the reactive nature of the public policing initiatives in the capital that had to be responsive to local conditions and concerns can be detected in other attempts by state and Church authorities to control behaviour. A good example, to set against blunter attempts to impose elite power, is the evolution of penal laws targeting Catholics, which occasioned fraught conversations about personal responsibility and public order. The Elizabethan regime famously prioritised political obedience over rigid religious conformity and introduced fines for non-attendance at divine service. The problems created by the peculiar status of married women, however, tied parliamentarians in knots. The original legislation targeted heads of household, on the assumption that they were responsible for the conformity of their families and servants, but staunchly Catholic elite women who organised celebrations of mass, aided and abetted seminary priests, and helped the 'old' religion not just stay alive but grow, became a thorn in the side of lawmakers. Attempts to extend existing legislation to apply to married women came up against practical problems created by the common law rules of coverture. These automatically transferred a wife's money and moveable property to her husband, leaving her no means of paying a fine.

From at least the 1570s, the solution of the Commissions for Ecclesiastical Causes, tasked with enforcing the reformation of religion, was to issue recognisances against the husbands of Catholic wives. These bonds put the onus on husbands to exhort their wives (or their whole families) to conform, on pain of a money penalty for non-compliance. This use of 'binding over' raised significant revenues, but husbands protested that it amounted to punishing one person for the crimes of another and complained that they could not be held responsible for their wives' beliefs. Recusant wives, meanwhile, played upon their diminished status to evade prosecution, as Elizabeth Moninge did in the early 1590s when she declared that 'she is a wife and under subjection and therefore of noe abilitie to give ayde' to Catholic priests. In seeking a long-term statutory solution, some members of Parliament favoured imprisonment as the punishment for married women recusants, but as one MP objected when debating the 1610 bill, 'I hold this remedy as bad if not worse than the disease.' Final resolution only came when Parliament retained imprisonment for married women but introduced the possibility of a husband paying a fee of £10 a month to purchase her freedom.[8] This measure increased the crown revenues resulting from recusancy, but as with the use of recognisances, the laws failed in their objective of having Catholicism die on the vine.

## Criminal Prosecutions

Where royal and ecclesiastical authorities met with greater success was in the accommodation of private prosecutions of crime and antisocial actions that could be labelled sinful. As the civil courts filled with litigation, so

criminal and ecclesiastical court caseloads swelled during the sixteenth
and early seventeenth century. In political circles the maintenance of order
was of paramount importance, reflected in the breathless language of the
burgeoning statutes outlawing the supposed catalysts of disorder. Statutes
not only created new felonies, but limited the application of the increasingly anachronistic legal fiction of benefit of clergy, which allowed convicted male felons to escape the death penalty if they could 'prove' they
were members of the clergy by passing a literacy test. The English legal
establishment also fulminated against the dangers of crime and disorder in
published judgments, commentaries and charges to juries. Yet state officials, such as the Attorney General, initiated a relatively small proportion
of criminal prosecutions, and the record levels of prosecutions witnessed
between 1580 and 1620 did not result from elite campaigns against criminal activities. Once again, the drivers of this growth were ordinary subjects seeking remedies or relief, either as victims of crime or as temporary
local officers charged with the presentment of offences. Royal and Church
officials took seriously the obligation to provide legal services, but it was
the people of England, from all but the lowest social ranks, who sought
out those services in record numbers.

The ideological underpinnings of the criminal law are well known,
laid bare in the common law's identification of the theft of goods worth
more than a shilling as a felony, attracting forfeiture of property and the
death penalty, while violent physical assault was merely a misdemeanour
attracting a fine. However, the changing patterns of criminal prosecutions
over time are revealing. For the reasons John Walter highlights in the next
chapter on 'Authority and Protest', the same population growth that produced economic change and inflation prompting the rise of civil litigation
also created a significant growth in poverty. This helped inspire various
forms of social protest and it also appears to have contributed to the rise
in criminal prosecutions, reflecting both a growth in the commission of
certain crimes, such as thefts, especially during desperate times brought
on by harvest failures, and heightened anxiety about the threat of crime.
The precise extent of crimes committed is impossible to discern, but it
is undeniable that during these years of social, economic and religious
upheaval more offences of all descriptions came before the courts in the
decades leading up to the 1640s, peaking sharply in the 1620s.

## Homicide, Violence and the Emergence of Manslaughter

Looking at long-term trends, it is clear that prosecutions for homicide
declined between the medieval and modern periods. However, that

decline was neither steady nor even, and indictments for homicide rose from the closing decades of the sixteenth century, reaching significant peaks in the 1590s and especially the 1620s. State executions of guilty felons followed a similar path, and in Cheshire in the 1620s there were on average 110 homicide indictments and 166 executions a year, when the population was probably no more than 80,000.[9] Killing during these unsettled years, in the form of murders and executions, was more frequent than during any decade of the preceding century or any time since.

After the 1640s there was a perceptible decline in prosecutions for homicide and for almost every other category of serious crime and offence. The Devon assizes, for example, heard around 250 cases a year between 1598 and 1640, but fewer than 40 cases a year between 1700 and 1710. In seventeenth-century London, homicides and other crimes against the person fell faster than crimes against property, which then began to rise again in the eighteenth century, suggesting shifts in sensibilities and behaviour in an increasingly commercial world of production and consumption. However, this increase in the prominence of property crime has not been so clearly detected in the rest of the country and it appears that growing political stability, state resources and levels of policing together produced a world in which fewer crimes were prosecuted and perhaps one in which fewer crimes were actually committed.

Questions remain, however, about the relationship between decreasing prosecutions for assault and homicide and how violence was (and should be) defined. There is no conclusive evidence, for example, that incidents of domestic violence declined over this period, but as the inflicting of physical harm became more unacceptable, greater numbers of husbands resorted to confining their wives against their wills, whether at home or in institutions, and refusing them necessities, a process that broadened the behaviours that we would label abuse.[10] Over the whole period the percentage of homicides that occurred within households rose – a trend that has continued to the present day. It is tempting to read this rise as clear evidence of an intensification of emotional attachments within marriages and families over time, but the totals these percentages are based on tell a more complicated story. Actual numbers of domestic homicides declined over time; it is just that homicides between unrelated parties declined faster, suggesting a change in attitudes to casual violence and advances in medical science that prevented victims of violent assaults from dying from their injuries more than a pronounced deepening of the emotional intensity of familial relationships. Overall, physical acts of violence did diminish, but further investigation is required of the shifting boundaries between violence and violation, and of changing attitudes to different manifestations of aggression, hostility and cruelty.

Alongside a growth and then subsidence in the number of indictments for inexcusable killings, there was a cultural as well as a legal shift in conceptions of homicide as a crime, seen most clearly in the formalisation in the sixteenth century of the categories of manslaughter and murder. The penalty for manslaughter remained death, but the sentence could more easily be evaded, whether by seeking a pardon, or by claiming benefit of clergy or pregnancy; or on the grounds that the accused killer had acted spontaneously, 'in hot blood', rather than with malice aforethought. In the seventeenth century this process of delineating differing categories and severities of homicide continued, with the addition of various provocation defences. Intervening when a family member was under attack, responding to assaults that compromised a person's honour, fighting off someone unlawfully depriving another person of their liberty, or killing a man caught engaging in adultery with one's wife all came to be recognised as extenuating circumstances that could be taken into account at sentencing. None of them justified homicide, but they provided courts with grounds to excuse killers from the death penalty, and they did so by shifting attention from the state of mind of the accused to the contributory behaviour of the victim.

## Gender and Crime

The categories of manslaughter and provocation described above all bear interesting signs of gender difference, grounded as they are in conceptions of masculinity and male honour. In Galen's model of the human body, which dominated medical understanding until the seventeenth century, females were considered colder than males, making it harder for women to claim they acted out of 'hot-bloodedness'. In fact, courts, and the population at large, usually associated female murderers with 'cold-blooded' killings that attracted the severest penalties. Similarly, the sexual double standard and gendered conceptions of honour ensured that the provocation defence a husband might claim if he killed his wife's lover did not apply to a wife if the roles were reversed. In these and other instances, focusing attention on gender is transforming understandings of the experiences of men and women both as perpetrators and as victims of crime. Women, then as now, made up smaller proportions of accused criminals, but long-held suppositions about the characteristics of female offenders when compared with their male counterparts have recently been called into question. Research on London after the Restoration reveals that women made up at least a third of Old Bailey defendants accused of property crimes, rising to a majority between 1690 and 1713.[11] Evidence from seventeenth-century Cheshire suggests that female criminals did not restrict themselves to petty theft and proportionately were just as likely as men to be indicted for committing grand larceny. Females also figured prominently in assault cases, often using knives and fists as weapons, belying long-held assumptions that women preferred verbal to physical violence.[12]

The classifications some historians employ help to explain a tendency to under-report the number and seriousness of indictments for crimes committed by female offenders. Homicide statistics, for example, regularly exclude deaths resulting from witchcraft and infanticide. This exclusion is understandable, for the purpose of comparing early modern with modern crime rates, but it is a distinction that does not exist in the records and would have made little or no sense to people living at the time. To early modern eyes female murderers were female murderers, and they figured large in the popular imagination through crime pamphlets that sensationalised female killers as monsters.

The idea that judges and juries showed lenience to female offenders, acquitting them in greater numbers than men and sparing more of them the death penalty out of paternalistic (and patronising) notions of chivalry, also appears misguided. Women may have been indicted less often than men for committing homicide, but those indicted were far less likely than men to have their killings defined as manslaughter, and in Cheshire a greater proportion of women than men indicted for homicide received death sentences. As Krista Kesselring affirms, 'women were vastly overrepresented amongst cold blooded killers'.[13]

Some women escaped conviction for felonies, and more female than male offenders received pardons, in part because benefit of clergy was unavailable to them for most of the period. However, if there is a pattern to be found it is in marital status or life situation rather than gender. The Old Bailey Sessions Papers reveal that mothers with dependent children evaded execution more often than single women (just as later in the eighteenth century married women might be transported with their guilty husbands). The thinking was predominantly pragmatic rather than sexist or sympathetic and the chivalry thesis appears to be largely an invention of twentieth-century historians.

Instances of leniency or compassion also need to be set against the parts of English law that betray raw discrimination, such as the 1650 law that made adultery a felony carrying the death penalty, but only for women, and the 1624 'Act to prevent the murdering of bastard children' that made it a crime to conceal the death of an illegitimate child. This law produced a rare and blatant reversal of the presumption of innocence that lies at the heart of English criminal law by presuming guilt unless the concealers (almost invariably unmarried women) could prove their innocence. More complex undercurrents of gender bias can be detected in the law of rape. Authorities consistently regarded rape as one of the most heinous felonies and took it very seriously – in 1602 Sir Edward Coke and his colleagues doggedly pursued a rape prosecution through Star Chamber over the course of many months – but indictments were rare and successful prosecutions rarer still, with only around 10 to 12 per cent producing guilty verdicts.[14] The problem was the rigid standard of evidence the law demanded and a reluctance to send accused rapists to the gallows unless their guilt was unequivocal. It is hard not to conclude that the failure of these cases resulted in part from a privileging of men's word over women's, yet at the same time community members and judges did not always equate acquittals with innocence. In a trial at the Old Bailey in 1675, for example, the court acquitted Edward Coker of raping an eleven-year-old girl because of the lack of the 'evidence the law requires', but then convicted him of assault and fined him the substantial sum of £16 13s 4d.[15]

## Exemplary Justice, Exemplary Mercy and Popular Participation

The paradox of English justice in the seventeenth and eighteenth centuries was that a growth of offences attracting the death penalty produced not a rise but a fall in the number of successful prosecutions and executions. The more that MPs railed against the dreadfulness of particular crimes, the more that constables, magistrates, witness, judges and juries worked to spare the lives of individuals accused of committing those crimes.

Parliamentarians and commentators observing this divergence between prescribed justice and actual practice lamented the inefficiencies of the system. Douglas Hay, however, has argued quite elegantly that this slippage was in fact a key element in the system's success. A regime lacking the resources required to solve crimes, capture perpetrators and maintain order through armed force had always made deft use of its control of three interrelated levers: terror, majesty and mercy.[16] The brutality of the justice meted out at public executions – especially the hanging, drawing and quartering reserved for treason convictions – was intended to act as a powerful deterrent to others in the crowd and the community. The orchestrated majesty of the occasion, and of the assizes and trials in Westminster Hall that produced the verdicts, harnessed rituals, symbols and speeches to imbue the justice system with an aura of power, mystery and divine authority far exceeding the actual resources at the state's disposal. Finally, the selective application of penalties and the pardoning of selected convicted felons provided an alchemy that could give the crown a reputation for mercy and fairness, draw gratitude from convicted felons and (ideally) transmute rebelliousness into deference. The theatricality of pardoning, seen in reprieves delivered at the gallows, heightened the majesty of the law, and the need for pardons grew as the number of statutory felonies expanded in and after the sixteenth century, as many of them excluded the possibility of claiming benefit of clergy. The provision of mercy therefore constituted a flexing of the royal prerogative that enhanced royal power and authority, through the deployment of the crown's dispensing power to override statutes that sought to ensure that sentences of death were carried out.

This application of available resources by elite officials was shrewd rather than simplistic, couched in the rhetoric of good order, obedience and deference as an antidote to chaos. Assize justices used their charges to juries to encourage the transformation of elite ideology into universal norms out of their desire to maintain a bulwark against violence, theft and disorder. The coercive goals of the Tudor, Stuart and Hanoverian regimes did not result from a crude conspiracy hatched by men of property, but from a coalescing of interests that could ebb and flow between elite groups or over time, as the deep divisions of opinion over law and judicial independence during the 1640s, and 1670s and 1680s, make clear. Their efforts proved successful because of the numbers of English men and women who acknowledged the extent to which the system delivered what it promised, bringing suspected offenders to justice and maintaining a semblance of order in uncertain times.

Popular acknowledgement of the benefits of the rule of law was crucial, given the reliance of the justice system on community co-operation. People from all backgrounds reported and prosecuted crimes and appeared as witnesses at trial; members of the community acted as constables; yeomen and gentlemen served on grand and trial juries in the complex process that governed the path from accusation to verdict and sentencing. Each of the individuals involved could exercise discretion, observable in witnesses who chose to turn a blind eye to certain offences or offenders, constables and magistrates who decided not to assist a prosecution, and jurors who reduced the value of stolen goods to attract a lesser penalty or risked judicial sanction by voting to acquit an offender they thought was guilty.[17]

Individuals who exercised their discretion in these ways showed their own support for exemplary justice and exemplary mercy, achieved through unofficial as well as official means. It was not just crown officials, in other words, who conspired to execute recalcitrant repeat offenders and the ringleaders of rebellions, while letting other accused felons or traitors go free. Jurors played a role in many of these decisions and they joined other members of society in seeing the merits of inconsistent prosecution and sentencing in a range of different settings. The fates of women accused of felonies at the Old Bailey, for example, appear to have depended on the women's life circumstances, marital status and demeanours as much as on their supposed crimes. Those that showed remorse and exhibited humility were more likely to go free than women who showed defiance, and as pointed out above, courts often proved more willing to execute a felon without a spouse or children than those with dependants. In these cases the sympathies of jurors and judges aligned, in not wanting to leave hungry widows and orphans to burden poor-relief, or indirectly to punish wives or husbands for the sins of their spouses.[18]

The vital role that non-elites played in sustaining the criminal justice system, especially by pursuing prosecutions, does not diminish the importance of the three levers of terror, majesty and mercy in maintaining legal as well as political order. This can be discerned from those instances where authorities misapplied them. In 1685, for example, James II and his justices made a series of decisions in the aftermath of the Monmouth Rebellion that undermined rather than reinforced popular commitment to the rule of law. First of all army officers promised troopers 5s or the forfeited goods of each rebel they apprehended, with the result that 'the militia hunted their quarry like game', implicating over 1,300 rebels. Chief Justice Jeffreys and his colleagues then set out to try these suspects in less than four weeks, in the infamous 'Bloody Assizes'. Regular trials would have taken months to complete so Jeffreys and his colleagues encouraged those accused to plead guilty and to give confessions implicating their accomplices, implying that they would receive mercy. However, that mercy never came. In the first weeks 81 were hanged, drawn and quartered, and most of the rest were sentenced to the same fate. Around 170 of these were executed and a further 70 or so died in prison awaiting execution. Only a handful received a full pardon and the king marked 850 or more of the remainder for transportation to the West Indies, parcelling them out to royal favourites to be sold to planters for £10 to £15 a head.

This was brutal rather than exemplary justice. Executioners performed the hangings and mutilations in thirty-seven different localities across Devon and adjoining counties, and revolted the local populations rather than ensuring their loyalty and obedience, especially given the absence of exemplary mercy.[19] The aftermath of these callous prosecutions helped to hasten the demise of King James II and contributed to procedural changes that permitted offenders accused of treason to be represented by legal counsel for the first time, a move that led eventually to the introduction of defence counsel for all felonies.

James II's mercenary impulse was hardly new. The crown had long been accustomed to selling pardons not simply to encourage loyalty but also to raise revenue, sometimes for astonishing amounts of money.[20] Nor was this impulse confined to the elites. The speed with which neighbours descended on and spirited away the personal possessions of an accused felon could be breathtaking, as they anticipated the forfeiture of all property to the crown that would follow a guilty verdict. The crown also 'farmed' out criminal forfeitures, allowing individuals to bid for the right to collect forfeited property in a certain jurisdiction to sell for a profit, leading to predatory practices and contests between greedy neighbours. Infighting, profiteering and the common refusal to return property if the accused was found innocent all reveal the nasty underbelly of community relations and belie visions of apparent cohesion.[21] While it is possible to posit two discrete conceptions of criminal justice – what rulers wanted and what the ruled would put up with – examples of greed and expediency from monarch and subject alike suggest a more dynamic and fluid mix of interests that overlapped or competed with each other depending on circumstance and the sway of pragmatism.

The ability of criminal prosecutions to fracture community solidarity can also be seen in witchcraft accusations. In England a substantial number of accused witches were not isolated figures living on the margins of society, but well-established and productive members of their communities who had known their accusers for years or even decades. Regardless of social status, most accusations of witchcraft emerged from broader, longstanding interpersonal conflicts of myriad kinds, stemming from property disputes, religious difference, master–apprentice or employer–servant relations, or attacks on honour, and represented a last resort in the midst of deteriorating personal relations. Those accused often mounted robust defences and some brought counter suits or sued for damages on the grounds of defamation occasioned by false accusations. These prosecutions therefore blurred the boundaries between criminal and civil actions, exposing complex reactions to breaches in customary expectations of sociability.[22]

## Change over Time

The undulating patterns of litigation levels and criminal and ecclesiastical prosecutions between 1500 and 1750 reveal only part of the history of popular interactions with systems of justice. English law also embodied or inspired wider cultural shifts in society, such as the slow move away from religion as the bedrock of all legal pursuits. In civil litigation the effectiveness of sworn oaths diminished as fears of eternal damnation lost some of their purchase on the minds of the unscrupulous. Complaints of perjury grew shrill and produced statutory interventions. The central courts ceased to allow the defence of compurgation or wager of law – where the sworn oaths of twelve acquaintances could be used to confirm not the innocence of defendants, but the integrity of their sworn oaths – because of the rising incidence of complete strangers charging money to swear to the honesty of defendants they had never met. Jacobean comedies foreground these and other cynical attempts to thwart justice at any cost, providing alternative visions of justice to set beside the idealised versions advertised by magistrates and assize justices.

In the criminal sphere the displacing of God's justice by crown justice can be detected in a turning away from Christian providence as a central explanatory motif. Crime pamphlets from the sixteenth and early seventeenth centuries emphasised how divine intervention would reveal or expose guilty criminals, even if earthly investigations did not. In this earlier period judges and juries appeared more interested in the moral guilt of individuals than in evidence of the crimes they were alleged to have committed, paying closer attention to local testimony of character and past reputation than to objective assessments of fact. By the later seventeenth century this was changing, with legal authorities raising the standards of acceptable proof, seen most clearly in the dramatic decline of successful witchcraft accusations after courts began demanding physical confirmation of harm caused rather than relying on hearsay evidence.

Crime went from something that anyone could commit, if they succumbed to sinfulness, into something criminals commit – a change that is apparent in the etymology of the word itself. According to the *Oxford English Dictionary* the first use of 'criminal' as a noun dates from 1626.

The move from sinner to criminal can also be sensed in the growing tendency to criminalise vagrancy and poverty more generally, as observers increasingly blamed the poor for their condition. This process was not helped when Parliament began to make crimes of longstanding customary practices the poor relied on, such as rights to gleaning, grazing livestock on the commons or gathering firewood from forests.

The same secularising impulse is also discernible in the trajectories of specific crimes such as rape. Depictions of rape in the sixteenth century focused on moral weakness and the corrupting power of sin, seeing the potential for any man to become a rapist. By the eighteenth century, the figure of the evil and depraved rapist had emerged, no longer an 'everyman' but now a 'monster', a characterisation that helped many guilty rapists who did not appear to fit this new stereotype escape conviction.[23] To make matters worse, the admittance of legal counsel for accused rapists led to a new focus on the character of victims and began the insidious process of shifting blame and attention from the indicted attacker to his accuser.

Focusing attention on the motivations of offenders produced other more positive changes, as we have seen with the emergence of manslaughter from a growing recognition that some homicides were more morally or socially abhorrent than others. New sensitivities to human motivation also led to a drop in successful prosecutions for the murder or concealment of newborns. By the eighteenth century juries regularly used loopholes in the 1624 statute to acquit women who had community support, almost regardless of their guilt, setting infanticide, as it was coming to be labelled, on its eventual course from being regarded as an unforgivable heinous crime to a human tragedy. The same kind of shift in sensibilities slowly transformed the crime of suicide.

Other changes resulted from the increased centralisation of state and legal authority, such as a 'growing awareness' from the early decades of the seventeenth century 'of a distinction between the private interests of individuals and the public interests of the state'.[24] As justice became more centralised it also became more impersonal, the conviviality of local manor and borough courts displaced by increasingly anonymous urban jurisdictions. Centralisation and an expanding commitment to law as a 'rational science' also encouraged further professionalisation, and the growth of legal formalism and reliance on established rules. These developments left less room for exceptions and for the employment of discretion by jurors, who became increasingly passive participants in the trial process.

The unique character and conditions of seventeenth- and eighteenth-century London produced a number of innovations that professionalised policing and prosecution and transformed the evolving criminal justice system. A new breed of active stipendiary magistrate dealt summarily with petty offenders without resort to trial, and used incentives to reward thief-takers and encourage prosecutions in the Old Bailey. The same court hosted the emergence of public prosecutors and the first appearance of solicitors acting as defence counsel.[25]

All of these various improvements and developments, from the reduced reliance on community testimony in felony trials and the growing importance and cost of lawyers, to the shrinking autonomy of trial jurors and the emergence of professional policing, came at a price in terms of popular engagement with the law. In 1500 community members from a range of backgrounds participated in the criminal process, as accusers, constables, witnesses, grand and trial jurors, and audience members at trials and executions. By 1750 a process of exclusion from these processes was well under way, with constables less answerable to their communities; paid informers and thief-takers hunting for criminals; imprisonment and transportation increasingly replacing public executions; and secularised, scientific approaches to justice privileging the word and work of professionals. On the civil, or non-criminal, side, sixteenth-century depictions of Westminster Hall show throngs of curious onlookers and even a few dogs crowding the public courts of Common Pleas, Chancery and Queen's Bench that operated alongside booksellers and market stalls. By the eighteenth century these courts had become more private, and the world of law had retreated into the studied decorum of the wood-panelled lawyer's office and judge's chamber.

Traditional admirers of the common law praised it as rational and to a large extent democratic, shaped and fired by the community in the organic kiln of custom and through the deliberations of juries. Modern historians are less optimistic, recognising the hierarchical nature of traditional justice and its vulnerability to corruption, prejudice, and class- and gender-bias, but there is no disputing that the displacement of common law by statute lessened its organic character. In all these different ways the law arguably was becoming more and more detached and distant from the populations it served.[26]

## Notes

1 C. W. Brooks, *Pettyfoggers and Vipers of the Commonwealth: The 'Lower Branch' of the Legal Profession in Early Modern England* (Cambridge: Cambridge

University Press, 1986), 77–8; C. W. Brooks, *Lawyers, Litigation and English Society since 1540* (London and Rio Grande: Hambledon, 1998), 29.

2  L. Knafla, *Kent at Law 1602*, Vol. II: *Local Jurisdictions: Borough, Liberty and Manor*, List and Index Society, Special Series, 45–6 (Kew: List and Index Society, 2011), xvii–xxii; W. A. Champion, 'Litigation in the boroughs: Shrewsbury's *Curia Parva* 1480–1730', *Journal of Legal History*, 15 (1994).

3  C. Muldrew, *The Economy of Obligation: The Culture of Credit and Social Relations in Early Modern England* (Basingstoke: Macmillan, 1998), 236.

4  L. Knafla, *Kent at Law 1602*, Vol. I: *The County Jurisdiction: Assizes and Sessions of the Peace*, List and Index Society, Special Series, 45–6 (Kew: List and Index Society, 2009).

5  W. Shakespeare, *Henry VI, Part II*, IV.ii.73.

6  S. Hindle, *The State and Social Change in Early Modern England, c. 1550–1640* (New York: St Martin's Press, 2000), 202.

7  P. Griffiths, *Lost Londons: Change, Crime, and Control in the Capital City, 1550–1660* (Cambridge: Cambridge University Press, 2008).

8  K. Peddle, 'In the name of the Father: The Elizabethan response to recusancy by married Catholic women, 1559–1586', *Feminist Legal Studies*, 15 (2007).

9  C. B. Phillips and J. H. Smith, *Lancashire and Cheshire from AD 1540* (London: Taylor and Francis, 1994), 7.

10 E. Foyster, 'At the limits of liberty: Married women and confinement in eighteenth-century England', *C&C*, 17 (2002).

11 J. M. Beattie, *Policing and Punishment in London, 1660–1750: Urban Crime and the Limits of Terror* (Oxford: Oxford University Press, 2001).

12 G. Walker, *Crime, Gender and Social Order in Early Modern England* (Cambridge: Cambridge University Press, 2003).

13 K. J. Kesselring, 'Bodies of evidence: Sex and murder (or gender and homicide) in early modern England, c. 1500–1680', *Gender and History*, 27 (2015); Walker, *Crime, Gender and Social Order*.

14 L. Knafla, *Kent at Law 1602*, Vol. III: *Star Chamber*, List and Index Society, Special Series, 51 (Kew: List and Index Society, 2012), xxv–xxvi, 30–67; G. Walker, 'Rape, acquittal and culpability in popular crime reports in England, c. 1670–c. 1750', *P&P*, 220 (2013), 126.

15 Walker, 'Rape, acquittal and culpability'.

16 D. Hay, 'Property, authority and the criminal law,' in D. Hay, P. Linebaugh, J. G. Rule, E. P. Thompson and C. Winslow, *Albion's Fatal Tree: Crime and Society in Eighteenth-Century England* (London: Allen Lane, 1975).

17 C. Herrup, *The Common Peace: Participation and the Criminal Law in Seventeenth-Century England* (Cambridge: Cambridge University Press, 1987).

18 M. Caswell, 'Mothers, wives, and killers: Marital status and homicide in London, 1674–1790', in R. Hillman and P. Ruberry-Blanc (eds.), *Female Transgression in Early Modern Britain: Literary and Historical Explorations* (Burlington, VT: Ashgate, 2014).

19  R. Clifton, *The Last Popular Rebellion: The Western Rising of 1685* (London and New York: Maurice Temple Smith and St Martin's Press, 1984).

20  K. J. Kesselring, *Mercy and Authority in the Tudor State* (Cambridge: Cambridge University Press, 2003).

21  K. J. Kesselring, 'Felony forfeiture and the profits of crime in early modern England', *HJ*, 53 (2010).

22  M. Gaskill, *Crime and Mentalities in Early Modern England* (Cambridge: Cambridge University Press, 2000).

23  G. Walker, 'Everyman or a monster? The rapist in early modern England, *c.* 1600–1750', *HWJ*, 76 (2013).

24  C. W. Brooks, *Law, Politics and Society in Early Modern England* (Cambridge: Cambridge University Press, 2008), 423.

25  Beattie, *Policing and Punishment in London.*

26  D. Lemmings, *Law and Government in England during the Long Eighteenth Century: From Consent to Command* (Basingstoke: Palgrave Macmillan, 2011).

IO

# *Authority and Protest*

## John Walter

Early modern government, conscious of its limited powers of repression and of the potential consequences of social and economic change, subscribed to the image of the people as 'the many-headed monster', 'likely to mutiny and rebel on the least occasion'.[1] Many historians, noting the grievances of the victims of change and subscribing to an economically determinist reading of the causes of protest, have shared this belief in the ubiquity of popular disorder. But the reality of protest was, nevertheless, rather different. Awareness of the limited coercive powers at their disposal meant that in their handling of the people and protest early modern governments and their local officers were capable of a more nuanced approach. The theoretical acceptance of a commercial society lagged behind the realities of economic change, and in consequence both Church and government could share popular hostility to the consequences of an increasingly capitalist economy. In turn, popular protest often defied the contemporary stereotype of collective violence unleashed in riot and rebellion. That protesters employed a broader range of tactics and strategies has encouraged more recent studies to emphasise the negotiative politics that lay behind protest and to talk of a popular political culture informing protest. And finally, and paradoxically, in the longer run the restructuring of society that economic change sponsored in this period helps to explain some marked changes in the pattern of collective protest, including the disappearance of large-scale rebellions and (arguably) the eventual 'pacification' of much of the countryside.

## Authority

Early modern governments lacked a substantial bureaucracy, professional police force and standing army. To govern the country, they were therefore forced to rely on the unpaid service of landed and civic elites such as sheriffs and magistrates, and parochial elites of farmers, traders and craftsmen as constables and churchwardens. Where rulers and ruled agreed about the proper priorities of government, this could be a very effective means of maintaining order – the gentry and middling sort lending their authority and power to implementing the orders of royal government. But early modern governments were aware that where class interest cut across consensus then a dependence on propertied elites could itself cause disorder.

In the early part of this period a landed class, dependant largely on wealth from its estates to maintain appropriate patterns of consumption and material display, sought to meet the challenge of inflation by appropriating more of the farmers' and smallholders' surplus. Seeking to achieve this either through changes to rents and tenures and/or the enclosure and engrossing of holdings in pursuit of direct farming and increasing rent rolls, the landed class might have to be persuaded to support the government's attempts to inhibit enclosure or to police the marketing of grain. This explains the government's recurring emphasis on the threat posed to the social order by 'the many-headed monster'. Similarly, the attitudes of 'middling-sort' parish officers were also critical. This was the group on which successive governments depended as local officials and members of juries and special commissions to present infringements of the laws relating to enclosure and the marketing of grain. But in periods or places where their own interests were threatened, they might use their local standing and the authority of manorial or royal office to lead protesting crowds. Lacking a standing army, early modern governments were forced to rely on locally recruited 'trained bands'. However, in regions where the causes of popular discontent were widely shared, members of the trained bands might side with rebels and rioters, or prove reluctant to suppress protests. From the rebellions of the Pilgrimage of Grace in the 1530s to the last agrarian rebellion in this period, the Midlands Rising of 1607, successive governments had the misfortune to realise the force of R. H. Tawney's observation that 'the reluctant militia of yesterday' might become 'enthusiastic rebels'.[2] Significantly, it was the presence of *foreign* mercenaries, assembled to fight in Scotland, which made possible the bloody suppression of the 1549 rebellions.

An important consequence of early modern government's potential weaknesses in repressing collective protest was its recognition of the importance of preventing it by *anticipating* and averting the causes of popular disorder. But early modern governments tended to mistake consequences for causes. Unaware of the dynamics of demographic and economic change, they believed that engrossing, enclosure and associated changes in farming practice – notably the conversion of arable to pasture – were the main causes of growing landlessness, scarcity and famine. Successive governments therefore introduced laws to regulate enclosure and engrossing. They also attempted to ameliorate prices by regulating the export of grain and policing the activities of middlemen in the grain trade and market, to regulate employment and to fix wages. All of these measures would be cited, and sometimes selectively (and knowingly) mis-cited, by protesters to legitimise their protests.

Lacking an extensive bureaucracy, but enjoying a united realm subject to royal law, the English crown also made important use of the law and law courts to publicise and prosecute its policies. This helps to explain the popular legalism that often shaped early modern protests. Collective protests were sometimes preceded or paralleled by the collection of common purses and the pursuit of remedy by waging law. But while knowledge of government policy might offer legitimation for popular protest, it might also help to contain the actions that protesters allowed themselves in an attempt to avoid charges of treason, riot or theft. And that popular grievances might also be pursued through the courts perhaps helped to moderate actual levels of disorder.

Early modern governments also made use of the Church, especially after the Reformation, to promote ideas about the social responsibilities of property-owners and power-holders. The Edwardian prayer book, for example, contained a prayer for 'good' landlords. At times of harvest failure, 'tuning the pulpits' to have sermons preached on the Christian duty of charity to neighbours and the poor, and the sinfulness of seeking to profit from scarcity, was common. Underlying these efforts was a continuing belief, reinforced by Renaissance civic humanism, in society as a commonweal or commonwealth. This was a protean concept in which the monarch had responsibility for the well-being of his or her subjects, and what would later be seen as purely economic relations should be guided by a shared responsibility for the good of fellow men and women. These ideas were always ideals, and they were increasingly challenged by the realities of economic change, which pitched the profits of commodity against the moral imperatives of commonweal. However, they continued to be important in the mental world of the people and, especially at times of economic crisis, received periodic restatement by government.

Despite the limitations they faced, early modern governments were capable of bloody repression, sometimes enforced by the more dependable private retinues of the landed class. Captured rebels could be subjected to the gory punishment of being hanged, drawn and quartered as traitors, or returned alive to their home towns or villages to be hanged on their doors.

But in the absence of readily effective forces of repression, royal governments promoted a culture of obedience. This was preached from the pulpit and promulgated in royal proclamations. It stressed that the monarch
ultimately derived his or her authority from God, that obedience was a
God-given obligation and rebellion a sin. Repression might be tempered
by the judicious dispensation of mercy to publicly penitent rebels. But the
public display of dismembered bodies preserved in pitch, such as the heads
of rebels that greeted travellers crossing London bridge, offered a powerful
reminder that within this culture of obedience there was no right to protest
against an authority ultimately derived from God. If anything, even worse
for men and women who believed in the physical reality of heaven and
hell was the message that even dissent by those who escaped detection and
detention would be known to an omniscient God and punished at death
by condemnation to the everlasting torments of hell. Within the belief
system of the early modern world, these were heavy threats, to which the
annual reading in the parish church of government-sponsored homilies –
on obedience, on rebellion – and the scripted (and often printed) 'last-
dying speeches' on the scaffold of convicted rebels gave repeated emphasis.[3]

Taken together, all these measures were designed to persuade the people
that monarchs used their power to protect the lives and livings of – especially the poorest – subjects. In creating this 'public transcript' of the good
king and loyal subjects, early modern governments sought to secure popular consent to their exercise of power as an authority legitimised by God (a
relationship that of course imposed further obligations) and exercised in
defence of its subjects. Royal protection, therefore, assumed popular obedience.[4] But, as will be seen, the creation of this transcript and the elaboration of laws and policies, whose explicit justification was the defence of
commonwealth and people, also opened up a space (at least in the eyes
of the people and protesters) for legitimate protest against the enemies of
commonwealth and people. This helps to explain why protest often took
the form of negotiating with, rather than trying to overthrow, authority,
and of enforcing rather than opposing royal policies. The evidence of sedition utterances suggests that there were always those willing to ground
their grievances in the language of class, but there was a discrepancy
between the full-blooded actions projected within these rhetorics of violence and the recoverable pattern of *collective* protest.[5]

## Protest

A series of factors appeared to make such protest more likely in this period.
Population growth between the early sixteenth and mid seventeenth

centuries created, both directly and indirectly, a significant growth in poverty. Directly, it led to the growth of a landless or land-poor population, while indirectly the pressures of a growing population on a pre-industrialised agriculture sector were the major cause of an inflation that saw the prices of basic foodstuffs increase perhaps eightfold in a little over 100 years. In turn, inflation and oversupply of the labour market saw real wages perhaps cut by half over a similar period. The impact of this inflation was all the greater on an early modern population that had been accustomed to a sustained period of lower prices, higher real wages and more plentiful land after the fall in population triggered by the Black Death and subsequent endemic plague.

Definitions of poverty vary, but by the mid seventeenth century close to half the population might be classified as poor. This was an alarming figure and reflected the structural weaknesses of a pre-industrialised economy. Nonetheless, it fails to register the even larger numbers who lived within the penumbra of poverty and who might find themselves plunged into poverty by conjunctural crises. Of these, the most threatening was harvest failure. When the harvest – the heartbeat of the economy – failed, which it did with worryingly but unpredictable regularity, there was a much larger group of 'harvest-sensitive' poor. Moreover, harvest failure was often symbiotically linked with trade depression, since high food prices diminished demand for cloth and other manufactures. While trade, and with it manufactures, experienced significant growth in this period, the nature of these sectors produced further instability. Overseas trade was vulnerable to the political dislocations, caused by currency manipulation and wars, over which the government had limited control. Manufacturing took place either in guild-controlled urban workshops or usually guild-free rural cottages, the latter notably in the major textile industries, which were located in pastoral rural economies with a surplus labour supply, with major centres in East Anglia, the West Country and West Riding of Yorkshire. Given the relative absence of fixed capital on which merchants organising the trade had to secure a return, a slump in the market saw them refusing to buy up the finished product, leading to the withdrawal of circulating capital. Thus, densely populated communities dependent on the state of the market for both work and food quickly became vulnerable to collective unemployment whenever the harvest failed or overseas markets were disrupted.

It is, then, easy to see why governments were quick to assume that economic change would produce growing disorder. But in reality there was a striking disparity between both the volume and nature of protest and those projected by a reading of the economic indices. Clearly, in the broadest terms, the map and pace of economic change determined where collective protests were likely to take place. Since it was the highly visible phenomenon of enclosure that generated riots in the countryside, such collective acts of protest were unlikely to be found in areas where enclosure was absent or took place either before or after this period. By contrast, grain riots, which in this period were almost entirely targeted against the export or internal movement of grain, were absent from upland pastoral-woodland areas that did not generate grain surpluses. In areas like the Lake District, harvest failure might produce famine but not crowd actions over food. This underlines the fact that it was not economic problems per se but popular understandings of the *causes* of those problems that determined whether or not grievance would lead to collective protest. For that to happen crowds needed to feel that any actions they took were not only strategic but also legitimate. Collective protest therefore, though frequent, was always exceptional and not everyday.

Protests took a variety of forms. These might run from seditious individuals giving voice to their grievances in anonymous written threats; through collective grumbling in the alehouse and market and the petitioning of the authorities; to collective crowd actions in riot and, in the sixteenth century, rebellion. They might also take the form of street theatre or of highly ritualised and symbolic adaptations of popular cultural and festive forms like the skimmington ride or Rogationtide procession.[6] In their uneven geography and discontinuous chronology, crowd protests also reflected the fact that change in early modern England was experienced locally and regionally, rather than nationally. Yet local and national sources of discontent could sometimes intersect. For example, the largest rebellion of the sixteenth century, the Pilgrimage of Grace, was a protest against the impact of royal policies and the Henrician Reformation, but in some areas, notably in the north-west, agrarian grievances help to explain why the rebel hosts were able to recruit crowds numbered in their thousands.[7] Popular memory might, with justice, associate the Reformation and dissolution of the monasteries with the seizure and exploitation of Church lands by crown and landed class.[8] Later, as England became a nation of protestants, anti-popery could licence attacks on Catholic members of the landed class who were unpopular, and enclosing lords of the manor. But most protests had their roots in economic and social grievance and operated within the politics of subsistence.

At the beginning of the period, in what was still a largely agrarian economy, it was access to land that prompted most protests. Later, as the proportion of the harvest-sensitive population dependent on the market for both employment and food increased, the emphasis began to shift to food riots, which by the harvest crises of the later seventeenth century had replaced enclosure riots as the most common form of collective protest. By the eighteenth century, the politics of the trade in which producers sought to defend the customs of their trade had become more important, anticipating their later predominance in the Industrial Revolution era.

## Agrarian Protest, Common Rights and Access to Land

With renewed population growth putting increased value on land, lords of the manor attempted to exploit their full range of rights over their tenants, seeking in particular to alter customs and tenure to raise rents and entry fines and so to appropriate more of their tenants' surplus. Given the variety and varying strength of tenures this was almost invariably a slow process and one that varied in success. At the same time, lords sought a return to direct farming by resuming their demesnes, which they had let out in the fifteenth century in response to late medieval population stagnation. This might involve enclosure, but it could also involve the intensification of other seigneurial rights. For example, in the sheep–corn region of East Anglia lords had the right, under a system known as foldcourse, to pasture (fold) their sheep flocks on the open fields, a right that they sought to exploit to profit from the buoyant market for wool. Such 'seigneurial reaction' had consequences for the authority of lordship. Whereas the aristocratic leaders of the 1536 Pilgrimage of Grace could mobilise many thousands, by the Northern Rising of 1569 their own estate policies had driven a wedge between such men and their tenants: they were able to recruit fewer and could more easily be suppressed by the government. It led to a series of mid-sixteenth-century rebellions, of which the best known is Kett's Rebellion, centred in the eastern counties of Norfolk and Suffolk.[9] In these rebellions, protesters took to direct action, throwing down enclosures and menacing unpopular landlords. But they also drew up articles of grievances and petitioned royal government for redress, expecting that the government under Protector Somerset would be sympathetic to grievances that both preachers and royal proclamations had attacked as destructive to the commonwealth.

Although an argument has been made that these rebellions could be seen as the last in the line of medieval risings by the commons, they also exhibited patterns of popular thought and behaviour that were to characterise much early modern protest. Despite their numerical superiority and rhetoric of violence, destruction was directed against property, not persons. In turn, this reflected the fact that although such large-scale gatherings doubtless encompassed a variety of opinions, the degree of leadership and control that the protesters achieved challenged the elite's stereotype of the violent and irrational 'many-headed monster'. Drawing on representations of the monarch as the fount of justice, the protesters sought to negotiate with, rather than oppose, royal government. They envisaged an alliance of the true commons with the just king against a landed class whose policies both threatened the commonwealth and challenged their own self-image as the good lord whose estate policies (supposedly) balanced the interests of lord and tenant.

The 1549 rebellions represented the largest outbreak of popular rebellion since the English revolt of 1381. But in many ways they were also the high water mark of agrarian rebellion. Kett's Rebellion ended in bloody suppression. The mid-century rebellions, especially when rewritten by government-authorised histories as bloody and violent expressions of class conflict, helped to further a change in the English landed class's attitude to their lands that contributed to the decline of rebellion as a form of protest. Increasingly, lords of the manor shifted from a traditional seigneurial policy of seeking to appropriate more of a limited tenant surplus to one in which they began to recognise the possibilities of securing a greater income through co-operation with their (larger) tenants in the more efficient farming of their lands. This was the beginning of a momentous change, since it signalled the transformation of the English landed class from seigneurs to agrarian capitalists and created an alliance of landlords and wealthy farmers that was to dominate much of the English countryside.

Since co-operation was increasingly between lords of the manor and their wealthier tenants in common pursuit of the profits of the market, this also contributed to a process of internal differentiation that saw middling-sort tenants switch from being the leaders of rebellion to the promoters of state authority in local society. Consequently, by the end of the sixteenth century, another attempted popular rising that sought consciously to draw on the legacy of 1549 – the so-called Oxfordshire Rising of 1596 – failed to mobilise those affected by enclosure. Nevertheless, this episode also reflected another striking characteristic of the relationship between government and protesters. Such was the government's fear of the threat of disorder in the hungry 1590s that knowledge of the attempted rising persuaded it to renew legislation policing enclosure.[10] This sensitivity to the threat of popular violence meant that government economic policy would continue to lag behind economic realities, prohibitive, rather than

permissive, of economic change. In turn, this meant that government policy continued to provide protesters with legitimation for their protests.

Change to tenures was a long-term process that continued to generate
conflicts in defence of custom, a potent but protean concept registering
the (past and present) balance of power between lords and tenants. These
could be fought out in both manorial and royal equity courts, the latter an
arena where tenants, if they could meet the costs of legal action and produce written records for the claimed rights (both large ifs), might enjoy
some success. But it was the visibility of enclosure, and popular belief in
its damaging effects, that produced open collective protest. After the mid
sixteenth century, the patchwork geography and chronology of enclosure
meant that continuing protests would take the form of riots, rather than
rebellions. The only exceptions to this were where the scale of enclosure
might pose an acute regional problem – as was the case with the Midlands
Rising of 1607 – or be imposed in a way that challenged the local interests
of middling-sort farmers and even local lords of the manor.[11] Thus, in the
1620s attempts by a financially strapped crown to drain the fens of eastern
England and to enclose the extensive royal forest in the West Country
both produced large-scale protests.[12]

With the withdrawal of wealthy men with natural authority like the
prosperous tanner and landowner Robert Kett, leadership for these later
large-scale protests was provided by men in a tradition of the charismatic
leader. In the Midlands Rising, the leader Captain Pouch claimed to be
sent by God and to have in his great pouch the power and authority to
protect his followers. His claim to have authority from the king to pull
down all enclosures from Coventry to York was taken up by his lieuten-
ants in the destruction of particularly notorious enclosures throughout
the Midland counties. The protests in the West Country against royal
deforestation and enclosure were led by the anonymous (and male) Lady
Skimmington. This was a name derived from the popular custom used
to police the gender order, by which crowds shamed and punished men
for failure to control wives who refused to obey their husbands. A ritual
intended to signify a world turned upside down, the skimmington was
clearly thought an appropriate symbol in actions intended to turn the
world right side up again by resisting those (often strangers to the local
community) who disrupted its economic and social order.

Riots against enclosure might occur wherever enclosure took place.
Enclosers who had purchased land from the profits of commerce, or
who sought to impose, rather than negotiate, enclosure (on both counts
not 'proper gentlemen') made protest more likely. Crowds sought to

defend common rights in the enclosed lands by means that suggested they better represented the interests of commons, community and commonwealth: they were 'good commonwealthsmen'. Protesters did not necessarily resort immediately to destruction of the enclosures, but deployed tactics that sought to avoid punishment for riot. Nevertheless, these hinted at the violence that would follow if enclosure continued. Libels were circulated, sometimes in rhyming verse, denouncing the enclosure. Graves were dug on the disputed lands, or gallows erected, from which would be hung a recognisable effigy of the encloser. Protesters adopted and adapted popular cultural forms to shape their actions. In the early seventeenth century, protesters in Lincolnshire adopted the text of the traditional play – the death of the summer lord – which ended May Day celebrations there. This helpfully incorporated a mock sermon and the execution of an effigy of a lord, which enabled them to act out a denunciation and symbolic decapitation of the deeply unpopular enclosing earl of Lincoln. In the north-west, where a form of the medieval miracle play persisted, protesters in the early 1620s staged a play in which enclosing landlords were depicted in hell's mouth, an essential prop of the miracle play, as a reminder of the punishment God might inflict on landlords for their greedy attempt to change tenurial customs.

When protesters turned to pulling down the hedges used to enclose land, they made good use of the licence afforded by significant moments in the traditional festive calendar. May Eve saw young unmarried males and females allowed to go into the fields to gather greenery to decorate church and houses on May Day. In areas where there was locally unpopular enclosure, the young of the community might prove hard to please, throwing down yards of enclosure hedges in search of the perfect branch. It was not by chance that the Midlands Rising began on May Eve. Similarly, Rogationtide, an event beginning with a sermon denouncing those who encroached on their neighbours' land and involving a procession to mark out the parish's boundaries, provided a ready-made text for an enclosure riot. Often, a popular legalism informed the actions of enclosure rioters. Contemporary definitions of riot stipulated that it was the act of three or more, so on occasion protesters were careful to go two by two to pull down the enclosure. Direct action was often accompanied by the collection of a common purse and the initiation of legal action in the manorial or royal courts. In early modern society, pulling down (a portion of) a hedge was the first step in a legal action to claim disputed lands.

Exploiting contemporary constructions of women as the weaker sex and the popular belief that women were 'without the law', women were often to the fore in protests over enclosure, complaining that the denial of common rights threatened their gendered responsibility to provide for their families. One encloser in moorland Yorkshire found himself surrounded by 100 or so women, on their knees and in tears, beseeching him to stay an enclosure that threatened their families' livelihoods. The noise they made with scraping their nailed boots hinted at the latent violence in this episode. Workers erecting enclosures found themselves threatened by women who offered, in mockery of the gendered division of responsibilities, to cut them 'as small as herbs to the pot'. The exhilaration and laughter that accompanied such exchanges between crowds and the targets of their hostility reflected the psychic relief and satisfaction that usually subordinated groups savoured in getting one over on their betters. Masculinity too was used to organise crowd actions. Called on to act the man and defend the community, young men and poor labourers were offered a chance to stake their claim to full manhood.

Protesters against enclosure could also derive legitimation from their belief that the government shared their hostility to a process that depopulated communities and, where it involved converting arable to pasture, increased the threat of dearth and harvest failure. Increasingly, however, enclosure represented a response to regional specialisation. For example, in the classic open field areas arable land was temporarily converted to pasture to improve soil fertility and increase grain yields. And, while the government's response to the Midlands Rising had been to issue further commissions to enquire into enclosure in the troubled areas, its policy had always been designed to police, not prohibit, enclosure.[13] Finally, existing discussions of enclosure riots have failed to recognise that their common form might conceal very different objectives. For the middling sort, whose office, wealth and status made them important leaders of opposition, the objective increasingly was not to oppose enclosure outright, but to negotiate concessions that recognised their interests in the land. Production for the market made yeomen farmers enclosers themselves and therefore increasingly willing to *negotiate* enclosure – by (their) agreement. In contrast, cottagers and smallholders with little or no hope of compensation for the loss of common rights were committed to *resisting* enclosure. But in forest and fen, middling-sort farmers and cottagers retained an interest in keeping these areas unenclosed. Under regional specialisation, the extensive wastes and commons served the interests of the capitalist farmers, while allowing the cottagers a reasonable subsistence and an independence that made their communities notorious as sites of what the propertied classes (mis-)characterised as idleness and disorder. The strength of this alliance of convenience meant that protests against enclosure in forests and fens, and in regions with similar social relations, could flare up again and again to the end of this period and well beyond.

But increasingly in the seventeenth century, would-be leaders of open protest in the countryside failed to secure support, their appeals to others to rise being prosecuted as sedition. While the political instability of the mid-century English revolution saw an increase in riots against enclosure and emparkment carried out by king, bishops and courtiers, the Midlands, previously the heartland of agrarian protest, saw little activity.[14] As this suggests, this temporary blip masked an underlying decline in the number of enclosure riots (and the authorities now had a standing army that it used to put them down). Thereafter, they were far fewer. But growing co-operation between gentry and middling sort did not signal an end to agrarian protest. The development of agrarian capitalism was gradual, rather than sudden. Even in 1700 there were areas of England, like Cumbria in the north-west, where lords and tenants were still locked in conflict over who would profit most from the product of the land. Nevertheless, in areas characterised by the consolidation of the tripartite structure of (often absentee) landlord, middling farmer and landless labourer, the labouring poor's dependence on their 'betters' for employment and poor-relief made them vulnerable to victimisation for any open shows of defiance. Hence, continuing and hard-felt grievances had to be expressed through the 'crime of anonymity' in the form of the anonymous threatening letter, poaching and animal maiming.[15]

## Moral Economy, Grain Riots and Access to Food

Crowd actions over food long pre-dated this period. This reflected the early development of both an urban system and 'grain-deficient' rural areas dependent on a market in grain. Interestingly, most medieval food riots, although directed against merchants and middlemen in the grain trade, had been triggered by the action of the crown in siphoning food from the local economy to feed troops engaged in its overseas military adventures.[16] The fragility of a pre-industrialised economy and the frequency of harvest failure meant that isolated protests were always possible. But it was only in the early modern period that crowd actions became prominent in the politics of subsistence. Their increasing incidence reflected the collision between a sharp increase in the vulnerable, harvest-sensitive population and the weak points in a developing national market in grain. Nonetheless, until the eighteenth century the number of *recorded* crowd actions over food was significantly less than the fears of early modern governments predicted, and they were absent throughout the period from many regions.

Despite its mushrooming growth, London experienced less than a handful of protests over food, with the last recorded episode taking place in the hungry 1590s. That the capital was largely free of protests over food was a reflection of the willingness of the government to risk disorder in the counties by licensing the transport of grain to the city in order to keep the capital fed. In rural areas, the labouring poor might secure access to food from employers, neighbours or parish authorities, and many were locked into forms of dependency that inhibited the possibility of collective protest.[17] Once again, it was not scarcity and absolute levels of deprivation that explain the pattern of protest, but popular understandings of the causes of scarcity and a strategic reading of the possibility and benefits of crowd action. Once again, a shared moral economy between government and people over the highly emotive and sensitive issue of the marketing of grain, the basic food staple in this society, helped to fashion protests.

From the harvest crisis of the 1580s onwards there was a well-established geography to crowd actions over food.[18] Riots occurred when grain was being moved out of the local economy, thereby threatening local subsistence, and where the social groups most affected by this were able to organise collective action. The export of grain triggered protests at port towns. The movement of grain required to feed England's cities, and above all London, provoked more protests, at ports in the south-east and East Anglia and in small towns in areas like the Thames Valley that served as bulking centres for the movement of grain to the cities by urban middlemen. Bristol's demands had a similar effect in the south-west. In these small towns and ports it was artisans and the labouring poor – those most at risk when the harvest failed and prices rose sharply – who formed the crowd. But their suspicions of, and sense of grievance at, the actions of outsiders might be shared by their employers and by local magistrates, who found themselves stuck with the consequences of a central government prepared to license contraventions of the marketing laws in order to feed and pacify the larger cities.

In the countryside, there were food riots, but these took place in areas of proto-industrialisation, above all in the textile districts. Here clothworkers and their families were the victims of a vicious combination of factors. Located in areas where the cloth industry had developed to absorb the surplus landless or land-poor labour in a predominantly pastoral, and therefore naturally grain-deficient, rural economy, clothworkers were dependent on the market for both food and employment. When the harvest failed, high food prices led to a slump in demand for both their product and labour and it left them without the money to feed themselves and their families. To add insult to injury, local middlemen on whom they depended for the supply of food now moved grain *through* their region in pursuit of higher urban prices. Finally, the absence of a resident magistracy where the industry was located meant they were forced to protest in order to alert the authorities to their plight and to try to stop the movement of grain.

In food riots, crowds acted in ways that suggest that, though driven by anger and desperation, there was a politics to their protests. The people thought hoarding by farmers and middlemen was one of the causes of dearth, driving up prices by creating an artificial scarcity. This was a belief to be found in popular ballads, and publicly endorsed from the pulpit and in royal proclamations issued in years of harvest failure that denounced hoarders as 'greedy cormorants'. But while individuals might be driven by hunger to steal food, with criminal courts showing a sharp increase in such crimes in years of dearth, crowds did not attack barns and granaries (with the partial exception of where grain was known to be stored for export). This again reflected popular knowledge of the law, for theft was a crime that could (and did) result in execution. But it also reflected a popular belief that the transport and, especially, export of grain in years of harvest failure were against the law. Since at least the early sixteenth century the government had issued measures to police the marketing of grain, requiring the licensing of middlemen, prohibiting the export and regulating the internal movement of grain when prices were high.

By the 1580s, administrative practice had been codified in Books of Orders, printed and distributed in years of dearth to the local magistrates. These required them to undertake surveys of grain stocks, and to order farmers to bring grain weekly to market where the magistrates were to see the poor served first and – a controversial measure – at below market prices. Outside years of dearth, these rules were only partially enforced, and even in such years the government was driven by fear of disorder in the capital to license their evasion to feed London. But the evidence suggests that in many counties they were dutifully enforced by magistrates, who also ordered local financial collections to purchase grain stocks that the poor might purchase at below market price or, on occasion, receive free.

Given that there was a public transcript that both Church and state publicly endorsed highlighting the corruption believed by the poor to have caused dearth, crowd actions over food were less an exercise in self-help than an appeal to the authorities to take the measures and enforce the laws that were intended to prevent dearth and starvation. While small amounts of grain might be taken, crowds more often mimicked the actions to be found in the Book of Orders. They did so in the knowledge that unless their actions triggered intervention by either the local or central authorities they would be self-defeating, frightening away the dealers upon whom grain-deficient communities depended. The politics of the crowd was, therefore, necessarily triangulated: they targeted middlemen, but their actions were designed to trigger intervention from authority (whose inactivity they also criticised). Crowds did not seize grain in the market, but waited until the grain had been sold and was being moved out of the local community. Then they might either 'stay' its transportation, or return it to market and organise its sale at a 'just price' – that is below the famine prices in the market. At Harwich in the early 1640s a crowd that had invaded a ship loaded with grain contented themselves with removing the sails, mimicking the action taken to impound vessels suspected of being involved in smuggling. In Kent, crowds who had seized grain shouted out that they had stayed it for the king and claimed half, the prescribed reward for those who prevented the illegal export of grain. In Somerset, crowds waited until grain was being moved by barge to the sea before hauling it back to where it had begun its journey, dumping the sacks of grain outside the houses of the local officials in a pointed criticism of what the crowd saw as their failure to enforce the law.

In protests like those at Norwich in 1532, or Maldon in Essex in 1629 led by 'Captain' Ann Carter, a butcher's wife, it was women who took the lead. This reflected their role as petty dealers and purchasers in the marketplace, responsible for buying the food the family needed and therefore sensitive to any malpractices there. But it also reflected, again, popular knowledge of the law. Married women turned their inequality before the law to their advantage, claiming, as their sisters in agrarian protest did, that that they were 'without the law' and that if they acted without their husbands' knowledge they could not be punished, a belief for which contemporary law manuals offered some support.[19]

After the mid seventeenth and into the eighteenth century, crowd actions over food became the most common form of collective protest within the politics of subsistence. This reflected the fact that government policy over dearth had shifted, loosening regulation of the market in grain

and, increasingly, encouraging its export. What had been a shared understanding between government and people was now becoming, in Edward
Thompson's striking phrase, 'the moral economy of the eighteenth century crowd'.[20] By the 1690s the geography of food riots had also changed,
shifting further west and north. With urban middlemen invading further
markets in order to feed not only the capital but also growing industrial
populations, areas like Worcester and Shrewsbury also experienced riots
directed against middlemen buying up grain for the industrial population
in the west Midlands.[21] Until the end of this period, high food prices saw
groups like weavers, tinners and miners at the centre of crowd actions
over food. Participation by these industrial groups in such crowd actions
reflected not just their dependence on the market for food (increasingly
in the form of milled flour or bread) and the sensitivity of demand in
their trade to harvest failure. It also reflected their own belief in their status as independent artisans, a belief increasingly challenged by economic
realities, but central to a third strand within the politics of subsistence: the
politics of the property of skill.

### The Property of Skill and the Politics of the Trade

Before the advent of full-blown industrialisation, most production took
place in urban workshops, in the mining villages of areas of coal, lead or
tin extraction, or in the producers' own cottage households in regions of
textile production or metal-working. The relationships of production were
not easily reduced to a simple division between employer and employee
and they continued to obscure the growing reality that workers in many
industries were selling their labour power for a wage. When demand was
high, for example, small masters could weave in their own right. And the
importance in many trades of subcontracting and a preference for payment by piece rate blunted recognition of the underlying loss of independence. All this helps to explain why many still thought of themselves as
independent producers, able to achieve control over the means and relationships of production – a control that varied both over time and by type
of industry. Nevertheless, in many rural industries, it was the merchants
or middlemen who played a controlling role in the trade. In the skilled
urban trades and, increasingly, rural industries it was the wealthier masters
who played a dominant role. In the extractive industries, it was the owners
of mining leases. Over time, the growing control exerted by mercantile
capital produced increasing points of conflict. Fluctuations in the state of
the trade might induce attempts by employers to reduce piece rates, alter

the terms of employment, challenge customs in the workplace, or employ more journeymen for whom the chances of setting up as their own masters became progressively harder. Wherever and whenever such changes occurred, there could be conflict. They challenged industrial workers' artisanal status as skilled and independent producers who controlled their work and the terms of employment. And it was that continued sense of their independence and rights as 'freeborn Englishmen' that helps to explain the forms that industrial protests took.[22]

If economic conditions provided the context for these outbreaks of collective action, it was the case, as in the other forms of protest within the politics of subsistence, that it was the workers' sense of their status and rights and their own explanation for their problems that determined the occasion and form that their protests took. Protests might take a wide variety of forms, including petitioning employers and authority and pursuing their rights through both the state's courts and, in areas such as Derbyshire lead- or Devon tin-mining, special courts particular to their industry.[23] The persistence and sophistication shown in these campaigns reflected the solidarities of mono-occupational industrial communities and the organisation that everyday patterns of working in the trade created. Where collective protests occurred they too might adapt popular cultural forms, for example subjecting unpopular employers or 'blacklegs' to shaming sanctions like 'riding the stang', a version of the skimmington ride in which targeted individuals were carried around the local community astride a pole. But while protesters in industrial disorders usually focused on the destruction of property, rather than persons, increasingly what set them apart into the eighteenth century was a level of violence against both that reflected their collective anger at underlying changes threatening their control of their working conditions.

As in other forms of protest within the politics of subsistence, industrial producers subscribed to a moral economy in which their customs should be respected and their rights to a wage reflecting their skill and needs acknowledged. Thinking of themselves as artisans and the holders of customary rights, they expected employers to recognise and respect this, and magistrates, and if necessary Parliament, to protect their 'property' in their skill. Thus, although wages (in whatever form) lay at the heart of industrial protests, they were always about more than this. Producers sought to retain a degree of control of the workplace. In the skilled trades of the urban workshops, the opacity of the workplace makes it harder, for this period, to recover a continuous history of the negotiations that took place and the intimidatory tactics that were used there. Occasionally, there are reports of secret combinations in a particular town and trade. But there were occasions when conflict in a trade became so general that the urban authorities were forced to take notice and to intervene. In areas of rural industry, the control that skilled workers could negotiate in the workshop, especially where the guilds retained some force, was harder to achieve. The dispersed nature of production in the putting-out system of the textile industries helps to explain why here protests often resorted to collective violence. Protesters attacked and destroyed the property of employers, and physically attacked and intimidated both employers and employees – blacklegs – who refused to join in their withdrawal of labour. Groups like the pitmen of the northern coalfield enjoyed a particular notoriety as disorderly and violent.[24] But behind such representations was the dislike propertied contemporaries had for all groups who continued to enjoy a measure of independence from the encroaching ties of labour discipline.

In reality, violence in industrial disputes represented a negotiating strategy. Angered by employers' attempts to reduce wages, to pay workers by 'truck' (payments in kind that took the form of food at prices determined by the employer), to increase the amount to be produced under the customary piece rate or to destroy controls on entry into the trade, groups like weavers and pitmen resorted to violence. But this was, or attempted to be, a controlled violence that, as in other forms of protest, was accompanied by the petitioning of magistrates and Parliament in which groups of workers made reference to the customs of the trade, to the protection of the statutory setting of wages and the famous statute of 5 Elizabeth, the Statute of Artificers, which they held guaranteed their status and skills. Violence in industrial disorders was then also an exercise in negotiation. In Hobsbawm's famous phrase, this was 'collective bargaining by riot'.[25]

By 1750 much had changed. Changes in the social relationships of production in agriculture and industry polarised communities, making the earlier potential for collective action *across* social groups harder to find. Government policy was now permissive, rather than prohibitive, of economic change, challenging the legitimation that protesters had earlier been able to derive from the 'public transcript'. The government was now more willing and able, with a standing army, to repress collective protests. The criminal law, with a reinvigorated Riot Act (1714), Combination Act (1721) against collective actions for better wages, and a string of capital statutes made it easier to criminalise and punish protest with transportation, imprisonment and the gallows. The experience of a world turned upside down in the English revolution of the 1640s challenged the wisdom of elites – landed or local – seeking to mobilise the people, and after 1660 refashioned the idea of the 'many-headed monster' into the new language of the *mob*.[26] Nevertheless, the authorities, both local and central, were selective in their use of these policies and, in the face of recurring crises, continued to be willing to mix repression with negotiation and accommodation. These changes, and with them the unmaking of an earlier tradition of protest, were ultimately to contribute to the making of an English working class. But to what extent they had, by 1750, created patterns of protest based on the politics of class remain problematic. The earlier evidence of sedition utterances suggests that there were always those willing to ground their grievances in the language of class.[27] There remained, however, an important discrepancy between those full-blooded rhetorics of violence and the recoverable pattern of social protest.

## Notes

1 C. Hill, 'The many-headed monster', in C. Hill, *Change and Continuity in Seventeenth-Century England* (London: Weidenfeld & Nicolson, 1974).
2 R. H. Tawney, *The Agrarian Problem in the Sixteenth Century* (London: Longman, Green, 1912), 322.
3 Ronald B. Bond (ed.), *'Certain Sermons or Homilies' (1547) and 'A Homily against Disobedience and Wilful Rebellion' (1570): A Critical Edition* (Toronto: University of Toronto Press, 1987).
4 J. Walter, 'Public transcripts, popular agency and the politics of subsistence in early modern England', in M. J. Braddick and J. Walter (eds.), *Negotiating Power in Early Modern Society: Order, Hierarchy and Subordination in Britain and Ireland* (Cambridge: Cambridge University Press, 2001).
5 A. Wood, '"Pore men woll speke one daye": Plebeian languages of deference and defiance in England, c. 1520–1640', in T. Harris (ed.), *The Politics of the Excluded, c. 1500–1850* (Basingstoke: Palgrave, 2001); A. Wood, 'Fear, hatred and the hidden injuries of class in early modern England', *Journal of Social History*, 39 (2006).
6 For a fuller discussion of the forms of protest to be found in the politics of subsistence, see Walter, 'Public transcripts'.
7 R. W. Hoyle, *The Pilgrimage of Grace and the Politics of the 1530s* (Oxford: Oxford University Press, 2001), 209–55. For an introduction to protests against the politics of Church and state, not discussed here, see A. Fletcher and D. MacCulloch, *Tudor Rebellions* (London: Longman, 1997); J. Walter, 'Crowds and popular politics in the English Revolution', in M. J. Braddick (ed.), *The Oxford Handbook of the English Revolution* (Oxford: Oxford University Press, 2015).
8 For this argument, see A. Wood, *The Memory of the People: Custom and Popular Senses of the Past in Early Modern England* (Cambridge: Cambridge University Press, 2013).

9  A. Wood, *The 1549 Rebellions and the Making of Early Modern England* (Cambridge: Cambridge University Press, 2007).

10 J. Walter, '"A rising of the people"? The Oxfordshire rising of 1596', in J. Walter (ed.), *Crowds and Popular Politics in Early Modern England* (Manchester: Manchester University Press, 2006).

11 J. E. Martin, *Feudalism to Capitalism: Peasant and Landlord in English Agrarian Development* (Basingstoke: Macmillan, 1983); R. B. Manning, *Village Revolts: Social Protest and Popular Disturbances in England, 1509–1640* (Oxford: Oxford University Press, 1988).

12 K. Lindley, *Fenland Riots and the English Revolution* (London: Heinemann, 1982); B. Sharp, *In Contempt of All Authority: Rural Artisans and Riot in the West of England 1585–1660* (Berkeley and London: University of California Press, 1980).

13 J. Thirsk, 'Changing attitudes to enclosure in the seventeenth century', in *The Festschrift for Professor Ju-Hwan Oh on the Occasion of His Sixtieth Birthday* (Taegu, Korea: Kyungpook National University 1991).

14 B. Manning, *The English People and the English Revolution* (London: Heineman, 1976), 112–227; J. Walter, 'The English people and the English revolution revisited', *HWJ*, 61 (2006).

15 E. P. Thompson, 'The crime of anonymity', in D. Hay, P. Linebaugh, J. G. Rule, E. P. Thompson and C. Winslow (eds.), *Albion's Fatal Tree: Crime and Society in Eighteenth Century England* (London: Allen Lane, 1975).

16 B. Sharp, 'The food riots of 1347 and the medieval moral economy', in A. Charlesworth and A. Randall (eds.), *Moral Economy and Popular Protest: Crowds, Conflict, and Authority* (Basingstoke: Macmillan, 2000).

17 J. Walter, 'The social economy of dearth in early modern England', in J. Walter and R. Schofield (eds.), *Famine, Disease and the Social Order in Early Modern Society* (Cambridge: Cambridge University Press, 1989).

18 J. Walter, 'The geography of food riots, 1585–1649', in Walter, *Crowds*.

19 J. Walter, 'Faces in the crowd: Gender and age in the early modern English crowd', in H. Berry and E. Foyster (eds.), *The Family in Early Modern England* (Cambridge: Cambridge University Press, 2007).

20 E. P. Thompson, 'The moral economy of the English crowd in the eighteenth century', *P&P*, 50 (1971).

21 M. Beloff, *Public Order and Popular Disturbances 1660–1714* (London: Oxford University Press and H. Milford, 1938), 79–80; J. Bohstedt, *The Politics of Provisions: Food Riots, Moral Economy and Market Transition* (Farnham: Ashgate, 2010).

22 J. Rule, *The Experience of Labour in Eighteenth Century Industry* (London: Croom Helm, 1981); J. Rule, 'The property of skill in the period of manufacture', in P. Joyce (ed.), *Work: The Historical Meaning of Work* (Cambridge: Cambridge University Press, 1987); A. Randall, *Before the Luddites: Custom, Community and Machinery in the English Woollen Industry, 1776–1809* (Cambridge: Cambridge University Press, 1991).

23 A. Wood, 'Custom, Identity and Resistance: English Free Miners and Their Law, *c.* 1550–1800', in P. Griffiths, A. Fox and S. Hindle (eds.), *The Experience of Authority in Early Modern England* (Basingstoke: Macmillan, 1996); A. Wood, *The Politics of Social Conflict: The Peak Country 1520–1770* (Cambridge: Cambridge University Press, 1999).

24 D. Levine and K. Wrightson, *The Making of an Industrial Society: Whickham 1560–1765* (Oxford: Oxford University Press, 1991), 375–427.

25 E. J. Hobsbawm, *Labouring Men: Studies in the History of Labour* (London: Weidenfeld & Nicolson, 1964), 7.

26 For a parallel study of these religious and political protests, see Walter, 'Crowds and popular politics in the English Revolution'.

27 See, e.g., the works cited in n. 5, above.

# 11

# Consumption and Material Culture

## Adrian Green

## Introduction

Human cultures generally revolve around food, clothing, shelter, work and worship. Associated activities form the routines of everyday life and entail acts of consumption that involve material artefacts. Material culture is core to creating and sustaining any given group. It rarely remains static over time, but goes through cyclical stages of development. Moreover, it regularly accrues symbolic value. In consequence, it can be understood as a form of communication, but the messages embodied in things may be implicitly coded as well as explicitly stated.

Objects deemed to be special tend to communicate their symbolic value explicitly – in art, court rituals or religious settings – and are often subject to overt rules. More everyday aspects of material culture communicate their significance implicitly, and are more likely to be structured by unspoken social codes, invariably understood by contemporaries but not always commented upon. Nevertheless, it is this configuration of materiality and coded behaviour that gives meaning to material culture as an aspect of social communication. The structuring role of material culture is embedded in the use of utensils, layout of rooms, choice of furnishings, distinctions in dress and experience of the built environment. Interpreting the world of things can provide profound insights into social behaviour and cultural values as well as economic production and exchange. This chapter focuses on the ways in which the consumption of special and everyday material culture was integral to social life in England between 1500 and 1750.[1]

## Methodology

The historical study of material culture is best based on two premises. Firstly, material culture needs to be studied as pattern, at a variety of scales. Only by studying the patterns in material culture can we make evidence-based historical claims about the role of materiality in cultural behaviour. Pattern applies not only to particular types of artefact but also to linked sets of artefacts that together constitute a material culture. For example, the material culture of the kitchen, dining table or bed chamber, through to the entire household's materiality including the house itself, were related to other households and formed larger sets. Patterns in defined sets of material culture may be discerned from documentary sources, such as inventories of household goods. Secondly, material culture needs to be interpreted in context. Only by establishing the significance of an artefact can scholars discover the ways in which objects were created and used. We should focus not only on objects but also on the contextual information provided by documentary and printed sources. In establishing pattern, scale and context, there are benefits to integrating the various categories of material culture traditionally the province of separate subdisciplines. Art and architecture were related to dress, diet, domestic life and the world of work. Art and craft were not a neat division, and objects occupied a spectrum from the special to the everyday. It was the users and consumers of objects as well as their producers that determined their symbolic and practical value. Connecting material culture together in context enables scholars to reconstruct historical behaviour. Such study may be applied at the scale of a single household or community, and to regional, national and trans-national patterns.[2]

## Consumption Cycles

Consumption is cyclical. 'Household stuff' and other goods are worn out and eventually return to dust. Yet man-made artefacts often outlasted the human life span, and material goods were too highly valued and too hard won to be easily disposed of, even at death. Consequently, goods were circulated within households and across generations. Clothing was frequently passed on within the family to children and servants, while goods identified as heirlooms were passed on to descendants, or handed over before death, particularly on the occasion of children leaving home or marrying. Beyond this circulation of goods within the family, clothing and artefacts were circulated via the market. There was a voracious trade in second-hand clothes, some of them stolen, while the probate inventories compiled at death were valued and then advertised for sale. This was an especially important mechanism, as second-hand household goods were inevitably purchased by somewhat lower-status couples embarking on marriage and setting up house. For moveable goods, the cycle of household formation and dissolution was central to their circulation, enabling a process of downward social diffusion as goods purchased new for more affluent households were used in time by the less affluent. The end for many goods is revealed by archaeological excavation, where middens and trash pits were informatively filled with food waste, broken ceramics and glass, tobacco clay pipes, and lost coins. Textiles rarely survive, except in water-logged conditions, and only clothing kept for best usually enters museum collections. Many items of clothing were recirculated, and the poor had worn and patched clothes until their raggedness disintegrated, with the rags sold to become paper or rugs.[3]

Grades of goods and clothing had a great deal to say about the status and standing of the household and person, both in small face-to-face communities, and in the somewhat more anonymous environment of towns. Poorer and smaller households were far from entirely reliant on hand-me-downs, however, and country folk purchased new goods at both traditional fairs and from the pedlars and chapmen who increasingly crisscrossed the realm. Pedlars started from wholesalers in the town at which they were licensed and took their ponies and baskets along regular routes, such that all of England potentially had access to the same consumer goods. Responding to the demand for clothing and accessories, carriers also provided mercer's wares to order and carried speculative stock. The cloth pieces, pins, handkerchiefs and ribbons that these carriers supplied led Margaret Spufford to identify a 'great reclothing' of the rural population, equivalent to the 'great rebuilding' of houses identified by W. G. Hoskins. Chapmen also provided a host of affordable items for the house, and took orders from country folk to bring specific goods on the next circuit through the village. The rapid expansion of the carrier network was symptomatic of a restructuring of England's economy around new centres of specialist production, and England's marketing system was transformed over the seventeenth century, as its fixed sites transmogrified into the county and market towns of late Stuart and Georgian England. Retail shops also emerged during the seventeenth century – most spectacularly in London, but also in provincial towns, such as Lancaster, where William Stout set up shop with the help of kin and credit links to London. Carriers and retail shops were the beginnings of a cycle that would lead to department stores, delivery vans and shopping malls.[4]

Material culture was also circulated by gift, including servants receiving clothing from their master or mistress and treasuring their own few possessions in locked boxes. In an age when the aristocracy frequently spent more on their head-dress than a servant might earn in several years, the inequalities in wealth were manifest. In some districts the parish also circulated goods among its settled poor, providing household equipment to aged pensioners that upon their decease was given out to another widow or widower. These goods for the deserving poor belonged to the parish and were documented in churchwardens and overseers' accounts. The undeserving poor, fallen into debt, prison or drunkenness, might lose their household goods as forfeit for unpaid rent and fines. Families that held on to their material assets either willed these to their descendants, or dispersed them to realise a cash bequest at death – or simply to clear outstanding debts and pay the funeral expenses. It was common for probate inventories to list furniture as 'old', while items identified as heirlooms, particularly silver and inscribed objects (including large pieces such as court cupboards or best beds as well as snuff boxes or portrait miniatures), did not feature in the probate valuation but were designated as bequests in the will. Even these vessels of family memory were valued not as antiques but as symbolic of the family. The lineage-conscious aristocracy and gentry frequently valued classical antiquities over the material antiquity of their own culture, and across society most of the material culture created further back than the previous reign became obsolete. Consumption cycles of material culture circulating through households in a process of accumulation and dispersal, along with the rebuilding and redecoration of the house and its fittings, typically involved only a couple of generations, so that the material culture of English houses in Good Queen Bess's day was a world away from George II's England.[5]

## Economic Expansion and Cultural Behaviour

English society was primarily orientated around the household and family. In the early sixteenth century it was common to grow food, keep livestock, make and mend furniture and clothes; coin was mainly reserved for rent and occasional expenditure on new livestock, crafted furniture or payments of parish dues. From the mid sixteenth century the commercial economy, orientated on the production and distribution of a widening range of consumer goods, underwent a decisive step-change. Dependency on wages increased exponentially over the period and cash or credit became vital to sustaining businesses and supplying material needs. Initially, this change in living habits was most prominent in south-east England. But the 'amendment of lodging' noted by William Harrison in Radwinter, Essex in 1577 was not equally spread across communities.

Only the affluent yeoman class participated in the first wave of Hoskins's 'great rebuilding of rural England', and Harrison comments that 'lodging' was 'not very much amended as yet in some parts of Bedfordshire, and elsewhere, further off from our southern parts'.[6] Yet those with equivalent means might by the end of Elizabeth's reign aspire to live in a comparable manner in the North Country and West Country. Stone-built statesman houses in Cumbria, or cob-and-thatch farmhouses in Devon, were ultimately comparable to a timber-framed Wealden in Kent, with local materials and craft traditions moulding the dwellings of the big yeomanry and parish gentry across England. Those of lesser means occupied 'clay dabbins' on the Solway plain or built cruck-framed cottages with mud walls in clay parts of the Midland shires, while looming over them were new houses for the gentry, such as Quenby Hall, built in brick between 1618 and 1636, for George Ashby and his London bride Elizabeth Bennett. To a large extent wealth as well as geography determined the new pattern of consumption. Documented consumption habits in Kent reveal a closer participation in London-based fashions, as location and wealth placed much of Kent in the orbit of the London economy, while remote Cornwall was less 'advanced', though no less interesting.[7]

Underpinning the commercial economy and spread of consumer goods for the home was an expansion in the volume and velocity of exchange, which required more coin. Whereas most folk in early-sixteenth-century England had limited access to cash and limited need for it, by the later sixteenth century cash or credit was necessary to maintain a household in which a new range of material goods was required. Increasingly over the seventeenth century, most aspects of life were supplied from afar, on the basis of monetary exchange or its equivalent in credit. England's economy, moreover, became regionally specialised, as goods produced in one place were marketed nationally. As Daniel Defoe observed in *The Complete English Tradesman* (1727), 'all our manufactures are used and called for by almost all the people, and that in every part of the whole British dominion, yet they are made and wrought in several distinct and respective Counties of Britain, and some of them are at the remotest distance from one another'.[8]

Defoe is among the best guides to the economy and culture of consumption in early-eighteenth-century England, with his novels offering acute insights into the social role of clothing. Novels, themselves among many innovations of commercial print in the period, enabled contemporary readers to imagine themselves in new ways in relation to material consumption: print was fundamental to the altered place of material culture in society. But well ahead of the 'explosion of print', the consumption of goods necessitated an expansion in the use of credit. For commercial households with their own craft or farming enterprise, and for lower-status households dependent on smaller-scale marketing of produce alongside waged income, credit became pervasive, with the consequence that debts had to be settled at death. This explains the increased practice of taking itemised probate inventories during this period. The goods of the deceased were listed in probate inventories valuing then selling the household goods so as to clear outstanding debts on the estate. As litigation over credit declined so too did the incidence of making probate inventories, such that the boom in inventories from the later sixteenth century through to around 1720 reflects the emergence then normalisation of credit. By the mid eighteenth century almost all acts of consumption and exchange involved money, in cash or its equivalent, and the fear of debt haunted eighteenth-century novels.[9]

For all the protean qualities of commercial innovation over this period, especially in London and other ports with continental links, the rigidity of England's settlement pattern and the persistence of its household forms meant that consumption practices very largely occurred within structures established earlier. The nuclear-family-with-servants household form was well established in fourteenth- and fifteenth-century England. Consumerism was already a feature of life in the Middle Ages, but neither as large in scale nor as socially spread as in later sixteenth-, seventeenth- and eighteenth-century England. Importantly, the sixteenth century witnessed a phase of product innovation, and improved techniques of production that, as Joan Thirsk argues, laid the basis for England's 'consumer society'. Jan de Vries points to the population increase of the sixteenth century as the trigger for this market-orientation on the part of producers, enabling profits to be orientated on household consumption: a phenomenon that occurred across north-western Europe, of which England – especially southern and eastern England – was only a part. Thirsk also shows the role of government in sponsoring economic improvement through 'projects' – a theme more recently amplified for policy-makers in seventeenth-century England by Paul Slack – by which time western England's commercial economy was being invigorated by Atlantic trade. The role of the state – or, more often, wealthy individuals close to the levers of power acting in their own interest as well as for the good of the 'commonwealth' – was critical to the expansion of the economy.[10]

Economic activity, however, remained very largely driven by the decisions of individual households to engage in production and consumption via the market. Jan de Vries formulates an 'Industrious Revolution' to explain the ways in which commercial households, especially housewives, produced craft and farming produce for the market so as to maximise household purchasing power and enable them to participate in the consumption of goods. This in turn generated a new relationship between work and leisure, as work was orientated towards the purchase of material things and leisure, potentially, for their enjoyment. All of this was achieved within the household structure established in the Middle Ages, where nuclear kin mattered most and servants were a subservient addition to the family rather than a separate class. The second structural continuity from late medieval England was the significance of urban places. These provided the infrastructure for short- and long-distance trade, in which England's commercial economy developed. What changed between 1500 and 1750 was the regional character of the economy, as certain districts specialised in particular goods or foodstuffs for a larger regional or national market. The urban hierarchy underwent change, as new proto-urban-industrial regions emerged – notably Newcastle and Sunderland for coal; Sheffield for steel; Leeds and the West Riding for cloth; Birmingham for metal goods; and Bristol, Whitehaven and Liverpool for the Atlantic trade. From these regional centres licensed carriers distributed consumer goods to the furthest reaches of the realm.

The carrier network gradually brought the whole of rural England – including upland districts – into the consumer society that Thirsk and de Vries identify as emerging from the mid sixteenth century. In the towns, meanwhile, shopkeepers switched from selling craft products from their workshops, to wholesaling goods to carriers and retailing to shoppers. Towns remained central to marketing, but the actual concept of the market underwent change. Over the seventeenth century, the term 'market' no longer referred necessarily to a fixed place of exchange, as it had since early medieval times, but now embraced the abstract notion of potential consumers anywhere. As Joyce Appleby demonstrates, a century and more before Adam Smith's *Wealth of Nations* (1776), economic thought in seventeenth-century England already acknowledged the advantages of the unfettered market. Print was fundamental to this revolution in understanding and experience of the market, as printed advertisements emerged during the seventeenth century as the basis for reaching anonymous consumers. Auctions were another innovation, especially for art and real estate; although widespread in ancient Rome, auctions were not used to establish price in the Middle Ages, when prices fixed by custom were the norm. By the later seventeenth century the commercial techniques for England's market society were fully in place. According to Neil McKendrick this set the scene for a 'consumer revolution', in which the culturally driven demand for goods provided the trigger for the supply-side Industrial Revolution later in the eighteenth century. For McKendrick the 'birth of a consumer society' only fully emerged with Wedgwood pottery and Manchester cotton factories after 1750. Yet, the making of a market society in the later sixteenth and seventeenth century through regional specialisation in production (including early industrialisation), product innovation, print, advertising, retailing, new systems of distribution and purchase on credit were at least as important as the further elaboration of commercial activity in the eighteenth century.[11]

## Material Culture and the Life-Cycle

While households formed the basic units of consumption and production, individual life experiences passed through stages of birth, childhood, adolescent subservience, youthful freedoms, adult householding, widowhood, death. Most aspects of material culture were geared to this life-cycle. Many individuals were subservient to the interests of the family, which remained central to the consumption of material goods throughout this period. Marriage and the establishment of an independent household formed the social ideal for most men and women, who spent their childhood and adolescence in a state of expectation, in training for adult life as masters and mistresses of a household.

Although toys and dolls were a feature of children's play in the sixteenth century they were heavily geared towards inculcating adult behaviour. Only in the eighteenth century did childhood become celebrated as a discrete episode in life, rather than being primarily regarded as a preparation for maturity. The commercialisation of childhood was an immediate manifestation of this cultural change. New forms of books and toys were evident from the later seventeenth century, as the print trade and particularly the metal trades around Birmingham responded to the childhood market, though it remained one highly attuned to conventional gender roles.[12]

Between childhood and adult independence, most men and women went through the service stage of the life-cycle, and some even enjoyed a period of youth relatively free of structures of authority and household responsibility. Apprentices were taught to learn the tools of their trade, and the material culture of work deserves as much attention as the domestic side of life. Sons inheriting farm-holdings underwent a parallel training in running a commercial enterprise. The material culture of workshop and farm was in part about rationalisation and improvement, with innovations in utensils and techniques, but also powerfully retained and recreated regional traditions in tools and craft techniques that would persist beyond 1750. While youths in stable households underwent some form of training, young maids often worked in the household of a family of somewhat higher status than their birth. For men and women alike, being placed in a household of higher stratus than their childhood home was an important mechanism for the diffusion of manners. This dynamic is too easily dismissed as social emulation. Common folk were wary of self-consciously aping the manners of their social superiors; masters and parents were concerned about servants getting above themselves. There were real thresholds that silently policed social stratification and its material expression. Cultural diffusion is not the same as social emulation. The closely stratified character of English society was a mechanism for both the diffusion and the differentiation of cultural practices, which in turn created tiers within society. The experience of higher-status households through domestic service and apprenticeship, and its elite equivalent in the patronage offered to well-placed youths in noble households, the universities and London Inns of Court, was an important mechanism for the diffusion of cultural habits. Direct experience early in life was required to inculcate new habits, with upbringing and education more important than indirect exposure via print or observation from a distance. The social capital acquired in childhood and youth mattered as much as cash and credit to the material culture of households. In this way, households of differing status and means, with different cultural trajectories behind them, created and consolidated class boundaries on the basis of material possessions and how to handle them. In his account of *The Birth of a Consumer Society* in eighteenth-century England, Neil McKendrick recognised the importance of this closely stratified society but overstated the role of emulation. Rather than following sociological attempts to model emulation, historians would be better advised to pay close attention to how contemporaries conceptualised consumption, in relation to keywords such as 'taste', 'politeness', 'property' and articulations of class.[13]

Preparation for marriage involved men and women accruing the resources to equip an independent household. Although most men and women only slowly accumulated the goods that would appear in the inventories made at the dissolution of their union at death, the need to save up and furnish a starter-home was sufficiently demanding to delay the average age of marriage until after the mid twenties. Marriage and the establishment of an independent household marked entry into full adult status as householder and housewife. The material form of the house itself embodied the social stratification of the community and nation – from a cottage or a husbandman's small house (with one or two hearths) to a yeoman's large house (with perhaps three or four hearths), to gentry and merchant families in well-heated homes with many more hearths. In rural and urban communities house size, and the resources on which the household was based, were tightly associated with social position.[14]

Houses embodied the household in a society of householders where companionate marriage was the avowed ideal, and where commercial enterprise involved co-operation between marriage partners. In courtship, while the educated might craft a poem or letter, country folk composed their love tokens by hand. They often followed regional traditions (such as carved love spoons), and this indicates the continued importance of self-made objects involving no money. In this context, well into the eighteenth century and beyond, there was a resistance to commodification and maintenance of a material culture not reliant on expenditure. For those from families of even small property, financial assistance from parents was often forthcoming at marriage, as were minor bequests from relatives: so much so that the high levels of mortality in the period would have been a blessing for some. Poorer couples with more fragile resources and no family safety net might be discouraged from marrying altogether and prohibited from setting up house in the village, lest they become a burden to the parish by claiming poor-relief. The problems of poverty and increasing dependence on waged income notwithstanding, the cultural ideal in early modern England was for the independence of the married couple. As a consequence, both relative and absolute poverty were increasingly defined in material terms, against the benchmark of the industrious commercial household earning a living through craft or farming enterprises.[15]

The union of the married couple found expression in the materiality of the marital home, with inscribed initials and date of marriage on ceramics, silver or pewter plate, and oak furniture. Many of these artefacts were given as wedding gifts, while goods acquired later often continued to commemorate the year of marriage, reinforcing its structural role in cementing the household as the primary arena for life. Even the fabric of the house might be inscribed with the dates and initials of marriage. These inscriptions announced the successful marriage to visitors and passers-by. Gentry families commemorated marriage in plaster ceilings and over-mantels, with heraldic devices enshrining the entwining of lineages. From the later seventeenth century, however, demonstrating learned taste rather than family lineage became the ideological basis for elite hegemony. Although aristocratic families continued to deploy heraldry as an emblem of family ties, the material culture of gentry households altered to express taste. The architecture of gentry houses shifted from an emphasis on markers of inherited status to the expression of classical taste. While the external façade received a classical makeover, the symbolism of lineage was often retained in the older fabric of the house, particularly where the core of the house remained the ancient hall, or a treasured piece of heraldic window glass was kept. Old England went together with a taste for the exotic, and imported porcelain from China was commissioned as gentry wedding gifts: demonstrating wealth and taste, but sustaining the emphasis on lineage and marriage by incorporating heraldry on dinner services and tea sets.

At both elite and middling social levels the material culture of marriage was ultimately an affirmation of patriarchy. This was subtly emphasised in the layout of heraldry and inscribed initials, where the standard form was the husband's initial on the left, with the surname initial raised in the centre, and then the wife's to the right. The habit of placing date and initial inscriptions on household goods, especially ceramics or plate for display; on expensive oak furniture; and on door lintels, fireplaces and plaster ceilings was distinctive to this period. It first emerges in the sixteenth century among the gentry, often with Latinate inscriptions, and spread to the middling sorts in the seventeenth century, increasing in frequency in the later seventeenth and early eighteenth century before tailing off as a cultural practice around the mid eighteenth century. Related to rising rates of literacy and mimetic upon print, the late-seventeenth-century peak coincides with the decline in the proportion of couples marrying across England. One way to interpret this pattern is to suggest that the force of inscriptions gained greater meaning when marriage and security of tenure were a rarer achievement. Cary Carson links dated inscriptions to 'possessive individualism', though community context was probably more critical.[16]

Not everyone, of course, married. Yet, the material culture of spinsters and bachelors was not markedly different from that of married couples. Spinsters usually lived as companions to other women, and frequently in occupations that created spinster-clusters in certain towns and neighbourhoods. Bachelors often lived as lodgers or wards in larger households, with only their chamber defined as personal space, and poorer lodgers shared access to cooking facilities with their landlady. While single folk may have had the opportunity for greater discretionary expenditure – on books and pictures, clothing or going out – in general the driver for the form and availability of material culture was the married household-based couple, which formed the main market for goods. Unmarried maids and bachelors were nevertheless an important subsection of the market for manufacturers and wholesalers, with cheap items consumed by single servants and wage-labourers. Manufacturers responded to demand, and England underwent a 'consumer revolution' on the basis of an expanding demand for household goods rather than consumerism centred on the self.

Wives led consumption, particularly in the purchase and care of textiles, especially window curtains, cushions, napkins for the table, and the hangings of the bed. As Carole Schammas has observed, dressing the bed and table was a strong female preference, exercised as part of both duty and fulfilment within the home. De Vries suggests this female agency encouraged women to maximise household purchasing power for the consumption of certain goods. Men were more involved in major purchases of expensive items, particularly furniture or plate, while men and women together mostly agreed on the installation of panelling, plaster and wall hangings, in conjunction with the recommendations of craftsmen and shopkeepers. By the eighteenth century the painted cloth hangings and painted wall decoration ubiquitous in sixteenth- and seventeenth-century England were being overlaid with wallpaper and fresh paint. Whatever their views on interior decoration, men usually had most say in the choice of the house itself, from starter-home on marriage to established middle age, and possibly a retreat in retirement to a smaller dwelling. There was, it seems, no separation of spheres before 1750, and men and women were both involved at home. For single men and women their material culture was an intensification of the preferences of the husband and wife; as with folk before marriage, they were able to exercise greater discretion in expenditure – pursuing interests in books, engravings or clothing – beyond what was expected to conform to the married household ideal. The materiality of the single life merits further research. John Styles found among the less affluent sections of the population that expenditure on clothing was higher before marriage than immediately after, when spending on the house and bringing up children took up more resources. Widows were similarly defined by the material culture that related to their former married status, which was often a visceral decline from the prime of life.[17]

Legally, the law of coverture made women's property the subject of their husband's authority, although the material culture of the wife – especially goods brought to the union at marriage – could be marked out as her own. Husbands and wives regarded certain possessions as relating to their side of the family, and distinct from goods assembled during marriage. Gender was subtly re-enforced through women's engagement with textiles, through sewing and mending as well as by purchase, reflecting a centuries-old culture of women engaging with fabrics. Cushions and curtains, and upholstered furniture for the wealthy, all heralded greater domestic comfort. For affluent men the comforts of home involved books, pictures, furniture and, by the eighteenth century, a dressing room in place of the closet. Piety was also an important element in household decoration and material culture, though only the godly had extensive scriptural decoration, and many people only gave a nod to biblical inscriptions on the chimney-piece, or preferred to observe older superstitions by burning marks onto the fireplace bresumer and banishing bad dreams with candle-marks on the ceiling. Further research is required to determine the relationship between household decoration and religion, which should embrace superstition as well as confessional differences. Potentially, Catholic houses had closer connections to the Continent, while Puritans and later Quakers were supposed to employ 'plain style' decoration in preference to the gaudy enrichment of Elizabethan and Jacobean interiors. While women as well as men led household prayers or withdrew to their closets, and larger houses had chapels, it can be difficult to identify a strongly gendered relationship in the use of religious space. Male and female spaces might seem apparent in the increasing specialisation of room use from the later seventeenth century. But the easy ascription of gender to household space is problematic, as in the *Spectator* magazine article on 'A lady's library', which satirises both the female taste for juxtaposing books and china ornaments, and male reactions to it. Even more problematic is the persistent misogynistic assumption that women have an innate appetite for consumption, related to an often unstated perception of female sexuality. McKendrick suggested that the 'consumer revolution' in eighteenth-century England was strongly associated with a female propensity to consume, which had hitherto been checked by historical circumstance, while de Vries offers a more compelling account of female agency. Consumerism and sexuality as a topic merits further research. Assuming an innate tendency among women to prefer shopping is unconvincing, and belies the evidence that affluent men enjoyed town as much as the ladies. Men nevertheless tended to hold a veto over expenditure, enforceable at law, especially noticeable when marriages unravelled and men issued advertisements to stop women's credit at the shops.[18]

Marriage was not the only life event marked out by material culture. Births and baptisms were commemorated: including, significantly, those of infants who died. Youngsters leaving home often made a gift or crafted a token for their parents. High levels of geographical mobility in early modern England (and beyond to New England and elsewhere) encouraged the marking of departure, especially the maintenance of kin-based relationships at a distance, with material culture.

Death was commemorated with memorials. External grave markers were a feature of pre-Reformation England, but were largely proscribed by the Protestant reformers in the sixteenth century. The habit resurfaced in the seventeenth century, as markers of the middling sorts proliferated on headstones in churchyards throughout England. Those unable to afford a carved stone had wooden grave boards, or simply planted flowers, to mark the spot. The gentry and upper-middling-sort professionals and merchants were buried inside the church, and a culture of material commemoration developed from the later sixteenth century that witnessed the installation of elaborate memorials mounted on the walls. These internal monuments, often with Latin inscriptions, proclaimed the achievements and character of the deceased as well as their family ties. Those buried outside in the churchyard more often had a simple epitaph drawn from scripture – which invariably emphasised mortality – and their family relationships recorded. As with the habit of inscribed initials on furnishings and buildings, the culture of erecting permanent grave memorials had a distinct period feel, beginning with the elites in the sixteenth century and spreading to the prosperous middling sorts in the seventeenth century; gravestones were a common aspiration after 1750. In the seventeenth century this culture of commemoration reflected in part the rising status – and literacy – of middling-sort families; it was the 'chief inhabitants' of each place who tended to be the first to erect a stone memorial amidst a churchyard of wooden grave boards. From the later seventeenth century it became increasingly common for such families to commemorate the dead with permanent memorials. Different in form from the lavish monuments to the gentry inside the church, the middling sorts had adopted aspects of elite commemoration (and employed the same craftsmen), but made this material practice their own. Memorials were about status, but they were also about mourning and memory, and it was not uncommon for survivors to commemorate their spouse or parent even decades after their death. They may also relate to expectations of resurrection among the religious. These monuments were created in a context of belief in an afterlife for the soul, yet reflect also an inclination to commemorate mortal remains and ensure enduring memory among the living. Movingly, many memorials were created to commemorate the married couple and their children, with names added over time as children predeceased their parents, and widows remembered their spouses.[19]

The material culture of the funeral and bereavement involved far more than just the gravestone, with mourning clothes, gloves and rings provided for in wills and commensality at funerals. The elite fashion for nocturnal funerals in the later seventeenth century was expressive of social relations – holding the community at a distance, while not wishing the gentry's death ritual to be a public spectacle. Institutions were also involved, with guild funerals as well as Church of England rites. Some of the deceased marked their piety by founding or endowing charitable institutions, particularly almshouses. The changing style of gravestones is, however, indicative of a further shift in sentiment. Seventeenth-century gravestones placed enormous emphasis on mortality, and this preoccupation with mortality was also a feature of contemporary art. This eased in the eighteenth century, as new forms of sentiment made it more appropriate to represent death indirectly – with urns, broken columns, weeping willows or representations of mourning female figures replacing the skulls, cross-bones, hour glass and scythe of 'Old Father Time' and Death himself. The English way of death, like the change in attitude towards childhood noted above, became more commercialised in the eighteenth century, but the changing forms of material culture still bear testimony to shifting cultural values.[20]

## Consumption and Class

Diet, furnishing and dress distinguished one class from another. As Adam Smith observed, this was not so much about differential access to resources as the quality of social distinction through taste. Smith's counter-intuitive observation that 'the rich consume little more than the poor' was based in part on the rising living standards of the lower ranks over the preceding century. Whereas Gregory King, in his social tables created in the 1680s, could point to those 'increasing the wealth of the kingdom' and those 'decreasing the wealth of the kingdom' through their consumption, Smith commented in *The Wealth of Nations* on the 'improvement in the circumstances of the lower ranks of the people' – observing that the common complaint 'that the labouring poor will not now be contented with the same food, clothing and lodging which satisfied them in former times, may convince us that it is not the money price of labour only, but its real recompense, which has augmented'.[21] Smith was writing before the miseries of the Industrial Revolution. The rich, we may add, also had a habit of extending their consumption to the limits of their income, in ways that could make their consumption as precarious as that afforded by the more meagre wages of the poor. Madame de Bocagradane, visiting Oxfordshire in 1750, observed that 'people of this class have their houses well furnished, are well-dressed and eat well; the poorest country girls drink tea, have bodices of chintz, straw hats on their heads and scarlet cloakes upon their shoulders'.[22] But historians should be wary of complacency in taking the testimony of the affluent as an adequate guide to the prevalence of cheer through material consumption; for all that Georgian swains and milk maids enjoyed colourful handkerchiefs and fresh bonnets as part of plebeian fashion, they were the object of an aristocratic perspective that saw them as pastoral figures in the landscape, preferably beyond the garden fence. Historians should be hesitant about taking material improvements in the standard of living as an index of happiness. Given the exploitation and exclusion active in England's economy and society there is arguably little to celebrate about the prevalence of poor-quality tea and cheap trinkets in English homes by 1750.

During the seventeenth century, England became a post-courtly society, orientated on London as a city rather than the location of the court, but this merely enabled the aristocracy (who preferred to shop in Paris) to reinvent themselves rather than cede power to the eagerly consuming middling ranks. Only in the 1740s, when Britain was at war with France, did English gentlemen's dress take inspiration from the plain style of servants (a far from unique instance of upward diffusion in fashion). Nevertheless, London's 'post-courtly' function as a city was a crucial feature of England's commercial society, which it shared with the Dutch, and contrasted England with France, where elite consumption by the court was more of a cultural focus. Sumptuary legislation governing status distinctions in dress, which had been repeatedly refined in Elizabeth's reign, was undone in the first English Parliament of King James in 1604, and Parliament came to prefer protectionist measures applied to manufactured goods rather than to police who was wearing what. London, with Paris beyond, was the focus of consumption for English people throughout the British world, and for metropolitan and provincial society alike. But this was still not fully a consumer society, and not everyone in the British Isles or the British Empire had an equal chance at eating a slice of the cake. Some could only pick at the crumbs. This was certainly not 'modern' mass consumption where objects are easily obtained and casually disposed of.[23]

Nevertheless, the relatively poor were participating in the same cultural changes as the affluent. And in many respects the later seventeenth and early eighteenth century was a time in England when there was a relative absence of acute poverty – compared to the poverty crises that triggered the Elizabethan poor law or its 'reform' in 1834. The poor in Georgian England took up tea-drinking, and came to eat with knives and forks, just as their wealthier neighbours adopted new modes of eating and drinking – with shared sets of cutlery, white china (or white glazed earthen-wares), cuts of meat for each place rather than a common pot dipped into with bread, and new cooking technologies associated with the adoption of new meals: notably the innovation of hobs and saucepans (introduced from France) in the later seventeenth century. All of which points to a change in the larger sets of material culture involved in consumption, which Jim Deetz described as the creation of 'the Georgian Order' in ways of living.[24] This was a deeply conformist culture, in which many people participated in the same trends for their own individual ends but avoided 'singularity'. Conformity and communal regulation may explain the particular prominence of public sociability, much of it commercialised, in framing consumption activities in seventeenth- and eighteenth-century England – from shopping arcades to coffee shops; theatres and assembly rooms; as well as public promenades and ticketed pleasure gardens. Occupation and status continued to govern people's clothing and behaviour, as well as life-cycle and place. Rare figures led taste, notably Beau Nash at the assemblies in Bath and Lord Burlington with William Kent at York. Most folk followed, and this was the logic of eighteenth-century ideas about taste, with intellectuals such as David Hume merely putting into words the codes of behaviour expressed more mutely through the consumption of material culture as core to social behaviour.[25] Dress, particularly, was not only about individual flair but also about being appropriately decked out for one's station in life, and many occupations were made visible through dress. Status and employment were embodied in clothes. Despite the elaboration of plebeian dress with buttons, bonnets, pins and ribbons, or men's hats and handkerchiefs, let alone the emergence of high fashion, with an annual London season from the seventeenth century and the arrival of the first fashion magazines from Paris by 1750, dress remained a conformist as well as a constructivist activity. So important was dress in eighteenth-century society that the poor had pieces of mirror in their homes to check their appearance before venturing into public, while affluent gentlemen and ladies had bedroom suites with adjacent dressing rooms in which to prepare themselves for the day. Ultimately, every group policed consumer behaviour. People were quick to detect when their social peers were acting without authenticity, and imaginative literature held lessons for those who stepped out of line.[26]

## Ideologies of Consumption

Innovation and a belief in progress – what contemporaries called 'improvement' – along with an increasingly materialist understanding of the world, defined what may be described as an ideology of consumption in England over the sixteenth to eighteenth centuries. This ethic of improvement – manifest in new foodstuffs, new utensils, newly rebuilt houses, newly hedged fields and changes of clothes – differentiated early modern English culture from the commercial economy of the Middle Ages. After all, England's expanding commercial economy involved no drastic alteration in the basic parameters of household and kinship structure. To differentiate the early modern household's culture of consumption from that of its medieval forebears we must look to the impact of other cultural influences, and their imperfectly understood relationship to material culture.

England's Reformation of religion was one. It had a direct bearing on how contemporaries understood materiality, and the importance placed upon material culture. The Protestant reform of worship focused on its material setting. It encouraged a change from contributing spare funds towards the fabric, furnishings and internal decoration of the parish church, to prioritising spending on one's own domestic comforts, including godly decoration of the dwelling. More profoundly, the Protestant Reformation and Catholic Counter-Reformation both indirectly sponsored a greater emphasis on the materiality of this world (including among the clergy) by contributing to a raised consciousness of the place of materiality in historical change, and ultimately to a process of secularisation. Witness the new interest of clerical antiquarians in the materiality of church architecture, such as Thomas Staveley's *History of Churches in England* (1712). Similarly, the seventeenth century witnessed an intensified engagement with the natural world, increasingly shorn of its magical qualities, pursued for its own sake, and fostered by the circulation of both manuscripts and print.[27]

Defined by its relationship to the household economy and the greater emphasis on materiality sponsored directly by expanding consumerism and indirectly by the Reformation, early modern consumption and material culture practices were quite distinct from both what came before in the Middle Ages, and what emerged later with further industrialisation. Early modern conceptions of materiality were different from those prevailing in later centuries. Material things were more directly related to their sources than is the case with modern alienated mass consumerism. This direct understanding of the creation of material things from the earth was still related to biblical conceptions of man's place in nature. As philosophers, notably Francis Bacon and John Locke, well understood, human artefacts were wrought from the earth. They were at once a product of nature and artificial. Common folk shared this perception, being necessarily familiar with the ways in which timber-and-brick houses with glass windows were created from carefully selected trees, earth and sand. Everyone was aware of the plant and animal source of the fibres that made up their clothing, the leather on their shoes or wooden clogs, the animal fat that produced the tallow for their candles, local sources of rushes cut for lights by those unable to afford tallow, and the laboriously collected wood and water used to fuel and clean the house. This places early modern perceptions of material culture in a different context from late modern capitalism, where the relationship among the natural sources for artefacts is generally much more attenuated and less familiar to consumers, and increasingly a source of anxiety over humanity's relationship to nature.

For most early moderns, God had endowed man with the capacity to make things, and Bacon believed that a total knowledge of the manmade and natural worlds would lead to man's recovery from the Fall, and perfection of the world. Bacon's influence is manifest in Randle Holme's *Academy of Armory* (1688), devised in the 1650s, with most of the artefacts illustrated by Holme having been invented in the preceding 100 years. Holme's encyclopedic documenting of the manmade and natural world was only published as part of the Royal Society's project on trades, directed at improving knowledge of man's manufacture of artefacts. Joseph Moxon's how-to manual *Mechanick Excercises* (1683) was part of the same enterprise, and a burgeoning 'how-to' literature in print. For Locke, man's capacity for crafting objects from the earth was the basis for man's property in things, and the basis for early modern conceptions of property rights in land and assets. Property's increasing importance in the seventeenth century (replacing an earlier emphasis on multiple use rights) went hand-in-hand with the increasing materialism of English culture. The eighteenth-century 'luxury debate' was about coming to terms with that change, in which religion was increasingly on the back foot, with economic expansion and household consumption widely recognised as the route to England's happiness. Print was central to this reconceptualisation of material culture, and Bernard Mandeville's *The Fable of the Bees* (1705) was the most prominent polemic to make the case for the public benefits of pursuing material interests and appetites.[28]

## Conclusion

The protean character of human materiality is specific to the context in which it is created, and thus for historians becomes a key diagnostic of periodisation. Material culture in England points to three sub-periods between 1500 and 1750, with an early-to-mid Tudor, then an Elizabethan–Jacobean phase before the civil war, and a later Stuart into Georgian 'style' thereafter. Particular political situations could give rise to particular moments in architecture and the decorative arts, and regnal labels are appropriate when considering material culture in this era, for even though England was increasingly focused on metropolitan London rather than upon the court, contemporaries still defined themselves and their material prosperity as reflecting the state of the realm under particular monarchs. They seldom thought in terms of decades or centuries, but were often aware of regional cultures and local traditions.

Specialist scholars can readily identify the place and date of an artefact and distinguish an original from a later reproduction. This specificity of materiality is central to our historical imagination; we can picture Henry VIII's court, and how this contrasts with the world of George II's London, or how a Cornish farmhouse differed from a Cumbrian. Across the period 1500–1750 the materiality of England changed several times. This stadial quality of material culture is usually referred to as 'style', but it is possible to be more direct and regard materiality as the expression of culture. Material culture does not alter at an even rate; although there is often a strong generational dynamic to the rhythms of change, similarities can be carried over more than one generation and more than one political ideology, as in the architecture and furnishing for parliamentarians and royalists before and after the Civil Wars, or the persistence of Georgian furnishings and fashions well beyond 1750. At differing scales, recognised through the emergence of distinct patterns, related sets of material culture metamorphosed from one way of doing things to another.

Diet, dress, housing and furnishings all altered as part of an expanding commercial economy linked to seaborne trade, and provided the material frame for an increasingly post-courtly and segregated society, with poverty defined by an acute or relative lack of material things. Yet it was unwittingly encouraged in the post-Reformation era by a greater concentration on the materiality of this world – what Max Weber called the 'Great Disenchantment'.[29] Consumerism, for all its techniques of rationalisation and opportunities for exuberance, may ultimately be motivated at the deepest level by a refusal to think about death. The culture of seventeenth-century England was certainly preoccupied with mortality – in art and commemoration – as the nation recoiled from the wars of religion in Europe and endured a civil war in Britain that appeared to many to herald the last days. The entrenchment of consumerism in the later seventeenth and early eighteenth century may in part have been a reflex against religious extremism. What certainly continued up to 1750 and after was the focus on the family as the basis for society and the household as the primary unit of production and consumption. In making themselves a home, at work, or enjoying themselves at leisure, English men and women ensured that material consumption was central in every sense to England's transformation and trajectory. Many aspects of material culture were also generated and consumed in ways that relied directly upon commercial print culture, and there is considerable scope for further research on both the linkages between material and print culture, and their trans-national character. As the diffusion of production techniques and consumption practices testify, southern and eastern Britain was directly engaged in a shared commercial culture with north-western Europe, particularly the Netherlands. The origins of a consumer economy were less tied to the genius of the English nation than to their geographical good luck to occupy a relatively prosperous part of the region of Europe that witnessed the emergence of a dignified and industrious trans-national culture.[30] The challenge for historians is to explain how and why their materiality changed over time.

## Notes

1  M. Douglas and B. Isherwood, *The World of Goods: Towards an Anthropology of Consumption* (London: Routledge, 1979).

2  I. Hodder (ed.), *The Archaeology of Contextual Meanings* (Cambridge: Cambridge University Press, 1987); I. Hodder (ed.), *The Meaning of Things: Material Culture and Symbolic Expression* (London: HarperCollins, 1989); I. Hodder, *Entangled: An Archaeology of the Relationships between Humans and Things* (Chichester: Wiley–Blackwell, 2012).

3  B. Lemire, *Dress, Culture and Commerce: The English Clothing Trade before the Factory, 1660–1800* (London: Macmillan, 1997); T. Arkell, N. Evans and N. Goose, *When Death Do Us Part: Understanding and Interpreting the Probate Records of Early Modern England* (London: Leopard's Head, 2000).

4  M. Spufford, *The Great Reclothing of Rural England: Petty Chapmen and Their Wares in the Seventeenth Century* (London: Hambledon Press, 1984); W. G. Hoskins, 'The rebuilding of rural England, 1570–1640', *P&P*, 4 (1953); A. Everitt, 'Country, county and town: Patterns of regional evolution in England', *TRHS*, 5th series, 29 (1979); J. Thirsk and J. P. Cooper (eds.), *Seventeenth-Century Economic Documents* (Oxford: Clarendon Press, 1972).

5 A. Vickery, 'An Englishman's home is his castle? Thresholds, boundaries and privacies in the eighteenth-century London house', *P&P*, 199 (2008); P. King, 'Pauper inventories and the material lives of the poor in the eighteenth and early nineteenth centuries', in T. Hitchcock, P. King and P. Sharpe (eds.), *Chronicling Poverty: The Voices and Strategies of the English Poor, 1640–1840* (Basingstoke: Macmillan, 1997); A. Green, 'Heartless and unhomely? Dwellings of the poor in East Anglia and north-east England', in J. McEwan and P. Sharpe (eds.), *Accommodating Poverty: The Housing and Living Arrangements of the English Poor, c. 1600–1850* (Basingstoke: Palgrave Macmillan, 2011); M. Spufford, 'The limitations of the probate inventory', in J. Chartres and D. Hey (eds.), *English Rural Society, 1500–1800: Essays in Honour of Joan Thirsk* (Cambridge: Cambridge University Press, 1990).

6 W. Harrison, 'Of the manner of building and furniture of our houses', in *The Description of England* (Ithaca, NY: Cornell University Press, 1968), originally published in 1577 and 1587; C. Dyer, *An Age of Transition? Economy and Society in England during the Later Middle Ages* (Oxford: Clarendon Press, 2005).

7 A. Green and R. T. Schadla-Hall, 'The building of Quenby Hall, Leicestershire: A reassessment', *Transactions of the Leicestershire Archaeological and Historical Society*, 74 (2000); M. Overton, J. Whittle, D. Dean and A. Hann, *Production and Consumption in English Households, 1600–1750* (London: Routledge, 2004).

8 D. Defoe, *The Complete English Tradesman in Familiar Letters* (1727), 2 vols. (New York: A. M. Kelley, 1969), Vol. I, 257; K. Wrightson, *Earthly Necessities: Economic Lives in Early Modern Britain* (New Haven and London: Yale University Press, 2000).

9 In addition to *Robinson Crusoe* (1719), *Moll Flanders* (1722) and *Roxana* (1724), see P. Earle, *The Making of the English Middle Class: Business, Society and Family in London, 1660–1730* (London: Methuen, 1989); C. Muldrew, *The Economy of Obligation: The Culture of Credit and Social Relations in Early Modern England* (Basingstoke: Macmillan, 1998).

10 J. Thirsk, *Economic Policy and Projects: The Development of a Consumer Society in Early Modern England* (Oxford: Clarendon Press, 1978); P. Slack, *The Invention of Improvement: Information and Material Progress in Seventeenth-Century England* (Oxford: Oxford University Press, 2015); J. de Vries, 'The industrial revolution and the industrious revolution', *Journal of Economic History*, 54:2 (1994).

11 J. O. Appleby, *Economic Thought and Ideology in Seventeenth-Century England* (Los Angeles: Figueroa Press, 1978); N. McKendrick, J. Brewer and J. H. Plumb, *The Birth of a Consumer Society: The Commercialization of Eighteenth Century England* (London: Hutchinson, 1982), critiqued by B. Fine and E. Leopold, 'Consumerism and the Industrial Revolution', *SH*, 15 (1990); and J. Brewer, 'The error of our ways: Historians and the birth of consumer society', Cultures of Consumption Working Paper no. 12 (Royal Society lecture, London, September 2003), www.consume.bbk.ac.uk/working_papers/Brewer%20talk.doc (accessed 17 October 2016).

12 L. Trusler, '"In play is all my mynde": Children and their toys in Renaissance England', *Things*, 13 (2001); J. H. Plumb, 'The new world of children in eighteenth-century England', *P&P*, 67 (1975); Philippe Ariès, *Centuries of Childhood* (London: Cape, 1962), criticised in A. Wilson, 'The infancy of the history of childhood: An appraisal of Philippe Ariès', *History and Theory*, 19 (1980); C. Heywood, *A History of Childhood: Children and Childhood in the West from Medieval to Modern Times* (Cambridge: Polity, 2001).

13 McKendrick, Brewer and Plumb, *The Birth of a Consumer Society*, 1–33; T. Veblen, *The Theory of the Leisure Class* (New York: Macmillan, 1899); C. Campbell, *The Romantic Ethic and the Spirit of Modern Consumerism* (Oxford: Blackwell, 1987); R. Williams, *Keywords: A Vocabulary of Culture and Society* (London: Fontana, 1983).

14 See www.hearthtax.org.uk (accessed 17 October 2016).

15 D. Cressy, *Birth, Marriage and Death: Ritual and the Life-Cycle in Tudor and Stuart England* (Oxford: Oxford University Press, 1997); S. Hindle, 'The problem of pauper marriage in seventeenth-century England', *TRHS*, 6th series, 8 (1998); L. Stone, *The Family, Sex and Marriage in England 1500–1800* (London: Weidenfeld & Nicolson, 1977); W. Gouge, *Of Domesticall Duties* (1622).

16 R. Machin, 'The great rebuilding: A reassessment', *P&P*, 77 (1977); C. Carson, 'The consumer revolution in colonial British America: Why demand?', in C. Carson, R. Hoffman and P. J. Albert, *Of Consuming Interests: The Style of Life in the Eighteenth Century* (Charlottesville: University of Virginia Press, 1994).

17 C. Schammas, *The Pre-Industrial Consumer in England and America* (Oxford: Oxford University Press, 1990); J. de Vries, 'Between purchasing power and the world of goods: Understanding the household economy in early modern Europe', in J. Brewer and R. Porter (eds.), *Consumption and the World of Goods* (London: Routledge, 1993); A. Vickery, *Behind Closed Doors: At Home in Georgian England* (New Haven and London: Yale University Press, 2009); J. Styles, *The Dress of the People: Everyday Fashion in Eighteenth Century England* (New Haven and London: Yale University Press, 2007).

18 A. Erickson, *Women and Property in Early Modern England* (London: Routledge, 1993); M. Pointon, *Strategies for Showing: Women, Possession and Representation in English Visual Culture* (Oxford: Clarendon Press, 1997); T. Hamling, *Decorating the 'Godly' Household: Religious Art in Post-Reformation Britain* (New Haven and London: Yale University Press, 2010); A. Green, '"A clumsey country girl": The material and print culture of Betty Bowes', in H. Berry and J. Gregory (eds.), *Creating and Consuming Culture in North-East England* (Farnham: Ashgate, 2004), discussing 'A lady's library', *Spectator*, 37 (1711); J. Bailey, *Unquiet Lives: Marriage and Marriage Breakdown in England, 1660–1800* (Cambridge: Cambridge University Press, 2003).

19 R. Houlbrooke, *Death, Religion and the Family in England, 1480–1750* (Oxford: Clarendon Press, 1998); S. Tarlow, *Ritual, Belief and the Dead Body in Early Modern Britain and Ireland* (Cambridge: Cambridge University Press, 2010).

20 J. Litten, *The English Way of Death: The Common Funeral since 1450* (London: Hale, 1991); N. Llewellyn, *The Art of Death: Visual Culture in the English Death Ritual, c. 1500–c. 1800* (London: Victoria and Albert Museum, 1991).

21 A. Smith, *The Theory of Moral Sentiments* (1759), Cambridge Texts in the History of Philosophy (Cambridge: Cambridge University Press, 2002), 215; A. Smith, *An Inquiry into the Nature and Causes of the Wealth of Nations* (1776), Oxford World Classics (Oxford: Oxford University Press, 1993), 70–2.

22 Cited in A. Buck, *Dress in Eighteenth-Century England* (London: Batsford, 1979), 130.

23 A. Ribiero, *Dress in Eighteenth Century Europe, 1715–1789* (New Haven and London: Yale University Press, 1984); A. Hunt, *Governing the Consuming Passions: A History of Sumptuary Law* (Basingstoke: Macmillan, 1996); D. Miller, *Material Culture and Mass Consumption* (Oxford: Blackwell, 1987).

24 J. Deetz, *In Small Things Forgotten: An Archaeology of Early American Life* (New York: Anchor, 1996); M. Johnson, *An Archaeology of Capitalism* (Oxford: Blackwell, 1996).

25 D. Hume, 'Of the standard of taste' (1757), in *David Hume: Selected Essays* (Oxford: Oxford University Press, 1993), 133–54; J. Brewer, *The Pleasures of the Imagination: English Culture in the Eighteenth Century* (London: HarperCollins, 1997).

26 T. Smollett, *The Expedition of Humphrey Clinker* (1771) (Harmondsworth: Penguin, 1985). For the scene at Newcastle see A. Green, 'The polite threshold in seventeenth and eighteenth century Britain', *Vernacular Architecture*, 41 (2010); and H. Berry, 'Creating polite space: The organisation and social function of the Newcastle assembly rooms', in Berry and Gregory, *Creating and Consuming Culture*.

27 C. Hill, 'The spiritualization of the household', in *Society and Puritanism in Pre-Revolutionary England* (London: Secker and Warburg, 1964); M. McKeon, *The Secret History of Domesticity: Public, Private and the Division of Knowledge* (Baltimore: Johns Hopkins University Press, 2005); K. Thomas, *Religion and the Decline of Magic: Studies in Popular Beliefs in Sixteenth and Seventeenth Century England* (London: Weidenfield & Nicolson, 1971); K. Thomas, *Man and the Natural World: Changing Attitudes in England* (London: Allen Lane, 1983); K. Thomas, *The Ends of Life: Roads to Fulfilment in Early Modern England* (Oxford: Oxford University Press, 2009); C. Taylor, *A Secular Age* (Cambridge, MA: Harvard University Press, 2007).

28 L. Cowen Orlin, *Private Matters and Public Culture in Post-Reformation England* (Ithaca, NY: Cornell University Press, 1994); P. Slack, 'The politics of consumption and England's happiness in the late seventeenth century', *EHR*, 122:497 (2007); J. Brewer and S. Staves (ed.), *Early Modern Conceptions of Property* (London: Routledge, 1995); J. M. Stafford (ed.), *Private Vices, Publick Benefits? The Contemporary Reception of Bernard Mandeville* (Solihull: Ismeron, 1997); J. Sekora, *Luxury: The Concept in Western Thought, Eden to Smollett* (Baltimore: Johns Hopkins University Press, 1977); A. O. Hirschman, *The*

*Passions and the Interests: Political Arguments for Capitalism before Its Triumph* (Princeton: Princeton University Press, 1977).

29  M. Weber, *The Protestant Ethic and the Spirit of Capitalism* (London: Routledge, 1992 [English trans. London: HarperCollins, 1930]); C. Taylor, *Modern Social Imaginaries* (Durham, NC: Duke University Press, 2004).

30  E. A. Wrigley, 'A simple model of London's importance in changing English society and economy, 1650–1750', *P&P*, 37 (1967); E. A. Wrigley, 'Urban growth in early modern England: Food, fuel and transport', *P&P*, 225:1 (2014); D. McCloskey, *Bourgeois Dignity: Why Economics Can't Explain the Modern World* (Chicago: Chicago University Press, 2010); J. de Vries, *The Industrious Revolution: Consumer Behavior and the Household Economy, 1650 to the Present* (Cambridge: Cambridge University Press, 2008).

# PART III

# Social Identities

# 12

# 'Gentlemen': Remaking the English Ruling Class

## Henry French

'Gentlemen' have been a problematic group in English social history, not least because they often elude easy definition in terms of their membership or common attributes.[1] These problems are compounded by contemporaries' willingness to use the term 'gentleman' in two, overlapping but distinct, ways: as an inclusive category, applied to all those of gentle birth and status (including the titular aristocracy); and as a term reserved specifically for 'lesser nobles', below the rank of 'baron' (baronets, knights, esquires and 'mere' gentlemen). This chapter will focus on the latter group, because non-titular landed gentlemen (the group referred to from the mid eighteenth century as 'the gentry') formed the core of the English landed elite from the sixteenth to the nineteenth centuries. Although the titled aristocracy expanded from 60 families in 1600 to over 600 by 1800, and accumulated a disproportionate share of wealth, status and power in Britain and Ireland, they shared many of their essential social and cultural characteristics with the wider swathe of landed society that will be considered here.

Social historians' problems with landed society reflect deeper ambivalences created by the inception and evolution of social history itself over the last century. This has produced a situation in which we know a huge amount about lives, experiences, opinions, actions and dynamics within this group, but where much of its *social* history still remains to be written. This chapter will consider three dimensions of this unfinished social history. Firstly, it will reflect upon the reasons why the group has proved problematic to social historians. Secondly, it will review the main conclusions that can be abstracted from the voluminous literature on the lives and activities of the gentry through the early modern period. Thirdly, it will suggest ways in which future studies might pursue the social history of this group, and, in particular, to integrate it further into the mainstream of analyses of early modern society.

For a century a simple, axiomatic question has bedevilled historical under-standings of the English gentry – should social history concern itself with a group of 10,000–20,000 families who constituted the ruling elite through the early modern period? Any possible answer bears directly upon the composition of the 'society' that social history professes to study, and on the nature of the 'history' that it seeks to write. There are three reasons why English social history has been very ambivalent about the gentry. Firstly, the late-nineteenth-century professionalisation of historical study, and its institutionalisation through university faculties, created a split between political/constitutional history and economic history (with some interest in 'class' formation) within academic circles. As Adrian Wilson has observed, the emergent academic economic and social history defined itself, in part, against the study of political history: 'the history of a people with the politics left out'.[2] The gentry were casualties of this split, because in the history of periods before the mid nineteenth century, the work-ing assumption was that the most important political actors were usually members of the landed elite.[3]

Secondly, as members of the historical section of the Communist Party of Great Britain, such as A. L. Morton, H. N. Brailsford, Maurice Dobb, Rodney Hilton, Christopher Hill, E. P. Thompson, George Rudé and Eric Hobsbawm, brought an ideological and methodological rigour in the two decades after 1945 to subjects previously studied as 'people's history', the evolving social history became construed very much as 'history from below'. This was institutionalised as academic social history in the 1960s. If social history had a duty, in Raphael Samuel's words, to be 'opposi-tional', and embedded in experience rather than ideology, then its practi-tioners argued that it should be concerned with 'ordinary people', not the social elite.[4] While the gentry featured extensively in Thompson's work on the law, poaching and riot; in Hill's explorations of the social con-text of the English Revolution; and in a host of other studies of popular protest, politics, and subversion; they did so primarily as 'class enemies'.[5] They were also included in the first generation of social history primarily either in the context of crime and social control,[6] or where their substan-tial archives allowed insights into topics that were difficult to study among other social groups, such as 'histories of family structure, marriage and childhood, adolescence, old age and death ... gender relations and sexual-ity',[7] sometimes with mixed results.[8]

Thirdly, and more prosaically, the heyday of this 'new social history' also coincided with a massive upsurge between 1960 and 1980 in research on the early modern English gentry, through the historiographical golden age of the 'county community' study of gentry politics, economic fortunes and social organisation in the century before 1640.[9] There was little need for social historians to work on this group, because so much research was already going on, even if much of it was on gentry politics. Conversely, since 1980 the rise of revisionist interpretations of the Civil War, and the tendency of detailed county studies to complicate rather than confirm the debates that initiated them, has led to a decline in regional studies of the group.[10]

The *social* history of the gentry – that is, the holistic consideration of the social and cultural identity, ideas, experiences, practices and power relationships of small, medium and large rentier landowners – really rests on three studies that complement a couple of older monographs.[11] These are the works of Felicity Heal and Clive Holmes, James Rosenheim, and Amanda Vickery.[12] While these studies provide a comprehensive overview of some of the most important attributes, influences and dynamics within the gentry, they also leave open some quite substantial thematic gaps for future researchers.

In the last two decades research into the composition, attributes, identity and dynamics within the gentry has been strongest among historians of the fourteenth and fifteenth centuries. It has revealed some of the very long-term continuities that characterised the gentry as a status group in English society, but also allows us to identify new developments in the early modern period.

Surprisingly, it has demonstrated that the term 'gentleman' and the idea of a collective group of 'gentlemen' or 'gentlewomen' came into currency in historical sources quite suddenly in the years between 1420 and 1440.[13] Christine Carpenter found that in Warwickshire, although 'by the 1420s esquires were beginning to be designated on private deeds with reasonable frequency', the term 'gentleman' was employed relatively infrequently until the 1440s to 'signal separation from the peasantry', and was rare in government documents until the 1460s.[14] She suggests that this descriptive change was triggered by the 1413 Statute of Additions, which 'finally produced the extrapolation from *gentil* for all well-born people to 'gentleman' for the lowest of the well born'.[15]

It is clear, too, that the group long preceded the term. Research by Coss has shown that by the late thirteenth and early fourteenth century non-titular landholders were increasingly able to assert their independence as minor territorial lords (firstly the esquires, then the gentlemen), and distinguish their authority from that conferred through their position as household officials or followers of the major aristocracy.[16] Even so, such minor landholders continued to derive much of their authority, status and patronage from their positions within larger aristocratic 'affinities'. Their clientage continued into the sixteenth century, with Thomas Howard, fourth duke of Norfolk (d. 1572), perhaps being the last English noble to command 'a neo-feudal loyalty from a tenantry which included many East Anglian gentry', by placing them on the bench, drawing them into his military retinues and requiring their votes for his parliamentary candidates.[17] The territorial power of magnates such as Edward Stafford, third duke of Buckingham, Thomas Percy, seventh earl of Northumberland, and Thomas Howard did not survive their fall. After its destruction, their gentry clients acquired more political and social autonomy, at the cost of greater local factionalism and competition for office.

From its origins, the gentry was a 'status' group rather than a more tightly knit social entity. Its members were united in the shared adoption of status-bearing social, cultural, economic and political characteristics, based on income derived primarily (but never exclusively) from the rents and services drawn from land. Yet, this status always encompassed a series of paradoxes. From the fourteenth century, gentlemen and -women constantly revered families of long lineage, but the gentry was always open to newcomers with sufficient wealth to acquire and sustain the status-bearing attributes sanctioned by the group.[18] 'Porosity, like adaptability, is a characteristic of the gentry which can certainly be traced to the period of origin.'[19] Gentility was portrayed as a fundamental status threshold, separating its possessors from all social groups beneath them, but gentry had only the heralds' visitations and their coats of arms to defend their status in law. As serfdom declined, it was more difficult for minor gentlemen and women to buttress their status by reference to the feudal prerogatives stemming from manorial lordship. Lordship remained important, but more as the means of access to demesnes to be rented out, than to bondmen who could be ordered about.[20]

This entrenched a further paradox, apparent until the end of the nineteenth century, in which landlords constantly traded the social prestige, power and influence of paternalist relations with tenants against the ever-present desire to maximise income.[21] In addition, while the extraction of unearned income from land remained the dominant status-bearing template among the gentry and aristocracy, the group was never averse to placing younger sons into learned professions (particularly the law) or higher-status distributive trades, or to receiving influxes of dowry income from marriages of daughters into such occupations, despite enduring snobbery about such connections. 'Studies of family settlements among the landed aristocracy from the twelfth to the nineteenth centuries reveal a remarkably consistent pattern, in which the heir's prospects take a normally unchallenged precedence.'[22]

If these concerns about lineage, arms, lordship, profit and primogeniture remained constants in the lives of all landowners from the central Middle Ages to Victorian England, what changed? We can identify four substantial developments: two of them, price inflation and religious reform, had their principal impact in the sixteenth and early seventeenth century; two others, changing social horizons and shifts in the bases of their social authority, began in that period but gathered pace after 1650. Price inflation began in the 1520s, and accelerated with population increases and coinage debasements in the 1540s and 1550s, with another sharp upturn triggered by harvest failures and wartime expenditure in the 1590s. More importantly, such rises came after 150 years in which rents, incomes, food prices, raw and manufactured materials had stagnated, particularly in rural areas. When landlords moved to increase rents, undermine long or perpetual tenures, secure higher prices and convert from arable to pasture or plough up commons, such activity violated the 'customs' established by tenants during three or four generations of low pressure. This explains why the apparent rapaciousness of 'rack-renting' landlords generated so much comment in the 1540s and 1550s, and so much real, and serious, popular unrest.[23]

At the same time as landlords awoke to the need to extract more rent from their land, the dissolution of the monasteries undoubtedly also increased the supply of land available for purchase by lesser families. Before this time, Carpenter's study of Warwickshire suggests that although some new families bought their way into the ranks of the county's gentry, most were 'royal or noble servants, lawyers, justices/judges', not rising yeomen. After 1480, most purchases were made by existing families, not by newcomers, in a land market that was increasingly fluid.[24] The dissolution brought 'fully a quarter of manors' in the county onto the land market, and opened up opportunities for new, as well as established, families.[25] By 1640, perhaps only 18 per cent of the county's gentry could claim to have held the status since the fifteenth century, which might explain why Carpenter found that by the early seventeenth century they exhibited 'often abysmal ignorance' of their late medieval ancestors.[26] By contrast, 27 per cent had achieved the status during the period 1500–59, and another 30 per cent during Elizabeth's reign.[27]

What was the net effect of this influx? The 'rise of the gentry' thesis that defined scholarly debate about the group between 1940 and 1965 revealed the heterogeneity of the gentry's composition and, consequently, no clear link to any patterns of allegiance during the Civil War, with social mobility and diversity within the group varying considerably among counties. In Kent and Cheshire, there appears to have been relatively little turnover of gentry families between 1500 and 1640. By contrast, 60 per cent of the gentry in Yorkshire, Leicestershire and Norfolk were newcomers since 1500, 70 per cent of those in Suffolk and Northamptonshire, and 85–90 per cent in the London hinterland counties of Essex and Hertfordshire.[28] The dissolution of the monasteries and chantries, and the sale and exchange of diocesan and dean-and-chapter lands into Elizabeth's reign transferred perhaps 10–20 per cent of the land area in England into private hands. While the hands at the front of the queue for royal largesse were usually those of courtiers (like Sir Thomas Audley or Sir Richard Rich) and aristocrats, the gentry featured heavily in the second tier of purchasers. Church land was used primarily to 'round out' existing holdings, and 'in no sense did the crown sales call into existence a new class of landowner'.[29] In Norfolk the gentry moved from holding 67 per cent of manors in 1535 to 78 per cent in 1565, where most other categories of landowners (the crown; aristocrats; and the Church, excluding monasteries) remained broadly stable.[30] In Yorkshire, over 25 per cent of Cliffe's 679 gentry families eventually owned some monastic land.[31] As Alan Simpson wrote in 1960, when the gentry debates still raged, 'as for "impoverished landlords" or "declining gentry", we do not doubt that they existed, but we cannot see why the agrarian history, per se, should have produced them in any great numbers'.[32] In an era when grain prices increased sixfold between 1500 and 1600, and rents increased perhaps six- to tenfold, while wage rates barely doubled, it was difficult *not* to increase profits on an estate of at least 500–1,000 acres.[33] Just as in more recent research on the thirteenth and fourteenth centuries, there is little evidence that smaller estates were more market-oriented, exploitative or grasping than larger ones, or that there were marked north–south variations or ideological differences between market-inclined 'puritans' and 'traditional' paternalists.[34] If the gentry got into financial difficulties, it was often more because they were unable to restrain increases in expenditure (on houses, jewels, clothes, household possessions, travel, dowries and jointures), rather than because they were unable to increase their rents.[35]

How intensive was such exploitation? Recent research by Richard Hoyle, Christopher Brooks and Andy Wood has illustrated how effective

tenants could be in launching collective legal defences against acquisi-
tive, profiteering or extortionate landlords, particularly in securing their
own, favourable understandings of manorial custom.[36] Although examples abound of vindictive, grasping landlords, like Henry, Lord Cromwell
in North Elmham, Norfolk, discussed in detail by Richard Hoyle, other
cases support Wood's view that 'the gentry also bought into custom, seeing it as a legal and cultural expression of a kind of social contract'.[37]
Sometimes this emollient behaviour was inspired by the desire to avoid
expensive legal proceedings initiated by their tenants, as in the case of
Henry Jernegan of Painswick, Gloucestershire, 'a gentle man well inclined
to a peaceable end', but only after receiving the symbolically 'dutiful and
submissive' deference of his tenants.[38]

From their origins, the gentry had always acted as brokers between localities and regional or national authorities, whether this was in the form of
connection to an aristocratic affinity, or involvement in royal administration or office, such as the commission of the peace.[39] The gentry gained
and maintained their importance to the Tudor polity by acting as reliable, trusted agents in the localities, as sheriffs, justices, militia captains,
hundred constables, and manorial lords.[40] 'Localism', Anthony Fletcher
has written, '... was by and large mastered and subsumed by the country gentry for the purposes of government. This in a sense was the very
essence of their achievement.'[41] The centrality of local office to the gentry's
self-identity is emphasised by the alienation and anger created by their
exclusion from power during the Civil War and the Cromwellian era.[42]
At such times, gentry on the wrong side probably agreed with Sir John
Oglander that, 'If thou hast not Somm Commande in thy cowntery, thou
will not be esteemed of the Common Sort of people, whoe hath more of
feare, then love in them.'[43] The deprivation of such supports turned many
royalist and moderate parliamentarian gentry into political recusants, who
focused their efforts on protecting their landed interests, social networks
and cultural capital in the localities.[44] The ostentatious celebration of
Christmas became both a symbolic oppositional act, and a demonstration
that the gentry still mattered in counties in which they had been deprived
of other significant authority.

The focus on the localities during the Interregnum was a volte-face,
after sixty-to-eighty years in which the gentry had begun to orient themselves more towards London, and as a political, social and cultural centre,
and increasingly sought to educate sons at distant schools, the two universities and the Inns of Court.[45] The resort to institutions of education

rather than household tutors may have been more important socially than intellectually. The late medieval gentry were probably already possessors of a literate, learned and socially distinctive culture, but it was one acquired *locally*.[46] The expansion of the numbers at public and grammar schools, and at university (after 1560), was driven as much by parents' desire for sons to leave behind their local roots as it was in the belief that social elevation demanded educational excellence.[47] This development also raised their social horizons, and in particular widened the geographical breadth of the 'pool of eligibles' from which they sought marriage partners. In the fifteenth and early sixteenth century, even in a relatively open county such as Warwickshire 'the lesser esquires and gentlemen, even heirs and heiresses, married locally, sometimes positively parochially'.[48] By the early seventeenth century, at least half the Warwickshire gentry looked outside the county for marriage partners. One-third of the county's more substantial gentry, and almost 20 per cent of its minor gentry, now sought partners from beyond the Midlands.[49] The development of the mature London 'season' after 1660 (already anticipated in the 1610s and 1620s),[50] and the concentration of elite sociability within regional centres such as York, Chester, Exeter, Gloucester or Winchester,[51] and emergent resort towns like Bath, Buxton, Tunbridge Wells and Scarborough, widened these horizons for less wealthy or well-connected landowners, too.[52]

At the same time, between *c.* 1600 and 1640, there was a growing emphasis on travelling as part of the gentleman's education.[53] Previously, the Reformation had exposed English travellers to danger, particularly after Elizabeth's excommunication in 1570, and hostilities with Spain between 1585 and 1604 made travel difficult for those not included in a diplomatic entourage.[54] Thereafter, a steady flow of gentry joined the higher nobility in travelling to Paris, and then on to the centres of classical and humanist scholarship and arts (as well as less licit activities) – Rome, Florence, Padua, Verona, Bologna and Milan – plus commercial and artistic centres such as Genoa and Venice.[55] Until the early eighteenth century, such gentry travellers tended still to be a fairly self-conscious *avant garde* of aesthetes, would-be courtiers and collectors.[56] However, they personified the more general emphasis on humanist cultural education, attributes and appreciation among the elite, which included a broadening of cultural horizons irrespective of actual patterns of travel.

There were other shifts in this period. In the 1620s and 1630s many English gentry persisted with customs of hospitality – of times of 'open house' to tenants and neighbours.[57] By the seventeenth century, such hospitality was increasingly discriminating, and tended to focus on feast days such as Christmas or Shrovetide, harvest-homes, or family events.[58] It was much less common for gentry to maintain an open hall, in which all their servants and any visitors or local paupers might be fed.[59] Some still fed the needy at their gates, but the gravitation of the gentry to London for part of the year, and the formalisation of relief through compulsory poor rates, diminished the symbolic and material significance of hospitality as an integral component of gentry identity. The Civil War accelerated these trends. Heavy taxation and sequestration of royalist families diminished the funds available for open hospitality. Once these values were disturbed and interrupted among the wartime generation, they were harder to revive organically after 1660.

As a status group, the gentry's economic fortunes tended to revive after 1660, even in the face of significant long-term declines in agrarian income in the period 1670–1730.[60] Similarly, they regained their control of the institutions of county, militia and national government, and held on to them determinedly until at least the late 1860s.[61] However, Rosenheim argues that in the century after 1660, there was a growing tendency for the landed elite to regard their estates more as places of leisure, recreation, peer-based sociability and artistic self-expression than as sacred trusts, seigneurial powerbases or governmental responsibilities. In particular, he suggests that through the eighteenth century, the gentry retreated from involvement in the magistracy and business of county government.[62] In their place came more minor local gentlemen, plus (as other studies have indicated) greater specialisation, with a few highly active magistrates acting as semi-permanent chairs of the county bench over many years, leading a larger group of justices who attended only once or twice a year.[63] This was compounded by changes in educational fashion. Falling gentry incomes, rising educational costs, the diminished reputation of the two universities and restrictions on the accessibility of tuition at the Inns of Court after 1680[64] meant that gentry sons (especially younger sons) were less likely to receive tertiary education, or even to be sent to a public school.[65] While a lack of legal knowledge was no bar to acting as a magistrate, a general decline in exposure to such training may have reduced the gentry's familiarity with, and appetite for, the role. Many more gentlemen participated in the expanded bureaucracy of the emergent 'fiscal-military' state, notably the 13,000 land tax commissioners in 1723 (perhaps triple the number of justices of the peace at the same time), or (open-field) enclosure commissioners, or as trustees of local charities, and eventually canal and turnpike trusts.[66] These roles were much narrower than the all-encompassing activities of the magistrate, and many who held them were inactive time-servers. Rather than rekindling gentry activism, these posts enabled aspirant lawyers, physicians, manufacturers and wholesale merchants, higher-status retail trades, and others among the 'middling' to lay claim to the status of gentlemen and to rub shoulders with landed society.[67]

Indeed, 'elite withdrawal' may have been exacerbated by a decline in the size of the landed gentry per se. As Clay has remarked, 'well before 1700 … the multiplication of the gentry, which had been so marked a feature of English society between 1540 and 1640 had ceased'.[68] This decline in numbers was the result of several concurrent trends: smaller completed family sizes and fewer male heirs in the three generations after 1660;[69] substantial increases in the value of marriage portions;[70] a decline in the volume of land for sale; and absolute declines in the value of returns on land, as well as their declining yield relative to an increasing range of other financial opportunities (government bonds, joint-stock companies and mortgages).[71] While a drop in the numbers of heirs tended to concentrate property in fewer hands, historians have been wary of linking this to the new, more prescriptive legal forms of inheritance that emerged after 1650. 'Strict settlements' allowed a landowner to specify, and thus control, the descent of his property at the time of his marriage, and to bind his as-yet unborn children into this legal agreement.[72] However, it is unclear whether their effect was to funnel landed property into fewer and fewer hands. As the Stones put it, 'The central significance of the strict settlement was that it was in practice not very strict.'[73] The rising proportion of surviving female heirs was probably of equal or greater importance in the amalgamation of gentry estates.[74]

At the same time, there are signs of greater social exclusivity in the lives of the gentry. While they sometimes maintained certain social set-pieces (notably feasting their tenants at harvest, at the heir's majority and at patriotic celebrations), and spectated at pastimes or spectacles attended by diverse audiences (cock-fighting, theatre, public executions, elections and parades), elite sociability was often within a bubble.[75] Literary societies, clubs of all kinds, hunts and masonic lodges were often joined by co-option.[76] Libraries, assemblies, balls, horse races, and other places or events were often policed by membership fees and rules to exclude the socially undesirable.[77] While this offered an access route for urban 'gentlemen-tradesmen', it created the powerful, but invisible, social thresholds that came to characterise English society into the twentieth century.[78] As Lawrence Klein, Peter Clark, and Markku Peltonen have demonstrated, it also enhanced concepts of social and personal civility or

'politeness' – manners that determined social acceptance, political organisation, economic worth and cultural standards, and controlled and
policed interactions between those who 'belonged' and excluded the 'vul-
gar', who made up most of the rest of society.[79] The landed elite had always
been marked out by diet, dress, equestrian culture, enhanced access to literacy and literate culture, the scale and permanence of their houses, their
retinues of servants, and their brokerage functions in political and social
networks. These remained, but were now buttressed by accent, manners,
early adoption of metropolitan fashions, greater cultural cosmopolitan-
ism and membership of a status group whose gatherings were national in
scope (the London season, winter in Bath, racing at Newmarket, summer
bathing at Scarborough or Weymouth).[80]

This change also affected the function and purpose of the landed estate.
The growth of the London season and of the resort towns transformed its
function into a centre of leisure and recreation, rather than of business,
government or authority. The remodelling of parks and the rebuilding of
houses reflected this. Influenced first by French and Dutch formality, and
then by new notions of the picturesque, parks became heavily designed
landscapes that embodied elite values (such as the classically informed
grottoes of Stowe, or parks designed to look like the landscapes of Claude
Lorrain).[81] Increasingly, country houses were designed for set-piece enter-
taining of peer-groups, particularly during parliamentary or legal vaca-
tions, including the late summer–autumn hunting season, rather than
year-round habitation. Their large, regular sash windows, high ceilings
and open rooms made these houses lighter, and accentuated views into the
park, but often at the expense of rendering their public quarters virtually
uninhabitable in winter.[82] The double-pile houses favoured by the late-
seventeenth-century author Sir Roger Pratt, and incorporated into the
eighteenth-century explosion of English Palladianism, did away with the
central dining hall, and instituted a separate 'servants' hall' below stairs,
and servants' accommodation in garrets served by back stairs.[83] While servants remained, in George Savile's words, 'the Wheels' of an elite household, increasingly the fashion was for these workings to be concealed.[84]
In addition, after the Restoration these servants were uniformly of non-
gentry origin, and (therefore) outside the social sphere of their employers.[85] While retained 'professionals', such as tutors, governesses, land
agents and surveyors, possessed education, and at least 'middling' origins,
there was no continuation of the training accorded to the sons of minor
gentry and local yeomen as servants in elite households in the fifteenth
and sixteenth centuries.[86] In this sense, the earlier 'great household' of

family, personal servants, household servants, tenants and retainers broke down, and the nuclear family and its social orbit were separated from all those who served it and generated its income.

As families were more often absent, in London, Bath, York or at a subsidiary property, they depended increasingly on local intermediaries: both professional estate stewards, and local attorneys and farmers who acted as rent collectors and local managers on outlying properties.[87] Full-time stewards tended to be confined to the larger gentry estates, but they offered a comprehensive service, in collecting rents, letting properties, bookkeeping, and corresponding with providers of goods and services. They wrote frequently to their employers, relating local news, but also details of 'best practice' in estate management, husbandry techniques, animal and crop varieties, and 'improvement' schemes (such as enclosure, drainage and crop rotations).[88] In this respect, while elite influence (or interest) in the localities did not decline in absolute terms, the more frequent absences of the gentry from their estates meant that the steward or bailiff became their most visible representative, and came to exercise much of their political, social, economic and cultural authority. The rule of the gentry remained a constant in English society from the fourteenth century until almost the beginning of the twentieth, but increasingly it was a rule by proxy, based on paternalist precepts that were remarkably consistent, but more and more hollowed out by market-based practices.

There are two substantial fields in which future research would be especially welcome: the social construction of gentry authority, and (as part of this) the detailed investigation of the functioning of gentry households and estates. There has been some excellent initial research on both subjects, but it has been conducted surprisingly recently, and points the way for more to be done.[89]

Existing research tends to assume that gentry power and authority were self-evident. The gentry were landholders, so they exerted control over tenants. They occupied various governmental offices, so they discharged the responsibilities that went with them. They were located within national-level networks of political, religious and cultural patronage, so they exploited them to bolster their own importance. However, although political and religious (and, to a lesser extent, cultural) patronage networks have been investigated in some depth, gentry power remains 'normalised' – the gentry were powerful *because* they were the gentry. Instead, this power deserves to be anatomised more carefully.[90]

In some respects, social history has treated gentry identity as either intrinsic to the social role of the group or best studied as it impacts other social groups. However, it is evident that this identity can be studied more effectively by disarticulating aspects of gentry power from the identity of the group. There is an obvious analogy with gender history. Histories of masculinity have interrogated male identity and norms by understanding them as social constructions, which have been depicted as 'natural' by being embedded deeply into assumptions about other valorised social concepts (honour, virtue, fraternal co-operation, fatherhood and so on). They have investigated maleness as a problematic, fractured and contradictory category, in the same way that the previous generation of gender historians split open patriarchy, and broader concepts of gender per se. The same process is beginning to be applied to gentry identity and authority – as a formulation that was always potentially unstable, needed constant reinforcement and was always in action against competing social formulations, *at the same time* as it was presented as permanent, inevitable and unchallenged.

This approach was pre-figured, slightly, by the Warwick School of historians of crime in the 1970s, particularly Douglas Hay's idea of a hegemonic 'elite conspiracy', as the basis for the wider social acceptance of a class-biased legal system in the eighteenth century. The benefit of this interpretation was that it interrogated the bases of elite power, and tried to show how it was constantly created and asserted in action. Subsequent research, notably by Peter King, has demonstrated that the criminal law and its institutions were dependent upon decision-making by a much wider section of the population – the top 40 per cent, at least, rather than the top 3 per cent – and involved constant negotiation of competing interests among a variety of different interest groups.[91]

Recently, Andy Wood's study of popular understandings of custom, rights and legality has identified a much subtler and more fruitful approach. The focus of Wood's study remains, broadly, 'history from below', and the investigation of mechanisms by which non-elite groups accessed the law, understood and articulated their rights, and defended or assimilated them in relation to the interests of propertied groups. Instead of a simple binary model of 'custom', which pits custom based on popular, oral memory against 'elite' rights determined by written records, he emphasises the overlap of interests and approaches. He shows that custom was a 'discursive field', in which socially (and legally) disadvantaged social groups could assert and prove their rights by working within and manipulating assumptions about property, resource entitlement, and precedent-based access-rights that were *shared* between propertied and property-less.[92] His study provides a template for how such an analysis could be read the other way, to think much more deeply about the ways in which the elite constantly fretted about, and worked hard at, the projection, justification and acceptance of their authority.[93] It highlights that there are other, as yet under-researched, 'discursive fields' in which the gentry struggled to assert their interpretations against those of other social groups, and through which some of the constituent elements of their identity might be revealed. These include socially inflected contests over the meaning of concepts such as honour and duty, leadership, cultural or intellectual authority, service, motherhood, family and household, landscape and spatial affinities.

Given the volume of research on gentry families, lives, marriages, inheritance, houses, estates, politics, religion, business interests, metropolitan connections and cultural horizons, what else can we study in order to develop our understanding of gentility as a socially constructed identity? Jane Whittle and Elizabeth Griffiths have provided one answer. Their systematic and exhaustive study of the remarkable (but not unprecedented) family and estate accounts kept by Alice Le Strange reveals new interpretative dimensions.[94] They demonstrate that historians' concentration on ostentatious, big-ticket purchases by the elite is misleading, because it ignores the wider web of small-scale household and estate production, exchange and reciprocity in which such purchases were situated.[95] These tie the gentry household much more deeply to its economic root-stock, and imply that the gentry, or their agents, needed to remember, service and manipulate hundreds of different social relationships, containing many subtle gradations of status, simply in order to supply a single, moderately large household.[96] Whittle and Griffiths's reconstruction of the human infrastructure of the gentry household provides a model for thinking about power and authority as they were embedded within day-to-day practices and ongoing relationships. It enables us to reconstruct the identity of a family who were socially distinctive, paternalist landlords and magistrates, but also debtors to their tenants, buyers in the local market; suppliers of goods and services, employers of labour, and consumers of specialist skills and knowledge – clients as well as patrons. By revealing the detail of resource-allocation within the family, it also allows us to say more about the other concealed mechanism of gentry survival through the period – provision for younger children (particularly wayward sons like Roger Le Strange) for lives at the margins of, or outside, the group – and its consequences in terms of social relations.[97]

Further closely observed analyses of social practices year-in, year-out would allow us to contextualise, recover and interpret the deeper 'discursive fields' of shared and contested understandings of power, identity and authority. Allied to recent studies of elite education, particularly through the medium of classical reception studies, research of this kind might supply a more detailed social history of gentility – that is, the active processes by which the landed elite conceived of their identity, and attempted to perpetuate it socially, economically, politically and culturally within immediate relationships, between centre and periphery, across generations and within six centuries of British (and Irish) history from 1300 to 1900.

This change of focus does not imply either that this group, or its values, should revert to being the primary focus, or the norm, for historical research. However, a better appreciation of the discourses and social practices that supported the gentry, and sustained an unequal distribution of power, authority and resources, is essential if we are fully to understand processes of causation and patterns of consequences, from whatever vantage point we choose, in early modern England.

### Notes

1  See P. C. Maddern, 'Gentility', in R. L. Radulescu and A. Truelove (eds.), *Gentry Culture in Late Medieval England* (Manchester: Manchester University Press, 2005); J. P. Cooper, 'Ideas of gentility', in G. E. Aylmer and J. S. Morrill (eds.), *Land, Men and Beliefs: Studies in Early Modern History* (London: Hambledon, 1983); P. Corfield, 'The rivals: Landed and other gentlemen', in N. Harte and R. Quinault (eds.), *Land and Society in Britain, 1700–1914: Essays in Honour of F. M. L. Thompson* (Manchester: Manchester University Press, 1996). For historians' efforts to define the group, see G. Mingay, *The Gentry: The Rise and Fall of a Ruling Class* (London: Longman, 1976); M. L. Bush, 'An anatomy of nobility', in M. L. Bush (ed.), *Social Orders and Social Classes in Europe since 1500: Studies in Social Stratification* (London: Longman, 1992); F. Heal and C. Holmes, *The Gentry in England and Wales, 1500–1700* (Basingstoke: Macmillan, 1994), 7, 14; L. Stone and J. C. F. Stone, *An Open Elite? England, 1540–1880* (Oxford: Oxford University Press, 1986); J. Cannon, 'The British nobility, 1660–1800', in H. M. Scott (ed.), *The European Nobilities in the Seventeenth and Eighteenth Centuries*, Vol. I: *Western and Southern Europe* (London: Longman, 2007); F. M. L. Thompson, *English Landed Society in the Nineteenth Century* (London: Routledge, 1963), 1–25, 109–50.

2  As described by G. M. Trevelyan, *English Social History* (London: Longman, 1973), vii.

3  A. Wilson, 'A critical portrait of social history', in A. Wilson (ed.), *Rethinking Social History: English Society 1570–1920 and Its Interpretation* (Manchester: Manchester University Press, 1993).

4  S. Hindle, A. Shepard and J. Walter, 'The making and remaking of early
   modern English social history', in S. Hindle, A. Shepard and J. Walter (eds.),
   *Remaking English Society: Social Relations and Social Change in Early Modern
   England* (Woodbridge: Boydell, 2013), 8.
5  Classic expositions of this approach are found in E. P. Thompson, 'Patrician
   society, plebeian culture', *Journal of Social History*, 7 (1974); E. P. Thompson,
   *Whigs and Hunters: The Origins of the Black Act* (London: Allen Lane, 1975);
   D. Hay, P. Linebaugh and E. P. Thompson, *Albion's Fatal Tree: Crime and Society
   in Eighteenth-Century England* (London: Allen Lane, 1975); and C. Hill, *Society
   and Puritanism in Pre-Revolutionary England* (London: Secker & Warburg,
   1964). Other studies include K. Lindley, *Fenland Riots and the English Revolution*
   (London: Heinemann, 1982); B. Sharp, *In Contempt of All Authority: Rural
   Artisans and Riot in the West of England 1586–1660* (Berkeley: University of
   California Press, 1980); P. Clark, 'Popular protest and disturbance in Kent, 1558–
   1640', *EcHR*, 2nd series, 29 (1976); D. Rollison, 'Property, ideology and popular
   culture in a Gloucestershire village 1660–1740', *P&P*, 43 (1981).
6  Again, E. P. Thompson's contribution was particularly important, codified in
   E. P. Thompson, *Customs in Common* (London: Merlin, 1991), Chapter 2. See
   also P. King, 'Edward Thompson's contribution to eighteenth-century studies: The patrician–plebeian model re-examined', *SH*, 21 (1996).
7  K. Wrightson, 'The enclosure of English social history', in Wilson, *Rethinking
   Social History*, 60.
8  The most controversial result was Lawrence Stone's 'trickle-down' theory of marital love in *The Family, Sex and Marriage in England 1500–1800*
   (London: Weidenfeld & Nicolson, 1977). Later, more nuanced and successful studies of gentry household and family structures have included
   L. Pollock, '"Teach her to live under obedience": The making of women in the
   upper ranks of early modern England', *C&C*, 4 (1989); V. Larminie, *Wealth,
   Kinship, and Culture: The Seventeenth-Century Newdigates of Arbury and Their
   World* (Woodbridge: Boydell, 1995); A. Fletcher, *Growing Up in England: The
   Experience of Childhood 1600–1914* (New Haven and London: Yale University
   Press, 2008); J. Whittle and E. Griffiths, *Consumption and Gender in the Early
   Seventeenth-Century Household: The World of Alice Le Strange* (Oxford: Oxford
   University Press, 2012).
9  A. Everitt, 'Suffolk and the Great Rebellion', *Suffolk Records Society*, 3
   (1960); A. Simpson, *The Wealth of the Gentry, 1540–1660: East Anglian
   Studies* (Chicago: University of Chicago Press, 1961); T. G. Barnes, *Somerset
   1628–1640: A County's Government during the 'Personal Rule'* (Cambridge,
   MA: Harvard University Press, 1961); A. Everitt, *The Local Community and
   the Great Rebellion* (London: Historical Association, 1969); J. T. Cliffe, *The
   Yorkshire Gentry from the Reformation to the Civil War* (London: Athlone Press,
   1969); J. Morrill, *Cheshire 1630–1660: County Government and Society during
   the English Revolution* (Oxford: Oxford University Press, 1974); A. Fletcher,
   *A County Community in Peace and War: Sussex 1640–1660* (London: Longman,
   1975); B. G. Blackwood, 'The Lancashire gentry and the Great Rebellion',

*Chetham Society*, 3rd series, 25 (1978); C. Holmes, 'The county community in Stuart historiography', *JBS*, 19:2 (1979–80); A. Hughes, 'Warwickshire on the eve of the Civil War: A county community?', *Midland History*, 7 (1982); W. Hunt, *The Puritan Moment: The Coming of Revolution to an English County* (Cambridge, MA: Harvard University Press, 1983); A. Hughes, *Politics, Society and Government in Warwickshire 1620–1660* (Cambridge: Cambridge University Press, 1987); P. A. Duffin, *Faction and Faith: The Politics and Religion of the Cornish Gentry before the Civil War* (Exeter: University of Exeter Press, 1996); M. Wolffe, *Gentry Leaders in Peace and War: The Gentry Governors of Devon in the Early Seventeenth Century* (Exeter: University of Exeter Press, 1997).

10  Increasingly, interest in the internal coherence and attributes of the gentry has shifted to the fifteenth century. See C. Carpenter, *Locality and Polity: A Study of Warwickshire Landed Society, 1401–1499* (Cambridge: Cambridge University Press, 1992); E. Acheson, *A Gentry Community: Leicestershire in the Fifteenth Century, c. 1442–1485* (Cambridge: Cambridge University Press, 1992); M. Aston and R. Horrox (eds.), *Much Heaving and Shoving: Late Medieval Gentry and Their Concerns. Essays for Colin Richmond* (Chipping: Aston and Horrox, 2005); Radulescu and Truelove, *Gentry Culture*; E. Noble, *The World of the Stonors: A Gentry Society* (Woodbridge: Boydell, 2009); P. R. Coss, *The Foundations of Gentry Life: The Multons of Frampton and Their World, 1270–1370* (Oxford: Oxford University Press, 2010); M. Mercer, *Medieval Gentry: Power, Leadership and Choice during the Wars of the Roses* (London: Continuum, 2010).

11  The older studies are Mingay, *The Gentry*; and Thompson, *English Landed Society*.

12  Heal and Holmes, *Gentry*; J. M. Rosenheim, *The Emergence of a Ruling Order. English Landed Society 1650–1750* (Harlow: Longman, 1998); A. Vickery, *The Gentleman's Daughter: Women's Lives in Georgian England* (New Haven and London: Yale University Press, 1998).

13  Maddern, 'Gentility'.

14  Carpenter, *Locality and Polity*, 45–7.

15  *Ibid.*, 45.

16  Coss, *Foundations of Gentry Life*, 4–5.

17  A. Hassall Smith, *County and Court: Government and Politics in Norfolk, 1558–1603* (Oxford: Oxford University Press, 1974), 36–43.

18  Carpenter, *Locality and Polity*, 255.

19  Coss, *Foundations of Gentry Life*, 4.

20  *Ibid.*, 115.

21  *Ibid.*, 106.

22  Carpenter, *Locality and Polity*, 248.

23  A. Wood, *The 1549 Rebellions and the Making of Early Modern England* (Cambridge: Cambridge University Press, 2007), 21–69.

24  Carpenter, *Locality and Polity*, 123–30.

25  Hughes, *Politics, Society and Government*, 28.

26  Carpenter, *Locality and Polity*, 255.

27  Hughes, *Politics, Society and Government*, 29.

28  C. G. A. Clay, *Economic Expansion and Social Change: England 1500–1700*, Vol. I: *People, Land and Towns* (Cambridge: Cambridge University Press, 1984), 154–5.
29  *Ibid.*, 146.
30  M. Overton, *Agricultural Revolution in England: The Transformation of the Agrarian Economy 1500–1850* (Cambridge: Cambridge University Press, 1996), 168–9.
31  Cliffe, *Yorkshire Gentry*, 15–16.
32  Simpson, *Wealth of the Gentry*, 212.
33  Clay, *Economic Expansion*, 147.
34  Coss, *Foundations of Gentry Life*, 106; see also n. 7 above.
35  Heal and Holmes, *Gentry*, 136–65.
36  R. W. Hoyle, 'Redefining copyhold in the 16th century: The case of timber rights', in Bas J. P. van Bavel and P. Hoppenbrouwers (eds.), *Landholding and Land Transfer in the North Seas Area (Late Middle Ages–19th Century)* (Turnhout: Brepols, 2004); R. W. Hoyle, '*Cromwell* v. *Taverner*: Landlords, copyholders and the struggle to control memory in mid-sixteenth-century Norfolk', in R. W. Hoyle (ed.), *Custom, Improvement and the Landscape in Early Modern Britain* (Farnham: Ashgate, 2011); C. W. Brooks, *Law, Politics and Society in Early Modern England* (Cambridge: Cambridge University Press, 2008), 285–93, 322–51; A. Wood, *The Memory of the People: Custom and Popular Senses of the Past in Early Modern England* (Cambridge: Cambridge University Press, 2013), 156–87.
37  Hoyle, '*Cromwell* v. *Taverner*'; Wood, *Memory*, 289.
38  Wood, *Memory*, 293.
39  Coss, *Foundations of Gentry Life*, 3; Carpenter, *Locality and Polity*, 85–6.
40  Heal and Holmes, *Gentry*, 166–89; A. Fletcher, *Reform in the Provinces: The Government of Stuart England* (New Haven and London: Yale University Press, 1986), 3–5, 31–42, 87–115, 282–316; M. J. Braddick, *State Formation in Early Modern England, c. 1550–1700* (Cambridge: Cambridge University Press, 2000), 27–46; S. Hindle, *The State and Social Change in Early Modern England, 1550–1640* (Basingstoke: Macmillan, 2000), 3–15.
41  Fletcher, *Reform in the Provinces*, 368.
42  Heal and Holmes, *Gentry*, 221–6.
43  A. Nicholson, *Gentry: Six Hundred Years of a Peculiarly English Class* (London: Harper, 2011), 117.
44  Fletcher, *Reform in the Provinces*, 11–19.
45  *Ibid.*, 140–1, 243–75, 307–18; F. Heal, *Hospitality in Early Modern England* (Oxford: Oxford University Press, 1990), 142; Whittle and Griffiths, *Consumption and Gender*, 191–4.
46  N. Orme, 'Education and recreation', in Radulescu and Truelove, *Gentry Culture*, 81.
47  This was the intention of some families. See Larminie, *Wealth, Kinship and Culture*, 142–51. On curriculum developments, see F. Cox Jensen, *Reading the Roman Republic in Early Modern England* (Leiden: Brill, 2012).
48  Carpenter, *Locality and Polity*, 99.

49  Hughes, *Politics, Society and Civil War*, 38–9.

50  Heal, *Hospitality*, 141–2; I. Warren, 'London's cultural impact on the English gentry: The case of Worcestershire, *c*. 1580–1680', *Midland History*, 33:2 (2008).

51  P. Clark, '"The Ramoth-Gilead of the good": Urban change and political radicalism at Gloucester, 1540–1640', in J. Barry (ed.), *The Tudor and Stuart Town: A Reader in Urban History 1530–1688* (Harlow: Longman, 1990); A. Rosen, 'Winchester in transition, 1580–1700', in P. Clark (ed.), *Country Towns in Pre-Industrial England* (Leicester: Leicester University Press, 1981).

52  See P. Borsay, *The English Urban Renaissance: Culture and Society in the Provincial Town, c. 1660–1760* (Oxford: Oxford University Press, 1989). Much of the activity that Borsay emphasises among the 'middle sort' post-1660 was pre-figured by smaller numbers of gentry in towns before 1640. Heal and Holmes, *Gentry*, 307–11.

53  E. Cheney and T. Wilks, *The Jacobean Grand Tour: Early Stuart Travellers in Europe* (London and New York: Palgrave Macmillan, 2014).

54  E. Cheney, *The Evolution of the Grand Tour: Anglo-Italian Cultural Relations since the Renaissance* (London: Cass, 1999), 203–5; J. Stoye, *English Travellers Abroad, 1604–1667: Their Influence on English Society and Politics* (New Haven and London: Yale University Press, 1989), 165–6.

55  J. Black, *The British Abroad: The Grand Tour in the Eighteenth Century* (Stroud: Sutton, 1992), 12–50.

56  Cf. Cheney and Wilks, *The Jacobean Grand Tour*, 25–57.

57  Sir Peter Leicester, Bt, of Tabley Hall, Cheshire, appears to have stopped feeding workers visiting his estate after 1642. C. F. Foster, *Seven Households: Life in Cheshire and Lancashire 1582 to 1774* (Northwich: Arley Hall, 2002), 75.

58  Heal, *Hospitality*, 148, 172, 187.

59  *Ibid.*, 172–4.

60  Clay, *Economic Expansion*, 158–63; Rosenheim, *Emergence of a Ruling Order*, 50–3.

61  Fletcher, *Reform in the Provinces*, 19–30, 316–48.

62  Rosenheim, *Emergence of a Ruling Order*, 117.

63  D. Eastwood, *Governing Rural England: Tradition and Transformation in Local Government 1780–1840* (Oxford: Oxford University Press, 1994), 77–8; C. Chalklin, *English Counties and Public Building 1650–1830* (London and Rio Grande: Hambledon, 1998), 28–36.

64  Rosenheim, *Emergence of a Ruling Order*, 36–7, 230.

65  Stone and Stone, *Open Elite?*, 170.

66  Rosenheim, *Emergence of a Ruling Order*, 113; W. E. Tate, *The English Village Community and the Enclosure Movement* (London: Gollancz, 1967), 173; J. R. Ward, *The Finance of Canal Building in Eighteenth-Century England* (Oxford: Oxford University Press, 1974); D. T. Andrew, *Philanthropy and Police: London Charity in the Eighteenth Century* (Princeton: Princeton University Press, 1989), 71–3; Vickery, *Gentleman's Daughter*, 302, 303, 346.

67  For one example, see H. R. French, *The Middle Sort of People in Provincial England 1600–1750* (Oxford: Oxford University Press, 2007), 212–23. For the extent of movement in the other direction, see R. Grassby, *The Business*

*Community of Seventeenth-Century England* (Cambridge: Cambridge University Press, 1995), 145–8, 150, 153–170.

68 Clay, *Economic Expansion*, 163.

69 The Stones note that 'between 1650 and 1740, just as nuptiality was declining and mortality, especially among children, was rising, marital fertility was falling to an all-time low, to judge from the mean number of children born per married couple'. Stone and Stone, *Open Elite?*, 61.

70 Rosenheim, *Emergence of a Ruling Order*, 54.

71 Clay, *Economic Expansion*, 163.

72 J. Habakkuk, *Marriage, Debt and the Estates System: English Landownership 1650–1950* (Oxford: Clarendon Press, 1994), 16–30; L. Bonfield, *Marriage Settlements, 1601–1740: The Adoption of the Strict Settlement* (Cambridge: Cambridge University Press, 2008), 93–121.

73 Stone and Stone, *Open Elite?*, 51.

74 *Ibid.*, 64.

75 Thompson, 'Patrician society, plebeian culture'.

76 E. Griffin, *Blood Sport: Hunting in Britain since 1066* (New Haven and London: Yale University Press, 2007), 128.

77 See Borsay, *English Urban Renaissance*, 332–49.

78 French, *Middle Sort*, 201–61.

79 L. E. Klein, 'Politeness and the interpretation of the British eighteenth century', *HJ*, 45:4 (2002); P. Clark, *British Clubs and Societies 1580–1880: The Origins of an Associational World* (Oxford: Oxford University Press, 2000); M. Peltonen, *The Duel in Early Modern England: Civility, Politeness and Honour* (Cambridge: Cambridge University Press, 2003). See Vickery, *Gentleman's Daughter*, 209–23 for Elizabeth Shackleton's adherence to such distinctions.

80 Borsay, *English Urban Renaissance*, 117–73; J. Brewer, *The Pleasures of the Imagination: English Culture in the Eighteenth Century* (London: HarperCollins, 1997), 1–51.

81 T. Mowl, *Gentlemen and Players: Gardeners of the English Landscape* (Stroud: Sutton, 2000), 149–62; J. Dixon Hunt, *The Figure in the Landscape: Poetry, Painting and Gardening during the Eighteenth Century* (Baltimore: Johns Hopkins University Press, 1976), 194–5; T. Richardson, *The Arcadian Friends: Inventing the English Landscape Garden* (London: Bantam, 2007), 306–28.

82 M. Girouard, *Life in the English Country House* (New Haven and London: Yale University Press, 1978), 181–212, 245–66.

83 Heal, *Hospitality*, 154–63.

84 G. Savile, *The Complete Works of George Savile, First Marquess of Halifax*, ed. W. Raleigh (Oxford: Clarendon Press, 1912), 24.

85 Heal, *Hospitality*, 165–7.

86 The late-sixteenth-century Lancashire judge and landowner Sir Richard Shuttleworth of Gawthorpe was attended by a number of gentry sons, placed in his household to learn the law. Foster, *Seven Households*, 53–5; Whittle and Griffiths, *Consumption and Gender*, 213.

87 D. R. Hainsworth, *Stewards, Lords and People: The Estate Steward and His World in Later Stuart England* (Cambridge: Cambridge University Press, 1992), 6–22; G. E. Mingay, 'The eighteenth-century land steward', in E. L. Jones and G. E. Mingay (eds.), *Land, Labour and Population in the Industrial Revolution* (London: Arnold, 1967).

88 See D. R. Hainsworth and C. Walker (eds.), 'The correspondence of Lord Fitzwilliam of Milton and Francis Guybon his steward 1697 to 1709', *Northamptonshire Record Society Publications*, 36 (1990).

89 See n. 13 above. See also Corfield, 'The rivals'; Vickery, *Gentleman's Daughter*, 13–36, 127–61.

90 For example, although the volume of essays edited by P. Griffiths, A. Fox and S. Hindle, *The Experience of Authority* (Basingstoke: Macmillan, 1996), demonstrated comprehensively that social historians now regarded power as a concept that was constantly negotiated in early modern society, its focus was on those who experienced authority, rather than those who experienced its exercise.

91 P. King, *Crime, Justice and Discretion in England 1740–1820* (Oxford: Oxford University Press, 2000), 357–67.

92 Wood, *Memory*, 286–97.

93 For a preliminary study of these processes of normative reproduction see H. French and M. Rothery, *Man's Estate: Landed Gentry Masculinities, 1660–1900* (Oxford: Oxford University Press, 2012).

94 Whittle and Griffiths, *Consumption and Gender*, 14–18.

95 *Ibid.*, 49–85.

96 *Ibid.*, 72–84, 97–111, 156–82, 210–38.

97 J. Thirsk, 'Younger sons in the seventeenth century', *History*, 54:182 (1969); Grassby, *Business Community*, 145–60; A. Dunan-Page and B. Lynch (eds.), *Roger L'Estrange and the Making of Restoration Culture* (Aldershot: Ashgate, 2008), 1–5.

# 13

# The 'Middling Sort': An Emergent Cultural Identity

## Craig Muldrew

Oh, what a pleasure is business! How far preferable is an active busy life (when employed in some honest calling) to a supine and idle way of life, and happy are they whose fortune it is to be placed where commerce meets with encouragement and a person has the opportunity to push on trade with vigour …[1]

Much of the work on 'sorts' of people and their place in the social order has focused on contemporaries' language of definition and identity – what individuals and groups meant by referring to themselves and others as 'middling', or as the 'better sort', 'chief inhabitants' or 'vestrymen'.[2] This reflected the so-called 'linguistic turn' of the 1980s, which focused on the importance of contemporary language to understanding the contours of society in the past, in reaction to anachronistic categorisations of people based on functionalist socio-economic groupings, or on modern concepts of class. The most comprehensive work on the nature of the middling sort, by Henry French, has concluded that there was most definitely a group of households upon whom we can look back and see that their relative wealth, material possessions, reputation and power in their communities marked them out. In contrast to their poorer neighbours, the middling sort resided in houses with more rooms, fireplaces and furniture, wore more expensive clothes, and occupied positions of authority. But despite these similar ways of living, and the associational business of involvement in local government and hospitality, French could find little evidence of a national as opposed to locally contingent self-identification.[3]

Contemporaries were in fact mostly uninterested in defining themselves as members of national social groups below the level of ethnicity. They were far more concerned with keeping a sharp eye out for a wide range of forms of behaviour among people they knew, which indicated, among others, noble, genteel, fine, pleasing, brave, honest, painstaking, laborious, industrious, poor, mean, roguish or base qualities. (All of these characteristics being further refined, on occasion, with such descriptions as vain, quarrelsome, self-interested, idle or beggarly.) In terms of collective designation, phrases like 'the better sort' or 'chief inhabitants' were more common usages than 'middling sort'.[4] This was because the economic world they lived in made their status relatively precarious and difficult to maintain over time, and adjectives like 'chief' or 'better' defined current inclusivity more effectively.

The term 'middle', or 'middling', sort was used by writers when they wanted to distinguish and characterise those who were neither the richest merchants or gentry, nor the poor: first in urban contexts, and then, especially from the civil war period, at county and even national level.[5] Historians have followed suit because we need to summarise and condense when describing change over time, and so the term 'middling sort' has stuck as a way to describe those who sought to differentiate themselves from the poor and who were in turn differentiated from the elites. Here, however, I intend to focus less on the group profile of such people than upon their emergent cultural identity: on the adoption among them of ethical positions that helped to form a distinctive identity, and that also facilitated social communication, providing a means of identifying similarities with others through the definition of acceptable behaviour. It will be suggested that these were initially developed in response to the combined effects of religious and demographic change, and subsequently the great disruption of the Civil War era. They helped people to deal with the challenges of changing social relations and governance created by those processes. But at the same time, and crucially, they justified household profit. It was the successful achievement of such profit that gave the middle sort their social identity, whatever name they chose to give themselves. They also acted together, in older urban bodies such as town councils and in newly established rural vestries, to decide how their wealth could be used and taxed to address social problems, in a way that was identifiably different from both the county gentry, and those too poor to be taxed. They participated extensively in governance, holding subordinate but vital offices as members of petty sessions, constables, churchwardens, overseers of the poor, tax collectors, councilmen and wardmote jurors. But if they exercised authority as the 'chief inhabitants' of their communities, they often remained dependent on the patronage of the titular gentry families for their offices. They were subordinate to those who lived in manor houses; socialised with other members of the gentry; derived income from rent; expected their deference; and, as magistrates, scrutinised their decisions.

In the early modern period the major historical change that contributed to the formation of middling-sort identity was the adoption of a new set of ethics to deal with the expansion of profit-oriented households created by the rapid growth of commercialisation after *c.* 1550. While there had been wealthier peasants in medieval vills, seigniorial control over village life, the communalism sustained by the common field system and a unified Church structure made for a local society based on hierarchy and reciprocity with *less* commercial development in the countryside.[6] Within this landscape, there were also, of course, important towns whose freemen and merchant elite already had an urban identity based on trading wealth. The middling identity that would develop from the later sixteenth century, however, was different in its nature. It was the result of a very distinct symbiosis with an emergent national trade system based on water transport – both coastal and on navigable rivers – and on London as a huge metropolitan entrepôt serving much smaller provincial towns.

Once population began its general rise from around 1530, a continually growing number of mouths to feed and bodies to clothe and house created more demand for goods than in any period hitherto. The price of grains rose sixfold between 1500 and 1640, creating an incentive for farmers to produce more. Networks of distribution and marketing became more complex as traders took advantage of the profits that could be made by shipping goods to places where prices were high because demand was greatest. This involved in particular the development of commercial agriculture in the south and coal production in the north-east to feed and fuel London, which had reached a population of 300,000 by the early seventeenth century. Larger farmers and yeomen who had sizeable crops became wealthier by selling on the market to townsmen, rural artisans and agricultural labourers, and used their new wealth to increase the size of their holdings. Much of this land was purchased from smallholders or other farmers who were unable to survive as independent producers. This led to a reduction in the size and number of smallholdings, and also in turn increased the number of agricultural labourers. This, then, led to a growing cycle of demand, as profits made from the increased sales of basic commodities such as food and clothing were invested in the purchase of more refined goods by wealthier individuals, in turn opening up more opportunities for employment in local manufacturing trades. It also created a widening social divide between an increasingly large body of poor who sold their labour on the market, and whose earnings were principally devoted to simply surviving, and yeomen, artisans or professionals like lawyers who profited by selling goods or services on the market.

Because commercialisation was so important to this process it makes sense to look first at the development of the middling sort in the towns where markets and shops were located and new goods imported and sold. Most larger towns were also incorporated boroughs, or became so during the sixteenth century. Corporations provided the status of freedom, or citizenship, which was not available in the countryside, and urban government, which provided an institutional structure for association. Jonathan Barry has argued that the associational institutions of urban life created what he has termed 'bourgeois collectivism'. The corporate identity of self-governance was expressed in the architecture of town halls, and in ritual processions of corporation members in their liveries during elections or celebrations. Guilds and companies, where they existed, added a further layer of inclusion and mutual support. In the commensality celebrating both, civic behaviour was practised and defined by wit in conversation, feast songs, and the consumption of wine in company halls, mayor's parlours or taverns. Towns also protected their rights at law against others, and developed corporate identities reflected in parliamentary representation. Citizenship of a borough also gave its members a cultural status based on republican ideas learned from classical texts such as Cicero or descriptions of Italian city states. Elections based on merit and esteem bred 'mutual trust'.[7]

But, the actual experience of being a successful citizen was that of a minority, and heavily concentrated in London and major provincial cities. As a percentage of England's total population, that of London rose from 2.5 per cent to over 11 per cent between 1520 and 1700, while the larger incorporated towns together only grew from 3 per cent to 7–9 per cent over the same period.[8] Also, within boroughs freedom was generally quite restricted to being earned through seven-year apprenticeships in a trade, purchase by those migrating into a town, or inheritance by the son of a freeman. The number of freemen was small in Bristol and Exeter – less than a fifth of adult males – and in Ludlow and Cambridge less than a tenth. In York and Norwich it was higher, approaching half. In the city of London it was as high as three-quarters of adult males (though a huge number of people lived outside the jurisdiction of the city). Increasingly urban government became more oligarchic and the high cost of the entertainment involved in office-holding made it possible only for those with money to spare. Trade identity centred on the guilds also underwent change. In London, as early as the late sixteenth century, the livery companies became less inclusive and more 'hierarchically oriented'. Elsewhere they might survive into the eighteenth century, but principally as associations of masters rather than as embodiments of a trade.[9]

In a landscape where the older institutional sources of urban identity
were becoming more restricted and exclusive, the formation of an alternative social identity – the means of thinking about being 'middle' – was
a process of justifying the social good of one's own and one's family's profits. This involved much anxiety about grace, public credit and success. It
ran counter to older Christian ideas, derived from Aristotle through St
Thomas Aquinas, that profit was a dangerous temptation to self-interest,
corroding the common social bonds, reciprocal duties and obligations of
a Christian community of both rich and poor. It was in towns, especially
London, that prosperous merchants and tradesmen, such as the draper
William Scott, turned to writing pamphlets to give moral justification
to trade as a form of material improvement. They argued that increased
trade would lead to more wealth for the nation, which would then be
available to be used in beneficial ways. As Scott put it, senators ought to
be rich … 'Wealth is a pledge … of their care of the Commonwealth …
he that hath done well for himself, will know how to do well for the public good.'[10] This argument shifted the meaning of commonwealth from
the idealisation of an organic society, as in Edmund Dudley's *The Tree
of Commonwealth*, to the social utility of household wealth gained from
application to business. This was done by using the word as a translation of *res publica* to mean 'public', referring as much to the collective
profit, in the sense of the common advantage of its individual members.[11]
As the cloth merchant Edward Missleden put it, 'Is it not lawfull for
Merchants to seeke their *Privatum Commodum* in the exercise of their
calling? Is not gaine the end of trade? Is not the publique involved in the
private, and the private in the publique? What else makes a Commonwealth, but the private-wealth … of the members therof in the exercise of
*Commerce* …?'.[12] In this way 'tradeful merchants' and 'gainful tradesmen'
justified themselves as a group defined by the activity of selling on the
market for profit, which produced the social good of monetised wealth,
which, they argued, was every bit as advantageous to the common good
as older notions of hierarchical gentry stewardship of land and local community.[13] They adopted the values of good credit and trust as opposed
to aristocratic profligacy and martial honour. Creditworthy behaviour,
temperance, moderation and quietness were the common aspirations
for the first generations of those who began to think of themselves as
achieving something new with their wealth. Also, most crucially, it was
in towns first that the idea of institutional redistribution of wealth was
introduced. This involved assessing proportionate rates of taxation on the
wealthiest part of the population, and was justified by being directed only

towards those deemed deserving.[14] This was wealth not to be shared indiscriminately and wilfully, but to be used proportionately and with a moral purpose to improve lives and create work. It was a way of defining and using wealth that would become enshrined in national poor law legislation by 1598, and then taken up with great social effect in rural parishes. But, at the same time, since many tradesmen remained unsuccessful or failed, the successful adopted the terminology of sorting from town grain markets – which commonly distinguished three sorts or qualities: better, middle and worst – to define those with wealth and credit from those without.

For R. H. Tawney the moral justification of profit and material wealth marked a fundamental change by which theology came to accommodate capitalism, following Max Weber's ideas about the Calvinist doctrine of profit and hard work and profit as justifiable evidence of salvation. Subsequent historians have developed this thesis to show how poverty without disability increasingly began to be stigmatised as a sign of sinfulness to be dealt with punitively. In contrast, being successful was seen as a sign of grace.[15] As we shall see below there is much truth to the contested adoption of these values when describing how the middling sort emerged in the sixteenth and early seventeenth century, but just considering them fails to do enough justice to the value of *trust* as a way of maintaining community and social bonds. This also contributed to the formation of middling identity through what we might call 'sorting'. Competitive households had to rely on one another to pay for goods sold on fairly long-term credit, and anxiety of loss led to households being classed according to their reliability, with the poor being most worrisome. All this is relevant to the relationship between identity and ideology as there is clear evidence in diaries that middling individuals thought about their financial success or lack of it. They did not abandon hospitality and concern for the poor, or the value of neighbourly activities such as attending funerals and christenings, but there was now a world of goods to be purchased by all classes, although in greatly differing amounts, and they were purchased on credit. Thus, a concurrent emphasis on household thrift developed as a support to good credit, and this had to temper hospitality.

The sheer complexity of chains of credit meant that there was a huge rise in litigation over unpaid credit from the mid sixteenth century, involving hundreds of thousands of suits per year.[16] This led to the rise of the attorney as a distinct profession whose income was based on fees earned by applying specialist training learned at the Inns of Court in London to process litigation through the many local and central courts.[17] The clergy, being trained at university and given livings supported by tithes and glebe land, were also a sort of profession, although they did not, of course, market their pastoral duties. Many, however, supplemented their earnings through local schools. In this way, the professions were closely related to the middling sort. Although not all attorneys were successful and wealthy, and many church livings were relatively poor, professional qualifications gave individuals the added security of a more regular income. This security was needed to ensure that litigation could proceed in a rule-based fashion, and that ethics could be preached in the parish church.[18]

Material social display was also considered to be part and parcel of a middling identity that reflected an Aristotelian mean between thrift and hospitality. A certain sobriety in dress reflected a household that was not overextended and at risk of going broke and endangering chains of credit in the community. But, at the same time a warm hearth, window curtains, comfortable chairs, pewter plates, candlesticks, knives and other tableware (made of silver if it could be afforded), and later porcelain tea services, together with the quality and amount of food served, were all necessary for reciprocal hospitality, upon which reputation also depended. This consisted of both arranged dinners, and the provision of food and lodging for neighbours and more distant tradesmen and farmers when travelling on the business that played an almost daily role in the lives of the middling sort. The inability to offer this was termed 'meanness', and while the 'meaner sort' could offer each other perfectly commensurable hospitality of plain fare or a drink at the alehouse, it was marked out as being different by its lower material value.

This can be clearly witnessed in the diary of Samuel Pepys, kept from 1660 to 1669. It is clear that Pepys was socially ambitious, and the entries in his diary show how he, and others in his estimation, judged his credit by the standards of his business diligence, and how this dramatically increased his success. Certainly one reason why Pepys kept the diary was to record the progress of his wealth, which he did often as in the following example from 1662: 'My mind is now in a wonderful condition of quiet and content, more than ever in all my life – since minding the business of my office ... For now my business is a delight to me and brings me great credit, and my purse encreases too.'[19] He is quite clear about the fact that he wanted a good reputation to achieve social status and to be accepted both at court as a loyal servant to the crown under his patron the earl of Sandwich, and amongst others working at the Navy office. He also socialised with many citizens and he clearly desired to rise to equal them in status. He wrote many times about the finery and material well-being of London citizens, and was quite clear about the material consumption needed to fit into this world: 'We had a very good and handsome dinner, and excellent wine. I not being neat in clothes, which I find a great fault in me, could not be so merry as otherwise, and at all times I am and can be, when I am in good habit.'[20] This was the cause of most of his extended descriptions of the goods he owned. Ordinary household objects such as cooking equipment or chairs were mentioned infrequently, but tableware and its social function is something that gets mentioned quite often, as on an occasion where he entertained his friends including Lord Brouncker, the Commissioner of the Navy; Sir William Batten, the Surveyor of the Navy; and William Penn:

> Anon comes our company ... I did make them all gaze to see themselves served so nobly in plate, and a neat dinner, indeed, though but of seven dishes. Mighty merry I was and made them all, and they mightily pleased ... at night to sup, and then to cards ... they full of admiration at my plate, particularly my flaggons (which, endeed, are noble), and so late home, all with great mirth and satisfaction to them, as I thought, and to myself to see all I have and do so much out-do for neatness and plenty anything done by any of them.[21]

Urban practices and writings were influential because of both the higher level of literacy in towns, and the overwhelming national influence of London. But if the development of an urban middling-sort identity can be quite clearly traced through an ideology of common profit, citizenship and success in business, with its institutional support, physical space and architecture, the experience of change in rural parishes and villages was much less unified. Andy Wood has characterised the contours of the rural practices and ideas that existed before the development of a middling-sort identity with great subtlety. This involved local identification of farming practices with environment under the paternalistic lordship of the manor. Here fields, pasture, woods, hedges, streams and hills were identified as both places of emotional significance and as common resources. While differences in wealth, status and occupation existed, as did many forms of social conflict, Wood argues that there was a unified culture of commensality and remembrance to deal with difference and dispute. This facilitated a slow process of use, adjustment and alteration that could accommodate much enclosure and consolidation of common fields while population and pressure on resources were low. It generated much of what was thought of as 'commonwealth' in rural society. There were well-developed moral guidelines of 'good lordship' and hospitality for wealthier farmers in which charity and common rights were exchanged for deference and the opposite behaviour was characterised as 'churlishness'.[22]

Commercialisation was not a process that could co-exist with this way of organising society. When it sat down at the village feast, it might have offered more exotic fare, but it had a price – a higher price that some were happy to pay, while others were not, and many could not. Food grown on smallholdings or fed by masters to servants might have been a more stable, less tempting, even Arcadian 'good', but it could not be monetised in a way that could purchase coal from Newcastle or tea from China. Inevitably success became in effect an aspect of identity, and 'honest profit' made without cheating or hard dealing towards the poor became a moral attribute to add to good neighbourliness and hospitality. While the rise in the price of basics like beer and bread was inevitable, given the rise in population, the extent of market purchase was not, as most labourers before the late sixteenth century were still hired as live-in servants, while smallholdings and access to commons could limit exposure to rising prices in the countryside. But, as explained in Chapter 7 of this volume, selling crops to towns led to wealth, and wealth led to a desire for new goods, and elaborating transportation links eventually led to the increased availabiity of things like textiles, metalwares, ceramics and coal, and imports such as oranges, raisins and tobacco, all of which came to be consumed extensively across the country.

A wide range of landholders availed themselves of growing market opportunities in the mid and late sixteenth century, helped in making a profit by such advantages as low and secure customary rents on manorial copyhold; access to the urban markets, especially that of London; and the possession of large sheep flocks to supply wool to the cloth industry. They came to be termed 'yeomen' in documents such as parish registers and probate records, in distinction from 'husbandmen' below them and the 'gentlemen' above. This was a term that also had connotations to national good, as its medieval origins referred to military service as archers. However, the practices they adopted were those of tradesmen. Yeomen also profited from selling on the market, and as long as food prices continued to rise, which they did until the mid seventeenth century, they were at much less risk of business failure. Increasingly also wealthier yeomen began to style themselves 'gentlemen' or even 'esquire' to denote the expansive lifestyles and civil behaviour that gave them acceptability among county elites as non-titled gentry. In Lancashire, for example, there were 763 gentle families in 1600, but in 1642 only 13 members were knights or baronets.[23]

The ideology of agrarian business and profitmaking also found expression in the new moralising language of 'improvement'.[24] It arose specifically not only to justify trade and creditworthiness, but also to challenge custom by arguing that the latter preserved poverty and created unemployment and vagrancy by preventing increased agricultural production. Instead of focusing on a morality that stressed paternalism and the responsibility of landlords to provide land and resources for the poor, improvement aimed to change the landscape to increase the common 'wealth'.[25] Improvement developed in a more Ciceronian vein of utility than the landscape farming described by Wood. Advocates of improvement saw land in terms of a productive resource given to mankind to be acted upon with industry to increase its productivity, rather than a space to be lived in and accessed through a complicated set of customary rights and agreements over its use mediated by law. By creating more produce for towns, and more employment for the poor, improvement justified profit just as wealthier townsmen had argued their wealth did. As one of the most widely read works on good farm management, Thomas Tusser's *Five Hundred Points of Good Husbandry*, put it, 'to follow profit earnestlie' resulted in 'treasure and pleasure' being richly acquired.[26]

Enclosure and its effects became the symbolic battleground between custom and improvement, and the ideological battle lines were nowhere more clearly drawn than in the pamphlet debate in the 1650s between the two ministers John Moore and Joseph Lee. On one side was Moore, who saw improvement as covetousness, and a means to take away land that gave sustenance to poor smallholders, and on the other Lee, who saw it as a way of producing more food to support employment in industry, thus creating more employment for the poor through growth and prosperity.[27] By the Restoration it was the latter discourse that had won out, having been promoted by the radical thinkers associated with the Hartlib circle, and taken up by philosophers such as John Locke and jurists like Mathew Hale, but it certainly did not go uncontested. Sermons continued to be made against covetousness, and even while industry advanced and the stock market was born in the 1690s, harvest shortages could still lead to criticism of capitalist farming.[28] Such disagreement continued because in truth there was little way of determining how far each case of engrossment or enclosure was motivated by personal profit, as compared to social good; they were supposed to go together.

Recent work has provided clear evidence that by the early seventeenth century the majority of land in most of southern England was being farmed by larger farmers on farms of 75 acres or more, which were clearly too large to have been worked without hiring labourers or servants.[29] Farms of such size had to be operating to make a profit, so most farmers must have come to believe in the ideology of profit, improvement, thrift, good credit and employment rather than older ideas of sufficiency. In the end there must have been few who could fully resist the pressures of the market and new spending patterns. These ideas all needed the promotion of wealthy households as desirable ends, but it was a different ethic than that of great and especially titled landlords, who frequently preferred to maintain paternalistic postures from a distance. The result was the creation of a distinctive middling sort in a rural society in which selling grain became like selling beer or drapery, and the poor were sorted from the rich in the sieve of reputation. Improvement took some time to increase employment, and the loss of rights and land by the poor created dependence on more variable and competitive day labour markets, adding pressure to abandon the 'idleness' of the cottage economy and become 'industrious'.[30] But, this was not a system of class interests ranged against older feudal social relations. It was a belief in the future and of change for the better to deal with problems, rather than an attempt to maintain the old, though the emotional power of 'social harmony' as a memory remained. It was in reaction to this language that custom came to be used by the poor to defend rights to common pasturage, gleaning, wood-gathering and other use-rights, which further accentuated differences in communities between the middling and labouring poor and smallholders.

It is also becoming increasingly clear that a divide was opening up between the farming regions of southern and northern England. In the north many smallholders and unimproved landholders remained; far fewer new multi-hearth houses were constructed.[31] The north had a different climate ecology in which rye and especially oats grew better and were cheaper than wheat, and attracted less-profit-oriented farmers. The difference between the experience of a farmer like Peter Walkden in northern Lancashire in the 1720s and that of Thomas Turner described below is striking. In terms of the amount of tax he paid, Walkden was undoubtedly middling sort. But the networks of credit he describes, and his material purchases, were much more basic and limited than in contemporary rural Sussex.[32] It was in the north, however, that an industrial society would flourish in the eighteenth century, with an urban middle class that did not develop around the workings of the vestry, but through the large-scale employment of labour in the cloth and mining industries.[33]

Meanwhile, one of the most decisive changes that moved the emphasis of middling-sort morality away from paternalistic relations to servants and hospitality to the poor was the establishment of the institutional structure of the poor law laid down in national legislation after 1598. In a landscape in which the older institutional securities like monastic charity had been disbanded almost overnight, this and subsequent statutes gave parish churchwardens and the newly created overseers of the poor the ability to enforce the collection of local taxation with the threat of fines. As a result, groups of householders deemed economically 'sufficient' were charged a tax to be redistributed according to a local need determined at the discretion of the aforesaid officers. Since most parishes were small enough for most leading householders to know each other, they banded together into bodies that became known as vestries to oversee this distribution, and increasingly, as expenditure rose, to contain or reduce it. This system increased the funds available for the dependent poor, but it also created a measured relationship of redistribution of monetised wealth to replace unequal participation in a common resource. 'Commonwealth' became the creation of abundance for redistribution. Moreover, this development further distanced the members of the middling sort from the dependent poor. The laws of settlement could be used to exclude potential 'charges' from other parishes, and some paupers were forced to wear badges as marks of their dependent identity. Their children could also be forced to take up apprenticeships elsewhere at the discretion of overseers.

The poor laws have been much studied, but we still need to know more about how large-scale estates interacted with the inhabitants of the parishes they dominated. Estate owners and manorial lords provided rental land and patronage. They hired many labourers. They sat on the local Bench as justices of the peace where appeals by poor appellants about vestry decisions were taken. The management policies of great estates, the degree to which they provided employment in a parish and the authority exercised by their owners could certainly affect the composition and attitudes of the middling sort. The parish commonwealth as a form of social/institutional organisation was most notable in the wealthier arable parishes of southern England. In Richard Gough's account of his Shropshire parish of Myddle, in contrast, the vestry and operation of the poor laws are almost entirely absent. Perhaps because it remained in 1701 a largely pastoral community with fairly abundant woodland, situated on the periphery of England, one does not get the sense from Gough of a parish divided between a middling elite and dependent poor.[34]

The best source for obtaining a sense of what it was like to participate in the social world of the rural middling sort in the wealthier, profit-oriented south can be found in the diary of the shopkeeper Thomas Turner of East

Hoathly in Sussex. The diary dates from 1754 to 1765, and Turner's comments on others' behaviour show that he was part of the new eighteenth-century world of sentimental rather than puritan self-examination. However, he still had constant worries about the liquidity of his shop and the long credit he had to extend to his customers. And most importantly he was continually involved in parish government, especially that of the poor law. Every year he kept parish accounts and distributed charity money, and he served three years as a churchwarden, four as an overseer of the poor, and six as collector of the land and window taxes.[35] This meant that both he and his wife Peggy were engaged in an almost daily round of socialising in which hospitality and local governance were mixed, and Turner commented on the morals and practices of this world.[36]

Although his accounts do not survive, the financial information in the diary indicates that Turner's retail trade was small and local, and his profit limited. His wife had to work at hop-picking to make extra money, and he continually worried about his financial stability. In August 1756 he fretted about the precariousness of trade in his small country town and estimated that, while previously his trade had been worth £15–30 a week, it had dropped to £5–10 in 1756. If this weekly estimate was roughly the same over the whole course of the year this represents average sales of £1,170 in a good year, which at a rate of profit of 10 per cent would have yielded Turner an annual income of about £117. However, in 1756 his sales would only have been £390, providing a profit of £39, which would have been earnings only £10 more than a well-off labouring family.[37]

The parish was under the lordship of Thomas Pelham, duke of Newcastle, and his estate was run by the steward Christopher Coates, who was styled a gentleman, and was clearly important in parish affairs, but whose character was less commented on than others, possibly because of his status and the importance of his patronage.[38] The three wealthiest families in East Hoathly were the farmers Jeremiah French and William Piper, together with the farming rector of the parish, Thomas Porter.[39] Elizabeth Browne was also a substantial landowner who owned the mill. Turner did her accounts and treated her with respect but did not socialise with her.[40] Then there was a group of tradesmen including Thomas Davey, a shoemaker who was Turner's best friend in the early years of the diary, and Charles Diggens, a tailor who was another close associate. In addition Joseph Fuller, a butcher, and Thomas Fuller, tallow chandler, were active in parish affairs and part of Turner's round of hospitality. Then there were somewhat less wealthy tradesmen such as Thomas Durrant, the younger son of the village blacksmith, whom Turner taught to read and write, and Robert Hook, a shoemaker, with whom Turner placed his nephew apprentice, and whose daughter he hired as a servant for a single month.

Turner described many dinners shared with various combinations of these individuals, with French, Piper, Porter and the Fullers being his most common companions. On each occasion he recorded his meals, perhaps as a record of hospitality, but probably also as a way of being paid shop debts, as he ate out more often than others ate at his house.[41] The busiest round of socialising took place in January as part of the Christmas season, and on many occasions the group also played at cards. In addition to this, tea and coffee were offered as hospitality, and cricket games were often played.[42] Alehouses were almost always frequented as places of business rather than relaxation, especially when travelling to neighbouring parishes. The vestry, rather ironically, was generally held at the crown tavern, and accompanied by drinking or eating.[43]

On many occasions Turner took his wealthier neighbours to task. In Jeremiah French's case it was for his heavy drinking, which led him to become quarrelsome – 'the noise of his clamour with the hoarse and grating sound of his huge big oaths almost deafens the ears of any of his audience' – and he was also given to 'obscenity and raillery'. But Turner also criticised his lack of charity because he continually attempted to avoid paying his proper share of the poor rates, and tried to remove paupers from the parish without proper regard to their character or circumstances.[44] Turner also commented on William Piper's meanness in offering hospitality, and lending to or doing favours for others, and the Revd Porter's acquisitiveness regarding land and recycling of old sermons.[45] He clearly enjoyed the socialising and especially the drinking with the local middling sort and took the laws of settlement for granted, but he was more at ease with other tradesmen and became friends with those who were not middling sort. When regarding the local wealthy farmers he was generally censorious of them in some way or another. Overall he was a critical, and self-critical, member of the middling sort, who portrayed the parish elite as self-interested and uncharitable, at the same time that he also enjoyed the pleasures of hospitality and conversation. Thus, in terms of a middling-sort experience, continual socialising around food and drink, together with the administration of the poor laws, also largely done in the context of eating and drinking, were the glue that permitted aspects of people's behaviour and character such as charity, honesty and hospitality to be assessed.

Turner also sympathised with the plight of the poor, often identifying more with them than with those he dined with, albeit through a prism of eighteenth-century writings on sensibility. He was also a close friend of Samuel Jenner, a bachelor who was poor enough to receive the Pelham charity when it was distributed in 1756, and who did odd jobs and ran errands for Turner. After the death of Turner's wife Peggy in June 1761, Jenner became perhaps Turner's closest friend. He often drank tea with Turner, stayed over at his house for dinner and slept in his bed, and accompanied him when he was looking for a new wife in 1764.

> Fri. 9 Mar. ... Sam. Jenner at work for me all day, dined with me on a light pudding, a piece of beef boiled and some Savoy greens. At home the whole day ... A very cold day. Sam. Jenner went away in the even. Perhaps it may appear odd, Sam. Jenner's being so much at my house, but he is a good-natured willing person and oft does my gardening etc. for nothing, and he is undoubtedly a worthy companion.[46]

A second example is James Merchant and his family. He first came to East Hoathly from the parish of Ticehurst 15 miles distant as an apprentice tailor to his uncle, but left because of a disagreement before his seven-year term was up. He too did odd jobs for Turner and always had dinner with his family on Christmas Day, together with the widow of his uncle and his sister Hannah, who became Turner's servant in 1758. However, when he married Elizabeth Mepham, who came from another poor family of the parish, members of which often did work for Turner and his wife, East Hoathly removed him back to his parish of birth as a pauper. Turner was involved in this, but did not make any comment on it. He presumably did not think it unjust. Thus, Turner is an interesting character who shows the range and nuances of middling emotional identity by this time. He certainly accepted the workings of the parish commonwealth as a normative way of dealing with poverty, but he was aware of his dependency compared to the wealthy farmers, and he felt that they acted too often out of self-interest and not charitable spirit.

Here I have traced the rise of a group of frequently insecure, commercially oriented families against the dissolution of older local hierarchies. These families created a new moral security for themselves through an ideology of profit earned by honest dealing and good credit, leading to improvement, which in turn led to employment and the relief of the poor. Although this process was driven by commercialisation, it was affected by such contingencies as the dissolution of the monasteries, by shifts in religious identity, by the elaborating local infrastructure of the English state, and by the survival of older values and the memory of former patterns of social relations. The experience of Richard Gough and the opinions of

Thomas Turner show this was not by any means a unified process. But, although there may have been little sense of national experience and identity among England's middling sort, there was a general belief in profit and commercialisation as a dynamic, ethically justifiable social system, even while there was a wide range of comfort or discomfort with how aggressive or disruptive such change should or could be.

The beginning of the eighteenth century witnessed a further move to a middling-sort ethics based more on financial security gained through greatly improved numeracy; the expansion of financial paper instruments such as stocks, bonds and promissory notes; and the increasing use of conveyancing to raise money on mortgages.[47] This allowed the development of a morality where wealth was seen as something to be used to help achieve individual happiness and security. This replaced much of the emphasis on litigation to enforce trust and credit. Although this change was a subtle one, it was bound up with the development of a sense of a self engaged in virtuous behaviour learned through reading and reflection on society, as opposed to expressions of anxiety about grace or public credit and success. This type of behaviour became easier to self-identify with as middling. Such was the case with the fictional father of Robinson Crusoe in Defoe's novel, published in 1719: 'I should always find ... that middle station ... were not subjected to so many distempers and uneasinesses either of body or mind ... that peace and plenty were the handmaids of a middle fortune; that temperance, moderation, quietness, health, society, all agreeable diversions, and all desirable pleasures, were the blessings attending the middle station of life.'[48] Another example can be found in the diary of an aspiring professional, the young Dudley Ryder, the son of a successful London linen draper of a dissenting background, who eventually became Attorney General under Walpole, and Chief Justice of the King's Bench in 1754.[49] In 1715 he had an allowance of £80 as well as extra money and clothes from his father's shop. Ryder's diary demonstrates a frame of thinking in which obligation remained important, but what was now stressed was that both parties should act to make each other happy, rather than to keep a legally binding contract. From the point of view of a philosopher or preacher, this was something open to all conscious beings, but in reality it was a behaviour particular to individuals with the time and money to read books and periodicals as a source of learning, and to engage in self-evaluation. Such self-identity could also be joined together in the many flourishing voluntarily societies, or periodicals could be used to create 'imagined' solidarity among disparate individuals.

Ryder's diary was an instrument of a new culture of self-reflection, sensibility and politeness that emerged in the early eighteenth century. Certainly he engaged in a very definite process of self-examination of his behaviour, not in relation to election or a desire to explicate sinfulness, but rather to create behaviour that would be pleasing to others and therefore also to himself. He read John Locke and Bishop Berkeley, and the *Spectator* and *Tatler*.[50] He continually analysed his own behaviour, especially when in the company of women, and talked about conquering his passions and feelings of resentment in conversation with others. After reading some of his own letters he noted directly that 'It is the most agreeable state of mind a man can be in to be pleased with his own performances.'[51] His concern was with the expression of feeling and behaviour towards others in conversation rather than with worries about how much he was trusted, or whether he would be paid what he was owed, and his judgement on others was about their politeness. Even a small shopkeeper like Thomas Turner, who never mentioned holding company stock as an investment, and had to worry continually about customers paying their debts, read the *Spectator* and Tillitson's sermons, and continually examined his own feelings. His comments on others' behaviour shows that he was part of the new eighteenth-century world of sentimental self-examination. He was also a member of a friendly society, a new eighteenth-century institution into which collective payments were made to help members in times of sickness and old age, which held an annual club feast. He formed part of a middling sort that by the mid eighteenth century had become a group of both wealthy farmers and lesser gentry families together with the wealthier urban tradesmen and merchants who had sufficient secured income financially to support sentimental education and polite behaviour in voluntary associations, at dinner, and at tea tables.

### Notes

1 T. Turner, *The Diary of Thomas Turner*, ed. D. Vaisey (Oxford: Oxford University Press, 1985), 238 [from 1761].
2 K. Wrightson, '"Sorts of People" in Tudor and Stuart England', in J. Barry and C. Brooks (eds.), *The Middling Sort of People: Culture, Society and Politics in England, 1550–1800* (London: Macmillan, 1994).
3 H. French, *The Middle Sort of People in Provincial England 1600–1750* (Oxford: Oxford University Press, 2007), Chapter 4.
4 Henry French, 'Social Status, Localism and the "Middle Sort of People" in England, 1620–1750', *P&P*, 166 (2000).
5 Wrightson, 'Sorts', 44–8.

6  C. Muldrew, 'From a "light cloak" to an "iron cage": An essay on histori-
   cal changes in the relationship between community and individualism', in
   A. Shepard and P. Withington (eds.), *Communities in Early Modern England*
   (Manchester: Manchester University Press, 2000), 156–59.

7  P. Withington, *The Politics of Commonwealth: Citizens and Freemen in Early
   Modern England* (Cambridge: Cambridge University Press, 2005), 51–74, 79.

8  Between 1520 and 1600 London grew from a size of 55,000 to 200,000
   people, while larger incorporated towns of over 5,000 people grew from
   nine towns containing just 70,000 individuals to nineteen towns with
   135,000 people. Over the course of the next century London added another
   375,000 people, while towns of over 5,000 rose in number to thirty.
   E. A. Wrigley, 'Urban growth and agricultural change: England and the
   Continent in the early modern period', in E. A. Wrigley, *People, Cities and
   Wealth* (Oxford: Blackwell, 1987), 159–63.

9  I. Archer, *The Pursuit of Stability: Social Relations in Elizabethan London*
   (Cambridge: Cambridge University Press, 1991), 111ff.; P. J. Corfield, *The
   Impact of English Towns, 1700–1800* (Oxford: Oxford University Press,
   1982), 86–90; R. King, 'The sociability of the trade guilds of Newcastle
   and Durham, 1660–1750: The urban renaissance revisited', in H. Berry and
   J. Gregory (eds.), *Creating and Consuming Culture in North-East England,
   1660–1830* (Aldershot and Burlington, VT: Ashgate, 2004), 58 and *passim*.

10 Withington, *Commonwealth*, 67.

11 C. Muldrew, *The Economy of Obligation: The Culture of Credit and Social
   Relations in Early Modern England* (Basingstoke: Macmillan, 1998), 130–7.

12 E. Misselden, *The Circle of Commerce* (London, 1623), 17.

13 J. McVeagh, *Tradeful Merchants: Portrayal of the Capitalist in Literature*
   (London: Routledge, 1981).

14 P. Slack, *Poverty and Policy in Tudor and Stuart England* (London: Longman,
   1985), 148–54.

15 R. H. Tawney, *Religion and the Rise of Capitalism* (Harmondsworth: Penguin,
   1926), Chapter 4.

16 Muldrew, *Economy of Obligation*, Chapter 8.

17 C. W. Brooks, 'Professions, ideology and the middling sort in the late sixteenth and early seventeenth centuries', in Barry and Brooks, *Middling Sort of
   People*, 113–40.

18 Physicians trained by universities and approved by the College of Physicians
   could similarly earn substantial fees with their professional qualification; *ibid.*

19 S. Pepys, *The Diary of Samuel Pepys*, ed. R. Latham and W. Matthews, 9 vols.
   (London: HarperCollins, 1970–83), Vol. III, 125.

20 *Ibid.*, Vol. II, 198–9; Vol. IV, 343.

21 *Ibid.*, Vol. VIII, 4.

22 A. Wood, 'Deference, paternalism and popular memory in early modern
   England', in J. Walter, S. Hindle and A. Shepard (eds.), *Remaking English
   Society: Social History and Social Change in Early Modern Society* (Woodbridge:
   Boydell, 2013), 233–34. A. Wood, *The Memory of the People: Custom and*

*Popular Senses of the Past in Early Modern England* (Cambridge: Cambridge University Press, 2013).

23 B. G. Blackwood, *The Lancashire Gentry and the Great Rebellion 1640–60* (Manchester: Manchester University Press for the Chetham Society, 1978), 4–11, 21. In Yorkshire the proportion was higher: 89 out of 649 families had titles. J. T. Cliffe, *The Yorkshire Gentry from the Reformation to the Civil War* (London: Athlone Press, 1969), 6.

24 See J. Whittle, Chapter 7 of the present volume.

25 R. W. Hoyle, 'Introduction', in R. W. Hoyle (ed.), *Custom, Improvement and the Landscape in Early Modern Britain* (Farnham: Ashgate, 2011), 17–19.

26 A. McRae, *God Speed the Plough: The Representation of Agrarian England, 1500–1660* (Cambridge: Cambridge University Press 1996), Chapters 1 and 5, and 145–51.

27 For a discussion see C. Warner, 'Enclosure, poverty and the public good in England, 1600–1660', unpublished M.Phil. thesis, Cambridge University (2012).

28 P. Slack, *The Invention of Improvement: Information and Material Progress in Seventeenth-Century England* (Oxford: Oxford University Press, 2014), Chapters 4, 7; B. Waddell, *God, Duty and Community in English Economic Life, 1660–1720* (*Woodbridge: Boydell, 2012*), Chapter 1.

29 J. Barker, 'The emergence of agrarian capitalism in early modern England: A reconsideration of farm sizes', unpublished Ph.D. thesis, Cambridge University (2012).

30 Growing industrial production and agricultural improvement increased employment in the period from 1660 to 1770. This created a category of the 'honest', 'industrious' or 'painful' poor who earned wages and were not middling or better, but who were no longer labelled with the opprobrium of derogatory characterisations like 'mean'. See C. Muldrew, *Food, Energy and the Creation of Industriousness: Work and Material Culture in Agrarian England, 1550–1780* (Cambridge: Cambridge University Press, 2011), 298–308.

31 L. Shaw-Taylor, 'The rise of agrarian capitalism and the decline of family farming in England', *EcHR*, 65 (2012).

32 R. W. Hoyle, 'Farmer, nonconformist minister and diarist: The world of Peter Walkden of Thornley in Lancashire 1733–34', *Northern History*, 48 (2011).

33 J. Smail, *The Origins of Middle Class Culture: Halifax, Yorkshire, 1660–1780* (Ithaca, NY: Cornell University Press, 1994), Chapters 5–6.

34 R. Gough, *The History of Myddle*, ed. D. Hey (Harmondsworth: Penguin, 1981).

35 Turner, *Diary*, xxii.

36 N. Tadmor, 'Where was Mrs Turner? Governance and gender in an eighteenth-century village', in Hindle, Shepard and Walter, *Remaking English Society*.

37 Turner, *Diary*, 31, 61, 137, 169.

38 *Ibid.*, 305–6.

39 *Ibid.*, Appendix B, 'Principal persons figuring in the diary'.

40 *Ibid.*, 223.

41  *Ibid.*, 131.

42  *Ibid.*, 173.

43  *Ibid.*, 302–3.

44  *Ibid.*, 67–8, 82–3, 91, 130–1, 176, 318–19.

45  *Ibid.*, 24, 45, 47, 50, 221–2, 271.

46  *Ibid.*, 287.

47  C. Muldrew, 'From credit to savings? An examination of debt and credit in relation to increasing consumption in England, *c.* 1650 to 1770', *Quaderni storici*, 137 (2011).

48  D. Defoe, *Robinson Crusoe*, ed. John Richetti (London: Penguin, 2001), 3–4.

49  D. Ryder, *The Diary of Dudley Ryder 1715–1716*, ed. W. Matthews (London: Methuen, 1939), 21–2, 326–7, 369–70; D. Lemmings, 'Ryder, Sir Dudley (1691–1756)', *ODNB*, online edn, May 2009, www.oxforddnb.com/view/article/24394 (accessed 25 July 2014).

50  Ryder, *Diary*, 38, 40, 223.

51  *Ibid.*, 31.

# 14

# The 'Meaner Sort': Labouring People and the Poor

## Jeremy Boulton

Who exactly were those whom contemporaries categorised as 'the meaner sort of people'? These were those people whom educated contemporaries such as William Harrison (1535–93) thought had 'neither voice nor authoritie in the common wealthe, but are to be ruled and not to rule other': day labourers, poor husbandmen, artificers and servants.[1] A more statistical account of the bottom of English society was devised by the political arithmetician Gregory King (1648–1712). King classified those who were, in his notorious phrase, 'decreasing the wealth of the nation' – by which he meant that their expenditure exceeded their income – into five groups: common seamen, labouring people and outservants, cottagers and paupers, common soldiers, and vagrants.[2] Such people are often grouped together as 'the labouring poor' – a term apparently coined by the prolific writer and (failed) businessman Daniel Defoe (1660?–1731). However, that phrase, which only came into general use in the late eighteenth century, should not be used in this period, since it conflates two overlapping social groups, labouring people and the poor, who really should be treated separately.

The key distinguishing feature of all labouring people was that they and their families earned part or all of their living by working for wages (usually money but sometimes wholly or partly in kind). For the majority, work started early in life. Where there was suitable industry, children as young as four could contribute to household income. The Norwich Census of the Poor (1570) listed 330 children and youths aged between four and twenty who worked to supplement household income. Many worked in the city's large textile industry, but a few helped their parents, such as the tinker's son who carried his father's bag.[3] Children could also work in the fields, scaring birds or picking up stones. Most children of the labouring sort would expect to leave home in their mid teens to go into service or apprenticeship; for many, being fed and housed as part of the family of a substantial farmer or middling artisan might well have been the material high point of their working lives. In the seventeenth and eighteenth centuries between a third and a half of all hired agricultural labour was supplied by unmarried 'servants in husbandry'. It is supposed to be during this relatively long, perhaps ten-year, period of servitude that labouring people saved up money to provide the start-up 'entry costs' to marriage and an independent life – although some have argued that for many of the labouring sort the prospect of steady employment at reasonable wages was enough to prompt a departure from service into marriage. All women in this social group worked, although their 'participation rate' (conventionally reckoned at 30 per cent of that of an adult male) was reduced significantly by the demands of childrearing. In Norwich in 1570 almost all women worked, mostly in the textile industry; petty retail; or 'domestic' tasks such as washing, cleaning or nursing. Because their ability to work partly depended on physical strength and their health status (including age-specific physical deterioration in eyesight and manual dexterity) exactly how (and how much) labouring people earned varied over the life course. In late-seventeenth- and early-eighteenth-century London, for example, 'charring, washing, nursing, and hawking tended to be the preserve of older women whose declining eyesight and arthritic fingers prevented them from maintaining themselves "by their needle" '.[4] Labouring work may have been part of a career that included a range of entirely different occupations. John Cannon (1684–1743), a member of the lower middling sort, recalled his career as a 'tennis ball of fortune', 'from a schoolboy to a ploughboy, and from a ploughboy to an excise man, and from an excise man to a maltster and from a maltster to an almost nothing except a schoolmaster'.[5]

This reliance on money wages has one huge advantage for historians. It is an odd fact that, although much of the social history of the wage-earning population is hidden from view, more is known about their earnings than for any other social group. Since the payment of money wages is often recorded in institutional accounts, historians have been able to construct time series based on wage rates paid by the day or week over very long periods. Henry Phelps Brown and Sheila Hopkins – to take the best known and still most useful dataset – constructed 'seven centuries' of daily wage rates of building craftsmen and their labourers paid by institutions in the south of England. This showed that a building craftsmen was receiving 6d a day in the early decades of the sixteenth century, compared to 4d received by a labourer. Between 1580 and 1629 the craftsmen were receiving 12d per day, compared to a labourer's 8d, and this had risen to 18d and 12d, respectively, between 1655 and 1687. By 1736–73 craftsmen received 24d per day and labourers 16d.[6] Wages varied region-ally and were notably higher in London, partly reflecting differentials in the cost of living. Agricultural labourers seem to have been paid at the same rate as building labourers, although the former were paid at higher rates for specialised seasonal tasks such as mowing and haymaking. There are, of course, many problems with these wage rates: they tell us nothing about the number of days worked, so estimates of income depend wholly on assumptions about levels of employment. Labouring work could also be intermittent and highly seasonal: the philanthropist Thomas Firmin (1632–97) wrote in 1678 of 'a poor woman that goes three dayes a week to wash or scoure abroad, or one that is employed in nurse-keeping three or four months in a year, or a poor market-woman who attends three or four mornings in a week with her basket, and all the rest of the time these folks have little or nothing to do'.[7] Wage-rate data, moreover, do not cover the earnings of women and children; whether families owned animals; or had access to land, grazing rights or other sources of support such as charitable handouts. Very, very occasionally censuses of poor drawn up by local officials reveal how the total earnings of labouring households were composed. Thus, Thomas Underhill, a sixty-six-year-old weaver living in Salisbury in 1635, was said to be earning 3s a week. His fifty-four-year-old wife Judith – despite her 'lame hand' – earned 10d a week. Their twenty-year-old daughter Eleanor earned 14d a week making bonelace; her sister Elizabeth (aged sixteen) earned 4d spinning. Three younger children (one aged seven who was at school, a five-year-old and one whose presence is likely but was not named) did not earn anything. Of the total fam-ily weekly income of 64d per week, therefore, Thomas's contribution was just 56 per cent. Even this income must have been thought insufficient to maintain three adults and two or three children, since the family was also receiving 6d per week in poor-relief.[8]

The labouring sort working in the countryside depended only partly on money wages to make ends meet. Their ability to earn a living depended on ownership of land and livestock (particularly cattle) and possession of common rights of grazing, gleaning (gathering corn left in the fields after harvest), fishing and fuel-gathering. Cattle were probably the single best guarantee of getting by: in the late eighteenth century the produce of one dairy cow kept on common land was supposedly equivalent to 40 per cent of an agricultural labourer's income. Possession of livestock was crucial. On the manor of Hartest near Lavenham (Suffolk) in 1608 it was reported that there were '40 small and poor copyholders, the best of them not having above two acres, the most of them being cottingers, and 35 other poor households that have no habitation of their own, nor cow nor calf' – a miserable experience that was diametrically opposed to that of fifty-two fortunate cottagers of Nassington (Northamptonshire), each allowed to pasture three cattle and ten sheep on common land, and thus supposedly able to 'live in such idleness upon their stock of cattle [that] they will bend themselves to no kind of labour'. Everitt has left the best description of this variety of experience:

> The lives of farmhands who lived with their master in the farmhouse bore little resemblance to those of labourers who lived with their wives and children in cottages in the village street. The economic standing of a skilled farmworker with a holding of his own and unstinted pasture rights on the common waste was altogether different from that of a disinherited day-labourer with no property but his wages, and a mere hovel of sticks and dirt to live in.[9]

All this means that to understand the history and fortunes of labouring people we need to know something (or guess) about levels of employment, access to land, customary rights and livestock, payments in kind (servants were paid wages that included board and lodging), and the earnings of women and children, as well as comparing the movement of wages to the prevailing cost of living. In general, however, the fortunes and life chances of the wage earner in this period were connected closely to trends in economic development and the movement of population.

Since wage earners formed a substantial and growing proportion of the total workforce, it is worth starting with modern estimates of the 'sectoral breakdown' of the English economy. Particularly influential have been E. A. Wrigley's estimates. He divided the English workforce according to whether it was employed in the urban, rural agricultural or rural non-agricultural (i.e. industry located in the countryside, cloth-making, mining etc.) sectors. In 1520 only 5.5 per cent of England's population lived in substantial towns, 18.5 per cent followed rural non-agricultural occupations and the remaining 76 per cent were rural agricultural. Thereafter the proportion of the population engaged in agriculture declined. By 1670, 13.5 per cent lived in towns and cities, 26 per cent were rural non-agricultural and the remaining 60.5 per cent in the rural agricultural sector. By 1750, 21 per cent of the population were urban, 33 per cent rural non agricultural and 46 per cent rural agricultural. Particularly in the seventeenth and early eighteenth centuries, then, there was a substantial move away from agricultural occupations: in *absolute* terms there were more people working in agriculture in 1600 than there were in 1750. It thus seems a reasonable supposition – if these estimates are anything like accurate – that more of the labouring sort were living in towns or worked in rural industries in the last half of our period.[10] This is vitally important. It means that a growing proportion became dependent solely on wages for a living and did not have access to land on which to grow their own food or keep livestock. The 'meaner sort', as a result of England's economic development, thus became more 'market sensitive' and (at least in theory) more vulnerable to periods of dearth and economic depression.

The fortunes of labouring people were ultimately determined by population trends. Broadly speaking the two-and-a-half centuries between 1500 and 1750 are best seen as two distinctive periods. The first, between 1500 and 1650, represents a period of rapid population growth. England's population grew very rapidly in the sixteenth century, from perhaps 2.4 million in 1520 to 4.11 million in 1600, and had reached around 5.23 million in 1650. The second period, 1650 to 1750, looks completely different: there was then demographic stagnation and even modest contraction until 1700, when the population stood at 5.06 million with only a modest recovery to 5.77 million by 1750.

Labouring people were at the sharp end of these demographic forces. This was a society in which productivity in both agriculture and industry was relatively low. As a result, the economy could not respond quickly – produce enough food and employment – to feed or employ extra mouths beyond very modest rates of population growth. Population growth thus produced rapid food-price inflation in the sixteenth and seventeenth centuries that drove down the purchasing power of money wages, since the overstocked labour market meant that wages did not rise as fast as food prices. For this reason 'real wages' – that is money wages deflated by a notional basket of prices representing the cost of living – fell, albeit unevenly from the early sixteenth century. The Phelps Brown–Hopkins real wage index shows a catastrophic fall in the purchasing power of building craftsmen whose money wages by the first decade of the seventeenth century had lost half of their purchasing power since the early sixteenth. A similar collapse in purchasing power is seen in the real wages of agricultural labourers. In addition to depressing the purchasing power of labour, rapid population growth also meant the emergence in the sixteenth century of serious (and noticeable) levels of under- and unemployment, in both the agrarian and industrial economies. This also greatly increased rates of migration in the economy: rather than eke out a living in such circumstances, increasing numbers of the labouring sort moved to areas of perceived economic opportunity such as towns and cities (particularly London), or agrarian regions with plentiful commons (such as wood pasture regions of England) or industry (such as mining or textiles). Long-distance 'subsistence' migration was therefore a feature of this period. It is no coincidence, either, that huge numbers of people emigrated in the seventeenth century, which further reduced rates of population growth. Emigration to the New World from all parts of the British Isles was something like 378,000 between 1630 and 1699. Large numbers may also have left England for Ireland: Carew Reynell (1636–90), writing in 1674, thought the 'want of people' at that time was also due to the fact that 'two hundred thousand more have been wasted in repopulating Ireland'.[11] Rapid population growth in an economy of low productivity and limited room for expansion meant increased competition for finite resources. This in turn meant that the period between 1550 and 1640 tends to see more attempts by parishes to regulate the behaviour of the poor; less tolerance to petty theft, bastardy and so on. It is also in this period that historians see the emergence of a new 'class' of landless wage labourers and rootless vagrants. It is also, of course, one of the reasons that poverty emerged as an urgent social problem. The relative position of the labouring sort vis-à-vis other groups was at its worst in the late sixteenth and early seventeenth century: dramatic social polarisation was the end result of rapid population growth, food price inflation and an overstocked labour market.

The period between 1650 and 1750 has a different character from the previous century. In the absence of population growth and with falling food prices, the purchasing power of money wages improved. The Phelps Brown–Hopkins real wage index stands at 39 for the difficult decade 1620–9, 49 in 1670–9 and 67 for the decade 1740–9 – which represented a recovery to levels not seen since the 1520s.[12] In real terms the median worth of labourers may have doubled between 1625 and 1649 and between 1657 and 1681, although this was subject to considerable geographical variation. It is not surprising, therefore, that it was after 1650 that contemporary writers increasingly condemned the English labourer for preferring leisure ('idleness') to working flat out for higher wages. Because there was more purchasing power for non-essentials, this period also saw more urban growth outside London – even a provincial 'urban renaissance' – and more demand for the products of industry. Generally speaking, for the labouring sort, it also meant that areas of economic opportunity were likely to be closer to home, so that the volume of long-distance 'subsistence' migration declined and anxiety about vagrants lessened.

Although such underlying trends are now reasonably clear, they are complicated by other distinguishing features of the early modern economy. Because only a proportion of corn harvested reached market (the rest being retained to feed the family of the producer) the price of grain sold was extremely volatile. This was especially serious for the market-sensitive labouring sort because the vast bulk of their household expenditure was spent on food, much of it on bread and grain. Notable years of high grain prices occurred in 1556, 1586, 1596, 1608, 1622, 1647, 1673, 1693 and 1697. Hardship, hunger and (at least until the mid seventeenth century) famine were particularly likely when poor harvests followed each other, such as in the mid 1590s, 1647–50 and the mid 1690s, or when they coincided with industrial depression, as in the 1620s.

If price shocks sometimes obscure or muddy underlying trends (and there were, of course, periods when prices were unusually depressed), one should also note that the experience of the wage earner was subject to huge regional variation. There were in England in this period about 9,000 parishes, ranging from huge, remote upland pastoral communities to small, compact settlements specialising in growing grain. Urban parishes could range from tiny, wealthy inner-city parishes to suburban giants. The process of economic development, increasing agricultural specialisation, developing rural industries and growing urbanisation also meant that parishes could change radically over this 250-year period. The social structure of Whickham (Co. Durham), for example, was literally turned upside down by the dramatic development of the coal industry in the sixteenth and early seventeenth century, which led to the immigration of hundreds of miners. At the national level, population pressure on limited resources, and the difficulty of maintaining viable holdings in a period of rising rents, also meant that many rural labourers and small husbandmen lost out, as enclosure eliminated and encroachment nibbled away cherished (and sometimes vigorously defended) common rights. A survey of the holdings of agricultural labourers from before 1560 and after 1620 found that the percentage who possessed only a cottage and garden nearly quadrupled from 11 to 40 per cent. It should also be noted that geographical location and settlement type dramatically affected the mortality experience of wage earners. Those moving to towns, and particularly to London, in search of employment and better prospects often paid the 'urban penalty' of much higher death rates caused by diseases to which they had not previously been exposed, such as tuberculosis, typhus and smallpox. The poor in overcrowded suburban tenements, as contemporaries observed, were also peculiarly likely to die in the frequently savage bubonic plague epidemics that were a regular feature of urban life until 1679. Even in the countryside, death rates varied hugely between remote, well-drained upland parishes and low-lying areas – particularly those in the malaria-ridden marshes on the south-east coast.

Recent research has highlighted other welfare implications of population change. Thanks to the work of the Cambridge Population Group we can now construct a 'dependency ratio': a comparative measure of the size of the productive age groups (conventionally those aged between fifteen and fifty-nine) to the rest of the population. This should not be pushed too far (since children and the elderly both produced something and consumed less than adults) but generally speaking this ratio was at its most unfavourable when the fertility of the population was high and population growth rapid in the late sixteenth and early seventeenth century, and most favourable in the late seventeenth century when the fertility of the population was relatively low, and when there were more elderly people. This suggests that being overburdened with children would have been more common in the late sixteenth and early seventeenth century, and, in crude terms, that the 'problem' of the elderly might have baulked larger as a welfare issue after 1640. Changing fertility also altered the number of close kin that people possessed. Computer modelling has demonstrated, for example, that a man born in 1550 and living to the age of sixty-five would have had more children and especially more grandchildren alive than a man born in 1650. The welfare implications of this are easier to model than to demonstrate from the historical record, however.

What proportion of the English population *were* wage earners in this period? Most historians would argue, given the development of rural industry, agricultural specialisation and substantial urban growth, that the absolute proportion must have been significantly higher in 1750 than it had been in 1500. Reasonable estimates have been made for particular communities, but for the national picture readers should be aware that we enter the realm of (highly) educated guesswork. There are very real problems of evidence. To begin with it is not a simple matter even to find out how most early modern people earned a living. The first national population census was held only in 1801, and the first that provides solid, reliable occupational information is usually held to be 1851. The labouring sort, too, rarely made wills or left probate inventories (both of which often contain occupational information) because they did not possess enough property and those that did were probably atypical. There are occasional sources that record occupations, but they tend to be one-off snapshots covering only particular counties (famously a muster roll for Gloucestershire in 1608, three from

Coventry, Rutland and part of Suffolk in 1522) or are based on records that might cover only taxpayers and that, anyway, more commonly survive in towns, particularly in the later seventeenth century. Parish registers, especially from the latter period, and again most often in urban settlements, can also sometimes contain illuminating occupational information. It goes without saying that none of the sources above says anything useful about female or child occupations. Alan Everitt thought that in the period 1500–1640 the labouring population made up about a quarter or a third of the rural population and argued that the proportion was certainly increased over the seventeenth century.[13] It is also exceptionally difficult to measure changes in the distribution of wealth, either nationally or at the local level, without very large margins of error. Two national taxes (the lay subsidy of 1524/5 and the late-seventeenth-century hearth taxes (1662–90) can provide a reasonable picture of the distribution of wealth – for those parts of the country where usable returns survive. At the local level it is possible to compare these sources to measure changes in the social structure over time, most notably in Wrightson and Levine's study of Terling (Essex), which concluded, after a comparison between the 76 taxpayers listed in the lay subsidy and the 122 households listed in the 1671 hearth tax, that the parish – in the early sixteenth century one of the wealthiest in Essex, itself one of England's wealthiest counties – 'filled at the bottom'. Their social group IV (labourers and cottagers) grew from 27.6 per cent of taxpayers in 1524/5 to 50.8 per cent of householders in 1671.[14] Unfortunately, their pioneering work has not been followed up at a national level, although there has been some (not terribly conclusive) work on the changing spatial distribution of wealth using these sources. Historians interested in England's social and occupational structure have been drawn to – and greatly influenced by – tables constructed by Gregory King in 1696 and Joseph Massie (d. 1784) in 1759. Although the content of both was shaped partly by the agenda of their authors, they purport to contain unique information about England's social structure, including the average income and family size of all social groups. King's estimate that common seamen, labouring people and out-servants, cottagers and paupers, common soldiers, and vagrants made up about half the English population has been particularly influential. King probably overestimated the number in these groups but even if revised downwards his estimates still suggest a significant increase in the proportion of the population working for wages since the early sixteenth century.[15]

Who were the poor? Contemporaries who attempted social classifications came up with different definitions. Daniel Defoe's sevenfold depiction of

English society in 1709 thought that group VI should be 'The Poor that fare hard', and below them at the bottom 'The Miserable, that really pinch and suffer want'.[16] Gregory King's enumeration of those 'decreasing the wealth of the nation' is sometimes equated with all those in at least intermittent poverty, but in fact King himself only labelled two groups explicitly as poor: 'cottagers and paupers' with an average income per head of just £2 per year (less than half that of labouring people and outservants whose per capita income was estimated to be £4 10s), and vagrants, who were also assumed to 'earn' just £2 per year per head.[17] The true importance of King's late-seventeenth-century guesstimates are that they demonstrate that 'the poor' were very far from being a homogeneous social group. Contemporaries agreed, however, that poverty was the condition of anyone unable to maintain him- or herself by their own labour. 'Those generally are to be deemed poore, which cannot live without reliefe of the lawe', it was stated in 1601: 'so long as there is any naturall or necessarie meanes left to live, none must depend upon the helpe of the lawe'.[18]

Classically the poor were also divided into the 'deserving' and the 'undeserving poor' a division that pre-dated the sixteenth century. The deserving poor were, from the mid sixteenth century at least, further divided into the poor 'by casualty' and poor by 'impotency'. The latter were the 'lame ympotent olde blynde and such other amonge them being poore and not able to worke'. The former were those cast into poverty by accident and sickness. By the end of the sixteenth century, the poor by casualty were also understood to include those willing to work, but unable to do so through want of employment, something that, as we have seen, was then an increasing problem. The 'undeserving' poor were those able to work but who chose not to: the wilfully idle and vagrant – mobile labouring people on the road who were encountered with increasing frequency and who were feared (and mythologised) as 'masterless men' with no social ties to any particular place. By the early seventeenth century the undeserving 'thriftless' poor were thought to contain a wide range of undesirables: including those increasingly subject to puritan campaigns to impose a 'reformation of manners': drunkards, prostitutes and petty thieves.

That lawmakers and writers focused increasingly on the poor is partly because of local policy responses to the demographic and economic developments of the sixteenth and early seventeenth centuries. In a sense, the period between 1500 and 1700 saw the discovery of the poor. One response to local political upheavals, economic and social dislocation, or perceived local increases in vagrancy or poverty was that a number of towns and cities took detailed censuses or listings of their poor. These included Worcester (1557), Norwich (1570), Warwick (1587), Ipswich (1597), Huddersfield (1622) and Salisbury (1635).[19] These were one-off snapshots. A unique *series* of detailed listings survives only for the town of Bolton (1674, 1686, 1699). Such counting was encouraged by the introduction of the Elizabethan poor laws – a 1601 manual contained a specimen template census. These counts revealed the extent of under- and unemployment produced by rapid population growth. The Norwich census found that one-third of poor men were unemployed, such as thirty-year-old Henry White, a 'laborer out of work' who lived with 'Margaret, his wyf, that spyn white warpe, & dwell together; and 2 sons, the eldest 9 yers that spin white warpe, the other 3 yere; & hir mayde, Elizabeth Stori of 16 yeris that spyn also'.[20]

The poor were not, however, a permanent underclass. Since the 1980s, historians have insisted on the predominance of 'life-cycle poverty'. The aged, sick, orphaned, widowed and those overburdened with children experienced poverty more frequently – rather as one might expect. Actually identifying the life-cycle component of poverty is technically difficult. There can be no doubt that widowhood and old age contributed disproportionately to those in poverty: old age was responsible for 16 per cent of poverty in Norwich in 1570 and no less than 39 per cent in Salisbury in 1635. In Hedenham, Norfolk, in the later seventeenth century most paupers fell onto regular relief in their fifties and sixties. Families overburdened with children seem to have been a more common feature of poverty in the early seventeenth century – precisely as predicted by the then prevailing demographic regime. That said, however, the actual contours of life-cycle poverty in any one community were shaped by demographic conditions and the nature of the local economy.

How many poor were there? If poverty varied over the life course, it also varied hugely across both time and space. The proportion of the total local population who were thought to be 'poor' in urban listings varied considerably, and, since such censuses coincided with particular periods of need, may not necessarily have been typical. In urban censuses the percentage ranged from as low as 5 per cent (Salisbury, 1635) to 12–13 per cent (Warwick, 1587; and Ipswich, 1597) to as high as 20–5 per cent (Norwich, 1570; Huddersfield, 1622). Such listings also show that the extent of poverty could vary considerably *within* towns and cities. In Norwich, which was divided into thirteen wards, the percentage of the population considered poor in 1570 ranged from as low as 7–8 per cent to as high as 36–41 per cent.[21] The Bolton listings demonstrate how problematic such statistics can be, since they vary considerably over a very short time period: the percentage of poor in Bolton was no less than 27 per cent in 1674, but only 12–14 per cent in the censuses of 1686 and 1699. What also now seems very clear is that exemption from national taxation is a misleading guide to levels of indigence. Recent studies have demonstrated, for example, that those exempted from the hearth tax were considered too poor to pay, but were unlikely to be in receipt of parish relief. In Bolton no less than 73 per cent of householders were exempt from the hearth tax, compared to the percentages of poor reported above. Although most people who experienced poverty were members of the labouring sort, this was a society that lacked safety nets: destitution could happen to almost anyone. A pamphlet attacking the peculiarly grim pauper burials in early-eighteenth-century London noted that those so interred 'died poor, tho perhaps part of their Time they lived plentifully, and served several Parish-Offices reputably, and to Satisfaction'.[22] The incidence of poverty also varied over the year, being higher in the winter months when employment was scarcer and illness more common. Poor-relief should 'somewhat be retained and reserved in sommer, that their releefe may be more liberall in winter'.[23] The last point that should be understood is that poverty is a relative, not an absolute, concept. Contemporaries unconsciously applied their own value judgements as to what poverty consisted of, what level of deprivation it implied and how much should be given to relieve perceived want. This means that over time more people might be considered as worthy of relief, not because absolute levels of need were greater, but because what was considered worthy of relief had expanded.

The social position of the English poor was dramatically altered by the Elizabethan poor laws. This legislation was introduced partly in response to the observable deterioration in the position of England's poor in the second half of the sixteenth century and often followed periods of extreme hardship after runs of bad harvests, such as the 1590s. The poor laws were also designed to fill the welfare gap created by the dissolution of the monasteries and hospitals, the abolition of chantries, and the supposed dilution of the charitable imperative (i.e. the switch from Catholicism espousing 'justification by good works' to a Protestant creed based on 'justification by faith alone') as a direct consequence of the English Protestant Reformation. Historians now believe that the loss of the charity of religious institutions was very serious – they are thought to have distributed £10,216–11,696 *per year* in alms in 1535, a sum not made good in real terms by the poor law until the early seventeenth century. The Elizabethan poor laws, too, were superimposed on an existing 'mixed economy of welfare', consisting of aid from hospitals and almshouses; and also informal private charity; neighbourly credit and support; and charitable doles of food, fuel or cash. It should also be noted that the poor laws were part of a larger package of welfare measures, which included legislation to encourage and protect charitable endowments (notably the Statute of Charitable Uses, 1601).

What then were the English poor laws? The term refers to a series of Acts of Parliament that by 1601 had introduced a system of parish-based poor-relief, funded by a compulsory local taxation on property (the poor rate); administered by local officials called overseers; and supervised, enforced and audited by local magistrates. The money raised was to be used to set the poor on work, apprentice their children, pay a select group of paupers a weekly cash pension and make less regular 'extraordinary' one-off payments. Statutes were passed in 1536, 1547, 1552 (this latter considered by some to be the real foundation of the Elizabethan poor law), 1555, 1563, 1572 and 1576. The two statutes that underpinned the poor law until 1834 were passed in 1598, confirmed with slight amendments in 1601. The poor law is sometimes known as the Old Poor Law, to distinguish it from the New Poor Law (which replaced it in 1834). The poor laws also included a sequence of clauses, and some separate statutes, directed against vagrants and beggars (dedicated Acts were passed in 1531, 1550, 1598, 1714, 1740 and 1744), which reflected the then perceived level of threat that such individuals were supposed to pose. The influential 1598 Act 'for the punishment of Rogues, Vagabonds and Sturdy Beggars' prescribed that vagrants should be whipped and passed back to their place of birth or last place of long-term residence with a special passport. Begging for food within one's home parish, allowed in 1598, was forbidden in 1601, although the prohibition was widely ignored. The Act of 1576 'for setting of the poor on Work, and for the Avoiding of Idleness' ordered the erection of houses of correction in every county to punish those refusing to be set on work (this was strengthened by another Act in 1610).

Although the basic Elizabethan framework remained until 1834, later legislation dealt with questions of eligibility and attempted to limit the rising costs of parish relief. Firstly, in the later seventeenth and eighteenth century, the poor became subject to what is known as the law of settlement. Although the poor law enshrined in law the notion that the parish was the basic unit of welfare responsibility, it had failed to define the criteria of belonging. This meant communities had a strong motive for ejecting those non-parishioners likely to be a welfare burden (such as pregnant single women): they sometimes appointed officials dedicated to the task of physically removing such people. The settlement laws (1662, 1692, 1697) attempted to fix this problem. The founding 1662 Act allowed the legal removal of newcomers 'likely to become chargeable' on complaint to two justices of the peace within forty days, if they rented houses worth less than £10 per annum. The Act also created a new legal class of poor – the 'certificate man'. Certificates allowed mobility between parishes: migrants were granted documents that confirmed they were the legal responsibility of their home parish. An Act of 1692 allowed newcomers to earn a settlement by paying parish rates, or serving an apprenticeship, or going into service for a year; and a clause in an Act of 1697 forbade the removal of certified poor unless they had actually become 'chargeable'. A lot of time and ink were spent at the time (and have been spent by historians since) on the mechanics of settlement law. Essentially parishes became engaged in a sometimes hectic 'zero sum game', examining those likely to need poor-relief, removing the unsettled and appealing removal decisions. The only sure winners were lawyers, since an arcane body of case law quickly built up, with some luckless paupers being transported back and forth, sometimes over quite long distances, as parishes disputed their legal responsibility to relieve them. Concern with rising costs at the end of the seventeenth century underlay the last really significant additions to the Old Poor Law. The Act of 1692 attempted to limit the ability of parishes to grant pensions without the authority of a justice, and one of 1697 sought to identify recipients of poor-relief by compelling the wearing of badges. The ultimate deterrent, however, was introduced by the so-called 'Workhouse Test Act' (1723), which encouraged the erection of parish workhouses and allowed parishes to deny poor-relief to any pauper who refused to enter them, foreshadowing a key feature of the New Poor Law. Only a minority of parishes, however – notably in London and its hinterland – had erected such institutions by 1750.[24]

What impact did the poor laws have on the lives of the poor? The poor laws delivered a potentially powerful administrative tool into the hands of local ruling elites, who sometimes used it to impose social and religious reform on the poor. Exactly *how* the poor were relieved under the poor laws was subject to huge variation. There was considerable local experimentation. This was particularly marked in some towns and cities, notably in the textile towns of south and eastern England before 1640, who attempted usually short-lived experiments in centralised systems. The wealthy Suffolk cloth town of Hadleigh, for example, ran a workhouse to discipline and train up to thirty of its poor children in the later sixteenth century. Salisbury opened a municipal brewery, a workhouse and a storehouse as part of an elaborate scheme of poor-relief between 1623 and 1628. Such initiatives were often devised by urban puritan elites seeking to reform the manners of their poor. London, whose poor-relief systems were always precocious, ran a partly centralised system of poor-relief based on large public hospitals in the second half of the sixteenth century, and constructed a city-wide London Workhouse in the 1640s, revived again in the later seventeenth century, a period when a number of other towns and cities attempted centralised poor-relief schemes based on municipal workhouses. In the end, however, such schemes broke down in the face of the inherent parochialism of the English poor law.

Many of England's parishes were initially slow to put the poor laws into operation, finding that customary welfare mechanisms were enough to support their local poor. Historians have, however, found more widespread and earlier implementation the harder they look. Implementation of the poor law is now thought to have been much more common, particularly in southern and central England in the second half of the sixteenth century, than thought previously, and it has been argued recently that, in contrast to previous estimates, most rural parishes had appointed overseers and introduced rates by the Civil War. By the 1690s almost every parish in the country was participating in this unique welfare system.

As far as it is possible to judge, the poor law played an increasing part in the household economies of the poor in the seventeenth and early eighteenth century. Most parish relief was delivered as a cash pension to the poor in their own homes. The amounts given varied widely according to the local cost of living, size and wealth of the parish tax-base and the life-cycle stage and circumstances of recipients. Although pensions could fall, on the whole the trend seems to have been upwards throughout the seventeenth century: in rural areas the most commonly paid pension in the first half of the seventeenth century was 6d per week, rising to 12d in the later part of the century, which suggests that pensions were then rising faster than money wages. By the end of the seventeenth century the poor rate in England and Wales was yielding some £400,000 per year, rising to an average of £689,971 in 1748–50 – a doubling in real terms. These figures suggest that the percentage of the total population who could have been maintained could have risen from 3.6 per cent to 7.9 per cent between 1700 and 1750. Local studies often find that the proportion of the population receiving regular pensions rose across the seventeenth century. The numbers relieved and the size of pensions paid, however, varied regionally, with significantly stingier poor-relief in northern counties of England.

Unfortunately very few sources record the total *incomes* of those in receipt of poor-relief. The few censuses that do (as, for example, Salisbury in 1635, and Bolton in 1686 and 1699) confirm the assumption of most historians that poor-relief was intended to *supplement* household income rather than provide total maintenance (see above for the case of Thomas Underhill of Salisbury). It also seems likely that an increasing proportion of the elderly population were being supported in the later seventeenth and early eighteenth century.

The increased spending on the poor and the growing numbers on relief in the later seventeenth and early eighteenth century are paradoxical, since we know that the period 1650–1750 was one when the living standards of wage earners *improved* significantly. Some of the increased spending may have derived from the fact that the relative *size* of the wage-dependent population was bigger, and that there were more elderly people who were most likely to need (and need more) poor-relief with fewer close kin to support them. It is also possible that the 'poverty line' – the minimum acceptable standard of living – had shifted upwards. Lastly, it might be that public poor-relief was actually taking a larger share of *total* welfare spending – that is that private charity and neighbourly support were diminishing as more and more people thought it not only 'needless but foolish to do that which is parish business'.[25] More work is needed on this question.

   How were the meaner sort and the poor perceived by the rest of society, and how did they see themselves? Their social superiors certainly recognised the fundamental part played in the social and economic order by the meaner sort: 'the rich cannot stand without the poor', pointed out the antiquary Robert Reyce in 1618.[26] Until the Protestant Reformation, too, the prayers of the poor (known to be especially efficacious) represented a considerable spiritual resource – most pre-Reformation funerals included a charitable dole of cash or food to attract as many poor as possible to pray for the soul of the departed in purgatory. Ultimately, however, this was a society in which manual labour of any description was considered a mark of inferiority: after all, university-educated physicians looked down on surgeons precisely because they worked with their hands. John Cannon, another educated man, did not look back on his period of agricultural work with pride: it was when he had 'become a mere clod hopper for a time'.[27] Most historians would argue that the social and cultural distance between the labouring sort and the 'better sort' increased over our period – by the end of the seventeenth century Richard Baxter (1615–91), the Presbyterian divine, could famously label ordinary villagers as 'the rabble that cannot read'.[28] Social superiors expected 'hat honour' from inferiors and would expect those in lowly social positions to dress appropriately and sit in the poorest and most humble pews in church. Social position was even reflected in the sort of food eaten. The meaner sorts had 'stomackes like ostriges, that can digest hard iron'; 'country persons and hard laborers' ate 'more gross, tough, and hard' foods – 'grosse meat is meete for grosse men', agreed the physician Thomas Cogan (c. 1541–1607).[29] The poor were dangerous, too, since it was widely recognised that they were especially prone to disease, notably plague. Social distance, snobbery and fear, however, did not eliminate paternalistic obligation and the need to exercise Christian charity, or remove the imperative to be a considerate master. In 1601 overseers of the poor – usually members of the middling sorts – when dealing with the poor were supposed to remember that poverty itself was a punishment from God: 'tender the poore but doe not tyrannize over them: for it is no more glorie to triumph over the poore, then to tread of a worm'.[30]

Recovering the attitudes and self-identity of the 'meaner sort' is complicated by the fact that their public utterances often conformed to their superiors' expectations of social relations (sometimes theorised as the 'public transcript') and may have masked very different private sentiments (the 'hidden transcript'). For this reason the deference and obsequious expressions of gratitude commonly found in petitions and requests for poor-relief and charity may well be misleading. That said, those whose livelihood depended solely on wages seem to have been (at least in what might have been the intimidating atmosphere of a Church court) conscious of their lowly position, like the Salisbury servant in husbandry (1590) who described himself as a 'poore hired servant & liveth onely by his hard labour not being otherwise any thing worth'.[31]

What is certain is that acceptance of alms or charitable aid of any description was *the* ultimate mark of poverty and dependence. Those reliant on alms were believed to be corrupted easily and lacked credit, authority and reputation. It is even possible that those in poverty internalised such values: 'If he be poore he will not be respected: for commonly the poore despise him that is poore.'[32] Acceptance of poor-relief or charity might also result in the public stigmatisation of distinctive clothing, a badge or, increasingly, a demeaning pauper funeral. Although poor people accepted charity, begged in the street (often using theatrical and even threatening behaviour) and applied for poor-relief, labouring people attempted to avoid such damaging dependency for as long as possible: witness the Wiltshire tailor in 1674 who 'thank's God that he Never yet received releife from the parish, & so long as he is able to work at his trade he hopes he shall not & also that he hath somthing of his owne to help to Maintaine him'. The poor seem to have valued a reputation for honesty and industriousness. In court they often stressed their 'honest endeavour': witness the poor wheeler who 'laboreth as a trewe poor man getting his lyving from hand to mouth', or the widow who admitted she was 'a poore woman but liveth in an honest way by her owne labour'.[33] Unsurprisingly, therefore, the poor were especially hostile to *total* dependency: many refused – despite losing their pensions – to enter the new parish workhouses in the early eighteenth century.

Many historians argue that those at the bottom of the social heap were far from powerless – that is they possessed some 'agency', an ability to negotiate with social superiors over the terms of their support or employment. There is some truth in this. Those asking for charity might threaten and curse those who refused them – something that is thought to have been behind many witchcraft accusations. Servants and apprentices, too, were sometimes far from deferential, relatively independent and quite capable of taking abusive employers to court. In particular historians have noted the skill and persistence with which individual applicants navigated their way through the poor laws, repeatedly appealing decisions made by overseers and magistrates and shaping testimonies to match the requirements of the law of settlement. In the end, however, such agency was limited: many applications were turned down and petitions and appeals were ignored or rejected. The poor laws, moreover, did not confer a 'right to relief' as some have argued – merely a right to *apply* for relief. Any agency exercised by the poor failed to mitigate their lowly social position significantly. What essentially happened to the labouring people of England between 1500 and 1750 was that a large proportion of them lost their ability to live independently, to 'make shift and mend', without the support of charity and public poor-relief.

### Notes

1 K. Wrightson, *English Society 1580–1680* (London: Hutchinson, 1982), 19.
2 J. Thirsk and J. P. Cooper (eds.), *Seventeenth-Century Economic Documents* (Oxford: Clarendon Press, 1972), 780–1.
3 J. F. Pound (ed.), *The Norwich Census of the Poor 1570* (Norwich: Norfolk Record Society, 1971), 17.

4 P. Earle, 'The female labour market in London in the late seventeenth and early eighteenth centuries', *EcHR*, 42:3 (1989), 343.

5 T. Hitchcock, 'Cannon, John (1684–1743)', *ODNB*, online edn, www. oxforddnb.com/view/article/66791 (accessed 24 July 2014).

6 E. H. Phelps Brown and S. V. Hopkins, 'Seven centuries of building wages', *Economica*, 22:87 (1955), 205.

7 Earle, 'Female labour market', 342.

8 P. Slack (ed.), *Poverty in Early-Stuart Salisbury* (Devizes: Wiltshire Record Society, 1975), 77.

9 A. Everitt, 'Farm labourers', in J. Thirsk (ed.), *The Agrarian History of England and Wales,* Vol. IV: *1500–1640* (Cambridge: Cambridge University Press, 1967), 402, 404, 396.

10 E. A. Wrigley, *People, Cities and Wealth: The Transformation of Traditional Society* (Oxford: Blackwell, 1987), 170.

11 Thirsk and Cooper, *Seventeenth-Century Economic Documents*, 758.

12 E. H. Phelps Brown and Sheila V. Hopkins, 'Seven centuries of the prices of consumables, compared with builders' wage-rates', *Economica*, 23:92 (1956), 312–13.

13 Everitt, 'Farm labourers', 398–9.

14 K. Wrightson and D. Levine, *Poverty and Piety in an English Village: Terling, 1525–1700,* 2nd edn (Oxford: Oxford University Press, 1995), 31–6.

15 For the growth and development of wage labour in the countryside, see Jane Whittle's chapter in the present volume, 163–165.

16 P. J. Corfield, 'Class by name and number in eighteenth-century Britain', *History*, 72:234 (1987), 50.

17 Thirsk and Cooper, *Seventeenth-Century Economic Documents*, 781.

18 *An Ease for Overseers of the Poore: Abstracted from the Statutes ... as a necessarie Directorie for Imploying, Releeving, and ordering of the poore* (Cambridge, 1601), 22–3.

19 P. Slack, *Poverty and Policy in Tudor and Stuart England* (Harlow: Longman, 1988), 73.

20 Pound, *Norwich Census*, 28.

21 *Ibid.*, 11, 107.

22 *Some Customs Consider'd, Whether Prejudicial to the Health of this City* (London, 1721), 11.

23 *An Ease for Overseers*, 4.

24 P. Slack, *The English Poor Law 1531–1782* (Basingstoke: Macmillan, 1990), 59–64.

25 Dudley North (1641–91), quoted in S. Hindle, *On the Parish: The Micro-Politics of Poor Relief in Rural England, c. 1550–1750* (Oxford: Oxford University Press, 2004), 144.

26 Everitt, 'Farm labourers', 396.

27 Hitchcock, 'Cannon, John (1684–1743)'.

28 Wrightson, *English Society*, 221.

29 A. Fox, 'Food, drink and social distinction in early modern England', in S. Hindle, A. Shepard and J. Walter (eds.), *Remaking English Society: Social Relations and Social Change in Early Modern England* (Woodbridge: Boydell, 2013), 166.

30 *An Ease for Overseers*, 28.

31 A. Shepard, 'Poverty, labour and the language of social description in early modern England', *P&P*, 201 (2008), 63.

32 *An Ease for Overseers*, 9.

33 A. Shepard, 'Language of social description', 58, 80, 89.

# 15

# Gender, the Body and Sexuality

## Alexandra Shepard

Gender constituted a fulcrum of difference in early modern English society, structuring identity and agency in myriad ways. The pervasive significance of gender as a category of identity did not, however, create a stable set of meanings associated with either masculinity or femininity. Gender difference, as understood by early modern people, was highly fluid, fluctuating in conjunction with other variants such as age, social status and marital status. It was also subject to change over time. According to some historians, concepts of gender difference, as well as categories of sexuality and attitudes towards sex, were fundamentally redrawn towards the end of the early modern period. One unchanging dimension, however, was the extent to which understandings of gender, the body and sexuality served patriarchal interests – through privileging men and masculinity – albeit not without multiple caveats and contradictions.

The gendered body and sexuality have only relatively recently become subjects of historical investigation. Of primary importance in stimulating exploration of these themes were, on the one hand, second-wave feminism (and its commitment to historicise patriarchy) and, on the other hand, the publication of the first volume of Michel Foucault's *History of Sexuality* in 1976, which argued that the very concept of sexuality is a construct of modern western scientific discourse. Challenging essentialist assumptions that sex, gender and sexuality are biologically produced, feminist and cultural historians have instead approached gender difference, sexual behaviour and related categories of identity as *culturally* created, in service to relations of power, and therefore subject to significant variation among societies and over time. More recently, scholars have begun to express caution against attributing categories of gendered identity entirely to cultural production, on the grounds that such an approach risks neglecting the agency of the body in shaping the experience and conceptualisation of gender difference and sexual desire.[1] Despite varied opinion as to the extent and nature of change over the course of the early modern period, as well as a more fundamental divergence over the somatic significance of the body, perhaps the most striking finding of research in this area is the central importance of concepts of sex and gender to the mental furniture of early modern people. Besides contributing vital components to the personal experience of difference, understandings of gender and sexual behaviour informed political and religious discourse and were extensively utilised, for example, in the conceptualisation of the state in terms of familial authority, in the demarcation of confessional boundaries disputed in the wake of the Reformation, and in response to cultural encounters with foreign 'others'. Sex and gender were deployed to make sense of a vast array of other differences, which in turn affected the ways in which they were experienced, and in that sense concepts of gender take on a double resonance in narratives of change associated with 'early modernity'.

## The Patriarchal Order

Early modern society was indisputably patriarchal in character. Patriarchal expectations were shored up by biblical injunction, enshrined in law, elaborated in medical theory and enmeshed in social practice. But the 'patriarchal edifice' was not without cracks and complexities.[2] It was founded upon the agency of some women, as well as undermined by varieties of female resistance; it did not privilege men either uniformly or unequivocally; and it depended on hierarchical distinctions within each sex as well as between men and women. Perhaps one of the explanations for ongoing 'patriarchal equilibrium', whereby men have consistently been privileged above women of comparable age and status, is the extent to which the patriarchal order left room for exceptions and contradictions as much as its enduring adaptability.[3] It is important, therefore, that our accounts of early modern patriarchy are alert to women's agency as well as their disadvantages, and mindful of men's varied access to patriarchal privilege, on the basis of age, social status, marital status and ethnic identity.

Although Protestant reform was in part founded upon ideals of spiritual equality, patriarchal norms nonetheless permeated early modern religious discourse. Clergymen continued to idealise femininity in terms of silence, chastity and obedience, in contrast to normative masculinity, which was associated with men's rational self-government, thrifty restraint and control of others as well as themselves. Despite their more positive attitudes to marriage as a public good (in response to Catholic approaches to marriage as a necessary container for sexual sin), Protestant reformers and puritan proselytisers remained heavily invested in maintaining distinct gender roles for spouses. The clergymen John Dod and Robert Cleaver outlined a clear division of labour between spouses in their 'how-to' guide to domestic harmony when they itemised the duties of a husband to 'get goods' to 'travell abroad, to seeke [a] living'; to 'get money and provision'; and to 'deal with many men', 'be entermedling', and 'skilful in talke' – in contrast to the duties of the wife to 'save' goods and 'keepe the house', and to 'talke with few' men and remain 'solitary and withdrawne', boasting of silence.[4] The flourishing genre of domestic conduct literature from the mid sixteenth to the mid seventeenth century to which Dod and Cleaver's tract belonged was nonetheless heavily preoccupied with the precariousness of husbandly authority and the limits of wifely subordination, and as a result its authors also conjured a range of negative male and female stereotypes as they elaborated patriarchal ideals. The domineering shrew (also a feature of the period's plays and ballads) who donned the breeches and overruled her husband at every turn, rendering him a cuckold through her sexual incontinence, is one such example. The uxorious husband, whose reason was imperilled by excessive affection for his wife, was caricatured as 'effeminately bewitcht', and risked becoming a 'milke-sop'.[5] At the other extreme, conduct writers disagreed about whether or not a husband's use of force was permissible, with most condemning heavy-handed tyranny as brutish and (perhaps more importantly) an ineffectual strategy for securing wifely obedience. Finally, the profligate wastrel (comparable to the spendthrift wife) was deemed a dangerous threat to his household's credit and his dependants' well-being.

This spectrum of deviation from patriarchal ideals represented by conduct writers can be placed alongside the even more varied range of social practice adopted by spouses. Conduct writers were ambivalent about the degree to which wives should exercise authority as joint or deputy governors of their households, but it is clear that in economic matters wives performed essential functions to keep households afloat (in contradiction to the neat gendered division of labour envisaged by Dod and Cleaver). Pragmatism and patriarchy were not always compatible. While in agricultural settings there was a greater spatial division of work, in both urban and rural settings there were many occasions on which spouses were necessarily interchangeable. Depending on local labour markets and the social status of the couple, husbands and wives might be involved in joint enterprise, contribute wage labour or establish a 'double business household'.[6] It is becoming increasingly evident that marriage (rather than widowhood), far from diminishing their economic agency, was the point at which women undertook more varied and independent forms of work, and that wives' participation was essential to the provision of their households and a contributory factor to the economic growth discernible from the early seventeenth century.[7] Despite a hostile legal context, in which women's trading rights and property ownership were curtailed by common-law dictates of 'coverture' (which assigned both marital property and liability for household debts to husbands), many wives nimbly took advantage of all available legal loopholes, undertaking wage labour and a wide range of productive enterprise, providing many services, and being responsible for a good deal of marketing. This was not simply craftily connived resistance (although there are certainly examples of wives undertaking clandestine measures to divert resources from their husband's control), but often part of carefully worked-out spousal strategies to maximise resources and diversify risk. It has even been hypothesised that an increase in wives' commercial production and wage labour contributed to an 'industrious revolution' from the mid seventeenth century that was a necessary precursor to industrialisation, and it is clear that in urban contexts at the very least married women's productive capacity remained significant into the nineteenth-century despite a growing discursive emphasis on female domesticity and separate spheres.[8] This does not, of course, mean that women and men enjoyed equal access to resources or economic opportunities. It does, however, debunk assumptions of female economic dependence, and it points to the necessity of a gender-inclusive approach to early modern economic development.

That marital relations figured so centrally in early modern social commentary is reflective of the importance of marital status in shaping gendered agency. Just as marriage involved the negotiation of authority and divisions of labour between spouses, so it was founded on varied forms of differentiation within each sex. Especially for women, age (and for many the associated marital status) figured prominently in establishing profound divisions, creating a 'gulf' between the 'never married' and 'ever married'.[9] Unmarried women were expected to remain firmly under the authority of their married counterparts, either in service or within their household of origin. While most young men were also temporarily denied the 'patriarchal dividends' associated with heading a household and governing others within, they nonetheless enjoyed a far greater degree of tolerance when they departed from the normative codes of behaviour expected of them with flamboyant displays of what might be described as 'anti-patriarchal' masculinity. Old age appears to have carried greater burdens and stigma for women than for men. Social status additionally contributed to distinctions within each sex, restricting the extent to which the growing population of labouring men from the early seventeenth century could aspire to normative manhood, and contributing in the longer term to the articulation of distinct working-class identities.[10] The patriarchal order was therefore founded on several axes of difference, the conjunction of which could create (and depended upon) substantial pockets of agency for some women as well as the subordination of some men, no matter how great the emphasis on the general principle of male privilege.

## The Gendered Body

Male privilege was equally central to, yet also complicated by, early modern approaches to the body. The social roles ascribed to men and women were underpinned by notions of what we would call 'biological determinism', albeit based on very different understandings of bodily difference. In the sixteenth and seventeenth centuries, a 'one-sex' model dominated medical theory. With roots in the ancient world, it was a product of humoral theory that originated with the Greek philosopher Hippocrates (460–371 BCE) but that was most commonly associated with the Roman physician Galen (130–200 CE). According to humoral theory, human bodies – like all matter – were composed of the four elements (air, water, earth and fire). These elements corresponded to the four humours represented in the body as blood, phlegm, black bile and yellow bile, and the balance of these four humours determined a person's temperament in relation to the combination of qualities associated with each of the humours. Different conjunctions of qualities – hotness, dryness, moistness and coldness – produced the temperamental characteristics labelled as sanguine, phlegmatic, melancholic and choleric. Humoral theory provided the framework for understanding illness and health, the temperamental differences among people, and the anatomical differences between men and women. Like most things in early modern culture, humoral differences were understood in hierarchical terms. Heat and moisture were life-giving, while coldness and dryness were life-sapping. When contrasted with women, men were characterised by their superior qualities of heat and dryness, whereas women were relatively cold and wet.

Humoral theory lent weight to male privilege in many ways. Men's claims to a superior rational capacity, for example, found justification in their humoral endowment with greater heat than women. By contrast, women were represented as victims of their cold, moist qualities, which rendered them sluggish, in thrall to their passions, and lacking control of their bodies. Men's aptitude for bodily self-government was one of the justifications for their advantageous political position. Men's capacity for self-control licensed them to control others – as household heads and in positions of wider authority. Analogies between the household and the state that elided kingship with 'fatherly rule', as well as metaphors that represented government in terms of taming the body politic, all proceeded from logic that gendered reason as male. More particularly, humoral theory provided an explanation for the anatomical variation between men and women. The premise of the 'one-sex' model was genital homology: that is, men and women possessed the *same genitals*. The anatomical basis of gender difference, then, was merely that men's genitals were on the outside, whereas women's reproductive organs remained inside their bodies. The vagina, ovaries and womb corresponded to the penis, testicles and scrotum. In fact, no distinct term existed for ovaries until the eighteenth century, before which point they were referred to as female testicles. Derived from Galen's *On the Usefulness of the Parts of the Body*, and circulated in diverse medical and anatomical tracts, the representation of male and female genitals as essentially the same, just differently located, was commonplace. Once again, it was heat that distinguished men above women. The womb, vagina and female testicles (ovaries) were an imperfect version of male genitalia because women lacked sufficient heat to push them out of their bodies.

Despite assumptions of male superiority, gender difference as medically categorised in terms of degree rather than kind was inherently unstable, admitting potentially fluid boundaries between the sexes. The consequent possibilities were sensationalised in stories recounting the sudden transformation of women into men, often following a moment of intense exertion that generated sufficient heat to push their inverted genitalia out of their bodies. Fears arising from notions of bodily mutability and the insecure boundary between female and male have been cited by some historians as a source of male anxiety in the early modern period. (Tellingly, this has not been explored as a cause of concern for early modern women.) Perhaps more profound, however, were assumptions that women were naturally sexually voracious and that sexual pleasure was necessary to their health and well-being. Unmarried women were deemed vulnerable to 'greensickness', a set of symptoms arising from an unfulfilled sexual appetite. Whether or not women experienced greater sexual pleasure than men was also the subject of learned medical theorising as well as popular debate. In a more sinister branch of thought, female sexuality was accorded dangerous potency in early modern witchcraft beliefs. More routinely, the female 'chastity' on which a successful marriage depended, in terms of a wife's exclusive sexual relations with her husband, hinged on her spouse's capacity to satisfy her desires, and a man could be vulnerable to humiliation if deemed incapable of taming his wife's lust.

Depictions of women as the lustier sex can be linked to reproductive theories that assumed that female as well as male orgasm was necessary for conception. Another product of Galenic notions of genital homology, the representation of conception in these terms reflected the parity between male and female testicles, both of which were assumed to produce 'seed', which then commingled to create an embryo. The Galenic version of the 'one-sex' model was therefore associated with a 'two-seed' theory of conception, which accorded women relative agency in the process. It contrasted with a model of conception derived from Aristotle, also in circulation in the early modern period, which ascribed generative agency to the male seed alone, depicting women's contribution in terms of providing the matter on which the male seed worked. Despite the co-existence of both theories, the Galenic version had gained greater currency among English medical writers by the end of the sixteenth century. We need to exercise caution, however, before assuming that the 'two-seed' model, with its allowance of comparable male and female pleasure and generative agency, represented a relatively favourable chapter in the history of female sexuality. We should not presume that orgasm – principally associated with the release of seed – meant the same in early modern medical discourse as it represents today in terms of a woman's experience of pleasure. Even in the Galenic model, male seed remained privileged above female seed, ascribed greater potency on account of its comparative heat, and the successful conception of an (implicitly superior) boy child was often credited to men's greater generative capacity. The gender parity implied by the 'two-seed' theory did not deliver uniform significance to generative partners, but rested on assumptions of inequality, which has led the cultural historian Patricia Simons to redub it the 'unequal two-seed theory'.[11]

The humoral economy was not meritocratic but sufficiently elastic to serve and compound the entrenched gender hierarchy. The cases of women who had apparently turned into men, or who (less sensationally) simply displayed levels of heat uncharacteristic for their sex, were not celebrated for achieving perfection but were represented as monstrosities. The ascendancy of the 'two-seed' theory during the early modern period did not preclude changes in the representation of reproductive agency that limited the role accorded to women. The civil wars that ravaged Britain in the 1640s had a significant impact on how the female body was represented in English health tracts over the course of the seventeenth century. A shift can be traced from a model of reproduction that afforded the female some agency, to the construction of conception in more masculinist terms. In response to the social and political turmoil associated with war, women's bodies were increasingly depicted in metaphorical terms as landscapes to be worked by men, such as fields to be ploughed and planted with seed, or fruit trees to be tended. And rather than being represented as the neck of the womb, the vagina became redescribed as a sheath for the penis in imagery that, it has been argued, served to reinscribe male authority after a period of social and political instability.[12]

The temptation to represent the 'one-sex' model of the body, with its associated 'two-seed' theory, in relatively positive terms has largely arisen from its significance as the backdrop in accounts of a fundamental transition in the eighteenth century to 'modern' concepts of bodily difference. In a pioneering work of cultural history, Thomas Laqueur argued that there was a fundamental turning point in western scientific discourse whereby the 'one-sex' model of gender difference was eclipsed during the eighteenth century by the ordering of men and women into two essentially 'opposite' sexes. When contrasted with the sexually passive female that Laqueur argues was a product of modernity, constructed as essentially different from the male in a biology of incommensurability, the characterisation of a shift from a 'one-sex' to a 'two-sex' model of difference in terms of its negative impact on women is undeniably beguiling – not least since it counteracts triumphalist notions of progress so often associated with the Enlightenment. The shift from a vertical ordering of male and female bodies differentiated by degree to a horizontal ordering of difference in terms of kind is attributed by Laqueur to the development of political theories of natural rights. The recasting of women as essentially different from men provided the necessary justification for their continued exclusion from the widening political arena. The denial of female sexual agency was therefore linked to the denial of female political agency.[13] Laqueur's claims have in turn been incorporated by several historians into accounts of the eighteenth century as a turning point in gender relations more generally, associated with a separation of the private and public spheres, the withdrawal of women from the workplace, and a subsequent closing down of possibilities for 'play' and overlap in gender roles.[14]

Many historians, however, have argued that early modern notions of reproductive biology, approached in terms of the 'before' to this development, have been over-simplified by Laqueur's investment in the profundity of the transition he strove to document. There are grounds for arguing that a shift towards a 'two-sex' model of bodily difference occurred much earlier than the eighteenth century. Many leading physicians were already insisting on the uniqueness of the female skeleton as well as the specificity of the female genital organs by the beginning of the seventeenth century. While such evidence does not dispute that a fundamental transition took place, it uncouples it causally from the Enlightenment, and resituates it in relation to new views of marriage and motherhood that became idealised by social elites in the wake of religious reform.

More profoundly, it is questionable whether the argument that a shift from a 'one-sex' to a 'two-sex' model is sustainable at *any point* during the early modern period in the face of contradictory evidence. If a broad source base is consulted, beyond Latin treatises for elite medical practitioners, to include genres such as erotic texts as well as regimens and health manuals for more popular consumption, representations of the gendered body become considerably more complex. A detailed study of erotica suggests that conflicting representations of sexual difference co-existed throughout the eighteenth century, which was characterised as much by persistence as by change. Entirely focused on bodies and sex, and often parodying the medical writing to which they were deeply indebted, erotic texts deployed bodily models constructed around similarity *and* difference selectively and interchangeably, depending on whether the emphasis was on pleasure or reproduction.[15] One-sex and two-sex versions of difference were not, it appears, mutually exclusive. Focusing on novelty at the expense of continuity has a distorting effect on narratives of change – a point reinforced by evidence for the longevity of humoral understandings of gender difference in popular opinion well into the nineteenth century.

Nor was the 'one-sex' model entirely watertight. Rather than a summation of a systematic theory of 'one-ness', the genital homology on which it rested was often only a starting point for more complex thinking about the bodily differences between the sexes. It served as a loose analogy, a device informing visualisation and memorisation exercises. Inclusion of references to a 'one-sex' model in a medical work did not rule out other theories, and inconsistent approaches regularly co-existed within the same treatise. James I's physician, Helkiah Crooke, for example, produced an encyclopedic work on the body that drew eclectically on a range of works representing several traditions.[16] Despite including images of generative homology, Crooke also questioned its basis by noting the many anatomical differences between men and women. Women do not have a prostate; the vagina is structurally different from the penis, and Crooke suggested that accounts of vaginas converting to penises through inversion were not credible. Discussions emphasising difference became more pronounced from the sixteenth century, as medical writers became more preoccupied with the newly 'discovered' clitoris and as gynaecology developed as an increasingly distinct branch of medicine.

Notwithstanding the commonplace inclusion of genital homology as a starting point for discussion of reproductive processes, medical writing more generally took a utero-centric approach to the female body that lacked any sustained male equivalent. Uterine disorders were accorded enormous influence over women's health and well-being more generally in medical discussion ranging well beyond reproductive issues. The assessment of women's mental health, for example, involved speculation about 'wandering wombs', a notion of uterine displacement that jeopardised women's entire bodily capacity. Menstrual irregularities were also deemed to have severe consequences for women's health in general. The assessment of reproductive functioning was much more central to appraisals of female than of male well-being. Reproductive capacity also undoubtedly loomed much larger in female rather than male embodied experience at a time when the majority of women spent as much as a third of their adult lives pregnant, when childbirth carried relatively high risks of maternal mortality, and when anxieties about controlling fertility abounded. For all the apparent parity between the uterus and the scrotum in models of genital homology, it must have been crushingly obvious to early modern people that the uterus exercised an influence on female health and the female life-cycle without any male parallel.

By contrast, in the representation of male sexual function, early modern authors adopted a 'semen-centric' framework. This is suggestive of a more profound difference between early modern and modern approaches to sexual difference than apparently represented by the one-sex and two-sex models of the gendered body. In a post-Freudian age, phallo-centric approaches to bodily difference have become the norm, and have arguably produced anachronistic assessments of pre-modern mindsets. As Patricia Simons has recently argued, the primary source of male virility in early modern culture was the *seed* or semen located in the testicles, not the phallus. Not without considerable significance, the penis nonetheless derived its potency as the delivery system for seed rather than in its own right. It was male seed, not sex per se, that was accorded healing properties in the treatment of 'greensick' women. Whereas the uterus was accorded primacy in discussions of the female body, the testicles – not the penis – occupied prime position in approaches to the male body, not just in medical writing but in broader cultural representations of male fertility more generally.[17]

Such arguments serve as a caution against adopting an anachronistically phallo-centric approach to early modern concepts of the gendered body, focusing exclusively on shifting explanations regarding genital anatomy and more particularly the presence/absence of a penis. Not only was the penis arguably accorded secondary importance in early modern culture compared with the testicles; the gendered differences associated with humoral theory also concerned a far broader range of attributes than genital anatomy. Facial hair, for example, was another central signifier of adult masculinity, similarly attributed to men's greater levels of heat. Heat pushed beards from male bodies, just as it made some men bald by forcing out the hair (understood as a form of excretion) from their heads. Facial hair not only established anatomical markers differentiating men from women, it also separated men from boys. Beards were associated with the social roles of fathering and soldiering, as well as with male wisdom, and they also functioned to signify a man's generative capacity. On the basis of the distinction lent to adult males by beards, Will Fisher has argued that boys, in fact, constituted a 'third gender' in early modern England.[18]

The categorisation of boys as a separate gender from men perhaps takes the significance of other anatomical markers a step too far. Boys shared some aspects of maleness with adult men, at the very least in anticipation of their maturation which led to their treatment as incipient men. The ritual practice of breeching – when boys around the age of seven discarded the petticoats worn by children of both sexes in order to assume specifically male attire that distinguished them from girls – was but one manifestation of expectations that placed them firmly on the pathway to adult masculinity. That boys appearing on stage could don false beards in order to play the man, as well as dresses to assume female roles, is suggestive of the fluidity of gender identities for young males rather than their fixity in terms of a separate category. Attending to the distinction between men and boys, however, nonetheless serves as an important reminder that humoral theory contributed as much to the elaboration of difference *within* the male sex as to the differences between men and women.

Medical theorists actually devoted more attention to the differences separating men than those distinguishing male from female. Medical writers normally assumed a male body as their subject, only rarely introducing explicitly gendered comparisons of men and women, usually inspired by the more specific discussion of conception and reproduction. The ideal male body, therefore, was most commonly imagined through comparisons with other kinds of men rather than in discussions of the differences between the sexes. Humoral theory was preoccupied as much with the *temperamental* differences among men as with the *anatomical* differences between men and women. The assumption of a male norm meant that the elaboration of the temperate ideal – the perfectly balanced body – proceeded through a series of comparisons with male deviations from it. Whereas men's superior capacity for rational self-control, for example, was straightforwardly claimed in male–female contrasts, the male ideal of reasoned self-governance unravelled in medical discussions of the many difficulties associated with achieving the requisite temperate moderation.

Men's superior propensity for bodily control was therefore repeatedly represented as being under threat from humoral imbalance associated not only with temperamental differences but also with age, diet, climate and environment, as well as the extremes of emotion produced by falling in love or experiences of grief, for example. Levine Lemnius, a Dutch physician, whose works circulated in Latin and in translation across Europe in the sixteenth and seventeenth centuries, elaborated many of the consequent dangers in his *Touchstone of Complexions*, which was first published in Antwerp in 1561, and which circulated in at least three English editions between 1576 and 1633. Lemnius depicted men's bodies as being in constant flux, and emphasised the difficulties associated with achieving the perfectly balanced temperate ideal. Age disqualified young men on the grounds of their surfeit of heat and moisture, which incited them to hasty, impetuous and lustful behaviour, and old men on account of their lack of heat and moisture, which rendered them weak, cautious and lacking vigour. Manhood itself – the pinnacle of the life-cycle during which men were most capable of achieving humoral balance – was restricted to a mere fifteen-year period between the ages of thirty-five and fifty. Even adult masculinity, however, was no guarantor of the bodily ideal, owing to men's temperamental differentiation. A hierarchy of 'complexions' divided men according to their humoral categorisation simply as hot, dry, cold or moist, or in compound form as sanguine, choleric, melancholic or phlegmatic. A hot complexion was deemed the healthiest, manifested by a hairy body and a courageous temperament, and was associated by Lemnius with 'manly dignity', whereas men with a cold complexion were represented as defective. Fat and sluggish, cold men possessed 'faltering tongues, and nothing ready in utterance, a nice, soft, and womanish voice, weake, and feeble faculties of nature, ill memory, blockish wit, doltish minde, courage (for lacke of heat and slendernesse of vitall spirit) fearefull and timorous, and at the wagging of every straw afraid'. Additionally portrayed as 'sleepy, slothfull, weaklings, [and] meycockes', such men were condemned by Lemnius as 'not apt nor able to beget any children'.[19]

The humoral differentiation of male bodies in such terms also proceeded along ethnic lines, traditionally attributed to the effect of climate on national character, and increasingly serving the incipient racial stereotyping attendant on colonial expansion in the British Atlantic world and on trading relations further afield. Humoral theory provided the justification for categorising indigenous men as either voraciously over-sexed or pathetically effeminate, and cultural encounters in the 'New World' no doubt contributed to the growing categorisation of men in terms of their sexual inclinations. Humoral theory thereby validated the superiority of European men, while also serving hierarchies of masculinity among them, implicitly eliding the characteristics of a hot or sanguine temperament with the attributes of social elites that no doubt established a satisfying set of norms with which the gentry readers of such texts could identify. However, the elaboration of humoral theory was nonetheless replete with images of men's bodily failings, with admissions that some men lacked the heat necessary to achieve manhood, while others lacked the ability to control it, undermining the claims made for men's powers of rational discretion and betraying expectations that not all men were capable of achieving the bodily control expected of them. When uncoupled from explicitly gendered comparisons, men's bodies (like women's bodies) were unpredictable, fluid and difficult to command.

The relationship between such representations of bodily mutability and men's experiences of masculinity is difficult to gauge. It might credibly be argued that the male bodily instability conceded by humoral theory was a further source of acute anxiety for at least some early modern men who may have felt insufficiently in control of their bodies or unable to match the physical expectations of manliness. There is some evidence, however, that some of the chaos associated with embodied masculinity – the bloodshed, vomiting, pissing and ejaculation – was actively celebrated in the riotous rituals that were vividly threaded through fraternal youth culture and that could also unite adult males. While the idealisation of the vigorous yet rationally self-governed man that proceeded through derision of the weak, soft and 'womanish' deviant clearly served hierarchies among men as well as the gender hierarchy, it is important to avoid creating false equivalences between these two forms of hierarchical ordering, not least since it was a function of male privilege that differences between men were so heavily elaborated. Gender saturated the representation of women, who tended to be lumped together as a sex, constructed in terms of the extent to which they differed from a male norm. Men, on the other hand, far from being reduced to their sex, could be represented in terms of the infinite variety of humankind. The representation of cold men as womanish also served to restate expectations of male superiority, which were not at all undermined by discussions that questioned the capacity of *all* men to achieve the ideal that was automatically assumed in male/female comparisons. Just as the early modern emphasis on female sexual agency should not inspire undue celebration, so we should remain cautious about the extent to which we depict men as the victims of early modern medical thinking. Irreducible to the 'one-sex' model, early modern models of gendered embodiment were profoundly shaped by patriarchal inflection. While involving potentially crippling distinctions among men, the consequent hierarchies of masculinity were firmly coupled to, and indeed served, more general assumptions that men were the superior sex.

## Sex and Sexuality

Medical representations of the gendered body entailed numerous assumptions about normative sexual behaviour associated with men and women's desire for each other. Generalising about sexuality in the past is notoriously difficult because of the partial quality of the available evidence on which we must base our conclusions. Quotidian sexual practices left little documentation. Samuel Pepys's coded allusions to sexual improprieties in the diary he kept in the 1660s were unusual in an age in which the confessional practices associated with diary keeping were in their infancy and highly socially restricted. Most of our evidence of sexual behaviour comes from disciplinary records kept by various jurisdictions that were empowered to punish sex and even speech about sex that occurred beyond prescribed boundaries. Charting the *regulation* of sex, while instructive, does not amount to the recovery of early modern sexual practices, licit or illicit. There are grounds nonetheless for investigating whether certain important changes took place in the regulation of sexual behaviour and the construction of sexual identities over the course of the early modern period.

According to the Christian morality that dominated approaches to sex until the later seventeenth century, having received renewed emphasis in the wake of the Reformation's focus on marriage as one of its battlegrounds, sexual relations outside marriage and without procreative potential were deemed sinful. The extent to which such prescriptions were taken seriously by those with prosecuting powers appears to have varied among places and over time, and often entailed different consequences for women and men. Pre-marital sexual relations appear to have been subject to harsher regulation from the later sixteenth century in Church courts, local borough courts and regional quarter sessions. That proscriptions against pre-marital sex had some impact on behaviour is suggested by the decline in illegitimacy ratios between the later sixteenth and the mid-seventeenth century, during which period there was also a reduction in the proportion of brides whose pregnancy at marriage can be confirmed from the timing of the subsequent baptism of their first child. Whether such trends, and their regional variation, should be related either to a more widespread internalisation of restrictive codes of sexual behaviour or to greater regulative zeal on the part of parish officials and those informing them (or both) is more debateable. It is also impossible to discern the extent to which heightened vigilance surrounding pre-marital sex was a product of hostile economic circumstances (rather than deepening piety) that were making it harder for young men and women to be confident of attaining the economic independence necessary for marriage, which in turn meant pre-marital pregnancy carried far greater risks of the economic burdens of illegitimacy. This did not, however, dampen expectations of sexual compatibility that informed judgements about a good 'match', since sexual pleasure retained its significance as one of the foundations of a stable marriage. To this end, the ritual of 'bundling' was customary in some regions, whereby future partners simulated a night in bed together (with each appropriately 'bundled' to restrict improper access) in order to confirm their suitability as partners. Rather than depending on repressive mechanisms associated with models of female sexual passivity, the containment of extra-marital sexual activity proceeded through communal vigilance of appropriate boundaries. At a time when long periods of sexual abstinence were theoretically demanded by a relatively late age at first marriage and a relatively high proportion of the population never marrying, female bodies were particularly vulnerable to the regulative touch of older women as well as to the predatory sexual advances of men.

As we have already seen, sexual desire on the part of women as well as men was readily admitted. However, the consequences of illicit sex between men and women were often much graver for the latter. Most obviously, the risks of an illegitimate birth were higher for women than for men, even if justices of the peace could and occasionally did require putative fathers of 'bastard' children to shoulder the practical as well as financial burdens of care. Mothers of illegitimate offspring were more likely to experience childbirth as a punitive ritual than their married counterparts, threatened with divine judgement against their unborn infant, and denied help by midwives and matrons until they had confessed its father's identity. Fathers of illegitimate children often sought to escape public responsibility for their offspring when they had sufficient resources and inclination to remain unburdened. One Norfolk curate even attempted to 'suffer' a boy who was only seven or eight years old 'to answere' for the illegitimate child the curate was suspected of fathering.[20] While some nonetheless privately acknowledged some pecuniary liability, others managed to flee or evade accountability altogether, sometimes enabled by the patronage of other men, and sometimes through exploiting their own position of authority to pass the blame. Stories of male servants being framed for the sexual exploits of their masters, often involving a fellow maidservant, abounded in litigation over disputed paternity. The options available to both men and women faced with illegitimate parenthood were therefore socially varied, depending on age and status as well as gender, but the physical realities of pregnancy, childbirth and (for many) feeding an infant must have served to confirm assumptions that the women concerned were much less likely than the men ever to shed the identity of a 'bastard-bearer'.

More generally, women in early modern England were vulnerable to the rich language of insult that labelled them as whores, 'jades' or 'queans', which lexicon was another manifestation of a deeply rooted double standard that rendered women more culpable for (hetero-)sexual licentiousness. Although the use of such labels was highly complex, and did not always function as a direct comment on a woman's sexual morality, the fact that there was no comparable term for a man is instructive. Men might be discredited as 'whoremongers', and later as 'libertines', but there was no explicit label to refer to a man who contravened expectations that sex should be contained within marriage. Such a divergent approach might be part of the explanation for why the prosecution of rape was relatively rare, and why convictions were largely restricted to cases in which the victim was a child. In terms of the labels attached to illicit sex between men and women, the most potent parallel for a man was to be stereotyped as a cuckold. Suspected cuckolds were subject to ridicule and some became targets of 'skimmingtons', which brought public humiliation through rough music, the parading of horns (the symbol of the cuckold) and effigies of befuddled husbands facing backwards on a horse. Such shaming rituals served to comment as much on the behaviour of a man's wife as on his failure to govern her, and derived some of their power from the fact that 'whore' was the most recognisable category of sexual deviance.

Women's adulterous behaviour was for the most part therefore treated much more seriously than men's in a further manifestation of the sexual double standard. Just as men were less likely to shoulder the burdens of illegitimacy than women, husbands also appear to have enjoyed more sexual licence than wives, with less at stake if discovered. Married men were much less likely than married women to seek legal redress against defamatory accusations of sexual wrong-doing. Wives who sought formal separation from a husband had a greater chance if they could prove his cruelty in addition to his infidelity, whereas husbands were better able to justify a suit for separation on the grounds of a wife's adultery alone. While moral commentary on adultery condemned it in either sex, reaching a fever pitch in the mid seventeenth century with the passage of legislation prescribing the death penalty for adulterers 'as well the man as the woman', the extent to which it exercised a prohibitive influence on men's behaviour is questionable.[21] The limits of moral discourse condemning sexual licence became increasingly evident from the later seventeenth century, alongside a sustained decline in formal regulative activity, albeit briefly punctuated by local campaigns for the 'reformation of manners'. As a 'culture of discipline' receded in the wake of religious toleration, Faramerz Dabhoiwala has argued that a 'sexual revolution' ushered in modern attitudes towards consensual sex between adult men and women as a matter of private conscience rather than public morality.[22] Approaches to adultery as a sin that universally threatened communal well-being gave way to a diversity of opinion that even included the celebration of adulterous behaviour by elite men as a form of gallantry, a shift aided by an expansion of print culture that sensationalised lurid details of cases of 'criminal conversation' whereby wronged husbands pursued their wives' lovers for substantial pecuniary damages in court. Such trends depended on shifting sexual norms, whereby female sexuality was recast in terms of passivity, requiring protection from the naturally predatory impulses assigned to men who were more definitively represented as the lustier sex. Whether all this constituted a revolutionary sexual 'liberty' (as Dabhoiwala has claimed), certainly for any beyond the propertied elite, remains questionable.

When *same-sex* relations were concerned, however, it was men rather than women who were at greater risk of both prosecution and, in a few cases, stigmatisation. This did not, though, rule out a far higher degree of tacit acceptance of sexual relations between men than of ('heterosexual') behaviour deemed to compromise female chastity. Sodomy was a capital offence in early modern England, and great symbolic significance attached to the image of the sodomite who was represented as a harbinger of disorder, corruption and divine wrath. Accusations of sodomy punctuated the anti-clericalism of Protestant propaganda, for example, which routinely represented the pope and Satan as sexual partners. Yet despite, and indeed perhaps because of, such negative imagery and the harsh penalties attached to penetrative sex between men, same-sex relations were arguably a routine part of male interaction, particularly in all-male settings such as schools and universities. Provided sexual behaviour between men was structured by hierarchies of age, which dictated a passive role for adolescents and an active, penetrative, part for adult males, it met with little resistance. This mismatch between the damning image of the sodomite and more permissive attitudes towards men's same-sex relations is in line with Foucault's assertion that the conceptualisation of sexuality as a category of identity is a distinctly modern phenomenon. Norms of 'heterosexuality' and its implied opposite 'homosexuality' were a product of nineteenth-century medical discourse, and, according to Foucault, were preceded by approaches to sex as a range of *acts* to which anyone might be drawn rather than as the foundation for differentiating between fixed *identities*.[23] Same-sex behaviour between men did not therefore preclude sexual relations between the men involved and women. The image of the sodomite derived its potency as a symbol of systematic depravity rather than as a category of sexual identity. The second earl of Castlehaven, for example, one of the few men actually prosecuted for sodomy in early modern England, was condemned as much for his failure to govern himself and his household in proper patriarchal fashion as for his specific indulgence in a range of extra-marital sexual practices that included rape as well as buggery.[24]

While the *potential* for very harsh treatment existed (and was occasionally applied), it appears that in practice the negative stereotype of the sodomite impinged less on the behaviour of men than the more damning figure of the whore shaped the possibilities available to women. For the most part, especially when approached in terms of acts, rather than as symptomatic of alternative identities, men's same-sex relations were an accepted part of a wider fraternal culture that tolerated and even expected a degree of intimacy between men that could rival conjugal ties. Ranging from the collective bonding characteristic of men's homosocial relations that facilitated fleeting bodily intimacy, to the longer-term partnerships that bound certain men together for the best part of their lives, homoerotic relations between men defied neat categorisation and met with varied responses. The concept of friendship was as important as the categorisation of sexual intimacy to the ways in which early modern people made sense of relationships between men. Friendship was celebrated as equivalent to marriage and kinship. Friends were mates, second selves and other halves. It was the reverence inspired by ideals of friendship that gave dignity to the long-term partnerships of certain men who chose to commemorate their relationships through joint burial. The monument to Sir John Finch and Sir Thomas Baines, for example, erected in Christ's College, Cambridge, celebrated their life-long partnership – described by Finch as a 'marriage of souls' – with reference to conjugal imagery that placed the depth of feeling between them on a par with marital intimacy.[25]

However much the idealisation of 'entire' friendship in such terms usually imagined relationships between men, women also pursued comparable emotional attachments as well as a range of behaviours that might usefully be described as 'lesbian-like' – in terms of departing from heteronormative expectations rather than reductively tied to the specifics of same-sex relations.[26] The tomb of Mary Kendall in Westminster Abbey, dated 1710, commemorates the 'close Union & Friendship, In which she liv'd with The Lady Catherine Jones' and Kendall's desire that 'even their Ashes, after Death, Might not be divided'. The figure of the 'female husband' was readily imaginable in early modern culture, providing the subject of a play by Henry Fielding (1746) and of numerous tales of women who 'passed' as soldiers or sailors. Court records detailing a marriage breakdown involving two women in London in 1680, as well as letters documenting romantic friendships between women who referred to each other as spouses, are further suggestive of a relatively flexible approach to concepts of conjugal relations. Such flexibility made for a complicated relationship between sexual acts and identities, which defy neat plotting on a linear, chronological trajectory. Nor was it without limits. Like the figure of the sodomite, the 'tribade' – a woman with an unusually large clitoris who sought to penetrate other women – could be conjured up in condemnation of female same-sex intimacy. Women who sought sex with other women might also be represented as 'hermaphrodites', medical anomalies of indeterminate sex whose sexual organs were neither properly inside nor sufficiently out of their bodies.[27]

The relatively commonplace ordering of same-sex relations along the lines of age therefore did not preclude the existence of identities associated with same-sex desire (largely expressed as negative stereotypes) or the possibility of long-term relationships between partners of the same sex, not least because such partnerships were more likely to be characterised – and characterised positively – as symbolic of faithful friendship rather than of *sexual* identities based on specific types of desire. It has nonetheless been argued that the period between 1700 and 1750 witnessed the emergence of categories of sexuality that fundamentally reordered approaches to same-sex relations. According to Randolph Trumbach, this transition was more broadly symptomatic of a shift from a 'traditional' to a 'modern' sexual system that increasingly treated sexual relations between the sexes and same-sex relations as mutually exclusive. Whereas adult men's desire for youths was traditionally treated as one of many alternatives to the only form of officially permissible sex – that is, within marriage – male–male desire became increasingly stigmatised as the characteristic of a minority of men whose sexual preferences precluded their entitlement to claim normative masculinity. Effeminacy began to take on new meanings associated with objects of sexual desire rather than deployed more generally to signify any man's lack of control over his appetite, sexual or otherwise. Most evident in London's 'molly-houses', a new sexual subculture emerged that placed 'mollies' (adult men whose sexual interests were restricted to men) in adversarial opposition to the male majority who were increasingly represented as desiring only women. This shift was mirrored by the slightly later emergence of a Sapphist identity for women who adopted masculine attributes and sought out more conventionally female partners. It may also have been accompanied by a heightened emphasis on penetrative sex and the privileging of male sexual agency in models and practices of 'heterosexual' intercourse.[28]

Growing rigidity in the categorisation of sexual desire can also be detected in the representation of prostitutes and in responses to cultural encounters with indigenous peoples in the wider world. The representation and treatment of prostitutes increasingly set them apart from other women. Partly a product of concerns about syphilis, and associated with the expansion of state-sponsored regulation, prostitution was gradually criminalised. As a result the prostitute's body was demarcated as essentially different, thereby separating her from other women. Categorising the differences that separated Europeans from non-European 'others' also involved the delineation of fixed sexual identities. Native American 'berdaches', for instance, who dressed and behaved as if they were women, were represented by European observers as effeminate sodomites, exclusively penetrated by other men. The cultures of China, India and the Ottoman empire were portrayed as sexually degenerate, while African men were characterised as hypersexual. Deviant sexualities, not just sexual acts, were readily attributed to non-Europeans in ways that are likely to have informed metropolitan understandings of sexual norms. A shift of emphasis from acts to identities was therefore at least partly born of the processes of differentiation inspired by global influence.

Just as a clear-cut shift from a 'one-sex' to a 'two-sex' model of the body is debateable, so a linear transition whereby sexual acts were superseded by sexual identities risks being over-schematic. This is especially the case if a search for coherent sexualities focuses anachronistically on identities that are recognisably modern rather than the sexual identities that may have resonated for early modern people. This is not to rule out fundamental changes in approaches to the gendered body and sexual relations over the course of the early modern period, but to recognise both their complexity and their partial character. Sex and gender were ever-present categories in early modern thought: of central importance in their own right; shaping hierarchies between men and women as well as within each sex; and threaded through the articulation of an infinite variety of differences founded on confessional identity, race and ethnicity, and informing the conceptualisation of power. Sex and gender were also embodied experiences, producing as well as reflecting understandings of difference in ways that require greater accommodation in our narratives of change.

## Notes

1 L. Roper, 'Beyond discourse theory', *Women's History Review*, 19:2 (2010).
2 B. Capp, *When Gossips Meet: Women, Family and Neighbourhood in Early Modern England* (Oxford: Oxford University Press, 2003), 3–14.
3 J. Bennett, *History Matters: Patriarchy and the Challenge of Feminism* (Manchester: Manchester University Press, 2006), Chapter 4.
4 J. Dod and R. Cleaver, *A Godlie Forme of Householde Government* (London, 1612), 167–8.
5 F. Lenton, *Characterismi; or, Lentons Leasures* (London, 1631), sig. B9; W. Gouge, *Of Domesticall Duties* (London, 1622), 286.
6 A. L. Erickson, 'Married women's occupations in eighteenth-century London', *C&C*, 23:2 (2008), 276.
7 J. Whittle, 'Enterprising widows and active wives: Women's unpaid work in the household economy of early modern England', *History of the Family*, 19:3 (2014); A. Shepard, 'Crediting women in the early modern English economy', *HWJ*, 79:1 (Spring 2015).
8 J. de Vries, *The Industrious Revolution: Consumer Behaviour and the Household Economy, 1650 to the Present* (Cambridge: Cambridge University Press, 2008).
9 L. Gowing, 'Ordering the body: Illegitimacy and female authority in seventeenth-century England', in M. J. Braddick and J. Walter (eds.), *Negotiating Power in Early Modern Society: Order, Hierarchy and Subordination in Britain and Ireland* (Cambridge: Cambridge University Press, 2001), 61; J. M. Bennett and A. M. Froide, 'A singular past', in J. M. Bennett and A. M. Froide (eds.), *Singlewomen in the European Past 1250–1800* (Philadelphia: University of Pennsylvania Press, 1999).
10 A. Shepard, *Meanings of Manhood in Early Modern England* (Oxford: Oxford University Press, 2003).

11 P. Simons, *The Sex of Men in Premodern Europe: A Cultural History* (Cambridge: Cambridge University Press, 2011), 142.

12 M. Fissell, 'Gender and generation: Representing reproduction in early modern England', *Gender & History*, 7:3 (1995).

13 T. Laqueur, *Making Sex: Body and Gender from the Greeks to Freud* (Cambridge, MA: Harvard University Press, 1990).

14 R. B. Shoemaker, *Gender in English Society 1650–1850: The Emergence of Separate Spheres?* (London: Longman, 1998); D. Wahrman, *The Making of the Modern Self: Identity and Culture in Eighteenth-Century England* (New Haven and London: Yale University Press, 2004).

15 K. Harvey, 'The substance of sexual difference: Change and persistence in representations of the body in eighteenth-century England', *Gender & History*, 14: 2 (2002).

16 H. Crooke, *Microcosmographia: A Description of the Body of Man* (London, 1615).

17 Simons, *Sex of Men*, Chapter 4.

18 W. Fisher, 'The Renaissance beard: Masculinity in early modern England', *Renaissance Quarterly*, 54: 1 (2001).

19 L. Lemnius, *The Touchstone of Complexions Expedient and Profitable for All such as be Desirous and Carefull of their Bodily Health*, trans. Thomas Newton (London, 1633), 61, 97, 104, 130.

20 Norfolk Record Office, DN/DEP30/32, fols. 54v–55v.

21 *An Act for Suppressing the Detestable Sins of Incest, Adultery and Fornication* (1650).

22 F. Dabhoiwala, *The Origins of Sex: A History of the First Sexual Revolution* (London: Penguin, 2013).

23 M. Foucault, *The History of Sexuality*, 3 vols. (New York: Pantheon, 1978–88).

24 C. B. Herrup, *A House in Gross Disorder: Sex, Law, and the 2nd Earl of Castlehaven* (Oxford: Oxford University Press, 1999).

25 A. Bray, *The Friend* (Chicago: University of Chicago Press, 2003).

26 Bennett, *History Matters*, Chapter 6.

27 L. Gowing, 'Lesbians and Their Like in Early Modern Europe, 1500–1800', in R. Aldrich (ed.), *Gay Life and Culture: A World History* (London: Thames & Hudson, 2006).

28 R. Trumbach, 'From age to gender, c. 1500–1750: From the adolescent male to the adult effeminate body', in S. Toulalan and K. Fisher (eds.), *The Routledge History of Sex and the Body 1500 to the Present* (London: Routledge, 2013).

# 16

# The English and 'Others' in England and Beyond

*Alison Games*

The English set themselves in opposition to a variety of European 'others' with the ebb and flow of European politics: first the Spanish in the sixteenth century, then the Dutch in the seventeenth century and finally the French in the eighteenth century. This protracted European quadrille coincided with a conceptual shift from a world divided between Christians and 'infidels', as Christians dubbed Muslims, to one of Christians and 'heathens', or 'savages', or 'pagans', as Europeans labelled the people they encountered in this era in America, Africa and Asia. England's global transition in these centuries created the conditions that defined English interactions with people around the world. Between 1500 and 1750 the English confronted an increasing number and variety of non-English people within and beyond England because of three factors: national consolidation, commercial and territorial expansion, and continental wars and the Protestant refugees they displaced. National consolidation shoved English, Welsh, Scots and Irish into sometimes uncomfortable proximity. Global expansion and continental warfare brought distant people to England, as refugees, traders, diplomats, slaves and curiosities, while hundreds of thousands of English people travelled overseas, as soldiers, mariners, traders and colonists, and as a result found themselves in face-to-face encounters with a wide array of foreign people. There were new spaces for interactions with others, and new kinds of others to be met. Places like the American continents, barely grasped in 1500, had become by 1750 both alluring places of settlement and cultural cauldrons where the English lived embroiled with other Britons, continental Europeans, Africans and Amerindians. These encounters produced new people, children of mixed race, whose existence fostered the emergence of new categories and laws to legislate as 'other' those children born of English parents in English domains.

Four trends have distinguished historical scholarship on 'others.' Firstly, scholars have tended to study these populations as discrete groups, exploring English interactions with single ethnic communities. One by-product of this attention to single populations is a tendency among some scholars to make claims for the exemplary 'otherness' of the population under study.[1] Edited compendiums on multiple populations compensate in some respects for this tradition of discrete historical enquiry, as do studies of single places, whether cities or colonies, with varied inhabitants.[2] A second important trend has been an emphasis on London. Both historical and literary scholars have tended to focus on the capital, historians because the city has some of the best extant sources and contained such large and significant foreign communities; literary scholars because of their concern with metropolitan culture produced in and for English consumers.[3] How the English reacted to strangers in other locales within England, especially in rural areas, is more difficult to discern, and is a fertile area for future research.

Thirdly, historians interested in the English and 'others' have for the most part focused on single geographic regions. Scholarship on 'alien' and 'stranger' communities in England, for example, rarely intersects with scholarship on the English beyond England (in Europe, Asia, Africa or the Americas); on stranger communities and non-English inhabitants in English territory overseas (in the British colonies of North America and the West Indies, for example); or on English interactions with the Welsh, Scots and Irish inhabitants of the British Isles. These separate treatments make it difficult to get a sense of whom, exactly, most English people encountered, and where, and how these experiences varied. English and Scots outside England, Nabil Matar has argued, were more likely in the seventeenth century to encounter a Muslim than an Amerindian or sub-Saharan African, largely because of the extent of Mediterranean trade and travel.[4] By 1750, the most numerically common other in territory claimed by the British state was African or Amerindian. Unfortunately, historians' knowledge of others sometimes tends to be in inverse proportion to their numbers, so that the minuscule numbers of Muslims or Africans who ended up in London in the sixteenth or seventeenth centuries are more familiar to scholars than the 2 million Africans ensnared in the slave trade to British colonies during the eighteenth century. This essay integrates these diverse populations and regions. Finally, over the past four decades historians have deployed different terms to describe non-English people, looking at 'others' and at 'difference' to talk about these populations, and shifting from a language of encounters to one of interaction, all inflected by contemporary scholarly interests in such overlapping categories as gender, class, status, religion, the body and race.

## The English and Others in the British Isles

The first 'others' that most English encountered were each other. A 'foreigner' in this period meant someone alien to a given locale. Profound regional differences in attributes including dialects, building practices, agricultural customs, dress and popular beliefs (to name only a few) characterised England. So John Smyth of Nibley believed when he made a record in 1639 of phrases unique to Berkeley Hundred (Gloucestershire), and that he would not expect to hear from the lips of a 'forraigner', by which he meant someone beyond the hundred.[5] These regional particularities, however, were only some of the many markers of difference that were important within England. After Henry VIII's separation from the Roman Catholic Church, religious differences severed friends and families, meaning that the 'other' might have resided in one's own family, whether a grandparent adhering to older practices or a sibling with the zeal of a convert to one of the new Protestant paths. Many converts deliberately set themselves apart from those around them, as the Quakers did when they adopted new habits of speech and manners. Religion might provide an English dissenter with greater affinity with a non-English person, turning the ethnic 'other' into a spiritual ally. Religious minorities sometimes fled England to find more sympathetic spiritual communities abroad, as about 800 Calvinists did during the reign of Mary; or as thousands of other Protestants did in the early seventeenth century, when they established English congregations in the Low Countries; or as Catholics did, when they left England to live and study and marry on the European Continent. In the western Atlantic, English Catholics relied on non-English priests for sacraments and succour.[6]

Although these examples of localism and religious difference intimate some of the many ways in which the English perceived each other as 'other', England was also inhabited by people born outside the kingdom, many of whom were defined legally as 'aliens' or 'strangers'. English subjects did not have to look far beyond the coin of the realm to see the visage of such people, including those who belonged to ethnic groups such as the Dutch, Scots and Germans, about which the English often had strong and disparaging sentiments. Nor did they have to look beyond that coin's face to understand how lineage linked England to Europe, and how England assimilated non-English people in a wide variety of ways, whether as the head of state, an urban artisan or at the lowest rung of newly emerging racial hierarchies. Between 1500 and 1760, five foreign-born monarchs governed the kingdom and reigned for a total of 105 years, or 40 per cent of the era. James I was a Scot, James VI of that kingdom; his son, Charles I, was also born in Scotland, although raised primarily in England. William III, James I's great-grandson, the Prince of Orange, was born in Holland. The Hanoverian George I came to the throne in 1714; his German-born son George II governed until 1760. The Scots, German and Dutch monarchs reflected some of the major non-English communities found within England.

By far the largest number of 'strangers' in England were other Protestant Europeans, primarily French, Dutch and German-speaking refugees from continental conflicts. While London and other important towns had long had communities of stranger merchants, in 1550, Edward VI established a 'Strangers' Church' in London to tend to the needs of foreign Protestants. This act reflected the rising number of Protestant refugees who poured into England, escaping in most cases a combination of religious persecution, wartime dislocation and economic reverses. Throughout the Elizabethan period, London's stranger population numbered about 8,000–10,000, and by the 1590s, the total population of 'strangers' in England may have totaled 23,000–24,000.[7]

The composition of this continental migration changed between 1500 and 1750. The sixteenth century saw high levels of migration from the Low Countries; such a large flow of refugees from the tumult of the Eighty Years War that people said that one-third of the people in the provincial town of Norwich were Dutch. Between 1660 and 1700, some 50,000 French Protestants settled in England, the largest cohort of European migrants, of whom about three-quarters settled in London. Second to the French population was that of Germans. Both the Dutch and German migrants assimilated to the extent that the number of congregations serving them declined as members shifted to the Anglican Church. As aliens, all suffered a variety of disadvantages, including being unable to own real property, or inherit or pass on property; they did not have political rights, could not trade overseas in English territory, and had to pay special customs. Aliens thus faced powerful incentives to acquire the rights of natural-born Englishmen, although most newcomers remained unnaturalised. They could achieve rights through two mechanisms: naturalisation, which required a private Act of Parliament, or denization, secured through a patent, or grant, from the monarch. Naturalised subjects possessed the same rights, theoretically, as natural-born subjects, while denizens had fewer privileges, but in both instances the status enabled the alien to buy and transfer real property.[8]

While continental wars produced large stranger populations in England, internal wars and national consolidation highlighted other non-English populations: Welsh, Irish and Scots. All three populations gained legal status equal to that of English subjects in this era. The Welsh were incorporated into the kingdom with the Acts of Union between 1536 and 1543. As for the Scots, in 1608, the Court of Exchequer determined in Calvin's Case that place of birth determined nationality, and thus (in the particulars of this case) that Scots born in Scotland after 1603 were English subjects. The case had implications for the Irish, who were also considered English subjects under its provisions.[9] In England, therefore, people such as the Welsh, Irish or Scots theoretically possessed the same legal rights as the English, as long as other impediments, particularly religion, did not disqualify them.

Distinctive social and political structures and cultural norms in the Gaelic and border regions of Britain and Ireland diverged enough from English norms that English observers readily dubbed their inhabitants as wild, barbarous and in dire need of a forced dose of English civility.[10] They justified incorporation of the Welsh into the English state in the sixteenth century because they decried them as a barbarous and murderous people who required the civilising process of the state. By the seventeenth century, the English no longer regarded the Welsh as foreign, but found them highly deficient, encumbered with peculiar customs, mired in poverty, and inhabitants of a 'repellent landscape of hills and mountains'.[11] English attitudes towards Gaelic Scots and Irish when they encountered them shared many of these features, in that the English perceived both populations as similarly barbarous, but with the added complexity that the English often faced them during times of war, as part of 'civilising' missions, during invasions and conquests, and often across a barrier of religious difference and incomprehension. Conquest and colonisation shaped and deepened English pejorative assessments of the Irish, especially between 1560 and 1641, when 100,000 English and Scots emigrated to Ireland. English soldiers and colonists tended to be ardent Protestants who regarded Irish practices as incomprehensible. Fynes Moryson, who served as a colonial official there from 1600 to 1603, found nothing to admire in Ireland apart from the whiskey. Common in all of these English perceptions was a model of social progress in which barbarous people might be yanked towards civility, a settled way of life, English laws and language, commerce, and Protestantism.[12] English settlement schemes often relied on English proximity to non-English people to provide models of civility, as was tried in places as diverse as Ireland and Acadia.

Welsh, Scots and Irish migrated to England, especially, like most English migrants, to the economic engine of London. Unlike communities of continental strangers, however, they lacked an institutional focus such as a separate church. Without legal or economic barriers to their participation in the institutional and economic life of England, for example, the Welsh left little evidence of collective presence. Migration enabled boys pursuing apprenticeships in London both to assimilate and to Anglicise, especially because most served English masters. The Welsh intermarried with English in London, and they adopted English naming practices, shifting from Welsh patronymics: David ap John ap Edward was also known in London as David Jones.[13]

The extent to which the English continued to regard the Welsh – the longest-allied unit in the kingdom – as alien suggests the challenges non-English groups faced in their assimilationist goals. Sons of Welsh gentry attended English universities, where they were derided for their accents and broken speech. From 1550 to 1750, the Welsh were ridiculed in English caricatures, mockery embodied in the character of 'Poor Taffy', a Welshman so impoverished that he rode a billy goat; was too poor to afford meat, so instead dined on Welsh rarebit or rabbit (a concoction of bread and cheese); and remained encumbered by his broken English. Not until 1750 did this disparaging image of the Welsh fade, replaced instead by a more admiring view connected to the rise of Romanticism and the resulting celebration of the remote and rugged landscapes abundant in Wales.[14]

## People from beyond the Seas

People from around the world appeared in England for reasons connected primarily to overseas trade, exploration and colonisation. The earliest English voyages to North America returned with Amerindian captives and visitors, a total of 175 altogether between 1500 and 1776. Many became celebrities wherever they went, presented at court; feted by prominent political figures; their likenesses captured by engravers and painters; their activities reported in newsletters and, later, newspapers. Amerindian visitors enabled interested Englishmen to study their languages, as Thomas Hariot did at Durham House in the late sixteenth century, and to promote overseas investment. In September 1603, fascinated Londoners thronged the banks of the Thames to watch Amerindians paddle their canoe in the river. Amerindians also came to England on diplomatic missions, some with real power, others with feigned authority. 'Four Indian Kings' enjoyed a sojourn in London in 1710, causing such a commotion when they attended *Macbeth* that the players could barely proceed. For their part, Amerindian visitors hoped to gather useful information about the English, especially in the early days of English efforts to occupy North American territory. A Powhatan delegation in 1608 included one man whose purpose was 'to know our strength', Captain John Smith recalled, 'and Countries condition'.[15] This accumulated knowledge shaped indigenous responses to the English in North America. The Powhatan leader Wahunsonacock, for example, insisted in 1610 that the English in Virginia show him the respect enjoyed by the 'great werowances [or leaders] and lords in England' by bringing him a coach and horses, to enable him 'to ride and visit other great men'. So he had been told by those who had been in England.[16]

When Amerindians arrived in such small numbers, they were oddities, curiosities, their cultural differences a source of fascination, not a threat to English customs. Similarly 'rare and costly objects' were lascars, or seamen from India, who travelled to London on East India Company vessels in the early seventeenth century. As early as 1667, however, these lascars seemed less precious to enterprising merchants, who sold them to America as slaves.[17]

The trade routes and territorial aspirations that brought visitors and captives from North America and mariners from India to England also created circuits through which sub-Saharan Africans travelled. These routes were invariably linked to the slave trade. Some visitors struck English hosts and observers as elite figures, men worthy of respect because of the class status the English projected on them. Ayuba Suleiman Diallo was one such visitor. A member of an elite family from Bondu, in Senegambia, Ayuba was captured in 1731 by slave traders, who sold him to an English merchant, who in turn shipped him to Maryland. He proved a hopeless agricultural worker, unaccustomed to such labour, and needing to withdraw regularly to pray. He ran away, was captured and demonstrated his ability to write before intrigued observers, who recognised the words 'Mahommad' and 'Allah' when Ayuba spoke and concluded he was Muslim. They assisted Suleiman in writing to his father asking to be redeemed. The letter found its way into the hands of James Oglethorpe, an English MP and philanthropist, who founded the colony of Georgia for debtors and who organised Ayuba's trip to England.

During his journey Ayuba mastered English, and after he arrived in April 1733, he met Hans Sloane, who arranged his presentation before the royal family. Thanks to the interest of the Royal African Company, which hoped to expand its trade and believed Suleiman might assist them in that endeavour, Suleiman travelled to Gambia in July 1734, completing his picaresque adventure.[18]

Apart from such visitors, small numbers of Africans and people of African descent lived in England, and, like so many other aliens, they dwelled primarily in cities. By the 1770s, they numbered between 3,000 and 15,000 in London.[19] Many of the people of African descent in Britain were free; others were enslaved. Slaves in Britain were often valued as prestige goods, adorned in meticulous livery, and young boys especially were featured prominently in portraits of the era, accompanying the women who were the paintings' subjects, including in multiple works by Anthony Van Dyck. As the law shaped the experience of Britons and European strangers in England, so too did it affect the status of slaves: the 1772 Somerset decision recognised them as free on British soil. Despite the small numbers of Africans in Britain, British people encountered their images everywhere, in shop signs and on stage, in novels such as Aphra Behn's popular *Oroonoko* (1688), and on textiles and tea trays. African characters, normally detached from any plantation context, often lone figures, occasionally costumed in Amerindian headdresses, also adorned tobacco advertisements.[20]

Aside from the Irish, Scots and Welsh, all of the 'others' discussed above were primarily urban residents. English people in rural areas were likely to encounter different kinds of strangers. Most were 'foreigners', people from other parishes, who could be required under laws governing vagrancy and poor-relief to return to their home parishes. Wanderers were suspect, none more so than 'Gypsies', as they were called in that era, a people whose first documented appearance in England dates to 1504 and who composed the tail end of a diaspora from India that reached England either from the Scottish north or across the channel. The case of the Gypsies exposes three key features of English encounters with others in this era. Firstly, migratory habits demarcated 'others'. Secondly, identities could change. One could *become* a Gypsy through garb and habits. And, thirdly, English-born Gypsies posed legal problems, since these subjects could not be deported. In 1563, Parliament decreed that it was a felony to look or act like a Gypsy, a status that one could cast off by promising to reform one's ways. Their services as entertainers and helpful tinkers made Gypsies useful to the people whose towns and villages they passed through, revealing the gap between multiple laws criminalising and disdaining their conduct, and local tolerance and appreciation for their services.[21]

## The English beyond England

English experiences with non-English people in England shaped in some – but not all – ways how they made sense of those they met beyond the kingdom. Evidence from the first decades of English activity in North America, for example, suggests that the English expected Amerindians to occupy a category similar to that of the Welsh, Irish and Scots. The illustrations of Picts in the final pages of Hariot's *Brief and True Report of the new found land of Virginia* (Frankfurt, 1590) conveyed this attitude: ancient Britons had become civilised, and so too could the people of Roanoke. But in many respects experiences within England were not portable. Strangers encountered by the English at home were primarily Protestant, town-dwelling Europeans, people interested in making a new home in England or benefiting financially there. The English met these people in a position of cultural, legal and political superiority, since English laws shaped the opportunities these strangers found to forge viable economic lives for themselves.

Beyond England it was the English who had to conform to the worlds others had made. Three variables shaped this culture of accommodation: diplomatic and commercial imperatives, curiosity, and physical vulnerability. Thousands of men left England, for example, as travellers and collectors. Students on the Grand Tour learned new languages; studied law, dancing, fencing and art; and mastered different national styles of sociability.[22] Their curiosity was echoed in the exploits of collectors and scholars, who studied languages and gathered manuscripts and art and ancient artefacts for English patrons. Oxford established a chair in Arabic in the seventeenth century, a reflection of this new kind of English engagement with the eastern Mediterranean.[23]

Travellers and collectors circulated through English merchant communities overseas. Small clusters of English traders lived together in European trading centres from Moscow to Lisbon. By the beginning of the seventeenth century, new locations, with more unfamiliar cultural settings, introduced more English traders to remote places, including Algiers, Istanbul, Aleppo, Surat, Cape Coast Castle, Hirado, Bantam, Hudson's Bay and Banda.[24] Traders pursued spices, gold, fabric, furs and slaves. Foreign polities gave English trading companies formal rights (known as capitulations) that permitted them to trade. These privileges included access to commodities, the right to residence in stipulated places, freedom to trade in restricted areas, permission to worship freely (although privately) in their own faith and the retention of legal rights (for punishing their own malefactors according to English law, for example).

In some posts, English merchants lived gently and discreetly, both a part of and apart from the dominant host culture. In early-seventeenth-century Lisbon, the Inquisition required Protestant English traders to demonstrate their public respect for Catholic rituals, doffing their hats even from inside buildings as processions passed.[25] Elsewhere, the English sought to immerse themselves in the varied opportunities of foreign ports, socialising with competitors. In 1616, when the wife of the Levant Company ambassador died in Istanbul, her funeral was attended by 'Most Nations under the Sunne', including people of different faiths – Christian (Protestant, Catholic, and Eastern Orthodox), Muslim and Jewish.[26] Some traders were drawn to join these foreign societies through religious conversion: to Catholicism in some locales, to Islam in others.

English vulnerability was especially acute in the Mediterranean, the first region where the English acquired familiarity with long-distance trade. Their travels in the Mediterranean gave the English experience living as outsiders, symbolised no more vividly than at the gate of Jerusalem, that most holy city which Christians could not enter without permission. The English in the region also risked enslavement, a status perhaps 15,000 to 20,000 English endured between 1600 and 1800 thanks to the raids of pirates based in North Africa, who seized ships and crews in the Mediterranean and launched raids on the English coast by 1625.[27]

In contrast to the legal, diplomatic, commercial and cultural dynamics of trade and travel, which often required the English to accommodate local mores, English officials had greater legal authority in territories the English claimed and governed. But this legal authority was not accompanied by an uncomplicated assertion of English cultural practices, nor an easy dominion over 'others'. Instead, it was others who defined the contexts within which the English established territories in the Americas. French, Spanish and Dutch activities and aspirations dictated the location of English settlements, and above all Amerindians often determined these settlements' initial geography and economy. Even after catastrophic epidemics, Amerindians still made up the majority of most colonies, especially those vast colonies with European-imposed political borders that stretched imaginatively from the Atlantic coast to the Pacific.[28] Roanoke's history symbolises how others shaped English experiences abroad in the

1580s: the English selected Roanoke's location to facilitate preying on the Spanish silver fleet, while the disappearance of Roanoke's English settlers signalled problematic relations with Amerindians. English inhabitants in some regions depended for their prosperity on tobacco, an Amerindian plant, while another New World plant, corn, kept colonists from starvation. Almost everywhere one looked, English settlements overseas perched on and prospered from the expertise and goods of others, even as the presence of others constrained these settlements.

Although some historians have suggested that the English replicated local English customs in some regions of North America, especially in the New England colonies, others have scrutinised the variety of English people, from all over the realm, who settled in new-found proximity overseas. English people from some thirty different English counties, for example, travelled from London to New England in 1635.[29] Moreover, even those from the same English region had trouble replicating their home cultures when confronted with the varied circumstances of life overseas. Buildings in the seventeenth-century Chesapeake resembled the kinds of huts built on wasteland and commons in England rather than the housing styles of the regions from which most migrants came.[30]

English migration comprised only one of many flows of people to English territory. In the seventeenth century, about 300,000 English people migrated to the Americas, primarily as bound labourers. They were accompanied by about 20,000 to 40,000 Irish and 7,000 Scots. After 1700, this migration from the British Isles shifted, becoming less English and more British, with about 70 per cent of some 270,000 migrants either Irish or Scots. In that century, about 100,000 German-speaking people also emigrated from the European Continent to American destinations in British territory. The colonies attracted the same refugee populations that reached England, although in much smaller numbers: some 1,500 to 2,000 Huguenots settled in British America from 1680 to 1700, compared to about 20,000 to 30,000 in that same period in England.[31] Altogether, before 1750, approximately 1,305,900 Africans and approximately 562,200 Europeans emigrated, or were forcibly transported, to English – later British – territory in the western Atlantic. As these figures suggest, the challenges for the English of understanding and living with others were particularly acute beyond England itself.[32]

Britons played a significant role in overseas activity. Overseas companies were under English control for the most part, but there were exceptions: the Scot William Alexander, who received a charter for Nova Scotia from James I; the Welshman William Vaughan's settlement in Newfoundland in 1616–25; the Scots proprietors of East New Jersey in the

1680s; and the Scottish Darien Company's settlement in the Isthmus of Panama in the 1690s.[33] Scots and Irish circulated through English colonies as traders, servants, agents and soldiers. Thanks to these migration patterns, the colonies were precociously British. This heterogeneity enabled the English governor of Providence Island (off the coast of Nicaragua) to attend a feast hosted by the island's Welshmen in January 1640.

Sometimes this ethnic diversity was a direct result of colonial strategies. The Virginia Company undertook reforms in 1620 that diversified the colony's economy and its population alike, recruiting glassblowers from Italy, silk experts from France, and millwrights from Hamburg.[34] Officials also sought non-English populations to help secure their borders: so the Trustees of Georgia did, in their recruitment of Highland Scots and Salzburgers in the 1730s.[35]

In many locales, the English were actually a minority population. The few English who lived in the English colony of Montserrat in the seventeenth century were surrounded by a Gaelic-speaking Irish majority.[36] By the late seventeenth century, English inhabitants of plantation societies generally lived as minority populations, outnumbered by African-born and African-descended enslaved labourers. Barbados had a slave majority by 1670, Jamaica by 1680, the Leewards by 1690 and South Carolina by 1708. In 1713, 89 per cent of Jamaica's population was enslaved.[37] In other colonies where the majority of the white population was European or of European descent, the English were nonetheless a minority. The English acquired a Dutch colony when they conquered New Netherland in 1664. The English remained a minority in New York City (outnumbered by Dutch-descended inhabitants) until the early eighteenth century, when they surpassed the Dutch, but were still outnumbered by all non-English whites.[38] Pennsylvania attracted such a diverse array of settlers – English, Welsh, Scots, Irish, Scots-Irish, German – that historians characterise it as anglophone America's first pluralistic society.[39] Some ethnic groups settled in separate enclaves, as many German-speaking migrants did in the eighteenth century and as the Scots did in New Jersey, and some ethnic ties intensified. Over the course of the eighteenth century, the German-language press in Pennsylvania *increased*, suggesting a different pattern of assimilation from that of continental migrants in England.[40]

### Contexts

This panorama of the wide variety of 'others' within and beyond England points to the centrality of some key themes, including local contexts, disease environments and gender, for assessing these English encounters with others in this period. The considerable diversity of English responses to any single alien group in different geographic, economic, cultural, religious and demographic contexts emerges clearly through an analysis of English–Jewish interactions. Before the 1650s, most English people who encountered Jews did so beyond England, since Jews had been expelled from England in 1290. In the first decades of the seventeenth century, English travellers remarked on the Jewish populations they saw. Their views of Jews varied depending on the status of the English and the relative privileges afforded Jews in different locales. In general, they demonstrated more sympathy for Jews in Catholic countries, where Jews suffered a range of legal and social penalties and, at worst, terrifying deaths in autos-da-fé, than in the Ottoman empire, where the privileges afforded Jews were the same as those given Christians. No monolithic anti-Semitism shaped English assessments; rather, responses ranged from compassion to jealous hostility.[41]

In 1656, although Jews were still officially banned from England, the state relaxed the longstanding prohibition, and a few Sephardic Jews emigrated from Holland. By 1695, the Jewish population of London was less than 1,000, and by 1750, there were perhaps 6,000 to 8,000 Jews in England, almost exclusively in London, and divided into Sephardic and Ashkenazi communities, with their own distinct languages and cultures.[42] Their legal status was uncertain, because the official ban had not been lifted, thus permitting governments to impose a variety of restrictions. Unable to become freemen of London, which required taking a Christian oath, Jews were consequently barred from certain trades, including opening shops within the city. By 1750, half of the Jews in England had been born there, so were no longer aliens, but they continued to suffer disadvantages because of their religious status. They could not be naturalised, for example, without performing Christian rituals.[43]

Conditions for Jews in the English colonies were measurably more advantageous. There, they were recruited by colonial officers eager for men with useful skills. The Suriname colonial government sought to attract Jewish immigrants in August 1665 by granting them a variety of rights, guaranteeing them all of the privileges and liberties other English inhabitants of the colony enjoyed. They were to be 'considered as Englishborn'.[44] Jamaica's government also recruited Jews in 1672 to bolster the colony's population. Jewish populations and synagogues existed in scattered ports, in Newport, Philadelphia, New York, Savannah, Charleston, Kingston and Bridgetown. Anti-Semitism endured – an unthinking part of a gentile's cultural baggage, William Pencak has suggested – but anti-Semitic stereotypes were less virulent than colonial hostility towards several other groups, including Catholics, French, Germans and Scots-Irish.[45] Their legal status in the colonies eased considerably in 1740, when Parliament passed a bill permitting foreigners who had lived in the American colonies for seven years to naturalise. The law exempted Quakers and Jews from receiving the sacrament and taking the oath of abjuration, which immediately facilitated the naturalisation of Jews, although Jews continued to face a range of legal and economic impediments in several colonies, including a ban on voting in New York and limitations on testifying in court.[46]

A second important context in which the English encountered others was disease environments. In North America, the English confronted an unexpected circumstance: the catastrophic deaths of Amerindians as endemic Eurasian diseases, such as measles, smallpox, mumps or diphtheria, became epidemic diseases among virgin-soil populations. English observers concluded not only that God intended them to occupy this territory, but also that the people of the Americas were weak. The tropics, too, posed challenges, this time for the English, especially on Africa's west coast. Mosquito-borne illnesses, such as malaria and yellow fever, killed high numbers of English – diseases to which some Africans who dwelled in regions where malaria and yellow fever were endemic possessed partial or complete resistance.[47] As the English assessed their own bodily infirmities in the tropics, and the relative salubrity of Africans, they concluded that Africans were unnaturally strong and hardy people – individuals well suited to labour, in contrast to the frail inhabitants of North America.[48] English encounters with others, in the specific disease environments of North America and coastal Africa, accelerated English reliance on Africans as slaves.

A third crucial context is gender. Most of the English people who travelled outside England were men: soldiers, mariners, fishermen, merchants, ministers, collectors and indentured labourers. English migration to the colonies was overwhelmingly dominated by male labourers: as high as 75 per cent of all migrants in the seventeenth century. English men derided Amerindian societies for what they regarded as perverse gender roles, with women performing agricultural labour while Amerindian men engaged in sporadic activities such as hunting that the English associated with recreational and noble pursuits.[49] The gendered assessments were mutual: on the battlefield, English and Amerindian men taunted each other about their manhood.[50]

The gender frontier was a place of sexual encounters, especially between English men and non-English women.[51] In the seventeenth century, overseas trading companies sometimes banned wives, with a variety of consequences for English social and sexual practices in overseas enclaves. Levant Company employees spoke frankly of prostitutes in their midst: in 1600 one merchant referred to the traders in Istanbul as a company of 'whoremongers'.[52] Some merchants formed long-term connections with indigenous women overseas. Job Charnock, the founder of Calcutta, lived with an unnamed female companion and their three children for many years until he died in 1693.[53] The East India Company merchants who traded in Japan (1613–23) quickly established long-term liaisons with Japanese women, who not only offered companionship, but also helped traders learn about the culture they had joined and taught them Japanese.[54] Even places where such informal sexual alliances are difficult to trace in extant records seem to have contained such unions. Surviving sources for Virginia, for example, contain few references to sexual or romantic relations with indigenous women (aside from the celebrated union of John Rolfe and Pocahontas), but one colonist's vocabulary list from the 1610s offers a clue: one Algonquin phrase he included was 'to lye with a woman'.[55] Sexual violence was often part of these interactions, especially for enslaved women, and there was a spectrum of sexual encounters, ranging from marriages between the English and non-English, to informal but long-term alliances, to transitory encounters, to gang rapes.[56]

One consequence of such sexual relations was mixed-race children. These children were, for the English, a new population, an unanticipated new 'other' that emerged in the early modern period because of England's new global orientation. They occupied a variety of statuses. In commercial entrepôts, many of these children stayed with their mothers, and became important in commercial and diplomatic ties between English traders and officials and indigenous people. The 'mulatto' population of the Gold Coast, for example, grew over the course of the seventeenth and eighteenth centuries, and these children became a vital part of the work force. Mixed-race men at the British trading forts on the Gold Coast occupied 'a semiprofessional middling sort' that facilitated relations between Europeans and Africans.[57]

Many such children found their way to England. One of the earliest was Thomas Rolfe, son of Pocahontas and John Rolfe, who was two when his mother died in England in 1617. Another early arrival was William Eaton, whose father had been an employee of the East India Company in Japan. The six-year-old child journeyed to England in 1623. He attended

Trinity College, Cambridge, and in 1639 he secured the legal status of den-izen.[58] As his denization suggests, these mixed-race children challenged the English to determine their legal and social status. Colonial governments passed a variety of laws to ensure that mixed-race children of English and African descent did not gain rights equal to children of European descent. The contrast with English-born children of 'strangers' in England is stark. Those children acquired the same legal rights as other English subjects. Over the course of the seventeenth century, English colonial polities with sizeable slave populations rejected patriarchal lineage and determined, gradually, that the children of enslaved women acquired the status of the mother. In December 1662, for example, 'Whereas some doubts have arisen whether children got by any Englishman upon a negro woman should be slave or Free', the Virginia colonial assembly determined that all children would follow the condition of the mother, whether slave or free.[59]

The complex manoeuvres undertaken to determine a child's status are particularly evident in the laws passed to govern free mixed-race people (often called 'people of colour' in the parlance of the time). These were generally the children of men who were European or of European descent and women who were African or of African descent. Colonial govern-ments – composed of the white kin of free mixed-race people – ensured that freedom did not promise legal equality. Colonial assemblies passed no laws to govern the sexual conduct of white men, which was what pro-duced this mixed-race population, but erected a variety of impediments to both manumission and full participation in colonial societies for their offspring. Jamaica banned 'mulattoes' (anyone with one African great-great-grandparent) from holding office in 1711. By 1733, mixed-race people could not vote, and within a decade, they could not testify against whites. Barbados passed comprehensive legislation in 1721 that imposed similar constraints. Many restrictions, including a cap on inheritance, hindered economic activity. In Jamaica, free people of colour had to wear a badge proclaiming their status; in Antigua, free people of colour needed a white sponsor, without which they risked re-enslavement. Legally, economi-cally and socially, free people of colour in British slave colonies faced sub-stantial barriers by the early eighteenth century to equal participation in colonial societies, and these impediments increased over the course of the century.[60]

Mixed-race children put pressure on early modern European ideas about identity, whether it was mutable or fixed. In the early mod-ern period, English people understood identity as something eas-ily changed by external factors. The line between English and other was not a clear border, but a space of transition, a zone easily crossed. English-born people became 'Gypsies' in the sixteenth century by choosing a wandering life; the English traveller Fynes Moryson returned from his continental travels in 1597 in a long traveling gown, and the nightwatchman at Gravesend thought he might be a Catholic or a priest until he heard Moryson speak English; English captives in the Mediterranean converted to Islam, becoming 'renegades'; English authorities in Virginia mistrusted their English child-interpreters who acquired Algonquian language skills and knowledge of Amerindian practices.[61]

If some people lost English identity through garb, habit, faith, language and demeanour, others could acquire or deepen it with similar external shifts. Those who aspired to royal patronage or office or to local power learned to adopt English dress, language and architecture. Irish lords invested vast sums in the seventeenth century in grand edifices in the English style with which to impress others and to demonstrate their attachment to English values and mores.[62] By the eighteenth century, prosperous white inhabitants of American settlements consciously aped and emulated English fashion, architecture and design, setting slaves and servants to work copying style books, erecting great houses, and filling them with European-made furniture and goods.[63] This surge of Anglicisation, in manners, law, fashion, sociability, religion and architecture, revealed that by 1750 English people and others of European descent in the western Atlantic self-consciously sought closer cultural ties with England, prodded in part by the presence of those many 'others' – essential manpower, free and enslaved, African and Amerindian – who had made English territories overseas so foreign from England itself. Those others were especially African or of African descent, people defined by law through slave codes and restrictions governing free people of colour as subordinate in their rights and privileges, with neither wealth nor English parentage sufficient to purchase the new identities available to prosperous white men; neither were they able to alter their identity as easily by donning new clothes, building a Palladian mansion or purchasing a Chippendale cabinet.

By 1750, ideas about identity – transformed slowly into ideas about race – became more fixed, and the encounters of English and others had played a vital role in this transition. It was an unimaginable and unforeseen transition from the English world as it had existed in the sixteenth century, where the other was likely to be a Protestant European artisan in a market town, someone whose children could be assimilated. The unassimilable other was a product of new environments and hierarchies and of choices English people made between 1500 and 1750 as they circled the globe and encountered new people.

## Notes

1  J. Selwood, *Diversity and Difference in Early Modern London* (Farnham: Ashgate, 2010), 7.
2  For edited collections, see B. Bailyn and P. D. Morgan (eds.), *Strangers within the Realm: Cultural Margins of the First British Empire* (Chapel Hill: University of North Carolina Press for the Omohundro Institute of Early American History and Culture, 1991); M. Daunton and R. Halpern (eds.), *Empire and Others: British Encounters with Indigenous Peoples, 1600–1850* (Philadelphia: University of Pennsylvania Press, 1999); R. Vigne and C. Littleton (eds.), *From Strangers to Citizens: The Integration of Immigrant Communities in Britain, Ireland and Colonial America, 1550–1750* (London: The Huguenot Society of Great Britain and Ireland, 2001); N. Goose and L. Luu (eds.), *Immigrants in Tudor and Early Stuart England* (Brighton: Sussex Academic Press, 2005). For exemplary studies of single places, see Selwood, *Diversity and Difference*; or J. D. Goodfriend, *Before the Melting Pot: Society and Culture in Colonial New York City, 1664–1730* (Princeton: Princeton University Press, 1992).
3  See E. Bartels's comprehensive survey of this scholarship in 'Shakespeare's "other" worlds: The critical trek', *Literature Compass*, 5:6 (2008), 111–38.
4  N. Matar, *Islam in Britain, 1558–1685* (Cambridge: Cambridge University Press, 1998), 2.
5  D. Rollison, *The Local Origins of Modern Society: Gloucestershire 1500–1800* (London: Routledge, 1992), 67.
6  S. H. Johnston, 'Papists in a protestant world: The Catholic Anglo-Atlantic in the Seventeenth Century', unpublished Ph.D. thesis, Georgetown University (2011), 99–101, 103, 108.
7  N. Goose, 'Introduction', in Goose and Luu, *Immigrants*, 14–18.
8  D. Statt, *Foreigners and Englishmen: The Controversy over Immigration and Population, 1660–1760* (Newark: University of Delaware Press, 1995), 29, 37, 31, 33.
9  *Ibid.*, 32–3.
10  J. H. Ohlmeyer, '"Civilizinge of those rude partes": Colonization within Britain and Ireland, 1580s-1640s', in N. Canny (ed.) *The Oxford History of the British Empire*, (Oxford: Oxford University Press, 1998), Vol. I, 127.
11  P. Morgan, 'Wild Wales: Civilizing the Welsh from the sixteenth to the nineteenth centuries', in P. Burke, B. Harrison and P. Slack (eds.), *Civil Histories: Essays Presented to Sir Keith Thomas* (Oxford: Oxford University Press, 2000), 270.
12  N. P. Canny, 'The ideology of English colonization: From Ireland to America', *William and Mary Quarterly*, 3rd Series, 30 (1973), 575–98.
13  K. W. Swett, '"Born on my land": Identity, community, and faith among the Welsh in early modern London', in M. C. McClendon, J. P. Ward

and M. MacDonald (eds.), *Protestant Identities: Religion, Society, and Self-Fashioning in Post-Reformation England* (Stanford: Stanford University Press, 1999), 252–5.

14 Morgan, 'Wild Wales', 269–70, 274, 276.

15 A. T. Vaughan, *Transatlantic Encounters: American Indians in Britain, 1500–1776* (Cambridge: Cambridge University Press, 2006), xi, 42, quotation 55; E. Hinderaker, 'The "Four Indian Kings" and the imaginative construction of the first British empire', *William and Mary Quarterly*, 3rd series, 53:3 (July 1996), 499.

16 L. B. Wright (ed.), *A Voyage to Virginia in 1609. Two Narratives: Strachey's 'True Reportory' and Jourdain's Discovery of the Bermudas* (Charlottesville: University Press of Virginia, 1964), 92.

17 M. H. Fisher, 'Bound for Britain: Changing conditions of servitude, 1600–1857', in I. Chatterjee and R. M. Eaton (eds.), *Slavery and South Asian History*, 189–90 (quotation 189).

18 P. D. Curtin, 'Ayuba Suleiman Diallo of Bondu', in P. D. Curtin (ed.), *Africa Remembered: Narratives by West Africans from the Era of the Slave Trade* (Madison: University of Wisconsin Press, 1967), 17–59; for a slightly later period, see R. J. Sparks, *The Two Princes of Calabar: An Eighteenth-Century Atlantic Odyssey* (Cambridge, MA: Harvard University Press, 2004).

19 The range in these numbers reflects the problems historians face both defining this population and grasping its size.

20 C. Molineux, *Faces of Perfect Ebony: Encountering Atlantic Slavery in Imperial Britain* (Cambridge, MA: Harvard University Press, 2012), esp. Chapters 1 and 5.

21 D. Cressy, 'The trouble with Gypsies in early modern England', paper presented to the Huntington Early Modern British History Seminar, November 2013.

22 B. Redford, *Venice and the Grand Tour* (New Haven: Yale University Press, 1996); A. Games, *The Web of Empire: English Cosmopolitans in an Age of Expansion, 1560–1660* (Oxford: Oxford University Press, 2008), Chapter 1.

23 Games, *Web of Empire*, 231–2.

24 On merchant diasporas, see P. D. Curtin, *Cross Cultural Trade in World History* (Cambridge: Cambridge University Press, 1984). See also D. Goffman, *Britons in the Ottoman Empire, 1642–1660* (Seattle: University of Washington Press, 1998).

25 Games, *Web of Empire*, 101–2.

26 W. Ford, *A Sermon Preached at Constantinople* (London, 1616), sig. A2v.

27 M. Guasco, *Slaves and Englishmen: Human Bondage in the Early Modern Atlantic World* (Philadelphia: University of Pennsylvania Press, 2014), 268 n. 12; R. C. Davis, 'Counting European slaves on the Barbary Coast', *P&P*, 172 (2001), 106, 118; R. C. Davis, *Christian Slaves, Muslim Masters: White Slavery in the Mediterranean, the Barbary Coast, and Italy, 1500–1800* (New York: Palgrave Macmillan, 2003), 3.

28 J. H. Merrell, ' "The customes of our countrey": Indians and colonists in early America', in Bailyn and Morgan, *Strangers within the Realm*, 152–6.

29 A. Games, *Migration and the Origins of the English Atlantic World* (Cambridge, MA: Harvard University Press, 1999), 28–9, 245 n. 15.

30 J. P. Horn, *Adapting to a New World: English Society in the Seventeenth-Century Chesapeake* (Chapel Hill: University of North Carolina Press for the Omohundro Institute of Early American History and Culture, 1994), 302–3.

31 J. Butler, *The Huguenots in America: A Refugee People in New World Society* (Cambridge, MA: Harvard University Press, 1983), 27, 47.

32 A. Games, 'Migration', in D. Armitage and M. Braddick (eds.), *The British Atlantic World, 1500–1800* (New York: Palgrave Macmillan, 2002), Chapter 2.

33 The Jersey colony was the most enduring. See Ned C. Landsman, *Scotland and Its First American Colony, 1683–1765* (Princeton: Princeton University Press, 1985).

34 K. O. Kupperman, *The Jamestown Project* (Cambridge, MA: Harvard University Press, 2007), 288, 301.

35 A. W. Parker, *Scottish Highlanders in Colonial Georgia: The Recruitment, Emigration, and Settlement at Darien, 1735–1748* (Athens: University of Georgia Press, 1997).

36 D. H. Akenson, *If the Irish Ran the World: Montserrat, 1630–1730* (London and Buffalo: McGill-Queen's University Press, 1997).

37 R. S. Dunn, *Sugar and Slaves: The Rise of the Planter Class in the English West Indies, 1624–1713* (Chapel Hill: University of North Carolina for the Omohundro Institute of Early American History and Culture, 1972), 312.

38 Goodfriend, *Before the Melting Pot*, 62, 75, 156–7.

39 S. Schwartz, *'A Mixed Multitude': The Struggle for Toleration in Colonial Pennsylvania* (New York: New York University Press, 1987).

40 A. S. Fogleman, *Hopeful Journeys: German Immigration, Settlement, and Political Culture in Colonial America, 1717–1775* (Philadelphia: University of Pennsylvania Press, 1996), 82–3, 149.

41 Games, *Web of Empire*, 55–7.

42 Statt, *Foreigners and Englishmen*, 30.

43 J. Roitman, 'Creating confusion in the colonies: Jews, citizenship, and the Dutch and British Atlantics', *Itinerario*, 36:2 (August 2012), 57.

44 'Privileges granted by the British Government to the Jews of Surinam', 7 August 1665, Appendix VII, in E. H. Lindo, *A History of the Jews of Spain and Portugal* (London: Longman, Brown, Green and Longmans, 1868), 381–3 (quotation 382).

45 W. Pencak, *Jews and Gentiles in Early America, 1654–1800* (Ann Arbor: University of Michigan Press, 2005), 3–4.

46 Roitman, 'Creating confusion', 58. On these impediments, see H. Snyder, 'English markets, Jewish merchants, and Atlantic endeavors: Jews and the making of British transatlantic commercial culture, 1650–1800', in R. L. Kagan and P. D. Morgan (eds.), *Atlantic Diasporas: Jews, Conversos, and Crypto-Jews in the Age of Mercantilism, 1500–1800* (Baltimore: Johns Hopkins University Press, 2009), 74.

47 On the importance of yellow fever in shaping colonial, military and commercial activities, see especially J. R. McNeill, *Mosquito Empires: Ecology and War in the Greater Caribbean, 1620–1914* (Cambridge: Cambridge University Press, 2010).

48 J. Chaplin, 'Race', in Armitage and Braddick, *British Atlantic World*, 161–2.

49 K. O. Kupperman, *Settling with the Indians: The Meeting of English and Indian Cultures in the Americas, 1580–1640* (Lanham, MD: Rowman and Littlefield, 1980), 60–2.

50 A. M. Little, *Abraham in Arms: War and Gender in Colonial New England* (Philadelphia: University of Pennsylvania Press, 2007), Chapter 1.

51 On gender frontiers, see K. M. Brown, 'Brave new worlds: Women's and gender history', *William and Mary Quarterly*, 3rd series, 50 (1993), 311–328.

52 Games, *Web of Empire*, 104.

53 D. Ghosh, *Sex and the Family in Colonial India: The Making of Empire* (Cambridge: Cambridge University Press, 2006), 246.

54 On such relationships in other places, see, for example, for Africa, G. E. Brooks, *Eurafricans in Western Africa: Commerce, Social Status, Gender, and Religious Observance from the Sixteenth to the Eighteenth Century* (Athens: Ohio University Press, 2003); for North America, S. Van Kirk, *Many Tender Ties: Women in Fur Trade Society, 1670–1870* (Norman: University of Oklahoma Press, 1983).

55 Games, *Web of Empire*, 131–2.

56 On sexual violence, see especially (for a slightly later period) T. G. Burnard, *Mastery, Tyranny, and Desire: Thomas Thistlewood and His Slaves in the Anglo-Jamaican World* (Chapel Hill: University of North Carolina Press, 2004).

57 S. P. Newman, *A New World of Labor: The Development of Plantation Slavery in the British Atlantic* (Philadelphia: University of Pennsylvania Press, 2013), 133.

58 Games, *Web of Empire*, 107.

59 W. W. Heninge (ed.), *The Statutes at Large: Being a Collection of All the Laws of Virginia, from the First Session of the Legislature, in the Year 1619* (New York, 1823), Vol. II, 170.

60 D. A. Livesay, 'Children of uncertain fortune: Mixed-race migration from the West Indies to Britain, 1750–1820', unpublished Ph.D. thesis, University of Michigan (2010), Chapter 2.

61 Games, *Web of Empire*, 25, 72–4, 130, 137.

62 Ohlmeyer, 'Civilizinge', 142.

63 P. W. Hunter, *Purchasing Identity in the Atlantic World: Massachusetts Merchants, 1670–1780* (Ithaca, NY: Cornell University Press, 2001); R. Isaac, *The Transformation of Virginia, 1740–1790* (Chapel Hill: University of North Carolina Press for the Omohundro Institute of Early American History and Culture, 1982).

# History, Time and Social Memory

### Andy Wood

The dangers of writing history in twenty-first-century Britain are not profound. The academic historian might incur a stinging book review, find it hard to place articles in leading journals, fail to attract research funding or, worst of all, find a secure teaching position. These things can be disappointing. But, there are no government spies leaning over our shoulders, no overt political scrutiny of our work, no conviction on the part of the state that, as Nikita Khrushchev observed, 'Historians are dangerous, and capable of turning everything topsy-turvy. They have to be watched.'[1] Yet it was not always so.

John Hayward discovered the ideological limits of historical writing the hard way. When he published his history of the reign of Henry IV in 1599, he dedicated it to the earl of Essex. The following year, when Essex launched his attempted coup against Elizabeth I, Hayward found himself in the Tower, accused of sedition. The affinity between Elizabeth I and Richard II, whom Henry had deposed, was too great to be ignored. Over and again Hayward's interrogators – leading members of the Privy Council – returned to his authorial intentions, especially the possibility of a link to Essex and to his apparent intention to stir trouble amongst what they called the common people.[2] What Hayward failed to recognise was that, when writing about certain historical subjects, he had to be very cautious. The next time that he wrote a study of a reign – this time that of Edward VI – he trod carefully. In particular, his presentation of the popular rebellions of 1549 was markedly hostile, depicting the rebels as irrational, base and senseless.[3] This time, Hayward uncritically reproduced the dominant values of his age, scripted into the historical past.

Richard Grafton's *Chronicle* (1569) provided a blunt statement of the intended effects of reading history. From the study of the past, Grafton wrote,

Kings maye learne to depende upon God, and acknowledge his governance in their protection: the nobilitie may reade the true honor of their auncestours: The Ecclesiasticall state maye learne to abhorre trayterous practices and indignities done against kings by the Popishe usurping clergie: high and lowe may shonne rebellions by their dreadfull effectes, and beware how they attempt against right, how unhable soever the person be that beareth it.[4]

In an economy that remained fundamentally rural, the common people of the countryside – 'country clowns' – were regarded within this paradigm as the epitome of crude, senseless vulgarity. The Latin history of Kett's Rebellion written by Alexander Neville in 1575, for example, denounced the brutish violence of those whom he called *plebs* and *agrestes*.[5] Reading such works sustained a broader elite sense that allowing the commons a space within the political order would usher in an age of chaos. These anxieties found clear voice in the months preceding the Civil War, as supporters of the crown and episcopacy argued that their puritan opponents – backed by threatening crowds of ordinary Londoners – were heirs to the rebel leaders of 1381, 1450 and 1549. In November 1641, the bishop of Exeter, Joseph Hall, warned the House of Lords:

My lords, if these men (sectaries and mechanical preachers) may, with impunity and freedom, thus bear down ecclesiastical authority, it is to be feared they will not rest there, but will be ready to affront civil power too. Your lordships know, that the Jack Straws, and Cades and Wat Tylers of former times, did not more cry down learning than nobility.[6]

The representation of history could therefore be highly political. Yet ideas are hard to nail down. For all the one-dimensional emphasis upon order, obedience to the crown and plebeian senselessness, there was no single tradition of early modern historical writing.[7] Importantly, the period saw a flowering of learned historical work that was dynamic, creative and ideologically unpredictable. Translations of classical works helped to underwrite a middling-sort participation in the English Renaissance. In works dealing with the classical past, for instance, William Shakespeare made extensive use of Sir Thomas North's 1579 translation of Plutarch's *Lives*. The feeling of a cultural and political inheritance from the classical past fed into a civic humanism emergent amongst urban propertied groups. *Holinshed's Chronicles* (1577 and 1587), a massive collaborative work that told the story of British history from its mythical foundations to the present, represented not just a landmark achievement in historical writing, but also another important foundation of a sense of citizenship amongst urban middling people. The collaborative team behind the *Chronicles* represented an emergent antiquarian movement that in its urban form provided a sharpened sense of the past, but also grew out of a longer-established tradition of town and city chronicles, manuscripts that were often carefully locked away in muniment boxes in guildhalls across the country.[8] Similarly, William Lambarde's history of Kent (1576) helped to spawn a tradition of county antiquarianism that was intimately interwoven with 'country' gentry identity.[9] Antiquarianism had its practical applications too. On the one hand, it could provide the basis for questioning the antiquity of their tenants' customary rights; on the other, an awareness of legal history served in the early seventeenth century to buttress the defence of parliamentary privilege against the crown.[10]

Much of the historical literature concerning early modern perceptions of the past has dealt with political philosophy, antiquarianism, historical scholarship and state-sponsored works on the protestant Reformation. Two things have flowed from this: firstly, the focus has been on the highly educated, leaving unaddressed the reception of this work by poorer and middling people; secondly, there has been a heavy dependence upon printed texts. It is only quite recently that historians have begun to study popular memory, drawing in particular on antiquarian writings and the depositions made by older people in legal cases. As yet this work remains patchy. There has been considerable interest in the use of memory as a legal resource in conflicts over customary law.[11] The interactions between oral and written tradition with regard to senses of the past have been explored.[12] The key subject of the relationship between landscape and memory has been addressed.[13] The study of early modern popular memory, then, is finally opening up. Nor has the 'popular' been seen as hermetically sealed: there has been an interest in the dynamic interchanges of ideas about the past between ordinary people and their lettered superiors – for instance, in the study of antiquarian writers who initially drew heavily upon local folkloric traditions.[14]

As a result, it is possible to illustrate two centrally important points about the popular sense of historical change in this period that constitute a distinctly *early modern* sense of the past. Firstly, by the early seventeenth century many English people felt that the past was slipping away from them, generating a sense that the fifteenth and early sixteenth centuries formed a separate world from that inhabited by the people of later Elizabethan and early Stuart England.[15] Secondly, the distinct and traumatic experience of the English Revolution came to create a sense of continuity between the later Stuart and early Georgian periods, as the women and men of that time constructed memories and representations of the 1640s that fed directly into the political struggles of later times. It was within this combined sense of change and continuity, I argue, that early modern English women and men came to understand themselves in time.

Like so much else in early modern England the popular sense of the past could be highly variable and localised. One way of remembering was plotted in the landscape. Writing around 1622, the Leicestershire antiquarian William Burton visited the location of the Battle of Stoke (1487) and was shown 'a little Mount cast up, where by common report is, that at the first beginning of the battaile, Henry Tudor made his Pataeneticall Oration to his Armie'. He was also shown a great store of the weapons, armour and arrow heads that every year were turned up by the plough.[16]

Popular rebellion also left its memories upon the land: Blackheath had been the location of rebel camps in 1381, 1450 and 1497; so had Mousehold Heath in 1381 and 1549. When an anonymous cartographer arrived in Norwich around 1590 in order to map Mousehold Heath, one of the historic landmarks he was shown was 'The Oke of Reformation so callyd by Kett the Rebell' – that is, the oak tree under which Kett's rebel council had met in 1549.[17] In Cumberland, Lord Howard noted in 1621 that, in the course of the struggles over tenant right, Cumberland tenants had gathered in an armed crowd at Geltebridge, the same place 'where themselves or there ancestors as rebells and before that tyme fought a sett battle againste the forces of the s[ai]d late Queene Elizabethe'.[18]

Events of national historical importance were of course known, but were often used by the common people as a temporal marker for events of distinctly local significance. In Queen Mary's reign, the seventy-three-year-old James Herdman remembered how, immediately after 'Kinge Ricards Field' (the Battle of Bosworth, 1485), the tenants of Bury (Lancashire) heard that the earl of Derby and a multitude of Welshmen were coming to plunder them, and so they brought their cattle into land held by the lord of Ashworth, who offered them 'savegard'.[19] The Battle of Flodden (1513), England's greatest victory over Scotland, was so widely remembered that it came to form a sharp point in otherwise local temporal measurements. Speaking in 1563, the sixty-year-old Gloucestershire labourer Walter Potter felt that the time of his remembrance (that is, his awareness of local affairs) coincided with 'the tyme of Skottyshe feld'.[20] A century later, the arrangement of the parish church of Lea (Lancashire) remained set by local participation at Flodden. Ellen Brabin recalled in 1664 how her father's place in church had been challenged, and 'upon inquirie was told (as he said) by auncient people that at flodden feild some of his Ancest[or]s who lived at Pinington Hall had furnished the then L[or]d of Atherton with eight or tenn men & horses against that battall and for that consideracion had leave given him to sitt & bury there.'[21] In 1612, a seventy-nine-year-old Lancashireman retained vivid memories of the return of his lord from Edward VI's later wars with the Scots:

> aboute threescore yeares since imediately after... S[i]r Thomas Talbott came home from Barwick hee uppon a Sondaie or hullidaie came to Blackbourne church and broughte w[i]th him a greate companie of his souldiers w[i]th syde coats some in blewe, some in white wi[th] red crosses on, the backe and breste and saith upon the said S[i]r Thomas his comeinge in to the saide Chappell there sate some people there amongste whome as this dep[onen]t hath heard was one of the Talbotts Lords of Sailsburie ... all the w[hi]ch people that were in the said Chapell the said S[i]r Thomas upon his comeinge discharged sayeinge there was noe [to sit] ... there butt for himselfe and his souldiers & whereupon all the people went awaie[.]

Still in his armour, Sir Thomas knelt and prayed, giving thanks for the safe return of his company. This was a memory that had a purpose: it allowed local inhabitants to identify their lord's ownership 'tyme past memorie of man before him' of the side chapel within which Sir Thomas had knelt.[22]

Memory, then, performed a function: it was what H. S. Commager calls a 'usable past'.[23] Such memories could be as varied and idiosyncratic as the local identities they enshrined and the local claims they legitimised. A common pattern that emerges, however, is that, by the late sixteenth century, there had emerged a popular sense of historical change that identified the Reformation and social and economic change as linked historical processes that fundamentally reshaped English society.[24]

The pre-Reformation church had its own memory culture. In its treatment of local saints, veneration of the memories of the founders of chantries, perambulation of parish boundaries, or the recitation of its bede rolls, pre-Reformation belief was highly localised.[25] The Henrician reformation picked away at some of this; the more aggressive Edwardian reformation swept away much more. During Elizabeth's long reign, a moderately Calvinist church succeeded in implanting a new religious culture in the minds of two generations of English people. The old religion seemed, by the end of the sixteenth century, to be as much part of the past as was the cosy paternalism of good lordship.

As we have seen, this was a slow process and there were those who clung onto the old ways. At the height of the Northern Rising of 1569, the old services were re-established in Durham Cathedral, hidden altar stones were dug up and re-established, and crowds gathered to hear the old services. One woman recalled that she could not find a seat in the nave, for 'the throng of people was so moch'. Witness statements taken in the aftermath point towards the continued affection of many people for the old ways. This memory was focused upon personal and paro-chial artefacts and upon old rituals. Many people mentioned their use of ritual objects that – under the Elizabethan settlement – were meant to have been set aside. Elizabeth Watson admitted that 'she used hir beads' during the service in the cathedral. Agnes Mixston had done the same, and while 'sorye for the offenc[e]s' confessed that 'she hath hir beads still'. Yet in emphasising those parts of the old service they had *not* followed, witnesses usually managed to imply an only partial commitment to the old religion. Agnes's husband, Gilbert Mixston, was also in the cathedral, heard the priest deliver a sermon to the effect that 'the old s[er]vys was the right waye' and admitted that 'he toke holly wayter'. Ralph Stevenson, however, 'toke holly water but no holly bred nor was shreven'. William Watson said that he took part in the celebration of mass out of fear, and that he 'bowed then downe of his knees but kno[c]ked nott & he toke holly water'. Members of the cathedral clergy were similarly selective and all denied knowledge of any old copes, relics, books or other objects that might sustain the supposedly vanished faith.[26]

Memories of the old religion, then, could in many places be fiercely retained – yet, when confronted by officialdom, be still capable of care-ful modulation. The important point was that the success of the English Reformation, in Durham as elsewhere, represented a triumph over local patterns of remembrance and the social organisation of ritual and local meaning. Yet there were those who, despite the steady wash of Elizabethan amnesia, still sought to communicate the memory of the old church to succeeding generations. As late as 1593 the author of the manuscript 'Rites of Durham' provides the fullest description that has survived of a pre-Reformation cathedral and the services that it sustained. As his mind's eye moved around the great romanesque cathedral, the author recalled the services and rituals that had once occurred there. His memories were deeply coloured, yet resonant of a sense of place and attachment that had been ruptured.[27] He was no antiquarian, recording a dead world as if it were some desiccated, empty entity. Rather, the 'Rites' remains full of vitality. The object, no less, was to provide a textual basis for the recre-ation of a lost world.[28]

The gradual transformation of religious identity and of the forms of worship that it entailed was perhaps the most obvious manifestation of the extent to which the mid sixteenth century represented a watershed. But the Reformation also broadly coincided with other forms of change (and directly contributed to them through the redistribution of former church property). And subsequent early modern memories of forms of rebellion against, or resistance to, such changes encapsulate memories of former ways of living and perceptions of what were conceived of as deleterious developments in both economic and social relations.

In 1573, aged witnesses from Middleham (Yorkshire) remembered that enclosing walls were established across their common some two years 'after the Scottishe felde called Floddam felde'.[29] In the last years of the sixteenth century, the tenants of Worsley (Lancashire) remembered that they had retained their rights of common on Walkden Moor until 'soone after Scotts Field, when their was a bickeringe betwixt the lords of worsley and the lords of Boothes upo[n] walkden moore'.[30] In 1554, witnesses from the Lancashire 'country' of Blackburnshire dated their ejection from the commons of Horelaw and Hollinhey by the powerful magnate Sir John Towneley to 'iiii years after the Scottes Feyld' or to 'aboute iiii or v years after Flowden Feyld'.[31]

In the Elizabethan West Country, there were sharp memories of the rebellions of 1549. The ninety-year-old yeoman Richard Clannaborough of Lustleigh (Devon) recalled in 1602 the customs he had known 'ever synce the Commotion in the tyme of the Raigne of the late Kinge Edward the Sixth' in the course of a dispute concerning the lord of the manor's claim to a monopoly over corn mills in the village.[32] In 1583, the Cornish yeoman Thomas Toser – 'borne about Christmas … twelve months after Blackheeth field [in 1497]' – remarked that a struggle over manorial boundaries in his home village of St Mellion had commenced shortly 'before the Comosyon in Cornwall last'.[33] In Norfolk, one way of recalling the events of 1549 was as an outright attack upon seigneurialism. In 1601, the eighty-year-old husbandman John Crosse remembered how, around 1540, Sir Edmund Bedingfield had constructed a lodge on the lordly rabbit warren (much hated by tenants because of the depradations of the lagomorphic inhabitants amongst their crops). As Crosse recalled things, the 'lodge was pulled downe in the comotion tyme': this was a direct attack upon the landscape of lordship.[34]

Such memories recorded not only grievance and subsequent resistance, but also repression. Kett's Rebellion, with its comprehensive indictment of landlord abuses, also entered local memory as a time of bloodshed. The Norwich authorities went out of their way to mark the city's relief from plebeian disorder, ordaining in 1550 that each year on 29 August ('Kett's

Day' – the anniversary of the rebel defeat) the bells of all the parish churches should be rung and prayers said, followed by a special sermon against rebellion preached at the cathedral.[35] In this way, the suppression of popular rebellion was scorched into official remembrance. Similarly, in 1537, the main urban centres of Norfolk – Norwich, King's Lynn and Yarmouth – were chosen as key sites at which rebels from Walsingham (Norfolk) who had plotted to murder the local gentry and to restore the monastic houses were to be hanged, drawn and quartered. A generation later, when the official chronicles of Norwich, Lynn and Yarmouth came to be written, the annihilation of these local opponents of Henry VIII's Reformation was given due prominence.[36]

The Northern Rising, like those of 1549, provided a marker in time according to which local events might be recorded. Powerful storms in Lincolnshire coincided with its suppression in 1570; local remembrance of the two events worked together.[37] Memories of the cruel aftermath of the rising were still strong in the Yorkshire 'country' of Kirkbyshire in 1601. In the course of large-scale crowd action against the enclosing landlord Sir Stephen Proctor, locals were called out in the queen's name to break down enclosures. Some warned their neighbours that 'we [were] commanded in the Rebell tyme in Gods name and the Queenes name, but we had like to have bene hanged in the devylls name at wch speches the people murmured saying then to themselves howe sholde we knowe when to obey in the queens name'. Yet despite these dark memories, some 300 or 400 Kirkbyshire folk gathered to break down enclosures on Thorpe More, 'the like whereof hath not there bene seene since the late rebellion in the North'.[38]

In 1620, giving evidence in a tithe dispute before the consistory court of Durham, the seventy-five-year-old Robert Darlinge recalled how 'he this ex[aminan]t was servant to and did dwell w[i]th one Mr Franckland att Cocken in the yeare of the insurreccon or rebellion in the north that last was'. Rebellion, Darlinge seemed to imply, might revisit the north: 1569 was the 'rebellion in the north *that last was*'.[39] In some places, the changes in landownership that followed the sequestration of rebel lords' estates following the 'last rebellio[n] in the north' formed as important a marker in time as the rebellion itself.[40]

In the Anglo-Scottish borders the militaristic culture of earlier times, fostered by the custom of 'tenant right', which ensured low rents and dues in return for the men's military service on the borders, was remembered into the seventeenth century as a past that had vanished, together with the social relations that had sustained it. The antiquarian Isaac Gilpin noted the 'Theevish' nature of the mid-Tudor border folk, observing that 'although they were amongst themselves very brutish and much addicted to robbing, stealing and so many other rude & disorderly Qualities, yet because of the name [of their landlords] they so loved their Landlord that they would unanimously rise' upon being so bidden.[41]

That sense of an ending was at its most powerful when the crown turned against tenant right following the union of the crowns in 1603.[42] Old Westmorland men giving testimony in support of tenant right in 1622 retained clear memories of their former service. One remembered how he had been called out by the warden on six occasions to fight the border reivers, 'furnished with a horse bowe and arrowes, steele cappe, a jacke and sword and dagger'. An eighty-year-old topped this: he remembered serving on the borders, a red cross stitched on his coat, on some twenty occasions.[43] Old John Askrigg looked back fondly on his warlike youth, a time when the crown protected the northern tenants; his neighbours remembered how he used to say that 'he hoped yet to see the border againe, & he stroakinge his beard he saide he hoped that gray beard shold once serve at Carlile again & Ryde before his master as of his white horse he was wont to do'.[44] These memories endured for generations, long after the border reivers had departed into the mist. In 1651, the ninety-seven-year-old James Taylor of Askgarth (Yorkshire) explained how, like the other men of his village, he had come to the borders when needed, riding his light horse and equipped with a coat of mail, a spear, dagger, sword and steel cap. He remembered that, early in Elizabeth's reign, when he and John Harth of Swaledale had served together against the Scots, fourteen of their neighbours had been killed and he was himself wounded. This was an old man looking back on the bloody skirmishes of youth. The struggles of John Harth, James Taylor and their neighbours had, by the end of Taylor's life, become part of local tradition. George Metcalfe explained that same year how he had been told by his grandfather about his service on the borders, the old man showing Metcalfe his withered arm, the use of which he had lost in the struggles with the reivers. Metcalfe's neighbour, the seventy-five-year-old John Kettlewell, well remembered how 'he heard his father name diverse of the said tenants who did goe in p[er]son to fight against the Scots, some of w[hi]ch said Ten[a]nts lost their lives there some others came wounded and lame home and some others never came home againe'.[45]

In the northern borders after 1603, then, there was a sense of an ending: of an old world passing away. Yet these memories were no mere whimsies; nostalgic they may have been, but as the contemporary historian Ben

Jones reminds us, nostalgia can represent a form of agency.[46] In recalling their border service, the old men of the north both reasserted a distinctly martial masculinity that had been lost following the Union of the crowns and reminded their younger neighbours of the bargain that had once existed between crown and border tenant: wartime service for secure copyhold tenures. Every time that northern women and men saw the scars on the bodies of their aged menfolk, they were reminded of that service, and how the bargain had been broken after 1603. In all these ways, ordinary people constructed a sense of change, one that carried with it distinct warnings for the future.

If the events and transformations of the sixteenth century retained their place in local memory, for the people of later Stuart and early Georgian England, the civil wars represented a profoundly traumatic body of memories. They remained divisive: recollections of violence, repression, destruction and atrocity committed by one's neighbours proved hard to forget.

Social historians have tended to avoid direct engagement with the historiography of the English Revolution, with far too many studies arbitrarily finishing in 1640.[47] Yet the civil wars and Interregnum were so powerful a force as to impose themselves on temporal registers across the country. They marked another watershed in time. The widowed Ellinor Sergeant of Harrogate (Yorkshire) recalled in 1669 how her husband had been the Forester of Knaresborough 'sev[er]all yeares before the Warrs began'.[48] Many were more impassioned in the terminology they used about the 1640s. One correspondent to John Walker, who was collecting memories of the sufferings of royalist clergy in the 1640s, referred to that decade as the 'wickedly wicked times'.[49] A Cambridgeshire witness of 1674 referred to the 1640s as 'the troublesome tymes', as did Elizabeth Fisher of Canterbury in the same year, and the aged Cheshire husbandman William Horton in 1701.[50] In some places, specific engagements – plunder, siege warfare, a skirmish or major engagement – stuck in local memory. In 1679, when William Stephenson gave evidence concerning a disputed watercourse in Hull, the clerk noted that he 'speaks to eight or nine years before the late siege'.[51] In 1697, a number of witnesses from Malmesbury (Wiltshire) dated local events in relation to the Restoration. One had a sharp memory of the most traumatic event of the English Revolution, dating an agreement about parish tithes to 'about the time that King Charles the first was beheaded'.[52] Derbyshire witnesses of the 1680s referred simply to the 'Late warr tyme'; others spoke of 'the souldering tymes'; the village gentleman George Hopkinson, whose home had been plundered by parliamentary soldiers, spoke pointedly of the 'late unhappy warres'.[53]

The intrusion of the wars into temporal registers that were otherwise profoundly local points to the significance of the English Revolution to ordinary people, being sufficiently powerful to stand as markers in time.[54] In this respect, they helped to validate individual and collective claims to local memory. One clear instance of this came in 1656, when a group of Weardale tenants recalled how they had served, under colour of their obligations to the crown under the custom of tenant right, for fourteen days on the Scottish border at the time of the Bishops' Wars. The effect was to legitimate claims to tenant right at a time when they were coming under threat from the local parliamentarian magnate, Sir Arthur Hesilrige.[55]

The 1640s were scorched into popular memory for good reasons. The wars brought with them slaughter, disease, plunder, impoverishment, hunger and atrocity. The records of quarter sessions administration are full of petitions from maimed soldiers or war widows seeking relief. Up until 1660, that relief was restricted to the injured men who had fought for the Parliament, and to parliamentarian soldiers' dependants. After the Restoration, it was the turn of former cavaliers and their wives and children.[56] The terms according to which parochial and county relief were administered to the victims of war, then, helped to perpetuate wartime divisions for generations to come. The disease and dearth that came with the disruption of trade and passage of marching armies was also burnted into people's memories. In the history that he wrote around 1700 of his home village of Myddle (Shropshire), Richard Gough recalled how the common had been

> cutt, and burnt, and sowed with corne in the later end of the warr time, temp. Car. I. The first crop was winter corne, which was a very strong crop; the next was a crop of barley, which was soe poore, that most of it was pulled up by the roote, because it was too short to bee cutt. That time there was a great dearth and plague in Oswaldstree.[57]

All of this mattered to ordinary people's experience of the wars, perhaps more so than the great issues of state that had provoked them.

For generations after the wars, their material destruction remained everywhere to be seen. In a set of notes that repeatedly reference the impact of the civil wars, the Lincolnshire antiquarian Abraham de la Pryme recorded in the 1690s that 'It was the L[or]d Kimbolton, Earl of Manchester's Regiment that defaced the Ch[urch] of Hatfield, they were exceeding rude people.'[58] He knew that he was traversing an ancient landscape. Some of the wayside crosses that de la Pryme passed denoted the bounds of land that had once been held by monastic houses; this land-scape had been disrupted by the wars. De la Pryme noted two such crosses, one of which was still standing in 1697; the other had been 'a stately cross [of] great height like a markate cross ... calld ... St Katherines – which was standing until Cromwell's days & then the soldiers pull'd it down to the bare ground'.[59]

Within a culture that understood the material world as a way of plot-ting local memory – in church seating plans, parish bounds, wayside crosses – the effects of wartime damage could be sharply felt. In 1705, the minister of Otton Belchamp (Essex) wrote an account of the parish boundaries, his intention being 'To describe the Bounds and limits of our Parish which are very obscure and to prevent encroachings of others'. This was a matter of special concern to him because 'in the times of the long Rebellion the landmarks of our Parish were cut downe, and it would be difficult for posterity to find out the proper precincts which our parish are incompassed withal'.[60] On the other hand, the civil wars might be com-memorated within the landscape. In 1674, it was recorded that in Wigan (Lancashire) there had been a battle at the northern end of the town in 1651 that ended in the death of the royalist Sir Thomas Tildersley, 'and as a memoriall of the place where S[i]r Thomas did fall ... a great Heap of stones [was] soon after laid together, by well affected persons'.[61]

Changes to parish churches – another memory site in local communi-ties – were also keenly felt. The shock of the destruction of their parish church remained powerful to the people of Pontefract in 1667. William Gates recalled how 'the p[ar]ish Church of Allhallowes was burnt and pulled downe in the late time of rebellion & that the steeple thereof onely is in part repaired'.[62] In 1686, William Walker, who had been a servant at Holford Hall for twenty-six years, remembered how he, his fellow servants and his masters –the Cholmondeleys, who had fought for the king in the 1640s – had always sat in the chancel of the church of Lower Peover (Cheshire). The chancel, Walker was sure, was the property of the Cholmondeleys. His seventy-year old neighbour, Richard Litter, was able to provide some historical context to the reflected pride that Walker seems to have felt in being a part of so prominent a household. He remembered how, back in 1625, one of the Cholmondeleys had passed away and was buried under 'a white gravestone in the same chancel'. Fifty years ago, he recollected, 'before the late unhappy warrs', the Cholmondeleys had financed the repair of the chancel and had renewed their heraldic arms, 'but in the s[ai]d warrs the same Coates were taken down by the soldiers (as this depo[nen]t hath heard) and were aft[e]r that … preserved by Peter Frodsham de[c]e[as]ed who was a tenant to the Lords of Holford'.[63]

Moreover, the social event that underwrote this reading of the landscape – the yearly Rogationtide custom that saw the perambulation of parish bounds, which many puritans saw as pagan – had in many parishes been discontinued during the Interregnum. In Kirkby-in-Ashfield (Nottinghamshire), there was a deep sense of landscape that reached back to before the dissolution of the local priory of Newstead: it was general knowledge before the wars came that certain fields had been held by the priory until its dissolution in the 1530s. These fields were taken in by the parish perambulation, and old folk would call out to their younger neighbours to take note of the boundaries and field names, 'and desired them to remember itt for the tyme to come'. All of this ceased when war came, after which the Rogationide processions were discontinued. Now, in 1664, the parishioners were attempting to recover their collective memories of the bounds.[64]

The land itself was also a bearer of memory: local inhabitants possessed an often intricate knowledge of the tenure that attached to different fields, to their prior occupancy, and to the entitlements and responsibilities that came with that occupancy. The English Revolution disrupted this too, not just with the seizure of the great estates of royalist gentry, but also with the sequestration of lands held by relatively humble people. William Shakespeare of Rowington (Warwickshire), for example, recalled in 1675 how 'in the time of the late warrs in the kingdome many of the coppyhold tenements' of Rowington 'were under sequestracon'; all of this led to confusion as to the precise pattern of tenure.[65]

In all of these ways, then, the civil wars proved highly disruptive of local ways of remembering. There is a certain irony to the searing of the English Revolution into popular memory. The Act of Indemnity and Oblivion (1660) enjoined subjects to erase the Interregnum from their recollections.[66] But both sides found this hard to achieve. One former cavalier, John Hague of Aston (Derbyshire), couldn't let go of his anger, finding himself in trouble for having 'tooke upon him to speake of the act of oblivion & said the Kinge was a foole & a knave if he made it not voyde & Hanged not upp all the Roundheads'.[67] Another Derbyshire man, Henry Alsibrooke of Church Broughton, wished that a local meadow 'were full of souldiers & he amongst th[e]m & th[a]t he should never be light at heart till th[a]t they may pull downe the higher powers (meaning the kinge)'.[68] The commemoration of Civil War struggles underwrote continued opposition to the Stuarts. The inhabitants of

Restoration Taunton (Devon), who had withstood a prolonged siege in the first Civil War, enjoyed a three-day festival to celebrate the defeat of their royalist besiegers. Beginning with drums sounding reveille in the dawn, pious sermons were followed by bonfires, drinking and dancing, at which members of the crowd chanted 'Rejoice you dogs, 'tis the eleventh of May, the day the cavaliers ran away.' In 1671, it was reported to the Privy Council that the people of Taunton performed this commemoration 'by which they glory in their rebellion (so far are they from repentance for it). This course they do also entail to their posterity'. Intergenerational continuity had already taken hold: the correspondent noted that the 'rejoicing' was 'kept by men, women and children throughout the whole town, many of which were not then born when the siege was raised'.[69]

The politics of later Stuart and early Georgian England were fought out under the shadow of the English Revolution. The 1640s represented as powerful a force in the politics of late-seventeenth- and early-eighteenth-century England as would the events of 1789, 1848 and 1871 in Third Republic France.[70] The Exclusion Crisis of 1678–81 was fought as if the party labels Whig and Tory represented synonyms for roundhead and cavalier. In the turbulent year of 1715, a Cheapside crowd marched behind effigies of Cromwell, William III and the duke of Marlborough, crying out 'Down with the Rump' and 'No Hanoverian, No Presbyterian Government'.[71] A similar set of analogies occurred to a Coventry crowd, who in 1736 cried out 'Down with the Rump, down with the Roundheads, no Hanover, down with the King's Head'.[72] Pursuing the same point, a Lancashire carpenter found himself in trouble in 1722 for having cried out during a riot 'Down with the Rump'.[73] Meanwhile, a rioting crowd at Harwich (Essex) in 1724 delighted in mocking George I: an outraged witness reported that the crowd was 'drumming a ridiculous Tune of Roundheaded Cuckolds &c'.[74] In a slippage that was indicative of the instability of straightforward party narratives, George Cleeve was presented to the assizes in 1716 for warning that 'King George must have a care what he did otherwise he would lose his head as King Charles had done.'[75]

The civil wars, then, represented a nightmare that loomed over later generations. But reconstructing those memories represents a methodological as well as an empirical challenge. There is no single, authoritative source that allows the historian entry into early modern popular memory. Perhaps more so than any other field in the social history of the 1500–1750 period, the evidence is both partial and fragmentary. Yet there are points of consistency and cohesion within the flux of remembrance. This chapter has tried to illuminate some of those points, especially where they help to mark out a distinctly *early modern* sense of time and place. All of this reminds us that popular memory is a field that is constantly 'crossed by competing constructions, often at war with each other'.[76] The study of social memory takes us into a contested, protean field. Understanding the constantly unpredictable eddies within popular memory will require the next generation of early modern social historians to transcend subdisciplinary boundaries and to rethink the nature of the social history project. There is everything to be gained, bringing us ever closer to the world we have lost.

### Notes

1  M. Ferro, *The Use and Abuse of History; or, How the Past Is Taught* (1981; English translation London: Routledge, 1984), 114.

2  J. Hayward, *The First and Second Parts of John Hayward's 'The Life and Raigne of King Henrie IIII'*, ed. J. J. Manning, Camden 4th series, 42 (London: Offices of the Royal Historical Society, University of London, 1991). For Hayward's interrogation, see TNA, SP12/274/58–62.

3  J. Hayward, *The Life and Raigne of King Edward the Sixth by John Hayward*, ed. B. L. Beer (Kent, OH: Kent State University Press, 1993).

4  F. Smith Fussner, *Tudor History and the Historians* (New York: Basic Books, 1970), 256.

5  A. Nevylli, *De furoribus Norfolciensium Ketto Duce* (London, 1575), 35, 42.

6  B. Manning, *The English People and the English Revolution*, 2nd edn. (London: Book Marks, 1991), 99. For an example, see BL, Add. MS 70520. Also anon., *The rebellious life and death of Wat Tyler and Jack Straw* (London, 1642); B. Stirling, 'Shakespeare's mob scenes: A reinterpretation', *Huntingdon Library Quarterly*, 3 (1945).

7  The foundational work is K. Thomas, *The Perception of the Past in Early Modern England*, Creighton Trust Lecture (London: University of London, 1983).

8  R. Tittler, 'Reformation, civic culture and collective memory in English provincial towns', *Urban History*, 24:3 (1997). For an overview, see A. Dyer, 'English town chronicles', *Local Historian*, 12 (1977).

9  For notable examples of county studies, see W. Lambarde, *William Lambarde: A Perambulation of* Kent, ed. R. Kent (Trowbridge: Adams and Dart, 1970); R. Carew, *The Survey of Cornwall* (1602; repr. Trowbridge: Adams and Dart, 1969); J. Norden, *Speculi Britaniae: The description of Hartfordshire* (1598; repr. New York: Da Capo, 1971). For the more fragmentary genre of county chorographies, see D. MacCulloch (ed.), *The Chorography of Suffolk*, Suffolk Record Society, 19 (Ipswich: Suffolk Record Society, 1976); C. M. Hood (ed.), *The Chorography of Norfolk* (Jarrold: Norwich, 1938).

10 D. R. Woolf, *The Idea of History in Early Stuart England* (Toronto: University of Toronto Press, 1990); G. Parry, *The Trophies of Time: English Antiquarians of the Seventeenth Century* (Oxford: Oxford University Press, 1995); D. R. Kelley, *The Writing of History and the Study of Law* (Aldershot: Ashgate, 1997); J. Broadway, *'No historie so meete': Gentry Culture and the Development of Local History in Elizabethan and Early Stuart England* (Manchester: Manchester University Press, 2006); R. Cust, 'Catholicism, antiquarianism and gentry honour: The writings of Sir Thomas Shirley', *Midland History*, 23 (1998); R. B. Manning, 'Antiquarianism and seigneurial reaction: Sir Robert and Sir Thomas Cotton and their tenants', *Historical Research*, 63:152 (1990).

11 A. Wood, *The Memory of the People: Custom and Popular Senses of the Past in Early Modern England* (Cambridge: Cambridge University Press, 2013); N. M. Whyte, 'Landscape, memory and custom: Parish identities *c.* 1550–1700', *SH*, 32:2 (2007); R. W. Hoyle (ed.), *Custom, Improvement and the Landscape in Early Modern Britain* (Farnham: Ashgate, 2011); S. Sandall, 'Custom, memory and the operations of power in seventeenth-century Forest of Dean', in F. Williamson (ed.), *Locating Agency: Space, Power and Popular Politics* (Newcastle: Cambridge Scholars, 2010).

12 A. Fox, *Oral and Literate Cultures in England, 1500–1700* (Oxford: Oxford University Press, 2000). For early work on the neglected subject of popular senses of time, see K. Wrightson, 'Popular senses of past time: Dating events in the North Country, 1615–31', in M. J. Braddick and P. Withington (eds.), *Popular Culture and Political Agency in Early Modern England and Ireland* (Woodbridge: Boydell, 2016).

13 N. Whyte, *Inhabiting the Landscape: Place, Custom and Memory, 1500–1800* (Oxford: Oxbow, 2009); A. Walsham, *The Reformation of the Landscape: Religion, Identity and Memory in Early Modern Britain and Ireland* (Oxford: Oxford University Press, 2011).

14 D. Woolf, 'The "common voice": History, folklore and oral tradition in early modern England', *P&P*, 120 (1988).

15 C. Brooks, 'Contemporary views of "feudal" social and political relationships in sixteenth and seventeenth-century England', in N. Fryde and P. Monnet (eds.), *Die Gegenwart des Feudalismus* (Göttingen: Vandehoeck & Ruprecht, 2002); M. Aston, 'English ruins and English history: The dissolution and the sense of the past', *Journal of the Warburg and Courtauld Institutes*, 36 (1973).

16 W. Burton, *A description of Leicestershire* (London, 1642), 47.

17 TNA, MPC/2787. One Restoration antiquarian was shown Kett's Oak, but garbled its significance. See R. Blome, *Britannia* (London, 1673), 169. I hope to write more fully about the Mousehold map in the future.

18 TNA, STAC8/161/16.

19 H. Fishwick, 'Disputed boundary in Ashworth', *Transactions of the Lancashire and Cheshire Antiquarian Society*, 15 (1897). For other mid-Tudor Lancastrians' mention of 'Kinge Ricards Field', see TNA, DL1/55/H2-3. See also P. Schwyzer, 'Lees and moonshine: Remembering Richard III, 1485–1635', *Renaissance Quarterly*, 63 (2010).

20 TNA, E134/7Eliz/East1.

21 Cheshire Record Office, EDC5 (1664), 69.

22 Cheshire Record Office, EDC5 (1612), 28. For other memories of Edward's Scottish wars, see TNA, E134/5JasI/Mich8.

23 H. S. Commager, *The Search for a Usable Past* (New York: Knopf, 1967).

24 Wood, *Memory*, 43–93.

25 Eamon Duffy has captured this localised memory with the greatest clarity. See, in particular, *The Voices of Morebath: Reformation and Rebellion in an English Village* (New Haven and London: Yale University Press, 2001).

26 DUL, DDR/EJ/CCD/1/2, fols. 177r, 1/8v, 200v, 201r, 201v–202r.

27 DUL, Cosin MS B.ii.11, p. 50. The earliest complete copy is DUL, Cosin MS B.ii.11. For an earlier copy, some sections of which have been lost, see Durham Cathedral Library, MS C.iii.23. For a good nineteenth-century copy, see DUL, CCB/B/175/57144/6. A definitive version of the 'Rites of Durham' is currently being prepared. For authorship, see A. I. Doyle, 'William Claxton and the Durham chronicles', in J. P. Carley and C. G. C. Tite (eds.), *Books and Collectors, 1200–1700* (London: British Library, 1997). I am grateful to Adrian Green for advice on this subject.

28 For the parochial equivalent of the 'Rites of Durham', see D. Dymond and C. Paine (eds.), *The Spoil of Melford Church: The Reformation in a Suffolk Parish* (Ipswich: Salient Press, 1989).

29 TNA, E134/17Eliz/East6.

30 Henry E. Huntington Library, Egerton MS, Ellesmere 5698f.

31 TNA, DL44/196. I hope to write more fully about this dispute.

32 C. Torr (ed.), *Wreyland Documents* (Cambridge: Cambridge University Press, 1910), 92.

33 Cornwall Record Office, CY/7189. For further mid-sixteenth-century memories of the Battle of Blackheath as an event around which to organise time, see M. McGlynn, 'Memory, orality and life records: Proofs of age in Tudor England', *Sixteenth Century Journal*, 40:3 (2009).

34 TNA, DL4/43/12.

35 A. Wood, *The 1549 Rebellions and the Making of Early Modern England* (Cambridge: Cambridge University Press, 2007), Chapter 6.

36 NRO, Y/D41/104, fol. 37r; NRO, NCR17A, 'Mayor's book', fol. 19r; BL, Add. MS 8937, fol. 2r; C. E. Moreton, 'The Walsingham conspiracy of 1537', *Historical Research*, 63 (1990).

37 TNA, E178/4036.

38 TNA, STAC5/P14/21; TNA, STAC5/A57/5.

39 DUL, DDR/EJ/CCD/1/11, fol. 75v (my emphasis). I am grateful to Megan Johnston for this reference.

40 TNA, E134/26Eliz/East4.

41 A. Bagot, 'Mr Gilpin and manorial customs', *Transactions of the Cumberland and Westmorland Antiquarian and Archaeological Society*, 2nd series, 57 (1962), 231.

42 R. W. Hoyle, 'Lords, tenants and tenant right in the sixteenth century: Four studies', *Northern History*, 20 (1984); R. W. Hoyle, 'An ancient and laudable

custom: The definition and development of tenant right in north-western England in the sixteenth century', *P&P*, 116 (1987). For a regional study, see J. L. Drury, '"More stout than wise": Tenant right in Weardale in the Tudor period', in D. Marcombe (ed.), *The Last Principality: Politics, Religion and Society in the Bishopric of Durham, 1494–1660* (Nottingham: University of Nottingham Press, 1987). For a description of tenant right dated 21 March 1582, based upon 'The reports & sayings of sundry aged persons touching the customarie service of the Inhabitants of the countie of Duresme & as they have seen it used in their tymes', see DUL, DCD/S/LP32/5(a).

43  TNA, STAC8/34/4.
44  TNA, STAC8/34/4.46; see also piece 54.
45  TNA, E134/1651/Mich17.
46  B. Jones, 'The uses of nostalgia: Autobiography, community publishing and working-class neighbourhoods in post-war England', *Cultural and Social History*, 7 (2010).
47  The social history of the English Revolution remains to be written.
48  TNA, DL4/111/15. See also TNA, E134/28ChasII/East20; Borthwick Institute for Archives, CP/H/3344.
49  F. McCall, 'Children of Baal: Clergy families and their memories of sequestration during the English civil war', *Huntington Library Quarterly*, 76:4 (2013), 618. See also A. Laurence, '"This sad and deplorable condition": An attempt towards recovering an account of the sufferings of northern clergy families in the 1640s and 1650s', in D. Wood (ed.), *Life and Thought in the Northern Church, c. 1100–1700: Essays in Honour of Claire Cross* (Woodbridge: Boydell, 1999). The Walker Manuscripts deserve systematic study.
50  Cambridgeshire Archives, P109/28/4; TNA, E134/35ChasII/Mich9; Cheshire Record Office, EDC5 (1701), 7.
51  East Riding of Yorkshire Archives and Records Services, DDBL/10/14.
52  TNA, E134/9WmIII/Trin9.
53  TNA, DL4/123/1685/2, DL4/123/1684/4, DL4/122/1683/1, DL4/109/8. For the interest displayed by William Hopkinson (father) in local history, see BL, Add. MS 6668, fol. 430r.
54  For the localism of temporal registers, see A. Wood, 'Popular senses of time and place in Tudor and Stuart England', *Insights*, 6:3 (2014).
55  DUL, WEC.145/12, 15; J. L. Drury, 'Sir Arthur Hesilrige and the Weardale Chest', *Transactions of the Architectural and Archaeological Society of Durham and Northumberland*, new series, 5 (1980).
56  M. Stoyle, '"Memories of the maimed": The testimony of Charles I's former soldiers, 1660–1730', *History*, 88:290 (2003); G. L. Hudson, 'Negotiating for blood money: War widows and the courts in seventeenth-century England', in J. Kermode and G. Walker (eds.), *Women, Crime and the Courts in Early Modern England* (London: UCL Press, 1994). Andy Hopper is currently engaged on a major study of this subject.
57  R. Gough, *The History of Myddle*, ed. D. Hey (London: Penguin, 1981), 63.
58  BL, Lansdowne MS 897, fol. 71r.

59 BL, Lansdowne MS 897, fol. 52v.
60 Essex Record Office, D/DU 441/96, 22–4.
61 Cumbria Record Office, DLONS/L12/2/18.
62 Borthwick Institite for Archives, CP/H/2836.
63 Cheshire Record Office, EDC5 (1686), 1.
64 Nottinghamshire Archives, DD/2P/24/5, 7.
65 TNA, E134/26ChasII/Mich32.
66 P. Aguilar, *Memory and Amnesia: The Role of the Spanish Civil War in the Transition to Democracy* (Oxford: Berghahn, 2002).
67 Derbyshire Record Office, Q/SB2/630.
68 Derbyshire Record Office, Q/SB2/631.
69 R. Clifton, *The Last Popular Rebellion: The Western Rising of 1685* (Hounslow: Martin Temple Smith, 1984), 44–5.
70 R. Gildea, *The Past in French History* (New Haven: Yale University Press, 1994).
71 N. Rogers, *Crowds, Culture and Politics in Georgian Britain* (Oxford: Oxford University Press, 1998), 31.
72 D. Rollison, *The Local Origins of Modern Society: Gloucestershire, 1500–1800* (London: Routledge, 1992), 219.
73 D. Woolf, *The Social Circulation of the Past: English Historical Culture, 1500–1730* (Oxford: Oxford University Press, 2003), 341.
74 E. P. Thompson, *Customs in Common* (London: Merlin, 1991), 69.
75 Rogers, *Crowds*, 57.
76 Popular Memory Group, 'Popular memory: Theory, politics, method', in R. Johnson, G. McLennan, B. Schwarz and D. Sutton (eds.), *Making Histories: Studies in History Writing and Politics* (Minneapolis: Minnesota University Press, 1982), 207.

# Further Reading

## 1 CRAFTING THE NATION

Anderson, B., *Imagined Communities: Reflections on the Origin and Spread of Nationalism*, new edn (London: Verso, 2006).

Brayshay, M., 'Royal post-horse routes in England and Wales: The evolution of the network in the later-sixteenth and early-seventeenth century', *Journal of Historical Geography*, 17 (1991).

'Waits, musicians, bearwards and players: The inter-urban road travel and performances of itinerant entertainers in sixteenth and seventeenth century England', *Journal of Historical Geography*, 31 (2005).

Colley, L., *Britons: Forging the Nation 1707–1837* (New Haven and London: Yale University Press, 1992).

Collinson, P., *Elizabethan Essays* (London: Hambledon, 1994).

Fox, A., *Oral and Literate Culture in England, 1500–1700* (Oxford: Oxford University Press, 2000).

Helgerson, R., *Forms of Nationhood: The Elizabethan Writing of England* (Chicago: University of Chicago Press, 1992).

Keenan, S., *Travelling Players in Shakespeare's England* (Basingstoke: Palgrave Macmillan, 2002).

Lake, P. and S. Pincus, 'Rethinking the Public Sphere in Early Modern England', *Journal of British Studies*, 45 (2006).

McMillin, S. and S.-B. MacLean, *The Queen's Men and Their Plays* (Cambridge: Cambridge University Press, 1998).

McRae, A., *Literature and Domestic Travel in Early Modern England* (Cambridge: Cambridge University Press, 2009).

Peacey, J., *Print and Public Politics in the English Revolution* (Cambridge: Cambridge University Press, 2013).

Seton-Watson, H., *Nations and States: An Enquiry into the Origins of Nations and the Politics of Nationalism* (London: Methuen, 1977).

Shrank, C., *Writing the Nation in Reformation England, 1530–1580* (Oxford: Oxford University Press, 2004).

Vallance, E., 'Loyal or rebellious? Protestant associations in England, 1584–1696', *Seventeenth Century*, 17 (2002).

Watt, J., '"Common weal" and commonwealth": England's monarchical republic in the making, *c.* 1450–1530', in A. Gamberini, A. Zorzi and J.-P. Genet (eds.), *The Languages of Political Society* (Rome: Viella, 2011).

Watt, T., *Cheap Print and Popular Piety, 1550–1640* (Cambridge: Cambridge University Press, 1991).

Withington, P., *Society in Early Modern England: The Vernacular Origins of Some Powerful Ideas* (Cambridge: Polity, 2010).

Woolf, D., *The Social Circulation of the Past: English Historical Culture, 1500–1730* (Oxford: Oxford University Press, 2003).

## 2 SURVEYING THE PEOPLE

Burke, P., *A Social History of Knowledge from Gutenberg to Diderot* (Cambridge: Polity, 2000).

Cassedy, J. H., *Demography in Early America: Beginnings of the Statistical Mind, 1600–1800* (Cambridge, MA: Harvard University Press, 1969).

Coleman, O., 'What figures? Some thoughts on the use of information by medieval governments', in D. Coleman and A. H. John (eds.), *Trade, Government, and Economy in Pre-Industrial England* (London: Weidenfeld & Nicolson, 1976).

French, H., *The Middle Sort of People in Provincial England 1600–1750* (Oxford: Oxford University Press, 2007).

Griffiths, P., 'Inhabitants', in C. Rawcliffe and R. Wilson (eds.), *Norwich since 1500* (London: Hambledon, 2004).

'Local arithmetic: Information cultures in early modern England', in S. Hindle, A. Shepard and J. Walter (eds.), *Remaking English Society: Social Relations and Social Change in Early Modern England* (Woodbridge: Boydell, 2013).

Harkness, D. E., 'Accounting for science: How a merchant kept his books in Elzabethan London', in M. C. Jacob (ed.), *The Self-Perception of Early Modern Capitalists* (Basingstoke: Palgrave Macmillan, 2008).

Innes, J., 'Power and happiness: Empirical social enquiry in Britain from "political arithmetic" to "moral statistics"', in *Inferior Politics: Social Problems and Social Policies in Eighteenth-Century Britain* (Oxford: Oxford University Press, 2009).

Kent, J., 'The rural "middling sort" in early modern England *circa* 1640–1740: Some economic, political, and socio-cultural characteristics', *Rural History*, 10 (1999).

McCormick, T., *William Petty and the Ambitions of Political Arithmetic* (Oxford: Oxford University Press, 2009).

McRae, A., *God Speed the Plough: The Representation of Rural England, 1500–1660* (Cambridge: Cambridge University Press, 1996).

Robertson, J. C., 'Reckoning with London: Interpreting the bills of mortality before John Graunt', *Urban History*, 23 (1996).

Rusnock, A. A., *Vital Accounts: Quantifying Health and Population in Eighteenth-Century England and France* (Cambridge: Cambridge University Press, 2002).

Scott, J. C., *Seeing like a State: How Certain Schemes to Improve the Human Condition Have Failed* (New Haven and London: Yale University Press, 1998).

Shurer, K. and A. Arkell (eds.), *Surveying the People: The Interpretation and Use of Document Sources for the Study of Population in the Later Seventeenth Century* (Oxford: Leopard's Head, 1992).

Slack, P., 'Government and information in seventeenth-century England', *P&P*, 184 (2004).

## 3 LITTLE COMMONWEALTHS I: THE HOUSEHOLD AND FAMILY RELATIONSHIPS

[Works published since 2000]

### *Household Formation*

Griffin, E., 'A conundrum resolved? Rethinking courtship, marriage and population growth in eighteenth-century England', *P&P*, 215 (2012).

McNabb, J., 'Ceremony versus consent: Courtship, illegitimacy, and reputation in northwest England, 1560–1610', *Sixteenth Century Journal*, 37 (2006).

O'Hara, D., *Courtship and Constraint: Rethinking the Making of Marriage in Tudor England* (Manchester: Manchester University Press, 2000).

Sharpe, P., *Population and Society in an East Devon Parish: Reproducing Colyton, 1540–1840* (Exeter: University of Exeter Press, 2002).

Stephens, I., 'The courtship and singlehood of Elizabeth Isham, 1630–1634', *HJ*, 51 (2008).

### *Marital Relations*

Bailey, J., '"I Dye [*sic*] by inches": Locating wife beating in the concept of privatization of marriage and violence in eighteenth-century England', *SH*, 31 (2006).

*Unquiet Lives: Marriage and Marriage Breakdown in England, 1660–1800* (Cambridge: Cambridge University Press, 2003).

Barclay, K., 'Negotiating patriarchy: The marriage of Anna Potts and Sir Archibald Grant of Monymusk, 1731–1744', *Journal of Scottish Historical Studies*, 28 (2008).

Barker, H., 'Soul, purse and family: Middling and lower-class masculinity in eighteenth-century Manchester', *SH*, 33 (2008).

Foyster, E. A., 'At the limits of liberty: Married women and confinement in eighteenth-century England', *C&C*, 17 (2002).

*Marital Violence and English Family History, 1660–1857* (Cambridge: Cambridge University Press, 2005).

Gowing, L., '"The manner of submission": Gender and demeanour in seventeenth century London', *Cultural and Social History*, 10 (2013).

Hunt, M. R., 'Wives and marital "rights" in the Court of the Exchequer in the early eighteenth century', in P. Griffiths and M. Jenner (eds.), *Londonopolis: Essays in the Cultural and Social History of Early Modern London* (Manchester: Manchester University Press, 2000).

Hurl-Eamon, J., 'Domestic violence prosecuted: Women binding over their husbands for assault at Westminster quarter session, 1685–1720', *JFH*, 26 (2001).

Keenan, S., '"Embracing submission"? Motherhood, marriage and mourning in Katherine Thomas's seventeenth-century "Commonplace Book"', *Women's Writing*, 15 (2008).

Kugler, A., 'Constructing wifely identity: Prescription and practice in the life of Lady Sarah Cowper', *JBS*, 40 (2001).

Perry, R., *Novel Relations: The Transformation of Kinship in English Literature and Culture, 1748–1818* (Cambridge: Cambridge University Press, 2004).

Pollock, L. A., 'Anger and the negotiation of relationships in early modern England', *HJ*, 47 (2004).

Shepard, A., *Meanings of Manhood in Early Modern England* (Oxford: Oxford University Press, 2003).

Stretton, T., 'Marriage, separation and the common law in England, 1540–1660', in H. Berry and E. Foyster (eds.), *The Family in Early Modern England* (Cambridge: Cambridge University Press, 2007).

Tague, I., 'Love, honor, and obedience: Fashionable women and the discourse of marriage in the early eighteenth century', *JBS*, 40 (2001).

　*Women of Quality: Accepting and Contesting Ideals of Femininity in England, 1690–1760* (Woodbridge: Boydell, 2002).

## Parents, Children and Siblings

Bailey, J., '"A very sensible man": Imagining fatherhood in England *c.* 1750–1830', *History*, 95 (2010).

Ben-Amos, I. K., 'Reciprocal bonding: Parents and their offspring in early modern England', *JFH*, 25 (2000).

Crawford, P., *Parents of Poor Children in England, 1580–1800* (Oxford: Oxford University Press, 2010).

Foyster, E., 'Parenting was for life, not just for childhood: The role of parents in the married lives of their children in early modern England', *History*, 86 (2001).

French, H. and M. Rothery, '"Upon your entry into the world": Masculine values and the threshold of adulthood among landed elites in England 1680–1800', *SH*, 33 (2008).

Harris, A., *Siblinghood and Social Relations in Georgian England: Share and Share Alike* (Manchester: Manchester University Press, 2012).

　'That fierce edge: Sibling conflict and politics in Georgian England', *JFH*, 37 (2012).

Levene, A., *The Childhood of the Poor: Welfare in Eighteenth-Century London* (Basingstoke: Palgrave Macmillan, 2012).

Newton, H., '"Very sore nights and days": The child's expereince of illness in early modern England, *c.* 1580–1720', *Medical History*, 55 (2011).

## Kin

Ben-Amos, I. K., *The Culture of Giving: Informal Support and Gift-Exchange in Early Modern England* (Cambridge: Cambridge University Press, 2008).

Botelho, L. A., *Old Age and the English Poor Law, 1500–1700* (Woodbridge: Boydell, 2004).

'"The old woman's wish": Widows by the family fire? Widows' old age provisions in rural England, 1500–1700', *Pergamon*, 7 (2002).

Lynch, K. A., 'Kinship in Britain and beyond from the early modern to the present: Postscript', *C&C*, 25 (2010).

Tadmor, N., 'Early modern English kinship in the long run: Reflections on continuity and change', *C&C*, 25 (2010).

*Family and Friends in Eighteenth-Century England: Household, Kinship and Patronage* (Cambridge: Cambridge University Press, 2001).

Wall, R., 'Beyond the household: Marriage, household formation and the role of kin and neighbours', *IRSH*, 44 (1999).

## Family Economy and Servants

Boulton, J., '"Turned into the street with my children destitute of every thing": The payment of rent and the London poor 1600–1850', in J. McEwan and P. Sharpe (eds.), *Accommodating Poverty: The Housing and Living Arrangements of the English Poor, c. 1600–1850* (Basingstoke: Palgrave Macmillan, 2011).

Erikson, A. L., 'Married women's occupations in eighteenth-century London', *C&C*, 23 (2008).

Healey, J., 'Poverty in an industrializing town: Deserving hardship in Bolton, 1674–99', *SH*, 35 (2010).

Hindle, S., 'Below stairs at Arbury Hall: Sir Richard Newdigate and his household staff, *c.* 1670–1710', *Historical Research*, 85 (2012).

'"Without the cry of any neighbours": A Cumbrian family and the poor law authorities, *c.* 1690–1730', in H. Berry and E. Foyster (eds.), *The Family in Early Modern England* (Cambridge: Cambridge University Press, 2007).

Hurl-Eamon, J., 'The fiction of female dependence and the makeshift economy of soldiers, sailors, and their wives in eighteenth-century London', *Labor History*, 49 (2008).

McIntosh, M. K., 'Women, credit and family relationships in England, 1300–1620', *JFH*, 30 (2005).

Muldrew, C., '"Th'ancient distaff" and "whirling spindle": Measuring the contribution of spinning to household earnings and the national economy in England, 1550–1770', *EcHR*, 65 (2012).

'"A mutual assent of her mind"? Women, debt, litigation and contract in early modern England', *HWJ*, 55 (2003).

## 4 LITTLE COMMONWEALTHS II: COMMUNITIES

Bossy, J., 'Blood and baptism: Kinship, community and Christianity in Western Europe from the fourteenth to the seventeenth centuries', in D. Baker (ed.), *Sanctity and Secularity: The Church and the World* (Oxford: Oxford University Press, 1973).

French, K. L., *The People of the Parish: Community Life in a Late Medieval Diocese* (Philadelphia: University of Pennsylvania Press, 2001).

Halvorson, M. J. and K. E. Spierling (eds.), *Defining Community in Early Modern Europe* (Aldershot: Ashgate, 2008).

Heal, F., *Hospitality in Early Modern England* (Oxford: Oxford University Press, 1990).

Hindle, S., *On the Parish? The Micro-Politics of Poor Relief in Rural England, c. 1550–1750* (Oxford: Oxford University Press, 2004).

Hindle, S., A. Shepard and J. Walter (eds.), *Remaking English Society: Social Relations and Social Change in Early Modern England* (Woodbridge: Boydell, 2013).

Kümin, B. A., *The Shaping of a Community: The Rise and Reformation of the English Parish, c. 1400–1560* (Aldershot: Ashgate, 1991).

Macfarlane, A., S. Harrison and C. Jardine, *Reconstructing Historical Communities* (Cambridge: Cambridge University Press, 1977).

McIntosh, M. K., *A Community Transformed: The Manor and Liberty of Havering, 1500–1620* (Cambridge: Cambridge University Press, 1991).

Muldrew, C., 'The culture of reconciliation: Community and the settlement of disputes in early modern England', *HJ*, 39 (1996).

Rosenwein, B. H., *Emotional Communities in the Early Middle Ages* (Ithaca, NY: Cornell University Press, 2006).

Sharpe, J. A., '"Such disagreement betwyxt neighbours": Litigation and human relations in early modern England', in J. Bossy (ed.), *Disputes and Settlements: Law and Human Relations in the West* (Cambridge: Cambridge University Press, 1983).

Shepard, A. and P. Withington (eds.), *Communities in Early Modern England: Networks, Place, Rhetoric* (Manchester: Manchester University Press, 2000).

Short, B., 'Images and realities in the English rural community: An introduction', in B. Short (ed.), *The English Rural Community: Image and Analysis* (Cambridge: Cambridge University Press, 1992).

Smith, R. M., '"Modernization" and the corporate medieval village community in England: Some sceptical reflections', in A. R. H. Baker and D. Gregory (eds.), *Explorations in Historical Geography: Interpretative Essays* (Cambridge: Cambridge University Press, 1984).

Thompson, E. P., *Customs in Common* (London: Merlin, 1991).

Waddell, B., *God, Duty and Community in English Economic Life, 1660–1720* (Woodbridge: Boydell, 2012).

Walsham, A., *Charitable Hatred: Tolerance and Intolerance in England, 1500–1700* (Manchester: Manchester University Press, 2006).

Wrightson, K., 'The politics of the parish in early modern England', in P. Griffiths, A. Fox and S. Hindle (eds.), *The Experience of Authority in Early Modern England* (Basingstoke: Macmillan, 1996).

Wrightson, K. and D. Levine, *Poverty and Piety in an English Village: Terling, 1525–1700*, 2nd edn (Oxford: Oxford University Press, 1995).

## 5 REFORMATIONS

Collinson, P., *The Religion of Protestants* (Oxford: Oxford University Press, 1982).

Duffy, E., *Fires of Faith: Catholic England under Mary Tudor* (New Haven and London: Yale University Press, 2009).

Durston, C. and J. Maltby (eds.), *Religion in Revolutionary England* (Manchester: Manchester University Press, 2006).

Green, I., *Print and Protestantism in Early Modern England* (Oxford: Oxford University Press, 2000).

Haigh, C. *The Plain Man's Pathways to Heaven: Kinds of Christianity in Post-Reformation England, 1570–1640* (Oxford: Oxford University Press, 2007).

Hamling, T., *Decorating the 'Godly' Household: Religious Art in Post-Reformation Britain* (New Haven and London: Yale University Press, 2010).

Hunt, A., *The Art of Hearing: English Preachers and Their Audiences, 1590–1640* (Cambridge: Cambridge University Press, 2010).

MacCulloch, D., *Tudor Church Militant: Edward VI and the Protestant Reformation* (London: Allen Lane, 1999).

Maltby, J., *Prayer Book and People in Elizabethan and Early Stuart England* (Cambridge: Cambridge University Press, 1998).

Marshall, P., *Reformation England 1480–1642* (London: Arnold, 2003).

Patterson, W. B., *William Perkins and the Making of a Protestant England* (Oxford: Oxford University Press, 2014).

Prior, C. W. A. and G. Burgess (eds.), *England's Wars of Religion, Revisited* (Farnham: Ashgate, 2011).

Ryrie, A., *Being Protestant in Reformation Britain* (Oxford: Oxford University Press, 2013).

*The Age of Reformation: The Tudor and Stewart Realms, 1485–1603* (Harlow: Pearson, 2009).

Shagan, E., *Popular Politics and the English Reformation* (Cambridge: Cambridge University Press, 2002).

Spurr, J., *The Post-Reformation: Religion, Politics and Society in Britain, 1603–1714* (Harlow: Longman, 2006).

Walsham, A., *Providence in Early Modern England* (Oxford: Oxford University Press, 1999).

Wood, A., *The Memory of the People: Custom and Popular Senses of the Past in Early Modern England* (Cambridge: Cambridge University Press, 2013).

## 6 WORDS, WORDS, WORDS: EDUCATION, LITERACY AND PRINT

Bernard, J. and D. F. McKenzie (eds.), *The Cambridge History of the Book in Britain,* Vol. IV: *1557–1695* (Cambridge: Cambridge University Press, 2002).

Charlton, K. and M. Spufford, 'Literacy, society and education', in D. Loewenstein and J. Mueller (eds.), *The Cambridge History of Early Modern English Literature* (Cambridge: Cambridge University Press, 2002).

Cranfield, G. A., *The Development of the Provincial Newspaper 1700–1760* (Oxford: Oxford University Press, 1962).

Cressy, D., 'Educational opportunity in Tudor and Stuart England', *History of Education Quarterly*, 16 (1976).

*Literacy and the Social Order: Reading and Writing in Tudor and Stuart England* (Cambridge: Cambridge University Press, 1980).

Fergus, J., *Provincial Readers in Eighteenth-Century England* (Oxford: Oxford University Press, 2006).

Fox, A., *Oral and Literate Culture in England 1500–1700* (Oxford: Oxford University Press, 2000).

Green, I., *Print and Protestantism in Early Modern England* (Oxford: Oxford University Press, 2000).

Harris, M., *London Newspapers in the Age of Walpole* (London: Associated University Presses, 1987).

Houston, R. A., *Scottish Literacy and the Scottish Identity: Illiteracy and Society in Scotland and Northern England, 1600–1800* (Cambridge: Cambridge University Press, 1985).

Laqueur, T. W., 'The cultural origins of popular literacy in England 1500–1850', *Oxford Review of Education*, 2 (1976).

Lawson, J. and H. Silver, *A Social History of Education in England* (London: Methuen, 1973).

O'Day, R., *Education and Society, 1500–1800: The Social Foundations of Education in Early Modern Britain* (London: Longman, 1982).

Porter, R., *Enlightenment: Britain and the Creation of the Modern World* (London: Allen, Lane, 2000).

Raven, J., *The Business of Books: Booksellers and the English Book Trade* (New Haven and London: Yale University Press, 2007).

Spufford, M., 'First steps in literacy: The reading and writing experiences of the humblest seventeenth-century spiritual autobiographers', *SH*, 4 (1979).

*Small Books and Pleasant Histories: Popular Fiction and Its Readership in Seventeenth-Century England* (London: Methuen, 1981).

Thomas, K., 'The meaning of literacy in early modern England', in G. Baumann (ed.), *The Written Word: Literacy in Transition* (Oxford: Oxford University Press, 1986).

Watt, T., *Cheap Print and Popular Piety, 1550–1640* (Cambridge: Cambridge University Press, 1991).

Whyman, S. E., *The Pen and the People: English Letter Writers 1660–1800* (Oxford: Oxford University Press, 2009).

## 7 LAND AND PEOPLE

Allen, R. C., *Enclosure and the Yeoman* (Oxford: Oxford University Press, 1992).

Brenner, R., 'The agrarian roots of European capitalism', *P&P*, 97 (1982).

Campbell, B. M. S. and M. Overton, 'A new perspective of medieval and early modern agriculture: Six centuries of Norfolk farming *c.* 1250–*c.* 1850', *P&P*, 141 (1993).

Dyer, C., *An Age of Transition? Economy and Society in England in the Later Middle Ages* (Oxford: Oxford University Press, 2005).

French, H. R. and R. W. Hoyle, *The Character of English Rural Society: Earls Colne, 1550–1750* (Manchester: Manchester University Press, 2007).

Muldrew, C., *Food, Energy and the Creation of Industriousness: Work and Material Culture in Agrarian England 1550–1780* (Cambridge: Cambridge University Press, 2011).

Overton, M., *Agricultural Revolution in England: The Transformation of the Agrarian Economy 1500–1850* (Cambridge: Cambridge University Press, 1996).

Shaw-Taylor, L., 'The rise of agrarian capitalism and the decline of family farming in England', *EcHR*, 65 (2012).

Tawney, R. H. *The Agrarian Problem in the Sixteenth Century* (New York: Harper and Row, 1967 [1912]).

Thirsk, J., *England's Agricultural Regions and Agrarian History, 1500–1750* (Basingstoke: Macmillan, 1987).

Whittle, J. (ed.), *Landlords and Tenants in Britain, 1440–1660: Tawney's Agrarian Problem Revisited* (Woodbridge: Boydell, 2013).

Whyte, N., *Inhabiting the Landscape: Place, Custom and Memory 1500–1800* (Oxford: Oxbow, 2009).

Williamson, T., *Shaping Medieval Landscapes: Settlement, Society, Environment* (Macclesfield: Windgather, 2003).

Wrigley, E. A., *Energy and the Industrial Revolution* (Cambridge: Cambridge University Press, 2010).

Yelling, J. A., *Common Field and Enclosure in England 1450–1850* (London: Macmillan, 1977).

## 8 URBANISATION

Barry, J. (ed.), *The Tudor and Stuart Town* (Harlow: Longman, 1988).

Barry, J. and C. Brooks (eds.), *The Middling Sort of People: Culture, Society and Politics in England 1550–1800* (Basingstoke: Macmillan, 1994).

Barry, J., 'Civility and civic culture in early modern England', in P. Burke, P. Harrison and P. Slack (eds.), *Civil Histories* (Oxford: Oxford University Press, 2000).

Borsay, P., *The English Urban Renaissance: Culture and Society in the Provincial Town, 1660–1770* (Oxford: Oxford University Press, 1989).

Borsay, P. (ed.), *The Eighteenth Century Town* (Harlow: Longman, 1990).

Clark, P. (ed.), *The Cambridge Urban History of Britain*, Vol. II: *1540–1840* (Cambridge: Cambridge University Press, 2000).

Clark, P. and P. Slack (eds.), *Crisis and Order in English Towns, 1500–1700: Essays in Urban History* (London: Routledge, 1972).

Collinson, P., *The Birthpangs of Protestant England: Religious Change in the Sixteenth and Seventeenth Centuries* (Basingstoke: Macmillan, 1988).

De Vries, J., *European Urbanization 1500–1800* (London: Methuen, 1984).

Griffiths, P., *Lost Londons: Change, Crime and Control in the Capital City 1550–1660* (Cambridge: Cambridge University Press, 2008).

Halliday, P., *Dismembering the Body Politic: Partisan Politics in England's Towns 1650–1730* (Cambridge: Cambridge University Press, 1998).

Horner, C. (ed.), *Early Modern Manchester* (Lancaster: Carnegie, 2008).

O'Callaghan, M., *The English Wits: Literature and Sociability in Early Modern England* (Cambridge: Cambridge University Press, 2007).

Phythian Adams, C., *Societies, Cultures and Kinship, 1580–1850: Cultural Provinces and English Local History* (Leicester: Leicester University Press, 1996).

Tittler, R., *Architecture and Power: The Town Hall and the English Urban Community, 1500–1640* (Oxford: Oxford University Press, 1991).

*The Reformation and the Towns in England: Politics and Political Culture, c. 1540–1640* (Oxford: Oxford University Press, 1998).

Withington, P., 'Intoxication and the early modern city', in S. Hindle, A. Shepard and J. Walter (eds.), *Remaking English Society* (Woodbridge: Boydell, 2013).

*The Politics of Commonwealth: Citizens and Freemen in Early Modern England* (Cambridge: Cambridge University Press, 2005).

'Public discourse, corporate citizenship and state-formation in early modern England', *AHR*, 112 (2007).

Wrightson, K., *Ralph Tailor's Summer: A Scrivener, His City and the Plague* (New Haven and London: Yale University Press, 2011).

Wrigley, E. A., 'A simple model of London's importance in changing English society and economy, 1650–1750', *P&P*, 37 (1967).

## 9 THE PEOPLE AND THE LAW

Beattie, J. M., *Crime and the Courts in England 1660–1800* (Princeton: Princeton University Press, 1986).

Brooks, C. W., *Law, Politics and Society in Early Modern England* (Cambridge: Cambridge University Press, 2008).

*Lawyers, Litigation and English Society since 1450* (London and Rio Grande: Hambledon, 1998).

*Pettyfoggers and Vipers of the Commonwealth: The 'Lower Branch' of the Legal Profession in Early Modern England* (Cambridge: Cambridge University Press, 1986).

Dolan, F. E., *Dangerous Familiars: Representations of Domestic Crime in England 1550–1700* (Ithaca, NY: Cornell University Press, 1994).

Gaskill, M., *Crime and Mentalities in Early Modern England* (Cambridge: Cambridge University Press, 2000).

Green, T. A., *Verdict According to Conscience: Perspectives on the English Criminal Trial Jury, 1200–1800* (Chicago: University of Chicago Press, 1985).

Halliday, P., *Habeas Corpus: From England to Empire* (Cambridge, MA: Belknap, 2010).

Herrup, C. B., *The Common Peace: Participation and the Criminal Law in Seventeenth-Century England* (Cambridge: Cambridge University Press, 1987).

Hindle, S., *The State and Social Change in Early Modern England, c. 1550–1640* (Basingstoke: Macmillan; New York: St Martin's Press, 2000).

Ingram, M., *Church Courts, Sex and Marriage in England, 1570–1640* (Cambridge: Cambridge University Press, 1987).

Kesselring, K. J. 'Felony forfeiture and the profits of crime in early modern England', *HJ*, 53 (2010).

*Mercy and Authority in the Tudor State* (Cambridge: Cambridge University Press, 2003).

Knafla, L. A., *Kent at Law* 1602, 6 vols (London: List and Index Society, 2009–2016).

Muldrew, C., *The Economy of Obligation: The Culture of Credit and Social Relations in Early Modern England* (Basingstoke: Macmillan, 1998).

Sharpe, J. A., *Crime in Early Modern England 1550–1750* (London and New York: Longman, 1999).

Shoemaker, R. B., *Prosecution and Punishment: Petty Crime and the Law in London and Rural Middlesex c. 1660–1725* (Cambridge: Cambridge University Press, 1991).

Walker, G., *Crime, Gender and Social Order in Early Modern England* (Cambridge: Cambridge University Press, 2003).

'Everyman or a monster? The rapist in early modern England, c. 1600–1750', *HWJ*, 76 (2013).

## 10 AUTHORITY AND PROTEST

Braddick, M. J. (ed.), *The Oxford Handbook of the English Revolution* (Oxford: Oxford University Press, 2015).

Braddick, M. J. and J. Walter (eds.), *Negotiating Power in Early Modern Society: Order, Hierarchy and Subordination in Britain and Ireland* (Cambridge: Cambridge University Press, 2001).

Fletcher, A. and D. MacCulloch, *Tudor Rebellions* (London: Longman, 1997).

Harris, T. (ed.), *The Politics of the Excluded, c. 1500–1850* (Basingstoke: Macmillan, 2001).

Levine, D. and K. Wrightson, *The Making of an Industrial Society: Whickham 1560–1765* (Oxford: Oxford University Press, 1991).

Lindley, K., *Fenland Riots and the English Revolution* (London: Heinemann Educational, 1982).

Manning, B., *The English People and the English Revolution* (London: Heinemann Educational, 1976).

Manning, R. B., *Village Revolts: Social Protest and Popular Disturbances in England, 1509–1640* (Oxford: Oxford University Press, 1988).

Martin, J., *Feudalism and Capitalism: Peasant and Landlord in English Agrarian Development* (Basingstoke: Macmillan, 1983).

Rule, J., *The Experience of Labour in Eighteenth Century Industry* (London: Croom Helm, 1981).

Sharp, B., *In Contempt of All Authority: Rural Artisans and Riot in the West of England 1585–1660* (Berkeley and London: University of California Press, 1980).

Walter, J., *Crowds and Popular Politics in Early Modern England* (Manchester: Manchester University Press, 2006).

Wood, A., *The 1549 Rebellions and the Making of Early Modern England* (Cambridge: Cambridge University Press, 2007).

*The Memory of the People: Custom and Popular Senses of the Past in Early Modern England* (Cambridge: Cambridge University Press, 2013).

*The Politics of Social Conflict: The Peak Country 1520–1770* (Cambridge: Cambridge University Press, 1999).

## 11 CONSUMPTION AND MATERIAL CULTURE

Berg, M., *Luxury and Pleasure in Eighteenth-Century Britain* (Oxford: Oxford University Press, 2005).

Brears, P., *Cooking and Dining in Tudor and Early Stuart England* (Totnes: Prospect Books, 2015).

Brewer, J., *The Pleasures of the Imagination: English Culture in the Eighteenth Century* (London: HarperCollins, 1997).

Brewer, J. and R. Porter (eds.), *Consumption and the World of Goods* (London: Routledge, 1993).

De Vries, J., *The Industrious Revolution: Consumer Behaviour and the Household Economy, 1650 to the Present* (Cambridge: Cambridge University Press, 2008).

Dyer, C., *An Age of Transition? Economy and Society in the Later Middle Ages* (Oxford: Oxford University Press, 2005).

Hamling, T., *Decorating the Godly Household: Religious Art in Post-Reformation Britain* (New Haven and London: Yale University Press, 2011).

Howard, M., *The Buildings of Elizabethan and Jacobean England* (New Haven and London: Yale University Press, 2008).

Johnson, M., *An Archaeology of Capitalism* (Oxford: Blackwell, 1996).

Lemire, B., *Fashion's Favourite: The Cotton Trade and the Consumer in Britain, 1660–1800* (Oxford: Oxford University Press, 1991).

Llewellyn, N., *The Art of Death: Visual Culture in the English Death Ritual c. 1500– c. 1800* (London: Reaktion Books, 1991).

McKendrick, N., J. Brewer and J. H. Plumb (eds.), *The Birth of a Consumer Society: The Commercialization of Eighteenth-Century England* (London: HarperCollins, 1982).

Overton, M., J. Whittle, D. Dean and A. Hann, *Production and Consumption in English Households, 1600–1750* (London: Routledge, 2004).

Peck, L. L., *Consuming Splendor: Society and Culture in Seventeenth-Century England* (Cambridge: Cambridge University Press, 2005).

Sekora, J., *Luxury: The Concept in Western Thought from Eden to Smollett* (Baltimore: Johns Hopkins University Press, 1977).

Spufford, M., *The Great Reclothing of Rural England: Petty Chapmen and Their Wares in the Seventeenth Century* (London: Hambledon, 1984).

Stobart, J., *Sugar and Spice: Grocers and Groceries in Provincial England* (Oxford: Oxford University Press, 2012).

Styles, J., *The Dress of the People: Everyday Fashion in Eighteenth-Century England* (New Haven and London: Yale University Press, 2007).

Trentmann, F., *The Oxford Handbook of the History of Consumption* (Oxford: Oxford University Press, 2012).

Thirsk, J., *Economic Policy and Projects: The Development of a Consumer Society in Early Modern England* (Oxford: Oxford University Press, 1978).

Weatherill, L., *Consumer Behaviour and Material Culture in Britain, 1660–1760*, rev. edn (London: Routledge, 1996 [1988]).

## 12 'GENTLEMEN': RE-MAKING THE ENGLISH RULING CLASS

Bush, M. L., 'An Anatomy of Nobility', in M. L. Bush (ed.), *Social Orders and Social Classes in Europe since 1500: Studies in Social Stratification* (London: Longman, 1992).

Cannon, J., 'The British nobility, 1660–1800', in H. M. Scott (ed.), *The European Nobilities in the Seventeenth and Eighteenth Centuries*, Vol. I: *Western and Southern Europe* (Basingstoke: Longman, 2007).

Carpenter, C., *Locality and Polity: A Study of Warwickshire Landed Society, 1401–1499* (Cambridge: Cambridge University Press, 1992).

Cooper, J. P., 'Ideas of gentility', in G. E. Aylmer and J. S. Morrill (eds.), *Land, Men and Beliefs: Studies in Early Modern History* (London: Hambledon, 1983).

Corfield P., 'The rivals: Landed and other gentlemen', in N. Harte and R. Quinault (eds.), *Land and Society in Britain, 1700–1914: Essays in Honour of F. M. L. Thompson* (Manchester: Manchester University Press, 1996).

French, H. and M. Rothery, *Man's Estate Landed Gentry Masculinities, 1660–1900* (Oxford: Oxford University Press, 2012).

Girouard, M., *Life in the English Country House* (New Haven and London: Yale University Press, 1978).

Habakkuk, J., *Marriage, Debt and the Estates System: English Landownership 1650–1950* (Oxford: Oxford University Press, 1994).

Hainsworth, D. R., *Stewards, Lords and People: The Estate Steward and His World in Later Stuart England* (Cambridge: Cambridge University Press, 1992).

Heal, F. and C. Holmes, *The Gentry in England and Wales, 1500–1700* (Basingstoke: Macmillan, 1994).

Larminie, V., *Wealth, Kinship, and Culture: The Seventeenth-Century Newdigates of Arbury and Their World* (Woodbridge: Boydell, 1995).

Maddern, P. C., 'Gentility', in R. L. Radulescu and A. Truelove (eds.), *Gentry Culture in Late Medieval England* (Manchester: Manchester University Press, 2005).

Mingay, G., *The Gentry: The Rise and Fall of a Ruling Class* (London: Longman, 1976).

Nicholson, A., *Gentry: Six Hundred Years of a Peculiarly English Class* (London: Harper, 2011).

Pollock, L., '"Teach her to live under obedience": The making of women in the upper ranks of early modern England', *C&C*, 4 (1989).

Rosenheim, J. M., *The Emergence of a Ruling Order: English Landed Society 1650–1750* (Harlow: Longman, 1998).

Stone, L. and J. C. F. Stone, *An Open Elite? England, 1540–1880* (Oxford: Oxford University Press, 1986).

Thompson, F. M. L., *English Landed Society in the Nineteenth Century* (London: Routledge, 1963).

Vickery, A., *The Gentleman's Daughter: Women's Lives in Georgian England* (New Haven and London: Yale University Press, 1998).

Whittle, J. and E. Griffiths, *Consumption and Gender in the Early Seventeenth-Century Household: The World of Alice Le Strange* (Oxford: Oxford University Press, 2012).

## 13 THE 'MIDDLING SORT': AN EMERGENT CULTURAL IDENTITY

Barry, J. and C. Brooks (eds.), *The Middling Sort of People: Culture, Society and Politics in England, 1550–1800* (London: Macmillan, 1994).

Blackwood, B. G., *The Lancashire Gentry and the Great Rebellion 1640–60*, Chetham Society, 3rd series, 25 (1978).

Campbell, M., *The English Yeoman under Elizabeth and the Early Stuarts* (New Haven: Yale University Press, 1942).

Earle, P., *The Making of the English Middle Class: Business, Society and Family Life in London, 1660–1730* (London: Methuen, 1989).

French, H., *The Middle Sort of People in Provincial England 1600–1750* (Oxford: Oxford University Press, 2007).

French, H. and J. Barry (eds.), *Identity and Agency in England, 1500–1800* (Basingstoke: Palgrave Macmillan, 2004).

Hunt, M., *The Middling Sort: Commerce, Gender and the Family in England 1680–1780* (Berkeley and London: University of California Press, 1996).

Kent, J. R., 'The rural "middling sort" in Early Modern England, c. 1640–1740: Some economic, political and socio-cultural characteristics', *Rural History*, 10 (1999).

McVeagh, J., *Tradefull Merchants: Portrayal of the Capitalist in Literature* (London: Routledge, 1981).

Muldrew, C., *The Economy of Obligation: The Culture of Credit and Social Relations in Early Modern England.* (Basingstoke: Macmillan, 1998).

Muldrew, C. and J. Maegraith, 'Consumption and material life', in H. Scott (ed.), *Oxford Handbook of Early Modern European History* (Oxford: Oxford University Press, 2015).

Prest, W. (ed.), *The Professions in Early Modern England* (Beckenham: Croom Helm, 1987).

Slack, P., *The Invention of Improvement: Information and Material Progress in Seventeenth-Century England* (Oxford: Oxford University Press, 2014).

Smail, J., *The Origins of Middle Class Culture: Halifax, Yorkshire, 1660–1780* (Ithaca, NY: Cornell University Press, 1994).

Weatherill, L., *Consumer Behaviour and Material Culture in Britain 1660–1760* (London: Routledge, 1988).

Withington, P., *The Politics of Commonwealth: Citizens and Freemen in Early Modern England* (Cambridge: Cambridge University Press, 2005).

Wood, A., *The Memory of the People: Custom and Popular Senses of the Past in Early Modern England* (Cambridge: Cambridge University Press, 2013).

## 14 THE 'MEANER SORT': LABOURING PEOPLE AND THE POOR

Arkell, T., 'The incidence of poverty in England in the later seventeenth century', *SH*, 12 (1987).

Barry, J. and H. French (eds.), *Identity and Agency in England, 1500–1800* (Basingstoke: Palgrave Macmillan, 2004).

Braddick, M. J. and J. Walter. (eds.), *Negotiating Power in Early Modern Society. Order, Hierarchy and Subordination in Britain and Ireland* (Cambridge: Cambridge University Press, 2001).

Clark, P. and D. Souden (eds.), *Migration and Society in Early Modern England* (London: Hutchinson, 1987).

Crawford, P., *Parents of Poor Children in England, 1580–1800* (Oxford: Oxford University Press, 2010).

Everitt, A., 'Farm labourers', in J. Thirsk (ed.), *The Agrarian History of England and Wales*, Vol. IV: *1500–1640* (Cambridge: Cambridge University Press, 1967).

Healey, J., *The First Century of Welfare: Poverty and Poor Relief in Lancashire 1620–1730* (Woodbridge: Boydell, 2014).

Hindle, S., *On the Parish: The Micro-Politics of Poor Relief in Rural England, c. 1550–1750* (Oxford: Oxford University Press, 2004).

Hitchcock, T., P. Sharpe and P. King (eds.), *Chronicling Poverty: The Voices and Strategies of the English Poor, 1640–1840* (Basingstoke: Macmillan, 1997).

Jordan, W. K., *Philanthropy in England 1480–1660: A Study of the Changing Pattern of English Social Aspirations* (New York: Russell Sage Foundation, 1959).

Lees, L. H., *The Solidarities of Strangers: The English Poor Laws and the People, 1700–1948* (Cambridge: Cambridge University Press, 1998).

McIntosh, M. K., *Poor Relief in England 1350–1600* (Cambridge: Cambridge University Press, 2012).

Pelling, M. (ed.), *The Common Lot: Sickness, Medical Occupations and the Urban Poor in Early Modern England* (London and New York: Longman, 1998).

Phelps Brown, H. and S. V. Hopkins, *A Perspective of Wages and Prices* (London and New York: Methuen, 1981).

Pound, J. F. (ed.), *The Norwich Census of the Poor 1570* (Norwich: Norfolk Record Society, 1971).

Rushton, N. S. and W. Sigle-Rushton, 'Monastic poor relief in sixteenth-century England', *Journal of Interdisciplinary History*, 32 (2001).

Shepard, A. *Accounting for Oneself: Worth, Status, and the Social Order in Early Modern England* (Oxford: Oxford University Press, 2015).

'Poverty, labour and the language of social description in early modern England', *P&P*, 201 (2008).

Slack, P., *The English Poor Law 1531–1782* (Basingstoke: Macmillan, 1990).

*Poverty and Policy in Tudor and Stuart England* (Harlow: Longman, 1988).

(ed.), *Poverty in Early-Stuart Salisbury* (Devizes: Wiltshire Record Society, 1975).

Snell, K., *Annals of the Labouring Poor: Social Change and Agrarian England 1660–1900* (Cambridge: Cambridge University Press, 1985).

Wales, T., 'Poverty, poor relief and the life-cycle: Some evidence from seventeenth-century Norfolk', in. R. M. Smith (ed.), *Land, Kinship and Life-Cycle* (Cambridge: Cambridge University Press, 1984).

Walter, J. and R. Schofield (eds.), *Famine, Disease and the Social Order in Early Modern Society* (Cambridge: Cambridge University Press, 1989).

## 15 GENDER, THE BODY AND SEXUALITY

Adair, R., *Courtship, Illegitimacy, and Marriage in Early Modern England* (Manchester: Manchester University Press, 1996).

Bennett, J., *History Matters: Patriarchy and the Challenge of Feminism* (Manchester: Manchester University Press, 2006).

Bray, A., *The Friend* (Chicago: University of Chicago Press, 2003).

*Homosexuality in Renaissance England* (London: Gay Men's Press, 1982).

Capp, B., *When Gossips Meet: Women, Family and Neighbourhood in Early Modern England* (Oxford: Oxford University Press, 2003).

Dabhoiwala, F., *The Origins of Sex: A History of the First Sexual Revolution* (Harmondsworth: Penguin, 2013).

Donoghue, E., *Passions between Women: British Lesbian Culture, 1668–1801* (London: Scarlet Press, 1993).

Fisher, K. and S. Toulalan (eds.), *Bodies, Sex and Desire from the Renaissance to the Present* (Basingstoke: Palgrave Macmillan, 2011).

(eds.), *The Routledge History of Sex and the Body 1500 to the Present* (London: Routledge, 2013).

Fisher, W., 'The Renaissance beard: Masculinity in early modern England', *Renaissance Quarterly*, 54 (2001).

Fissell, M., 'Gender and generation: Representing reproduction in early modern England', *Gender and History*, 7:3 (1995).

*Vernacular Bodies: The Politics of Reproduction in Early Modern England* (Oxford: Oxford University Press, 2004).

Fletcher, A., *Gender, Sex and Subordination in England 1500–1800* (New Haven and London: Yale University Press, 1995).

Foucault, M., *The History of Sexuality*, Vol. I: *An Introduction*, trans. Robert Hurley (New York: Vintage, 1980).

Foyster, E. A., *Manhood in Early Modern England* (London: Longman, 1999).

Gowing, L., *Common Bodies: Women, Touch and Power in Seventeenth-Century England* (New Haven and London: Yale University Press, 2003).

   *Domestic Dangers: Women, Words and Sex in Early Modern London* (Oxford: Oxford University Press, 1996).

   'Lesbians and their like in early modern Europe, 1500–1800', in R. Aldrich (ed.), *Gay Life and Culture: A World History* (London: Thames & Hudson, 2006).

Gowing, L., M. Hunter and M. Rubin (eds.), *Love, Friendship and Faith in Europe, 1300–1800* (Basingstoke: Palgrave Macmillan, 2005).

Harvey, K., 'The substance of sexual difference: Change and persistence in representations of the body in eighteenth-century England', *Gender and History*, 14 (2002).

Herrup, C. B., *A House in Gross Disorder: Sex, Law, and the 2nd Earl of Castlehaven* (Oxford: Oxford University Press, 1999).

Hitchcock, T., *English Sexualities, 1700–1800* (Basingstoke: Macmillan, 1997).

Hubbard, E., *City Women: Money, Sex and the Social Order in Early Modern London* (Oxford: Oxford University Press, 2012).

Ingram, M., *Church Courts, Sex and Marriage in England, 1570–1640* (Cambridge: Cambridge University Press, 1987).

Laqueur, T., *Making Sex: Body and Gender from the Greeks to Freud* (Cambridge, MA: Harvard University Press, 1990).

McKeon, M., 'Historicizing patriarchy: The emergence of gender difference in England, 1660–1760', *Eighteenth-Century Studies*, 28 (1995).

Mendelson, S. and P. Crawford, *Women in Early Modern England* (Oxford: Oxford University Press, 1998).

Park, K., *Secrets of Women: Gender, Generation, and the Origins of Human Dissection* (New York: Zone Books, 2006).

Paster, G. K., 'The unbearable coldness of female being: Women's imperfection and the humoral economy', *English Literary Renaissance*, 28 (1998).

Phillips, N., *Women in Business 1700–1850* (Woodbridge: Boydell, 2006).

Probert, R. (ed.), *Cohabitation and Non-Marital Births in England and Wales, 1600–2012* (Basingstoke: Palgrave Macmillan, 2014).

Roper, L., 'Beyond discourse theory', *Women's History Review*, 19 (2010).

Shepard, A., 'Brokering fatherhood: Illegitimacy and paternal rights and responsibilities in early modern England', in S. Hindle, A. Shepard and J. Walter (eds.), *Remaking English Society: Social Relations and Social Change in Early Modern England* (Woodbridge: Boydell, 2013).

   'Crediting women in the early modern English economy', *HWJ*, 79 (2015).

   *Meanings of Manhood in Early Modern England* (Oxford: Oxford University Press, 2003).

Shoemaker, R. B., *Gender in English Society 1650–1850: The Emergence of Separate Spheres?* (London: Longman, 1998).

Simons, P., *The Sex of Men in Premodern Europe: A Cultural History* (Cambridge: Cambridge University Press, 2011).

Stolberg, M., 'A woman down to her bones: The anatomy of sexual difference in the sixteenth and early seventeenth centuries', *Isis*, 94 (2003).

Toulalan, S., *Imagining Sex: Pornography and Bodies in Seventeenth-Century England* (Oxford: Oxford University Press, 2007).

Trumbach, R., *Sex and the Gender Revolution* (Chicago: University of Chicago Press, 1998).

Turner, D., *Fashioning Adultery: Gender, Sex and Civility in England, 1660–1740* (Cambridge: Cambridge University Press, 2002).

Wahrman, D., *The Making of the Modern Self: Identity and Culture in Eighteenth Century England* (New Haven and London: Yale University Press, 2004).

## 16 THE ENGLISH AND 'OTHERS' IN ENGLAND AND BEYOND

Bailyn, B., and P. D. Morgan (eds.), *Strangers within the Realm: Cultural Margins of the First British Empire* (Chapel Hill: University of North Carolina Press, 1991).

Daunton, M. and R. Halpern (eds.), *Empire and Others: British Encounters with Indigenous Peoples, 1600–1850* (Philadelphia: University of Pennsylvania Press, 1999).

Games, A., *The Web of Empire: English Cosmopolitans in an Age of Expansion, 1560–1660* (Oxford: Oxford University Press, 2008).

Ghosh, D., *Sex and the Family in Colonial India: The Making of Empire* (Cambridge: Cambridge University Press, 2006).

Goffman, D., *Britons in the Ottoman Empire, 1642–1660* (Seattle: University of Washington Press, 1998).

Goodfriend, J. D., *Before the Melting Pot: Society and Culture in Colonial New York City, 1664–1730* (Princeton: Princeton University Press, 1992).

Goose, N. and L. Luu (eds.), *Immigrants in Tudor and Early Stuart England* (Brighton: Sussex Academic Press, 2005).

Guasco, M., *Slaves and Englishmen: Human Bondage in the Early Modern Atlantic World* (Philadelphia: University of Pennsylvania Press, 2014).

Johnston, S. H., 'Papists in a Protestant World: The Catholic Anglo-Atlantic in the Seventeenth Century'. Unpublished Ph.D. thesis, Georgetown University (2011).

Kidd, C., *British Identities before Nationalism: Ethnicity and Nationhood in the Atlantic World, 1600–1800* (Cambridge: Cambridge University Press, 2006).

Landsman, N. C., *Scotland and Its First American Colony, 1683–1765* (Princeton: Princeton University Press, 1985).

Matar, N., *Islam in Britain, 1558–1685* (Cambridge: Cambridge University Press, 1998).

McClendon, M. C., J. C. Ward and M. MacDonald (eds.), *Protestant Identities: Religion, Society, and Self-Fashioning in Post-Reformation England* (Stanford: Stanford University Press, 1999).

Molineux, C., *Faces of Perfect Ebony: Encountering Atlantic Slavery in Imperial Britain* (Cambridge, MA: Harvard University Press, 2012).

Selwood, J., *Diversity and Difference in Early Modern London* (Farnham: Ashgate, 2010).

Statt, D., *Foreigners and Englishmen: The Controversy over Immigration and Population, 1660–1760* (Newark: University of Delaware Press, 1995).

Vigne, R. and C. Littleton (eds.), *From Strangers to Citizens: The Integration of Immigrant Communities in Britain, Ireland and Colonial America, 1550–1750* (London: Huguenot Society of Great Britain and Ireland, 2001).

## CODA: HISTORY, TIME AND SOCIAL MEMORY

Fentress, J. and C. Wickham, *Social Memory* (Oxford: Oxford University Press, 1992).

Fox, A., *Oral and Literate Cultures in England, 1500–1700* (Oxford: Oxford University Press, 2000).

Misztal, B., *Theories of Social Remembering* (Maidenhead: Open University Press, 2003).

Thomas, K., *The Perception of the Past in Early Modern England*, Creighton Trust Lecture (London: University of London, 1983).

Tittler, R., 'Reformation, civic culture and collective memory in English provincial towns', *Urban History*, 24 (1997).

Walsham, A., *The Reformation of the Landscape: Religion, Identity and Memory in Early Modern Britain and Ireland* (Oxford: Oxford University Press, 2011).

Whyte, N., *Inhabiting the Landscape: Place, Custom and Memory, 1500–1800* (Oxford: Oxbow, 2009).

Wood, A., *The Memory of the People: Custom and Popular Senses of the Past in Early Modern England* (Cambridge: Cambridge University Press, 2013).

Woolf, D., *The Social Circulation of the Past: English Historical Culture, 1500–1730* (Oxford: Oxford University Press, 2003).

# Index